INSIGHT GUIDES

GREAT BRITAIN

Discovery CHANNEL

APA PUBLICATIONS
Part of the Langenscheidt Publishing Group

INSIGHT GUIDE
GREAT BRITAIN

Editorial
Editor
Brian Bell
Picture Editor
Steven Lawrence
Series Editor
Dorothy Stannard

Distribution
UK & Ireland
GeoCenter International Ltd
Meridian House, Churchill Way West
Basingstoke, Hampshire RG21 6YR
Fax: (44) 1256 817988

North America
Langenscheidt Publishers, Inc.
36–36 33rd Street, 4th Floor
Long Island City, New York 11106
Fax: (1) 718 784 0640

Australia
Universal Publishers
1 Waterloo Road
Macquarie Park, NSW 2113
Fax: (61) 2 9888 9074

New Zealand
Hema Maps New Zealand Ltd (HNZ)
Unit 2, 10 Cryers Road
East Tamaki, Auckland 2013
Fax: (64) 9 273 6479

Worldwide
**Apa Publications GmbH & Co.
Verlag KG (Singapore branch)**
38 Joo Koon Road, Singapore 628990
Tel: (65) 6865 1600. Fax: (65) 6861 6438

Printing
Insight Print Services (Pte) Ltd
38 Joo Koon Road, Singapore 628990
Tel: (65) 6865 1600. Fax: (65) 6861 6438

First Edition 1984
Eighth Edition 2009

CONTACTING THE EDITORS
We would appreciate it if readers would alert us to errors or outdated information by writing to:
Insight Guides, P.O. Box 7910, London SE1 1WE, England. Fax: (44) 20 7403 0290. insight@apaguide.co.uk

www.insightguides.com

ABOUT THIS BOOK

A region with such a rich history and culture as Great Britain lends itself especially well to the approach taken by the award-winning Insight series.

The first Insight Guide pioneered the use of creative full-colour photography in travel guides in 1970. Since then, we have expanded our range to cater for our readers' need not only for reliable information about their chosen destination but also for a real understanding of that destination.

Now, when the internet can supply inexhaustible – but not always reliable – facts, our books marry text and pictures to provide that much more elusive quality: knowledge. To achieve this, they rely heavily on the authority of local writers and photographers.

How to use this book

The book is carefully structured to convey an understanding of Great Britain and its culture and to guide readers through its sights and attractions:

◆ The Features section, which has a red colour bar, covers the region's history and culture in lively authoritative essays written by specialists.

◆ The Places section, with a blue bar, provides full details of all the sights and areas worth seeing. The chief places of interest are coordinated by number with specially drawn and cross-referenced maps.

◆ The Travel Tips section, with a yellow bar, at the back of the book, offers a point of reference for information on travel, accommodations, restaurants and other practical aspects of the region. Information may be located quickly using the index printed on the back cover flap, which also serves as a bookmark.

Left: enjoying the beach at Wells-next-the-Sea, Norfolk.

The contributors

Because Insight Guides' editorial headquarters is located in London, expert contributors were not hard to find. This edition's project editor, **Brian Bell**, wrote for the first edition back in 1984 and later served for 17 years as Insight Guides' editorial director. He was born in Northern Ireland, which is not part of Great Britain but is part of the United Kingdom – one of those consequences of a complex history that often baffle the inquiring visitor.

It is the aim of this guidebook to throw light on such complexities, and the A–Z section on British culture, ranging from tradtional pubs to the current obsession with surveillance, enabled the editors to examine some peculiarities of the British way of life and, in doing so, give full rein to their hobby-horses. Several experienced freelance journalists also contributed to this section; they included **Richard Johnson, Roger Williams**, **Angela Wilkes**, **Alan Hamilton** and **Daniela Soave**.

You certainly can't understand the country today without some knowledge of its turbulent past, but how do you squeeze several thousand years of British history into a manageable size? The task fell to Insight regular **Pam Barrett**, who has a history degree from London University. She also updated several Places chapters for this edition.

Such is the density of sites and attractions in Britain that each area of the country is worth a book in its own right – and indeed many have been covered fully in individual Insight Compact Guides. In the present book, we concentrated on must-see sights and events, with a generous sprinkling of lesser known but rewarding destinations.

Many writers brought their local knowledge to bear on the Places chapters. They include **Rebecca Ford**, **Paula Soper**, **Dorothy Stannard**, **Alyse Dar**, **Alexia Georgiou**, **Rachel Lawrence**, **Andrew Eames**, **Roland Collins**, **Iain Crawford**, **Penny Phenix**, **Darroch MacKay**, **Roger Williams** and **Marcus Brooke**.

The fact-packed Travel Tips section was updated by **Catherine Dreghorn**. **Zoë Goodwin** was the book's cartography editor, and the index was compiled by **Isobel McLean**.

Map Legend

- International Boundary
- National Boundary
- County Boundary
- National Park
- Ferry Route
- Underground
- Airport: International/ Regional
- Bus Station
- Tourist Information
- Church/Ruins
- Monastery
- Archaeological Site
- Mansion/Stately home
- Castle/Ruins
- Mosque
- Synagogue
- Cave
- Statue/Monument
- Place of Interest

The main places of interest in the Places section are coordinated by number (e.g. ❶) with a full-color map, and a symbol at the top of every right-hand page tells you where to find the map.

Contents

Introduction

History

Culture from A to Z

Photo Features

Places

Information Panels

LEFT: view of Somerset from Glastonbury Tor.

Travel Tips

Maps

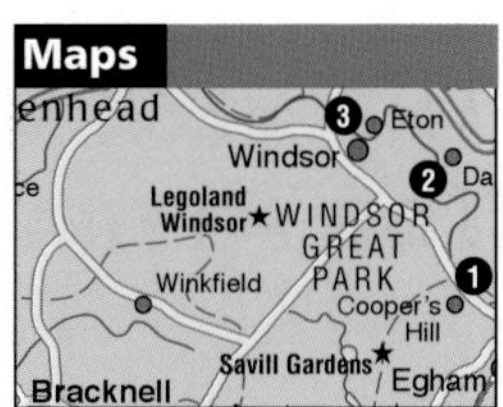

The Best of Great Britain: Top Attractions

Packed into this compact island are hundreds of things worth seeing and doing. Those shown here give a taste of the rich and varied fare on offer

Above: The Tower of London is one of the capital's great icons – packed with history dating back to 1078 and housing the crown jewels. *See page 136.*

Below: The Mersey Ferry is the way to see the fine waterfront of Liverpool, the Beatles' home town. *See page 278.*

Above: Cornish beaches are where the surfers head for, to ride Atlantic rollers. Dizzy cliffs and pristine sands bring walkers and holiday families, too. *See page 239.*

Left: The Edinburgh Festival is the world's largest arts festival, filling the Scottish capital with music, comedy, drama and eccentricity every August. *See page 327.*

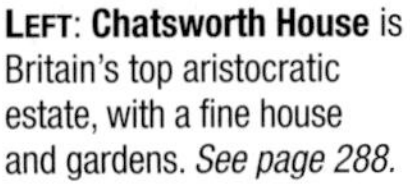

Left: Chatsworth House is Britain's top aristocratic estate, with a fine house and gardens. *See page 288.*

ABOVE: **Stratford-upon-Avon** is Shakespeare's birthplace, shown above, and is a good base from which to explore the beautiful and historic Warwickshire countryside. *See page 182.*

ABOVE: **The Scottish Highlands** are as wild as Britain gets: deer roam the hills, salmon leap in the rivers and eagles soar overhead. *See page 339.*

RIGHT: **Oxford**'s dreaming spires have represented one of Europe's most renowned places of learning since the 12th century. *See page 169.*

ABOVE: **Snowdonia**'s mountainous magnificence is the high spot in Wales. Walk, drive, or take the Ffestiniog railway to the heights. *See page 268.*

RIGHT: **Durham Cathedral** is indisputably the finest Norman building in the country, dramatically perched above the River Wear. *See page 303.*

The Best of Great Britain: Editor's Choice

Setting priorities, the sights worth seeing, best pubs and pageants, unique attractions... here, at a glance, are our recommendations, plus tips even the locals may not know

Top Attractions for Families

- **Alton Towers, Warwickshire** Britain's best-known theme park has wild white-knuckle rides and other thrills. Not cheap. *Page 286.*
- **Beamish, County Durham** This open-air museum in 300 acres tells the social history of the North-East, with tram rides, working farm and collier village. *Page 304.*
- **Ironbridge Gorge Museums, Telford** Award-winning string of museums on the River Severn celebrating the "birthplace of industry". *Page 282.*
- **Jorvik Viking Centre, York** Take an underground ride into the world of Vikings – complete with smells – in this innovative museum. *Page 299.*
- **Legoland, Windsor** Rides, shows and multiple attractions. *Page 161.*
- **Longleat Safari Park** The first safari park outside Africa in the grounds of a stately home. *Page 237.*
- **Maritime Museum, Greenwich**. Recalling when Britain ruled the waves. *Page 151.*
- **Museum of Childhood, Edinburgh** Toys, games and nurseries add up to "the noisiest museum in the world." *Page 325.*
- **SS Great Britain, Bristol** A brilliant re-enactment of life on the world's first iron-hulled ship with a screw propeller. *Page 235.*

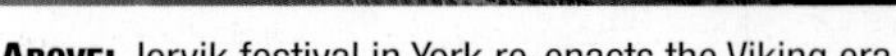

Above: Jorvik festival in York re-enacts the Viking era.

Best Festivals and Pageants

- **Chinese New Year** London's Chinatown explodes with fire-crackers and dancing dragons. *Page 123.*
- **Edinburgh Military Tattoo** The largest event of its kind in the atmospheric castle. *Page 324.*
- **Mela Festival** The Asian festival celebrating Bangla New Year in several dozen venues, from Edinburgh to London, at various times of the year.
- **National Eisteddfod of Wales** This annual celebration of Welsh culture dates from the 12th century. *Page 270.*
- **Notting Hill Carnival** Exuberant August parade, with West Indian bands and floats, is Europe's largest street festival. *Page 147.*
- **Trooping the Colour** Britain honours the Queen's birthday in Horse Guards Parade, London. *Page 117.*
- **Up Helly Aa** Fire festival in Lerwick celebrates the Viking past of the Shetland Islands. *Page 345.*

Left: the Queen rides out in Trooping the Colour.

THE TOP ROYAL HOMES

- **Balmoral** The royals' Scottish home since 1848. *Page 348.*
- **Buckingham Palace** Their London base, with Changing of the Guard. *Page 117.*
- **Caernarfon Castle** The fortress where Charles became Prince of Wales. *Page 265.*

ABOVE: Guards parade at Buckingham Palace.

- **Edinburgh Castle**: This one-time Scottish royal residence is still keeper of the nation's crown. *Page 324.*
- **Hampton Court Palace, Surrey** Henry VIII's magnificent Surrey palace has magnificent gardens. *Page 155.*
- **Kensington Palace** Birthplace of Queen Victoria. *Page 146.*
- **Palace of Holyroodhouse, Edinburgh** The Queen's Scottish residence in early summer. *Page 325.*
- **Sandringham House** Norfolk base for the royals at Christmas. *Page 196.*
- **Windsor Castle** The Queen's official residence, a day-trip from London. *Page 160.*

THE BEST GARDENS

- **Eden Project, Cornwall** Futuristic glass domes are the hot houses in this award-winning, eco-friendly extravaganza. *Page 242.*
- **Powis Castle**, Tuscany comes to Wales in fine Italianate gardens. *Page 270.*
- **RHS Gardens, Wisley** The Royal Horticultural Society's showcase. *Page 210.*
- **Royal Botanic Gardens, Kew** Fine day out from central London to legendary gardens first planted in 1759. *Page 153.*
- **Sissinghurst Castle, Kent**: Vita Sackville-West's charming garden. *Page 213.*

RIGHT: the futuristic Eden Project in Cornwall.

ABOVE: the Great Court of the British Museum.

ENTHRALLING MUSEUMS

- **Ashmolean, Oxford** A peerless museum of art and archaeology collected by scholars from around the world. *Page 173.*
- **British and Commonwealth Museum** The port of Bristol recalls the ships and traders that built the Empire. *Page 235.*
- **British Museum, London** Embraces no less than the history of civilisation. *Page 130.*
- **Merseyside Maritime Museum** Slavery and emigration are the abiding themes in this evocative museum in Liverpool. *Page 278.*
- **Museum of Scotland, Edinburgh** Attached to the Royal Museum, this new building gives a history of the nation. *Page 326.*
- **Museum of Welsh Life, Cardiff** Welsh culture is celebrated in this museum of social history. *Page 256.*
- **National Media Museum, Bradford** Covers history of film, television and photography. *Page 295.*
- **National Motor Museum, Hampshire** Beaulieu Abbey, home of the aristocratic Montagu family, puts veteran cars on show. *Page 228.*
- **Science Museum** London's utterly engrossing displays of inventions. *Page 145.*

Top Traditional Pubs

● **Brown's Hotel,** King Street, Laugharne. Brown's was called "home" by local writer Dylan Thomas who spent rather too much time in the snug here.
● **George Inn,** Borough High Street, Southwark. London's only remaining galleried coaching inn dates from 1676 and was a haunt of Charles Dickens.
● **Globe Inn**, High Street, Dumfries. "...the Globe Tavern here, which these many years has been my Howff [haunt]" wrote the Scottish bard, Robert Burns, whose memorabilia fills this 17th-century pub.
● **Old Spot Inn**, Hill Road, Dursley, Gloucestershire.This award-winning country pub in the heart of the Cotswolds is as good as county pubs get.
● **Ye Olde Gate Inn**, Well Street, Brassington. This Derbyshire pub has been described as the "cosiest pub in Britain". One for cold winter evenings.
● **Philharmonic**, Hope Street, Liverpool. One of the city's many Victorian glories (and John Lennon's favourite); ladies are invited to inspect the elaborate tilework in the gents if there is nobody using it.
● **Pot Still**, Hope Street, Glasgow. This famous whisky pub has more than 500 different labels in store.
● **Tan Hill Inn**, Richmond, Swaledale. In the Yorkshire Dales National Park, this is the highest pub in Britain, and full of pets, from ducks to ponies.
● **Ye Olde Trip to Jerusalem**, Brewhouse Yard, Nottingham. Built into the cliffs of the town's castle, this is reputed to be England's oldest pub, dating from the 12th century when ale was healthier than most drinking water.

Above: the George, London's oldest coaching inn.

The Finest Stately Homes

● **Alnwick Castle** Home of the Dukes of Northumberland; Harry Potter flew around here in the movies. *Page 305.*
● **Apsley House** "No 1, London" has been the London home of the Dukes of Wellington for 200 years. *Page 147.*
● **Blenheim Palace, Oxfordshire** This vast, English baroque pile is the family home of the Dukes of Marlborough; Winston Churchill, an offspring, was born here. *Page 174.*
● **Chatsworth House, Derbyshire** Seat of the Dukes of Devonshire. *Page 288.*
● **Castle Howard, Yorkshire** The *Brideshead Revisited* TV series and movie were filmed here. *Page 301.*
● **Hopetoun House** Echoing the style of Versailles, the Scottish house was built for the forebears of the current resident, the Marquess of Lithgow. *Page 328.*
● **Inveraray Castle** Scottish home of the Duke of Argyll, chief of the Clan Campbell. *Page 340.*
● **Woburn Abbey, Bedfordshire** Home of the Dukes of Bedford, who installed a safari park to attract visitors. *Page 98.*

Left: Blenheim Palace's sumptuous interior.

THE TOP ART GALLERIES

● **Baltic Exchange, Gateshead** The largest contemporary arts venue outside London. *Page 304.*

● **Barbara Hepworth, St Ives** The sculptor's home in an attractive Cornish fishing village. *Page 240.*

● **Constable Country, Suffolk** Follow the trail of Britain's great landscape painter. *Page 200.*

● **David Hockney Gallery, Saltaire**: Britain's most famous living artist has a permanent gallery in this splendid old mill in his native Bradford. *Page 295.*

● **National Gallery, London** Treasures from the Renaissance to the Impressionists – and it's free. *Page 113.*

● **National Gallery of Scotland, Edinburgh** World-class display of European art. *Page 326.*

● **Tate Modern, London** Wildly popular gallery in a former power station. *Page 138.*

● **The Walker, Liverpool** Great collection of Victorian and Pre-Raphaelite paintings. *Page 279.*

ABOVE: Sir Henry Raeburn's *Rev. Robert Walker Skating on Dunningston Loch*, National Gallery of Scotland.

ABOVE: Orkney's Ring of Brodgar, dating from 2300BC.

BEST ANCIENT SITES

● **Cerne Abbas Giant, Dorset** The massive naked figure carved into a hillside is thought to be a pagan fertility symbol. *Page 240.*

● **Chester, Cheshire** The most important Roman town outside London contains the largest amphitheatre in Britain. *Page 280.*

● **Hadrian's Wall** Britain's top Roman monument, popular with walkers. *Page 304.*

● **Fishbourne Roman Palace, Sussex** The large archaeological site includes magnificent floor mosaics. *Page 209.*

● **Orkney** There is evidence on the island of Neolithic farmers, dating from around 3000 BC. *Page 345.*

● **Stonehenge, Wiltshire** Nobody is certain how or why this huge stone circle was erected. *Page 222.*

● **Sutton Hoo, Suffolk** Burial site of Anglo-Saxon kings. *Page 200.*

MONEY-SAVING TIPS

● **Travel** Rail travel in Britain is expensive. You could make a saving with a GB Flexi Pass, which allows travel throughout Britain over a certain number of days in a one-month period. Fares are Adult, Child, Senior, Youth, Family, Guest and Party, First or Standard Class, and are cheaper in Low Season (1 Nov–28 Feb). Much cheaper but more time-consuming are buses, which cover the country. Most are run by National Express and Megabus, whose competitive bravura can reduce some tickets to £1. *See page 355.*

● **London Transport** The cheapest and easiest way to travel around is by using an Oyster card, which you can buy in advance from abroad *(see page 356)*. Children under 11 and wheelchair users travel free.

● **Eating out** The standard of pub food is generally decent enough, but not always cheap. In cities, lunchtime menus can be good value, as can early evening, pre-theatre meals. A tax (VAT) is levied on food consumed on the premises, so it is slightly cheaper to take away the food, perhaps to a nearby park (prices are listed).

● **Museums** One of the best things about visiting Britain is its many free museums. Some have late evening openings once or twice a week. City churches in London and elsewhere often put on free lunchtime concerts.

Grannie's

RONGBOW

THE BRITISH CHARACTER

If the English are ambiguous, the Welsh loquacious and the Scots cantankerous, how do they all manage to get along on the same overcrowded island?

Millions of people in Britain, wrote George Orwell in 1947, "willingly accept as their national emblem the bulldog, an animal noted for its obstinacy, ugliness, and impenetrable stupidity." A foreigner, he went on, would find the salient characteristics of the common people to be "artistic insensibility, gentleness, respect for legality, suspicion of foreigners, sentimentality about animals, hypocrisy, exaggerated class distinctions, and an obsession with sport."

The Welsh and the Scots would point out that Orwell was thinking primarily of the English who, to the fury of the Welsh and Scots, persistently equate the terms "British" and "English".

The contradictory English

But then the English have a gift for ambiguity. As a character in Alan Bennett's play *The Old Country* put it: "When we say we don't mean what we say, only then are we entirely serious." If that seems contradictory, there's worse to come. The British embrace marriage more frequently than any other European nation, yet their divorce rate is second only to Denmark's. On average, they work more hours per week than any other European Community country (43.9 hours for men), yet their productivity is lowest. They have 54,600 churches, but by far the lowest active church membership in Europe (14 percent of the total population). They laud family life, yet many prefer to send their children off to boarding school as soon as possible and park their aged parents in old people's homes. They pride themselves on their solidarity in war, yet cling to a divisive class system in peacetime.

> *To understand Great Britain, its people will tell you, will take many visits. This, bearing in mind their inability to say exactly what they mean, translates as: "Although we regard tourism as terribly vulgar, we do rather need the repeat business."*

They are also famed for their tolerance and sense of humour, yet, as the writer Paul Gallico observed: "No one can be as calculatedly rude as the British, which amazes Americans, who do not understand studied insult and can only offer abuse as a substitute." Britain's nearest neighbours can be just as amazed as Americans. André Maurois

LEFT: London mayor Boris Johnson aboard a classic Routemaster, now used only for tourist purposes.
RIGHT: Napoleon called the English "a nation of shopkeepers" – and shopping remains popular.

advised his fellow countrymen: "In France it is rude to let a conversation drop; in England it is rash to keep it up. No one there will blame you for silence. When you have not opened your mouth for three years, they will think, 'This Frenchman is a nice quiet fellow'."

The truth, as always, is more complicated. If Maurois had been in Liverpool or in Leeds, in Glasgow or in Cardiff, he might not have got a word in. The Englishman who has "all the qualities of a poker except its occasional warmth" probably lives in the overcrowded southeast, where standoffishness is a way of protecting precious privacy.

But certain generalisations can be made. Because Britain is an island its people have retained their bachelor outlook despite marrying into the European Union. Because it has not been successfully invaded for nearly 1,000 years, Britain remains deeply individualistic. On the one hand, its people perhaps overvalue tradition – a substitute for thought, critics say; on the other hand, they tend not to kill one another in civil conflict and they have absorbed, with relatively little civic pain, large numbers of their former imperial subjects.

The voluble Welsh

To the English, the Welsh appear a much more homogeneous group than themselves: ebullient, warm-hearted and emotional but also rather sly and extremely garrulous. A certain amount of antipathy exists. Evelyn Waugh, for instance, claimed in his novel *Decline and Fall*: "We can trace almost all the disasters of English history to the influence of Wales." And Shakespeare poked fun at Welsh hyperbole by having the Welsh hero Owain Glyndwr boast, in *Henry V*, "I can call spirits from the vasty deep" – only to be put down by Hotspur, who replies, "So can any man; but will they come?" The Welsh, for their part, have had to work hard, like many minority nations, to protect their self-esteem and culture from a strong neighbour, but have been wary of independence.

Within Wales itself, the people seem anything but homogeneous. Many in North Wales, where Welsh is still widely spoken, look down on people from South Wales whose blood is much more mixed and whose habits are thought too anglicised. Naturally, South Walians return the compliment by regarding North Walians as less progressive and less sociable.

The gift of the gab was nourished in the 19th century, when Wales was fertile ground for preachers and trade union leaders.

Whether their preferred tongue is English or Welsh, however, there is no point in denying that most of the Welsh are extremely voluble. "It is not so long ago," remembered the poet Dannie Abse, "that the trains leaving from London for

South Wales consisted of separate carriages – that is, they were not open-planned. Then, half a dozen strangers would look out of the window, or suck their mints, or read their newspapers, but they would not speak to each other. It was not the 'done' English thing. The English are happy with few words and like to keep strangers at a comfortable distance from themselves. And in a train leaving England for Wales, who knows who is not English? Only when the train had passed through the Severn Tunnel, only when the passengers felt themselves to be safely in Wales, only then would the carriage suddenly hum with conversation."

The uncompromising Scots

In contrast, the Scots are seen by the English as "dour", though they'd be hard put to justify the claim in a noisy Glasgow pub. English literature is peppered with anti-Scots aphorisms, such as P.G. Wodehouse's observation that "it is never difficult to distinguish between a Scotsman with a grievance and a ray of sunshine."

The Scots' principal grievance is that the London-based parliament treats them as second-class citizens, especially when implementing its economic policies. This is far from being a new complaint, having been echoed long before the two nations united in 1707 in what most Scots still regard as a shotgun marriage. Indeed, when the future Pope Pius II visited the country in the 15th century, he concluded: "Nothing pleases the Scots more than abuse of the English."

That's not to say that the Scots can't cooperate with the English when it suits them: the work ethic and ingenuity of Scots played a major role in creating the British Empire. But the differences in character are long-established. Unlike the English and Welsh, the Scots were never conquered by the Romans, and they also avoided Norman centralisation after the Conquest in 1066. Their religious experience also set them apart: while England absorbed the Reformation with a series of cunning compromises, Scotland underwent a revolution, replacing the panoply of Roman Catholicism with an austere Presbyterianism designed to put the people directly in touch with their God. No man was deemed inherently better than the next.

In many ways, the Scots character baffles the English. It combines sourness and humour, meanness and generosity, arrogance and tolerance, cantankerousness and chivalry, sentimentality and hard-headedness. That's a potent broth.

In 1997 the Scots voted to set up their own parliament in Edinburgh. This has given them a certain degree of independence – but a divorce from England, most insist, remains unlikely. ❑

LEFT: celebrating the historical role of Welsh archers, Carew Castle. **ABOVE:** Sir Sean Connery became a firm supporter of the Scottish National Party.

1
2
3
4
5
6
7
8
9
10
11
12
13
14
15

DECISIVE DATES

PREHISTORY

250,000 BC
First evidence of human life in far west of Europe.

5000 BC
Britain becomes an island.

3000 BC
Stone-age people arrive, probably from Iberia.

2300 BC
Stonehenge is built.

700 BC
Celts arrive from central Europe.

ROMAN OCCUPATION

55 BC
Julius Caesar heads the first Roman invasion.

AD 61
Rebellion of Boudicca, Queen of Iceini in East Anglia, is crushed.

AD 119
Romans build Hadrian's Wall to keep back the Picts and Scots in the north.

ANGLO-SAXONS AND DANES

449–550
Arrival of Jutes from Jutland, Angles from Denmark and Saxons from Germany.

563
St Columba establishes monastery on island of Iona, Scotland.

597
St Augustine comes as a missionary and ends up first Archbishop of Canterbury.

LEFT: medieval costumes.

A Pict as subsequently imagined.

779
King Offa builds a dyke to keep out the Welsh.

897
Danish Vikings are defeated at sea by Alfred the Great, generally regarded as having founded the British navy.

980–1016
Viking invasions renewed.

1017
Canute, first Danish king, chosen by Witan (council).

THE NORMANS

1066
William, Duke of Normandy, conquers England and gives authority and parcels of land to Norman barons.

1080–1100
Great monastery and cathedral building begins.

1086
Domesday Book, a complete inventory of property in Britain, is completed.

1124
David I succeeds to Scottish throne.

1167
Oxford University founded.

THE PLANTAGENETS

1154
Henry II, descendent of Geoffrey of Anjou, inherits

BELOW: the Battle of Hastings as portrayed in the Bayeux Tapestry.

London's mayor and aldermen.

the throne, thus starting the line of Angevin kings. He owned more land in France than he did in Britain.

1170
Archbishop Thomas Becket, having defied Henry II, killed in Canterbury cathedral.

1215
Barons force King John to sign Magna Carta guaranteeing freedoms.

1265
First House of Commons meets at Westminster Hall.

1277–88
English conquest of Wales. Llewellyn ab Gruffydd, its last prince, is killed.

1306
Robert Bruce is crowned King of the Scots.

1348–49
The Black Death plague kills nearly half the population.

1337–1453
Hundred Years' War with France drags on.

1381
Peasants' Revolt marks the erosion of serfdom.

1387
Chaucer's *Canterbury Tales* is published.

HOUSES OF LANCASTER AND YORK

1415
Owain Glyndwr, the Welsh hero, dies.

1455–85
Wars of the Roses between the competing Houses of York and Lancaster.

1412
St Andrew's University is founded in Scotland.

1476
William Caxton sets up Britain's first printing press.

THE TUDORS

1485
Henry VII, grandson of the Welsh Owain Tudor, crowned.

1509
Henry VIII begins his reign at the age of 17.

1534
Henry abolishes Papal authority in England.

The Peasants' Revolt in 1381 saw the serfs revolt against authority.

ENGLISH MONARCHS SINCE THE NORMAN CONQUEST

Norman
William 1066–87
William II 1087–1100
Henry I 1100–35
Stephen 1135–54
Plantagenet
Henry II 1154–89
Richard I 1189–99
John 1199–1216
Henry III 1216–72
Edward I 1272–1307
Edward II 1307–27
Edward III 1327–77
Richard II 1377–99
Lancaster
Henry IV 1399–1413
Henry V 1413–22
Henry VI 1422–61
York
Edward IV 1461–83
Edward V 1483
Richard III 1483–85
Tudor
Henry VII 1485–1509
Henry VIII 1509–47
Edward VI 1547–53
Mary 1553–58
Elizabeth I 1558–1603
Stuart
James I 1603–25
Charles I 1625–49
[Commonwealth 1649–53, Protectorate 1653–60]
Charles II 1660–85
James II 1685–89
William and Mary 1689–1702
Anne 1702–1714
Hanover
George I 1714–27
George II 1727–60
George III 1760–1820
George IV 1820–30
William IV 1830–37
Saxe-Coburg-Gotha
Victoria 1837–1901
Edward VII 1901–10
Windsor
(so called from 1917)
George V 1910–36
Edward VIII 1936
George VI 1936–52
Elizabeth II from 1952

The Great Fire of London, 1666.

1535
Henry becomes Supreme Head of Church of England.

1536–39
Henry VIII destroys or closes 560 monasteries and religious houses.

1536
Act of Union joins England and Wales.

1558
England's last possession in France, Calais, is lost.

1558
Elizabeth I begins her 45-year reign.

1580
Sir Francis Drake completes his three-year voyage round the world.

James I of England.

1585
William Shakespeare begins his career in London.

1587
Mary, Queen of Scots, is executed.

1588
Spanish Armada defeated.

THE STUARTS

1603
James VI of Scotland, son of Mary, Queen of Scots, is crowned James I of England, uniting the kingdoms.

1605
Guy Fawkes tries to blow up parliament.

1620
Pilgrim Fathers set sail for America.

1642–49
Civil War between Royalists and republican Roundheads. Many castles and fortified houses razed. Charles I is beheaded and the country effectively becomes a republic.

1660
Monarchy is reinstated with Charles II.

1665
The Great Plague of London.

1666
The Great Fire of London.

1672–1700
Following the fire, St Paul's Cathedral is built.

1694
Bank of England set up.

Charles II restores the monarchy.

THE HOUSE OF HANOVER

1714
George I of Hanover, Germany, is invited to take the throne. He speaks no English and shows very little interest in his new subjects.

1721
Sir Robert Walpole becomes Britain's first prime minister, a new British concept.

1739
Wesley begins to preach Methodism.

1746
Battle of Culloden is final defeat for Stuart dynasty.

1775
James Watt makes the first steam engine.

1805
Admiral Lord Nelson is killed at Battle of Trafalgar.

1807
Abolition of the slave trade.

1815
Duke of Wellington defeats Napoleon Bonaparte at Waterloo in today's Belgium.

1830
A railway is opened from Liverpool to Manchester.

Queen Victoria and Prince Albert.

THE VICTORIAN AGE

1837
Victoria becomes Queen, aged 18. She marries Albert of Saxe-Coburg in 1840.

1851
The Empire-boosting Great Exhibition held in London.

British prime minister William Pitt and Napoleon carve out their empires.

1876
The Queen becomes Empress of India.

1890–96
Cecil Rhodes, founder of Rhodesia, becomes prime minister of Cape Colony, South Africa.

1898–1902
British fight Dutch in Boer War to settle South Africa.

THE EDWARDIAN ERA

1909
Old-age pensions are introduced by the Chancellor, David Lloyd George.

1914–18
World War I. More than 1 million Britons and Allies die, mainly in northern France.

HOUSE OF WINDSOR

(so named from 1917)

1918
Universal suffrage (except for women under 30).

1926
General Strike by workers paralyses the nation.

1927
The BBC is founded.

1936
Edward VIII abdicates so that he can marry a divorcée, Mrs Wallis Simpson.

1939–45
World War II. Fewer military casualties than World War I, but many civilians die in heavy bombing.

1946
Labour government sets up National Health Service.

1947
Edinburgh Festival is begun, and the Welsh Eisteddfod re-established.

1947
India and Pakistan gain independence.

Britain's leader in World War II.

1951
Festival of Britain lifts spirits after postwar austerity.

1953
Queen Elizabeth II crowned at the age of 27.

1961
Commonwealth ejects South Africa because of its apartheid policy.

1962
The Beatles enter the pop charts with their first hit, Love Me Do.

1965
Capital punishment ends.

1969
Troops sent to Northern Ireland to tackle Unionist/nationalist sectarian strife.

1972
Northern Ireland government replaced with direct rule from Westminster.

1973
Britain joins the European Community.

1979
Margaret Thatcher is UK's first woman prime minister.

North Sea oil, an economic boon.

Charles and Diana wedding coin.

1981
Prince of Wales marries Lady Diana Spencer.

1982
Argentinian troops beaten off the Crown Colony of the Falkland Islands.

1984
IRA bomb aimed at the Conservative government in conference at Brighton kills five people.

1990
Tory party votes Margaret Thatcher out of office.

1994
First trains run through the Channel Tunnel.

1996
Shakespeare's Globe, a replica of the 16th-century theatre, opens in London.

1997
Labour wins its first general election since 1974. Diana, Princess of Wales, dies in a car crash in Paris.

1998
Northern Ireland peace accord signed.

1999
Scottish and Welsh assemblies begin to exercise a limited degree of devolution.

2003
A congestion charge of £5 a day is made on cars entering central London on weekdays. Britain joins the US in going to war with Iraq.

2005
On 6 July London is chosen to stage 2012 Olympic Games. The following day bombs explode on three Tube trains and a bus, killing more than 50 people.

2006
In January a bottlenose whale is found swimming up the Thames in central London. Attempts to save it fail.

St Pancras Eurostar terminal.

2007
The new Wembley Stadium opens four years late and more than £470 million over budget. In November the new Eurostar terminal opens at St Pancras.

2008
The long boom in the stock market and house prices comes to an abrupt end.

BEGINNINGS

One wave of immigrants followed another, creating a truly mongrel breed. Then came the conquerors: the Romans, Saxons, Angles and Normans

When French and British construction workers met beneath the English Channel in 1990, Britain became linked to Continental Europe for the first time in 7,000 years. For it was then, when the last Ice Age ended, that melting ice flooded the low-lying lands, creating the English Channel and the North Sea, and turning Britain into an island. This fact of being "set apart" from Europe was one of two seemingly contradictory factors which would affect every aspect of the country's subsequent history. The other was a genius for absorbing every invader and immigrant, creating a mongrel breed whose energies would establish an empire incorporating a quarter of the population of the planet.

Early settlers

A race of nomadic hunter-gatherers were the earliest inhabitants. By about 3000 BC tribes of Neolithic people had crossed the water from Europe, probably from the Iberian peninsula, now Spain. They were farming folk who kept animals and grew crops. The barrows which can still be found, mostly in the chalky lands of Wiltshire and Dorset, were their huge communal burial mounds.

More dramatic monuments were the henges, the most important of which was Stonehenge in Wiltshire, constructed before 2000 BC. Exactly why it was built is unknown, but it must have had religious and political significance; the massive undertaking involved in bringing bluestones all the way from Wales for part of its construction suggests that its builders had a substantial power base.

The Celtic tribes are ancestors of the Highland Scots, the Irish and the Welsh, and their languages are the basis of both modern Welsh and Gaelic.

The next wave of immigrants were the Celts. They began to arrive about 700 BC and kept coming until the arrival of the Romans. They may have come from eastern and central Europe and they probably became dominant because, being ironworkers, their weapons were superior.

The Romans

British recorded history begins with the Roman invasion. Julius Caesar first crossed the English Channel and arrived in Britain in 55 BC but, meeting resistance and bad weather, he returned to Gaul. The successful invasion did not take place until nearly a century later, in AD 43, headed by the Emperor Claudius. This time, the land they knew by its Greco-Roman name, Pretani, was subdued with relative ease, apart from the country in the far north they called Caledonia (now Scotland). To repel persistent raids by the warlike Picts, or "painted ones", the Emperor Hadrian had a wall built right across the north of England.

When the Romans left, nearly 400 years later, to defend Rome against the barbarians, they left behind a network of towns, mostly walled, many on the sites of Celtic settlements or their own military camps, and a good road network. Yet their influence faded surprisingly fast. Buildings crumbled through lack of repair and language, literacy and religion soon disappeared.

Anglo-Saxon assault

The new wave of invaders from central Europe, Saxons, Angles and Jutes, gradually pushed the native Celts westward into Wales and north into Scotland. The Saxons established their kingdoms in Essex, Sussex and Wessex (which covered most of the West Country), the Jutes were confined to Kent, and the Angles settled in East Anglia, Mercia (the Midlands and the Welsh borders) and Northumbria, which reached to the Scottish border. In Scotland, the Picts and Scots were eventually united under King Kenneth MacAlpine.

In the mid-9th century the Danes or Norsemen, popularly known as Vikings, who had been raiding the country for almost a century and taking their booty home, decided it was time to settle. Of the local leaders, Alfred of Wessex (AD 871–901) was the only one strong enough to defeat them and come to a relatively amicable agreement. The Danes, who established a large settlement in York, were to control the north and east of the country, ("the Danelaw"), while Alfred would rule the rest. Alfred is known as "the father of the British navy" as he founded a strong fleet which first beat the Danes at sea, then protected the coasts and encouraged trade.

Alfred, said to have taught himself Latin at the age of 40, translated Bede's work into English. A learned man himself, he encouraged learning in others, established schools and formulated a legal system and built up the army and navy, earning his title "Alfred the Great".

After the great king's death, trouble broke out again. His successors reconquered the Danelaw, but in 980 Viking invasions recommenced. King Ethelred tried paying them to stay away by imposing a tax, called the *danegeld*, on his people. But Ethelred, whose title "The Unready" was as well earned as Alfred's, was a poor psychologist. The Danes merely grew more predatory while he grew more confused.

When his death left no strong Saxon successor, the Witan chose Canute, the Danish leader, as king. Canute proved to be a wise ruler. He divid-

LEFT: Pict warrior. **ABOVE:** Roman mosaic found in Dorset.

ed power between Danes and Saxons and, to protect his northern border, compelled Malcolm II, king of the Scots, to recognise him as overlord.

Had Canute's sons, Harold and Hardicanute, not died within a few years of him, the whole history of Britain might have been very different. As it was, the succession passed to Edward, son of Ethelred, who had spent most of his life in Normandy, the part of France settled by the Vikings.

The Norman Conquest

Edward (1042–66), known as the Confessor, was a pious man who built Westminster Abbey to the glory of God. He was also far more Norman than Saxon and soon upset his father-in-law, Earl Godwin, by filling his court with "foreign" favourites and appointing a Norman priest Archbishop of Canterbury. He is also said to have promised the English throne to William, Duke of Normandy. But, when Edward died, the council advising the king chose Harold, son of Godwin, as monarch.

Harold's reign lasted less than a year. In October 1066 William of Normandy came to claim the throne. He landed at Pevensey on the Sussex coast and defeated Harold in battle on Senlac Field, near Hastings. William was crowned king in Westminster Abbey on Christmas Day and set out to consolidate his kingdom. Many Saxon nobles had died in battle while others fled to Scotland. William filled the vacuum with Norman barons and strengthened and formalised the feudal system which had begun before his arrival.

His barons received their land in return for a promise of military service and a proportion of the land's produce. The barons then parcelled out land to the lesser nobles, knights and freemen, also in return for goods and services. At the bottom of the heap were the villeins or serfs, unfree peasants who were virtually slaves.

William's influence was strongest in the south. Faced with combined Saxon-Danish rebellion in the north, he took swift and brutal action, devastating the countryside and destroying much of the Roman city of York. He then built a string of

THE DOMESDAY BOOK

William needed to know exactly who owned what in his new kingdom, the amount of produce he could expect and the taxes he could demand. So he sent out his clerks to compile a meticulous property record. How much land did an archbishop have? How many oxen did a ploughman own? Nobody was to escape the great reckoning. The massive survey, called the Domesday Book because it seemed to the English not unlike the Book of Doom to be used by the greatest feudal lord of all on Judgment Day, was completed in 1086. Today, it is kept in the Public Records Office in London, and is a fascinating document of early social history. An online version is available at nationalarchives.gov.uk.

defensive castles, and appointed a Great Council consisting of his new tenants-in-chief, which met three times a year in the southern cities of Winchester, Westminster and Gloucester.

The early Norman kings had trouble keeping peace on their borders. William's son, Henry I, tried a pacific approach to Scotland: he married King Malcolm III's daughter, Matilda. He died in 1135, leaving no male heir. His daughter, also called Matilda, had married Henry Plantagenet, Count of Anjou, and became embroiled in a civil war against the followers of her cousin, Stephen. This war ended in 1153 with Stephen in control of the Crown but forced to accept Matilda's son, Henry, as joint ruler. When Stephen died the following year, Henry, founder of the Angevin dynasty (the dynasty of Anjou), usually known as the Plantagenet dynasty, became king and went on to rule for 35 years.

The great monasteries

While battles raged and kings connived, there was another side to life in this period, which has been described as "the flowering of Norman culture on English soil". The monasteries, both Benedictine and Cistercian, formed the new cultural centres; Canterbury, Westminster and Winchester were among the most active in the south, as were Fountains Abbey and Rievaulx in the north and Strata Florida in mid-Wales.

In Scotland the great monasteries at Melrose, Dryburgh, Jedburgh and Kelso were all built in the reign of Malcolm III's son, David I (1124–53), who also established a capital at Edinburgh.

These great houses produced erudite historians and scholars, some of whom went in search of other branches of learning in European monasteries, but they made no attempt to educate those outside the Orders. Benedictine monasteries were a vital part of the feudal system, some gradually becoming almost indistinguishable from the great landed estates. Their abbots lived very well indeed, eating and drinking with great abandon.

King Arthur and Albion

But Chaucer's knight, his "verray parfit gentil knight", shows another side of medieval life: the courtly tradition and the code of chivalry. The highly exaggerated, romantic ideals of knights who would fight and die to win a smile from their pure and unblemished ladies first gained popularity in the 12th century at the time of the Crusades. From this tradition sprang the Arthurian myth.

Arthur probably existed and may well have been a Celtic leader of the 6th or 7th century. But it was Geoffrey of Monmouth, a 12th-century historian, who invented many Arthurian legends: his magical sword, Excalibur, and the wizard Merlin. Tintagel Castle in Cornwall, supposedly Arthur's birthplace, was not built until the 12th century – but there is no need to let historical facts spoil a good story.

As more people learned to read, curiosity about the history of Britain grew and writers were tempted to embellish, romanticise and quite simply invent. Geoffrey attributed one of Britain's early names, Albion, to the fact that the country had first been ruled by Albina, daughter of a Roman Emperor, Diocletian. More sober writers believe the name comes from the Latin for white, *alba*, and refers to the cliffs at Dover, the Romans' first sight of Britain.

In the 15th century William Caxton, the printing pioneer, blended historical fact and fantasy, myth and legend, in a fascinating account called *The Description of Britain*. A century later, Raphael Holinshed compiled his *Chronicles*; this work featured the story of King Lear, later dramatised by Shakespeare, who relied heavily on Holinshed's work for several plays. ❑

LEFT: a panel from the Bayeux Tapestry shows William the Conqueror setting sail for England in 1066.
RIGHT: pilgrims on their way to Canterbury.

Prehistoric Times

Of all Britain's historic places, it is the prehistoric sites that are the most evocative – the legacy of ancient and mysterious cultures

It is impossible to travel far in Britain without seeing some evidence of the peoples who settled the land in the far-off centuries before history was recorded. These sites are not always immediately apparent – only a grassy bank between two fields may remain, perhaps, or a series of ridges around the summit of a prominent hill. These ridges were the banks and ditches which defended the hill-top forts of Iron-Age tribes, who could watch over the lower ground from behind the encircling wooden pallisades. Maiden Castle in Dorset is a particularly fine example, and Cadbury Castle, just off the busy A303 in Somerset, has been linked to Arthurian legend as the possible site of Camelot.

Circles of stone

While the hill-forts were obviously places of habitation, the enigmatic stone circles that loom on many a remote hillside still lack a definitive explanation. Were they temples of ancient religions, places for pagan sacrificial rituals, meeting places, monuments celebrating some wonder of nature...?

Stonehenge is the most famous site, and remains a remarkable place in spite of the many visitors who are drawn to it at the height of the season. Many maintain that Castlerigg Stone Circle, high up on remote moorland in the Lake District, has the most picturesque setting, while the standing stones and ancient burial cairns of Orkney have a very special atmosphere. Cornwall and Wales, last strongholds of the Celtic tribes of Britain, are littered with cairns and standing stones.

Above: Even without his obvious charms, the **Cerne Abbas Giant** is an impressive sight. Standing 180ft (55 metres) tall, he was carved into the turf of Dorset's chalk down-land, probably during the Roman occupation or earlier. No-one can be certain of his significance, though legend has understandably endowed him with powers of fertility. Some locals refer to him as "the Rude Man."

Below: The neolithic village of **Skara Brae**, on the Orkney islands off Scotland, was Inhabited between 3200BC and 2200BC. There are eight houses, linked together by low alleyways.

Below: a dolmen at **Lanyon Quoit** in Cornwall known as "the Giant's Table."

THE MAGIC OF THE DRUIDS

The original Druids, spiritual leaders of the Celts, were a far cry from the present-day variety, who don flowing robes and gather at Stonehenge to celebrate dawn on midsummer's day. Now largely based in Wales, these Druids appear principally to be a society for promoting Celtic culture.

Druidism was a pre-Christian religion which formed the cornerstone of Celtic society and its priesthood held tremendous power and influence. The Celts were volatile and warlike, but they were also hospitable, extremely artistic and very spiritual. They worshipped gods who controlled nature and the seasons, having a direct bearing on their day-to-day lives, and the Druids were the fount of all knowledge.

Well versed in magic, the Druids revered the oak tree and mistletoe, and held their rituals in oak forests. They probably used dolmens (stone monuments) as temples and altars, though Stonehenge itself predates them by many centuries.

The Druids, who acted not only as priests but also as religious teachers and judges, maintained their power by creating an aura of mystery. They committed their knowledge to memory. Thus it was literacy as much as the conversion of many of them to Christianity that ultimately eroded the influence of the Druids in the 2nd to 4th centuries AD.

ABOVE: The **Callanish Stones**, on the Isle of Lewis in Scotland's Outer Hebrides, form a spectacular megalithic monument, built around 2000BC. There are 13 primary stones.

BELOW: Stonehenge, in Wiltshire, doesn't impress from a distance because the stones are visually diminished by the surrounding plain. Close up, they are awesome. They were assembled between 3000 and 2300 BC – but how, why and by whom? The axis of Stonehenge is aligned with the sunrise on 21 June, the longest day of the year, so some believe it may have been used to calculate the passing of time.

RIGHT: Maiden Castle in Dorchester, Dorset, is the largest and most complex Iron Age hill fort in Britain. The castle was first laid out in 600BC over the remains of a Neolithic settlement. Several hundred people lived here from 800BC until 43AD, after which the site was occupied by the Roman army. The ramparts, English Heritage estimates, enclose a total area equivalent to 50 football pitches.

SHAKESPEARE'S KINGS

Threatened at home by powerful barons and abroad by fragile alliances and the power of the Pope, England's monarchs were a dramatist's dream

For his Histories, William Shakespeare drew on the lives of the Plantagenet and Tudor kings who ruled from 1154 to 1547, and his stirring dramas colour our view of them today. These were the King Henrys, the Richards and King John, around whom he wove fanciful plots, bloody deeds and heroic tales. He did not tackle the first of the Plantagenet kings, Henry II: that was left for T.S. Eliot, in the 20th century, who made a classic drama out of the king and his archbishop in *Murder in the Cathedral*.

Henry cemented the Anglo-Norman state. Through his mother's line he was the rightful king of England and through his father he inherited the title Count of Anjou. With his marriage to Eleanor of Aquitaine he also gained control of her lands, which stretched to the Pyrenees. But Scotland, Ireland and Wales formed no part of his kingdom.

Church versus State

Relations between Church and State became increasingly strained during Henry's reign. He tried to end the Church's monopoly of jurisdiction over members of the clergy who committed secular crimes, and to bring clerics under the law of the land. Thomas Becket, his strong-willed Archbishop and erstwhile friend, resisted this and was berated by the king. In 1170, four knights of the royal household took literally Henry's wish that someone would "rid me of this meddlesome priest" and murdered Becket on the altar steps of Canterbury Cathedral.

When Henry II died in 1189, his son Richard came to the throne. Richard has always been one of England's most popular kings even though – or maybe because – he spent most of his time in the Holy Land fighting Crusades against the Infidel. Known as Coeur de Lion (Lionheart) for his bravery, he was deeply mourned when killed in France, despite the domestic mess into which his prolonged absence and expensive exploits had plunged the country. It was the injustice at home, presided over in part by Richard's brother and successor John, that produced the legendary Nottingham outlaw, Robin Hood, who, with his Merry Men, preyed on the rich to give to the poor.

Magna Carta

King John scores poorly among English monarchs. He quarrelled with the Pope over his practice of siphoning off the revenues of ecclesiastical estates and over the Papal appointment of Stephen Langton as Archbishop of Canterbury. This resulted in another Interdict and John's excommunication.

To consolidate his power, Henry II made administrative reforms and instigated the system of common law which operates today, distinguishing English from Continental and Scottish legal systems.

He also caused a rising tide of resentment among the barons, chiefly because he failed to protect their Norman lands from the advances of the French king, Philip Augustus. Another important grievance was that John had imposed high taxes, undermined the power of the feudal courts and taken for himself the fines of offenders which had previously been part of the barons' income.

Angered by the king's contempt of them, the barons threatened to take up arms against John unless he agreed to a series of demands on behalf of the people. These became the basis of the Magna Carta (Great Charter) signed at Runnymede near Windsor in 1215. Under its terms, the Church was given back its former rights. The Charter also limited royal power over arrests and imprisonments and prevented the king from expropriating fines. For the barons the main interest was to stop him encroaching on their feudal rights and privileges.

Although history sees the Charter as a milestone, the document on which British freedoms are based, it brought no immediate solution. The Pope condemned it and John defied it and his barons; as soon as he could, he raised troops and ravaged the north. The barons retaliated by turning to Louis of France for help, but John died in 1216 before he could cause any more trouble.

Battles with the barons

John's son, who became Henry III, proved little better. He gave most of the top jobs to foreign favourites who flocked to England after his marriage to Eleanor of Provence and, in 1242, he embarked on a disastrous war with France which ended with the loss of the valuable lands of Poitou. The barons, under Simon de Montfort, rebelled and the king was defeated at the Battle of Lewes (now the county town of East Sussex). In 1265 de Montfort summoned a parliament, which represented the chief towns and boroughs and has been called the first House of Commons, although anything like a fair system of representation was still centuries away. But de Montfort's lust for power soon lost him the support of the barons. In 1266 Henry was restored to the throne where he reigned peacefully, if not very well, until his death in 1272.

Under Edward I, Henry's son, Wales was con-

LEFT: King John stirred the barons to revolt.
ABOVE: a romanticised 19th-century view of Robin Hood and his Merrie Men, the mythical Nottingham outlaws who took from the rich and gave to the poor.

quered. Llewellyn, Prince of Wales, was killed in the Battle of Builth on the River Wye and his brother David was captured and executed. The Statute of Wales in 1284 placed the country under English law and Edward presented his newborn son to the Welsh as Prince of Wales, a title held by the heir to the throne ever since.

The Hundred Years' War

In England, the reign of Edward II had little to commend it. His defeat by Bruce paved the way for a Scottish invasion of Ireland. He lost Gascony and upset his own barons by appointing his unsuitable friends to high office. Even his wife deserted him and joined his enemy, Roger Mortimer. The pair assumed power and in 1327 Edward was deposed by Parliament, who named his young son king. Edward was later murdered, unmourned, in Berkeley Castle in Gloucestershire.

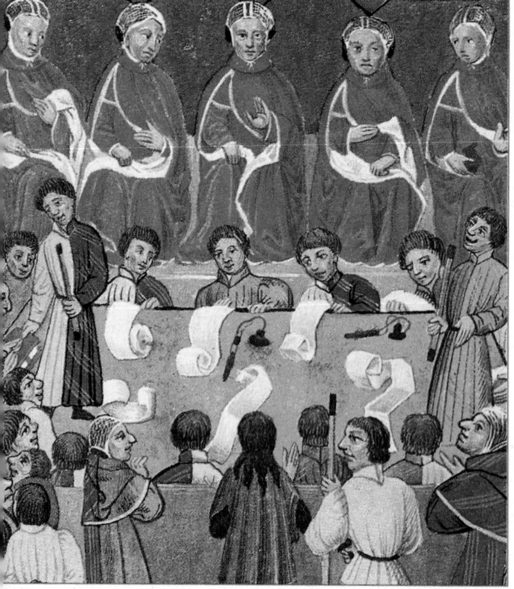

As soon as he was old enough, young Edward III, showing little filial loyalty, had his mother incarcerated for life in Castle Rising, Norfolk, and Mortimer executed. Much of his long reign was spent fighting the Hundred Years' War with France, which actually lasted from 1337 to 1453 with several periods of peace.

These protracted hostilities began when Edward, whose maternal grandfather was Philip IV of France, claimed the French throne. The fortunes of war shifted from one side to the other. At the Battle of Crécy more than 30,000 French troops were killed and the Massacre of Limoges, led by England's Black Prince, left 3,000 dead. But by 1371 the English had lost most of their French possessions.

After a long peaceful lull, Edward's claim was revived by his great-grandson, Henry V, immortalised by Shakespeare as the heroic Prince Hal. With miraculously few English casualties – although rather more than Shakespeare claimed – Henry defeated the French at Agincourt, starved Rouen into submission four years later, and made a strategic marriage to a French princess. By the time of his death in 1422 he controlled all of northern France.

Plague and Poll Tax

On the domestic front, times were also hard. The Black Death, which reached England in 1348, killed nearly half the population. Followed by

THE STRUGGLE WITH SCOTLAND

Scotland became a united country in the 12th century – apart from the islands, still controlled by the Danes. Gaelic was still the language of the Highlands, but elsewhere most people spoke English and trade links with England had been established. But this didn't mean that the Scots had to like the English.

When Alexander II died in 1286, rivals claimed the throne. The first, John Balliol, son of the founder of Balliol College, Oxford, was persuaded to accept the throne as England's vassal. But he resented owing allegiance to England and made a treaty with King Edward I's enemy, the king of France, then crossed the border and ravaged Cumberland. Edward fought back, Balliol was captured and imprisoned and the sacred kingmaking Stone of Scone was taken to Westminster Abbey.

The struggle against English domination was later renewed by Robert Bruce (1274–1329), one of Scotland's greatest heroes. Through his aristocratic father he was distantly related to the Scottish royal family, and his mother had strong Gaelic antecedents.

Defeated by the Earl of Pembroke, Bruce became a fugitive but re-emerged to be crowned at Scone, and in 1314 defeated the English at Bannockburn in Stirlingshire. Scottish independence was recognised. Robert's daughter Margery married Walter Stewart and their son Robert II came to the throne in 1371, the first Stuart King.

lesser epidemics during the next 50 years, it had reduced Britain's population from 4 million to 2 million by the end of the century. This had far-reaching effects. By leaving so much land untended and making labour scarce, it gave surviving peasants, and those who came after them, a better bargaining position. But it also meant that some landlords, unable or unwilling to pay higher wages, tried to force peasants back into serfdom. The more affluent peasants of Kent and East Anglia began to flex their economic muscles and when a Poll Tax was introduced in 1381 they rose in rebellion, both against the tax and against the landlords' oppressive treatment.

Wat Tyler and Jack Straw were the most prominent leaders of the Peasants' Revolt, which gained the support of the urban poor and briefly took control of London. Soon the rebellion was brutally suppressed and Richard II reneged on his promise to abolish serfdom. But this manifestation of the power of the people had made their lords and masters nervous and landlords became more wary about enforcing villeinage. Gradually the feudal system withered until it died.

The "Yeomen of Old England" who feature in some patriotic songs also emerged as a result of the 14th-century plagues. Landlords found it more profitable to rent out much of their land rather than pay labourers to tend it and in so doing they created a whole new class of yeomen farmers. The name originally meant simply "young men", presumably those with the energy to scratch a living from the often poor pieces of land and convert them, as they gradually did, into valuable smallholdings.

In 1399 the Lancastrian Revolution overthrew Richard II and put Henry IV, Duke of Lancaster, on the throne. It was during his reign that the first English heretic was burned at the stake. He was William Sawtrey, Rector of Lynn, in Dorset, and his heresy was preaching the Lollard Doctrines. Lollards were the followers of John Wycliffe, who rejected the Pope's authority and had the Bible translated into English so that any literate person could understand it. The persecution of the Lollards continued into the next reign when the movement, not organised enough to withstand the pressure, went underground. The demands for change and reform in the Church would resurface successfully 100 years later, when they suited the purposes of the king.

LEFT: a trial takes place in Westminster Hall.
ABOVE: Wat Tyler was beheaded by the Lord Mayor of London after the Peasants' Revolt, watched by King Richard II (seen on the right inspecting his troops).

The Wars of the Roses

Times were rarely peaceful during these centuries. Foreign wars were fought to gain or retain land and glory, while at home periodic attacks on the throne by rival contenders were equally bloody. Henry IV had to contend with the Rebellions of the Percys, a powerful Northumberland family, and the guerrilla warfare conducted by Owain Glyndwr (Owen Glendower, 1354–1416), a self-declared prince who was pressing hard for independence for Wales.

Henry IV's son, Henry V (1413–22), faced a conspiracy led by the Earl of Mortimer and, in 1455, after Henry VI had gone insane and government put into the hands of a Protector, rivalries between the powerful Dukes of York and Somerset led to the Wars of the Roses. This name was, in fact, coined by the 19th-century novelist Sir Walter Scott, but it is a convenient shorthand for these battles between the great House of York, symbolised by the white rose, and that of Lancaster, symbolised by the red.

Edward IV (1461–83) reigned for most of the duration of these wars. He has been called "a man of gentle nature and cheerful aspect", although he did not extend his gentleness towards his brother, the Duke of Clarence, who incurred the king's displeasure, was found guilty of treason in 1478 and drowned in a butt of Malmsey wine.

One of the nastiest things about these wars was the number of people who were executed, with or without a trial, off the field of battle. Perhaps the best known of these murders was that of the young princes, Edward and Richard, said to have been smothered while imprisoned in the Tower of London in 1483. The guilt of their uncle, Shakespeare's hunchbacked Richard III, has never been proven and there is today a society dedicated to proving his innocence. Certainly, he's unlikely to have been as black as he was painted by Shakespeare – who, after all, was writing a melodrama calculated both to entertain and to conform diplomatically to the prejudices of his own time.

A pub, Jack Straw's Castle, commemorates the leader of the Peasants' Revolt and does a thriving trade on London's Hampstead Heath.

The circumstances of Richard's own death are also well known. He was killed during the Battle of Bosworth, in Leicestershire, where Shakespeare had him offering his kingdom for a horse, while his crown came to rest ignominiously in a nearby hawthorn bush.

The wars ended with the marriage of Henry VII (1485–1509), part-Welsh grandson of Owen Tudor and descendant of John of Gaunt, Duke of Lancaster, to Elizabeth of York. This united the opposing factions and put the country under the rule of the Tudors. Henry was something of a financial wizard and, determined to enrich a throne impoverished by years of war, proceeded to extort money wherever possible.

Through loans, subsidies, property levies and fines he refilled the royal coffers but, regrettably, most of the money was squandered by his son, Henry VIII on a series of French wars. These renewed hostilities gave the Scots an opportunity to ally themselves with the French and invade England. But they were terribly defeated at the Battle of Flodden Field, where James IV and 10,000 of his men were slaughtered.

The break from Rome

Henry VIII is the most famous of British kings. He was the hugely fat, gluttonous and licentious ruler who married six times, divorced twice and beheaded two of his wives. He is also famous as the man who brought about the Reformation, which made England a Protestant rather than a Catholic country, because the Pope refused to annul his marriage to Catherine of Aragon, who could not oblige him by producing a male heir.

There are other well-known characters in this drama: one is Thomas Wolsey, Archbishop and Lord Chancellor, who had Hampton Court Palace built as an exhibition of his wealth and who was later charged with high treason for not giving sufficient support to his King. Another is Sir Thomas More, beheaded for refusing to recognise Henry as Supreme Head of the Church of England; and a third is Thomas Cromwell who, between 1536 and 1539, carried out the King's drastic wish to destroy the country's monasteries. But he made the mistake of taking Protestantism too far for Henry's liking and was rewarded with decapitation on Tower Hill, while all the monastery lands and riches went to his ungrateful monarch.

The causes of the English Reformation were not, of course, quite so simple. Papal dispensation for the divorce was only withheld because Pope Clement VII was living in fear of Charles of Spain, the Holy Roman Emperor and Europe's most powerful monarch, who happened to be Catherine's nephew. A desire for Church reform had been growing for many years and now, encouraged by the success of Martin Luther (1483–1546), the great German reformer, many believed its time had come. The privilege and wealth of the clergy were also resented, even by those who had no doctrinal quarrels with the Church. And, of course, Henry needed the money to be made from the vast amounts of seized monastic lands and property.

"Bloody Mary"

Under Henry, Wales was joined with England in the 1536 Act of Union, which gave it representation in parliament. When he died in 1547, Henry was succeeded by his only male heir, Edward, a sickly 10-year-old who died six years later. His half-sister Mary then came to the throne and won herself the nickname "Bloody Mary", proving that a woman could be just as ruthless as a man when the occasion demanded. A devout Catholic, she restored the Old Religion and raised fears that her

marriage to Philip II of Spain would lead to undue Spanish inteference and the introduction of the dreaded Inquisition. During her rule the Marian Persecution, as it was called, saw at least 300 Protestants burned as heretics, including Archbishop Cranmer, who died at Oxford after first thrusting into the flames "the unworthy hand" which had earlier signed a recantation.

Mary is also remembered as the monarch who lost the French port of Calais, the "brightest jewel in the English crown" and the last British possession on the Continent, during a renewed war with France. More remorseful about the loss of land than the loss of so many lives, she declared that when she died the word "Calais" would be found engraved on her heart. ❑

FAR LEFT: Henry V, Shakespeare's most heroic king.
LEFT: beheading was the punishment for traitors.
RIGHT: Henry VIII as Holbein's paintings portray him.

The Golden Age

Under Elizabeth I, Britain ruled the waves and produced great literature. But then power began to shift from the monarch to the politicians

The Elizabethan Age has a swashbuckling ring to it: the Virgin Queen and her dashing courtiers, the defeat of the Spanish Armada, and the exploits of the "sea dogs", Frobisher and Hawkins. Sir Walter Raleigh brought tobacco back from Virginia; Sir Francis Drake circumnavigated the world.

In this age of the renaissance man, even the great poets Sir Philip Sidney and John Donne spent time before the mast – although William Shakespeare, born six years after Elizabeth had been crowned queen, stayed at home, entertaining the crowds at the Globe Theatre in London's Southwark. Poetry, plays and pageants were the thing, and they accompanied the Queen on her tours of the country.

Conspiracies against the Queen

Elizabeth I, Henry VIII's daughter by Anne Boleyn whom he beheaded, may have had an interesting life at court but in fact she spent nearly 20 years of her long reign (1558–1603) resisting Catholic attempts to either dethrone or assassinate her. She had re-established Protestantism but was constantly challenged by those who wished to put Mary Stuart, Queen of Scots, on the throne and return to the Old Religion.

Mary had a colourful background. Sent to France as a child, she returned a young widow and in 1565 married her cousin, Lord Darnley. But she became far too friendly with her secretary, Rizzio, who was stabbed to death by her jealous husband at the Palace of Holyroodhouse in Edinburgh (tour guides point out the exact spot where it happened – some can even discern traces of faded bloodstains). Shortly afterwards Darnley himself was killed and, as Mary rather too swiftly married Lord Bothwell, suspicions were aroused, a rebellion mounted and Mary had to abdicate in favour of her son, James.

On fleeing to England, however, she was promptly incarcerated by Elizabeth and languished in prison while plots were fomented, mostly involving the assistance of Spain. The trial and execution of Mary in 1587 removed the conspirators' focal point and the defeat of the Spanish Armada the following year put an end to Catholic conspiracies against Elizabeth.

When Elizabeth died without an heir she was succeeded by Mary's son, James. He was James VI of Scotland, but James I in England, where he was the first of the Stuarts to take the throne. His succession brought a temporary union of the two countries but his reign, too, was bedevilled by reli-

Defeating the Spanish Armada gave England naval supremacy, which laid the foundations for a future of flourishing trade, expansionism and colonisation.

gious controversy. The Puritans became prominent, believing that the Reformation had not gone far enough and calling for a purer form of worship. And the Catholics engineered a number of plots, one of which resulted in Sir Walter Raleigh's 13-year imprisonment in the Tower of London (his well-appointed rooms can be visited). Ironically, Raleigh was released by James who was short of money and sent in search of gold in Guiana. The expedition failed and Raleigh, accused of treason, was executed.

The Gunpowder Plot

The most famous of the Catholic conspiracies was the Gunpowder Plot of 1605, when Guy Fawkes attempted to blow up the Houses of Parliament. The immediate result was the execution of Fawkes and his fellow-conspirators and the imposition of severe anti-Catholic laws. Curiously, people today, however sceptical of politicians, burn effigies of Fawkes on the night of 5 November, and set off thousands of pounds-worth of fireworks.

LEFT: Elizabeth I, the "Virgin Queen".
ABOVE: the defeat of the Spanish Armada in 1588.

The Puritan protests were more peaceful, but James had little sympathy with their demands. A new translation of the Bible into English (the "Authorised" or "King James" Version) was a rare concession. James said he would "make them conform or harry them from the land". Some left voluntarily. Going first to Holland, a small group who became known as the Pilgrim Fathers set sail in the *Mayflower* in 1620 and founded New Plymouth in North America, Britain's first toe-hold in the New World.

Meanwhile, in Ireland, events were taking place which would leave a long and bloody legacy. The lands of northern Irish lords had been seized in Elizabeth's reign after a series of rebellions had been brutally suppressed. Now they were redistributed among English and Scottish settlers. The county of Derry was divided up among 12 London merchant guilds and renamed Londonderry. Ulster became England's first important colony.

The Stuart period was one of conflict between Crown and Parliament. James I, a staunch believer in the Divine Right of Kings, a belief held by most European rulers of the time, would have preferred no Parliament at all and actually did without one for seven years. But, once recalled in 1621, the House of Commons renewed its insistence on political power in return for the taxes it was constantly asked to raise.

The Civil War

Under Charles I, relations with Parliament went from bad to dreadful. In 1628 he reluctantly accepted the Petition of Right, one of the most important documents in British history, which forbade arbitrary arrest and imprisonment and deemed that taxes should be raised only by an act of Parliament. But a year later he dissolved Parliament and initiated 11 years of absolute rule.

Surprisingly, he managed very well and might have continued indefinitely had it not been for the over-zealous attempts of William Laud, the anti-Puritan Archbishop of Canterbury, to impose the English Book of Common Prayer on the fero-

ciously independent Scottish Church, or Kirk.

Influenced by the great French theologian, John Calvin (1509–64), the Scottish Church had embraced Puritan values, and was referred to as Presbyterian because its elders were known as Presbyters, not Bishops. Laud's intransigence provoked a massive popular rebellion. The Covenanters, so-called because they had signed a National Covenant "to resist Popery", formed an army and invaded England.

Short of money and trained men, Charles was unable to cope. He had to summon a Parliament, but King and Commons were constantly at each other's throats and in 1641 discontented Irish Catholics took advantage of their disarray to attack the settlers who had taken their land. Thousands were massacred and the outcry in England was heightened by a belief that Charles had backed the Irish Catholic side. This belief, together with Charles's attempt to arrest the five members of Parliament most openly opposed to him, precipitated the Civil War.

> *The English Civil War of 1641–53 has become romanticised, and today a society flourishes which re-enacts the principal battles for fun.*

Charles gained the support of the north and west of the country and Wales. Oliver Cromwell, member of Parliament for Cambridge and a stout defender of the Puritan cause, became leader of the Ironsides, backed by London and the southern counties and later joined by Scottish troops. Enormous damage was done to castles, churches and fortified houses during the war and when it was over many were "slighted" – either destroyed completely or made indefensible. Today the King and his Cavaliers are shown more sympathy than Cromwell and his Roundheads – so called because of their short haircuts.

Cromwell's republic

King Charles's execution in 1649, on a scaffold erected outside Inigo Jones's new Banqueting House in Whitehall, has also become the stuff of which legends are made. He reputedly wore two shirts, so that he would not shiver in the January cold and cause people to think he was afraid. The poet Andrew Marvell, deeply moved by the event, wrote: "He nothing common did or mean/Upon that memorable scene."

As so often in politics, making a martyr of the enemy proved a big mistake. There was public outrage at home, while in Scotland Charles's son and namesake was crowned king. Young Charles, however, was not happy with the Presbyterian religion he was pledged to uphold. He marched into England where he was defeated at Worcester, was pursued south and, after many adventures, finally escaped to France.

Meanwhile, Cromwell and "the Rump" – the Parliamentary members who had voted for Charles's execution – declared England a Commonwealth. One of Cromwell's first acts was to exact reprisals for the massacres in Ireland by killing all the inhabitants of the towns of Drogheda and Wexford. Another was the suppression of the Levellers, a group within his own army who did not believe that his democratisation had gone far enough. In 1653 Cromwell dissolved Parliament, formed a Protectorate with himself as Lord Protector and ruled alone until his death in 1658. Without him republicanism faltered and, in 1660, Charles II was declared king.

Britain prospered under Charles (1660–85), who, it was said, "never said a foolish thing nor ever did a wise one". True or not, one unwise thing Parliament was afraid he would do was become a Catholic. They therefore passed the Test Act, which excluded all Catholics from public office of any kind. In 1678 Titus Oates (whose house can still be seen in the narrow high street in Hastings in Sussex) disclosed a bogus "Popish Plot" to assassinate the king. In the resultant hysteria, thousands of Catholics were imprisoned and no Catholic was allowed to sit in the House of Commons – a law that was not repealed for nearly 300 years.

Whigs and Tories

Fear of the monarchy ever again becoming too powerful led to the emergence of the first political parties. Both were known by nicknames: Whigs was a derogatory name for cattle drivers, Tories an Irish word meaning thugs. Loosely speaking, the Whigs opposed absolute monarchy and supported the right to religious freedom for Nonconformists, while Tories were the upholders of Church and Crown, the natural successors of Charles I's Royalists. The Whigs were to form a coalition with dissident Tories in the mid-19th century and become the Liberal Party. The Tories were the forerunners of the Conservative Party, which retains the nickname.

In 1685 Charles was succeeded by his brother. James II (1685–89) was not a success. Within a year he had imposed illegal taxation and tried to bring back absolute monarchy and the Catholic religion. Rebellions were savagely put down, with

LEFT: Oliver Cromwell, who ruled Britain as Lord Protector from 1653 to 1658. **ABOVE:** the monarchy restored, Charles II walks out on Horseguards Parade.

SIR CHRISTOPHER WREN

Although Wren (1632–1723) was renowned in his day as an astronomer, it is his architectural achievements that have gained him immortality. He designed 53 London churches and replaced many other prominent buildings after the devastating Great Fire in 1666, influencing generations of architects. St Paul's Cathedral, which took 36 years to build, remains his greatest achievement – a plaque in the crypt displays the words: "Reader, if you seek his memorial – look around you."

hundreds being hanged and many more sold into slavery to the West Indies.

In desperation, Whigs and Tories swallowed their differences and in 1688 offered the crown to James's daughter, Mary, and her husband, the Dutch prince William of Orange. This became known as the Glorious Revolution and, although bloodless, a revolution it certainly was. By choosing the new monarch, Parliament had proved itself more powerful than the Crown. This power was spelled out in a Bill of Rights, which limited the monarch's freedom of action and ushered in a new era in which Divine Right and Absolute Monarchy had no place.

But James II had not yet given up hope. Backed by the French, he landed in Ireland in 1689, believing that the disaffected Irish Catholics would support him. This they did, but with disastrous results for both sides. At Londonderry 30,000 pro-William Protestants survived a siege lasting 15 weeks, but were finally defeated. Their Loyalist descendants still call themselves "Orangemen", and "No Surrender" is the Protestant rallying cry heard in Ulster's streets today. The next year, William's troops defeated James at the Battle of the Boyne. James fled to France, the south of Ireland was subdued and Protestant victory complete.

WILLIAM OF ORANGE

William the Conqueror's 1066 invasion of England was a hostile one, but William of Orange's 1688 invasion was by invitation. England's Protestant establishment saw the Dutch ruler as being the best means of overthrowing the Catholic James II, whose daughter, Mary, William had married. As a child, William (1650–1702) had been taught by Calvinist preachers and he gained his military experience in wars against France. Though he ruled England tolerantly, his heart remained in the Netherlands.

War with France dragged on, to be transformed in Queen Anne's reign into the War of the Spanish Succession, its aim being to put Charles, Archduke of Austria, on the Spanish throne. John Churchill, Duke of Marlborough, won a famous victory at Blenheim in 1704, for which he was rewarded with Blenheim Palace in Oxfordshire. In the same year Gibraltar was taken. Still in British hands, this remains a source of dispute with Spain today. The Treaty of Utrecht ended the war in 1713 and the Queen died without an heir the next year.

ABOVE: Scotland's Catholic clansmen face defeat at Culloden in 1746. **RIGHT:** William Hogarth's painting *Gin Lane* depicts the squalor of slums in London.

The birth of Great Britain

It was during Anne's reign that the name Great Britain came into being when, in 1707, the Act of Union united England and Scotland, largely for economic reasons. Under the Act the two countries were to share the same monarch and parliament while trade and customs laws were to be standardised, though Scotland was to retain its own Church and legislature. The Act did not, however, bring about instant friendliness and accord between the two nations, and it was largely the cause of the Jacobite Rebellions a few years later.

On Anne's death, a reliable Protestant monarch was needed in a hurry and George of Hanover, great-grandson of James I on his mother's side, but a Hanoverian through his father's line and German in language, upbringing and outlook, was invited to Britain. Throughout his 13-year reign he never learned to speak English fluently, nor did he have any great liking for his subjects.

Hanoverian Britain

The Hanoverian dynasty, under the four Georges, spanned a period of nearly 115 years. It was a time of wars with France and Spain, of expanding empire, industrialisation and growing demands for political reform. It also saw the last violent attempts to overthrow a British monarch, in the shape of the two Jacobite Rebellions in support of the "Pretenders", descendants of James II.

The first rebellion, in 1715, in support of James, the "Old Pretender", was defeated near Stirling and its leaders fled to France. Thirty years later English war with France encouraged the Jacobites to try again. Charles, the "Young Pretender", popularly known as Bonnie Prince Charlie, raised a huge army and marched into England. Finding little support from English Jacobites, he returned north of the border where in 1746 his Highland troops were savagely defeated at Culloden. The power of the clan chiefs was destroyed.

No more "Pretenders" arose. From then on power struggles would be political ones, for it was with politicians and Parliament that real power lay. Monarchs were gradually becoming titular figures. Historians may talk about the reign of George III, but it was the policies of William Pitt or Lord Liverpool which mattered. Similarly, the Victorian Age was really the age of Peel and Palmerston, Gladstone and Disraeli. ❑

THE GROWTH OF LONDON

London was partially rebuilt after the Great Fire of 1666, which started in a baker's shop in Pudding Lane and destroyed two-thirds of the cramped, timber-built city. But the subsequent elegant buildings of Sir Christopher Wren (1632–1723), such as St Paul's Cathedral, were a far cry from the overcrowded and insanitary slums in which most people lived. In the more affluent areas, some streets were widened to allow carriages to pass and rudimentary street lighting was introduced in the mid-18th century.

London was then, as now, the country's leading commercial centre and fortunes were made in colonial trade which stimulated banking, insurance and share dealing. A flourishing trade and financial sector also created work for craftsmen and artisans, to furnish homes, build carriages and make clothes. At the same time it brought in service industries to cater for the habitués of the theatres, concert halls and newly fashionable coffee houses.

London was also the centre of court life and the seat of political power. The royal families spent their time at Buckingham House, Kensington Palace and at Hampton Court. George III was the first monarch to live in Buckingham House and George IV had it redesigned by John Nash into a Palace. A system of patronage flourished around Parliament, which met at Westminster, although not in the present building, which was built after a serious fire destroyed its predecessor in 1834.

Britannia Rules

Trade boomed, cities burgeoned, railways spread, the Empire swelled. It was a great time to be British – unless, that is, you were poor

The treaty signed at the end of the Seven Years' War with France in 1763 allowed Britain to keep all its overseas colonies, making it the leading world power. The empire had been growing since 1607 when Virginia, the first British colony in America, had been established. In 1620 English Puritans had settled in Massachusetts and other settlements were made later in the century. By 1700 most were governed by a Crown official and incorporated into Britain's Atlantic Empire.

Throughout the 17th century the demand for goods – furs, rice, silk, tobacco, sugar – led to a series of wars with the Dutch and the French from which Britain emerged in control of much of West Africa, Newfoundland and Nova Scotia and some of the Caribbean islands. French and English battled for supremacy in Canada and India during the 18th century. By 1760 England had proved the clear winner: General James Wolfe's capture of Quebec ended French power in Canada and Robert Clive had beaten both Indians and French for control of the Indian subcontinent, a victory which made the East India Company a private colonial power.

Attempts to wreck the hated power looms were made by "Luddites", named after Ned Ludd of Leicestershire. But the rebels lost the fight.

Convicts and slaves

Britain's loss of its American colonies in 1783 was eased by the opening up of the Pacific. Captain Cook reached Tahiti in 1768 and then went on to New Zealand and Australia, where he landed at Botany Bay. When American Independence deprived Britain of a place to send its convicts,

the harsh, undeveloped lands of Australia were the obvious alternative.

Colonial trade, unfortunately, went hand in hand with slavery. European traders bought slaves in West Africa, shipped them to the Americas under appalling conditions and sold them to plantation owners, often in exchange for produce which they took back home. The raw materials would then be converted into finished products and exported to other parts of the Empire. It was a neat trade triangle which meant high profits for some, misery and degradation for others. It was not until 1807 that the tireless efforts of William Wilberforce made the trade illegal and another 27 years before slavery itself was finally abolished in all British colonies.

The agricultural revolution

Radical changes took place in the English countryside in the late 18th century. Since Saxon times, large areas of land had been cultivated in narrow strips by tenant farmers, and common land had been used for grazing. Little was known about crop rotation or fertilisation and land would be worked until it was exhausted.

During the late 18th and early 19th centuries this system ended when the Enclosure Acts empowered wealthier landowners to seize land to which tenants could prove no legal title and to divide it into enclosed fields. This explains the patchwork quality of much of Britain's countryside, and the paintings of Suffolk by John Constable (1776–1837) show that in some parts of the country little has changed.

A system of crop rotation meant land could be exploited to the full while the cultivation of fodder crops enabled livestock to be kept through the winter months. Artificial fertilizer and new agricultural machinery, such as the seed drill invented by Jethro Tull, also made arable farming more efficient and more profitable. But for the tenants evicted from their lands by the enclosures and the labourers thrown out of work by mechanisation, it was a disaster. Riots erupted in many areas but they could not prevent the march of progress. Many dispossessed peasant farmers had to leave their homes and look for work in the towns, which became hopelessly overcrowded. In Ireland and the Scottish Highlands the agricultural revolution led to mass emigration, particularly to America, and to lasting resentment.

Those who had done well out of new farming methods began to look for ways to invest their capital. They soon joined flourishing city bankers and merchants who had been made prosperous by international trade, to finance what we now call the Industrial Revolution.

This surfeit of capital was one reason why Britain was the first country to industrialise, but it was also helped by relative political stability, the security which came from being an island, from natural resources and from good trade arrangements. These fortunate circumstances combined to produce a genuine revolution, so rapid and complete were the changes it made.

LEFT: Bristol traded profitably with the New World.
ABOVE: coal mines stoked the Industrial Revolution.

The Industrial Revolution

The first steam engine was devised at the end of the 17th century but it was only when the Scottish inventor James Watt (1736–1819) modified and improved the design in the 1770s that steam became an efficient source of energy, which would power trains and ships as well as factory machinery and make many later developments possible. The new steam pumps, for example, allowed speculators to drain deep coal mines, which vastly increased coal production, an important factor when opencast and shallow mines were nearly exhausted.

Textiles had long been a vital part of Britain's economy and the invention of the Spinning Jenny and the power loom in the 1770s and 1780s opened the way to mass production. As in agriculture, mechanisation destroyed the livelihood of those who could not invest in it. Handloom weavers, many of them women and children, were obliged to leave their homes and work in these "dark satanic mills".

Perhaps the most important element in speeding industrialisation was the breakthrough made by Abraham Darby of Coalbrookdale, Shropshire, who succeeded in smelting iron with coke, instead of charcoal. This hugely increased the production of iron which was used for machinery, railways and shipping. Here, in 1776, the world's first cast-iron bridge was built and can still be seen. Cast steel was first produced in the mid-18th century but it was another 100 years before the Bessemer process made possible the cheap mass production of steel.

It was, of course, pointless to produce goods or materials unless they could reach a market, so improved transportation ran parallel with production. The 18th century saw massive outlay on canal building. By 1830 all the main industrial areas were linked by waterways and Scotland was sliced in two by the Caledonian Canal. Unfortunately, most of these would fall into disuse when the new railways proved faster and more efficient, but today, cleared out and cleaned up, they provide thousands of miles of leisure boating. There are more miles of canal in Birmingham than there are in Venice.

New roads were built. A process involving crushed stones and a layer of tar was named after its inventor, the blind Scot John Macadam, and gave us the road surface called "tarmac". By the early 19th century, men such as Macadam and Thomas Telford, whose masterpiece is the magnificent Menai Strait Bridge in North Wales, had created a road network totalling some 125,000 miles (200,000 km).

The Railway Age

But above all this was the age of the railways, when iron and steam combined to change the face of the country, and were romanticised in such vivid paintings as *Rain, Steam and Speed* by J.M.W. Turner (1775–1851). Isambard Kingdom Brunel (1806–59), who also designed the elegant Clifton Suspension Bridge across the Avon Gorge, laid down the Great Western Railway, consolidating a reputation that led him to being voted the second greatest Briton in a 2002 historical poll by the BBC *(see page 77)*. The Stockton and Darlington line, designed by George Stephenson, inventor of the *Rocket*, was the first steam line to open, in 1825, followed five years later by the first inter-city line, from Liverpool to Manchester. This historic occasion was marred when William Huskisson, the President of the Board of Trade, was accidentally killed while officiating at the opening.

In the 18th and 19th centuries a whole new class of industrialists and entrepreneurs made fortunes to rival those of the aristocracy, who in turn looked down on them as *nouveaux riches*, with no breeding. But what about the workers? The new factories and mines certainly provided employment, but working conditions were dreadful. Fatalities in the new deepcast mines were high and those who survived sudden death often had their lives shortened by pneumoconiosis. Children as young as four were employed underground and women worked alongside the men. In factories, too, employees of all ages were treated abominably, working 15-hour days in poor light and deafening noise.

It was not until 1833 that the first Factory Act made it illegal to employ children under nine and for women and under-18s to work more than 12 hours a day. Sixty years were to pass before another act dealt with health and safety at work, and then in a very minor way.

These early industrial reforms were the initiatives of enlightened, liberal-minded men, acting on behalf of the under-privileged, often arousing great opposition from members of their own class for their "interference". It would be some time before working people would be able to achieve benefits on their own behalf.

The Combination Acts of 1824 allowed workers to "combine" together to improve wages, but nothing else. The case of the Tolpuddle Martyrs, six Dorset men sentenced to deportation for their attempts to organise a more comprehensive union, demonstrated the need for workers to protect themselves against exploitation, but it was not until 1868 that the first Trades Union Congress met. Unions then went from strength to strength, although for a long time they largely benefited the so-called "Triple Alliance" of miners, railwaymen and transport workers, and they did little for workers in other areas.

The fear of revolution

The two events which most alarmed the British ruling classes in the closing decades of the 18th century were the American War of Independence and the French Revolution. In the former, people proved themselves willing to fight and die for equality, national identity and political representation. In the latter, they were prepared to remove the heads of the aristocracy and anyone else who denied them liberty, equality and fraternity.

The fear of revolution was exacerbated by wars with France and Spain and the dissatisfaction provoked by the heavy taxes and loss of trade they caused. Known as the Napoleonic Wars, these

LEFT: the coaches of the 1830s were soon to be made redundant by the railways. **ABOVE:** labouring on London's Bankside as trade continued to expand.

RADICAL THINKERS

Radical thinkers such as Edmund Burke (1729–97) and Tom Paine (1737–1809) enthused over the American people's struggle and Paine also supported the ideals of the French Revolution, although he later became sickened by its excesses. *The Rights of Man*, which he published in 1792, defended the people's right to reform what was corrupt. It seriously worried the government. Freedom of the press was suppressed, many radical leaders imprisoned, and Paine escaped to France.

Tom Paine

hostilities began with the threatened French invasion of Belgium and Holland in 1793 and rumbled on, with only three years' break, until 1815.

These were wars which gave Britain two of its greatest heroes, Admiral Lord Nelson (1758–1805) and the Duke of Wellington (1759–1852) and some of its most famous victories. There was the Battle of the Nile in 1798, when Nelson annihilated the French fleet; the Battle of Trafalgar, where he himself was killed after reminding his men that "England expects that every man will do his duty"; Sir John Moore's inspired strike at Corunna, and Wellington's victory at Waterloo, which ended Napoleon's career in 1815.

But political change in England was to come not through revolution but gradual reform. Between 1832 and 1884 three Reform Bills were passed. The first abolished "rotten boroughs", places which returned members to Parliament but had few or no inhabitants, and redistributed parliamentary seats more fairly among the growing towns. It also gave the vote to many householders and tenants, which was based on the value of their property.

The later reform acts extended the franchise more widely, but it was still property-based. Only in 1918 was universal suffrage granted and, even then, it was not quite universal: women under 30 were excluded and had to wait another 10 years. It is unlikely that women would have been enfranchised until much later had it not been for the determined and sometimes violent efforts of the suffragettes, led by Emmeline Pankhurst, and the role women had played in the workforce during World War I.

The 1829 Emancipation Act, which allowed Catholics to sit in Parliament, was another measure which frightened many of the old school, who feared it might pave the way for Popish plots and undermine both Church and State. And the controversial Repeal of the Corn Laws – the heavy taxes on imported corn which were crippling trade and starving the poor – split the ruling Conservative Party. The "Peelite" faction, followers of the pro-repeal Prime Minister Sir Robert Peel, joined

TRAFALGAR'S HERO

Remembered for his stirring words before the 1805 Battle of Trafalgar, in which he died – "England expects that every man will do his duty" – Vice-Admiral Horatio Nelson is credited from saving Britain from an invasion by Napoleon. Born in Norfolk in 1758, he joined the navy at the age of 12 and was a captain by 20. Later, as head of the navy, he was known as an inspiring leader. History also remembers him for his long and romantic affair with Emma, Lady Hamilton, an ambassador's wife.

with Whigs to form the embryonic Liberal Party. This new grouping was committed to free trade, religious tolerance and a growing conviction that Ireland should be granted Home Rule.

The trouble with Ireland

The "Irish Question" was one to which no satisfactory answer could be found. The resentment of centuries bubbled to the surface after the potato famine of 1848, when about 20 percent of Ireland's population died of hunger and more than a million people emigrated to escape a similar fate. Hostility to Britain and all things British manifested itself in sporadic outbreaks of violence over the next decades. In 1885, after the extension of the franchise, 86 members of the Irish Party were elected to Parliament.

Under the leadership of Charles Parnell, the "Uncrowned King of Ireland", and with the backing of Prime Minister Gladstone and many of his Liberal Party, it seemed that their demands for Home Rule would be met. But Gladstone's bills were defeated and Parnell brought down by a personal scandal. It was not until 1914 that Britain agreed to establish an Irish parliament. But World War I intervened, delaying action, and Irish nationalists, tired of waiting, decided to fight.

At Easter 1916 a group of nationalists staged a rebellion. It was savagely repressed and the ringleaders executed. The severity of the reprisals swung Irish public opinion firmly behind the rebels, who established their own parliament, the Dail, and fought a guerrilla campaign against the British. This prompted a compromise: in 1921 Ireland was partitioned. The Irish Free State in the south was given Dominion status, not full independence, and obliged to accept the loss of six counties in the north which remained under British rule as Northern Ireland. Partition led to civil war in Ireland. In 1932, a new party, Fianna Fáil, won the election and five years later the Prime Minister, Eamon de Valera, declared southern Ireland a Republic.

The age of Dickens

In 1848, as famine raged in Ireland, revolution broke out all over Europe. In Britain, once fear of the Chartists was quashed, the country entered a period of self-confidence and relative domestic harmony, despite the polarisation of rich and poor which Benjamin Disraeli, a later Conservative prime minister, called "the two nations" in his mid-century novel, *Sybil*. Poverty was nowhere more evident than in London, for many of whose citizens the squalor and crime which Charles Dickens (1812–70) portrayed so evocatively in his novels – which were first written for serialisation in popular newspapers – were all too real.

Dickens was not the only one who saw a need for improvement. Change, although slow, was on the way. The idea that public health was a public responsibility was gradually taking hold. After a cholera epidemic in 1832 claimed thousands of lives, health officials were appointed and measures taken to provide drainage and clean water.

LEFT: an election meeting in Blackburn, in the new industralised Midlands. **RIGHT:** a *chiffonier*, or rag gatherer, portrayed in Charles Dickens's novels.

The police force which Sir Robert Peel had established in 1829, and which took the nickname "bobbies" from him, was helping combat crime in London and other large towns. At the same time, Peel had abolished the death penalty for many petty crimes, such as pocket-picking, influenced perhaps by the ideas of Jeremy Bentham, the utilitarian thinker who believed there should be a balance between reward and punishment. Bentham founded University College, London and his corpse, fully clothed, still sits in a glass case in the entrance hall.

A new class of clerks, trades-people and artisans were adopting the values of thrift, sobriety and self-improvement which Samuel Smiles exhorted in his famous work, *Self-Help*. The Co-Operative Movement, which began in 1844 in Rochdale, Lancashire, was run on self-help lines, providing cheap goods and sharing profits with its members. Methodism, founded by John Wesley (1703–91), who established the first Methodist chapel in Bristol, had become the religion of the working class. It is often said that the British Labour Party owes more to Methodism than to Marxism.

The working class

It is certainly true that working-class people, on the whole, were not attracted by revolutionary struggle and preferred to pursue their aims through trade union organisation and representation in Parliament. The first working-class member of Parliament in 1892 was John Keir Hardie, the Scottish miners' leader, and 14 years later the British Labour Party won its first parliamentary seats. Although Karl Marx (1818– 83) lived and worked in London for much of his life – his tomb can be seen in London's Highgate Cemetery – his ideas were known and shared only by a relatively small group of middle-class intellectuals.

Also largely ignored by the working man for whom he hoped to speak was John Ruskin (1819–1900), one of the founders of the Pre-

THE COMPLACENCY OF THE VICTORIAN MIDDLE CLASSES

Funded largely by the wealth of the Empire, middle-class life had become comfortable and pleasant. Improved transport – including the world's first underground railway, opened in London in 1863 – enabled people to work in towns but live in leafy suburbs. Most of their new homes had bathrooms and the majority employed a maid.

Skating in London's Regent's Park.

Art and drama flourished. Aubrey Beardsley's fluid, sensual drawings were creating a stir. The Art Nouveau movement influenced the work of Charles Rennie Mackintosh (1868–1928), who founded the Glasgow School.

At the theatre, audiences were being entertained by the plays of two Anglo-Irish writers: George Bernard Shaw, who believed in combining education with entertainment and introduced radical politics into his work, and Oscar Wilde, who poked sophisticated fun at London's high society in plays such as *The Importance of Being Ernest* but who ended his glittering career in a prison cell on charges of homosexuality.

Married women were finally allowed to control their own property in 1882 and were soon permitted to vote in a few local elections. Social reformers were making some progress in alleviating poverty. All in all, Britain was feeling quite pleased with itself by the end of the century.

Raphaelite Brotherhood of painters and writers which flourished in the late 19th century. William Morris, who devoted himself to the revival of medieval arts and crafts, shared Ruskin's anger at the social deprivation caused by capitalism. Examples of his decoration and furnishings can be seen at Kelmscott Place, near Oxford, which was for a time the centre of the Brotherhood's activities. Fellow Pre-Raphaelites were Edward Burne-Jones, John Millais and Dante Gabriel Rossetti, artists who were perhaps less concerned with the social ills of the 19th century but equally convinced of the need to return to pre-Renaissance art forms. They eventually became establishment figures and their work is spread through galleries in London, Birmingham, Manchester and Liverpool.

Ruskin and Morris were among a growing number of those who believed that the lot of working people would only be improved through education. Despite fears in some quarters that education for the masses was a dangerous thing, two Education Acts were passed towards the end of the century which made schooling free and compulsory up to the age of 13. The educational provision may have been rudimentary, but at least it was there – which put England on a more equal footing with Scotland, which had had state education since 1696.

Working-class life improved considerably during the last quarter of the 19th century. Many homes had gas lighting and streets were cleaned by the new municipal councils. The music hall provided inexpensive entertainment in towns. Bicycles became a common method of transport, and day trips by train to seaside resorts were the highlight of summer, even if most excursionists could not afford the bathing machines which allowed more affluent visitors to get into the water without any great loss of modesty.

LEFT: a painting by Phoebus Leven shows Covent Garden market in 1864. **ABOVE:** the princess who became the long-reigning Queen Victoria. **RIGHT:** the Crystal Palace, built for the Great Exhibition of 1851.

Celebrating the empire

Queen Victoria's Diamond Jubilee in 1897 celebrated 60 years on the throne for the woman who had spent much of her reign as a black-clad widow and who had given her name to the age. She ruled over the biggest empire in the world. Atlases of the time showed vast areas coloured red, signifying that they were British colonies. The Punjab and much of Southern Africa had been added to earlier possessions. Egypt and the Sudan had become colonies – in practice if not in name – after Britain invaded in 1882 to protect its shipping routes to India through the newly built Suez Canal. Britannia did indeed rule the waves.

Like most empires at their peak, Britain's seemed unassailable. Then came the 20th century… ❑

MODERN TIMES

The British won their wars but lost their empire and then faced the big question: did they really and truly want to join a United States of Europe?

All good things must come to an end. The Boer War of 1899–1902 ended in victory for Britain in South Africa but damaged its international reputation. France, Germany and America were competing for world markets. The newly united German state was the biggest threat, its education system putting it far ahead of Britain in scientific and technological developments. It had good reserves of coal and iron and was becoming the world's biggest producer of steel, which it was using to build battleships to rival those of the British navy.

Fear of Germany's growing strength forced Britain and France into an alliance. This, together with an earlier treaty which promised to guarantee Belgium's neutrality, plus the fear that Germany would overrun Europe and gain control of parts of the Empire, brought Britain into World War I in 1914. The Edwardian era, sandwiched between the turn of the century and the outbreak of war, is remembered as the zenith of prosperous stability, but its foundations had been shifting for some time.

The scale of the carnage on the French battlefields in World War I shocked even such patriots as the writer Rudyard Kipling (1865–1936) who had been firmly committed to the aims of the war.

The Roaring Twenties

World War I claimed over a million British casualties, most of them under the age of 25. But had the sacrifice been worth it? Men who had fought in France and been promised a "land fit for heroes" were disillusioned when they found unemployment and poor housing awaited them at the war's end in 1918. Women who had worked in factories while the men were away were not prepared to give up any of their independence.

There were strikes on the railways and in the mines and political unrest led to four general elections in just over five years, including one which brought the Labour Party to power for the first time. In 1926 a general strike paralysed the country but the unions' demands were not met and the men returned to work, much disgruntled and worse off than before.

There was another side to life, of course. For some, unaffected by gloomy financial reality, these were the Roaring Twenties. Women with cropped hair and short dresses drank cocktails and danced to the new music, jazz, which had crossed the ocean from America. Silent films, another US import, were the wonder of the age. Writers such as Virginia Woolf and D.H. Lawrence were opening new horizons for the curious and daring – although it would be another 30 years before Lawrence's *Lady Chatterley's Lover* could be published in Britain.

The New York Stock Market crash of 1929 looked as if it would bring the party to an end. The effects soon spread throughout Europe and by 1931 Britain was entering the Great Depression. It ruined a few fortunes, but the principal victims of the recession were in the industrial areas of northern England, south Wales, and Clydeside in Scotland. Three million people lost their jobs and suffered real misery with only the "dole", a limited state benefit, to keep them from starvation and homelessness. British cinema thrived as people sought an escape from reality.

In the south of England and the Midlands, the depression hit less hard and recovery was faster, mainly due to the rapid growth of the motor, electrical and light engineering industries. The bold, geometric designs of Art Deco, which began in Paris in 1925, could soon be seen adorning the spanking new factories which lined the main roads, roads which were starting to fill with small, family cars.

World War II

With memories of the "war to end all wars" still fresh in people's minds, there was great reluctance to enter another conflict. But by 1939 the policy of appeasement of German aggression was no longer tenable. Although Britain's island status saved it from invasion, the war involved civilians in an unprecedented way. German bombing raids tore the heart out of many cities. Coventry was particularly badly hit; its present cathedral, with its renowned John Piper windows, was built to replace the one that was lost. Ports and shipyards around the country were battered by repeated raids. Much of the modern building in British

LEFT: bathing belles in the 1920s. **ABOVE:** London's Underground stations became bomb shelters in 1940.

THE ABDICATION

In 1936, following the death of George V, the country was rocked by an unprecedented crisis. Edward VIII succeeded his father but was obliged to abdicate when family, Church and Government united in their refusal to let him marry a twice-divorced American, Mrs Wallis Simpson. The British public was kept in the dark about the matter. The couple married in France and remained in permanent exile as the Duke and Duchess of Windsor.

Edward's brother came to the throne and, as George VI, became a popular monarch, not least for the solidarity which he and his Queen, Elizabeth, later the Queen Mother, showed to their subjects during the Blitz, as the German bombing raids were called.

towns, not always blending too harmoniously, has been erected on former bomb sites.

Many London families spent their nights in the Underground stations, the safest places during an attack, and a lot of people from cities and industrial areas were evacuated to the countryside during the worst of the Blitz. For children, sent to live with strangers while their parents remained behind, it was both a time of great loneliness and the first glimpse many of them had ever had of green fields and woodlands. For some of the country families on whom they were billeted, it may have been their first glimpse of the effects of urban deprivation.

Sir Winston Churchill had received massive popular support as an inspirational war leader, and is still regarded by many people as Britain's greatest prime minister. But when hostilities ended in 1945 the electorate, to his surprise and dismay, declined to re-elect him and voted overwhelmingly for a Labour government. It wasn't that they weren't grateful for his wartime leadership; but the war effort had fostered egalitarianism and many returning servicemen felt that electing a Conservative government again would simply resuscitate the old class differences.

The problems of the war-torn country proved intractable. For one thing, the war effort had left it virtually bankrupt and deeply in debt financially to the United States. But the Labour government laboured to keep its promises. The basis of the welfare state was laid, providing free medical care for everyone and financial help for the old, the sick and the unemployed. The Bank of England, coal mines, railways and steelworks were nationalised. These were hard and joyless years, however, and wartime rationing of food, clothing and fuel continued into the early 1950s.

The end of empire

One of the most far-reaching consequences of the war was that it hastened the end of Britain's empire. Starting with India's independence in 1947, the colonies one after another achieved autonomy during the next two decades, although many remained in the Commonwealth, with the Queen as their titular head. Jamaica and Trinidad did not gain independence until 1962, but they were two islands whose people were among the first black immigrants to Britain in the early 1950s, when work was plentiful and immigrants were welcomed to fill the labour gap. Newcomers from the Caribbean settled mainly in London at first, while later immigrants from the Indian sub-continent made their homes in the Midlands, where textiles and the motor industry offered employment.

The post-war years were ones of uneasy peace. Britain joined the war against North Korea in 1950 and its troops, still a conscripted army, fought there for four years. In 1956, following Egyptian nationalisation of the Suez Canal, British and French forces conspired to attack Egypt, pleading bogus provocation. The action was widely condemned both at home and particularly in the United States, and it represented an ignominious end to Britain's imperial ambitions.

These were also the years of the Cold War between the Soviet Union and the West, which prompted Britain to become a nuclear power. The first British hydrogen bomb was tested in 1957, two years after the world's first nuclear power station had opened in Cumberland (now Cumbria). The Campaign for Nuclear Disarmament was born in response and organised large protest marches.

A new Elizabethan Age

All was not gloom and doom. In 1947 Edinburgh staged a highly successful festival of music and drama, which has gone from strength to strength. At the same time the first annual International Music Eisteddfod was held in Llangollen in Wales. Four years later the Festival of Britain was held in the newly built Royal Festival Hall on

London's South Bank – the National Theatre was added to the concrete complex in 1964.

The Festival was designed to commemorate the Great Exhibition 100 years earlier and strongly signalled the beginning of the end of postwar austerity. In 1953, a new Elizabethan Age began as Elizabeth II was crowned in Westminster Abbey. Britain's Television Age began in earnest too that day, too, as millions watched the coronation live on tiny flickering screens.

By the latter half of the decade things were definitely looking up. Harold Macmillan, the Conservative prime minister, declared in a famous speech that people had "never had it so good": unemployment was low, average living standards were rising. New universities were built, with the aim of making higher education a possibility for more than just the privileged elite. Most people had two weeks' paid holiday a year and, alongside the traditional seaside resorts, holiday camps blossomed, offering cheap family vacations.

Social attitudes were changing too, reflected in the rise of a group of writers known as "angry young men", including John Osborne and Arnold Wesker, whose plays challenged conventional values. Their popularity marked the beginning of a move away from middle-class and American dominance in literature and popular culture.

The Swinging '60s

The 1960s saw an explosion of new talent, much of it from the north of England. Alan Sillitoe and Stan Barstow wrote about working-class life in a way no one had done before. Northern actors, such as Albert Finney and Tom Courteney, achieved huge success and, in the cinema, directors Lindsay Anderson and Karel Reisz (best known for *If...* and *Saturday Night and Sunday Morning*) made British films popular box-office attractions. Pop music, as it was now called, underwent a revolution when a group from Liverpool, the Beatles, became world celebrities and turned their home town into a place of pilgrimage.

The introduction of the contraceptive pill prompted a revolution in sexual attitudes, and the laws relating to abortion, homosexuality and censorship were liberalised. It was a decade of optimism and national self-confidence was infectious: in 1966 England's footballers even beat Germany to win the World Cup.

The subdued '70s

It was during the winter of 1973, when an oil embargo and a miners' strike provoked a State of Emergency and brought down Edward Heath's Conservative Government, that the self-confi-

LEFT: Churchill appeals to the electorate in 1945.
ABOVE: the climax of *If...*, Lindsay Anderson's 1968 allegorical film pitting youth against the establishment.

dence collapsed. In the same year, with mixed feelings, Britain finally became a full member of the Common Market (now the European Union). Rising oil prices pushed up the cost of living, high inflation took its toll, and unemployment soared.

Oil was discovered in the North Sea. But, although building oil rigs provided jobs, the oil revenues were largely soaked up in payments to the jobless. There was no economic miracle.

To deepen the gloom, English cities were again bombed. This time the perpetrators were the IRA, who were fighting to end British rule in Northern Ireland, which spent most of the 1970s and '80s in a state akin to civil war as a dispute over the unfair allocation of public housing spiralled into a bitter struggle over national identity.

The 1970s also saw nationalism flourish in Wales and Scotland. Plaid Cymru (pronounced *Plyed Cumree*) became a political force in Wales, where TV and radio channels in Welsh were launched. In Scotland, support grew for the Scottish National Party *(see panel on opposite page)*.

The Thatcher years

By 1979, unemployment had reached 3½ million and a wave of strikes plunged the country into what was called "the winter of discontent" – the media has a tendency to quote Shakespeare in times of crisis. The country lost confidence in its Labour government and an election returned the Conservatives to office under their new leader, Margaret Thatcher.

The impact of the West's first woman prime minister was enormous, but her personal popularity soon began to fade as the economy remained weak. But her political stock was dramatically strengthened in 1982 by the Falklands War when an invading Argentinian force was beaten off these South Atlantic islands, remnants of the empire.

For many, the 1980s meant increased prosperity. The most ambitious development was the renewal of London's derelict docklands area into a new industrial site, with its own small airport and light railway system and prestige housing for young urban professionals. Docklands' Canary Wharf development was dubbed Chicago-on-Thames. For many people, however, the dream of living in London faded as the strong economy pushed up the capital's house prices and rents.

The nervous '90s

As the 1990s began, the economy was no longer riding so high. A long and acrimonious miners' strike in 1984 had weakened the unions, and coal mines, including most of those in the closely knit mining communities of South Wales, were subsequently closed. Most of Britain's nationalised industries were privatised, a move which a former Conservative prime minister, Harold Macmillan, likened to "selling the family silver".

After 11 years of Thatcherite rule, people began to tire of the Iron Lady's uncompromising style and she was finally voted out in November 1990 – not by the electorate, but by her own party. The Conservatives believed she had lost touch with the country, particularly over its role within the European Union, and that they might therefore lose the next election. She was replaced by a less combative leader, John Major.

Britain's technical status as an island was removed in 1994 when the first fare-paying passengers travelled by rail to Paris and Brussels through the long-awaited Channel Tunnel. But the big question remained: did Britain really feel European enough to be part of a full monetary union – perhaps even, one day, a political union?

That *fin de siècle* feeling

Two events in 1997 shook the nation out of its wary complacency. In a general election the Conservative Party was swept from power after 17 years as the Labour Party roared in with an unassailable overall majority of 179 seats in the House of Commons. The Conservatives were left without a single seat in either Scotland or Wales, both of which voted in subsequent referenda for a greater degree of self-rule; this limited devolution took effect in 1999 with the setting up of new assemblies in Edinburgh and Cardiff.

But Tony Blair's new government soon disappointed many by abandoning its socialist roots, promoting unexpectedly conservative economic policies with evangelical fervour, and by showing equally unexpected enthusiasm for the NATO bombing of Serbia in 1999.

The second defining event in 1997 was the death in a car crash in Paris of Diana, Princess of Wales. The wave of grief that swept the country took everyone by surprise, both the grievers who mourned all night outside Kensington Palace in London and the cynics who found echoes of *Evita* in the insistent public anguish. Some attacked the royal family for failing to display sufficient anguish – a predicament dramatised in a 2006 movie when Helen Mirren portrayed *The Queen*.

To mark the new century, a huge Millennium Dome was built at Greenwich in London, but the pedagogic exhibition it contained failed to catch the public imagination and it lost a fortune. The London Eye, a giant revolving wheel on the south bank of the Thames in London, was a far greater success and became a permanent fixture. In June 2001 the Labour Party won another landslide election victory, despite a great deal of voter apathy. The crucial question of whether Britain should embrace the single European currency, the euro, totally divided public opinion, and effectively the issue was put on the back burner.

The American connection

Europe remains an issue that can still destroy governments because it forces people to confront questions of identity and loyalties. For centuries

LEFT: as prime minister, Margaret Thatcher inspired great loyalty and great antagonism.
RIGHT: grief for the dead Diana, Princess of Wales.

SCOTLAND'S FUTURE

Scots have been an integral part of the United Kingdom since the 1707 Treaty of Union, yet talk of independence has never really ceased. Many Scots feel that the English take them for granted and were particularly incensed that, when oil was discovered in the North Sea in the 1970s, making Aberdeen the "Oil Capital of Europe", the proceeds flowed into the national coffers in London. Yet, when a Scottish Parliament was set up in 1999 to run domestic affairs, only three out of five Scots bothered to vote. In 2007's elections, however, the Scottish National Party took power, challenging the status quo. Economists argue that Scotland is probably better off within the UK, but national pride doesn't always heed economists.

Britain had warred with Spain, France and Germany, and, although Britons today are happy to holiday in a *gîte* in Normandy or a resort on the Costa del Sol, most still regard Europe as "foreign". Because of ancestral links and a shared language, many feel more comfortable with the United States, even though its values and attitudes are often far more "foreign" than those of, say, Germany or Italy.

Tony Blair argued that Britain is ideally placed to be a bridge between America and the European Union, but European politicians regularly accused Britain of being a less than faithful partner as it professed eternal love for its fellow Europeans but remained reluctant to learn their languages, wouldn't accept the euro as national currency, and continued to cast come-hither glances towards its muscular friend across the Atlantic.

This conflict came to a head when George W. Bush's administration determined to invade Iraq. While much of Europe opposed the war, Tony Blair made Britain a full coalition partner. The issue divided the country – and the Labour Party. When a BBC reporter implied that the government had exaggerated the threat posed by Saddam Hussein, the ensuing row led to the eventual resignations of the BBC's chairman and director-general.

The failure to find the much touted weapons of

The Struggle for Power that Dominated Britain's Government

The Labour Party's success in divesting itself of any policy that might be remotely construed as socialist and morphing itself into "New Labour" was the work of two men, Tony Blair, a lawyer, and Gordon Brown, a researcher with Scottish Television. It had been assumed that Brown, the more intellectual of the two, would one day be Labour's leader but, when that position became vacant in 1994 on the premature death of John Smith, Blair persuaded enough colleagues that he and not Brown had the necessary charisma to win an election. It was rumoured that the two did a power-sharing deal whereby Blair, if he became prime minister, would hand over after a few years to Brown, who would in the meantime control the country's finances as Chancellor of the Exchequer.

But Blair, after Labour's landslide win in 1997 and its subsequent win in 2001, showed little inclination to hand over the reins, and the fractious relationship between the two men came to dominate the country's politics. After a less spectacular Labour general election win in 2005, Labour MPs finally persuaded Blair to hand over the premiership to his unrelenting rival.

The change of face was at first welcomed, but soon Brown was accused of being indecisive and lacking in the charisma required of a leader in the television age. His popularity slumped, though his experience of having run the Treasury for a decade was reassuring during the world financial markets' turmoil in 2008.

mass destruction in Iraq severely dented Blair's reputation for trustworthiness, according to opinion polls, and, although Britain's economy had remained more robust than most European economies, criticism mounted that Labour had failed to deliver adequate public services and had no answers to chronic problems such as traffic congestion and threats to the environment.

Yet Labour's hold on power remained secure, because the Conservative Party had failed to heal the splits (especially over Europe) that had forced Margaret Thatcher from power and the acrid arguments between the Thatcherite sympathisers and their opponents made them look unfit to govern.

London is targeted

In July 2005, London surprised itself by winning its bid to host the 2012 Olympic Games. The building programme needed to accommodate the games would, it was promised, rejuvenate rundown areas of East London.

On the very next day, the jubilation ceased as suicide bombings killed 52 people and injured more than 700 on three Underground trains and a bus. Two weeks later, other bombers failed to detonate four more devices on the city's transport network. These attacks raised the question of how to make such a sprawling cosmopolitan city more secure, particularly since the bombers were not foreign terrorists who had evaded the country's border checks but hitherto blameless British-born Muslims protesting against the country's involvement in Iraq and Afghanistan.

The insecure society

As in the United States after 2001, security became a major issue. Yet, curiously for such a reserved people, the British were already, per capita, the most spied-on people on the planet. In addition to a forest of speed cameras – designed, some thought, as much to raise revenue as to cut road accidents – surveillance cameras had sprung up in town centres, often as a response to local people's demands to curb late-night violence as pubs disgorged youths increasingly dedicated to "binge drinking" *(see Surveillance, page 92)*.

Visitors were even more bemused by the heat generated by a ban on hunting foxes with hounds – a debate that consumed more than 700 hours of parliamentary time. The issue divided town dwellers from country people but was also presented as part of the class struggle, with working-class Labour supporters avenging themselves on upper-class supporters of fox-hunting. In a country that clings to traditions, categorisation by class remained in robust health in the 21st century. ❑

LEFT: the uneasy relationship between Gordon Brown, left, and Tony Blair dominated British politics for more than a decade. **ABOVE:** as Heathrow's Terminal 5 opens, environmental protesters have their say.

NO SMOKING

CULTURE FROM A TO Z

Like an iceberg, the British psyche is mostly hidden from view. In a series of penetrating essays, we reveal what lies beneath the surface

The British take a masochistic delight in hearing how bleak their outlook is. As Sir Winston Churchill put it, they "are the only people who like to be told how bad things are – they like to be told the worst." And it's certainly a conspicuous characteristic. Noël Coward lampooned it in the song "There are bad times just around the corner" – which, of course, became immensely popular.

Visitors find it hard to accept this self-deprecation, suspecting that it is really a cloak for rampant arrogance and discovering that few countries are as rewarding to dip into. Take a pin and put it down on a map of Britain and you will find a different experience each time: different people, different houses, different scenery, different accents, different values, different views. Together they make up an astonishing island race, in whom the culture and customs are inextricably mixed; a character that is the sum of so many parts.

The A to Z of the nation and its foibles on the following pages can also be dipped into. These short essays look at the ruling establishment of government, knights, lords and monarchy, and the role of the BBC. They examine the country's preoccupations with sex, the weather and official secrets. They look at its hang-ups about accents, class and sex. They extol its games, its theatre and its pubs. They explain the particular peculiarities of tea-drinking and forming queues. The nation's notorious xenophobia is confronted head on. And the section finishes by trying to analyse the peculiar zeitgeist that has gripped post-imperial Britain – this "soggy little island huffing and puffing to keep up with Western Europe", as the American novelist John Updike once characterised it.

This alphabetical analysis does not explain everything that goes on either in public or behind closed doors between John O'Groats and Land's End. But it may shed light on the shadier areas of a society renowned for curious customs, mild eccentricities and a confusion about whether it's European. ❑

PRECEDING PAGES: exuberant audience at the Last Night of the Proms, the annual musical festival staged by the BBC at London's Royal Albert Hall.
LEFT: accompanying the Changing of the Guard ceremony at Buckingham Palace.
TOP: patriotic sandcastle. **RIGHT:** examining the art at London's Tate Modern.

ACCENTS

When, in *Pygmalion* (later to be reborn as *My Fair Lady*), George Bernard Shaw set Professor Henry Higgins the task of passing off Eliza Doolittle, a common Cockney flower-seller, as a duchess at an ambassador's dinner party, there was no question about Higgins's first priority: he had to change her accent. Then, as now, a person's origins, class as well as locality, could be identified by the way he or she speaks and, as Shaw wisely observed, "it is impossible for an Englishman to open his mouth without making another Englishman despise or hate him."

ALLOTMENTS

Gardening is a wildly popular pastime, but what if you don't have a garden? Around a quarter of a million people rent allotments, small parcels of land on which to grow vegetables and fruit. They also provide opportunities to exchange tips with other gardeners. Allotments, which are grouped together and average 250 sq metres, are generally owned by local town or parish councils. Their popularity peaked during World War II, though the practice can be traced back a thousand years to when Saxons would clear a piece of woodland and allocate portions to local citizens. In the 19th century, the government made it obligatory for local authorities to provide allotments when there was a demand for them.

Although such snobbery is most associated with the English, the Welsh and Scots are not immune. The linguistically alert can detect a range of class differences between the North Welsh and the South Welsh, for instance, and the ambassador would much prefer a dinner party guest who greeted him in the soft-spoken tones of middle-class Edinburgh than in the rough vernacular of working-class Glasgow.

It is remarkable – given these social pressures, the small size of Britain and the smoothing influence of television – that a vast variety of regional accents continue to flourish. Yet they do: two Britons, one with a strong West Country accent and the other from Newcastle upon Tyne, would scarcely understand each other.

With Asian and West Indian immigrants having added to the variety of speech patterns in Britain, consensus about what constitutes "proper English speech" remains as elusive as ever. Pity the manufacturers of digitised voice generators: who in Glasgow wants their cooker to inform them in a Surrey accent that their roast is ready, or what Oxfordshire driver wants his car to tell him in a Norfolk accent to fasten his seat-belt? The same unsatisfactory solution again presents itself and machines, like BBC announcers, embrace Received Pronunciation.

BBC

Depending on your viewpoint, the BBC is either the world's biggest and best broadcasting organisation, or a power-crazed and profligate monster that's out of control. Since it is a public service organisation funded through an annual licence fee that must be paid by everyone who owns a TV set – whether they watch BBC channels or not – public opinion cannot be ignored.

It's certainly big. It runs eight advertising-free TV channels in the UK, including children's channels and a politics channel, a similar number of ad-free national radio channels, a host of local radio channels, several choirs and orchestras, and Europe's biggest website. It also publishes books and magazines, which commercial publishers regard as unfair competition because of the free on-air publicity these products receive.

In addition, it runs commercial operations overseas, such as BBC America, and is paid by the government to promote Britain's image and values by broadcasting BBC World Service radio around the world in 32 languages. Its costume dramas are not only popular at home but make a lot of money in export sales. Crucially, it nourishes emerging talent – actors, writers, directors, executives – who often go on to form the creative backbone of many of its commercial rivals.

The BBC's powers and obligations are vested in a trust of 12 worthy and theoretically independent people appointed by the government. These powers are exercised through a permanent staff headed by a director-general and a board of management. The government confines itself to insisting that the BBC, which was established in 1927, must be impartial and free from political interference and must stay within its budget.

lent and edifying rather than what people necessarily want to watch, but audience ratings matter. If the BBC appeals to too few people, the universal annual licence fee could no longer be justified. But if it dumbs down too much in pursuit of ratings, its commercial rivals – and in particular Rupert Murdoch, who controls Sky TV's satellite channels – would say it is no longer fulfilling its public-service purpose. It's a truism to say the BBC can never win. In an age of proliferating digital channels, the licence fee is increasingly under attack, and the Corporation is constantly looking at ways of financing its output, from index-linked licences to pay-as-you-view TV.

That's the theory. In practice, the political parties tot up the number of minutes' reporting of each side of an issue, looking for bias – and usually claim to find it. When in 2003 a reporter seemed to allege on an early-morning radio news programme that Tony Blair's government, in order to justify going to war with Iraq, had exaggerated the threat from Saddam Hussein, all hell broke loose and both the BBC chairman and its director-general eventually resigned.

Unconcerned with pleasing advertisers, the BBC could ration its audience to what is excel-

LEFT: he loves boating and is bound to have an Oxford accent. **ABOVE:** filming one of the BBC's celebrated costume dramas, Charles Dickens's *Little Dorrit.*

CLASS

A newspaper cartoon cunningly caught the British confusion over its social attitudes. "I don't believe in class differences," its well-heeled gentleman was explaining, "but luckily my butler disagrees with me."

The implication is that the lower classes, far from being revolutionaries, are as keen as anyone to maintain the status quo, and that they still embody the attitude to the upper classes parodied more than a century ago by W.S. Gilbert in the comic opera *Iolanthe*:

Bow, bow, ye lower middle classes!
Bow, bow, ye tradesmen, bow, ye masses!

From time to time, the class rigidities seem set

to crumble, but the promise is never quite fulfilled, mainly because the British have a genius for absorbing dissenters into "the system" as surely as a spider lures a fly into a web. The 1960s promoted a new egalitarianism; but it wasn't long before such former threats to civilised society as Mick Jagger were consorting with the royal family. In the 1980s, the consensus among classes seemed again to be threatened, this time by Thatcherism, whose economic policies created stark inequalities between the regions and swelled the ranks of the disgruntled unemployed; worried about their election prospects, the Conservative Party replaced Mrs Thatcher in mid-term with the more emollient John Major.

Mr Major's humble origins suggested that any working-class boy who applied himself diligently could become prime minister – surely a threat to the power of the upper classes? And what about the supposedly left-wing traditions that nurtured Tony Blair and Gordon Brown? In reality, however, the true aristocrat is unperturbed by such irrelevancies, regarding a prime minister as the nation's equivalent to his butler.

The monarchy cements the social hierarchy; fringe aristocrats define their social standing in relation to their closeness to royalty, and the elaborate system of honours – from peerages and knighthoods to Companionships of the British

Empire – transform achievement into much sought-after feudal rank because the titles (even though generally decided by the politicians of the day) are bestowed in person by the monarch.

The ruling class is a pragmatic coalition of middle and upper-class members. Generally, "they" (the people who seem to make all the decisions) remain strangely amorphous; common speech refers constantly to the fact that "they" have built an inadequate new motorway or that "they" have allowed some hideous glass skyscraper to be placed next to a Gothic cathedral – a peculiar dissociation from power in an avowedly democratic society. But "they" have certain characteristics in common: they tend to have been educated at any one of a dozen public schools and then to have

THE CHANNEL ISLANDS

Victor Hugo called the Channel Islands "pieces of France which fell into the sea and were gathered up by England." Best known as tax havens, the two main bank-laden islands are Jersey (45 sq miles/117 sq km) and Guernsey (24 sq miles/62 sq km). The 2 sq-mile (5 sq-km) island of Sark is a feudal remnant, ruled over by an hereditary seigneur. The islands lie in the Gulf of St Malo just off the French coast and constitutionally are not part of the United Kingdom, yet their ambience is resolutely British. English holidaymakers like the slightly French ambience combined with the familiar English language.

progressed to either Oxford or Cambridge universities. From then on, the network is firmly in place and, with the help of dinner parties, country-house weekends and college reunions, the bush telegraph of power keeps lines of communications open. The "old school tie" has a durable knot.

Cricket

It's playing the game that counts, as the old saying (or excuse) goes, not the winning. That's certainly true of cricket, which has been described as "a game which the British, not being a spiritual people, had to invent in order to have some concept of eternity." The main purpose is simple: a bowler hurls a leather-covered ball at three wooden stumps in order to dislodge two strips of wood (bails) resting on top of them, and the batsman tries to deflect the ball with a paddle-shaped piece of willow.

But the byzantine rules, first laid down by London's Marylebone Cricket Club in 1788, are best captured by a satirical definition: "You have two sides, one out in the field and one in. Each man that's in the side that's in, goes out and when he's out he comes in and the next man goes in until he's out. When they're all out, the side that's out comes in and the side that's been in goes out and tries to get those coming in out. Sometimes you get men still in and not out. When both sides have been in and out, including the not-outs, that's the end of the game."

Not surprisingly, an international match can take from three to five days to complete.

Crime

The incidence of most kinds of crime, from burglary to serious assault, are falling, according to government statistics. The trouble is, according to a survey by National Statistics, a government body, most people don't believe the figures.

People don't have much faith in newspapers either, but dramatic crime reporting does make an impact. A spate of teenage knifings in 2008, for example, gave the impression that such crime was out of control. Yet when London police conducted a six-week shakedown of youths, only 500 of the 27,000 people frisked were carrying knives – less than 2 percent. And an analysis of hospital admissions found that the vast majority of violent crimes occur in Britain's most impoverished areas.

The unsurprising moral: it's best not to wander through a deprived inner-city are late at night looking like an affluent tourist.

LEFT: classic image of the "two nations" as working-class boys in the 1930s watch Eton pupils wait for their chauffeurs at the start of their vacation.
RIGHT: icons of Englishness, cricken and warm beer.

Drama

In spite of its reputation, the West End of London is not always the place to find the country's dramatic cultural pearls. Here the tradition is as much of the theatre as of performances. This is where velvet and gilt Victorian playhouses were

designed so that most of the audiences would peer down over the cast, where "the gods" (the seats high at the back) bring on vertigo and a concern that, had the buildings been conceived today, fire regulations would have ensured they never left the architects' drawing boards.

Nevertheless, the West End is still a theatrical magnet, because that is where the money is. Catering for audiences by the coachload, impresarios look to musical spectacles, revivals, and to plays that will please the widest range of tastes. As a result, such middle-of-the-road creative persons as composer Andrew Lloyd Webber (now Lord Lloyd-Webber) and the playwright Alan Ayckbourn have become both famous and very rich.

Traditionalists claimed that the mania for musicals squeezes out new drama productions. Yet a glance at the theatre listings in *Time Out* magazine doesn't entirely bear out this claim. Classics continue to be staged at the National Theatre and the Old Vic, new writing is still put on at the Royal Court and the Bush, experimental work and alternative comedy are mounted at the fringe theatres, and playwrights such as David Hare, Tom Stoppard and Terry Johnson attract an audience.

As well as locally grown stars such as Michael Gambon, Ian McKellan, Maggie Smith, Diana Rigg and Judi Dench, American actors have never been strangers to the West End – Dustin Hoffman appeared as Shylock in *The Merchant of Venice* in 1989, for example – but recently a flood of Hollywood actors have been keen to enhance (or revive) their careers in London. Kathleen Turner, Linda Gray and Amanda Donohoe took turns to disrobe as Mrs Robinson in a stage version of *The Graduate*, and Nicole Kidman was described as "theatrical Viagra" when she briefly appeared naked in David Hare's *The Blue Room*. After Kevin Spacey scored a hit in *The Iceman Cometh* at the Old Vic, he accepted the job of part-time artistic director of the venerable theatre, helping to raise funds to repair its leaky roof and cracked walls and promising to act as well as direct there.

Shakespeare is certainly alive and well. The replica of Shakespeare's Globe on London's South Bank has been a triumph of culture over commercialism, with audiences paying to savour the 16th-century ambience by standing for hours in front of the stage or sitting on rock-hard benches. The Royal Shakespeare Company, based in Stratford-upon-Avon, takes much of its repertoire to London and several regional cities, and the National Theatre, which has three auditoria on the South Bank, regularly features the Bard. The National's current director, Nicholas Hytner, has produced more innovation (he brought in the outrageous *Jerry Springer – The Opera*) and, with the help of business sponsorship, made many seats available for just £10. Notable productions can regularly be found at the Young Vic, the Gate, the

ECCENTRICS

In *English Eccentrics*, the poet Edith Sitwell (1887–1964), stated that the English were prone to eccentricity because of "that peculiar and satisfactory knowledge of infallibility that is the hallmark and the birthright of the British nation." Perhaps for this reason, the aristocracy has provided many of the single-minded hobbyists and enthusiasts such as the 8th Earl of Bridgewater, who organised banquets for dogs, or the 5th Earl of Portland, who like to live underground, unseen. Rather than being genuine oddballs, today's eccentrics are often publicity-seekers such as David Sutch, whose Official Monster Raving Loony Party contested general elections. A more genuine article might be the monocled astronomer Patrick Moore.

Almeida and the Royal Court, nurturer of radical writers such as David Hare and Caryl Churchill.

The backbone of British theatre lies beyond London, in the repertory companies of the provinces. The Manchester Exchange, Leicester Phoenix, Glasgow Citizens' and Edinburgh Traverse all have good reputations and in Liverpool a hive of talent has included the playwright Willy Russell and the actress Julie Walters. And the Fringe Festival in Edinburgh every August is where myriad actors and comedians clamour to show their earliest promise.

Britain's tradition of acting excellence is a boon for television drama producers and for Hollywood. Who would have thought that Sir Ian McKellan, who has graced many a Shakespearian stage, would finally make his fortune as Gandalf in the *Lord of the Rings* trilogy?

ELECTIONS

There are three significant parliamentary political parties in Britain, Labour, Conservatives, and Liberal Democrats, with Plaid Cymru (Welsh nationalists), the Scottish Nationalists and Ulster Unionists trailing a long way behind. The House of Commons, parliament's Lower House, is furnished with green seats, which distinguishes it from the red seats of the Lords in the Upper House (where some peers are hereditary and others are appointed, not elected). The Commons can just about hold all 650 MPs, though the amount of committee work means there are often no more than a handful of members in the chamber at any one time. Like most British institutions, parliament is male dominated and the frequently raucous behaviour is reminiscent of an elite public school.

Unpardonable sins include accusing fellow MPs of lying (though they can be mendacious or "economical with the truth"). As recompense, they are free to libel members of the public without fear of prosecution – so long as they don't repeat the libel outside the House. The ministers are answerable to the House, and the prime minister, relying on quick wit and practised evasiveness, answers questions in person on Wednesdays.

Parliament has no written constitution. It relies on statutes and acts which have been passed over the centuries. The monarch has a right of veto but, wisely, none has used it since the 18th century. The Queen is not allowed to set foot in the chamber unless she is invited – which she is at the start of each session in November, when she reads a speech prepared by ministers and civil servants outlining her government's plans for the nation's future.

A government may be in office for five years and the prime minister can call an election at any time within that period, giving six weeks' notice of the date. A prime minster who hangs on until the last possible moment has probably got good reason to feel insecure, and most premiers pick an opportune moment after about four years. The prime minister is not chosen by the people: after

LEFT: Jeff Goldblum and Kevin Spacey in *Speed the Plow* at London's Old Vic. **RIGHT:** 10 Downing Street, the address every British politician would like to have.

THE LUNATIC FRINGE

Anyone in Britain can form a political party. All that is required is a name for the party and a person to second the registration – and a £500 deposit, which is forfeited if the party receives less than 5 percent of the constituency vote. This stipulation is intended to deter frivolous candidates – but it doesn't. There are numerous hopeful parties, including the Greens, The Monster Raving Loony Party, the Natural Law Party (which runs on a platform of peace through meditation) and Sausages Against HP Sauce. On election night, candidates of all these parties appear briefly on television as the results are announced. It all adds to the gaiety of life and preserves the country's reputation as a safe haven for eccentricity.

an election, the leader of the party which ends up with the most elected MPs is invited by the Queen to form a government and so becomes PM.

Elections for the European Parliament stir fewer passions than domestic polls, and a surprising number of voters are unable even to say who their member for Europe is.

FILM INDUSTRY

Is a car assembled by British workers at Nissan's Sunderland factory a British car? To most people, it is a Japanese car made in Britain. Similarly, films such as *Match Point* (2005) made by Woody Allen in London using mainly English actors and technicians are not generally regarded as British. Even the James Bond and Harry Potter movies, despite their English backgrounds, have the flavour of international productions. On the other hand, Hugh Grant's caricature Englishness stamps films such as *Four Weddings and a Funeral* (1994) and *Notting Hill* (1999) as British even though his American co-stars (Andie MacDowell and Julia Roberts) signal a desire for international appeal.

So, regardless of where the production and distribution finance comes from, what *is* a "British" film? It's a much debated question. A more rewarding one is to ask well-informed locals what they regard as their favourite (as opposed to "best") British film. This was what the British Film Institute did by surveying 1,000 people in the UK's cinema and television industries. Of the 820 films nominated, these were the top 10:

❶ *The Third Man* (1949). Although set in post-war Vienna and starring two Americans (Joseph Cotton and Orson Welles), director Carol Reed and writer Graham Greene brought a very British sensibility to the film.
❷ *Brief Encounter* (1945). Celia Johnson and Trevor Howard repress their middle-class emotions in a Noël Coward story directed by David Lean.
❸ *Lawrence of Arabia* (1962). David Lean's Oscar-winning blockbuster with the tall Peter O'Toole playing the short, eccentric Arabist.
❹ *The 39 Steps* (1935). Alfred Hitchcock's take on John Buchan's spy adventure, starring Robert Donat, makes good use of Scottish locations.
❺ *Great Expectations* (1946). David Lean again, directing a mesmerising black-and-white version of the Charles Dickens novel.
❻ *Kind Hearts and Coronets* (1949). Robert Hamer's dark Ealing comedy with Alec Guinness playing eight aristocrats murdered by the ninth in line to the dynasty.
❼ *Kes* (1969). Ken Loach's unsentimental story of a Northern working-class boy who finds meaning in caring for a kestrel.
❽ *Don't Look Now* (1973). Nicholas Roeg's terrifying tale places Julie Christie and Donald Sutherland in a sinister Venice.

❾ *The Red Shoes* (1948). The team of Michael Powell and Emeric Pressburger, who made a string of classic 1940s films, tell the story of a young ballerina and a megalomaniac impresario.
❿ *Trainspotting* (1996). Danny Boyle's tough portrayal of a group of Scottish junkies made a star of Ewan McGregor.

FOOD

Few people contemplating a first visit to Britain would cite the cuisine as a major attraction. They may have heard disconcerting reports of soggy vegetables, tinned sauces and artificially flavoured puddings, and will certainly be aware of beef contaminated by "mad cow disease". But Britain has a sophisticated culinary tradition going back to the days of the grand Victorian country houses, and even earlier. In the Brighton Pavilion, visitors today can not only see the enormous kitchen and its elaborate implements and fine copper serving dishes, but can read the menu for a banquet given in in 1817. More than 100 dishes feature, from delicate soups (a choice of four) to every kind of meat or game, including quail and wood pigeon. Puddings included miniature soufflés – chocolate, apple or apricot.

Victorian culinary knowledge was codified by a Mrs Beeton, who published her renowned *Book of Household Management* in 1861. She provided expert advice on everything from how to dry herbs to judging the age of a partridge, and her book, having been updated many times over the years, is still in print.

How, then, did the country acquire its reputation as a culinary wasteland? Britain's indigenous foodstuffs – lamb, potatoes, apples and pears, herbs, fish, eggs and cheeses – can be of very high quality, but they must be very fresh or stored under controlled conditions, and must be skilfully prepared. In Victorian times, most middle-class families employed servants, including a cook. But in the years leading up to World War II, changing social conditions led most people to give up their servants. Then came the wartime rationing of meat, eggs and butter. By the time these basic items were available once again, many traditional ways of cooking had been forgotten or, without servants, were no longer practical.

LEFT: Hugh Grant impersonates the quintessential Englishman in *Four Weddings and a Funeral*.
ABOVE: Gordon Ramsay, doyen of celebrity chefs.

In their place came an emphasis on convenience, with time-saving appliances and the modern supermarket with its rows of tinned and frozen foods. The neighbourhood grocer, butcher and fishmonger began to disappear – and with them, the attention to freshness and understanding of ingredients which had been taken for granted.

But the supermarkets had their advantages. Thanks to modern modes of transport, they could bring produce from sunnier parts of the world to the British masses, and at a reasonable price. Oranges, avocados and olive oil were once luxury items, and could now be afforded by all. Very gradually, British chefs – and humble dinner party

hosts – have learned how to incorporate the full flavours of the Mediterranean into the wholesome staples of the British diet. An army of foodies has goaded the supermarkets into providing fresh herbs year round, bread baked on the premises, and organic produce and meats.

Today, from Cornwall to Caithness, you will find upmarket restaurants and "gastropubs" offering "Modern British" dishes such as roast cod with basil mash, roast rack of lamb with Provençale herbs, and raspberry profiteroles. And chefs such as Gordon Ramsay, Anthony Worrall-Thomson and Jamie Oliver have become ubiquitous television celebrities.

If, however, you don't fancy a seared tuna steak drizzed with a sun-dried tomato coulis, you can still find the fish-and-chip shops and kebab stalls which have made British food famous the world over. The trouble is that most of them deserve notoriety, not fame.

FOOTBALL

Britain's most popular sport fields three national teams: one for England, one for Scotland, and one for Wales. England pioneered "the beautiful game" – the first known written reference to "football" dates to 1409 and the rules of the modern game were codified in London in 1863 – and has more clubs than anywhere else in the world,

including amateur teams and youth leagues as well as internationally known clubs.

Unlike the national teams, whose players must have been born in the country, the Premier League teams can shop for talented players from around the world. This has turned the major clubs into wealthy corporations glamorous enough to attract rich patrons, with the result that half the Premier League teams are now foreign-owned. US sports tycoon Malcolm Glazer paid £790 million in 2005 to take control of Manchester United. Manchester City was bought by Thailand's former prime minister Thaksin Shinawatra, who then sold it on to a group of Arab billionaires led by Abu Dhabi's Sheikh Mansour bin Zayed al Nahyan. Since 2003 Chelsea has been the plaything of Russia's Roman Abramovich.

It helps to be wealthy if you're a fan, too. Ticket prices for top games are on a par with those for West End musicals and the souvenir market is a money-spinner. Manchester United, for example, has an online megastore offering a vast range of branded items, from pyjamas and ear-rings to fleece blankets and beanie bears.

The injection of capital vastly improved facilities at major football grounds and halted the fall in attendances caused by endemic hooliganisim in the 1980s. But it also polarised the game, with smaller clubs seeing potential revenues siphoned off by the big-name clubs.

The hope is that, in addition to spending millions buying international stars such as Cristiano Ronaldo, the big clubs will develop more home-grown talent to replace the likes of David Beckham and Michael Owen. Doing so might help them achieve the football fan's greatest dream: to bring the World Cup back to England, which last won it way back in 1966.

GOLF

The Scots can lay claim to inventing the game in the 14th or 15th century, and the Royal and Ancient Golf Club of St Andrew's remains one of the golf world's governing bodies. An ambition of many golfers is to play the Old Course at St Andrew's, where rounds are allocated by daily ballot as well as advamce request.

The Scottish Parliament banned the game (along with football) in 1457 on the grounds that it was distracting youth from archery practice. Mary, Queen of Scots took the game to France, where her attendants were known as cadets, hence "caddies". The links on which she played, at Musselburgh, are still in operation – the world's oldest.

Today the UK has more than 5,000 golf courses. A concentration of courses between Liverpool and Blackpool – the "Golf Coast" – includes three famous Royal links courses: Birkdale, Liverpool, and Lytham & St Annes.

HERITAGE INDUSTRY

One reason why the British appear to live so much in the past is that they've got so much of it. Yet not until the 1980s, when corporatism and Margaret Thatcher took Great Britain Ltd by the throat, did anyone realise that The Past needed to be ruthlessly revalued on the national balance sheet. What's more, it needed a bright new image. So it changed its name. It became Heritage, and the tourist map of Britain took on a new aspect. Instead of the familiar counties and areas, there appeared Robin Hood Country, James Herriott Country, Rob Roy Country, Jane Austen Country… Soon any area without such slick identification sought it. The depressed northeast, for instance, baptised itself Catherine Cookson Country – much to the confusion of tourists who turned up in South Tyneside in search of the mean streets that Ms Cookson had captured so well in her novels, only to find that they had long since been bulldozed.

Almost every week, somewhere in this economically declining country, a new museum opens. No aspect of life can escape being removed, rearranged, sanitised and preserved for profit. As the iron and steel industries wither away, the Ironbridge Gorge Museum flourishes. As coal mines close throughout Wales, the Big Pit mining museum at Blaenavon kits out tourists in hard hats and miners' lamps.

Critics complain that recreated "heritage" is often bogus history. Many new-wave industrial entertainments, said a former director of the Ironbridge Gorge Museum, tend to create a "curious, nostalgic, rose-coloured picture of a sort of Pickwickian industrial past which bears no relation to reality, but which we like to imagine. A lot of what is presented isn't based on scholarship at all but on attitude and emotion."

In the end, there are distinctions to be drawn. "Places like Jorvik in York, Beamish industrial museum in Durham and Ironbridge in Shropshire offer you 'real' artefacts as well as reconstructions," said Gordon Marsden, editor of *History Today* magazine. "But a themed museum like, say, the Oxford Story in Oxford is more like an Easter egg – hollow inside. You get a quick whisk through the past but then come out with nothing real to relate to."

LEFT: England's capture of the World Cup in 1966 was marked by a commemorative stamp. **ABOVE:** heritage replaces heavy industry in Ironbridge in Shropshire.

GREAT BRITONS

The BBC broadcast a TV series in 2002 on *Great Britons*, starting with 100 names and inviting the public to rank them. These were the results:

1. Sir Winston Churchill, (1874–1965), statesman
2. Isambard Kingdom Brunel, (1806–59), engineer
3. Diana, Princess of Wales (1961–97)
4. Charles Darwin (1809–82), naturalist
5. William Shakespeare (1564–1616), playwright
6. Sir Isaac Newton (1643–1727), scientist
7. Queen Elizabeth I of England (1533–1603)
8. John Lennon (1940–80), musician
9. Vice Admiral Horatio Nelson (1758–1805), naval hero
10. Oliver Cromwell (1599–1658), Lord Protector

It's all becoming rather Orwellian, people sometimes say. But even George Orwell might be taken aback to find that the subject of his 1930s study of recession in *The Road to Wigan Pier* has now become –what else? – the £3.5 million Wigan Heritage Centre.

ISLANDS

Great Britain is the largest of the British Isles, an archipelago made up of around 2,000 islands. It is distinguished from the United Kingdom (of Great Britain and Northern Ireland) by the specific exclusion of any part of Ireland, and from the British Isles by the exclusion of the self-governing Isle of Man and Channel Islands.

The Isle of Man, in the Irish Sea midway between England and Ireland and 16 miles (25 km) from the Scottish coast, has a population of some 50,000. Its parliament, the House of Keys, is said to be the world's oldest. The Manx language, from the same root as Gaelic, was spoken by half the inhabitants at the end of the 19th century, but it has now died out. The island is famous for the tail-less Manx cat, and for its relaxed tax regime.

The idea of being a king of an island is clearly attractive and whole islands do occasionally come up for sale. The reclusive Barclay brothers, owners of the *Daily Telegraph* and *The Scotsman* newspapers, bought Brecqhou, one of the Channel Islands, and fortified it to keep their castle-like mansion private. But most marketable islands are on the western side of Britain, from the Isles of Scilly off Land's End in Cornwall, past Anglesea in Wales to the more prolific Western Isles of Scotland. In the far northwest are the Hebrides; flying off the northeast are Orkney and the Shetland islands, where Britain's most northerly inhabited island, Muckle Flugga, is manned by brave lighthouse keepers.

Inter-island transport in these remote places is sometimes difficult and often exhilarating. With Caledonian MacBrayne, the Scottish ferry company, it is possible to island-hop through 22 of the Western Isles. Loganair has the shortest scheduled flight in the world – a two-minute flight between two Orkney islands – and uses fields and even beaches as landing strips.

Some of the Scottish islands are getting their own private airstrips for the use of new owners. From having been traditionally the property of the landed aristocracy, many are now being bought by film stars, rock musicians, property speculators and tycoons who don't seem to mind the often grim weather. Accordingly, prices have spiralled. The islanders have grown nervous; when an island is sold, the futures of its residents hang in the balance. (In 1997, the islanders of Eigg breathed a sigh of relief when they finally managed, with the help of a benefactor, to pool together enough money to buy the island for themselves.)

One word of caution: when a new owner has taken possession of an island, he is only the lord of all he can see when the tide is high; when the tide is low, he is surrounded by the Crown, because the monarch owns the foreshore.

Jokes

For a slightly objective view of something so intensely subjective as humour, one could do worse than seek the opinion of George Mikes, a Hungarian who moved to England where he became a humorous writer. "Britain is the only country in the world which is inordinately proud of its sense of humour," he said. "In other countries, if they find you inadequate or they hate you, they will call you stupid, ill-mannered, a horse-thief or hyena. In England, they will say that you have no sense of humour. That is the final condemnation, the total dismissal."

Yet no monolithic British sense of humour exists. There are many varieties, of which five are most common:

• **Irony.** To justify their view of themselves as good losers, to whom playing the game is more important than winning it – fortunately, given their usual performance – the British have developed a sophisticated self-mockery. It is a virtue to be able to laugh at oneself. Losers loom large in British television sitcoms, from the rag-and-bone men of *Steptoe and Son* (translated to the US as *Sanford and Son*) to Ricky Gervais's cringe-inducing *The Office* (which also spawned a US version).

• **Satire.** The satirist, who laughs at others, is nourished by the prevalence of hypocrisy in national life. Also, given the rigidity and conservatism of most national habits and institutions, it's easier to joke about them than to change them. Political pamphleteering nourished that habit, which continued in such TV programmes as *Yes, Prime Minister*. The great visual tradition of vicious caricature, which reached its peak in the 18th and 19th centuries with James Gillray, George Cruikshank and William Hogarth, was continued in the TV puppet show *Spitting Image*.

• **Smut.** Farces in which hilarity often relies on males losing their trousers remain popular theatre and stand-up comedians rely heavily on lewdness. Because the British are repressed about sex, dirty jokes abound and TV hits such as *Little Britain* seem obsessed with bodily functions. "Mark my words," warned playwright Alan Bennett, "when a society has to resort to the lavatory for its humour, the writing is on the wall."

• **Absurdity.** Perhaps as a palliative against the national failings of formality and pomposity, sur-

LEFT: Winkle Street cottages in Calbourne, Isle of Wight. **ABOVE:** writer and comedian Ricky Gervais.

real humour is highly developed. Lewis Carroll is the greatest literary exemplar, and there is a long tradition of nonsense verse. Modern examples are the radio *Goon Shows* of the 1950s (in which Peter Sellers made his name) and the *Monty Python's Flying Circus* TV comedies of the 1970s. Cruelty and sadism figure heavily in this form of humour, allowing people to channel nastiness and frustration into a socially acceptable outlet, smiling politely. John Cleese perfected this technique.

● **Wit.** Shakespeare is full of it and Dr Johnson is still endlessly quoted ("A second marriage is the triumph of hope over experience"). The richness of the English language, with its wealth of

homonyms and synonyms, encouraged verbal acrobats such as Oscar Wilde ("He hasn't a single redeeming vice.") and George Bernard Shaw ("An Englishman thinks he is moral when he is only uncomfortable."). But there's also ready wit to be found in most areas of national life, even in Parliament. In one famous exchange, Lady Astor spat at Sir Winston Churchill: "If the Rt. Hon. Gentleman were my husband, I'd put poison in his tea." To which Churchill replied: "If the Hon. Lady were my wife, I would drink it."

KNIGHTS

Twice a year, at New Year and on the Queen's official birthday in June, British newspapers carry two pages of tiny type – the Honours List of medals given out to the good, the worthy, the dedicated, the long-serving, the self-important. Most simply receive medals (Order of the British Empire or Commander of the British Empire), a few are made lords, others will be made knights, to be called, for ever after, Sir or Dame.

This is what is left of the system of patronage and chivalry upon which wars were fought, taxes levied and monarchs, however mad or bad, could guarantee a faithful following. In the Middle Ages there were two kinds of knight: religious and secular. Religious orders, such as the Knights Templar, took monastic vows and devoted themselves to crusades against the infidel, while the secular knights enrolled in the services of noblemen.

By the 14th century, however, knights had become merely wealthy landowners and anyone holding property worth more than £20 a year could buy a title.

Today titles are not bought as such, but there is a remarkable correlation between knighthoods and generous donations to political parties. The Honours List is compiled by the civil service for the government of the day, although the public can also nominate worthy recipients in their communities. The Queen turns the winners into knights by dubbing them on each shoulder with a cermonial sword.

The recipients are something rather predictable,

for the most part unknown beavers, busybodies and bureaucrats. Headlines focus on the sprinkling of knighthoods for people in the arts and sport, since the public might at least have heard of them. The lack of patriotism involved in having been a tax exile didn't stop Sean Connery or Michael Caine from being knighted, and Sir Anthony Hopkins chose to become an American citizen. The actor and gay activist Ian McKellen was rebuked for accepting a knighthood in Margaret Thatcher's final Honours List, as she had done so little to support gays. But few minded Elton John becoming Sir Elton after he sang "Candle in the Wind" at the Princess of Wales's funeral service.

There are 10 different orders of knighthood. There is a better chance of becoming a lowly Knight Batchelor than joining one of the more obscure orders, such as The Most Eminent Order of the Indian Empire, a title not conferred since 1947. Most would be content with a less chivalrous Baronetage or Knightage with a title of Sir and, for Sir's wife, Lady, and the knowledge that they have joined an exclusive club of around 4,500. Membership is for life unless, as in the case of the odd businessman, they are jailed ("detained at Her Majesty's pleasure" is the euphemism), in which case Her Majesty can show her displeasure by demanding the title back.

Lords

Some Britons are born lords (by heredity), some achieve their lordships (by doing something remarkable, or simply making a lot of money), and some have lordships thrust upon them (by passing their sell-by date as a member of parliament and being shoved into the House of Lords by the prime minister).

The pecking order of the nation's nobility, at last count, goes like this: royal dukes 5 (Edinburgh, Cornwall, York, Gloucester, Kent), ordinary dukes 24, marquesses 35, earls 204, viscounts 127 and barons 500. Kindly address a duke as "Your Grace" and a marquess as "Most Honourable". For the rest, "Right Honourable Lord" will do. In general, English lords take precedence over Scottish lords, of whom there are a disproportionate number; they include the Duke of Atholl, the only man in the realm allowed to keep a standing army, which he does in his 100-strong Atholl Highlanders.

Left: Sir Elton John is a knight of the realm.
Right: Lord (Andrew) Lloyd-Webber is a peer.

The stately homes of many lords can now be visited. The burden of death duties, and of maintaining these crumbling piles, turned some of them into theme parks from the 1960s onwards. Otherwise, floating the odd Old Master or piece of furniture on to the art markets keeps them going for a year or two.

There are some 800 peers of the realm in all. With few exceptions their titles pass through the male side of the family. The heirs to a large chunk of Britain will undoubtedly attend a top public school, but not go to university, preferring instead officer training at the Royal Military Academy, Sandhurst, after which they would hope to join

one of the army's prestigious Guards regiments. Until 1999, all were entitled to sit in the House of Lords, where they were able to review government legislation and, if they wished, block it. But the Labour government, deeming this process to be inegalitarian, removed the right of all but 92 hereditary peers to sit in the House of Lords, and further legislation is needed to improve on this fudged compromise. Satirists warn that the reform has made Britain a less amusing place.

There are around 600 Life Peers, created in the Honours List (*see Knights*). They are entitled to sit in the House of Lords, as are the Archbishops of Canterbury and York plus 24 bishops, making up the Lords Spiritual, and 19 Law Lords, judges who are Lords of Appeal. Life Peers, more properly called Life Barons, are not entitled to pass their title to their children.

In theory, the wisdom and experience of the current 700 or so members of the House of Lords enable them to improve the legislation sent to them from the more turbulent House of Commons. Unhappily, genes can pass on stupidity from generation to generation as easily as intelligence, an argument used to justify the erosion of hereditary peers' influence.

Some democrats argue for the popular election of Life Peers, but others say that the public would tend to vote for celebrities rather than wise legislators. However, since the government elevated the maestro of the West End musical to become Lord Lloyd-Webber, that precedent has already been set.

MONARCHY

"Her majesty's speech delivered upon the reassembling of parliament was, as usual, insipid and uninstructive. Its preferred topic was her majesty's approaching marriage, a matter of little importance or interest to the country, except as it may thereby be burdened with additional and unnecessary expense." That curt dismissal of Queen Victoria was written by a correspondent of *The Times* a century and a half ago. Since then the tribes of Britain have become noticeably more democratic, more pluralistic, more educated, more informed and far more reverential to the family whom they continue to crown with the world's most valuable single piece of jewellery.

Her Majesty Queen Elizabeth II, descendent of both Kings Egbert of Wessex (AD 827–39) and McAlpine of Scotland (1057–93), and relative of the half-dozen remaining monarchs of Europe, earns around £1.8 million a day. It takes only the briefest whistle-stop tour of Britain's major palaces to realise that she is the world's richest woman and is the custodian of the world's largest private collection of art. Conscious of certain criticism, she recently began to pay tax and many "lesser" royals were removed from the Civil List, which provides public money towards their expenses.

Sometimes there is an outcry if lesser royals are seen to be living off the fat without putting in time on what can be an arduous stream of official engagements. But the British still regard the monarchy as a useful and desirable institution. By its very age it is a potent symbol of national identity; by being above party politics and not subject to election, it provides the State with a sense of last-bastion hope against the incompetence of often uninspiring politicians; and not least it is a darned good show.

Unlike Queen Victoria, who tried to interfere with her democratically elected prime ministers and became so disenchanted with the whole business of politics that she seriously considered packing her bags and ruling the Empire from Australia, her descendents who have reigned this century as the House of Windsor have been adept at keeping clear of the political arena. Never mind that, as builders, art patrons or setters of style, they have often seemed uninspired dullards.

The Queen passed retiring age in 1986 and she has made it known that, should the public want it, she would go. But opinion polls show that she retains broad support. The same cannot be said of her son and heir, Charles III (as he would be), who often seems ill-at-ease in public. Much mud was flung during the break-up of his marriage to Diana, Princess of Wales, and her tragic death in 1997 led to more calls that Charles should stand aside from the succession in favour of his eldest son, Prince William.

The ideal "image" of the royals in the 21st century is a matter of debate. Nobody wants them to return to being the remote figureheads they were until the 1960s; Diana's overwhelming popularity certainly stemmed from her rejection of formal protocol and willingness to express her emotions as well as from her glamour.

But many also question whether Britain's tabloid press's portrayal of the family as the cast of an action-packed soap opera has destroyed the mystique that a hereditary monarchy needs to prosper in a democratic age. A savage TV puppet show, *Spitting Image*, lampooned them mercilessly, depicting the late Princess Margaret as a gin swiller and Prince Charles as an ecology freak. After the scandals surrounding Andrew and Fergie and Charles and Diana, the tabloids turned their attention to Princes William and Harry. So what other sexual scandals are still to be revealed? Will Charles ever make it to the throne? Will the republican cause ever triumph? Stay tuned for tomorrow's exciting episode…

LEFT: the Queen and Prince Philip at the annual Braemar Highland gathering in Scotland.
ABOVE: top newspaper proprietor Rupert Murdoch.

NEWSPAPERS

After listening to a journalist passionately defending the importance of a politically free and unfettered press in a modern democracy such as Britain, a character in Tom Stoppard's play *Night and Day* replied: "I'm with you on the free press. It's the newspapers I can't stand."

Many share that ambivalence because, while Britain has some of the world's best newspapers, it also has some of the worst. By "worst", one means that objective news is consistently subordinated to highly imaginative stories about the sex lives of TV personalities, pop stars, footballers and the royal family, and that the few columns of genuine news are grotesquely sensationalised.

The saving grace is the diversity of Britain's papers. Ten national dailies (total daily sale: 10.8 million) and nine Sundays (total sale: 10.1 million) are distributed nationwide, augmented by a host of regional dailies, local weeklies and urban freesheets.

Circulations have shrunk alarmingly as readers and advertising migrate to the internet and most papers have tried to broaden their appeal. But the wide choice still makes possible the facile characterisation of people according to what they read. Thus *Guardian* types are held to be arrogant, soft-centred liberals who value rehabilitation of wrong-doers above punishment, and *Daily Mail* types are

flag-waving patriots who would crack down on immigration and bring back the death penalty.

One worry is concentration of ownership: Rupert Murdoch alone owns four national best-sellers: *The Sun*, the top daily tabloid; *The Times*, now also tabloid but retaining a little of its old cachet; the *News of the World*, the top Sunday scandal-sheet; and the quality *Sunday Times*. If Murdoch decides to throw his weight behind one political party, the influence is significant.

North-south divide

The Scots and Welsh have their distinctive cultures *(see pages 21–3)* and a degree of self-government. But the English are remarkably heterogeneous and, as in many European countries, there is a tendency to differentiate broadly – and controversially – between northerners and southerners.

The stereotype portrays notherners as being more outgoing, forthright and gregarious; southerners as being more wary, noncommittal and reserved. Join a bus queue in London, it's said, and you'll stand in silence; join one in Liverpool and you'll soon strike up a conversation.

Even allowing for wide individual differences, the usefulness of that broad distinction is undermined in areas with large numbers of immigrants who have added a touch of their own cultures to the mix. In addition, there is debate of whether the Midlands, the area centred on Birmingham, belongs to "the North" or "the South".

Danny Dorling, professor of human geography at the University of Sheffield, cut through this confusion by drawing a diagonal line from the Bristol Channel in the west to the fishing port of Grimsby in the east. "'The South has a few pockets of poverty in a sea of affluence," he said, "whereas the North has a few pockets of affluence in a sea of poverty." The decline in manufacturing, weighted towards the north since the Industrial Revolution, has emphasised the gap, as has the sky-high cost of housing in the crowded southeast.

Health statistics bring little cheer to people living in northern England – they are more likely than southerners to smoke and drink to excess, their mental health is poorer, and their life expectancy is up to three years less.

Such news, of course, emanates from London, where government and the national media are based, as are most of the big cultural institutions. If a northern city is flooded, said one cynic, it's a weather story; if Chelsea or Westminster were flooded, it's a national emergency. But then the London elite have been canny enough to build the Thames Barrier to help minimise that risk.

Outdoor activities

Despite living on an island notorious for inhospitable weather, the British seem to enjoy spending a great deal of time out of doors – in their gardens or, increasingly, following more energetic outdoor pursuits. Exactly why they should prefer golf to basketball, and mountaineering to gymnastics, even after successive cold, damp sporting holidays, is a mystery.

Apart from gardening, the nation's most popular leisure activity is walking – or rambling, as it is often known. During the Industrial Revolution, workers in the polluted northern mill towns fought for the right to roam the countryside on their days off. Rights of way from time immemorial were legally enshrined as public footpaths – which is just as well, as even in 1908 a member of the Commons and Footpaths Preservation Society complained in *The Times* that the motor car had made walking on narrow country roads too dangerous to contemplate.

Today, the Ramblers Association and affiliated groups have nearly 200,000 members and wage recurring battles against landowners who erect barbed-wire fences, plough up footpaths, or apply to abolish historic rights of way. Every local tourist authority can supply information on attractive walks in its vicinity, which generally happen to pass conveniently close to a good pub.

Cyclists, too, are increasingly well catered for. Britain chose to celebrate the Millennium by criss-crossing itself with cycle routes from Elgin to Eastbourne and from Fishguard to Felixstowe. The routes are a combination of traffic-free paths and quiet roads, and are sometimes established on disused railway lines, now paved over.

For those of hardier disposition, there is also skiing in Scotland's Cairngorms, surfing and scuba-diving in the West Country, hang-gliding in any coastal or hilly area, and horse riding everywhere. Many Britons find that the best way to meet nature on its own terms is simply by heading towards the nearest body of water and sinking a rod – if you are so tempted, do remember to buy a fishing licence.

LEFT: a friendly teashop welcome in North Yorkshire.
ABOVE: an abortion rights group takes its campaign to the House of Commons.

PARTY POLITICS

The two major parties have clung to power longer in recent years than was traditionally the case. Founded in the 18th century, the Conservative Party (familiarly known as the Tories) held power from 1979 until 1997. The Labour Party, formed in the late 19th century, then took over and won subsequent elections in 2001 and 2005. The old stereotypes of the Tories as "the toffs' party" and Labour as "the working-class party" eroded as both sought the "middle ground". Thus Labour behaved like capitalist magnates in selling off nationalised assets, and the Tories sounded almost like socialist sympathisers in condemning the bankers who triggered the 2008 financial crisis.

The "first past the post" electoral system (as opposed to proportional representation) gives the third party, the Liberal Democrats, fewer Members of Parliament than the number of votes cast for them would justify. Although denied real power, they can usefully curb the excesses of the two main parties, and could be a coalition partner if an election ended in stalemate for the big two.

The Scottish National Party, often accused of being anti-English, won control of the Scottish Parliament, which runs domestic affairs in Scotland, in 2007. In Wales, Plaid Cymru is a significant force in the Welsh Assembly.

Both Scotland and Wales also elect MPs to the Westminster parliament where they are allowed to vote not only on national and international questions but also, anomalously, on the domestic affairs of England, which does not have a separate regional parliament.

PUBS

The best pub in England is called The Moon Under Water, and it hides down an unprepossessing side street in an old northern industrial town not far from Manchester. It has that indefinable richness of atmosphere that comes in part from its customers, who are mostly regulars and who attend not only for the beer but equally for the conversation, and in part from its uncompromisingly Victorian architecture and fittings, its dark-grained mahogany, ornamental mirrors and sparkling etched glass, its cast-iron fireplaces and ceiling stained yellow-brown by decades of nicotine, all combining to create the solid comfortable ugliness that often characterised the 19th century.

It has games, particularly darts, in its public bar, and good solid plain food at prices that would bankrupt a restaurant. It has barmaids who know everyone by name, and a delightful garden where, in summer, the customers drink under the shade of plane trees, while their children play at a decent distance on thoughtfully provided swings and slides.

The Moon Under Water is entirely free from modern miseries: from piped music, from plastic panels masquerading as oak, from the flashing lights of video games. It is always quiet enough to talk, if only to praise the excellence of the fine traditional English ale.

The Moon Under Water does not exist, and never did (although a modern chain of pubs usurped the name). It was a figment of the imagination of George Orwell, the author of *Nineteen Eighty-Four*, who 50 years ago played a round of that perennially popular English game – dreaming

POPULATION: HOW GREAT BRITAIN IS A MELTING POT

Great Britain has 58.8 million people, 86.3 percent of whom live in England, 5 percent in Wales, and 8.7 percent in Scotland. By 2021 the population is expected to have grown by 11 percent and by 2031 may top 71 million. This growth is seen as a challenge, particularly to the creaking transport infrastructure.

At Notting Hill Carnival, London.

Nine percent of England's population is non-white, compared with 2 percent in England and Wales. Nearly half (45 per cent) of non-whites live in the London region, where they make up 29 per cent of all residents.

London is the base for 78 percent of Black Africans and 61 percent of Black Caribbeans. More than half of the Bangladeshi group (54 percent) also lives in London. Other ethnic minority groups are more dispersed. Only 19 per cent of Pakistanis live in London, while 21 per cent live in the West Midlands, 20 per cent in Yorkshire and the Humber, and 16 per cent in the northwest.

The Irish have traditionally found it easy to settle – and even vote – in Britain while retaining their Irish nationality. Almost a third (32 per cent) of the 691,000 Irish in Britain live in London, making up 3 per cent of the population. These days citizens of any European Union country can settle in Britain, and recent years have seen a large influx of Poles and other eastern Europeans.

of the perfect pub. There are 57,000 pubs in Britain – though dozens close every week, hit by a fatal combination of cut-price competition from supermarket alcohol, drink-driving laws and the ban on smoking indoors. Some of the survivors are a great deal closer to perfection than others.

Perfection is in the eye of the beholder, of course, and just as many "Irish pubs" round the world bear only the faintest resemblance to a traditional Gaelic boozer, many an "old-worlde" English pub may not be true to pub traditions.

What, then, makes a good traditional pub? There are certain well-defined ground rules. In the English beer-drinker's Bible, the annual *Good Beer Guide,* author Michael Jackson wrote*:* "In a good pub, the greatest attention is given to the drink, and in particular to the beer. Sociability, on both sides of the bar, comes a close second. A good pub encourages social intercourse, and is not dominated by cliques. A good pub has a caring, responsive landlord, not an uninterested time-server or an arrogant buffoon. In a good pub, whatever further services are offered, there is always one bar (and preferably two) to accommodate those people who simply want to drink and chat without the distraction or inhibition induced by overbearing decor, noisy entertainment, or intrusive dining."

Most pubs have at least two bars: the "public bar" which is the basic drinking shop; and the "lounge bar". There may be a difference of a few pence in the drink prices; all pubs are required by law to put their price lists prominently on display.

Some would say that the public bar is for serious, usually male, drinkers, or for workers in dirty overalls. It will probably have a bare floor and a dartboard, or a pool table. Conventionally, the lounge bar is for sitting down, for entertaining women, for an evening out. It may have a piano or piped music.

LEFT: multiracial Britain waves the flag.
ABOVE: voting at a general election becomes a pleasure when a pub doubles as a polling station.

The word "pub" is merely a shortened form of "public house", an indication that the earliest ale houses were simply private homes where the occupant brewed beer and sold it at the front door or across a table in the living room. To indicate that the house sold ale, the owner would hang out a sign, not saying "Ale", as the average Saxon peasant never graduated to literacy, but a pole topped with a bough of evergreen.

There is no shortage of claimants to be the Oldest Pub in Britain, but one with a stronger case than most is the Trip to Jerusalem, hacked into the rock beneath the walls of Nottingham Castle, and certainly in business at the time of the 13th-century Crusades, hence its name. Like so much else in British life, the pub reached its zenith in Victorian times and the country is still immensely rich in opulent pub interiors from that period, despite all the efforts of philistine pub-owning corporations to rip them out in the name of "modernisation".

Pubs have been changing over the past few decades. More and more of them sell good, inexpensive food and some ("gastropubs") are competing strongly with restaurants. Tea and coffee are often on offer and children are being made more welcome. A variety of "theme pubs" have sprung up to woo younger drinkers.

The law says that no one under 14 may enter a pub, and between 14 and 18 they must be accompanied by an adult and may not buy or consume liquor. In reality some pubs, especially in country districts, welcome whole families. Some set aside special rooms for children, and where there are gardens they are almost always welcome. It is, in the end, up to the absolute discretion of the landlord, and how strictly the local police chief applies the law. In bigger cities, certain pubs have a predominantly gay clientele.

A radical change came about with recent laws which allowed pubs to open not just at lunch time and in the evening, but largely to set their own opening hours, depending on the habits of their customers. About a third of pubs take advantage of this. Twenty minutes' "drinking up" time is still allowed after the closing time.

QUEUES

"A man in a queue is as much the image of a true Briton as a man in a bull-ring is the image of a Spaniard or a man with a two-foot cigar of an American," wrote humorist George Mikes. "An Englishman, even if he is alone, forms an orderly queue of one."

Queue-jumping incurs severe social disapproval. This can be a torrent of abuse, though usually it takes no more serious form than tut-tutting and loud remarks such as: "I say, don't they know there's a queue?" The easiest response is to pretend one is a foreigner; the affronted queuers will then sigh, knowing that you know no better, poor soul, having been deprived of their cultural conditioning.

Some think that the orderly behaviour of most crowds is the only rational behaviour when one lives in a small, overpopulated island. Others see such conspicuous respect for order as the Germanic traits never far below the surface in the British character.

Ralf Dahrendorf, a German who became head of the London School of Economics, may have got to the heart of the matter when he said: "I have a feeling that this island is uninhabitable, and therefore people have tried to make it habitable by being reasonable with one another."

Don't all rush to agree – there's a queue!

RACE

Britons have the blood of many people coursing through their veins. Even before history was written, tribes were coming in from Iberia, central Europe and the Indian subcontinent. Romans were followed by waves of Jutes, Angles, Saxons, Scandinavians and Normans (originally Scandinavian Norsemen). What Prince Llewellyn was fighting for in Wales was not the original Celtic heritage, but the last bastion of a tribe driven up from Iberia and finally stopped by the Irish Sea. Robert the Bruce, champion of the Scots, was descended from Robert de Bruis, a French Norman knight who arrived with William the Conqueror.

Trade, persecution and war brought Flemish weavers, French Huguenots, Chinese sailors, White Russians, patriotic Poles and German Jews. Hunger brought, among others, the Irish. In the 1950s Commonwealth citizens were enticed to Britain with job offers, but when they arrived, mostly from the West Indies, they found a welcome not quite as warm as they had been led to expect. There are around half a million West Indians now; many have been assimilated, although some of the latest generation have begun to reassert their Afro-Caribbean heritage.

Asians came, too, from Africa and the Indian subcontinent, heading for the manufacturing cities of Birmingham, Bradford and Leicester. In 1972 Asians thrown out of Uganda were reluctantly allowed into Britain: increasingly, Her Majesty's Principal Secretary of State for Foreign and Commonwealth Affairs did not want to allow its Commonwealth citizens the right of abode – as many Hong Kong Chinese discovered when the colony reverted to China in 1997 – and the word "immigrant" became a euphemism for coloureds or blacks.

Many Ugandan Asians were professional businessmen and, though they had to start their lives again with nothing, some were able to build up highly successful companies which their sons are now inheriting. On a smaller scale, newsagents and local grocers' shops with long opening hours are often Asian-run; in towns and villages everywhere there are Indian restaurants, usually owned or managed by people from Pakistan or Bangladesh. Chicken tikka is the nation's favourite dish.

There are more than 1 million Indians in Britain, 747,000 Pakistanis, 283,000 Bangladeshis, 1.1 million blacks (mainly from the Caribbean and Africa) and 247,000 Chinese. That sounds a lot of people, but these and all other non-white ethnic groups in the country added together still make up less than 8 percent of Britain's 59.6 million population.

Racial intolerance is not endemic, but some nasty incidents are reported and paranoia about terrorism has caused concern in Muslim communities. This magnified when it emerged that three of the four men who suicide-bombed London's transport system in 2004 had been born in Britain.

Many surveys suggest that race is seen as a diminishing social problem, but the financial benefits provided to immigrants – not least to those Eastern Europeans now entitled to enter the UK as citizens of the European Union – remains a hotly debated political topic.

LEFT: a private bar is a little more ornate than the adjacent public bar. **ABOVE:** an orderly bus queue.

RELIGION

"What a pity it is that we have no amusements but vice and religion," said Sydney Smith. As a journalist as well as a clergyman, Smith, who was born in Essex in 1771, knew both the failings and the predelictions of the British. And, nearly two centuries after his death, the vicar is still portrayed as an object of affectionate ridicule. He is the stuff that farces are made of: a blathering, upper-class nincompoop who regularly looses his trousers or is otherwise compromised through misunderstandings. Or he is the sorry figure the tabloid press triumphantly unveils from time to time, accused of committing sins of the flesh.

In reality, the vicar who pops in for afternoon tea and lives in a large grace-and-favour vicarage is a disappearing breed. Although a slight upturn was detected in congregations in the early 1990s, they have dwindled, and Britain is no longer a nation of churchgoers. The Church is, however, a microcosm of society. Mosques, synagogues and temples co-exist beside cathedrals, churches and chapels. But it is the Church of England, with the

Queen as its head, that is the backbone of Britain's moral society. The sovereign's role, established by Henry VIII, gives her power to appoint (these days to approve) the two archbishops, of Canterbury and York, who are in turn responsible for their bishoprics and for the church's ruling body, the General Synod, which regulates church matters subject to parliament and royal assent.

On the whole, the Church of England, though rather stuck with a typically British misogynous establishment, is pretty easy-going. It has a liberal, ecumenical approach and prefers compassion to fire and brimstone. The ordination of women was one important issue on which some establishment figures could not yield – but instead of digging in their heels when women donned dog collars, they walked out and became Roman Catholic. The question of gay clergy provoked another heated controversy, particularly from affiliated churches in Africa and the Caribbean, and some believed the Church of England might split in two.

The church's Welsh and Scots counterparts are less flexible. The Scots Presbyterian Church is a stern church, Calvinist in its beliefs. Worshippers in the remoter parts of the country still regard cooking, washing up or reading a newspaper on Sundays as a cardinal sin. Scots Catholics, too, are far stricter than English ones.

Nor is there such a liberal tradition among the ministry of Wales, where the utilitarian "chapel" is well attended. The chapels are Methodist, a movement founded by the 18th-century evangelist John Wesley, which urged thrift and hard work and appealed to the working class. It took hold in the working populations of northeast England, parts of Cornwall and, particularly, Wales where, linked with the Welsh language, Calvinistic Methodism evolved.

Rugby

Rugby, it has been said, is a thug's game played by gentlemen, while soccer is a gentleman's game played by thugs. Rugby Union (largely an amateur sport) and Rugby League (the professional variant) are both played with an oval ball and supposedly originated in England's Rugby School in 1823 when a pupil playing football picked up the ball and ran with it. Rugby's rules are relatively simple, but it involves a lot of body contact.

In England, though not in Wales, Rugby Union was historically a participatory sport rather than a spectator sport. The Six Nations Championships each year involve teams from England, France, Ireland, Italy, Scotland and Wales.

Sex

Time to consult George Mikes again. "Continental people," he said, "have a sex life; the English have hot-water bottles." The description is probably just as true of the Scots and Welsh, though of course there are exceptions, and the nation did have a brief affair with sex in the Swinging Sixties. But in the Aids era, the pendulum has swung back: *No Sex, Please, We're British* enjoyed an exceptionally long run in the West End.

Britons prefer their sex to be safe, a bit of a naughty joke rather than a dangerous affair. A classic example was the wheeze dreamed up by a group of Yorkshire women, members of the normally staid Women's Institute, who posed for a nude calendar to raise money for cancer research. The idea so caught the imagination that it was made into a film, *Calendar Girls*, with Helen Mirren in 2003 and subsequently became a stage play.

There is a parallel between Britain's attitude to sex and the country's traditional eating habits: performed when needs dictate, with minimum flair.

Just as Continental caterers have found scant competition in setting up the smaller, best-run restaurants and cafés, so generations of Continental men, faced with the British female on holiday, must wonder when their luck is going to run out. Why should the most insincere, banal compliment, even when garnished with a foreign accent, produce such instant success year after year? It must be because, whatever other qualities it may possess, British sexuality is sorely lacking in flattery and flirtation. More often an initial encounter will involve insulting banter. Two young men, for instance, may approach two young women in the following manner. One youth will target the woman of his choice and give his companion a grotesque nudge. "Here!" he will shout merrily. "Don't think much of your one!" From this exchange, the young lady in question will understand that her swain fancies her very much indeed.

Traditionally, the attitude of the British to sex is prudish and repressive. They are supposed to be secretly addicted to spanking and other forms of corporal punishment for which public school has instilled a taste. They mail childish postcards showing, perhaps, a puny, henpecked husband, his fat and unattractive wife and a beautiful big-busted bikini-clad passer-by. The printed jest is double entendre of the "Ooh, what a lovely pear" variety.

This is by no means old-fashioned humour, as any click of the radio or television switch will reveal. There is no better crash course of British sexuality than the *Carry On* films (28 in all, full of sexual stereotypes, from tarty, pneumatic blondes to outrageously effeminate homosexuals). More recently, television sitcoms such as *Little Britain* have carried on this tradition, more outrageously.

LEFT: the Archbishop of Canterbury, Dr Rowan Williams, meets Prince Charles, in line to head England's established church. **ABOVE:** the older woman's sex symbol, Helen Mirren, in *Calendar Girls*.

Sex has never been a legitimate excuse for a crime of passion in Britain, but it haunts politicians. In 1963 the Profumo Scandal hastened the end of Harold Macmillan's Conservative government. The country was enthralled by the saga ("War Minister shares delights of call girl with Soviet naval attaché") and it still excited enough interest to become a successful film, *Scandal*, a quarter of a century later.

Surveillance

No democracy in the world turns more surveillance cameras on its citizens than Britain. It's impossible to count them all – estimates put the figure between 4 and 5 million – and lax controls on who is given access to the resulting data has led some to fear a serious erosion of civil liberties. The country's information commissioner, who monitors such dangers on behalf of parliament, warned that the country was "sleepwalking into a surveillance society."

The cameras photograph you in department stores and tiny corner shops, in airports and railway stations, in car parks and housing estates. They track your progress in city streets and along the nation's motorways. London's congestion zone alone has 340 camera sites to record the number plates of every vehicle that enters, triggering fines for those that don't pay the charge.

Some taxis have installed cameras to deter passengers from assaulting the driver. Speakers have been incorporated in a few cameras so that remote operators can instruct pedestrians to pick up litter they have just dropped – the disembodied voice is felt to embody authority. Some "lollipop ladies" – the women who carry signs on lollipop-like poles to shepherd children across roads near schools – had cameras fitted to their headgear to record uncooperative drivers.

Critics draw parallels with the repressive society imagined by George Orwell in *Nineteen Eighty-Four*. Yet across the country citizens' groups have enthusiastically lobbied their local councils to install cameras in town centres to help curb vandalism and violence. The police point to their usefulness in tracking criminals, including terrorists, and in finding lost children.

The cameras that attract most venom – to the extent that they have been attacked with axes and petrol-bombed – are speed cameras, which account for the vast majority of more than 2 million speeding tickets issued a year. Opponents claim that many cameras are sited not at known accident spots but on stretches of road likely to maximise revenue from the typically £60 fines.

Orwell was again invoked when government ministers, citing the need to counter terrorism, proposed a massive database detailing all telephone calls and emails sent in the UK. Given the state's traditional inability to set up computer systems that worked properly, this was felt to be a rash proposal.

The law-abiding, argued the government, have surely nothing to worry about. Nigel Shadbolt, a computer scientist at the University of Southampton, responded: "If you keep within the law, and the government keeps within the law, and its employees keep within the law, and the computer holding the database doesn't screw up, and the system is carefully designed according to well-understood software engineering principles and maintained properly, and the government doesn't scrimp on the outlay, and all the data are entered carefully, and the police are adequately trained to use the system, and the system isn't hacked into, and your identity isn't stolen, and the local hardware functions… well, you have nothing to fear."

TEA

On average, Britons drink five cups of tea a day, consuming about one third of the total tea export market every year. The "real" cup of tea is, however, not always easy to find. Places to go looking are posh hotels that cater for the better-off tourist, low-budget cafés of the fish-and-chip variety that thrive in seaside towns, and native British homes that have not gone over to teabags.

The finest tea is made from the bud and first two leaves of the tea bush. They should be steeped in boiled water for between three and five minutes. Traditionally, very strong Indian tea, rigid with tannin and probably jaw-clenchingly sweet, is favoured by burly men who work with their hands, while women, children and effete males like their cuppa watery-weak and China. But an occasional macho workman called out to fix something in a British home has reportedly voiced approval of delicately scented, pale Earl Grey.

There are as many ways of making a cup of tea properly as there are British residents and all methods involve mysterious and magical warmings and stirrings of the pot, exact timings and individual blends. Up North, they tend to put the tea in first, then add milk; down South they do the reverse and both halves of the country swear blind that theirs is the only way to make tea. Anyone with Far or Near East connections may well add a sneaky pinch of cardamom.

Diarist Samuel Pepys found his first cup of China tea such a novelty in 1660 that he gave it a special entry. In its early days, it was so expensive that it was locked away in metal caddies to stop the servants helping themselves. Adding to the price was the cost of transportation from the Far East on such speedy clippers as the *Cutty Sark*, now in dry dock at Greenwich, in London.

A cup of tea, without sugar or milk, contains only about four calories. Its stimulating effect is due to caffeine (weight for weight, tea leaves contain more than twice the caffeine of coffee beans). Its astringency and colour come from the tannin content, its flavour from volatile oils.

The habit of afternoon tea with cakes was started around 1840 by the Duchess of Bedford. The West Country's rich cream teas, with scones, jam, clotted cream and cakes to accompany the pot of tea, is inexpensive, delicious in a sickly way and packed with cholesterol. For a traditional afternoon tea, try a big hotel like the London Ritz, though you have to book. To work one off, find a Tea Dance where you can do the foxtrot to such nostalgic inter-war orchestral numbers as *Blue Moon* and *Smoke Gets In Your Eyes*. Such dances were once highly fashionable and are still popular with older people, the occasional member of parliament and anyone else with a little free time in the afternoon.

LEFT: police monitor surveillance cameras in London.
RIGHT: an olde-worlde tearoom in East Anglia.

UNION JACK

The flag of Great Britain is the same as the flag of the United Kingdom, which includes Northern Ireland. The Union Flag is a bit lopsided and may only be flown one way up. If hoisted incorrectly, particularly at sea, where mariners are well informed in these matters, it may be taken for a distress signal. The flag of any country hoisted on the jackstaff of a ship's bows is called the Jack, hence the flag's popular name of Union Jack.

The Union Flag was designed after the union between England and Scotland in 1606, combining the red cross of St George (heraldically speaking, cross gules in a field argent) with Scotland's cross of St Andrew, a white diagonal cross on a blue background (saltire argent in a field azure). In 1801 the red diagonal cross (saltire gules in a field argent) of Ireland's St Patrick was added. No room is left for Wales's St Dewi, or David, whose emblem is a dove.

The constituent parts of the kingdom also have animals and plants for their own flags and heraldic devices: lions for both England and Scotland and a dragon for Wales; a rose for England, a thistle for Scotland and a leek for Wales.

U AND NON-U

U is the correct vocabulary used by the upper classes, and non-U embraces the vulgarities of the tediously aspiring middle classes. That was the view of the upper-crust author Nancy Mitford, who in 1954 laid down a few rules. You gaze into a looking-glass, not a mirror; you wear false teeth rather than dentures; you sit in a drawing-room, not a lounge; you wear scent rather than perfume; you say "What?" rather than "Pardon?"; and you die rather than pass on. Crucially, you go to the lavatory or the loo but never to the toilet. Today's dilemmas are no less puzzling. One etiquette expert, for example, has suggested that a gentleman never pushes a trolley in a supermarket, he always uses a basket.

V-SIGN

In World War II, that master of morale-boosting, Winston Churchill, signalled eventual Victory by raising two fingers with the palm facing outwards. A more familiar modern gesture is to raise two fingers with the back of the hand facing outward; this is an uncompromising expression of abuse and often provokes a fracas. Care is needed here.

WEATHER

"When two Englishmen meet, their first talk is of the weather," wrote Dr Samuel Johnson. Two centuries later, this relatively harmless national obsession is still going strong and no weather-related phrase is considered too banal or boring to merit use as a conversational opening gambit between strangers. Try "Hot/cold enough for you, then, is it?" "Looks like rain", "All right if you're a duck" and "Don't suppose this will hold much longer." All of these are useful, widely used phrases.

Why should the British be so interested in the vagaries of their climate? The key lies in its unpredictability. Its swings of mood don't bear out its dull reputation at all. Far from always having the drizzly, mediocre summers and mild, wet winters, British weather can switch rapidly from drought to flood, damp cold to oppressive heat. Each dramatic change catches Britons on the hop.

In August 1990 temperatures reached the highest ever recorded: 98.8°F (37.1°C). Hurricanes in 1987 and 1990 caused several deaths and uprooted thousands of trees, Western film-style dust "devils" have blown through the lanes of Surrey, and waves higher than a double-decker bus submerged a seaside town in Wales.

Such violent extremes are made all the harder to bear because national habits, buildings and clothing are simply not designed to cope with them. Few homes or offices have fans or air conditioning to alleviate the summer's heat. In winter, heating and insulation systems work at half-cock, while road and rail networks inevitably come to a standstill in anything more than an inch of snow (one railway company, brought to a halt by one light snowfall, asserted – to general hilarity – it was the "wrong kind" of snow). Unwary motorists, villagers and livestock disappear under mounds of drifting snow in a manner that puzzles Continentals, who are used to handling such seasonal hazards.

They would prefer to pit themselves against the worst the elements can throw at them, rather than make themselves comfortable, which would be wimpish. So, in summer's oven heat, they do not hide in tree-shaded piazzas or close their shutters to keep the tiled floor cool. Their cities are designed to ensure that streets become sweltering canyons, while overfurnished homes become more stuffy.

Hats (other than those expensive designer creations shown off at Ascot) are generally not taken seriously. Anyone spotted wearing something large and shady to fend off sunstroke or stop precious body heat seeping away is probably foreign.

Global warming may change British weather forever, creating hot, dry summers. The writer Virginia Woolf thought that such weather might turn us all into outgoing Mediterraneans. But relentless, reliable sunshine is far more likely to provoke deep Scandinavian gloom, making us all sadder than SAD – Seasonal Affective Disorder, a condition diagnosed by doctors and normally produced by too little, rather than too much light.

For although the British have always dreamed of an empire upon which the sun never sets, dependable good weather spoils their "just-in-case" philosophy. Umbrellas, extra woollens and fold-up plastic raincoats are much-loved accessories. British women might have been considered as chic as Parisiennes were it not for their just-in-case cardigans flung inelegantly over summer dresses. In the days before golfing umbrellas were big and country people waxed their coats, ugly folding plastic macs used to make rainswept holidaymakers look like film-wrapped, self-basting chickens. The small plastic rainhat, furled down to the size of a condom and secreted in the handbag, is still favoured today by older ladies with tightly permed, snowy hair.

Britons today keep a keen weather eye on their climate by frequently tuning in to radio and television forecasts. Traditionally, TV weathermen and women have been civil servants from the Meteorological Office in Bracknell, Berkshire, and some have compensated for their lack of media background by cultivating eccentricity. One cut-price cable channel carried the whole business to its absurd extreme by appointing a blonde with compelling physical attributes to read the weather in Norwegian.

LEFT: the nation's flag keeps off the nation's rain at Tunbridge Wells. **ABOVE:** when your home is flooded, what you need is a nice cup of tea.

WHISKY

The earliest known reference to whisky occurred in 1494 when Scottish Exchequer Rolls record that Friar John Cor purchased a quantity of malt "to make aquavitae". It's not a hard drink to make, and by 1777 Excise officers estimated that Edinburgh had eight licensed stills and 400 illegal ones. Today more than 2,500 brands of Scotch whisky, one of Britain's top five export items, are sold around the world.

Yet something as easy to make cannot be made authentically outside Scotland. Many have tried, and the Japanese have thrown the most modern technology at the problem; but the combination of damp climate and soft water flowing through the peat cannot be replicated elsewhere.

These days there are two kinds of Scotch whisky: *malt*, made from malted barley only; and *grain*, made from malted barley together with unmalted barley, maize or other cereals. Most popular brands are blends of both types of whisky – typically 60 percent grain to 40 percent malt.

A single malt, the product of one distillery, has become an increasingly popular drink, thanks largely to the aggressive marketing by William Grant & Sons of their Glenfiddich brand. But sales of single malts still account for only one bottle in 20 sold around the world, and most of the production of single-malt distilleries is used to add flavour to a blended whisky.

The Scots themselves tend to favour Glenmorangie, which is matured in old Bourbon casks, charred on the inside, for at least 10 years to produce a smooth spirit with hints of peat smoke and vanilla. The most popular malt in the United States is The Macallan, which is produced on Speyside and matured in 100 percent sherry casks seasoned for two years in Spain with dry oloroso sherry; connoisseurs argue that the 10-year old is a better drink than the more impressive-sounding 18-year old.

The brave should sample Glenfarclas (with over 60 percent alcohol). Those desiring a more diluted sample need only take one of the many distillery tours on the Scotch Whisky Trail or enjoy the annual Speyside Whisky Festival (May). Because whisky "breathes" while maturing in its casks, up to 4 million gallons (20 million litres) evaporate into the air each year. All you have to do is inhale.

XENOPHOBIA

Like many island peoples, the British – and especially the working classes – have a profound distrust of outsiders, perhaps equating them unconsciously with invaders. It is not by chance that it took them so long to agree, reluctantly, to help finance a tunnel beneath the English Channel. The writer Nancy Mitford expressed an extreme version of this narrow-mindedness: "Abroad is unutterably boring and foreigners are fiends." The actor Robert Morley was more circumspect: "The British tourist is always happy abroad so long as the natives are waiters."

Even when dealing with their fellow Europeans, the British fall back on stereotypes. David Frost and Anthony Jay, in their book *To England With Love*, definitively summed up hell for the British as "a place where the Germans are the police, the Swedish are the comedians, the Italians are the defence force, Frenchmen dig the

WINE

Climate change may give a boost to home-grown wine, but there are already 400 vineyards, mostly in the southern parts of England and Wales, producing 2 million bottles a year. Many are tiny affairs, often run as a hobby. The biggest, at 250 acres (100 hectares), is Denbies (London Road, Dorking, tel: 01306-876616 for details of tours), about 20 miles/32km south of London.

Today's vineyards are dominated by the German vines planted in the 1950s and '60s. Around 90 percent of production is white wine, described as having a floral bouquet, a fresh taste and an acidic finish. English wine is quite distinct from "British wine", fermented and bottled in Britain from imported grape juice – not recommended.

roads, the Belgians are the pop singers, the Spanish run the railways, the Turks cook the food, the Irish are the waiters, the Greeks run the government, and the common language is Dutch." Any odds on a federal Europe?

Youth

In a word-association test, "youth" is often paired with "crime" – which may have more to do with middle-aged news values than with reality. One generation's threat to middle-class morality – the Beatles in the 1960s, punk in the 1970s – lose their power to shock with the passing of time and somehow become quaintly endearing.

These days, knife crime makes the headlines, though it is confined largely to certain inner-city areas and certain ethnic groups. For the most part, teenagers are criticised for being indifferent to social or political commitment and for being too eager to reciprocate the interest shown in them by car manufacturers, music companies, movie producers, fashion firms and food chains. Otherwise, they can join the army or get married at 16, the age of consent, and at 18 they can vote and get drunk.

LEFT: a glass of malt in good hands. **ABOVE:** young drinkers maintain an old British tradition of spending a considerable amount of time in pubs.

Zeitgeist

Taking a nation's spiritual temperature is as precise an art as palmistry, but a clue to Britain's confusing symptoms since World War II was provided by Dean Acheson, a US Secretary of State, who declared: "Great Britain has lost an Empire and has not yet found a role."

Instead, it has embraced a wide repertoire of roles: in the 1950s, that of a respectable, middle-class spinster, strapped for cash but determined to maintain her dignity in difficult circumstances; in the 1960s, that of a buoyantly optimistic, fashion-conscious good-time girl screaming for the Beatles; in the 1970s, that of a lonely woman beset by financial worries, spurned by America and regarded by Europe as hopelessly dowdy and old-fashioned; in the 1980s, a determined career woman, inspired by Margaret Thatcher to embrace a red-blooded success ethic; and in the 1990s and early 21st century along came some promising high-profile supporting roles in America's all-action blockbusters *Save Kuwait, Bomb the Balkans, Aid the Afghans* and *Invade Iraq*.

But where are the future good roles for an ageing player on the world stage? Her future is most likely to lie in European co-productions, sharing the smaller-print billing with her Continental counterparts. It hasn't the glamour of Hollywood, but times change – and, well, a girl's got to eat. ❑

Stately Homes

They reflect more than privileged lives. They also illustrate centuries of social history, and of great artistic and architectural achievement

Britain's stately homes have a fascination that attracts visitors in their millions every year. Many have embraced the tourist theme enthusiastically, with such added incentives as safari parks, transport museums, historical re-enactments and adventure playgrounds, but at the heart of them all lies a house with a story. It may tell of great achievement in a palatial mansion crammed with priceless works of art; it may reflect centuries at the heart of a close-knit country community in the form of a rambling old manor house, crammed with centuries of acquisitions; it may even show how the servants and estate workers would go about their daily duties.

Changing times

A house that may appear to be pure 18th-century neo-classical may well be hiding a medieval core and perhaps a Tudor fireplace where Elizabeth I once warmed her toes. Victorian high-flyers often confused the issue by building convincingly fanciful medieval-style castles, complete with every convenience that Industrial Revolution technology provided.

The short Edwardian era saw both the carefree heyday of the country house party and the onset of World War I, which marked the demise of stately homes in their traditional role. Maintaining them was costly, and an ingenious solution was provided in 1953 when the 13th Duke of Bedford, faced with huge death duties when he succeeded his father, was faced with the prospect of donating Woburn Abbey in Bedfordshire to the National Trust. Instead, he opened it to the public, charging them to view the 12th-century building and its contents. He later added a safari park to its grounds, enabling visitors to view from the safety of their cars lions and tigers, giraffes and elephants roaming freely. A golf club and antiques centre, plus wedding and conference facilities, were later added to the menu (details at woburnabbey.co.uk).

Initially, many fellow aristocrats condemned the Duke's ideas as crass commercialism, but soon many followed his example.

Left: The statues, figurines, iron benches and sundials that grace the gardens of stately homes have not escaped the attention of professional thieves, who have been known to peruse *Country Life* magazine to identify opportunities.

Above: Knole in Kent, birthplace of the writer Vita Sackville-West, was built by an Archbishop of Canterbury in 1456–86 and is surrounded by a 1,000-acre (400-hectare) deer park.

Below: Lyme Park in Cheshire, used in the BBC's 1995 version of Jane Austen's *Pride and Prejudice*, began as a hunting lodge in about 1400. The current hall was built in the 16th century.

ABOVE: Elton Hall, a romantic, part-Gothic baronial home in Cambridgeshire, has belonged to the Proby family since 1660. Sir Peter Proby, Lord Mayor of London, had previously been granted land and property at Elton by Queen Elizabeth I.

ABOVE: Lady Henrietta Spencer-Churchill, daughter of the 11th Duke of Marlborough and an interior decorator and author, at her family home, **Blenheim Palace** in Oxfordshire.

THE POWER OF THE NATIONAL TRUST

It sounds like another stuffy government institution, but in fact the National Trust, founded in 1895, is a registered charity and receives no state grant. Covering England, Wales and Northern Ireland – Scotland has its own independent National Trust – it initially protected open spaces and threatened buildings, but soon it began preserving places of historic interest or natural beauty for the enjoyment of future generations.

It now cares for 1,000 ancient monuments, over 300 historic houses and gardens such as Coughton Court in Warwickshire *(above)*, industrial sites, 700 miles (1,100km) of coastline and 970 sq miles (2,520 sq km) of countryside. Many country houses and gardens were donated to it by their owners who could no longer afford to maintain them or to pay death duties. Broadening its heritage ambitions, it even acquired the childhood homes of John Lennon and Paul McCartney.

The Trust is funded entirely by membership subscriptions and donations from its 3½ million members, by legacies, and by admission charges. It relies heavily on close to 50,000 volunteers who staff its ticket offices and gift shops.

BELOW: Castle Howard in Yorkshire, built between 1699 and 1712 for the 3rd Earl of Carlisle, is a country house rather than a true castle. It is a popular film location (*Brideshead Revisited, Barry Lyndon*).

PLACES

A detailed guide to the entire country, with principal sites clearly cross-referenced by number to the accompanying maps

In the early 1960s, before jogging and trainers were invented, Dr Barbara Moore began a brief craze of walking the length of the country, 874 miles (1,408 km) from John O'Groats in the northeast of Scotland to Land's End in Cornwall. (Even in this land of eccentrics she was thought rather crazy.) Though it took several weeks, it made the island seem small. Today a motorist could make the trip in not much more than a day, and it seems to have shrunk still further. But within that short distance there is an extraordinary variety of landscape, of peoples and places to see.

Apart from winter in the blizzard-blown Highlands of Scotland, getting around the country is very easy, particularly by car, and minor roads have always been good. Britain is, however, a crowded island: traffic can be bumper to bumper on motorways, while in London the average speed of traffic is the same as it was in the days of horse-drawn carriages.

Britain has its own favourite holiday haunts: the Lake District in the northwest, the Peak District in the Midlands, Devon and the Cornish Riviera in the West Country and the Pembroke Coast in South Wales. The Scots tend to head for the West Coast, while Blackpool, Britain's favourite traditional seaside resort, creaks a bit under its 6 million annual visitors.

The tourist, rightfully, wants to see the classic sites, to visit the historic buildings, the university towns, to go on literary and artistic pilgrimages, to enjoy the splendour of castles, gardens and country houses. But there is pressure on these places and there is a continuing debate about limiting numbers.

While this book gives all the necessary information about these important and popular historic centres, it also suggests a host of other places to visit, places often missed but which give just as much insight into the life and culture of Britain. The chapters have been divided geographically in a way that makes each area easy to explore, and the Travel Tips section at the back of the book has further recommendations that will help you gain an insight into Britain both on and off the beaten track. ❑

PRECEDING PAGES: Snowshill village in the Cotswolds; Eilean Donan in the Scottish Highlands; Big Ben, at London's Houses of Parliament. **LEFT:** the village green at Cavendish in Sussex. **ABOVE:** traditional town crier; country pub in Warwickshire.

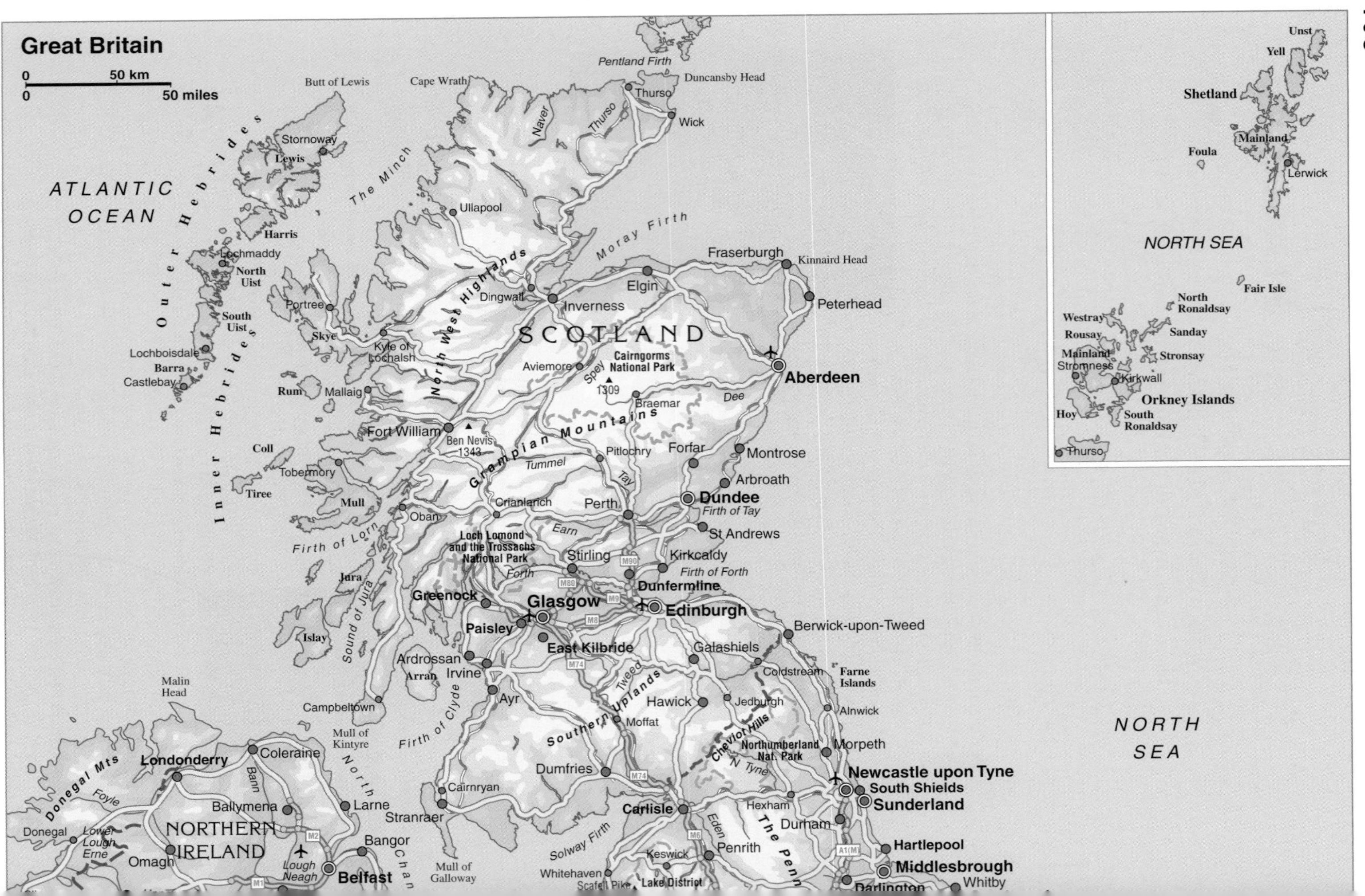

Great Britain
0 50 km
0 50 miles
ATLANTIC OCEAN
Outer Hebrides
Inner Hebrides
Butt of Lewis
Cape Wrath
Pentland Firth
Duncansby Head
Thurso
Wick
Naver
Stornoway
Lewis
The Minch
Ullapool
Harris
Lochmaddy
North Uist
South Uist
Lochboisdale
Barra
Castlebay
Moray Firth
Fraserburgh
Kinnaird Head
Peterhead
Elgin
Inverness
Dingwall
North West Highlands
Portree
Skye
Kyle of Lochalsh
SCOTLAND
Aviemore
Spey
Cairngorms National Park
1309
Braemar
Dee
Aberdeen
Rum
Mallaig
Fort William
Ben Nevis 1343
Grampian Mountains
Pitlochry
Forfar
Montrose
Arbroath
Coll
Tobermory
Tiree
Mull
Tummel
Tay
Dundee
Firth of Tay
Crianlarich
Perth
Oban
Earn
St Andrews
Loch Lomond and the Trossachs National Park
Firth of Lorn
Stirling
Kirkcaldy
Firth of Forth
Forth
Jura
Dunfermline
Greenock
Glasgow
Edinburgh
Berwick-upon-Tweed
Islay
Sound of Jura
Paisley
East Kilbride
Galashiels
Ardrossan
Arran
Irvine
Coldstream
Farne Islands
Malin Head
Campbeltown
Firth of Clyde
Ayr
Tweed
Southern Uplands
Hawick
Jedburgh
Alnwick
Moffat
Mull of Kintyre
Cheviot Hills
Northumberland Nat. Park
Morpeth
Donegal Mts
Londonderry
Coleraine
North
Dumfries
N Tyne
Newcastle upon Tyne
South Shields
Sunderland
Cairnryan
Foyle
Bann
Ballymena
Larne
Stranraer
Carlisle
Hexham
Durham
Donegal
Lower Lough Erne
NORTHERN IRELAND
Omagh
Bangor
Lough Neagh
Belfast
Mull of Galloway
Solway Firth
Eden
Penrith
The Penn
Keswick
Hartlepool
Middlesbrough
Whitehaven
Scafell Pike
Lake District
Darlington
Whitby
Unst
Yell
Shetland
Mainland
Foula
Lerwick
NORTH SEA
Fair Isle
North Ronaldsay
Westray
Rousay
Sanday
Mainland
Stromness
Stronsay
Kirkwall
Orkney Islands
Hoy
South Ronaldsay
Thurso
NORTH SEA

IRISH SEA
CELTIC SEA
English Channel
St George's Channel
Bristol Channel
Cardigan Bay
Strait of Dover
ENGLAND
WALES
Dundalk
Drogheda
Longford
Kells
Lough Ree
Mullingar
Boyne
Erne
Suck
Dublin
Dún Laoghaire
Bray
Portlaoise
Lough Derg
Barrow
Nore
Slaney
Kilkenny
Clonmel
Suir
Wexford
Blackwater
Waterford
Rosslare
Carnsore Point
Youghal
Douglas
Barrow-in-Furness
Heysham
Yorkshire Dales Nat. Park
Ripon
Lancaster
Harrogate
York
Flamborough Head
Bridlington
The Wolds
Kingston upon Hull
Blackpool
Ribble
Burnley
Leeds
Bradford
Huddersfield
Preston
Blackburn
Southport
Wigan
Bolton
Barnsley
Scunthorpe
Grimsby
Doncaster
Anglesey
Holyhead
Llandudno
Conwy
Liverpool
Manchester
636
Sheffield
Warrington
Stockport
Peak District Nat. Park
Worksop
Lincoln Wolds
Caernarfon
Betws-y-coed
Ruthin
Chester
Lincoln
Skegness
Snowdon 1085
Dee
Wrexham
Stoke-on-Trent
Boston
The Wash
Cromer
Snowdonia Nat. Park
Cambrian Mountains
Derby
Nottingham
Trent
Loughborough
King's Lynn
Swaffham
Great Yarmouth
Shrewsbury
Dolgellau
Machynlleth
Leicester
Stamford
Nene
Ouse
The Fens
Wolverhampton
Birmingham
Peterborough
Norwich
The Broads
Aberystwyth
Coventry
Corby
Lowestoft
Llandrindod Wells
Severn
Thetford
Waveney
Leominster
Worcester
Warwick
Northampton
Newmarket
Bury St Edmunds
Wye
Cambridge
Fishguard
Teifi
Stratford-upon-Avon
Banbury
Bedford
Ipswich
St David's Head
Llandovery
Usk
Hereford
Milton Keynes
Stour
Felixstowe
Pembrokeshire Coast Nat. Park
Carmarthen
Tywi
Brecon Beacons Nat. Park
885
Cheltenham
Harwich
Gloucester
Oxford
Luton
Colchester
Cotswold Hills
Cirencester
St Albans
Chelmsford
Pembroke
Tenby
Chiltern Hills
Watford
Basildon
Swansea
Cardiff
Newport
Swindon
London
Southend-on-Sea
Bristol
Reading
Margate
Weston-super-Mare
Bath
North Downs
Canterbury
Lundy
Exmoor Nat. Park
Bridgwater
Basingstoke
Guildford
Maidstone
Dover
Barnstaple
Bideford
Avon
Taunton
Salisbury
Test
Winchester
Crawley
Royal Tunbridge Wells
Folkestone
Calais
Taw
Arun
South Downs Nat. Park
The Weald
Dungeness
Bude
Southampton
South Downs
Brighton
Hastings
Exe
Yeovil
New Forest Nat. Park
Chichester
Tamar
Bournemouth
Portsmouth
Eastbourne
Exeter
Beachy Head
Boulogne
Dartmoor Nat. Park
Poole
Weymouth
Isle of Wight
Bodmin
le Touquet-Paris-Plage
Torquay
Bill of Portland
Truro
St Austell
Plymouth
Berck
Penzance
Isles of Scilly
Land's End
Falmouth
Start Point
M1
M4
M5
M6
M6 Toll
M11
M18
M20
M25
M27
M40
M42
M53
M54
M55
M56
M58
M61
M62
M69
M180
M2
M3
A16
A26

London Zoo
Hampstead 39
Euston Station
EUSTON
Camden Lock 40
Camden Town Hall
Argyle St
Acton St
King's Cross Rd
REGENT'S PARK 22
Inner Circle
Outer Circle
Broadwalk
Albany Street
REGENT'S PARK
Hampstead Road
Euston Mosque
Eversholt St
Euston Road
Judd Street
Holy Cross
ST PANCRAS
St Anne
Euston Tower
EUSTON SQUARE
Woburn Pl.
Upp. Woburn Pl.
Tavistock Sq
British Medical Association
Foundling Museum 32
Madame Tussauds
Holy Trinity
Euston Centre
Percival David Foundation of Chinese Art
Brunswick Sq
CORAM FIELDS
Gray's Inn Road
Doughty St
PARK SQ GARDENS
Euston Rd
WARREN ST
University College Hospital
Gower Street
University College
Woburn Pl.
Bernard St
Guilford Street
30 Dickens House Museum
23
REGENT'S PARK
Park Cr.
Fitzroy Square
Tottenham
Charlotte St
University of London
Russell Square
RUSSELL SQ
Gt Ormond St Hospital for Sick Children
RUSSELL SQ GDNS
Southampton Row
Portland
Great Portland St
Telecom Tower
Gower St
Theobald's Road
MARYLEBONE
Place
St Charles
American Church in London
GOODGE ST
Court
BLOOMSBURY
Harley Street
Broadcasting House BBC
Goodge St
Bedford Square
Bloomsbury Sq
British Museum 31
HOLBORN
Wallace Collection 24
Langham Pl.
All Souls
Mortimer Street
Road
St George
Bloomsbury Way
HOLBORN
Sir John Soane's Museum
High Holborn
Wigmore Hall
Wigmore Street
TOTTENHAM COURT RD
Cartoon Museum
New Oxford St
High Holborn
Kingsway
LINCOLN'S INN FIELDS
Cavendish Sq
Regent
OXFORD CIRCUS 21
Oxford Street
Soho Square
Charing Cross Road
St Giles High St
Endell St
Great Queen St
John Lewis
Selfridge's
Oxford
Street
Palladium Theatre
Photographers' Gallery
Phoenix Theatre
Neal St
Neal's Yard
Drury La
Old Curiosity Shop
Street
Wardour St
Berwick St
Dean Street
Frith St
Monmouth St
Royal Opera House 4
Bow St
Theatre Royal
Aldwych Theatre
New Bond St
Hanover Square
Liberty
Carnaby St
5
Old Compton St
COVENT GDN
St Clement Danes
26 Handel House Museum
St George
29 SOHO
Long Acre
Covent Garden Market
Aldwych
Bush House
Conduit St
Regent Street
Golden Square
Shaftesbury Ave
St Paul
3
London Transport Museum
Somerset House 7
Roosevelt Memorial
Sotheby's
Savile Row
Brewer St
LEICESTER SQ
Chinatown
St Martin's La.
COVENT GARDEN
Courtauld Institute
Lancaster Pl.
25
MAYFAIR
Piccadilly Circus
Trocadero Centre
6 Leicester Sq
London Coliseum
Strand
The Savoy
Gilbert Collection
Immaculate Conception
Berkeley Square
Faraday Museum
Old Bond St
Royal Academy of Arts 27
28
PICCADILLY CIRCUS
Haymarket
National Portrait Gallery
St Martin-in-the-Fields
Adelphi Theatre
Waterloo Bridge
Grosvenor Chapel
Piccadilly
St James
National Gallery 2
Trafalgar Square
CHARING CROSS
VICTORIA EMBANKMENT GARDENS
Embankment
Jermyn St
Fortnum & Mason
Nelson's Column 1
Charing Cross Station
EMBANKMENT
Queen Elizabeth Hall
British Film Institute
The Dorchester
ST JAMES'S
Admiralty Arch
Northumberland Ave
Curzon Street
The Ritz
St James's St
Christie's
ICA 11
Trafalgar Studios
Park Lane
Shepherd Market
GREEN PARK
Pall Mall 8
Duke of York Column
The Admiralty
Whitehall
Old War Office
Royal Festival Hall
58
Piccadilly
Chapel Royal
Marlborough House
18 Banqueting House
Hispaniola
Christ Church
St James's Palace 9
Guards Memorial
Horse Guards Parade 10
Tattershall Castle
GREEN PARK 14
Clarence House
The Mall
Horse Guards Road
Ministry of Defence
Victoria Embankment
JUBILEE GARDENS
Wellington Museum, Apsley House
Lancaster House
17
Downing St
London Eye 60
Wellington Mon.
ST JAMES'S PARK 13
Foreign Office
Cenotaph
Dali Universe
York Road
Wellington Arch
Constitution Hill
Queen Victoria Memorial
Parliament St
County Hall 61
BUCKINGHAM PALACE GARDENS
Buckingham Palace 12
Cabinet War Rooms & Churchill Museum
Treasury
WESTMINSTER
London Aquarium
Grosvenor Place
Birdcage Walk
Gt George St
Big Ben
Westminster Bridge
Central Hall
Wellington Barracks
WESTMINSTER
16 Houses of Parliament
Florence Nightingale Museum
Queen's Gallery
Guards' Chapel & Museum
ST JAMES'S PARK
Broad Sanctuary
15 Westminster Abbey
St Margaret St
St Thomas' Hospital
Buckingham Gate
Royal Mews
Westminster Chapel
New Scotland Yard
Victoria Street
Thames
Upp. Belgrave St
Hobart Pl.
Westminster City Hall
Church House
Jewel Tower
VICTORIA TOWER GARDENS
Palace Road
LAMBETH
Grosvenor Gdns
Belgrave Pl.
Belgrave St
Street
St Matthew
Great Peter St
Abingdon St
ARCHBISHOP'S PARK
VICTORIA
Victoria
Buckingham Palace Rd
19
Westminster R.C. Cathedral
St John's Concert Hall
Millbank
Lambeth Road
62 Lambeth Palace
Eaton Square
Eccleston St
Victoria Station
Vauxhall Br. Rd
Rochester Row
Horseferry Road
Lambeth Bridge
Garden Museum
Page Street
Tate Britain 20

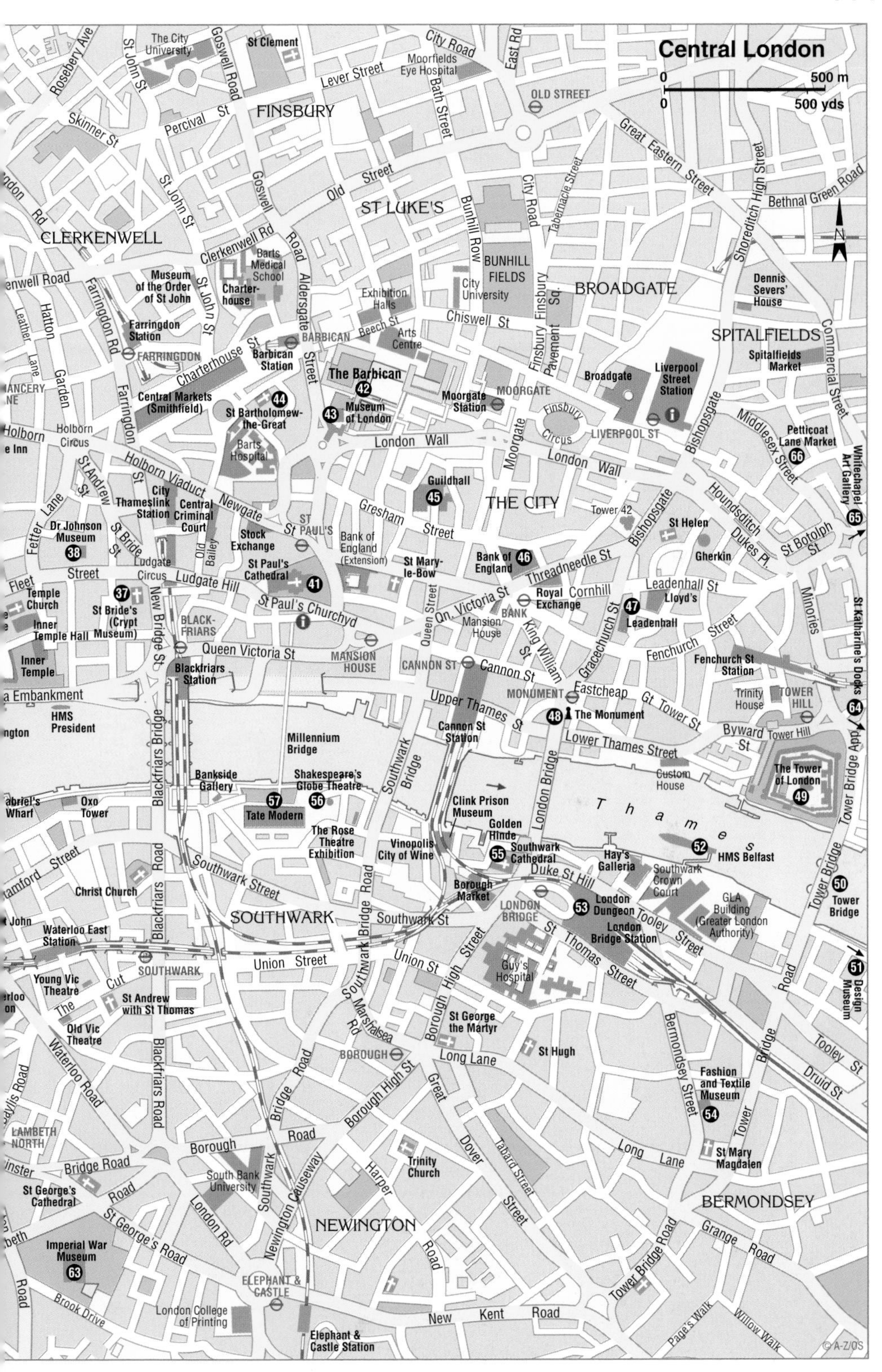
Central London
0 500 m
0 500 yds
FINSBURY
ST LUKE'S
CLERKENWELL
BUNHILL FIELDS
BROADGATE
SPITALFIELDS
THE CITY
SOUTHWARK
NEWINGTON
BERMONDSEY
The Barbican 42
Museum of London 43
St Bartholomew-the-Great 44
Guildhall 45
Bank of England 46
Leadenhall 47
The Monument 48
The Tower of London 49
Tower Bridge 50
Design Museum 51
HMS Belfast 52
London Dungeon 53
Fashion and Textile Museum 54
Southwark Cathedral 55
Shakespeare's Globe Theatre 56
Tate Modern 57
Dr Johnson Museum 38
St Bride's (Crypt Museum) 37
St Paul's Cathedral 41
Imperial War Museum 63
Tower Hill 64
Whitechapel Art Gallery 65
Petticoat Lane Market 66
Dennis Severs' House
Spitalfields Market
Liverpool Street Station
Broadgate
Moorgate Station
Barbican Station
Farringdon Station
Charterhouse
Museum of the Order of St John
Barts Medical School
Central Markets (Smithfield)
Barts Hospital
Central Criminal Court
City Thameslink Station
Stock Exchange
Temple Church
Inner Temple Hall
Inner Temple
Blackfriars Station
Cannon St Station
Royal Exchange
Mansion House
Lloyd's
Gherkin
Tower 42
St Helen
Fenchurch St Station
Trinity House
Custom House
Millennium Bridge
Bankside Gallery
Oxo Tower
The Rose Theatre Exhibition
Vinopolis City of Wine
Clink Prison Museum
Golden Hinde
Borough Market
Hay's Galleria
Southwark Crown Court
GLA Building (Greater London Authority)
London Bridge Station
Guy's Hospital
St George the Martyr
St Hugh
St Mary Magdalen
Trinity Church
South Bank University
St George's Cathedral
London College of Printing
Elephant & Castle Station
Christ Church
Waterloo East Station
Young Vic Theatre
Old Vic Theatre
St Andrew with St Thomas
HMS President
Moorfields Eye Hospital
The City University
St Clement
City University
Exhibition Halls
Arts Centre
Thames
© A-Z/OS

PUBLIC
UNDERGROUND
1911
GO
TO McDONALD'S
SAMSUNG
Budweiser
2006 FIFA WORLD CUP GERMANY
TDK
SANYO
local
taxi
Mon - Sun
pharmacy
beauty
BAKERLOO LINE
PICCADILLY LINE
PUBLIC TOILETS
TRAVEL INFORMATION
The last entrance to close is the one outside Lillywhites
PICCADILLY CIRCUS STATION

Recommended Restaurants and Pubs on pags 128–9

CENTRAL LONDON

It's a surprisingly walkable city – just as well, given the traffic congestion. It's also a largely unplanned metropolis, which means you never know what you'll find round the next corner

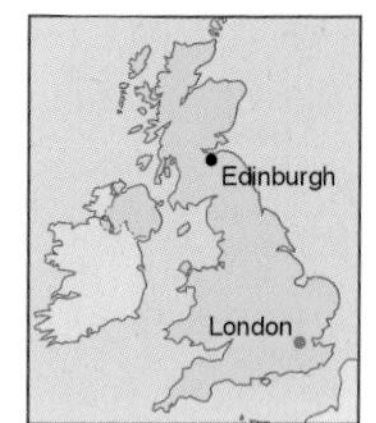

No one has captured in words the excitement of London as well as Samuel Johnson, the doctor who had a literary cure for just about everything: "When a man is tired of London he is tired of life, for there is in London all that life can afford." Today, over 250 years later, Johnson's words still ring true. London's variety is inexhaustible.

A good starting point is **Trafalgar Square ❶**. Sitting at the core of London as one of the most impressive public squares in the world, it was laid out in the 1830s and '40s by Sir Charles Barry and dedicated to the memory of Admiral Lord Nelson and his decisive victory over Napoleon's fleet off Cape Trafalgar in 1805.

The square is a paragon of the Classical style, enclosed by graceful white facades and dominated by the 162-ft (50-metre) **Nelson's Column** and four bronze lions. This is the strategic heart of London. The financial wizards of the City of London work to the east; the main shopping centres are to the west; the entertainment empire of the West End lies directly to the north; and the government palaces of Whitehall and Westminster stretch to the south along the River Thames.

The square has long been the site of public gatherings, political demonstrations and New Year celebrations. A mayoral campaign to rid it of its traditional plague of pigeons was largely successful, and in 2003 the north side of the square was pedestrianised to give people a sporting chance of reaching the fountains without being mown down by traffic. Every Christmas a 70-ft (20-metre) Norwegian spruce is erected in the square, a gift from the city of Oslo in recognition of the protection given by Britain to members of the Norwegian royal family in World War II.

The National Gallery

Running along the north flank of Trafalgar Square is the **National Gallery ❷** (Mon–Sat 10am–6pm, Wed until 8pm, Sun noon–6pm; tel: 020-7747 2885; nationalgallery.org.uk; free). Founded in

Main attractions

- TRAFALGAR SQUARE
- COVENT GARDEN
- CHARING CROSS ROAD
- PALL MALL
- BUCKINGHAM PALACE
- HOUSES OF PARLIAMENT
- OXFORD STREET
- REGENT'S PARK
- MAYFAIR
- PICCADILLY CIRCUS
- BLOOMSBURY
- HOLBORN
- HAMPSTEAD

LEFT: Piccadilly Circus. **BELOW:** Nelson's Column.

The Hay Wain, *John Constable's classic 1821 painting that has decorated a million chocolate boxes, is on show in the National Gallery.*

1824, the gallery has grown into one of the most outstanding and comprehensive collections in the world, with a list of masters ranging from Leonardo and Rembrandt to El Greco and Van Gogh. The collection is arranged chronologically, from the 13th century to the end of the 19th century. The modern "Sainsbury Wing", designed by Robert Venturi, houses the rich Renaissance collection.

Around the corner, established in 1856, is the superb **National Portrait Gallery** (daily 10am–6pm, Thur until 9pm; tel: 020-7312 2463 npg.org.uk; free). Presenting an illustrated British history, it contains the faces of the nation's illustrious men and women by the nation's illustrious artists and photographers. Only a fraction of the collection's 10,000 paintings, drawings, sculptures and half a million photographs, is on display at any given time.

To the right of the National Gallery is **St Martin-in-the-Fields** church, the oldest surviving structure on Trafalgar Square, built along simple but elegant lines by James Gibbs in 1722–6. The church became well-known during World War II when its crypt was a refuge from the Blitz. St Martin's is still the parish church for Buckingham Palace, with royal boxes at the east end.

BELOW: Trafalgar Square, looking towards the National Gallery.

Covent Garden

Northeast of Trafalgar Square begins the maze of narrow streets and tiny alleys called **Covent Garden ❸**. There has been some type of market on this spot for more than 300 years, but the name actually derives from the convent garden that occupied the area until Henry VIII's Dissolution. At the centre of Covent Garden lies a cobblestone piazza, designed by Inigo Jones, and superb steel-and-glass market pavilions constructed in the 1830s to house flower, fruit and vegetable stalls. The market was moved to new quarters south of the river at Nine Elms in 1974, and in the early 1980s Covent Garden was refurbished into an area of restaurants, shops and cafés. It's now a tourist-oriented showplace for buskers, or street entertainers, and a summer mecca for shoppers, office workers at lunchtime and tourists.

The market and boutique-lined streets are popular for afternoon shopping, especially cobbled **Neal Street** which is home to a few specialist shops such as The Kite Store, the Astrology Shop and The Tea House. **Neal's Yard**, at Earlham Street, with an apothecary, bakery and natural food shops, is gathered around a tiny square full of potted trees.There is an antiques market on Mondays, and the popular Jubilee Market on weekends offers a colourful hotchpotch of arts and crafts, food stalls and puppet shows. But the action really heats up at night. Those with a taste for English tradition might imbibe at the many ancient pubs in the area such as the **Lamb and Flag** (on Rose Street, off Floral Street), a 17th-century pub once frequented by prizefighters and known as the "Bucket of Blood".

Used as a backdrop for the movie *My Fair Lady* in 1964, Covent Garden is also

Recommended Restaurants and Pubs on pages 128–9

synonymous with British theatre. Some of the names associated with its past are Sarah Bernhardt, Charlie Chaplin, Richard Brindsley Sheridan and George Bernard Shaw. Dominating the west end of the piazza, **St Paul's Church** (1633), by Inigo Jones, is known locally as the actor's church. On the second Sunday in May a service commemorates the Punch and Judy puppet tradition, first noted here in 1662 by diarist Samuel Pepys. There's a brass-band procession of Mr Punches around the area at 10.30am and puppetry performances in the afternoon.

The **Theatre Royal** was established on Drury Lane in 1663 and is still a showcase for musicals. In 1733, another theatre was built nearby, on the site now occupied by the majestic **Royal Opera House** ❹ (box office tel: 020-7304 4000; royaloperahouse.org), home of both the Royal Opera and Royal Ballet companies. You can now have lunch here, drink in the bar, view exhibitions, and take in views of London's skyline from the magnificent Floral Hall.

The old flower market, in the southeastern corner of the square, is now home to the impressive **London Transport Museum,** which has a big collection of horse-drawn coaches, buses, trams, trains, rail carriages, and some working displays (daily 10am–6pm; tel: 7565 7299; ltmuseum.co.uk; entrance fee to adults but free to accompanied children under 16). It effectively traces the social history of modern London, whose growth was powered by transport, and deals intelligently with issues such as congestion and pollution. Facilities for children are especially good: there are extensive play areas, simulators to allow them to "drive" a Tube train, and actors playing early tunellers or 1930s ticket clerks who are prepared to describe yesteryear's working conditions.

London Transport Museum has 20 road and rail vehicles on show in Covent Garden, covering two centuries of the city's public transport.

Charing Cross Road

Bibliophiles usually make haste for **Charing Cross Road** ❺, which marks the western boundary of the Covent Garden district with a solid wall of bookshops. They range from **Foyle's** (the largest bookstore in London) to such spe-

Below: riding a carousel in Covent Garden.

Charlie Chaplin statue in Leicester Square. The comic was born in Walworth, south London, in 1889.

cialist enclaves as **A. Zwemmer** (graphic design and photography). A few second-hand bookshops remain. Those seeking maps should head for **Stanford's** treasure trove at 12–14 Long Acre (off Covent Garden, to the north of the Piazza).

Charing Cross Road is on the east side of **Leicester Square** ❻. This is the domain of tourists, pigeons and buskers, a gaudy place filled with flashing neon and throbbing music. Many cinemas are scattered around its leafy confines, the larger ones hosting important premieres. There's a statue of London-born Charlie Chaplin as The Little Tramp, and a Shakespeare fountain in its centre.

Somerset House

To the south of Covent Garden lies the Strand. Here, by Waterloo Bridge, is the neoclassical **Somerset House** ❼ (tel: 020-7845 4600; somersethouse.org.uk), built in 1770–1835. It now houses three attractions: the superb **Courtauld Institute** (Mon–Sat 10am–6pm, Mon until 2pm, Sun 2–6pm) collection of Impressionist paintings with works by Van Gogh, Gauguin and Cézanne; the **Hermitage Exhibition** (daily 10am–6pm) featuring works from the St Petersburg gallery shown in temporary exhibitions; and, downstairs, the **Gilbert Collection** (daily 10am–6pm), a treasure trove of European silverware, clocks, jewellery, and micro-mosaics. The Seaman's Hall gives access to the splendid River Terrace, which in summer has a café with great river views.

BELOW: keeping cool in the fountains of Somerset House – in winter the courtyard becomes a skating rink.

St James's Palace

A much different atmosphere is found in **Pall Mall** ❽, on the west side of Trafalgar Square, a sedate and elegant avenue that runs through the heart of the St James's district. This is London's "Club Land" – the exclusive gathering place of English gentlemen behind the closed doors of the Athenaeum, White's, the Carlton and a dozen other private enclaves. The street takes its name from *paille maille*, a French lawn game imported to England in the 17th century and played by Charles I on a long green which once occupied this site.

Wedged between the wood-panelled halls of Pall Mall and the leafy landscape of Green Park are a number of stately homes. The most impressive of these, built by Henry VIII in the 1530s, is **St James's Palace** ❾, which was an official royal residence until the 19th century. It is now occupied by the Princess Royal and royal servants. A cluster of royal mansions here includes **Marlborough House**, **Clarence House** and **Lancaster House** where Chopin once played a royal-command performance for Queen Victoria.

The Mall

The Mall is London's impressive ceremonial way, a broad tree-lined avenue that runs from Buckingham Palace to Admiralty Arch. The spectacular Trooping the Colour takes place on the Mall each June, as Queen Elizabeth II rides sedately down the avenue in a horse-drawn carriage with an escort of Household Cavalry as part of a 300-year-old ceremony to mark the official birthday of the monarch. The legions mass on **Horse Guards Parade** ❿, a huge open

Map on pages 110–1

Recommended Restaurants and Pubs on pages 128–9

space behind Whitehall, where a royal unit troop their regimental flags to the tune of marching music and thundering drums. The Household Cavalry can also be seen at 11.30am daily (alternative days in winter), as they ride down the Mall on their way to and from the Changing of the Guard at Buckingham Palace. They also mount a guard outside the old palace entrance on Whitehall.

Overlooking the Mall is the **Institute of Contemporary Arts** ⓫ (noon–9.30pm), the cutting edge of modern painting, sculpture and the performing arts. It also shows art-house movies.

Scots Guards on duty at Buckingham Palace.

Buckingham Palace

Londoners have a love-hate relationship with **Buckingham Palace** ⓬. To some, the Queen's home is one of the ugliest buildings in the capital, but it's also held in esteem as the symbol of Britain's royalty. The palace arose within a mulberry grove in the early 18th century as a mansion for the powerful Duke of Buckingham. It was purchased in 1762 by George III (who preferred to live in St James's Palace). However, it wasn't grand enough for George IV (the Prince Regent), and soon after the building came under his control in 1820 he commissioned his favourite architect, John Nash, to rebuild it on a more magnificent scale. Despite costly alterations, the palace wasn't occupied until Victoria became queen in 1837 and made it the official royal residence in London.

In front of the palace, the **Queen Victoria Memorial**, built in 1901, encompasses symbolic figures glorifying the achievements of the British Empire and its builders.

Visitors gather in front of Buckingham

Below: Buckingham Palace.

The Grand Staircase of Buckingham Palace.

Palace for the Changing of the Guard and perhaps to snatch a glimpse of the Queen, who is in residence when the flag is flying. The more dedicated may pay a visit to the **State Rooms** (Aug–Sept daily until 4.15pm; tickets at Green Park underground station from 9am), which are open in the autumn when the Queen is not in residence. Otherwise, only two sections of the palace are open to the public. The first is the **Royal Mews** (Tues–Thur noon–4pm, Oct–Dec Wed only, closed Jan–Mar), which contain royal vehicles from coaches to Rolls-Royces; the golden State Coach, built for George III in 1762, is still used by the Queen on major occasions.

The second venue, the **Queen's Gallery** (10am–5.30pm), displays a rotating sample of art from the fabulous Royal Collection. These include Leonardo da Vinci drawings, paintings by Holbein and Rubens, and sketches by Hogarth.

Bounding Buckingham Palace on the north and east are two of London's renowned green spaces – the arboreal tracts of St James's Park and Green Park. **St James's** ⓭ in particular has lush vegetation and a tranquil lake. Indeed, the park provides a haven for a multitude of water birds, office workers and civil servants. The wooden footbridge across the lake gives a superb view of Buckingham Palace.

Green Park ⓮ is a wild and rugged contrast. There are no tidy flower beds or ornate fountains – just rolling expanses of grass and woods where Charles II used to take his daily stroll.

Westminster Abbey

A short walk from the southeast corner of St James's Park is **Westminster**, the seat of English government for nearly 750 years. Westminster is also a holy place – the burial ground of English monarchs, the site of one of the greatest monasteries of the Middle Ages and the location of the most inspiring Gothic architecture in London. The area was a marshy wasteland inhabited by lepers until the 11th-century reign of Edward the Confessor, who built both a great church and a palace upon the reclaimed land.

BELOW: Westminster Abbey. **BELOW:** one of the Abbey's oddest monuments shows a noblewoman's husband trying to fend off Death as he tries to claim her.

Recommended Restaurants and Pubs on pages 128–9

Westminster Abbey ⓯ (Mon–Fri 9.15am–3.45pm, Sat 9am–1.45pm) was consecrated on 28 December 1065; Edward died nine days later and was buried before the high altar. In December 1066, the ill-fated Harold (soon to lose his throne to William the Conqueror) was crowned as the new king in the Abbey. This set yet another precedent: since that day, all but two English monarchs have been crowned here.

Little remains of Edward's Saxon abbey; it was completely rebuilt under the Normans and then redesigned in flamboyant French-Gothic style 200 years later. The **Henry VII Chapel** is a 16th-century masterpiece of fan-vaulted ceilings in pure white stone, decked out in the colourful medieval banners of the Knights Grand Cross of the Order of the Bath. Behind lies the Royal Air Force Chapel, with a stained-glass window containing the badges of every squadron which fought in the 1940 Battle of Britain. **Poets' Corner** contains the graves of Chaucer, Tennyson and Dryden, plus monuments to Shakespeare, Milton, Keats, Wilde and many others. The abbey also houses the **English Coronation Chair**, built in 1300 for Edward I and still used for the installation of new monarchs.

The Houses of Parliament

On the river side of Westminster Abbey rise the **Houses of Parliament** ⓰, an intrepid Gothic structure designed in the 1830s by Charles Barry and August Pugin to replace the old Westminster Palace built by Edward the Confessor. The building is one of the triumphs of Victorian England: 940 ft (280 metres) long with 2 miles (3 km) of passages and more than 1,000 rooms.

At the south end is **Victoria Tower**, from which a Union flag flies whenever Parliament is in session, while on the north flank rises the majestic Clock Tower, commonly known as **Big Ben** after the massive bell, cast in 1858, that strikes the hours. Facing Big Ben is **Portcullis House**, a modern office block for members of parliament; its much criticised "chimneys" form part of the air-conditioning system.

Within Parliament convene the two governing bodies of Great Britain, the House of Commons and the House of Lords, which moved into the old Palace of Westminster after Henry VIII vacated the premises in the 16th century. The Commons, comprised of the elected representatives of various political parties, is the scene of both lively debate and loutish heckling as MPs (Members of Parliament) wage verbal battle across their wood-panelled hall. You can watch proceedings from the safety of the **Visitors' Gallery** (when Parliament is in session, queue at St Stephen's Gate; entry begins 4pm Mon, 1pm Tue–Thur, 10am Fri).

One of the few relics of the old Westminster Palace to withstand a devastating fire in 1834 is **Westminster Hall**, a 240-ft (72-metre) long room built in 1099 with a sturdy hammer-beam roof of ancient oak. The hall has seen some of English history's most dramatic moments – from the tragic trial of Sir Thomas More in 1535 to the investiture of Oliver Cromwell as Lord Protector in 1653.

A small museum of Parliament Past

The name Big Ben, commonly used for the clock tower of the Houses of Parliament, properly refers only to the 13-ton bell. If you want to climb the 393 steps to see it, and enjoy a fantastic view, you will need to be a UK resident and contact your MP to arrange a tour. Children under the age of 11 are not admitted. Tours last around 1 hour.

BELOW: Richard Lionheart, King of England from 1189 to 1199, inspires the Houses of Parliament.

The Central Map Room of the Cabinet War Rooms, restored to its 1940s state.

and Present is housed in the **Jewel Tower** (daily Apr–Sept 10am–1pm, 2–6pm, Oct–Mar 10am–1pm), a moated keep beside Westminster Abbey that held the king's jewels, clothing and furs until the reign of Henry VIII.

Whitehall is the broad and busy avenue that runs north from the Houses of Parliament to Trafalgar Square. Once the fulcrum of British colonial power, it is still home to the Foreign and Commonwealth offices, the Treasury, Admiralty and Ministry of Defence – and the Prime Minister's 17th-century residence at **No. 10 Downing Street** ⑰, now protected by gates for security reasons.

At the end of King Charles Street, down Clive Steps, a small wall of sandbags identities the **Cabinet War Rooms** (daily 9.30am–6pm; tel: 020-7930 6961; cwr.iwm.org.uk), the underground nerve-centre from which Churchill directed Britain's war effort. Using old photographs for reference, the rooms have been meticulously restored to their 1940s state and the tour through this claustrophobic bunker is compelling enough to have attracted two US presidents, Bill Clinton and George W. Bush. The newly incorporated **Churchill Museum** dedicates itself to the life of the great statesman, with letters and memorabilia.

For a startling contrast to the drab architecture of modern government take a detour into the **Banqueting House** ⑱ (Mon–Sat 10am–5pm) on the other side of Whitehall, a brilliant relic of the old Whitehall Palace and a masterpiece of the English baroque. Inigo Jones built the hall in 1622 at the request of James I. A decade later Peter Paul Rubens added the lovely allegorical ceiling.

Surprising modernity

Victoria Street shoots southwest from Parliament Square as an unexpected corridor of steel and glass skyscrapers in the heart of neo-Gothic London. Tucked back off the street is the terracotta bulk of **Westminster Cathedral** ⑲, England's premier Roman Catholic church. It arose in the 1890s in a bizarre Italo-Byzantine style, with a lavish interior of multicoloured marble and an exterior in alternating red and white bricks. The **Campanile Tower** offers a superb view.

Millbank follows the gentle curve of the Thames to the south of Parliament Square, first passing the **Victoria Tower Gardens** (home of Rodin's *The Burghers of Calais*) before sweeping round to the grand neoclassical mansion which is **Tate Britain** ⑳ (daily 10am–5.50pm; tel: 020-7887 8888; tate.org.uk/britain; free). The Tate, founded in 1897 by Henry Tate, of the Tate & Lyle sugar empire, holds the world's greatest collection of British art.

Among the outstanding British paintings are attractive portraits by Thomas Gainsborough (1727–88), evocative views of the English countryside by John Constable (1776–1837) and intensely dramatic and impressionistic seascapes and landscapes by the prolific J.M.W. Turner (1775–1851) which are housed in the Clore Gallery. These are the paintings Turner bequeathed to the nation on his death, with the stipulation that they should all be hung in one place, and

BELOW: Westminster Cathedral, Britain's leading Roman Catholic church.

should be available for the public to see, without charge.

In 2000 the gallery's modern collection moved across the river to a converted power station, becoming Tate Modern *(see page 138)*.

Oxford Street

Just three stops on the tube from Pimlico station is Oxford Circus and London's busiest shopping street, **Oxford Street** ㉑, which marks the boundary between Marylebone and the exclusive district of Mayfair. The western half of Oxford Street contains most of London's top department stores, including the capacious **Selfridge's**; the eastern end has some much tackier trading outlets as you get towards **Tottenham Court Road**, a centre for electronics stores.

For a change of scene, take a stroll through the **Photographer's Gallery** at 16–18 Ramillies Street, which has regular exhibitions (Mon–Sat 11am–6pm, Thur until 8pm, Sun noon–6pm; tel: 020-7831 1772; photonet.org.uk). The gallery, which sells limited-edition prints, doubles as a café, so it's also a good place to quench a thirst or rest tired feet.

The **Marylebone** (pronounced *marly-bun*) district sprawls along the southern edge of Regent's Park. Infamous in the 18th century for its taverns, boxing matches and cockfights, it is also associated with Arthur Conan Doyle's fictitious detective, who is celebrated at the **Sherlock Holmes Museum** (239 Baker Street; daily 9.30am–6.30pm; tel: 020-7935 8866; sherlock-holmes.co.uk; charge). It recreates Victorian rooms and has waxwork tableaux.

Regent's Park

Regent's Park ㉒ is a massive green space with a long and chequered history. Henry VIII established a royal hunting ground here on land seized from the Abbess of Barking. Later, in the early 19th century, the park became part of the Prince Regent's (later George IV) great scheme for a huge processional thoroughfare and palace complex to stretch from Pall Mall to Primrose Hill. The Prince commissioned John Nash to design and develop the scheme, but the dream got only as far as the famed Regency terraces on the southern fringe of the park, which represent Nash at his best.

Selfridge's imposing frontage.

BELOW: David Hockney with a massive canvas he donated to Tate Britain, *Bigger Trees Near Warter*, a scene from his native Yorkshire.

A falconry display in London Zoo.

BELOW: it can take Madame Tussauds 500 hours of specialist sculpting to create figures such as Princes William and Harry.

London Zoo (9am–5.30pm; tel: 020-7722 3333; zsl.org/london-zoo charge) was founded in Regent's Park in 1826 by Sir Stamford Raffles, who also founded Singapore. Among the zoo's features are the aviary designed by Lord Snowdon, the 1930s penguin pool and a glass pavilion housing the ecologically oriented Web of Life Exhibition.

Madame Tussauds

For waxworks aplenty, there's **Madame Tussauds** ㉓ (Marylebone Road; daily July–Sept 9am–5.30pm, Oct–June 10am–5.30pm, from 9.30am at weekends; tel: 020-7935 6861; madame-tussauds.co.uk; admission fees are at West End theatre levels). The exhibition was founded in 1802 by Marie Tussaud, a tiny woman who learned her craft in post-Revolution Paris – making wax effigies of the heads of guillotine victims.

Today's effigies, which vary from the breathtakingly lifelike to the barely recognisable, relentlessly concentrate on celebrities from pop stars and sports heroes to popes, and anyone who fades from the headlines is soon melted down. The key to the waxworks' popularity is that the models are no longer roped off or protected by glass cases – you are encouraged to put your arms round the Queen or give Mick Jagger a peck on the lips, and be photographed doing so.

The Chamber of Horrors re-creates various none-too-scary tableaux of torture. At extra cost, you can enter a dark section of the chamber where actors portraying deranged serial killers lunge at you. A better bet is the audio-animatronic Spirit of London ride, which carries you past well-made historical tableaux.

Hereford House in nearby Manchester Square contains the superb **Wallace Collection** ㉔ (Mon–Sat 10am–5pm, Sun noon–5pm tel: 020-7563 9500; wallacecollection.org; free), a treasure chest of 17th- and 18th-century art and ornaments, including Sèvres and Limoges porcelain, antique French furniture and works by Titian, Rubens and Holbein.

Mayfair

Exclusive **Mayfair** is the hub of English wealth, the home of oil barons and property giants, of landed aristocrats and self-made nabobs. By the mid-18th century, the powerful Grosvenor family had purchased the land and developed Mayfair into an elegant Georgian housing estate. This enticed the wealthy of dreary inner London to move out and settle in one of the city's first suburbs.

Today, Mayfair is known for its stylish shops and lavish auction houses. **Bond Street** ㉕ brings together all the big names – the Louis Vuittons, the Calvin Kleins, the Patek Philippes – and is the street where you can buy something for that person who already has everything.

Mayfair antiques and art are world-famous. **Christie's** in King Street auctions more than 150,000 objects a year, including furniture, armour, jewels and paintings, while **Sotheby's** in New Bond Street has been the scene of some of the most important deals in art history.

For a quiet walk, try one of Mayfair's elegant Victorian arcades, the tiny covered streets lined with a startling array of unique and interesting shops. The **Royal Opera Arcade** is the oldest, but the **Piccadilly**, **Prince's** and **Royal arcades** are just as elegant. **Burlington Arcade** with its uniformed doormen is the most famous. **Savile Row** is the traditional home of bespoke tailoring.

At 25 Brook Street, the composer of the *Messiah*, who lived here from 1724 to 1759, is celebrated in the **Handel House Museum** ㉖ (Tues–Sat 10am–6pm, Sun noon–6pm; tel: 020-7495 1759; handelhouse.org; charge).

A few doors from Burlington Arcade is the **Royal Academy of Arts** ㉗ (Piccadilly, daily 10am–6pm, Fri until 10pm; tel: 020-7300 8000; royalacademy.org.uk; charge except for permanent collection). The Academy has changing exhibitions of major artists and its Summer Exhibition of amateur and professional artists provides light entertainment and perhaps the chance to pick up a bargain.

Soho

John Nash's curving **Regent Street**, with classy shops ranging from Aquascutum and Liberty's to Hamleys and the Apple Store, divides Mayfair from **Soho** as effectively as if there were an ocean between the two. Soho, long known for its low-life bars and sex clubs, has returned to being a neighbourhood of cosmopolitan foodshops and restaurants, with a population of East European émigrés, French, Italian and Greek restaurateurs and a thriving Chinese community. Chinatown's restaurants are centered on **Gerrard Street** and **Lisle Street**.

The sleazy side of Soho has largely gone, though there are still some tasteful strip shows, and a few hole-in-the-wall dens offer "live" entertainment designed to part customers from their money in the blink of an eye.

Piccadilly Circus ㉘ is the spiritual heart of Soho, once a roundabout and now a frenzied junction which is crowded with black cabs, red buses and awe-struck tourists. The bronze statue of Eros stands atop a fountain on the south side.

The **Britain and London Visitor Centre**, 1 Regent Street, is the major central source of tourist information on London and Britain; it contains an accommodation and travel ticket booking service, and bureau de change.

Nearby in Holland Street is the **Trocadero Centre**, a complex of shops and

Mayfair was once farmland outside London. The name derives from the medieval May Fair, which took place each spring. For two weeks, the otherwise tranquil pastures sprang to life with fire eaters and eel divers, sausage tables and hasty-pudding stands.

BELOW: the Royal Academy of Arts.

A Night on the Town

The West End is synonymous with evening entertainment, whether a show, a club, a restaurant, a bar or a Leicester Square cinema.

Soho is still the most fashionable area, and is still the sex centre of London, although smut is on the retreat. Some of the best food and the trendiest clubs are here, including Ronnie Scott's jazz club in Frith Street and for clubbers with a sense of fun, Madame Jo Jo's on Brewer Street. Soho entertains a real cross section of Londoners, from the casually-dressed lager drinkers packing out the more traditional pubs, to the city boys swilling champagne in their private members' bar before hitting a lap-dancing club such as Stringfellow's in Upper St Martin's Lane.

Old Compton Street is the centre of the gay scene, with pubs such as the Admiral Duncan and Comptons drawing big crowds. In nearby Wardour Street, Village Soho is another popular gay venue with unthreatening clientele and a sprinkling of glam.

Most of the so-called "super-clubs" in the area have now closed down but one hanger-on is Cirque at the Hippodrome (Cranbourne Street). The celebrated gay disco: G-A-Y (the Astoria, 157–65 Charing Cross Road) continues to entertain, sometimes with live pop acts that have included the Spice Girls, Kylie Minogue and Madonna.

With the new late-licensing laws many bars stay open until at least 3am, which has removed much of the 11pm rush towards neighbourood clubs. Some bars can be difficult to get into – more because of capacity than the dress codes. Many of the cafés also stay open into the small hours and do a roaring trade in the *de rigueur* post-bar coffee and snack.

The evening promenade

Londoners get a buzz from being in the company of the countless nationalities that throng Leicester Square, Piccadilly Circus, Trafalgar Square and Covent Garden. These are the best-known central areas for evening promenading. London may not seem to offer a conducive climate, but 84 percent of all overseas visitors describe their evening activities as "just walking around".

Further afield

Apart from Soho, the King's Road in Chelsea, Notting Hill and Queensway, Camden and Islington are lively in the evenings. More offbeat places can be found in the east end of town, such as Farringdon, Brick Lane and Hoxton Square. For a glamorously old-fashioned evening, head for Mayfair and St James's. Here you'll find discreet restaurants and exclusive nightclubs such as Annabel's in Berkeley Square, appealing to an older crowd which doesn't need to ask the price.

The choice of evening entertainment in London is vast, and is best explored in the pages of the weekly listings magazine, *Time Out.* ❑

ABOVE: pouring a drink at Wardour Street's Freedom Café-Bar, a popular venue with gays.
LEFT: an evening of jazz at Ronnie Scott's in Soho.

restaurants whose attractions include **Funland**, a huge hi-tech indoor entertainment centre (10am–midnight weekdays, 1am weekends).

In the heart of Soho is **Berwick Street** 29, the site of a fruit and vegetable market. Karl Marx lived around the corner on **Dean Street** in the building now inhabited by the Quo Vadis restaurant.

Bloomsbury

For yet another drastic change in mood, hop on the tube at Piccadilly Circus and ride four stops on the Piccadilly Line to Russell Square. This will deposit you in **Bloomsbury**, the intellectual and scholastic heart of the city. Many University of London colleges have buildings in this area, including the **School of Oriental and African Studies**, and **University College** in Gower Street. Bloomsbury was the address of such intellectual figures as John Maynard Keynes (1883–1946) and Virginia Woolf (1882–1941).

Charles Dickens lived with his family at 47 Doughty Street for almost two years (1837–39), during which time he wrote parts of *Oliver Twist*, *Nicholas Nickleby* and *Pickwick Papers*. His home, now **Dickens House Museum** 30 (Mon–Sat 10am–5pm; tel: 020-7405; charge), is filled with portraits, letters, furniture and other personal effects of the famous novelist.

Bloomsbury is dominated by the **British Museum** 31 (Sat–Wed 10am–5.30pm, Thur–Fri 10am–8.30pm; free), one of the world's greatest collections. Its Great Court, a large covered square containing the majestic Lion of Knidos and an Easter Island statue, is worth a visit in itself. Don't expect to see everything in a day; a month wouldn't be time enough. *Detailed coverage: pages 130–1.*

At 35 Little Russell Street, which runs off Museum Street, the **Cartoon Museum** (Tue–Sat 10.30am–5.30pm, Sun noon–5.30; tel: 020-7580 8155; charge) highlights the work of top British cartoonists, past and present.

Northeast of Russell Square, at 40 Brunswick Square, is the **Foundling Museum** 32 (Tue–Sat 10am–6pm, Sun noon–6pm), home of a fine art collection built up by a philanthropic sea captain who started a hospital and school for foundlings and encouraged artists, includ-

Eros presides over Piccadilly Circus.

BELOW: Berwick Street market in Soho.

The spire of Wren's St Bride's Church in Fleet Street is said to have inspired the first tiered wedding cake.

BELOW: Sir John Soane's Museum.

ing William Hogarth, to donate works to raise funds. Other artists featured include Gainsborough and Reynolds.

Holborn

In **Holborn**, which centres on the busy street and tube station of the same name, **Staple Inn** ㉝, a timber-framed Elizabethan structure that once served as a hostel for wool merchants, survived the Great Fire of London. It shows how much of the city must have looked before the 1666 fire devastated it.

Legal London

Lying between Holborn and the Thames are the prestigious **Inns of Court** – the confluence of London's legal world since the Middle Ages. There were originally 12 inns, founded in the 14th century for the lodging and education of lawyers on "neutral" ground between the merchants of the City and the monarchs of Westminster. Today only four remain, and no one can enter the legal profession in London without acceptance into one of them.

Gray's Inn ㉞ has a garden designed by Francis Bacon in 1606, a haven of plane trees and smooth lawns that provides a tranquil lunchtime retreat away from the hustle of the City. **Lincoln's Inn** ㉟, north of Fleet Street, has a medieval hall and a 17th-century chapel by Inigo Jones. The leafy expanse called **Lincoln's Inn Fields**, once a notorious venue for duels and executions, attracts summer picnickers and sunbathers.

On the north side is the **Sir John Soane's Museum** (13 Lincoln's Inn Fields, tel: 020-7405 2107; soane.org; Tue–Sat 10am–5pm; free), an outlandish mansion which is a sort of British Museum in miniature. Soane, a celebrated 19th-century architect, lived here and built up a remarkable collection of antiquities and paintings – and even a sarcophagus. A highlight of its art gallery is Hogarth's satirical *Rake's Progress.*

The most fascinating of the inns is the twin complex of the **Inner** and **Middle Temples** ㊱. The name derives from the Knights Templar, a medieval religious fraternity that occupied this site until the early 14th century. The temple has changed little: it is still a precinct of vaulted chambers, hammerbeam roofs and lush wood panelling. In the 16th-century Middle Temple Hall, Shakespeare's own company once performed *Twelfth Night* for the Elizabethan court.

The 12th-century **Temple Church** is one of only four "round churches" left in England. It contains a number of knights' tombs and a tiny punishment cell.

Fleet Street

In **Fleet Street**, centre of the national newspaper industry until the 1980s, **St Bride's** ㊲ is still the parish church of journalists. It is an impressive 17th-century church by Sir Christopher Wren, and its crypt contains remnants of Roman and Saxon London. At 17 Fleet Street, **Prince Henry's Room** (Mon–Sat 11am–2pm) contains artefacts relating to the diarist Samuel Pepys (1633–1703).

Just north of Fleet Street at 17 Gough Square is the **Dr Johnson Museum** ㊳, (Mon–Sat 11am–5.30pm), where the great man of letters and compiler of the first English dictionary, Samuel Johnson, lived from 1748 to 1759.

Recommended Restaurants and Pubs on pages 128–9

NORTH LONDON

To visit one of London's most historic "villages", head north on the London Underground Northern Line from Waterloo Station. For more than 300 years **Hampstead** 39 has attracted writers, artists and actors to its elegant Georgian and Regency mansions.

Keats House (Keats Grove; May–Oct Tue–Sun noon–5pm; tel: 020-7435 2062; keatshouse.gov.uk) is where the poet John Keats wrote much of his work, including *Ode to a Nightingale* (1819).

Sigmund Freud briefly lived here too after fleeing the Nazis in 1938; the **Freud Museum** preserves his house at 20 Maresfield Gardens much as he and his daughter Anna left it (Wed–Sun noon–5pm, tel: 020-7435 2002; freud.org.uk).

Despite the encroachment of suburbia, the area retains a village atmosphere, aided by the proximity of 790-acre (310-hectare) **Hampstead Heath**. An 18th-century decree forbade building on the Heath, thus preserving a rambling tract of dark woods and lush meadows where the only large structure is **Kenwood House**. Within its walls is the Iveagh Bequest, a rich collection of British and Dutch paintings that includes works by Vermeer and Reynolds (daily Apr–Sept 10am–6pm, Oct–Mar 10am–4pm; free).

Camden Lock.

Haverstock Hill runs from Hampstead into Camden Town, where weekend crowds flock to markets. Since 1972, **Camden Lock Market** 40 has featured antiques, crafts, old clothes – and talented buskers. The Dingwalls music venue and Jongleurs comedy club are sited here, and a traditional canal water boat runs trips from the West Yard area along the Regent's Canal to Little Venice (daily Apr–Sept, reduced winter service; tel: 020-7482 2660). **Stables Market** has vintage clothing, esoteric record stores and unusual furniture. ❑

BELOW: an autumn afternoon on Hampstead Heath.

RESTAURANTS, PUBS AND BARS

Restaurants

Prices for a three-course dinner per person with a half-bottle of house wine:

£ = under £20
££ = £20–30
£££ = £30–50
££££ = over £50

Soho

Alastair Little
49 Frith St, W1. Tel: 020-7734 5183. L & D Mon–Fri, D only Sat. £££
Its eponymous chef no longer mans the stoves, but the service and Modern European cooking remain excellent.

Gay Hussar
2 Greek St, W1. Tel: 020-7437 0973. L & D Mon–Sat. ££ (set menu), £££
In polished, gentleman's club surroundings, a mix of hearty British and Hungarian dishes are served. Pork and potatoes are prominent.

Harbour City
46 Gerrard St, W1. Tel: 020-7439 7859. Daily, all day. £–££ (set menu), ££
Good Chinese choice with a window table overlooking Chinatown. Dim sum noon–5pm.

Joy King Lau
3 Leicester St, WC2. Tel: 020-7437 1133. Daily, all day. ££ (set menu). £££
Chinese. Set menus from around £28 feature sizzling veal with black-pepper sauce, a range of noodle dishes, and dim sum until 4.45pm.

Kettners
29 Romilly St, W1. Tel: 020-7734 6112 Daily, all day. ££
This sprawling *grande dame* fuses an extensive champagne list with a pizza menu. Piano bar too. Always busy.

L'Escargot
48 Greek St, W1. Tel: 020-7437 6828. L & D Mon–Fri, D only Sat, Sat lunch in the Picasso room. £££ (set menu) ££££
The *grand-p re* of London's French restaurants, with its lovely 1920s decor, is now run by Marco Pierre White. Choose between the exciting hubbub of the ground floor or the more intimate Picasso room upstairs, with à la carte and set menus.

Covent Garden

Christopher's
18 Wellington St, WC2. Tel: 020-7240 4222. L & D Mon–Sat, Br Sat/Sun. ££ (set menus), £££
The dishes on the contemporary American menu are imaginative and usually well prepared, but the elegant dining rooms are the main attraction. Good-value pre- and post-theatre menus.

J. Sheekey
28–32 St Martin's Court, WC2. Tel: 020-7240 2565. L & D daily. ££ (weekend lunch menu), ££££
Think chargrilled squid with gorgonzola polenta, Cornish fish stew and New England baby lobster, followed by rhubarb pie, or the famed Scandinavian iced berries with white-chocolate sauce. Impressive wine list. Chic. Booking essential.

Joe Allen
13 Exeter St, WC2. Tel: 020-7836 0651 Noon–midnight Mon–Sat, D only Sun. ££ (brunch, pre-theatre and late supper menus. £££
Tucked away below street level, this relaxed diner has a predictable enough menu – salads, steaks, spareribs, pecan pie – and average-quality food, but it's ever popular with diners, who sip cocktails until 12.45am.

Rules
35 Maiden Lane, WC2. Tel: 020-7836 5314. L & D daily. ££ (pre-theatre menu) ££££
Rules, established in 1798, is London's oldest restaurant, and the decor, notably the wonderful Art Nouveau stained-glass ceiling and the wood panelling, reflects its heritage. The robust food is very English, with beef, lamb and a variety of game from Rules' own estate in the Pennines.

Sarastro
126 Drury Lane, WC2. d7836 0101 aL & D daily. £ (set-lunch menu), ££
"The show after the show" is this restaurant's slogan. The flamboyant decor, with velvet drapes, golden chairs, opera boxes, chandeliers and props, is a stage set in itself. The menu is more straightforward, offering basic fish, meat and vegetarian options.

LEFT: the Gay Hussar, long established in Soho.

Mayfair

Benares
12a Berkeley Square House, Berkeley Square, W1. Tel: 020-7629 8886. L & D Sun–Fri, D only Sat. **££** (set lunch and early dinner) **£££**
Hits on the Indian menu include Goan-style lobster Masala in coconut, clove and cinnamon sauce. Recipient of a Michelin star.

Hard Rock Café
150 Old Park Lane, W1. Tel: 020-7629 0382. L & D daily. **££**
Expect long queues, huge portions and homage to rock 'n' roll memorabilia. Nachos, chicken wings, sundaes and hamburgers with every possible trimming. Guitar museum next door.

Mirabelle
56 Curzon St, W1. Tel: 020-7499 4636. L & D daily. **£££** (set lunch), **££££**
A classic restaurant, reinvented by Marco Pierre White. Dishes include parfait of foie gras with truffles in aspic and gratinée of cod with champagne sabayon. Lovely terrace.

Marylebone

Orrery
55 Marylebone High St, W1. Tel: 020-7616 8000. L & D daily. **£££** (set menu) **££££**
Dinner here is a romantic gastro experience. Barbary duck with *pain d'épice*, foie gras *tarte tartin* and *banyuls* jus are typical dishes.

Bloomsbury

Cosmoba
9 Cosmo Place, WC1. Tel: 020-7837 0904. L & D Mon–Sat. **££**
A hidden gem in an alley connecting Southampton Row and Queen Square. Plain, family-run and specialising in homely Italian food.

ABOVE: Soho bars provide the latest mix of cocktails.

Wagamama
4a Streatham St, WC1. Tel: 020-7323 9223. L & D daily. **£**
This was the original of the Japanese chain. Canteen-like basement with communal tables and bench seating, serving wholesome budget noodles and garnishes such as dumplings, salads, soups and juices.

Holborn

Gaucho
125–126 Chancery Lane, WC2. Tel: 020-7242 7727. B, L & D Mon–Fri. **£££**
Argentinian-style chain specialising in steaks, but good fish and chicken are also available. Good for special breakfasts too.

Westminster

Boisdale
15 Eccleston St, SW1. Tel: 020-7730 6922. L Mon– Fri, D only Sat. **£££**
Scottish dishes such as lobster bisque, haggis, and Aberdeen Angus steaks. There is always fresh fish and game and a full malt whisky line-up.

Goring Dining Room
Goring Hotel, Beeston Place, SW1. Tel: 020-7390 9000. L & D Sun–Fri, D Sat. **£££**
Traditional fare such as lobster omelette thermidor, roast beef and Yorkshire pudding, filet of venison and proper puddings. Sunday roast lunch is a speciality.

Pubs

For those who like their ale from a barrel and not a bottle, Soho has plenty of classic Victorian pubs – **The Argyll Arms** *(18 Argyll St)*, **the Coach & Horses** *(29 Greek St)*, **the Dog & Duck** *(18 Bateman St)* are just three. Also in Soho, **Couch** *(97–9 Dean St)* is a popular post-work pub with plenty of seating (but only three couches) and superior bar food. **Bar Code** *(3–4 Archer St)* is a late-night funky gay dance and cruise bar.

Historic pubs around Covent Garden include the **Lamb and Flag** *(33 Rose Street)*, tucked away down the tiniest of alleyways, and **The Punch & Judy**, on the upper level of the Market itself.

In Fitzrovia, they still display George Orwell's journalists' union card at the **Fitzroy Tavern** *(16 Charlotte St)*. The **Newman Arms** *(23 Rathbone St)* is famed for its pies and **The Marquis of Granby** *(2 Rathbone St)* offers many varieties of British sausage.

Around Fleet Street, **Ye Olde Cheshire Cheese** *(145 Fleet Street)* was frequented by Dickens and Samuel Johnson. The **Black Friar** *(174 Queen Victoria St)* is worth seeing for its Arts and Crafts interior, but it also has a good choice of ales.

Bars

If you're in search of a hip hang-out, head for West Soho and **Alphabet** *(61–3 Beak St)*. Arranged over two floors, it caters for a media in-crowd. A quality martini and an excellent selection of wines can be found at **Café Bohème** *(13–7 Old Compton St)*. For a touch of class, the very grand **Atlantic Bar & Grill** *(20 Glasshouse St)* in the refurbished ballroom of the Regent Palace Hotel, is perfect for a champagne cocktail.

Mayfair has grand hotel bars. Try the stately **American Bar at the Connaught** *(Carlos Place)*, the mirrored piano **Dorchester Bar** *(53 Park Lane)*, the fashionable deco **Claridges' Bar** *(55 Brook St)* or the **Rivoli Bar** at The Ritz *(150 Piccadilly)*.

THE BRITISH MUSEUM

Founded in 1759, this world-class institution on Great Russell Street contains some 6½ million objects

Devote just 60 seconds to each object owned by the British Museum and you'd be there, without sleep or meal breaks, for more than 12 years. Even though only 50,000 objects are on display at any given time, this is not a place to "do" in a couple of hours. It is a treasure house that caters for scholars as well as tourists and, as the scholars do, it is best to concentrate initially on what interests you most. A tour of the highlights is a good start (see right-hand column or join one of the organised tours). As you seek out any particular objects in the 100 or so galleries, you will be diverted by enough intriguing displays to justify future visits.

The British Museum, founded in 1753, is the most traditional of institutions, with most objects in glass cases and few buttons and levers for children to manipulate, but it is rarely boring. The best time to visit is soon after opening at 10am, before the crowds begin aiming their flashguns unwisely at the reflective glass cases and panning their video cameras. This is also an ideal time to appreciate the Great Court, a dramatic glassed-over space in the heart of the complex, added for the millennium, and the round Reading Room, where Marx and Lenin once studied and which is now an information and research centre. Entry to the museum is free.

● **Tours worth taking:** Ninety-minute tours of the museum's highlights (charge payable) take place daily at 10.30am, 1pm and 3pm. Free "eye-opener" tours (30–40 minutes) are also held, and a variety of audio sets can be hired, including one for children.

LEFT: Assistant to the Judge of Hell, a 16th-century stone figure from China's Ming Dynasty. The bunch of scrolls he is holding record the sins of the dead.

ABOVE: the celebrated Reading Room, where Karl Marx researched *Das Kapital*, was added to the museum's central courtyard in 1857. In 1997, when the British Library relocated its books to new premises, the Great Court was glassed over to create Europe's largest covered public square. Touchscreens in the Reading Room enable visitors to plan a tour of the galleries.

ABOVE: a section from the north freize of the Parthenon. Often known as the Elgin Marbles, these 5th-century sculptures, whose muscular detail and fluidity of movement transcend their origins as blocks of marble, were removed from Athens to decorate his Scottish mansion by Lord Elgin (1766–1841). The Greek government has long demanded their return.

ABOVE: Tsuki-no-Hikari, a 1991 bronze by Igor Mitoraj, sits outside the museum's main entrance on Great Russell Street.

BELOW: double-headed wooden serpent from Mexico, with a mosaic in turquoise – a symbol of fertility to the Aztecs.

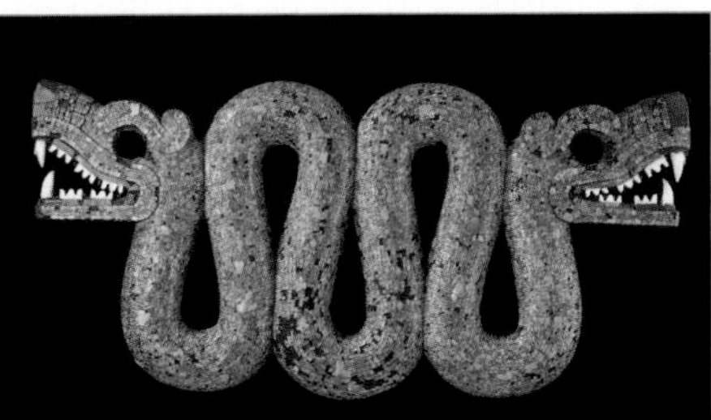

THE TOP 10 HIGHLIGHTS

The Egyptian mummies
The museum has the richest collection of Egyptian funerary art outside Egypt.

The Sculptures of the Parthenon
Commonly known as the Elgin Marbles, these 5th-century BC sculptures have a wondrous muscular detail.

The Rosetta Stone
This granite tablet from the 2nd century BC provided the elusive key to deciphering ancient Egypt's hieroglyphic script.

The Nereid Monument
The imposing facade of this 4th-century monument from Xanthos in Turkey was reconstructed after an earthquake.

The Mausoleum of Halikarnassos
This giant tomb, finished around 351 BC in southwest Turkey, was one of the seven wonders of the ancient world.

The Sutton Hoo Ship Burial
The richest treasure ever dug from British soil, an early 7th-century longboat was probably the burial chamber of an East Anglian king.

The Lewis Chessmen
82 elaborately carved 12th-century chess pieces, found in the Outer Hebrides, off the Scottish coast.

Lindow Man
A well preserved 2,000-year-old body found in a peat bog in England and dubbed Pete Marsh.

The Benin bronzes
Brass plaques found in Benin City, Nigeria, in 1897. They depict court life and ritual in extraordinary detail.

Cassiobury Park Turret Clock
This intricate 1610 weight-driven clock is part of a rich collection of timepieces.

TOP: horse's head from the Parthenon Gallery (Room 18).
CENTRE RIGHT the gilded wooden inner coffin of Henutmehyt, a Theban princess (c.1290BC).
RIGHT: a ceremonial helmet from the Sutton Hoo treasure.

LONDON: THE CITY AND SOUTHWARK

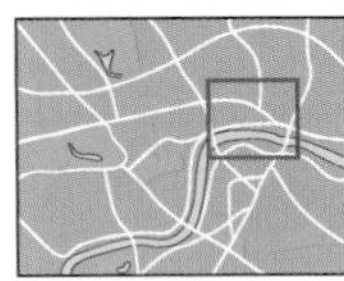

The City is the oldest part of London, where Britain's financial institutions are tightly packed. Across the river, Southwark has revived its ancient role as an entertainments centre

Main attractions
ST PAUL'S CATHEDRAL
MUSEUM OF LONDON
BANK OF ENGLAND
LLOYD'S OF LONDON
THE TOWER OF LONDON
HMS BELFAST
THE LONDON DUNGEON
SOUTHWARK CATHEDRAL
SHAKESPEARE'S GLOBE
TATE MODERN
SOUTH BANK CENTRE
THE LONDON EYE
IMPERIAL WAR MUSEUM
THE EAST END

Fleet Street sweeps from London's theatreland into Ludgate Hill and the **City of London**, that history-packed square mile that sits atop the remains of both Roman and medieval towns. "The City" was for centuries the domain of merchants and craftsmen, a powerful coalition of men who helped force democracy upon the English monarchy and then built the world's largest mercantile empire.

Despite the encroachment of modern office blocks and computers, the area retains something of its medieval ways: the square mile is still governed separately from the rest of London, by the ancient City Corporation and its Court of Common Council – relics of the medieval trade and craft guilds. Outside the jurisdiction of London's popularly elected mayor, it has its own separately elected Lord Mayor, who rides through the City each November in a golden coach.

BELOW: St Paul's Cathedral.

Wren's masterpiece

Sitting at the top of Ludgate Hill is **St Paul's Cathedral** ❹❶ (Mon–Sat 9.30am–4pm), dominating the skyline of the City like no other structure, the massive dome punching upward through the forest of highrises that has come to surround it since World War II. After the Norman St Paul's was destroyed in the Great Fire of 1666, Charles II asked Christopher Wren to design a new cathedral to befit the status of London. Wren's first plan was rejected as too radical, but he responded with a brilliant blend of Italian baroque and classical influences – a huge cruciform building whose stone cupola takes it to a height of 365 ft (111 metres). Only St Peter's in Rome has a bigger dome.

St Paul's arose in 1675–1710 as the first cathedral built and dedicated to the Protestant faith. It played host to Queen Victoria's Diamond Jubilee ceremonies in 1897, Winston Churchill's funeral in 1965, and the wedding of Prince Charles and Lady Diana Spencer in 1981. The cathedral miraculously survived the Blitz, though the neighbourhood around it was destroyed by German bombs and missiles.

Recommended Restaurants and Pubs on page 141

St Paul's is also a notable burial place; among those entombed within are Wellington, Nelson, Reynolds, Turner and Wren himself. Its interior displays the work of the finest artists and craftsmen of the late 17th century: iron grillework of Tijou, wooden choir stalls by Grinling Gibbons, and the murals inside the dome by Sir James Thornhill.

The cathedral's appearance is deceptive. The famous dome viewed from afar would look over large if seen from inside the building. The dome you look up at from within is in fact a much smaller dome, on top of which is built a brick cone. The cone's purpose is to support the massive weight of the external Portland stone dome, which weighs more than 50,000 tons.

Around the inside of the dome stretches the **Whispering Gallery**, so called because you can easily comprehend the voices of anyone standing on the opposite side of the void. A winding stairway leads to the outside of the dome, where there is a panoramic view of London.

A chapel behind the High Altar, damaged during the Blitz, was restored as the American Chapel, with a book of remembrance paying tribute to the 28,000 American citizens based in the UK who died in World War II.

To the north of St Paul's is the **Barbican Centre** 42, a startling contrast to the maze of twisting streets and ancient buildings that surround the cathedral. This urban renewal project arose from the rubble of an old neighbourhood that had been destroyed in the 1940–41 Blitz.

Museum of London

The nearby **Museum of London** 43 (London Wall, Mon–Sat 10am–5.50pm, Sun noon–5.50pm; tel: 0870-444 3852; museumoflondon.org.uk; free) is an essen-

The acoustics of St Paul's Whispering Gallery mean that a faint whisper can be heard across the gallery, 107 ft (33 metres) away.

BELOW: George William Joy's 1895 oil painting *The Bayswater Omnibus*, from the Museum of London.

The Lord Mayor's Show begins at the Guildhall each November, as the newly elected mayor rides through the City in a golden coach. Thousands of spectators line the route to watch the colourful procession.

tial stop for understanding how the City developed. There are models of old buildings, reconstructed shop fronts, audio-visual shows, a reference library, antique vehicles and a number of historic artefacts such as the Lord Mayor's state coach. The museum holds 1 million objects in its stores, but only a small proportion are on permanent display. From late 2009, many exhibits, including those relating to the 1666 Great Fire of London, will move into new galleries.

The museum's highlights include:

- *London Before London.* This surveys life in the Thames Valley from 450,000 BC–AD 50. The centrepiece of the exhibition is the "River Wall" displaying 300 artefacts found in the Thames.
- *Roman London.* This gallery has a hoard of gold coins (1st–2nd century AD) found buried in a safety deposit box near Fenchurch Street, and the gilded arms of what must have been a life-size statue of a god or emperor.
- *Tudors to the early Stuarts.* The civil war collection includes Oliver Cromwell's death mask and Bible, but more captivating is the cabinet filled with the glittering Cheapside Hoard. In 1912, a workman digging in London hit on a box containing 230 pieces of finely crafted jewellery set with precious stones. The treasure may have belonged to a goldsmith who hid his stock during the civil war of 1642–49.

Also within the complex is the **Barbican Arts Centre**, home of the London Symphony Orchestra. It has an art gallery, theatre, cinema and concert hall.

Nearby is **St Bartholomew-the-Great** ㊹, a Norman church which has also served as a stable, factory, wine cellar, coal store, and even as Benjamin Franklin's London printworks during its 1,000-year history.

The Guildhall

In the shadows of the Barbican's skyscrapers is the **Guildhall** ㊺ (Gresham Street; 9am–5pm; tel: 020-7606 3030; cityoflondon.gov.uk; free) one of the few buildings to survive the Great Fire and now the home of the City government. This ornate Gothic structure was built in 1411 with funds donated by various livery companies, the medieval trade and craft guilds that held sway over the City. Within the Guildhall is the famous **Great Hall**, decorated with the colourful ban-

BELOW: the Lord Mayor's Parade.

Recommended Restaurants and Pubs on page 141

ners of the 12 livery companies and the shields of all 92 guilds.

The Lord Mayor's Show *(see margin note)* sets off from the Guildhall and ends at **Mansion House**, the official residence of the Lord Mayor since the 1750s.

Britain's financial heartland

A short walk east along Gresham Street brings you to a bustling intersection dominated by the **Bank of England** ㊻, a building of powerful classical design. The Bank still prints and mints all British money, administers to the national debt and protects the country's gold reserves.

It contains the **Bank of England Museum** (entrance in Bartholomew Lane, Mon–Fri 10am–5pm; tel: 020-7601 5545; free). While the waxwork mannequins of clerks and customers carry on their business, the presentations narrate how the bank helped to finance Britain's war effort against France in 1688, how it became one of the first institutions in the City to employ women and how it controlled government borrowing during World War II.

Nearby stands the old London **Stock Exchange**, founded in 1773. The trading floor is no longer used as shares are now traded electronically.

Lloyd's of London

The computerisation of the Stock Exchange brought demands for office buildings purpose-built for modern communications. One of the first, and most dramatic, is the 1986 **Lloyd's of London** building in Lime Street, designed for the insurance group by Richard Rogers. It is not open to the public.

Beside this modern building is the more accessible **Leadenhall** ㊼. Once the wholesale market for poultry and game, the magnificent Victorian structure has been converted into a handsome commercial centre, with a collection of stylish restaurants, sandwich bars and shops which attract city workers at breakfast and lunchtime.

London's other steel-and-glass Victorian constructions – the railway stations – were also given facelifts during the 1980s building boom. **Liverpool Street** was overhauled and Fenchurch Street acquired a 1930s Manhattan-style office block, **1 America Square**, over its railway lines. **Broadgate**, a complex of 13 office blocks around three squares, includes an ice rink (for lessons, ring 020-7505 4068) and a voluptuous sculpture, Fernando Botero's *Broadgate Venus*.

The most distinctive new structure is **30 St Mary Axe**, a 40-storey tapering glass tower designed by Lord Foster and known affectionately as "the erotic gherkin".

Gracechurch Street leads south to London Bridge and the Thames. Just before you reach the river, a huge fluted column peers over the helter-skelter of rooftops: the 202-ft (60-metre) **Monument** ㊽ (Apr–Sept Mon–-Fri 9am–5.40pm, Sat–Sun 2pm–5.40pm, Oct–Mar Mon–Sat 9am–3.40pm). This is Sir Christopher Wren's memorial to the Great Fire of 1666 which destroyed more than 13,000 houses. You can climb 311 steps to a small platform, from which the view is memorable.

The tapering tower at 30 St Mary Axe, nicknamed the Gherkin.

BELOW: Lloyd's of London.

The Imperial State Crown, with 2,868 diamonds, was made in 1937 and is on display in the Tower of London.

BELOW: attired in Tudor uniforms, Yeoman warders ("Beefeaters") have been guarding the Tower of London for 500 years.

The Tower of London

Lower Thames Street traces the medieval banks of the river past the old Billingsgate Fish Market and the elegant Custom House. A squat stone building commands this southeast corner of the City, a pensive medieval fortress known as the **Tower of London** ❹❾ (Nov–Feb Tue–Sat 9am–5pm, Sun–Mon 10am–5pm, Mar–Oct Mon–Sat 9am–6pm, Sun 10am–6pm; tel: 0870-756 6060; hrp.org.uk/tower; charge).

The Tower has served, over the centuries, as fortress, palace, prison and museum, as well as arsenal, archive, menagerie and treasury. Because its buildings were functional and frequently remodelled, many interiors look comparatively modern and, overall, the Tower somehow lacks the romantic aura that many of its millions of visitors expect. But how could the boards that Henry VIII trod hope to survive the footfalls of 2½ million tourists a year?

William the Conqueror built the inner keep (the **White Tower**) as both a military stronghold and a means of impressing his new subjects in England. Constructed between 1078 and 1098, it was the largest building in Britain and soon symbolised royal domination. It remained a royal residence until the 16th century, when the court moved to more comfortable quarters in Westminster. The Tower then became the storehouse for the Crown Jewels and the most infamous prison and execution ground in London. After 1747 it became the Royal Mint, Archive and Menagerie. German spies were executed here in both world wars.

The White Tower houses the diminutive **St John's Chapel**, built in 1080 and now the oldest church in London. Beneath Waterloo Barracks is a vault containing the **Crown Jewels**, including the Imperial State Crown, which sparkles with 3,000 stones, and the **Royal Sceptre**, which centres around a 530-carat diamond called the Star of Africa. A moving walkway ensures that visitors cannot linger long over the principal exhibits.

Also worth seeing are the **Crowns and Diamonds** exhibition in the Martin Tower, and the **Royal Fusiliers Museum's** permanent display of weapons from the mid-17th to mid-19th centuries.

The Tower is protected by the Yeomen Wardens or Beefeaters, so-called not because of their carnivorous habits, but because they were founded in the 16th century as the *buffetiers* or guardians of the king's buffet.

An authentic chopping block sits upon Tower Green – yes, you may place your head on it for photographs. Acting as tour guides are the Beefeaters, some of whom display a limited gift for theatrical melodrama. You can skip their one-hour tour by hiring an audio guide. Note, though, that the spiral staircases in some of the towers require a degree of agility.

The most spectacular of London's many spans is **Tower Bridge** ❺⓿, a striking Gothic structure that isn't as old as it looks – it opened in 1894. Its bascules still rise frequently – four or five times on some days – to let tall vessels through. The Tower Bridge Experience (Apr–Sept 10am–6.30pm, Nov–Mar 9.30am–5.15pm; entrance near north end; charge) offers a tour of the inside of the bridge, as well as superb views.

Recommended Restaurants and Pubs on page 141

Bankside

On the south side of Tower Bridge is the restaurant-lined **Butler's Wharf** and the **Design Museum** 51 (daily 10am–5.45pm; tel: 0870-833 9955; designmuseum.org; charge), which displays influential design and artefacts, mainly 20th-century, and has changing exhibitions.

The riverside walk between Tower Bridge and London Bridge passes by **HMS *Belfast*** 52 (May–Sept 10am–6pm, Oct–Apr 10am–5pm; tel: 020-7940 6300; http://hmsbelfast.iwm.org.uk). Commissioned in 1939, it is now a maritime museum. A tour ranges from the bridge to the engine rooms, capturing the cramped facilities endured by its 950-man crew.

Continuing past more renovated warehouses towards London Bridge, cut through **Hay's Galleria**, a small shopping mall carved out of a former tea wharf, to reach Tooley Street. Here, the **London Dungeon** 53 (daily Sept–Jun 10am–5.30pm, Jul–Aug 9.30am–6pm; tel: 020-7403 7221; thedungeons.com; charge) provides a gruesome, actor-led account of London's history, including the Black Death, the Great Fire and the grisly deeds of Sweeney Todd and Jack the Ripper – children love it, but be prepared for long queues.

To its left is **Winston Churchill's Britain at War Experience** (Apr–Sept 10am–6pm, Oct–Mar 10am–5pm; britainatwar.co.uk; charge), which includes a simulation of a World War II bombing raid and lots of 1940s memorabilia.

Nearby, at 83 Bermondsey Street, is the **Fashion and Textile Museum** 54 (Mon–Fri 10am–5pm; ftmlondon.org), created by Zandra Rhodes to honour 1950s British designers and to teach students.

Southwark Cathedral

Just to the south of London Bridge rises the imposing **Southwark Cathedral** 55,

The cruiser HMS Belfast, *which served in World War II and the Korean War, is Britain's only surviving example of the big-gun armoured warships built during the first half of the 20th century.*

BELOW: Tower Bridge, whose bascules rise several times a day to let through ships.

Southwark Cathedral.

(southwark.anglican.org/cathedral), where Shakespeare was a parishioner. Augustinian canons erected the original church in the 13th century, but the cathedral has been much altered since then, and now has a sensitively designed refectory, library, conference centre and shop. It holds free organ recitals on Mondays (1.10–1.50pm) and free classical concerts on Tuesdays (3.15–4pm).

Adjacent is **Borough Market**, a wholesale fruit and vegetable market whose history dates back 1,000 years. On Thursday and Friday afternoons and on Saturdays (9am–4pm) crowds flock – despite its reputation for being pricey – to a retail market offering a wide range of gourmet and organic products, not just fruit and veg.

Beyond the cathedral, by the Thames in the St Mary Overie Dock, is a full-size copy of Sir Francis Drake's galleon, the ***Golden Hinde*** (tours daily 10am–6pm; tel: 0870-011 8700; goldenhinde.org; charge). The original circumnaviged the globe in 1577.

Just to the west, the **Clink Prison Museum** features old armour and torture instruments.Beyond it, **Vinopolis** runs audio tours of vaults portraying the world's wine-producing regions, and the **Anchor Inn** is an historic pub.

Shakespeare's Globe

Continue westwards along the river to reach a replica of the 1599 **Shakespeare's Globe** ❺❻. This open-roofed theatre-in-the-round stages the Bard's plays close to where they were first performed (performances in summer; guided tours every half hour 9.15am–12.15pm). **Shakespeare's Globe Exhibition** is well worth a visit – there are traditional displays, but it's the touch screens and hands-on exhibits that are fun, enabling you to speak some of the playwright's greatest lines in response to the recorded voices of great actors and then listen to the result.

Tate Modern

Beyond the Globe, a towering brick chimney identifies **Tate Modern** ❺❼ (Sun–Thur 10am–6pm, Fri–Sat 10am–10pm; tel: 020-7887 8888 tate.org.uk; free), whose large collection of international modern and contemporary art is

BELOW: Shakespeare's Globe theatre. **RIGHT:** gallery in Tate Modern.

Recommended Restaurants and Pubs on page 141

housed in the former Bankside Power Station. The massive turbine hall gives temporary installations and major sculptures room to breathe. Displays in the gallery's main rooms are arranged thematically rather than chronologically, mixing the work of Picasso, Matisse, Mondrian, Dalí, Bacon, Pollock, Rothko, Warhol and many others. The intention is that juxtaposing work produced before the 1970s (an imprecise dividing point) with contemporary work will show how artists have learnt from one another since 1900. The gallery, with 5 million visitors a year, is one of London's top attractions.

Tate Modern is linked to St Paul's across the river by the **Millennium Bridge**, a slender footbridge.

The South Bank

The **South Bank Centre** 58 (bookings 0871-663 2500; southbankcentre.co.uk), across Waterloo Bridge from Somerset House, is Europe's largest arts complex.

The **Royal Festival Hall** plays host to the London Symphony and Philharmonic orchestras, a spacious arena that is famed for its acoustics and visibility. Next door are the **Queen Elizabeth Hall** and the **Purcell Room**, used for events from chamber music to poetry readings. On the upper level of the complex is the **Hayward Gallery**, which has changing exhibitions of contemporary art.

BFI Southbank, in the shadow of Waterloo Bridge, presents a repertory of vintage and foreign-language films as well as the London Film Festival each November. The British Film Institute also runs **London IMAX Cinema** 59, which rises like a behemoth from the roundabout at the south end of Waterloo Bridge.

Back by the river is the concrete bulk of the **National Theatre** – three theatres under one roof – known for the high quality of its drama productions. For a peak behind the scenes, book a backstage tour (tel: 020 7452 3400).

The London Eye

To the west is the immensely popular 450-ft (135-metre) **London Eye** 60 observation wheel erected for the millennium (to book, tel: 0870 5000 600). The 32 enclosed capsules take 30 minutes to make a full rotation, and on a clear day, you can see for 25 miles (40 km).

Next to it is the majestic **County Hall** 61, built in 1909–33 and until 1986 seat of the Greater London Council. It now contains two hotels and several restaurants; the **London Aquarium** (tel: 020-7967 8000; londonaquarium.co.uk; 10am–6pm), whose 41 exhibits range from sharks to stingray; the **Dalí Universe** (10am–5.30pm), which displays more than 500 of Salvador Dalí's works; and **Namco Station**, a games and entertainments centre (admission free).

Upriver from the South Bank complex, beyond Westminster Bridge, is **Lambeth Palace** 62, which has been the London residence of the Archbishop of Canterbury for nearly 800 years. It is seldom open to the public. The garden and deconsecrated church of St Mary nearby are home to the lovely **Garden Museum** (Mon–Sun 10.30am–5pm; tel: 020-7401 8865; gardenmuseum.org.uk; charge).

The London IMAX cinema to the south of Waterloo Bridge.

BELOW: the London Eye and County Hall.

The Imperial War Museum houses weapons, tanks, paintings, uniforms, scale models, and an extensive Holocaust Exhibition. There are recreations of World War I trenches and the impact of a World War II bombing raid.

The Imperial War Museum

Another landmark south of the river is the imaginative **Imperial War Museum** ❻❸, situated on Lambeth Road in a building opened in 1815 as a hospital for the insane (10am–6pm; tel: 020-7416 5320; iwm.org.uk; free). The museum's excellence lies in its success in being thought-provoking, not sensational.

The East End

Back on the north bank of the river, downstream from Tower Bridge, lie **St Katharine's Docks** ❻❹. Built in 1828 as a shipment point for wool and wine, the docks were renovated in the early 1980s and have become a posh residential and commercial district. The complex contains a shopping arcade, a yacht harbour, pub, hotel and several old warehouses (such as the Ivory House), now converted in to modern offices and flats. It is the most successful of the docklands developments which extend east from here to the Isle of Dogs where the **Canary Wharf** complex (Britain's tallest office block) marks their modern ambitions.

Mansell Street leads north from the Tower into the warren of narrow streets that marks the start of London's **East End**, traditionally the City's working-class district. **Whitechapel** and **Spitalfields** – both at the north end of Mansell Street – are where 19th and early 20th-century European immigrants settled.

The **Whitechapel Art Gallery** ❻❺ (Tue–Sun 11am–5pm, Wed until 8pm; free) in Whitechapel High Street is one of London's most exciting galleries, hosting exhibitions by living artists. **Spitalfields Market**, a wholesale fruit and vegetable market until 1991, is now awash with antiques and crafts stalls, and surrounded by trendy boutiques.

Nearby, **Petticoat Lane** ❻❻ is the most famous East End market. Today, the traders – a mixed bag of Cockneys, West Indians and Asians – prove every Sunday morning that racial harmony is possible. The stalls along Middlesex Street are a chromatic jumble of clothes, antiques, food and much more besides. ❑

How the 2012 Olympics are transforming east London

The construction of a new Olympic Park in Stratford has brought much needed investment to the area. Situated in the Lower Lea Valley, the 500-acre (200-hectare) site will house nine purpose-built sporting venues, a media centre and an Olympic Village providing accommodation for all of the athletes. The centrepiece of the park will be an 80,000-seat athletics stadium which will also be the setting for the opening and closing ceremonies. A state-of-the-art aquatics centre is planned, as well as a hockey centre, a velopark and four multi-sports arenas for fencing, volleyball, basketball and handball.

ABOVE: how the main stadium is likely to look.

Existing sports venues in other parts of London will also be used for the games, with football matches at the new Wembley Stadium, tennis at Wimbledon and archery at Lord's Cricket Ground. Some of London's many parks have been incorporated into the extensive network of venues. Greenwich Park will provide a picturesque backdrop for equestrian events, while the Triathlon will take place in Hyde Park and a road-cycling course will be created in Regent's Park. Horse Guards Parade, a parade ground usually reserved for royal occasions, will be transformed into a beach volleyball pitch.

The recession that began in 2008 tightened budgets. But London's ailing transport network is being extended and improved in order to accommodate the 500,000 spectators expected to travel to the Olympic Park each day. Many of these visitors will probably travel on the Javelin, a high-speed shuttle which will whizz passengers from central London to the Olympic Park in 7 minutes. Extensions to the East London line and the Docklands Light Railway are being built, as is a Channel Tunnel rail link from Stratford.

After 2012, the main site will become a large public park, and the Olympic Village will be converted into apartments.

RESTAURANTS AND PUBS

Restaurants

Prices for a three-course dinner per person with a half-bottle of house wine:

£ = under £20
££ = £20–30
£££ = £30–50
££££ = over £50

The City

Carravagio
107 Leadenhall St, EC3. Tel: 020-7626 6206. L & D Mon–Fri. **£££** (set menu) **££££**
Grand and rather showy Italian restaurant in a converted bank. Fish is a good option and the fillet steak with aubergine and gorgonzola is a carnivore's dream. But the bill is likely to he high.

The Eagle
159 Farringdon Rd, EC1. Tel: 020-7837 1353. L & D Mon–Sat, L only Sun. **££**
This was the pub that launched a thousand gastropubs with its pioneering menu of inventive dishes. The food has a Mediterranean bias. A good choice of European beers is also available.

St John
26 St John St, EC1. Tel: 020-7251 0848. L & D Mon–Fri, D only Sat. **££££**
This little restaurant close to Smithfield's meat market, is a Clerkenwell favourite. Simple but curious dishes such as Middlewhite belly and dandelion or pigeon and rabbit.

Sweetings
39 Queen Victoria Street, EC4. Tel: 020-7248 3062. L only Mon–Fri. **££**
First-rate fish restaurant with bags of traditional City atmosphere, and well-prepared dishes such as grilled skate, turbot in mustard sauce or dressed crab, and old-fashioned puddings such as treacle tart.

The South Bank

RSJ
33a Coin St, SE1. Tel: 020-7928 4554. L & D Mon–Fri; D only Sat **££–£££**
This pretty restaurant offers pleasant dishes such as Gressingham duck with beetroot salad, but the real attraction is the excellent selection of wines from the Loire.

Southwark

Le Pont de la Tour
Butlers Wharf Building, 36d Shad Thames, SE1. Tel: 020-7403 8403. L & D daily. **££££**
Prime ministers and presidents have enjoyed the splendid view of Tower Bridge from this upmarket Conran restaurant, where the stress is on seafood. Impeccable but very expensive.

Masters Super Fish
191 Waterloo Rd, SE1. Tel: 020-7928 6924. L & D Tue–Sat, D only Mon. **£**
Need a taxi? You'll find cabbies galore tucking into huge portions of fish and chips in this old-fashioned eatery.

Mesón Don Felipe
53 The Cut, SE1. Tel: 020-7928 3237. L & D Mon–Sat, D only Sun. **££**
Londoners in the know flock to this excellent tapas bar. Tables fill up fast, but there's often room at the bar. The juicy fresh anchovies are great.

ABOVE: Café du Marché on Charterhouse Square.

Tas
33 The Cut, SE1. Tel: 020-7928 2111. L & D daily. **££**
Turkish-flavoured venue, good for vegetarians. It's easy to go overboard on the *meze*, so save room for the equally tasty mains. Branches at 72 Borough High St (Tel: 7403 7200) and 20–2 New Globe Walk (Tel: 7633 9777).

Pubs

In the City, **Jerusalem Tavern** *(55 Britton Street)* is an intimate little pub dating from 1720, with cubicles, Georgian-style furniture and a selection of real ales and fruit beers. **The Counting House** *(50 Cornhill)* is a bank-turned-pub, which still has its high ceilings and chandeliers.

In Southwark, The **George Inn** *(77 Borough High St)*, owned by the National Trust, is London's only galleried coaching inn. The **Market Porter** *(9 Stoney St)* is famous for opening its doors 6–8.30am for Borough Market workers.

The **Boot and Flogger** *(10–20 Redcross Way; closes 8pm)*, is a traditional wine bar named after a corking device. Reminiscent of a gentleman's club, it trades as a Free Vintner, meaning that it doesn't need a licence.

LONDON: CHELSEA AND KENSINGTON

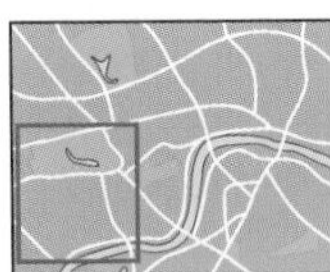

Home to some of Britain's best and brightest – and wealthiest – Chelsea and Kensington offer the visitor fine museums, lovely streets to stroll along, and superlative shopping

Main attractions

KING'S ROAD
CHELSEA ROYAL HOSPITAL
KNIGHTSBRIDGE
VICTORIA AND ALBERT MUSEUM
NATURAL HISTORY MUSEUM
SCIENCE MUSEUM
ROYAL ALBERT HALL
HYDE PARK
HOLLAND PARK
NOTTING HILL
LITTLE VENICE

In the 19th century Chelsea was an avant garde "village" just outside the sprawl of central London. Among its more famous residents were Oscar Wilde, John Singer Sargent, Thomas Carlyle, Mark Twain and T.S. Eliot. Cheyne Walk, a row of elegant Georgian terraced houses just off the river, has long been Chelsea's most popular residential street. George Eliot, Turner and Carlyle lived here in the 19th century; J. Paul Getty and Mick Jagger in the 20th. Chelsea is where England swung in the 1960s and where punk began in the 1970s.

BELOW: a stroll down King's Road.

King's Road ❶ is Chelsea's famous thoroughfare. It started life as a tranquil country lane but was later widened into a private carriage road from St James's Palace to Hampton Court on the order of King Charles II. It rose to its pinnacle of fame in the 1960s, when ground-breaking designers Mary Quant and Ossie Clark set up shop here, and it was in its boutiques that the miniskirt first made its revolutionary appearance. In the 1970s Vivienne Westwood and Malcolm McLaren took up the avant-garde baton, dominating the punk scene with their boutique "Sex". Today the street still attracts a trendy young crowd, but it has become more mainstream.

Soldiering on

Down on the riverfront is **Chelsea Royal Hospital** ❷, (daily, 10am–noon, 2–4pm; chelsea-pensioners.org.uk; free), Sir Christopher Wren's masterpiece of the English baroque style, opened as a home for invalid and veteran soldiers in 1682. A few hundred army pensioners still reside here, and parade in their famous scarlet frockcoats on Oak Apple Day (29 May). Visitors can see the Great Hall, Octagon and Chapel and the museum.

On Royal Hospital Road, tracing the history of the British military from the 15th century, is the **National Army Museum** (daily 10am–5.30pm; tel: 020-7730; national-army-museum.ac.uk; free). You can feel the weight of a Tudor cannonball, try on a soldier's helmet, and view some flamboyant paintings.

Ranelagh Gardens stands adjacent to the Royal Hospital, the site of the Chelsea Flower Show (rhs.org.uk.chelsea), dating from 1862 and held each spring by the Royal Horticultural Society.

On Royal Hospital Road is the historic **Chelsea Physic Garden** (Apr–Oct Wed noon–5pm, Sun 2–6pm; tel: 020-7352 5646; chelseaphysicgarden.co.uk; charge), a botanical laboratory founded in 1676 from which cotton seeds were taken to the American South in 1732. It's a pretty place for a stroll and afternoon tea.

Cross either Albert or Chelsea bridges and enjoy the lush expanse of **Battersea Park** ❸ on the south bank, with gardens designed as part of the Festival of Britain in 1951 and the Buddhist Peace Pagoda, commemorating the 1985 Year of Peace.

Belgravia

Having crossed the Thames again and returned to King's Road, leave Chelsea by proceeding east, crossing Sloane Square and entering the elegant district of **Belgravia**. The area was used for grazing until Thomas Cubitt developed it as a town estate for aristocrats in the early 19th century. The district retains this exclusive quality as the home of diplomats, senior civil servants, celebrities and the occasional duke or baron. Belgravia is littered with grand Regency terraces and squares, bound by cream-coloured mansions and carefully tended gardens. Behind the grand facades lie the diminutive mews, tiny cobblestoned alleys that once served as stables. This is London's most expensive residential district.

North of Belgravia via Sloane Street is the bustling neighbourhood of luxury shops and first-class hotels at **Knightsbridge**. This is the home of **Harrods** ❹, London's most famous department store, owned by the flamboyant Egyptian,

Harrods employs more than 5,000 staff from 50 countries to serve as many as 300,000 customers on peak days. At night its exterior is lit up with 11,500 energy-efficient lightbulbs.

BELOW: Founder's Day parade at the Chelsea Royal Hospital.

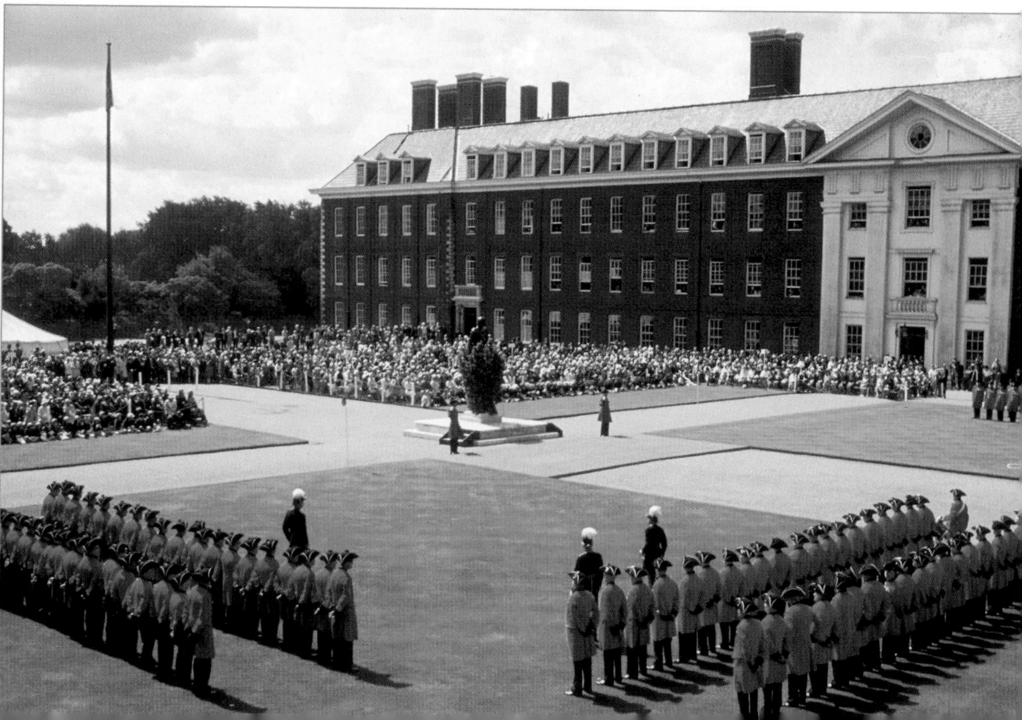

The Victoria and Albert Museum's British galleries trace the country's changing taste from 1500 to 1900.

Mohamed Al-Fayed. At night, its light-spangled facade resembles an enormous Victorian birthday cake. The tiled food halls, which display more than 500 varieties of cheese, 140 different breads and 160 brands of whisky. Visitors are asked to dress "presentably" and wear shoes.

Victoria and Albert Museum

South Kensington tube station (one stop after Knightsbridge) is the jumping-off point for Exhibition Road's cluster of fine (and free) museums. The **Victoria and Albert** ❺ (Cromwell Road; tel: 020-7942 2000; vam.ac.uk; daily 10am–5.45pm, until 10pm Wed; free) is the most famous of these, housing a marvellous collection of 5 million items dedicated to the fine and applied arts of all nations, eras and styles. Some see it as a vast box of delights, others as a confusing mish-mash. The maze-like interior includes 7 miles (11 km) of galleries, with exhibits ranging from exquisite Persian miniatures to a whole room designed by Frank Lloyd Wright. One minute one can be admiring the 1515–16 Raphael Cartoons drawn for the tapestries in the Sistine Chapel, and the next examining E.H.

Kensington and Chelsea

0 500 m
0 500 yds

Recommended Restaurants and Pubs on page 149

Shepard's illustrations for Winnie-the-Pooh or admiring a plaster cast of Michelangelo's *David*. Other highlights include an outstanding collection of Indian art in the Nehru Gallery, fashion from the 17th century to the present day in the Fashion Galleries, and the British Galleries, which trace the country's taste ("what was hot and what was new") from 1500 to 1900.

Natural History Museum

If any of London's museums encapsulates the Victorians' quest for knowledge and passion for cataloguing data, it's the **Natural History Museum** ❻ (Cromwell Road; tel: 020-7942 5000; nhm.ac.uk; daily 10am–5.50pm; free). Occupying an extravagant Gothic Romanesque building, it has one of the best dinosaur and prehistoric lizard collections anywhere. The highlight is a full-scale animatronic T-Rex that roars and twists convincingly.

The Life Galleries section of the museum also has fascinating exhibits on early man, Darwin's theory of evolution, human biology, birth and whales (including a life-size model of a blue whale). In the Earth Galleries (geology section) you can experience a simulated earthquake, or examine a piece of the moon. The Creepy Crawlies section demonstrates how many uninvited housemates occupy an average home. In the basement, children can touch, weigh and examine specimens under a microscope.

Ancient fish skeleton in the Natural History Museum.

Science Museum

With more than 10,000 exhibits, plus attractions such as an IMAX theatre and an interactive play area for children, the **Science Museum** ❼ (Exhibition Road; tel: 0870-870 4868; sciencemuseum.org.uk; daily 10am–6pm; free) could take days to explore, so it's wise to set priorities.

The Making the Modern World gallery includes the world's oldest surviving steam locomotive, the coal-hauling Puffing Billy (circa 1815), Stephenson's Rocket passenger locomotive (1829), a Ford Model T (1916), a Lockheed Electra airliner hanging in silvery splendour from the ceiling (1935), a copy of Crick and Watson's DNA spiral model (1953) and the Apollo 10 command module (1969).

The popular Exploring Space gallery houses the huge Spacelab 2 x-ray telescope – the actual instrument flown on the

Although national museums and galleries are free, most others have entrance charges. The London Pass allows free entry to many attractions and includes free travel on the Underground and buses. www.londonpass.com

Below: the Science Museum's Making of the Modern World gallery.

The Royal Albert Hall, opened by Queen Victoria in 1871, has accommodated as many as 9,000 people, though today's safety regulations limit the number to 5,544.

BELOW: the Albert Memorial.

Space Shuttle – and full-size models of the Huygens Titan probe and Beagle 2 Mars Lander. The replica of the Apollo 11 lunar excursion module has been reconfigured to a new level of accuracy.

The Flight Gallery's exhibits range from a seaplane to a Spitfire, from hot-air balloons to helicopters. The 1919 Vickers Vimy in which Alcock and Brown made the first non-stop transatlantic flight is here, as is Amy Johnson's *Gipsy Moth Jason*, and there's a replica of the Wright Flyer in which Wilbur and Orville Wright pioneered powered flight in 1903.

The Wellcome Wing, linked to the main building, concentrates on information technology, hums with hands-on displays relating to the human experience.

Royal Albert Hall

One of Victorian England's greatest monuments also lies within South Kensington. Queen Victoria laid the foundation stone for the **Royal Albert Hall** ❽ (tickets and tours: 020-7589 8212) in 1867 in memory of her late husband, Prince Albert, who was responsible for many of the South Kensington institutions. The circular 8,000-seat auditorium, one of the largest theatres in London, stages a varied programme from pop concerts to the BBC-sponsored summer Henry Wood Promenade Concerts – the Proms – a marvellous annual showcase of both classical and more modern music.

Across Kensington Gore sits the **Albert Memorial** ❾, a flamboyant – even vulgar – Gothic monument that rises suddenly from the plane trees of Kensington Gardens and Hyde Park. Prince Albert sits under a lavish canopy, forever reading the catalogue from the 1851 Great Exhibition. Marble figures on the lower corners of the steps depict America, Asia, Africa and Europe.

Palaces and gardens

A short walk through the tranquil gardens is **Kensington Palace** ❿. Christopher Wren refurbished the mansion for William and Mary in the 1690s, and for nearly 100 years it served as the principal royal residence in London. Today it is the London residence of some minor members of the royal family. Many of the first-floor State Apartments can be

Recommended Restaurants and Pubs on page 149

viewed (tel: 0870-751 5170; hrp.org.uk; 9am–5pm, Sun from 11am). You can also see the Royal Dress Collection, a presentation of royal, court and ceremonial dress dating from the 18th century to the present day, including some of Princess Diana's gowns. On the first floor are the State Apartments, displaying paintings from the Royal Collection.

In **Hyde Park**, the **Princess Diana Memorial Fountain** is a somewhat underwhelming circular ring of flowing water which, when it opened in 2004, proved hazardous to some children who slipped while paddling. The **Serpentine Gallery** ⓫ (10am–6pm; free), a tiny art museum beside a bird-filled lake, stages adventurous exhibitions.

At the southeast corner of Hyde Park, a museum dedicated to the Duke of Wellington, who defeated Napoleon at Waterloo in 1815, is located in **Apsley House** (149 Piccadilly, tel: 020-7499 5676; english-heritage.org.uk; Tues–Sun 10am–5pm). It has notable collections of furniture, silver, porcelain and paintings.

In the northeast corner of Hyde Park is **Speakers' Corner** ⓬, where, particularly on Sundays, orators and idiots passionately defend their beliefs. This tradition began when the Tyburn gallows stood here (1388–1783) and felons were allowed to make a final unexpurgated speech to the crowds before being hanged.

Close by, on a central reservation in Park Lane, is a striking monument to **Animals in War**, with sculptures marking the role played by horses and other animals on history's battlefields – 8 million horses alone died in World War I.

Leighton House

Holland Park ⓭, just west of Kensington Palace via Kensington High Street, is one of London's least known but more interesting green spaces. It includes a Japanese garden, an adventure playground and a youth hostel. In summer an open-air theatre stages opera and drama.

At 12 Holland Park Road, a rather plain red-brick house contains one of the most extraordinary interiors in London. **Leighton House** ⓮ (Wed–Mon 11am–5.30pm; tel: 020-7602 3316; charge) was the home of the Victorian artist Lord Frederic Leighton from 1866 until he died in 1896 and is a mix of lavish Orientalism and conventional Victorian comforts – a private palace in intense, jewel-like colours. The *pièce de résistance* is the Arab Hall, inspired by a Moorish palace in Palermo.

You can hire boats to row on the Serpentine Lake in Hyde Park.

Notting Hill

North of Holland Park is **Notting Hill**, one of London's most highly sought-after residential districts with handsome white stucco Victorian terraces and villas. On the last Sunday and Monday of August the narrow streets explode with music and colour as the city's huge West Indian population stages Europe's largest street carnival, complete with ambitious floats, steel bands and extravagant costumes. It's mostly a good-natured affair, but don't flaunt anything that may tempt the inevitable petty thieves.

BELOW: Notting Hill Carnival, held at the end of August.

Searching for a bargain at Portobello Road market. The merchants know their antiques, so although fine objets d'art can be found, they are seldom cheap.

BELOW: cricket at its balletic best during an England versus New Zealand Test match at Lord's.

The district's other famous attraction is the **Portobello Road Market** ⓯. On Saturdays the street becomes jammed. At the more genteel top end, vast numbers of tourists browse through the antiques. Further north, under the Westway fly-over, a flea market mixes junk, cutting-edge fashion and arts and crafts (Fri–Sun). Between these two, the traditional fruit, veg and flower stalls have been joined by traders selling foodstuffs from around the world.

East of Notting Hill and on the north side of Hyde Park is **Bayswater**, whose grand mansions are now mostly hotels. Leading off it, **Queensway** has many ethnic restaurants.

Little Venice

The posh residential district of **Little Venice** ⓰ lies at the junction of the Grand Union, Regent's and Paddington canals and residential moorings for barges here are much sought after.

Refurbished canal barges operated by the **London Waterbus Company** (Apr–Oct daily, Nov–Mar Sat–Sun; tel: 020-7482-2660) run east from Little Venice to Regent's Park through another exclusive residential neighbourhood, **St John's Wood**, home of the celebrated Abbey Road recording studios.

Lord's Cricket Ground ⓱ is tucked away in the heart of the Wood. Lord's is the grand shrine of cricket, the world's best-known ground and home of the famous Marylebone Cricket Club (MCC), the governing body of the quintessentially English sport. The **Cricket Museum** (entrance on St John's Wood Road; two-hour guided tours: Apr–Sept at 10am, noon, 2pm, Oct–Mar noon, 2pm; tel: 020-7432 1033) is filled with two centuries of memorabilia.

The nearby **London Central Mosque**, completed in 1977, incorporates an Islamic Cultural Centre. ❑

RESTAURANTS AND PUBS

Restaurants

Prices for a three-course dinner per person with a half-bottle of house wine:

£ = under £20
££ = £20–30
£££ = £30–50
££££ = over £50

Chelsea

Cheyne Walk Brasserie
50 Cheyne Walk, SW3. Tel: 020-7376 8787. L & D Tue–Sat, L only Sun, D only Mon. **££** (weekday lunch menu) **£££**
The flavours of Provence are cooked up over the central grill of this Belle Époque dining room. Also offers views of the Albert Bridge and a sumptuous cocktail lounge.

Eight Over Eight
392 King's Rd SW3. Tel: 020-7349 9934. L & D Mon–Sat, D only Sun. **£££**
This stylish restaurant in a former pub offers Asian dishes with a modern twist. Salad of rare salmon, green mango and palm, duck and foie gras shu mai, and chocolate pudding with green tea ice cream are just some of the delights on offer.

Gordon Ramsay
68 Royal Hospital Rd, SW3. Tel: 020-7352 4441. L & D Mon–Fri. **£££** (lunch menu) **££££**
The celebrity chef's gastronomic offerings – such as roasted sea scallops with octopus, black pudding tempura, cauliflower purée and parmesan velouté – are exquisite. The lunchtime set menu costs £40 for 3 courses.

Poissonnerie de L'Avenue
82 Sloane Avenue, SW3. Tel: 020-7589 2457. L & D Mon–Sat. **££–£££** (set menu) **£££**
Run by the same family for over 40 years, it serves fresh fish and seafood from the adjoining fishmonger's. Dishes are old-school French, although some come with an Italian flourish.

Kensington

Bibendum
Michelin House, 81 Fulham Road, SW3. Tel: Restaurant: 020-7581 5817; Oyster Bar: 7589 1480. L & D daily. **£££** (set lunch) **££££**
Opened by Sir Terence Conran and Paul Hamlyn in 1987, Bibendum continues to thrive; there's an oyster bar on the ground floor and a restaurant on the first floor of this individual Art Deco-style building.

Bombay Brasserie
Courtfield Rd, SW7. Tel: 020-7370 4040. L & D daily, last orders midnight. **££** (set lunch) **£££**
This upmarket Indian has rejuvenated its classic menu and deserves its reputation for good, if expensive, food. Try to book a table in the conservatory.

Brasserie St Quentin
243 Brompton Road, SW3. Tel: 020-7589 8005. L & D daily. **££** (set meal served until 7pm) **£££**
Small suppliers provide seasonal produce, so depending on the time of year you'll find smoked Irish eel, English asparagus, oysters and partridge alongside snails and seared foie gras.

ABOVE: taking afternoon tea at Harrods.

Kensington Place
201–9 Kensington Church St, W8. Tel: 020-7727 3184. L & D daily. **£££**
A trailblazer of the Modern European scene, it still serves simple yet inventive good food. Noise levels are high.

Pizza on the Park
11 Knightsbridge, SW1. Tel: 020-7235 7825. L & D daily. **££**
This flagship restaurant of the Pizza Express chain offers live jazz on Wednesday to Saturday evenings, plenty of space and very good pizzas.

Pubs

The King's Road has several good watering holes. There is the **Chelsea Potter** *(119 King's Rd)* or **Henry J Beans** *(195–7)*, an American bar and grill with the lure of a beer garden. But head off its well-trodden track to unearth some of the area's best pubs. These include the **Pig's Ear** *(35 Old Church St)*, lacking in authenticity after a continental-style refit, but with a fine real ale to its name; the **Surprise** *(6 Christchurch Terrace)*, a small local with stained glass and bar billiards; the **Cooper's Arms** *(87 Flood St)*, upholding the Campaign for Real Food; the **Cross Keys** *(1 Lawrence St)*, dating from 1765 and worth a visit for its gorgeous rooms; and the **Lots Road Pub and Dining Room** *(114 Lots Rd)*, a good gastropub.

Closer to Belgravia, the **Orange Brewery** *(37–9 Pimlico Rd)* has remnants of its former brewery

Good food is to be found in pubs these days, especiallly in "gastropubs". Here are a few of the best: **Anglesea Arms** *(15 Selwood Terrace, South Kensington)*, the **Cross Keys** *(1 Lawrence St, Chelsea)*, **The Abingdon** *(54 Abingdon Rd)*, **Churchill Arms** *(119 Kensington Church Street)* **Windsor Castle** *(114 Campden Hill Road)*, **The Cow** *(89 Westbourne Park Road*, **The Fat Badger** *(310 Portobello Road).*

DAY TRIPS ALONG THE THAMES

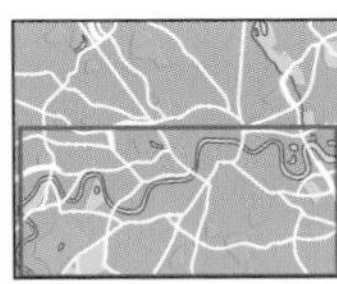

The Thames has played a central role in London's history, and you can travel along it by boat to a variety of fascinating places, including Greenwich, Kew Gardens and Hampton Court

Main attractions
GREENWICH
NATIONAL MARITIME MUSEUM
ROYAL OBSERVATORY
THE O2 ARENA
BATTERSEA PARK
HOGARTH'S HOUSE
KEW GARDENS
RICHMOND
TWICKENHAM
HAMPTON COURT PALACE

The capital spreads out from the centre seemingly for ever, as more than 7½ million people find space to live over 610 sq miles (1,570 sq km). Liberally sprinkled among this human mass are many parks, palaces and museums which offer rest and respite from the hustle and bustle of the big city. The River Thames is its biggest breathing space.

From Greenwich to Richmond, every suburb along the river has its own personality, and each can be reached by local London transport, as well as by riverboats. Eastwards, London's Docklands have been greatly renovated, but beyond a few remaining local pubs, it will be a long time before they find any real character. To the west, however, the river is a focus of pleasure: in summer, oarsmen and yachtsmen pit their wits against its tides, people stroll along its towpaths and the pubs are wet with warm beer and enlivened by warm company.

BELOW: the Royal Observatory and Flamsteed House.

Royal Greenwich

Greenwich ❶ can best be reached by train from Cannon Street, Victoria or London Bridge train stations. Alternatively, a boat service runs downriver from Westminster (tel: 020-7930 4097) and Charing Cross piers (tel: 020-7839 3572), leaving every 40 minutes in peak season and taking about an hour. Or take the Docklands Light Railway (DLR) from Bank tube station to Cutty Sark station, which is a five-minute walk to Greenwich town. A good time to visit Greenwich is at the weekend when there are craft and antique markets.

There have long been settlements here. In the 11th century Vikings pulled their longboats ashore, slew Archbishop St Alfege, and ravaged London. In 1427 Bella Court Palace was built on the riverside and it became a royal retreat. Henry VI made it his favourite residence and subsequent Tudor monarchs – Henry VIII, Elizabeth I and Mary – were all born at Greenwich, and it was here that Sir Walter Raleigh is supposed to have laid his cloak over a pool of mud so that Queen Elizabeth would not get her feet wet.

James I had the old palace demolished and commissioned Inigo Jones to build a new private residence for Queen Anne. The result was the **Queen's House**, completed in 1637, a masterpiece of the Palladian style and perhaps the finest piece of Stuart architecture in England.

Next door is the **National Maritime Museum**, an excellent seafaring collection, swelled with Millennium funds. Here the 1805 Battle of Trafalgar is relived and the glory of the nation's maritime tradition unfolds, with boats, paintings, and memorabilia from heroic voyages. A short distance up the hill (by foot or shuttle bus) is the **Royal Observatory**, constructed at Greenwich by Charles II in 1675 in order to perfect the arts of navigation and astronomy. Since that time, the globe's longitude and time zones have been measured from the Greenwich Meridian, which cuts right through the middle of Flamsteed House, now a museum of astronomical instruments and timepieces. (The Royal Observatory, Maritime Museum and Queen's House are open daily 10am–5pm, last entrance 4.30pm; combination entrance tickets available.)

The **O_2 concert arena** ❷ (North Greenwich tube station; tel: 020-8463 2000; theo2.co.uk) was built as the Millennium Dome and is now named after the mobile phone company that bought the naming rights. It is a massive entertainments centre hosting top rock concerts and sports events, with lots of eating places both inside and around it.

Greenwich has been associated with British sea power for the past 500 years. Just downstream is the Royal Navy's **Historic Dockyard** at Chatham *(see page 215)*, which flourished under Henry VIII and Elizabeth I. In the late 17th century, Sir Christopher Wren built the **Royal Hospital for Seamen** at Greenwich, an elegant complex in the baroque style that became the **Royal Naval College**. Its highly decorated chapel and Painted Hall, decorated in the early 18th century by Sir James Thornhill, are open to the public (daily 10am–3.30pm).

On the waterfront are anchored two of England's most famous ships. The ***Cutty***

The Painted Hall of the Royal Naval College, Greenwich.

BELOW: looking towards Docklands from Greenwich Park.

The Royal Naval College, begun by Christopher Wren in 1696, was designed as two halves to preserve the view from Queen's House to the river. It was originally a royal palace but was given over to the training of naval officers in 1873.

Sark, built in 1869 and now being rebuilt after a damaging fire, was the last of the great China clippers, a speedy square-rigger that once ran tea from the Orient to Europe. When reopened, it will contains a collection of ship figureheads, its own being the witch who pursued Tam O'Shanter in the Robert Burns poem, getting so close she pulled off his horse's tail: she is wearing a "cutty sark" – a cut-down shift. During rebuilding, an adjacent exhibition is open to visitors.

Nearby sits the tiny ***Gipsy Moth IV***, the yacht in which Sir Francis Chichester sailed solo round the world in 1966.

Take the river boat further downstream to catch a glimpse of the **Thames Barrier** ❸ *(see caption, opposite page).*

Upstream: gardens and grand houses

River boats go upriver from Charing Cross, too, past Westminster and Lambeth to Battersea and Chelsea, followed, on the north bank, by the District tube line, and on the south bank by the overground train line from Waterloo. Opposite the Peace Pagoda in **Battersea Park** ❹, erected for the 1985 Year of Peace by Japanese Buddhists, is Sir Christopher Wren's **Chelsea Hospital** ❺ and beyond, the upmarket development at **Chelsea Harbour** ❻. But the leafy riverbank does not really begin until **Putney** ❼, where the university boat race between Oxford and Cambridge universities begins each March. Putney can be reached by river boat, or by taking the District Line to Putney Bridge.

Beyond is Hammersmith Bridge. The Piccadilly and District tube lines go to Hammersmith, the starting point of a riverside walk that leads to Chiswick and has a number of popular riverside pubs, such as the Dove on Upper Mall; this historic 18th-century tavern is where the words of *Rule, Britannia* are supposed to have been written by James Thomson.

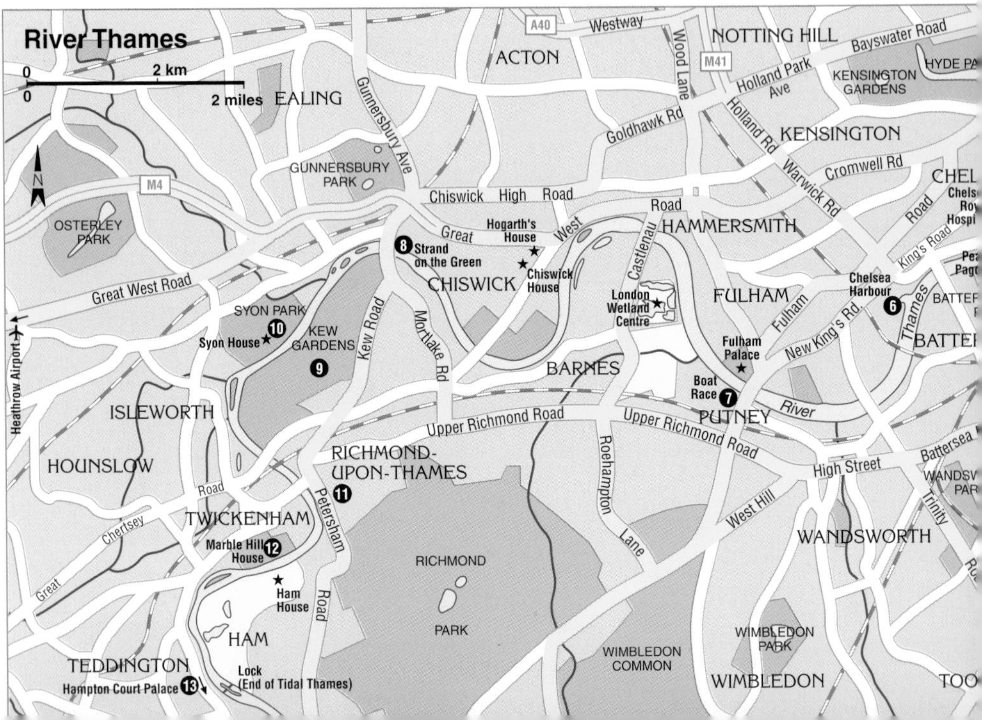

River Thames

0 2 km
0 2 miles

EALING
ACTON
NOTTING HILL
KENSINGTON
HAMMERSMITH
CHISWICK
FULHAM
BARNES
PUTNEY
WANDSWORTH
ISLEWORTH
HOUNSLOW
TWICKENHAM
RICHMOND-UPON-THAMES
HAM
TEDDINGTON
WIMBLEDON
GUNNERSBURY PARK
OSTERLEY PARK
SYON PARK
KEW GARDENS
RICHMOND PARK
WIMBLEDON COMMON
WIMBLEDON PARK
KENSINGTON GARDENS
❽ Strand on the Green
Hogarth's House
Chiswick House
❾
❿ Syon House
⓫
⓬ Marble Hill House
Ham House
⓭ Hampton Court Palace
Lock (End of Tidal Thames)
London Wetland Centre
Fulham Palace
Boat Race ❼
Chelsea Harbour ❻
Heathrow Airport
Great West Road
Chiswick High Road
Upper Richmond Road
Goldhawk Rd
Cromwell Rd
Westway
Wood Lane
Holland Park Ave
Bayswater Road
Gunnersbury Ave
Kew Road
Mortlake Rd
Roehampton Lane
West Hill
High Street
New King's Rd
Petersham Road
Chertsey Road
Castelnau
King's Road

Recommended Restaurants and Pubs on page 155

Strand on the Green ❽, just beyond, has lively Georgian houses and charming fishermen's cottages. After your walk, try one of the good riverside pubs, including the Bull's Head and City Barge, both nearly 400 years old.

A further diversion at Chiswick is **Hogarth's House** (Tues–Sun pm only; tel: 020-8994 6757), a 17th-century mansion now filled with engravings and personal relics of one of England's most famous artists. **Chiswick House**, an early 18th-century Palladian villa designed by the third Earl of Burlington, is even more delightful. (Overground train from Waterloo to Chiswick, or District or Piccadilly tube lines to Turnham Green; Easter–Oct Wed–Sun 10am–5pm; tel: 020-8995 0508).

Tropical house in Kew

Kew, a quiet suburb upstream and across the Thames from Chiswick, plays host to the Royal Botanic Gardens, often called simply **Kew Gardens** ❾, 300 acres (120 hectares) of exotic plants from around the world (daily; tel: 020-8332 5655). The gardens were first planted in 1759 under the direction of Princess Augusta, who was then living on the site. In 1772, George III put Kew in the hands of botanist Sir Joseph Banks, who had just returned from a round-the-world expedition to collect plant specimens with Captain Cook, and the collection grew and grew. There are special areas given over to redwoods, orchids, roses, rhododendrons, alpine and desert plants and Kew is now a Unesco World Heritage site.

The most famous of Kew's nurseries is the **Palm House**, a vast Victorian pavilion of steel and glass that contains hundreds of tropical plants. The ecologically correct and energy-saving **Princess of Wales Conservatory**, opened in 1987, has 10 climatic zones, ranging from arid to moist tropical, under one roof.

The Thames Barrier, with the O_2 arena in the background. The barrier, a steel wall stretching 1,700 ft (520 metres) across the Thames, protects London from the danger of flooding. (visitor centre at 1 Unit Way open Apr–Sept 11am–4pm, Oct–Mar 10.30am–4pm; tel: 020-8305 4188; nearest train station is Charlton, 20 minutes' walk.)

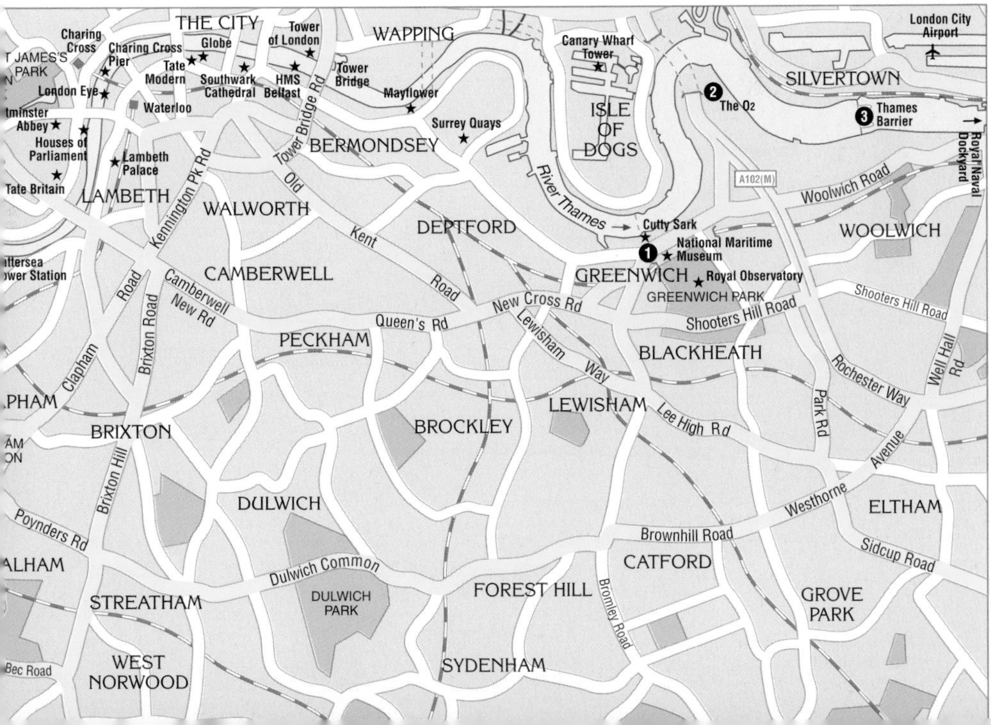

Ham House, built in 1610, has delightful gardens. Cavaliers and Roundheads do fierce battle each spring on the Ham House grounds as part of a three-week Richmond Festival.

BELOW: 19th-century glasshouses at Kew Gardens, a leading centre for botanical research.

Across the Thames from Kew is another famous botanical centre – **Syon Park** ❿. The Dukes of Northumberland built a great mansion here in the 16th century while the lush gardens were added by the great English landscape gardener, "Capability" Brown *(see page 219)*. **Syon House**, a neo-Classical building remodelled in the 18th century by Robert Adam, has a lavish baroque interior and vivid conservatory (house open Mar–Oct Wed, Thur, Sun 11am–5pm; tel: 020-8560 0881).

In Syon Park's **Tropical Forest** (daily 10am– 5.30pm) in Syon Park, children can have a "close encounter" with a variety of exotic animals (snakes, toads, tarantulas, caiman). Feeding time is at 1pm at weekends and during school holidays, and other wildlife includes marmosets, parrots and a raccoon.

To reach Syon Park from central London, take the District Line to Gunnersbury, then the 237 or 267 bus to Brent Lea Gate. From Kew, cross Kew Bridge and take the bus.

Richmond-upon-Thames

Reachable by overland train from Waterloo or via the District tube line, or on foot along the towpath from Kew, **Richmond-upon-Thames** ⓫ retains its village atmosphere with its cluster of book and antique shops, tea salons and charming riverside pubs; the Three Pigeons and the White Cross are two of the most popular. The Victorian-style **Richmond Theatre** sits on the edge of the green and is an important showcase for big-name productions on their way to the West End. **Richmond Park** was enclosed by Charles I as a royal hunting estate and is now the only royal park that keeps a large stock of deer. On the way to the park, a walk up Richmond Hill from the centre of town leads to a magnificent view west over the Thames.

Bus 65 or 371 from Richmond will take you to the flamboyant 17th-century **Ham House**, an annexe of the Victoria and Albert Museum (Easter–Oct Sun–Mon and Wed 1–5pm; tel: 020-8940 1950). Ham House contains a rich collection of period paintings (including Reynolds and Van Dyck), tapestries, furniture, carpets and clothing.

Recommended Restaurants and Pubs below

Richmond Bridge leads across to **Twickenham**, known for its many mansions. It is also the home of English rugby (international games are staged in winter at the huge Twickenham Rugby Football Ground). The 18th-century **Marble Hill House** ⓬ on Richmond Road is a Palladian-style dwelling that has long provided a retreat for the secret affairs of the Crown. Both George II and George IV kept their mistresses in this mansion. Today the house contains a fine picture gallery and a lovely garden, the scene of outdoor Shakespeare productions and concerts in summer (Mar–Oct Sat 10am–2pm, Sun until 5pm). Riverside Twickenham offers a number of worthy pubs including the White Swan, the Eel Pie and the Barmy Arms.

Hampton Court Palace

Above Twickenham is Teddington, the first lock that marks the end of the tidal Thames, and then **Hampton Court Palace** ⓭. Its two distinctive architectural styles make it both the paragon of the Tudor style and the self-proclaimed English version of Versailles (Mon 10.15am, Tue–Sun 9.30am winter closing 4.30pm, summer 6pm; tel: 020-8781 9500). In the early 16th century, Hampton Court was built by Cardinal Wolsey as the finest and most flamboyant residence in the realm. When Wolsey fell from grace, he gave the palace to Henry VIII in a futile attempt to regain favour. The king instantly fell in love with it and moved there with Anne Boleyn. He ordered the construction of the Great Hall, the Clock Court and the Library, and enlarged the gardens. It is said that Elizabeth I used Hampton Court as an illicit love nest away from the prying eyes of Westminster. She also planted the gardens with exotic trees and flowers brought to England from the New World by Sir Francis Drake and Sir Walter Raleigh.

In the 1690s, the sumptuous **State Apartments** were designed by Wren for William and Mary, who also commissioned the famous Maze and the Tijou grillework atop the entrance gates. Today the 1,000 rooms are filled with paintings, tapestries and furnishings from the past 450 years. ❑

The King's Staircase in the State Apartments of William III, Hampton Court Palace. The paintings are by Antonio Verrio (c.1639–1707).

RESTAURANTS

Greenwich

Davy's Wine Vaults
159–161 Greenwich High Road, SE10. Tel: 020-8858 7204. L & D Mon-Sat, L only Sun **££**
Informed wine, good food. Sunday lunch until 5pm.

Inside
19 Greenwich South Street, SE10. Tel 020-8265 5060. L & D Tue–Sat, Br Sat, L Sun. **£££**
Reliable local serving Modern European dishes, such as pan-fried sea bass and barbary duck.

SE10 Restaurant & Bar
62 Thames Street, SE10. Tel: 020-8858 9764. L & D Mon–Sat, L only Sun. **£££**
Popular place specialising in good fish and shellfish.

The Spread Eagle
1–2 Stockwell Street, SE10 Tel: 020-8853 2333. L & D daily. **£££**
French restaurant in a 17th-century coaching inn. Excellent wine list.

Kew

The Glasshouse
14 Station Parade, Kew, TW9. Tel: 020-8940 6777. L & D daily. **££** (set lunch), **££££**
One of SW London's culinary hotspots. Modern French-inspired cuisine.

The Orangery
Kew Gardens, TW9. Tel: 020-8332 5655. 10am till one hour before Gardens close. **£**
Enjoy coffee, lunch or afternoon tea in this elegant Grade-I listed building.

Richmond

Chez Lindsay
11 Hill Rise, TW10. Tel: 020-8948 7473. L & D daily. **£** (set lunch), **££**
Breton fishing village atmosphere, with superb fish, shellfish, *galettes*, *crêpes* and *steak-frites*.

H_2O
Floating Restaurant, Richmond Riverside, TW10. Tel: 020-8948 0220. L & D daily. **££**
The roof of this old bridge-side barge is a great lunch spot. The Italian food isn't as good as the location.

Petersham Nurseries
Off Petersham Road, TW10. Tel: 020-8605 3627. Seasonal – call for details. **£££**
Enchanting café with tables around a greenhouse.

Tootsies
Hotham House, Riverside Richmond, TW9. Tel: 020-8948 3436. L & D daily. **£**
Good burgers and steaks and a great location.

The Richmond Café
58 Hill Rise, TW10. Tel: 020-8940 9561. L & D daily. **£** (set lunch), **££**
Good-value Thai food and friendly service.

Prices for a three-course dinner per person with a half-bottle of house wine:
£ = under £20
££ = £20–45
£££ = £45–60

The English Season

The Season is when high society is on display. The events are mostly sporting, but a sense of style is more important than a sense of fair play

The English Season was an invention of upper-crust Londoners as a series of mid-summer amusements. This was the time when young girls "came out" at society balls, at which eligible young men would be waiting to make a suitable match. Mission accomplished, the families would repair to their country homes. The presence of royalty is an important ingredient, and the royal family has long taken a keen interest in the sports highlighted by the Season.

The events, cynics say, are completely insignificant compared to their importance as social gatherings. People who care nothing for rowing attend Henley Regatta in the first week of July; philistine amateurs flock to the Royal Academy's Summer Exhibition; the musically challenged die for a ticket to Glyndebourne's opera season on the south coast; and ill-informed people queueing for tickets to Wimbledon seem to think it's the only tennis tournament in the world.

Above: blazers are donned for Cowes Week, held off the south coast in August, the peak of the sailing season.

Above: Bein tennis umpire Wimbledon at end of June c take nerves steel as the play fight it out in game's championsh

Left: George Bernard Shaw's Eliza Doolittle, playe here by Audrey Hepburn in *A Fair Lady*, faced her big test Royal Ascot, held in June. Her task? To convince fashionable society that she was a lady, nc a cockney flower seller.

ABOVE: Life's a picnic at the Henley Regetta, held in the Oxfordshire town at the beginning of July. Some people even take an occasional break to watch the rowing championships.

ABOVE: The Chelsea Flower Show in May has everything you need for the garden – and a few things you probably don't.

BELOW: International Polo Day is held at the Guards Polo Club, Windsor Great Park, in July. Cartier's sponsorship sets the tone.

THE ALTERNATIVE SEASON

Muddy fields and dripping camp sites don't dampen the spirits of those attending the "alternative" season – the annual round of music festivals. The larger ones attract the best bands from around the world and you don't have to be a hippy, crustie or a member of a youth tribe to attend. Many people take a tent to the large weekend events.

The largest rock event, the Glastonbury Festival *(above)* in Somerset, takes place at the end of June. More than 1,000 performances are given on 17 stages by more than 500 bands, and attracts big names from Amy Winehouse to Leonard Cohen. Tickets can sell out quickly.

If you can't get to Glastonbury, try the two-day Big Chill festival which takes place in early August in the rolling Herefordshire hills. This is a family-oriented, eco-conscious event, with a wide variety of music vying with art, dance and film.

The best world music festival is Womad, held in Malmesbury, Wiltshire, in mid-July. There are workshops and arts and crafts, with good facilities for families. The Reading Festival in late August attracts some of the best US rock groups, and the Cambridge Folk Festival takes place in July.

BELOW: Glyndebourne, a summer opera location charmingly set on the South Downs near Brighton, is renowned as much for its lavish picnic hampers as it is for the performances of its star singers.

Recommended Restaurants and Pubs on page 165

THE THAMES VALLEY

Winding its way across the western Home Counties of Buckinghamshire, Berkshire and Oxfordshire, the Thames crosses some of the gentlest and most quintessentially English of landscapes

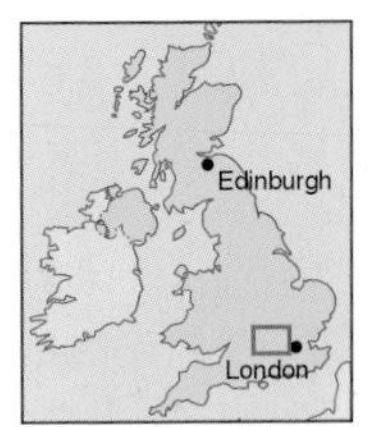

The banks of this historic waterway have seen civilisations come and go. On the twin hills of Sinodun, south of Dorchester-on-Thames, the early Britons built a major camp as early as 1500 BC. (*Dun* means fort in Celtic.) After the arrival of Caesar, the Romans did the same, and the remains of both settlements can be seen today. The Thames is a river of plenty and has made its valley a fertile farmland. In the Middle Ages the river was so thick with salmon even the poor ate it as a staple. Great abbeys and monasteries flourished here, and kings and queens have made it their home.

Runnymede

To fly-fishermen, the Thames Valley begins at Bell Weir Lock just a mile north of **Staines**, south of the M4 beside the orbital M25. From Bell Weir north to the river's source (a muddy patch in a field near Coates in Gloucestershire), the river is bordered almost continuously by hills. On the west side of the motorway is Egham and the riverside meadow at **Runnymede** ❶ where, on 15 June 1215, King John signed the Magna Carta. Tradition maintains that the barons encamped on one side of the Thames while the king's forces occupied the other. Magna Carta Island, the larger of the two river islands, was the neutral ground on which they met. Above is **Cooper's Hill**, which affords a panoramic view of Windsor Castle to the north.

At the bottom of the hill lies the Magna Carta Memorial, an uninspiring structure presented by the American Bar Association in recognition of the charter's influence on the American Constitution. Nearby is the John F. Kennedy Memorial, standing in the plush acre that, in 1965, the Queen gave to the United States in perpetuity.

A pleasant diversion from Runnymede follows the riverside road from Staines to **Datchet** ❷. This was once the Datchet Lane mentioned in Shakespeare's comedy *The Merry Wives of Windsor*, along which Sir John Falstaff

Main attractions

RUNNYMEDE
WINDSOR CASTLE
LEGOLAND
ETON
MAIDENHEAD
COOKHAM
HENLEY-ON-THAMES
SONNING
DORCHESTER
ABINGDON

LEFT: Windsor Castle. **BELOW:** the Queen owns unmarked Thames swans.

Like Buckingham Palace in London, Windsor Castle has a Changing of the Guard ceremony (Apr–June Mon–Sat 11am, alternate days July–Mar).

was carried in a basket of dirty linen to be ducked in the Thames.

Windsor's royal castle

England's most famous castle lies across the river from Datchet at **Windsor** ❸, 50 minutes by train from London's Waterloo (direct) or Paddington (change at Slough; daily Mar–Oct 10am–5.30pm, Nov–Feb 10am–4pm; tel: 01753-831118). Since the reign of Henry I in the 12th century, Windsor Castle has been the chief residence of English and British sovereigns. William the Conqueror founded the original structure, a wooden building that consisted most likely of a motte and two large baileys enclosed by palisades. The stone fortifications were built in the 12th and 13th centuries. Rising dramatically on a chalk cliff, the castle you see today incorporates additions by nearly every sovereign since. In the 19th century, George IV and Queen Victoria spent almost £1 million on additions. The late 20th century saw great restoration of the interior, in particular of **St George's Chapel** (closed Sun except for worship), the worst casualty of a disastrous fire in 1992.

Part of the Lower Ward, St George's Chapel is one of the finest examples of Perpendicular architecture in England (rivalled only by King's College Chapel at Cambridge and the Henry VII Chapel at Westminster). Dedicated to the patron saint of the Order of the Garter, the chapel displays in the choir stalls the swords, helmets, mantles and banners of the respective knights.

In the Upper Ward are the **State Apartments**. These serve as accommodation for visiting foreign sovereigns and are occasionally closed to the public. Lavishly furnished, they include many important paintings from the royal collection, including works by Rubens, Van

BELOW: Windsor Castle has extensive gardens.

Recommended Restaurants and Pubs on page 165

Dyck, Canaletto and Reynolds. There are also drawings by Holbein, Michelangelo, Leonardo and Raphael.

The Round Tower is what everyone thinks of as Windsor Castle. Climb the 220 steps for the wide valley view, but don't try to see the east side of the Upper Ward which houses the Queen's private apartments. Instead, venture outside and south of the castle to the **Great Park**, more than 4,800 acres (1,920 hectares) of lush greenery. The **Savill Garden**, renowned for its rhododendrons, incorporates a landscaped garden created to mark the Queen's Golden Jubilee.

Legoland

As a complete contrast, there is **Legoland Windsor** (mid-Mar–end Oct, variable opening days/hours, mid-July–end Aug, until 7pm; tel: 08705-040404). Some 2 miles (3 km) from the town centre on the B3022 Windsor/Ascot road, this is a popular (and expensive) theme park based around the children's building blocks – in this case, millions of them. Its 150 acres (60 hectares) of wooded landscape includes rides, shows and workshops. Lego is a contraction of two Danish words, *Leg Godt*, meaning "play well" and the park puts a worthy emphasis on learning as well as having fun. (Shuttle buses run from Windsor; Greenline buses run from London Victoria, tel: 0870-608 7261.)

Eton

Across the river from Windsor is **Eton College**, that most famous of English public schools, founded in 1440 by 18-year-old Henry VI. The original set of buildings included a collegiate church, an attached grammar school and an almshouse. It was Henry's intention that the church and school become a place of pilgrimage and devotion to the Virgin.

The Thames between Windsor and Eton. The river, which rises in Gloucestershire and flows into the North Sea, is 215 miles (346km) long. In London, where it is tidal, the level rises at high tide by 23 ft (7 metres) and the currents are strong enough to drown most people who fall in before they can be rescued.

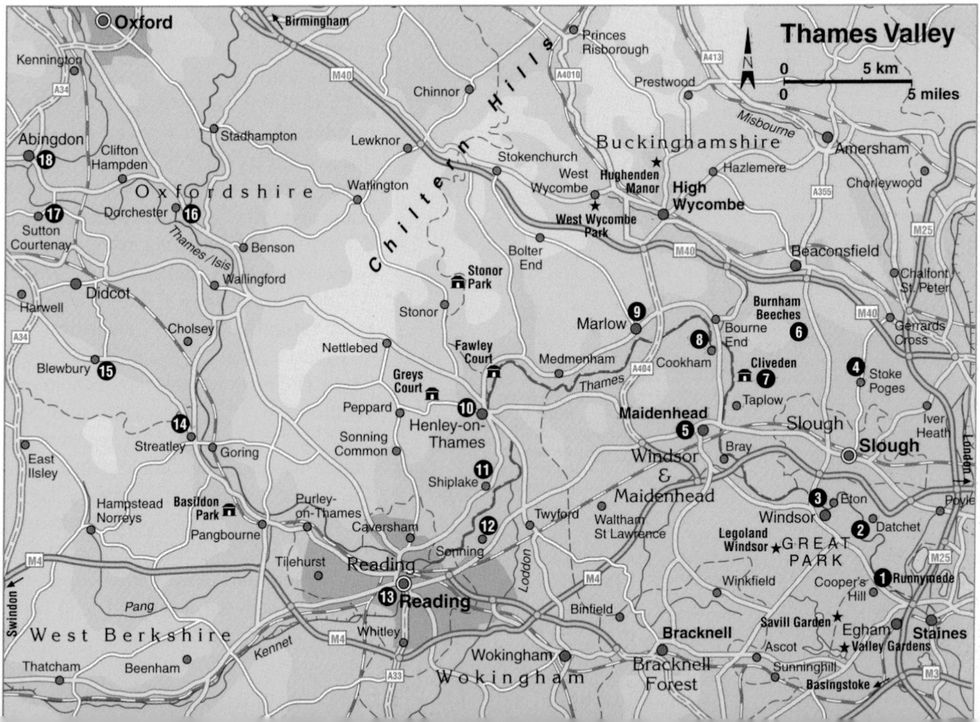

In the Middle Ages, all swans on the Thames belonged to the Crown. Two London guilds were later allowed to own swans as well. Each July, in the ceremony of "Swan Upping", the beaks of cygnets are marked to show ownership by the Crown.

The Wars of the Roses cut him short. He was murdered in the Tower of London and every year on the anniversary of his death an Etonian lays a wreath of lilies in the cell in which he died.

To the visitor, Eton is a cluster of red-brick Tudor buildings with little towers and hulking chimneys. The **School Yard** (the outer quadrangle), the **Long Chamber** and the **Lower School** all date from the 15th century. The chapel, in Perpendicular style, has 15th-century wall paintings depicting the miracles and legends of the Virgin. Most of the windows were damaged in World War II, but some of the modern installations are interesting. The cloisters dating from the 1440s are stunning; beyond them stretch the fields on which, according to the Duke of Wellington, the Battle of Waterloo was won.

Eton, described as "the chief nurse of England's statesmen", boards 1,300 boys and the pupil-teacher ratio is 10 to one.

Stoke Poges ❹, north of Eton and beyond **Slough** (a dull commuter town to avoid) is the final resting place of the poet Thomas Gray and the inspiration for his *Elegy Written in a Country Churchyard*. The monument erected in 1799 commemorates him with a maudlin inscription, but the sheer beauty of the churchyard – its old lychgates, its rose bushes and its garden of remembrance – is what attracts visitors.

BELOW: Cliveden, former seat of the Astors and now a luxury hotel.

Maidenhead

Half a dozen miles (10 km) upriver from Eton lies **Maidenhead ❺**, the starting point of some of the most beautiful countryside in the valley. Known in medieval times as "Maydenhythe", one suggested meaning being maidens' landing place, its bridges are its most interesting feature: the 128-ft (38-metre) arches of Brunel's Railway Bridge are the largest brick spans ever constructed.

From Maidenhead the A4130 goes 8 miles (13 km) directly to Henley, but there are several picturesque villages and towns clustered on either side of the river nearby. **Bray**, nestled in a bend in the Thames just south of Maidenhead, has a lovely church that dates from 1293. The **Jesus Hospital**, founded in 1627, is also interesting, and still cares for 26 older citizens from a trust set up by its originator.

Taplow is another pretty village on the north side of the Thames opposite Maidenhead. From here, a road runs through Burnham to **Burnham Beeches ❻**, a pastoral stretch of 375 wooded acres (150 hectares).

Upstream from Maidenhead is **Cliveden Reach**, another wooded tract, this one owned by the National Trust. The house called **Cliveden ❼**, once the home of a Prince of Wales, several dukes and the Astor family, is poised dramatically above cliffs. Before World War II Nancy Astor turned it into a meeting place for politicians and celebrities.

Today, Cliveden is run as a luxury hotel. The main rooms are viewable part of the year (Apr–Oct Thur and Sun 3–5.30pm). The gardens are open to the public and are decorated with Roman fountains, temples and topiary (mid-Mar–Oct daily 11am–6pm, Nov until 4pm; tel: 01628-605069). Maps, available at the entrance, show suggested walks through the woodland with spectacular views of the Thames.

Recommended Restaurants and Pubs on page 165

Cookham

Cookham ❽ is yet another picturesque riverside village, though it is best known as the home of the artist Stanley Spencer (1891–1959). Spencer's painting of Cookham Bridge hangs in London's Tate Britain. The Stanley Spencer Gallery, dedicated to his work, is housed in the King's Hall on Cookham High Street where he attended Sunday School (Easter–Oct daily 10.30am–5.30pm, Nov–Easter Sat–Sun 11am–4pm).

A copy of his painting of the *Last Supper* hangs in Holy Trinity Church, parts of which date from the 12th century. The 15th-century tower is unusual; it is one of the few church towers with both a clock and a sundial.

Six miles (9 km) upriver is **Marlow** ❾, the market town in which Mary Wollstonecraft wrote *Frankenstein*. In 1817 she lived in West Street ("Poets' Row") with her husband, the poet Shelley, while he was writing the poem, *The Revolt of Islam*. In Saxon times, Marlow was known as "Merelaw" but what you see today is comparatively new: the suspension bridge and **All Saints Church** date from the 1830s. The rustic walks along the river below Marlow Lock are refreshing, as is **Quarry Wood**, 25,000 acres (10,000 hectares) of beechwoods on the Berkshire bank.

Henley-on-Thames

Henley-on-Thames ❿, a small market town with many old buildings, has been known for its races since 1839, when it hosted the world's first river regatta. The four-day Henley Royal Regatta, usually held in the first week of July *(see page 156)*, attracts rowers from all over the globe. It also attracts an audience of near-Edwardian elegance – white linen dresses, straw hats and bottles of bubbly. Less celebrated regattas are held at weekends throughout the summer.

As its name implies, the **River & Rowing Museum** in Mill Meadows (summer Mon–Sun 10am–5.30pm, winter until 5pm; tel: 01491-415600) casts its net wider than just rowing to include a recreation of *The Wind in the Willows*, Kenneth Grahame's much-loved children's classic, published in 1908.

Watchful umpires at Henley's regatta.

BELOW: the Henley Royal Regatta, started in 1839, attracts more than 100 crews from outside Britain.

Through Streatley runs the Ridgeway, one of Britain's most ancient paths, still popular with visitors, going north over the Berkshire Downs to Dunstable and west through the Vale of the White Horse to the magic stone circles of Avebury and Stonehenge.

There are several stately homes around Henley, but the most exquisite is **Greys Court**. West of Henley on the road to Peppard, this well-preserved Tudor house has remains of an earlier manor house dating from the 14th century (Apr–Sept Wed, Thur and Fri 2–5pm; tel: 01491-628529). There is a crenellated tower, a huge wheel once used for drawing water using donkey-power and a maze.

Shiplake ⓫ is a sprawling village notable for its church, rebuilt in 1689, but housing excellent 15th-century stained glass from the abbey church of Saint-Bertin in Saint-Omer, France. Tennyson was married here in 1850.

Sonning

Shiplake is best visited en route to **Sonning** ⓬, considered by many as the prettiest of Thames villages. The little islands that rise here in the river make the views especially pastoral. In Saxon times, Sonning was the centre of a large diocese, with a Cathedral, a Bishop's Palace and a Deanery. Today, only parts of the Deanery garden walls remain, though the present church incorporates fragments of Saxon work. The old houses in the village are well preserved. The half-timbered **White Hart Inn** is 500 years old and has a lovely rose garden. The bridge at Sonning is one of the oldest on the river and, on the Oxfordshire side, there is a picturesque mill.

Reading ⓭ is the single industrial town in the lower valley; an important traffic hub and retail centre and famous for its annual rock festival, but a somewhat dreary place capitalising on the Thames Valley's aspiration to be Silicon Valley. The playwright Oscar Wilde (1854–1900) was broken by two years' hard labour in the red-brick jail.

Streatley ⓮ and **Goring**, 10 miles (16 km) north of the A329, face each other on either side of the river. Streatley is the prettier of the two, situated at the foot of the Berkshire Downs. Five miles (8 km) northwest is **Blewbury** ⓯, a lovely town with thatched cottages, watercress beds and winding lanes.

Upriver about 8 miles (13 km) is **Dorchester** ⓰. This ancient town was, at different times, a Roman fort (Durocina) and a cathedral city. The abbey church was spared demolition at the Dissolution by a local resident who

BELOW: Sonning, which Jerome K. Jerome in his humorous 1889 novel *Three Men in a Boat* called "the most fairy-like little nook on the whole river."

Recommended Restaurants and Pubs below

bought it from the Crown for £140. The stained glass in the nave dates from the 14th century. In the chancel is a Jesse Window in which Jesse, Christ's ancestor, lies on the sill with a fruit vine springing from his belly. The High Street, which follows the line of the Roman road to Silchester, is lined with timber-framed buildings.

Sutton Courtenay ⓱ and **Clifton Hampden** are riverside villages with lush willow trees hanging low over the banks. There's good swimming here in summer. Sutton Courtenay is especially interesting, with a well-preserved Norman church and a cluster of medieval houses nearby. In the graveyard is the resting place of Eric Blair (1903–50), better known as the writer George Orwell.

Abingdon

After Sutton Courtenay the river turns north, on its way to **Abingdon** ⓲ on the doorstep of Oxford. This old town sprang up in the 7th century around a powerful Benedictine mitred abbey. In the 14th century the townspeople led a bloody uprising against the monks, though it was not until the Dissolution that the abbey lost its power. Most of the ecclesiastical buildings were destroyed – don't be fooled by the 19th-century artificial ruins in the abbey grounds. But there are some authentic remains. These include the abbey **Gateway**, the 13th-century **Checker** (with its idiosyncratic chimney) and the 15th-century **Long Gallery**.

Dating from 1682, Abingdon's Town Hall, of the open-ground-floor type, was built by Sir Christopher Wren's mason, responsible for the dome of St Paul's Cathedral in London. East Saint Helen's, with the church at the foot, is perhaps the prettiest street. ❑

Dorchester Abbey. Today's building was begun in the 12th century, replacing two earlier Saxon cathedrals, and was enhanced over the next 500 years. It is still used for worship and for concerts.

RESTAURANTS

Bray

The Fat Duck
1 High Street
Tel: 01628-580333 ££££
Heston Blumenthal creates complex, adventurous dishes such as snail porridge and nitro-scrambled egg-and-bacon ice cream. His brand of modern British cookery and quest for new taste sensations earned him three Michelin stars. There's a sample menu.

The Waterside Inn
Ferry Road
Tel: 01628-620691 £££
In an idyllic spot overlooking the Thames, this is one of England's most exceptional restaurants. Three Michelin stars.

Epsom Downs

Le Raj
211 Firtree Road
Tel: 01737-371064 £
Stylish Bangladeshi cuisine with a good reputation.

Goring-on-Thames

The Leatherne Bottel
On the B4009 north of Goring
Tel: 01491-872667 ££
An old riverside inn. Excellent food, imaginatively produced, fresh ingredients.

Henley-on-Thames

La Bodega
38 Hart Street
Tel: 01491-578611 ££
Spacious tapas bar and restaurant with comprehensive menu and good choice of Spanish wines.

Shinfield

L'Ortolan
The Old Vicarage, Church Lane
Tel: 01189-888500 £££
Innovative Anglo-French cuisine. Stunning flavours and a feast for the eye as well as the tastebuds.

Sonning Eye

The Mill at Sonning
Sonning Eye, Reading
Tel: 0118-969 8000 ££
Theatre/restaurant in old mill. Combined price for lunch and matinee or dinner and evening show. Nice setting, average food.

Windsor

Browns
The Promenade, Barry Avenue
Tel: 01753-831976 ££
Although part of a chain, this bar and brasserie is reliable. Many cocktails.

Carpenters Arms
Market Street. £
Victorian-style family pub. Good ales, affordable food.

Oakley Court
Windsor Road, Water Oakley
Tel: 01753-609988 £££
Elegant and formal, with wood panelling, high ceilings. Modern European food.

Prices for a three-course dinner per person with a half-bottle of house wine:
£ = under £25
££ = £25–50
£££ = £50–100
££££ = +£100

City & Rail Stn 5

Recommended Restaurants and Pubs on pages 186–7

OXFORD TO STRATFORD

The triangle of Britain between Oxford, Warwick and the River Severn contains history, culture and architectural style which seem to grow out of the ground. At its heart are the Cotswolds

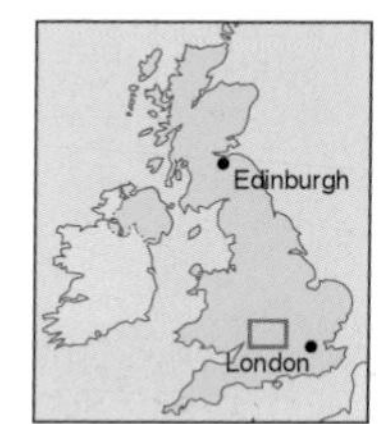

The Cotswolds are part of a range of limestone hills which stretch from the Dorset coast northeast to Lincolnshire. What distinguishes them here is oolite. Oolite, called egg-stone because it looks like the roe of a fish, is the fine-grained freestone that has given a special character to the houses, barns, churches and pigsties from the hills' edge above Chipping Camden to the southern full stop at Bath. More than in any other region of Britain, the buildings here are organic, shaped by local hands.

The stone takes on colours from gold to blue-grey, and responds with different hues to changing weather conditions in a quite remarkable way. In Oxford these stones glisten wet after a noontime shower, and none of their warmth has left those that were used to build the rose-covered cottages of Stratford-upon-Avon, or Warwick Castle and the timbered Tudor houses that still nestle beneath the castle.

As if to reinforce the idea of a natural triangle, this area of the west Midlands is now enclosed by motorways on its three sides: the M4 from London to Bristol at its base; the M40 from London to Birmingham via Oxford and Warwick on the eastern side; the M5 from Birmingham to Bristol on the west. A good hopping-off point to the region is Oxford, which is about one hour's drive (60 miles/95 km) from both London and Birmingham. London's Paddington Station serves the region.

City of dreaming spires

When Britain's noblest river passes through **Oxford ❶**, it is not called the Thames as it is everywhere else. Instead it is called the Isis. Another river flows into it, the Cherwell (pronounced *Charwell*), and rising from the confluence of these muddy banks are the spires of that most mythologised of English cities.

However you arrive, you will see

Main attractions

OXFORD
BLENHEIM PALACE
BURFORD
BIBURY
CIRENCESTER
GLOUCESTER
CHELTENHAM
BROADWAY
CHIPPING CAMPDEN
STRATFORD-UPON-AVON
WARWICK
COVENTRY
BIRMINGHAM

PRECEDING PAGES: Chipping Steps, Tetbury.
LEFT: Oxford's High Street.
RIGHT: Magdalen College, Oxford.

Busts such as the Emperors' Heads (or Bearded Ones) put up in 1669 outside the Sheldonian Theatre were often used in antiquity to create boundaries.

them: the spire of Christ Church Cathedral, Tom Tower and Magdalen Tower. This is Oxford, the city that has given its name to many things from marmalade to movements, where undergraduates, cycling around corners, trail their gowns in the wind. But Oxford is also the site of the first Morris Motors works and since World War II it has been an industrial city as much as an academic one. Yet the twain all too rarely meet and, despite the inevitable arrival of a McDonald's in Cornmarket Street, Oxford has reached the 21st century amazingly unscathed.

A tour of Oxford is essentially a tour of the colleges, and a good starting point is **Carfax** Ⓐ. (The name derives from the French, *Quatre Voies*, "four ways".) This is the old centre of the city, around the pedestrianised area, where the four main streets meet: Cornmarket, High Street, Queen Street and St Aldate's. The tower at the northwest corner, all that remains of St Martin's Church, dates from the 14th century, and from the top of it you take in a good view of the city (daily Apr–Oct 10am–5.30pm, Nov–Mar 10am–3.30pm). From Carfax, walk south along St Aldate's (passing the impressive, neo-Jacobite Town Hall on the left) to **Christ Church** Ⓑ, the grandest of the colleges (Mon–Sat 9am–5.30pm, Sun 1–5.30pm).

Known simply as "The House", Christ Church was founded in 1525 by Cardinal Wolsey (his pointed hat is The House's insignia), on the site of an old priory said to have been established by the Saxon princess, St Frideswide. **Tom Tower** was built by Sir Christopher Wren in 1681. **Tom Quad**, the largest quadrangle in Oxford, has splendid grace and magnitude, and it was in the pool here, which is known as Mercury, that Anthony Blanche was dunked in Evelyn Waugh's influential 1945 novel, *Brideshead Revisited.*

Christ Church chapel is also the **Cathedral** of Oxford. The 144-ft (43-metre) spire is one of the earliest in England, dating from the 13th century. As well as the reconstructed tomb of St Frideswide, the cathedral also contains some exquisite stained glass, including works by the Pre-Raphaelite artist, Edward Burne-Jones. Lining the south side of the Tom Quad is the enormous **Hall** of Christ

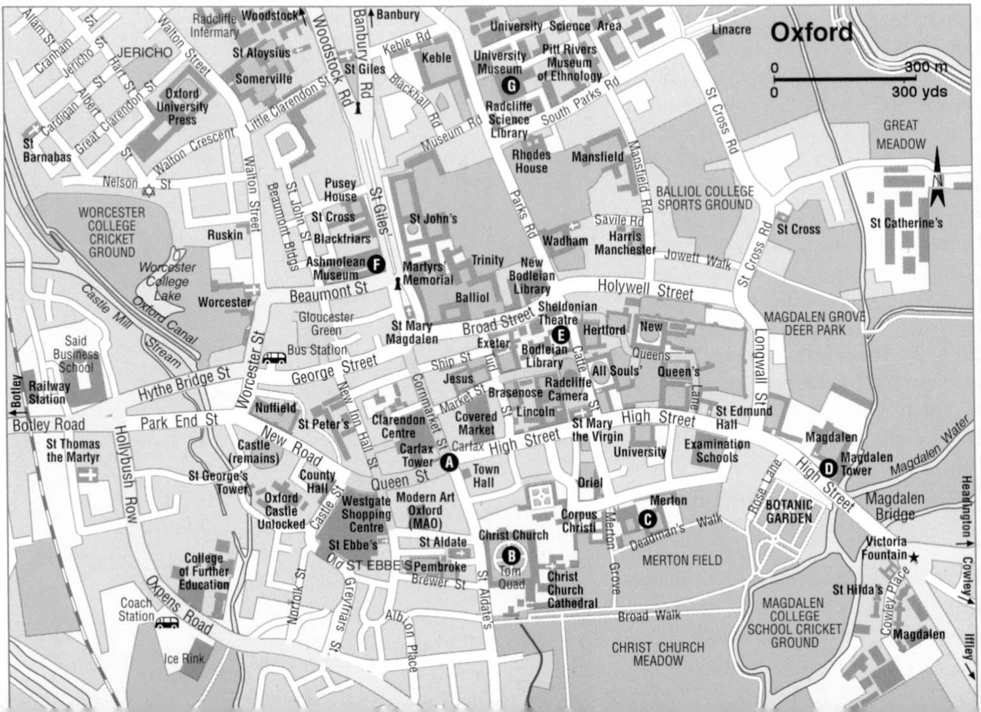

Recommended Restaurants and Pubs on pages 186–7

Church, with its magnificent hammerbeam ceiling, while away to the north is the neoclassical Peckwater Quad and the smaller Canterbury Quad, where the **Picture Gallery** has a fine collection of Renaissance paintings and drawings (Mon–Sat 10.30am–5pm, Sun 2–4.30pm). South of the college, extending down to the confluence of the Isis and Cherwell rivers, is the glorious **Meadow** where cows graze. Along the Isis are the university and college boathouses. It's here, in Eights Week at the end of May, that the summer college races take place.

College tour

From the Broad Walk, the wide path running east–west across the Meadow, there's a path cutting north to **Merton College** **C** (Mon–Fri 2–4pm, Sat–Sun 10am–4pm; free). Founded in 1264, Merton has some of the oldest buildings in Oxford. Its library in Mob Quad (the oldest complete quadrangle in Oxford) was built in the 1370s (guided tours daily at 2, 3 and 4pm. In winter tours might get cancelled). The library's 16th-century bookshelves make it the first Renaissance library in England, one where the books were set upright instead of being kept in presses. One of Merton's illustrious graduates was the writer and caricaturist Max Beerbohm (1872–1956), and in Mob Quad is a set of rooms decorated with a selection of his memorabilia.

Opposite Merton are **Corpus Christi** (1.30–4.30pm except during conferences; free) and **Oriel** (daily 1–4pm; buildings by guided tour only), smaller colleges both, though no less picturesque. The chapel at Corpus has an altarpiece ascribed to Rubens. Merton Street turns left at the top and into the **High Street** where the landmark **Magdalen Tower** **D** (pronounced *maudlin*) rises to the right.

Magdalen was founded in 1458 by William of Waynflete. The chapel is a fine example of Perpendicular architecture and the cloisters are stunning. Behind them is the **Grove**, Magdalen's deer park, and the lovely **Water Walks**, a maze of garden and stream-side paths. On the opposite side of High Street is the

Magdalen College and its celebrated bell tower, from the top of which choristers sing a Latin grace at dawn on 1 May – a tradition that dates to the tower's inauguration in 1505.

BELOW: Oxford's Bridge of Sighs.

The Radcliffe Camera. It was built in 1737–1749 to house the Radcliffe Science Library and was absorbed as a reading room of the Bodleian in 1860. Its subterranean storage space can cope with 600,000 books.

BELOW: tour in progress in the Divinity School. **RIGHT:** Blackwell's.

rose-rich **Botanic Garden** (daily 9am–5pm, until 4pm in winter).

Walking west along High Street you pass on the left the **Examination Schools**, built in 1882 in the style of a Jacobean country house with classical and Gothic elements, and on the right **St Edmund Hall** (entrance in Queen's Lane; open during daylight hours; free). This was incorporated as a college in 1957. Before that, it remained the sole survivor of the once numerous residential halls of the medieval university. The name of St Edmund Hall, founded in the mid-13th century, honours Edmund of Abingdon, who died in 1240 and was the first Oxford graduate to become Archbishop of Canterbury and be canonised.

Further west along High Street are **University College** on the left (with a Shelley memorial) and **All Souls** on the right, the only college with no undergraduates (Mon–Fri 2–4.30pm, until 4pm in winter; free). But a winding stroll along Queen's Lane will take you to the rear of **New College**. The chapel and cloisters of both are stunning, as is the garden with the remains of the medieval town wall. The lane curves and suddenly you stand beneath the Venetian bridge (built in 1903) that connects the new and old buildings of **Hertford College**.

The Bodleian Library

From here there is a lovely view of the round **Radcliffe Camera** (1749) on the left and Wren's **Sheldonian Theatre** (1669) straight ahead. Dominating the scene, however, with the magnificent **Old Schools Quadrangle** as its centrepiece, is the **Bodleian Library** **E**. This is one of the world's largest libraries, founded in 1602 by Sir Thomas Bodley. Having agreed to receive a copy of every book registered with Stationers' Hall in 1610, the library now houses more than 6 million volumes, including 50,000 precious manuscripts.

The Bodleian has never been a lending library; even Charles I was once refused the loan of a book. Beyond the main entrance of the library is the old **Divinity School**, with its fine vaulted ceiling. Although the library is not open to the public, tours can be booked at the Divinity School which include a brief look into the main hall.

Recommended Restaurants and Pubs on pages 186–7

If you actually want to buy a book rather than just look at them, **Blackwell's** in Broad Street, which started in a small room in 1879, stocks 200,000 titles. Its vast Norrington Room, carved out beneath Trinity College, has the largest display of books for sale in one room anywhere in the world.

Opposite **Balliol College** (daily 2pm–5pm) a cross in the road marks the point where the Protestant Martyrs, bishops Cranmer, Latimer and Ridley, were burnt at the stake in 1555 and 1556. Around the corner at the top end of St Giles, they are further commemorated by the **Martyrs' Memorial**, erected in 1841.

The neoclassical building opposite the Martyrs' Memorial, and the oldest public museum in Britain, is the **Ashmolean Museum** **F** (Tue–Sat 10am–5pm, Sun 2–5pm; tel: 01865-278000; free). It houses a superb collection of Italian Renaissance, Dutch still-life and modern French painting. It also has an impressive collection of 16th- and 17th-century tapestries, bronzes and silver; Greek, Roman and Egyptian sculpture; a Stradivarius, ceramics and jewellery. Between 2006 and 2009, much of the museum was rebuilt to incorporate 39 new galleries.

North along St Giles is **St John's College**, founded in 1555. Its lovely gardens, landscaped by "Capability" Brown, rival those of Wadham and Trinity as the prettiest in Oxford (daily 1–5pm; free). Behind St John's is the **Oxford University Museum** **G**, built in 19th-century neo-Gothic to the taste of the art critic John Ruskin (1819–1900). The museum is a storehouse of zoological, entomological, mineralogical and geological odds and ends (daily noon–5pm; free).

Around Oxford

There are several villages worth visiting nearby. **Iffley**, south of the city, has a well-preserved Norman church that dates from 1170 and stands gracefully and timelessly above the river. The thatched cottage is the old church school. Some 16 miles (25 km) further southwest is the market town of **Wantage** **2**, birthplace of King Alfred (AD 849–99), and 3 miles (5 km) further west is **Uffington** where the 360-ft (110-metre) **White Horse** was carved in the Iron Age at the highest point in the Berkshire Downs.

Eynsham **3**, 8 miles (13 km) west of

Most of the colleges are open daily to visitors (usually in the afternoons). However, they tend to close at exam times, and some close at the end of term when conferences are held. Check noticeboards outside each college for opening times.

BELOW: Oxford University Museum.

Sir Winston Churchill was born on 30 November 1874 in a simple room to the west of Blenheim Palace's Great Hall. It was at Blenheim that Churchill proposed to his future wife, Clementine, in the Temple of Diana. The house acted as inspiration for several of his paintings, some now on show.

Oxford along the A40, is a picturesque village with the remains of a once famous abbey. Further northwest via Witney is **Minster Lovell** ❹, which has a 15th-century cruciform church and the romantic moated ruins of Minster Lovell Hall. The remains of this 15th-century manor house stand above the Windrush River with a gloomy beauty. Francis, the 9th Baron Lovell, went into hiding here and starved to death in 1487.

Eight miles (13 km) north of Oxford on the A34 is **Blenheim Palace** ❺ (Mar–Oct daily 10.30am–5.30pm; park open all year; tel: 08700-602080; www.blenheimpalace.com), the destination not only of admirers of Sir Winston Churchill, but of those who like the natural-style gardens of Britain's best-known landscape gardener, "Capability" Brown. An afternoon stroll at Blenheim, with tea afterwards in the handsome village of Woodstock, is a quintessentially English country excursion.

Britain's largest private house, covering 7 acres (2.8 hectares) including the courtyards, the Churchills' family home is the masterpiece of the playwright and architect John Vanbrugh (1664–1726). The exterior of the palace is an orgy of the baroque style, with both Doric and Corinthian columns. Inside is a maze of magnificent state apartments and, on the ground floor, the small bedroom where Winston Churchill was born in 1874. There's also an exhibition of Churchilliana, including photographs and letters. When the house is closed, there is still the 2,500-acre (1,000-hectare) park to enjoy. Originally designed in the ornate French style by Henry Wise, the landscaping was completely redone in 1764 by Brown, who constructed a dam across the River Glyme and created the majestic lake seen today.

Cotswolds villages

Shaking off the clay of Oxford's vale, the roads west climb gradually to the heights of the edge facing the Severn and the distant mountains of Wales. Here are the Cotswold hills, broken by steep wooded valleys and rushing streams, Coln and Churn, Windrush, Dikler, Leach and Evenlode. They thrust out like fingers and detach themselves in isolated humps. Height and defensibility made their upper slopes the settlements of prehistoric man.

BELOW:
Blenheim Palace.

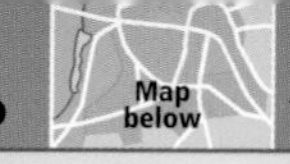

Recommended Restaurants and Pubs on pages 186–7

Their pastures and rivers provided subsistence in Roman times, and wealth for medieval peoples in the production of wool and cloth. Cirencester, 40 miles (65 km) west of Oxford, was second only to London in size in Roman Britain, and Burford, half way between the two, had its wool-merchants' guild before the Norman Conquest. Thus, the architecture of Cotswold villages was subsidised by the profits of the clothing industry. With its collapse, the Cotswolds went to sleep till pricked awake by the tourist.

The churchyard at **Burford** ❻ has tombs in the shape of wool bales. Wool merchants' houses of the 14–16th century can often be found hiding behind later fronts. Just south of Burford, at Filkins, is **Cotswold Woollen Weavers**, a traditional working mill where you can watch craftsmen spinning and weaving fleece using age-old skills (Mon–Sat 10am–6pm, Sun 2–6pm; free).

South of Filkins, **Lechlade** ❼, 22 miles (36 km) west of Oxford on the A420/A417, on the upper Thames, makes a good starting point for a circuitous tour. Below St John's Bridge cabin cruisers pass, and trout wait beside the 13th-century **Trout Inn**. No doubt William Morris, the utopian craftsman, dropped in here from his house just downstream at **Kelmscott Manor** (Apr–Sept Wed 11am–1pm, 2–5pm, various Sat; tel: 01367-252486, www.kelmscottmanor.co.uk). A typical Cotswold stone-built house, the manor has a roof of split stones, of which Morris said: "It gives me the same sort of pleasure in their orderly beauty as a fish's scales or a bird's feathers." Morris took the house with Dante Gabriel Rossetti, in 1871, and it became a centre for the pre-Raphaelite

An Edwardian steam launch cruises along the Thames towards Lechlade.

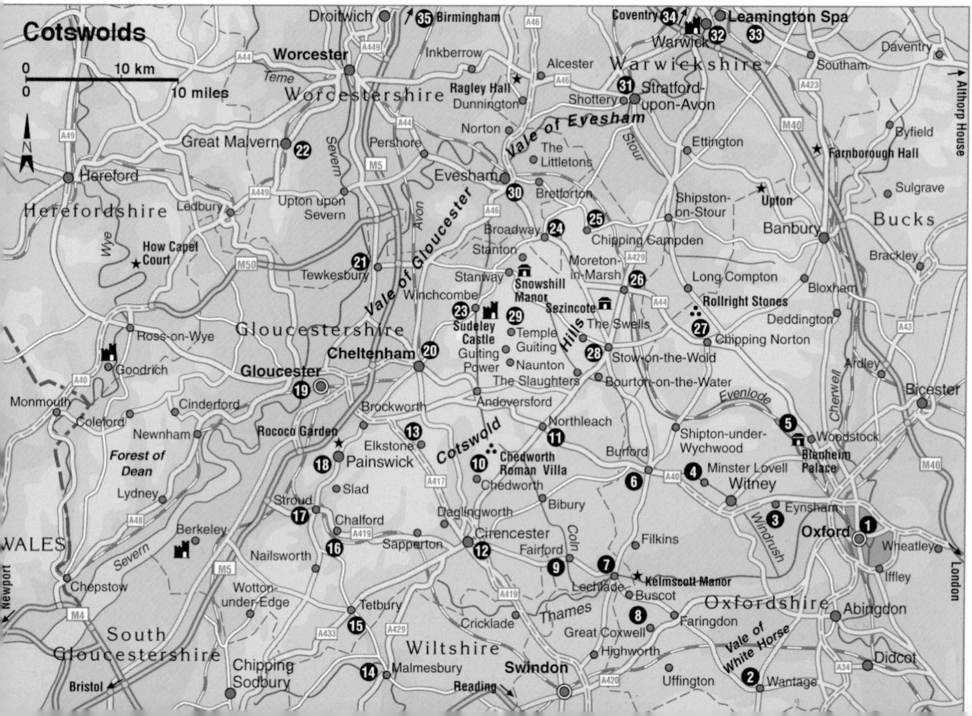

movement. His body was carried from here to the churchyard in 1896.

Morris delighted in taking friends to the tithe barn at **Great Coxwell** ❽ (daily until dusk). This cathedral among barns owes its importance to the 13th-century monks at Beaulieu Abbey in Hampshire. The great oak timbers that support the roof rest on pillars of stone taller than a man. The nave, aisles and transept convey the message that this is indeed a house of God.

Just across the river from Kelmscott is **Buscot Park** (Apr–Sept Wed–Fri and 2nd and 4th Sat–Sun in month 2–6pm; tel: 0845-3453387, www.buscot-park.com). Lord Faringdon enlarged the Adam-style house in the late 19th century, engaging the pre-Raphaelite artist Edward Burne-Jones to paint panels for the saloon and design the glass for the east window in the church.

William Morris was the leading light of the Arts and Crafts Movement. He considered the machine-made products of the Industrial Revolution sterile and ugly, and founded a company to produce hand-made textiles, wallpaper and furniture.

Rare stained glass

Mysteries you can see through right away are rare. The windows of St Mary's Church at **Fairford** ❾ (for services), 5 miles (8 km) west of Lechlade, are one of them. Was this fantastic stained glass the work of Henry VIII's master glass painter, the man who worked on King's College Chapel, Cambridge? Or was it a prize taken from a captured ship? Did it come, perhaps, from the Netherlands, and did Dürer have a hand in it? Was the glass made for the church, or the church built for the glass? How did it survive the Civil War? Speculation aside, the "Last Judgment" is a masterpiece, and the red and blue devils, all with spiked teeth and yellow horns, are wonderfully frightening.

Five miles (8 km) north of Fairford, up the River Coln, is the beautiful village of **Bibury**. William Morris is credited with having discovered it, but Bibury's beauty has been there for all to see since the 17th century. **Arlington Row's** gables and high-pitched roofs are the very essence of the Cotswolds. These stone-built cottages, beside a stream running from the mill, once housed weavers, who dried the cloth on Rack Isle, now a wild fowl reserve. The nearby 17th-century **Arlington Mill** (daily 8am–6pm) still has its working machinery, and has a fine display of Arts and Crafts furniture.

To the west of Bibury, the Cirencester–

BELOW: Bibury, described by The artist and craftsman William Morris (1834–96) as "the most beautiful village in England."

Northleach road (A429) follows the route of the original Roman road, the Fosse Way. **Chedworth** ❿, on the left, 5 miles (8 km) north of Cirencester, has cottages scattered in terraces above the river. The woods below shelter what is probably the country's best-preserved **Roman villa** (Tue–Sun Apr–Oct 10am–5pm, Mar and early Nov 11am–4pm), dating from AD 180 and covering an area of 6½ acres (2.6 hectares). The baths are especially well preserved, and the mosaics are made from two varieties of local Cotswold stone.

The church tower at **Northleach** ⓫, 10 miles (16 km) northeast of Cirencester, soars above the rooftops in the Perpendicular style. The wool merchants who built the church are remembered in the fine memorial brasses dating from the 15th and 16th centuries. In the town centre, **Keith Harding's World of Mechanical Music** (daily 10am–6pm) is concerned with the intricacies of antique musical boxes and clocks, gramophones and self-playing pianos.

Cirencester

The Fosse Way leads south to join two other Roman roads, the Icknield Way and Ermin Street, in **Cirencester** ⓬, which some would have you say "Cissiter" and the Romans "Corinium", though locals call it Ciren. Second only in size and importance to London under the Romans, its fortunes flourished under the wool merchants, and floundered during the 19th century. Today, the medieval character of this "capital of the Cotswolds" is remarkably preserved.

One of the best examples of Perpendicular style in the country, the porch of the parish church of St John the Baptist (daily), once doubled as the town hall. Of the 12 bells in the tower, the ninth is called the "Pancake Bell", because it is always rung on Shrove Tuesday.

The story of Roman Cirencester is compellingly told at the **Corinium Museum** (Mon–Sat 10am–5pm, Sun 2–5pm) and substantial remains of the town walls are still in evidence, along with a well-preserved amphitheatre.

Ermin Street is now the A417 leaving the town to the northwest, where two village churches are not to be missed. First is **Daglingworth**, 4 miles (6 km) away, with Saxon sculptures, including a crucifixion of compelling simplicity. Then, high up, 5 miles (8 km) further on, is **Elkstone's** church ⓭, with a view from its east window under low Norman arches like a limestone cave.

Malmesbury ⓮, 12 miles (20 km) southwest of Cirencester on the A429, is known for two distressing incidents: the killing of a woman by a tiger from a visiting menagerie and the conversion of the abbey into a factory. The woman was Hannah Twynnoy, who died in 1703. Her tombstone records: "For Tyger fierce took life away … And here she lies in bed of clay". At the Dissolution a rich clothier bought the abbey in a package deal which allowed him to convert it into a weaving shed, and the parishioners to use the nave for services. Enough remains, especially a richly decorated porch, to give a good idea of the abbey's former glory.

Five miles (8 km) northwest of Malmesbury, in **Tetbury** ⓯, a fine 17th-

TIP

If the tower of Cirencester's parish church is open when you visit, it is worth climbing to the top for a view of Cirencester Mansion, built by the first Earl Bathurst between 1714 and 1718, and hidden from view at street level by the world's tallest yew hedge. Beyond the mansion are the broad tree-lined avenues of Cirencester Park, which is open to the public.

BELOW: Tetbury, an important market for Cotswold wool and yarn in the Middle Ages, has a population today of more than 5,000.

Painswick's bowling green, Britain's oldest, dates to 1554, though dwindling interest in recent years has threatened the club's future.

century market hall recalls the bustle of trading in wool once conducted in the pillared open space beneath it.

Gorgeous valley

Returning north 6 miles (10 km) beyond Tetbury, the A46 arrives at Nailsworth and the start of the gorge-like valleys of Stroudwater, of wheels now still and looms long silent. There are still one or two cloth mills here, and cottages hug the terraces above the steep streets. At **Chalford** ⓰, off the A419, the descent into the **Golden Valley** begins.

Curiosities are both here and further east at **Sapperton**. One is a round house with conical roof and Gothic windows on the banks of the canal that opened in 1789 to link the Thames with the Severn. At Sapperton the canal disappears into the hillside under a triumphal arch.

From where the River Frome breaks through the western wall of the Cotswolds, **Stroud** ⓱, on its hill, looks across to the mountains of Wales. The country's cloth industry was concentrated here in the Stroudwater valley in the 16th century, and England's armies went to war in uniforms of scarlet and blue cloth from these mills.

Take to the heights to the east of the A46, and you are in a land of swift-flowing streams and wooded ravines. **Slad**, on the B4070, is the village on which Laurie Lee based his novel, *Cider With Rosie*. Lee was born and died here. His cottage and pub are still there, but the school has taught its last children.

On the A46, 3 miles (5 km) north of Stroud, is **Painswick** ⓲, whose traditions

What gives Cotswolds buildings their distinctive look

The Cotswolds' architectural style is simple yet effective. Roofs are very steeply pitched – they have to be to carry the weight of the stone tiles. The tiles are applied in a fish-scale pattern, starting with the smallest, hand-sized tiles at the ridges and descending to table-sized tiles at the eaves. The eaves overhang the walls because, in the absence of guttering, this was the best way of carrying rainwater well away from the walls. Other features that look decorative but which are entirely practical do the same job of shedding water, especially the drip moulds found around the chimney stack and above windows and doors.

Window frames are also made of stone, usually with a cross-shaped mullion (upright bar) and transom (horizontal bar) dividing the space into four, with two tall lights in the bottom half and two smaller lights above.These are the basic ingredients of almost all Cotswold architecture.

Some buildings have extra features – dormer windows or Italianate details such as round or lozenge-shaped windows or rusticated quoins and door and window surrounds – but by and large this simple style was used on every type of building, from barns and churches to cottages and manors. A grand Elizabethan building like Bibury Court is essentially a larger version of the nearby Arlington Row weavers' cottages.

The principal difference between the houses of the rich and the poor is that grander buildings were constructed of cut-stone (known as ashlar), with mortar joints so narrow as to be almost invisible. Humbler buildings were made of rubble – stones of random size – cemented by thick beds of lime mortar. Adding colours to the limewash resulted in an attractive poylchromatic look.

Map on page 175

Recommended Restaurants and Pubs on pages 186–7

include weaving, tomb-carving and "clipping". The mills have closed and the masons have put down their tools, but the clipping (meaning "embracing") service is still held every September when children join hands to encircle St Mary's Church. Just north of Painswick on the B4073 is the **Rococo Garden** (Jan–Oct daily 11am–5pm), restored to its former glory as depicted in a painting of 1748.

Kings, queens and tailors

The nearby county town of **Gloucester** ⓳ is a cathedral city and inland port and has been a strategic centre guarding the route to Wales since Roman times. King Alfred held a parliament here in AD 896, Canute signed a treaty and William the Conqueror ordered the Domesday survey from the Chapter House. Henry I died here of eating lampreys (a kind of eel), Henry III was crowned and crook-backed Richard III reputedly ordered the murder of his nephews. Charles II took out his spite on the city for opposing his father, by having its walls demolished.

Of the Roman walls, vestiges remain; of the medieval town, very little. The old docks have been renovated and include the excellent and child-friendly **National Waterways Museum** (daily 10am–5pm), which tells the story of England's waterways and offers cruises around the docks.

The **Cathedral** remains the city's focal point. The nave is Norman, and the windows in the south transept are in earlier Perpendicular style. Fourteenth-century stained glass fills the largest east window in England and over the choir is a complicated cross-ribbed vault. Pilgrims once came to the richly ornamented tomb of Edward II, murdered at nearby Berkeley Castle. There is marvellous fan vaulting in the cloisters and even the Monks' Lavatory has its appeal.

In the town there is a **Folk Museum** packed with displays on local history (Tue–Sat in school holidays; tel: 01452-396868; free). There are Turners and Gainsboroughs in the **City Museum and Art Gallery** (Tue–Sat 10am–5pm; free). The **House of the Tailor of Gloucester** (Apr–Oct daily 10am–5pm, Nov–Mar Mon–Sat 10am–4pm) recalls Beatrix Potter's famous story, which was based on real people and events.

Gloucester Cathedral, which doubled as Hogwarts School of Witchcraft and Wizardry in the Harry Potter movies.

BELOW: Cheltenham is a major race centre.

Sudeley Castle, a great, castellated house, just south of Winchcombe, was built in the 1440s. It has been carefully restored, and displays a fascinating collection of royal relics and paintings.

Just 8 miles (13 km) northeast is **Cheltenham** ⓴, a spa town which makes a good base for the Cotswolds. Lord Byron came here, as did George III. The discovery of the mineral spring in 1718 started it, but it was the visit of George III and his queen 70 years later that made the spa fashionable as a summer resort. Like Bath, it was fortunate in its architects, J.B. Papworth and J.B. Forbes, who chose Cotswold stone or stucco, and in the lightness and gaiety of the Greek Revival style. Graceful terraces and squares form a backdrop to the **Rotunda** and the **Pittville Pump Room** (Wed–Mon 10am–4pm) where the waters can be tasted. The elegant **Promenade** and **Montpellier** are the places to shop, while aficionados of the Arts and Crafts Movement should not miss the outstanding collection at **Cheltenham Art Gallery and Museum** (Mon–Sat 10am–5.20pm; free).

Cotswold limits

The Cotswolds's western limit is 10 miles (16 km) north at **Tewkesbury** ㉑ where the Avon joins the Severn. Here stone gives way to attractive timbered cottages, many of them serving as pubs, such as the 17th-century Bell Inn. In 1473 the Battle of Bloody Meadow, the last of the Wars of the Roses, was fought here, spilling over into the **Abbey** itself. Even the monks took a hand. From the Abbey's square tower there are views over the river valleys to the Malvern Hills and the mountains of Wales.

Twelve miles (20 km) northwest of Tewkesbury is **Great Malvern** ㉒, from which there are magnificent views over 10 counties. This is another health resort here and the hills are the source of a reputable bottled mineral water.

If ghosts walk at all, they must walk at **Sudeley Castle** ㉓ (mid-Mar–Oct; gardens 10.30am–5pm; castle 11am–5pm), 6 miles (10 km) northeast of Cheltenham on the B4632 *(see margin note)*.

Two villages further along this road to Broadway are **Stanway**, with scallop shells over the rather pretentious gateway to the manor, and **Stanton**. Nearly every cottage here was built during the best period of Cotswold architecture, from the mid-16th to the mid-17th century. **Snowshill Manor** (late Mar–Apr Thur–Sun, May–Oct Wed–Sun; manor noon–5pm; gardens 11am–5.30pm), an attractive Tudor mansion, in a valley south of Broadway, houses an eclectic collection from musical instruments to toys.

Broadway ㉔ is the Cotswolds' show village. Houses and cottages face one another across an expanse of green on the road from London to Worcester, all in the same style and honey-coloured stone. The **Abbot's Grange** dates from the 14th century and the **Lygon Arms** (one of the Cotswolds' best restaurants) from the 16th. Charles I and Cromwell stayed here, but not, of course, at the same time.

Broadway Tower (Apr–Oct daily 10.30am–5pm, Nov–Mar Sat–Sun until 4pm) on the escarpment above is the second-highest point in the Cotswolds and has splendid views.

Chipping Campden ㉕, 5 miles (8 km) northeast of Broadway, has a long main street lined with fine stone houses

BELOW: a cottage in Chipping Campden.

Recommended Restaurants and Pubs on pages 186–7

dating from before the 17th century, when this was one of the most prosperous wool towns. Especially interesting are the almshouses and church, the town hall, and the house of William Grevel, a wool merchant, who died in 1401, and to whom there is a brass memorial in the church.

Sezincote

Turning east towards Oxford on the A44, the circuitous route reaches **Moreton-in-Marsh** 26, which took to linen weaving when the woollen industry failed. Every Tuesday, the town hosts the largest open-air market in the Cotswolds. Nearby is **Sezincote** (house May–July and Sept Thur–Fri 2.30–5.30pm; garden Jan–Nov Thur–Fri 2–6pm or dusk), a house in the Indian style, which gave the Prince Regent his ideas for Brighton Pavilion *(see page 211)*.

Eight miles (13 km) further on is **Chipping Norton** 27 ("Chipping" means market). Alongside many 18th-century houses is **Bliss Tweed Mill**, looking like a country mansion crowned with a factory chimney (now luxury apartments). The town is handy for an excursion 3 miles (5km) northwest to the **Rollright Stones**, a large circle of 70 Bronze Age standing stones known as the King's Men, a smaller group called the five Whispering Knights and a lone menhir, the King (site open all year; rollrightstones.co.uk; small fee). Their origins are unknown, but, according to legend, a local witch turned the king and his knights to stone.

Indian influences at work at Sezincote.

Secret valleys

The hill town of **Stow-on-the-Wold** 28, 4 miles (6 km) south of Moreton-in-Marsh, was once the scene of great sheep fairs. Writer Daniel Defoe recorded as many as 20,000 sheep being sold on one occasion. Like sheep, 1,000 defeated Royalists were penned in the church after the last battle of the Civil War in 1646. To the west of the town are the Swells, **Upper Swell** and **Lower Swell**, pure Cotswold villages on the River Dikler.

Temple Guiting 29 and **Guiting Power**, in thick woods on the Windrush a few miles further west, are a little too perfect. Between them, the **Cotswold Farm Park** (mid-Mar–mid-Sept daily

BELOW: Broadway has been called "the Jewel of the Cotswolds."

10.30am–4pm, mid-Sept–Oct Sat–Sun 10.30am–4pm), a rare breeds centre, offers a chance to see local domestic animals such as Cotswold lions – sheep with fleeces like lions' manes – and pigs such as Tamworth Gingers.

Over the hill, just below the Swells, are **Upper Slaughter** and **Lower Slaughter**, with fords on the tiny Slaughterbrook, dovecotes and mills. Nearby is **Bourton-on-the-Water**, one of the best of the Cotswold stone villages. Set on the River Windrush, it has all the ingredients of fairyland: miniature footbridges over streams and under willow trees, sweet smells in the perfumery, a motor museum in a barley mill, a model railway, and a model village.

Also nearby, **Birdland** (Apr–Oct 10am–6pm, Nov–Mar 10am–4pm) is the home of hundreds of species of exotic birds, many of which were bred at the park and roam freely.

On their northern side, the Cotswolds merge into the **Vale of Evesham**, part of the Avon valley where the climate is ideal for growing fruit and vegetables which has given the town of **Evesham** ㉚ a prosperous air.

Stratford-upon-Avon

Above Evesham the A439 follows the Avon for 14 miles (22 km) to **Stratford-upon-Avon** ㉛. William Shakespeare was born here in Henley Street on 23 April 1564. He was christened in the local Holy Trinity Church and went to the local school; at 18 he married 26-year-old Anne Hathaway and they had three children. In 1597, after his extraordinary career as a playwright in London, he bought New Place in Chapel Street to where he retired. He died on his 52nd birthday and is buried at Holy Trinity.

In spite of the numbers of tourists, the town, of half-timbered buildings beside the river, still manages to evoke the atmosphere of Shakespeare's times. His birthplace is the starting point for a tour of the town. The entrance is through the modern **Shakespeare Centre** Ⓐ on Henley Street (daily, summer 9am–5pm, winter 10am–4pm).

Shakespeare's granddaughter married Thomas Nash in 1626, and they lived in **Nash's House** Ⓑ on Chapel Street, which is now a town museum (summer Mon–Sat 9.30–5pm, Sun 10am–5pm, winter 11am–4pm). Nash's House was

Sudeley Castle saw Tudor history pass like a pageant. Catherine Parr lived here after Henry VIII's death, and was married again to Thomas Seymour. Lady Jane Grey stayed here, and Queen Elizabeth I was a frequent visitor.

BELOW: Shakespeare's Birthplace in Stratford-upon-Avon.

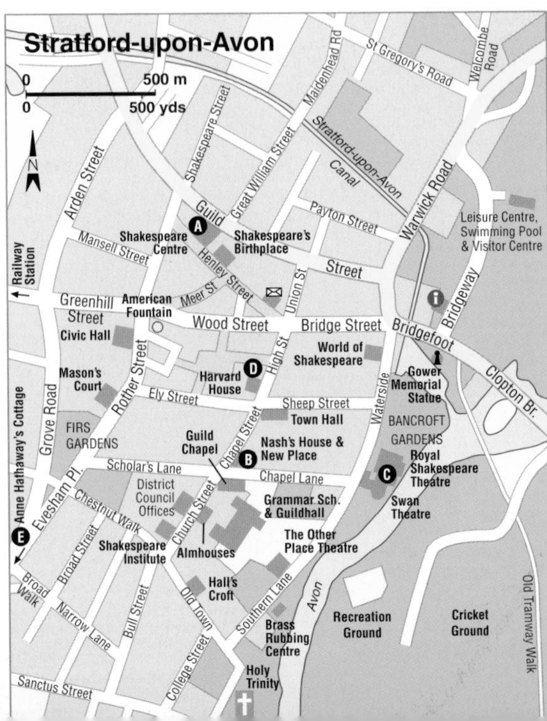

Recommended Restaurants and Pubs on pages 186–7

next door to New Place, of which only the foundations remain, preserved in a delightful, Elizabethan-style garden.

The living legacy of the playwright can be found at the **Royal Shakespeare Theatre** C, where a remodelling of the auditorium will include an extensible thrust-stage; the smaller, galleried **Swan Theatre**, where the Royal Shakespeare Company stages its often controversial performances; and The Other Place. Backstage tours run 2–4 times daily (to book tel: 01789-403405).

Between Shakespeare's birthplace and Nash's House is **Harvard House** D (for hours tel: 01789-204016). Built in 1596, this was the home of Katherine Rogers, whose son, John Harvard, funded the famous US university. It now houses the Museum of British Pewter.

In **Shottery**, a mile or so west of the town, is **Anne Hathaway's Cottage** E (daily, summer 9am–5pm, winter 10am–4pm). Anne lived in this thatched cottage during the many years Shakespeare was in London.

Three miles (5km) northwest of Stratford, in **Wilmcote**, the childhood home of Shakespeare's mother has been restored as **Mary Arden's House**. The timber-framed farmhouse has been furnished in keeping with the tastes of a wealthy Tudor family.

Warwick

Eight miles (13 km) north of Stratford, just off the A46, is **Warwick** 32. Despite a serious fire in 1694, many buildings from the Tudor period remain standing. First fortified in 914 by Ethelfleda, the daughter of Alfred the Great, **Warwick Castle** (daily, summer 10am–6pm, Aug weekends until 7pm, winter 10am–5pm; tel: 01926-495421) has had a rich history. Although only a mound of earth remains of the original Saxon structure, the 14th-century towers standing today are the proud features of England's finest medieval castle. For centuries England's most powerful families lived at Warwick. A collection of paintings, including portraits by Rubens, Van Dyck and Holbein, is complemented by sets of arms and armour. The graffiti in the dungeon and torture chamber is attributed to Royalist soldiers from the Civil War. Bordering the River Avon, the

The Gower Memorial to Shakespeare in Stratford-upon-Avon.

BELOW: Mary Arden's house in Wilmcote.

Lord Leycester Hospital.

Althorp Park (July–Aug only 10am–5pm; booking advised; tel: 0870-167 9000) lies off the A428 northwest of Northampton. This is the family estate of the Earl of Spencer and the burial place of his sister Diana, Princess of Wales.

BELOW AND RIGHT: Warwick Castle exterior and historic tableau.

castle's 60-acre (25-hectare) gardens, landscaped by "Capability" Brown, are well kept.

Lord Leycester Hospital by Warwick's West Gate was founded as a guildhall in 1383. In 1571, Robert Dudley, Earl of Leicester, had the buildings renovated as almshouses. Today, the hospital is a museum and the home of ex-servicemen.

Adjacent to Warwick, **Royal Leamington Spa** ㉝ is a spacious Regency and Victorian spa town that has prided itself on its amenities since it began to develop bath houses and other amenities around its saline springs in the late 18th century.

Coventry

The A46 continues for 8 miles (13 km) to **Coventry** ㉞, through whose streets the 11th-century Lady Godiva rode naked in protest against her husband's imposition of taxes. This is a car-manufacturing town that was terribly bombed during World War II. The **New Cathedral** stands strikingly juxtaposed with the beautiful, ruined shell of the old. By Sir Basil Spence, it was completed in 1962 and is highly imaginative with immense stained-glass windows and a richly coloured interior; Epstein's sculpture of St Michael and the Devil is among the stunning works here.

Near the cathedral is the **Herbert Art Gallery and Museum** (Mon–Sat 10am–5.30pm, Sunday 2–5pm; tel: 024-7683 2386; theherbert.org; free). Permanent collections cover natural history, social history and art, and it has has an innovative resident theatre company, Triangle. There's background on Coventry's most famous daughter, Lady Godiva, the wife of a powerful 11th-century Saxon earl, Leofric. A dispute provoked Godiva into riding naked through the streets, her modesty just about preserved by her long hair and the tact of the citizenry who stayed indoors.

The redesign of the city centre's open spaces has created a corridor linking up the cathedrals to the futuristic Whittle Arch and the **Coventry Transport Museum**, refurbished to include four new galleries (daily 10am–5pm; free). The peaceful canal towpath provides a very different kind of exhibition setting, with 5½ miles (9 km) of waterside art making up the **Coventry Canal Art Trail**.

Birmingham

To the west of Coventry, **Birmingham** ㉟ was a manufacturing centre long before the Industrial Revolution of the late 18th century. The canals and railways of that era confirmed its importance. In the 1960s, the construction of the Bullring Shopping Centre became one of the country's most famous examples of revolutionary urban planning at the same time as the city became the focus of the national motorway network. However by the 1990s, Birmingham, affectionately known as Brum, was in dire need of a facelift.

In recent years, it has been much improved and is emerging as a great centre for services, shopping and cultural activities, as exemplified by the new **Bullring**. This dramatic redevelopment has brought modern, attractive retail space into the city while retaining existing landmarks such as St Martin's Church and the circular Rotunda building.

At the centre is **Victoria Square**, an enormous pedestrian esplanade dotted with contemporary sculptures and flanked by the classical **Town Hall**, modelled on the Temple of Castor and Pollux in Rome, and the Renaissance-style **Council House** with its mosaic and pediment relief entitled *Britannia Rewarding the Manufacturers of Birmingham*. The nearby **Museum and Art Gallery** (Mon–Sat 10am–5pm, Sun 12.30–5pm; free) is famous for its matchless collection of pre-Raphaelite paintings. Waterloo Street climbs to **St Philip's Cathedral**, built in 1715 and a fine example of English Baroque, with the glorious stained-glass windows designed by Edward Burne-Jones (1833–98).

The canalside developments to the west of the centre have as their focus **Brindleyplace**, where elegant office buildings give way to a cluster of restaurants and bars. Also in this area are the **International Convention Centre**, with its acclaimed Symphony Hall, and the **National Sea Life Centre** (daily Mon–Fri 10am–4pm, Sat–Sun until 5pm). On a more intimate scale, the **Ikon Gallery** (Tue–Sun 11am–6pm; free) is a laid-back venue for contemporary art with a good café-cum-tapas bar. The waterside theme extends to the **Mailbox**, an exclusive complex of designer shops and eateries.

Further south, on the fringes of Chinatown, the National Trust's **Back to Backs** (opening times vary; by guided tour only, booking recommended, tel: 0121-666 7671) is Birmingham's last surviving court of houses built literally back to back, a common feature in the industrial towns of 19th-century Britain. Visitors are taken through four of the dwellings, restored and decorated to reflect the lives of chosen inhabitants from the 1840s, 1870s, 1930s and 1970s. The retro, fully operational sweetshop hugging the end of the row is a great touch. Three more houses can be rented as holiday accommodation.

Near the east gate of the University of Birmingham, at Edgbaston, is the **Barber Institute of Fine Arts** (Mon–Sat 10am–5pm, Sun noon–5pm; free), an Art Deco building housing a fine collection of works ranging from Rembrandt and Rubens to Monet and Magritte. ❑

The futuristic Selfridges department store in Birmingham's Bull Ring.

BELOW: the water sculpture in front of Birmingham's Council House represents youth and eternity.

RESTAURANTS, TEAROOMS AND PUBS

Restaurants

Prices for a three-course meal per person with a half-bottle of house wine:
£ = under £25
££ = £25–50
£££ = £50–100
££££ = £100+

Arlingham

The Old Passage Inn
Tel: 01452-740547 **££**
Fresh seafood is a speciality at this award-winning restaurant on the banks of the River Severn. Also organic meat and vegetarian dishes and a mouthwatering selection of puddings. Friendly welcome.

Barnsley

The Village Pub
Tel: 01285-740421 **££**
An upmarket gastropub decorated in country-house style, and serving European cuisine using top-quality local organic ingredients, including vegetables grown in Barnsley House Garden across the road.

Bibury

The Swan
Tel: 01285-740695 **££**
In a stunning location by the bridge over the River Coln, this charming stone hotel puts a stylish European twist on modern British dishes.

Birmingham

Rajnagar International
256 Lyndon Road, Olton, Solihull
Tel: 0121-742 8140. **££**
Said to be the best Bangladeshi restaurant in the country with pleasant decor and service and authentic food, especially fish.

V2 Chinatown Eating Place
73–75 Pershore Street
Tel: 0121-666 6683 **£**
Laid-back café serving authentic Cantonese food to a studenty crowd. Tasty one-pot meals and fresh roasts daily. East Asian TV and a small library of Manga comic books provide diversion between courses.

Broadway

The Lygon Arms
High Street
Tel: 01386-840318 **££**
Committed foodies will not begrudge the cost of a meal in the barrel-vaulted Great Hall of the Lygon Arms. Attention to every detail ensures that even straightforward sounding dishes are given gourmet appeal.

Cheltenham

Le Champignon Sauvage
24–26 Suffolk Road
Tel: 01242-573449 **££–£££**
Interesting menu including wild mushrooms, the food has a touch of class, and chef David Everitt-Matthias has won awards for his desserts. Two Michelin stars.

Chipping Campden

Red Lion
High Street
Tel: 01386-840760 **£–££**
The emphasis at this popular old coaching inn is on fresh local produce. Daily specials may include chicken and mushroom crêpes or Gloucestershire Old Spot loin of pork. Vegetarian dishes. Children are welcome.

Frampton Mansell

The White Horse
Tel: 01285-760960 **£–££**
First-rate gastro-pub in a rural setting between Cirencester and Stroud.

Great Milton

Le Manoir aux Quat'Saisons
Church Road
Tel: 01844-278881 **££££**
Raymond Blanc's award-garlanded French restaurant sources 90 types of vegetable and over 70 varieties of herb from its own kitchen garden. Sated guests can stay overnight in deluxe rooms or suites.

Leamington Spa

Love's Restaurant
15 Dormer Place
Tel: 01926-315522 **££**
Simple but accomplished, French-inspired dishes from young chef Steve Love, crowned National Chef of the Year 2004. Attentive service.

Northleach

Old Wool House
Market Place
Tel: 01451-860366 **££**
Authentic French cuisine in the heart of the Cotswolds. Game is a speciality in season. Dinner only (lunch by special arrangement).

LEFT: Raymond Blanc's Manoir aux Quat' Saisons in Great Milton.

ABOVE: Oxford students celebrate the end of their exams at the King's Arms.

Oxford

Browns
5–11 Woodstock Road.
Tel: 01865-511995 **££**
Breakfast, light lunches and three-course meals in a relaxed atmosphere (11am–11.30pm). Bookings only taken for parties of 8 plus, Mon–Thur, so expect queues.

Chiang Mai Kitchen
130a High Street
Tel: 01865-202233 **££**
Top-quality Thai cuisine at very reasonable prices in one of the city's finest 17th-century houses.

Gee's Brasserie
61a Banbury Road
Tel: 01865-553540 **££**
Well-established restaurant in the Raymond Blanc tradition in a beautiful, airy conservatory.

Le Petit Blanc
71–2 Walton Street
Tel: 01865-510999 **££**
Raymond Blanc's latest venture in Oxford. Light but traditional French dishes in an airy atmosphere – open all day, including for breakfast.

Pizzeria Mama Mia
8 South Parade,
Summertown
Tel: 01865-514141 **£**
Pleasant and long-established restaurant with excellent pizza.

Paulerspury, nr Northampton

Vine House
100 High Street
Tel: 01327-811267 **££**
Old stone farmhouse with some fine modern English dishes.

Tetbury

Calcot Manor
Tel: 01666-890391 **£–£££**
Choose between the romantic candle-lit restaurant, or the unpretentious, friendly Gumstool Inn. Menus change with the seasons, but perennial offerings include roast duck, chargrilled sole.and pasta.

Thame

The Old Trout
29–30 Lower High Street
Tel: 01844-212146 **£–££**
Brasserie-style restaurant, especially good for fish.

Tearooms

Bo-Peep Tea Rooms and Restaurant
Riverside,
Bourton-on-the-Water
Tel: 01451-822005

The Marshmallow
High Street,
Moreton-in-Marsh
Tel: 01608-651536

Pubs

Oxford has many delightful old pubs. These include arguably the town's best pub, the **Turf Tavern**, hidden down an alley almost under the Bridge of Sighs (or via Bath Place off Holywell Street), which has a beer garden, good selection of real ales and food. **The Eagle and Child** on St Giles is famous as the pub where the Inklings literary group used to meet up. The **King's Arms** on the corner of Parks Road and Holywell Street is large and popular with students and locals, and has a good lunchtime buffet. The **Rose and Crown** on North Parade is another good choice, with a good selection of real ales.

There are a number of well-known pubs right on the city's doorstep. They include the **Trout Inn** on the Thames at Godstow, which featured in the Inspector Morse TV series. It serves a good choice of food and has the added attraction of peacocks in the garden. The **White Hart** at the picturesque village of Whytham, just off the western ring road, focuses more on food than drink, as does **The Fishes** at nearby North Hinksey. Still retaining its pub atmosphere, though serving decent food as well, is **The Plough** at Wolvercote; a visit here can be combined with a pleasant walk along the adjacent canal.

In Stratford-upon-Avon, the **Dirty Duck** on Waterside is a classic actors' pub, often full of theatre types. In Warwick, the **Old Fourpenny Shop** on Crompton Street has well-chosen guest beers.

In the Cotswolds, the **Old Spot Inn** at Dursley has been voted pub of the year by the Campaign for Real Ale. In Cheltenham, the **Adam & Eve** on Townsend Street is an old-style pub with skittles and darts.

RIGHT: the Rose and Crown on Oxford's North Parade.

CAMBRIDGE AND EAST ANGLIA

Once cut off from the rest of England by forest and uncrossable marshland, the countryside and historic towns of East Anglia have managed to retain their other-worldliness

East Anglia, the four counties of Norfolk, Suffolk, Cambridgeshire and Essex, bulging into the North Sea between the Thames estuary and the Wash, has the least annual rainfall in all of Britain. You would not know this, however, since it is also a region of fens and great rivers, of lakes, called meres or broads, and bird-filled coastal marshes. The beauty of East Anglia is not a typical one. Few places rise higher than 300 ft (90 metres) above sea level.

No one passes through East Anglia; nowhere lies on the other side. Road and rail connections with the rest of the country are limited. To the south the A12 leads northeast from London to Colchester, famed for its oysters, and on to Ipswich before heading north to the seaside towns of Lowestoft and Great Yarmouth. From east London the M11 runs up to Cambridge 53 miles (85 km) directly north, from where the A11 goes northeast to Norwich and the A10 continues to King's Lynn and the fenlands around the Wash. The main rail routes run from London's King's Cross and Liverpool Street stations.

A rich heritage

In the 11th century, when the area was surveyed by the compilers of the Domesday Book, the counties of East Anglia were some of the richest and most highly populated in the country. Later, the region became a sanctuary from the power struggles that wracked the rest of the emerging kingdom, and it was to East Anglia that many religious orders fled for peace. They left a legacy of churches, cathedrals and abbeys; in Norfolk alone there are 600 churches.

The houses once occupied by the gentry still mark the landscape much as the churches do. **Audley End ❶** (Apr–Sept Mon, Wed–Sun, house noon–5pm, garden 10am–6pm; tel: 01799-522399) in

Main attractions

- SAFFRON WALDEN
- CAMBRIDGE
- ELY CATHEDRAL
- SANDRINGHAM
- NORWICH
- NORFOLK BROADS
- WELLS-NEXT-THE-SEA
- GREAT YARMOUTH
- SOUTHWOLD
- ALDEBURGH
- IPSWICH
- FLATFORD
- LAVENHAM
- BURY ST EDMUNDS

PRECEDING PAGES: Old Moot Hall, Aldeburgh.
LEFT: punting on the Cam in Cambridge.
RIGHT: waiting for the tide to come in at Wells-next-the-Sea.

The Imperial War Museum's outpost at Duxford.

the medieval town of **Saffron Walden**, 15 miles (24 km) south of Cambridge, was built for a Lord Treasurer and said by James I to be "too large for a king". As it stands today the house is large, but it is only a fraction of the original; much of it was demolished in 1721. The interior decoration, by Robert Adam, and the immaculate gardens, landscaped by "Capability" Brown, are classics of English country design. The thriving organic kitchen garden, with its 170-ft (52-metre)-long vine house, is much as it was in its Victorian heyday. Just across the road is a miniature railway (tel: 01799-541354).

East Anglia is still a region of wealth. Farmers drive luxury cars, and the modern gentry host grouse shoots for their southern cousins. University brainpower has been harnessed in the hi-tech industries of Cambridge's science parks. But what the visitor feels most in East Anglia is the sense of isolation. It has changed little for centuries. Undisturbed by both the sooty touch of the Industrial Revolution and the bombs of World War II, many villages and towns remain unspoiled, apart from noise pollution around the airforce bases at Mildenhall and Lakenheath. The only element that destroys East Anglia is the sea, which is devouring the eastern shores. East Anglia harbours myriad landscapes that range from the flat wilds of north Norfolk to the rolling green tranquillity of south Suffolk. Gainsborough and Constable both declared that the beauty of Suffolk landscapes – the winding lanes, sloping fields and still waters – was what spurred them to paint.

Eight miles (13km) northwest of Saffron Walden is the small village of **Duxford** ❷, which has two 12th-century churches, a 14th-century chapel, picturesque inns – and Europe's biggest air museum, **Imperial War Museum Duxford** (daily 10am–6pm in summer, 10am–6pm in winter; tel: 01223-837267; duxford.iwm.org.uk; free to under-15s). As well as a collection of classic British warplanes such as a Spitfire and a Lancaster, it has a Comet and a Concorde, plus tanks, trucks, midget submarines and naval helicopters. A separate building houses the American Air Museum,

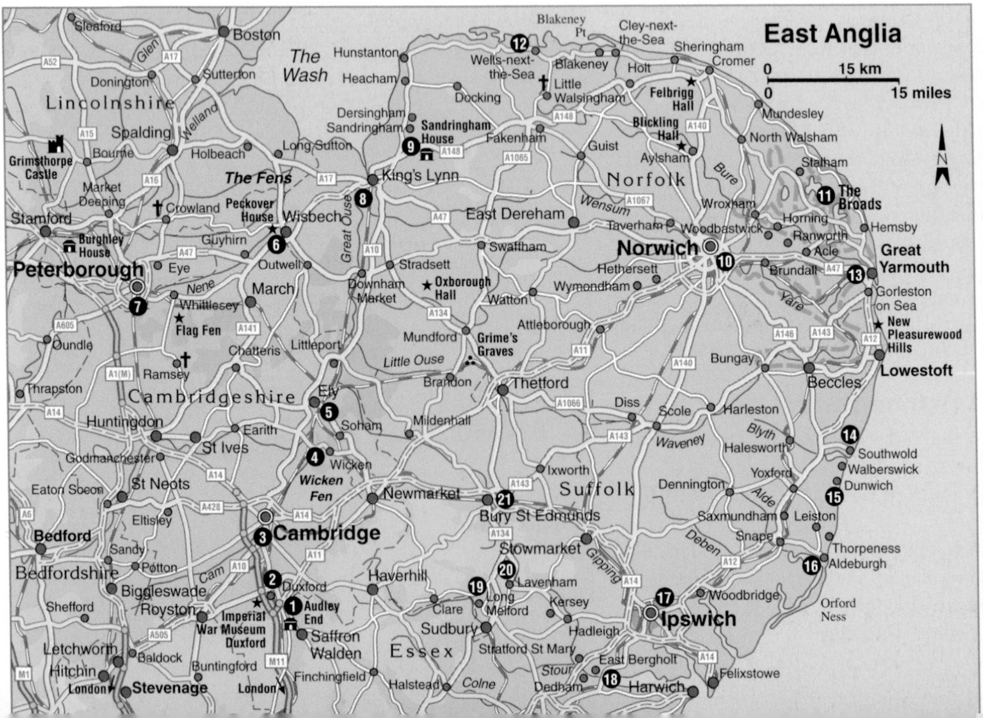

Recommended Restaurants and Pubs on page 203

with such classics as a B-17 Flying Fortress and a B-52 Stratofortress.

Cambridge

An Elizabethan historian once described the fen dwellers as "brutish, uncivilised and ignorant". Today's Oxford undergraduates invoke this claim when they scornfully refer to the university at **Cambridge** ❸ as the "Fenland Polytechnic", but some of the world's finest thinkers, artists and architects matured in this fenland town.

Cambridge, which takes its name from the River Cam, was founded in the 12th century by a settlement of Franciscans, Dominicans and Carmelites. In 1209, a handful of scholars hurriedly fled Oxford after a disagreement with the town authorities and settled in Cambridge. It was this – and the founding in 1284 of the first college, Peterhouse, by Hugo de Balsham, Bishop of Ely – that established the university.

Other colleges were soon founded under the patronage of local gentry and a succession of monarchs. On King's Parade and central to the University is **King's College** Ⓐ, founded in 1441 by Henry VI. Five years later, **King's College Chapel** – considered the glory of Cambridge – began construction, which took nearly 70 years. Chapel services are open to visitors, and it is a worthwhile experience to stand in the ancient pews alongside Rubens' *Adoration of the Magi*, listening to the voices of the famous choir float up the curves of the magnificent fan-vaulted ceiling and gazing at the series of 25 16th-century stained-glass windows, which portray the story of the New Testament.

Next door is the dignified **Senate House** (closed to the public), the university parliament, built by James Gibbs between 1722 and 1730. From the top of **Great St Mary's Church** Ⓑ opposite the Senate House visitors can see the whole of Cambridge, including the distant gaunt tower of the **University Library**. Like the Bodleian at Oxford, the University Library at Cambridge by law receives a copy of virtually every book published in the United Kingdom.

The beauty of Cambridge is its compactness; a few steps in any direction will take you past a piece of history, whether it be the Anglo-Saxon tower of the tiny church of St Bene't's (eclipsed by the col-

Visitors are generally free to walk through the college grounds. Colleges on King's Parade have a small entrance charge; others, on the town's outskirts, are free. For savings on other attractions, there is the Cambridge Visitor Card, available for £3 from the Grafton Centre Shopping Centre information desk and Borders bookshop (www.visitorcards.co.uk/cambridge).

BELOW: King's College.

Stone carving on St John's College, whose alumni include William Wilberforce and William Wordsworth.

lege buildings, but older by at least 250 years) or the Cavendish Laboratory, the site of the first splitting of the atom.

In the gardens of **Christ's College** C a tree said to have shaded the poet John Milton (1608–74) as he worked still stands. The Great Court at **Trinity** D is the largest university quadrangle in the world, but look closely at the figure of its founder, Henry VIII, above the gateway: instead of a sceptre he holds a chair leg. Trinity's library, seen from the riverfront, was built by Sir Christopher Wren. Further north is **St John's** E, founded in 1511. Its three-storey gatehouse, decorated with carvings of heraldic beasts, is magnificent. Behind it is the **Bridge of Sighs** (1831), loosely modelled on its more famous namesake in Venice. Across Bridge Street from St John's is the **Church of the Holy Sepulchre** F, one of only four Norman round churches in England. This one was founded in 1130, possibly in connection with the Crusades. The shape is based on that of the Holy Sepulchre in Jerusalem.

Queens' College G, hidden behind St Catharine's, has an unusual and seemingly rickety half-timbered President's Lodge. A little beyond the town centre along Trumpington Street stands **Peterhouse** H, the oldest, smallest and reputedly most conservative of the colleges. Next door is the **Fitzwilliam Museum** I (Tue–Sat 10am–5pm, Sun noon–5pm; Greek/Roman and Cypriot galleries closed until summer or autumn 2009; free), a spectacular collection of art, books and antiquities including works by Turner, Titian and Rembrandt, and the original manuscripts of William Blake's poems.

Beyond the Fitzwilliam the **Botanic Gardens** make a haven for tired visitors and students alike. In Castle Street is a delightful **Folk Museum** (Mon–Sat 10.30am–5pm, Sun 2–5pm, Oct–Mar closed Mon), and around the corner, **Kettle's Yard** J (house Tue–Sun summer 1.30–4.30pm, winter 2–4pm; gallery Tue–Sun 11.30am–5pm; free). The former home of Tate gallery curator Jim Ede, this unusual museum in four cottages is filled with Ede's eclectic collection of modern works by artists such as Ben Nicholson and Henry Moore.

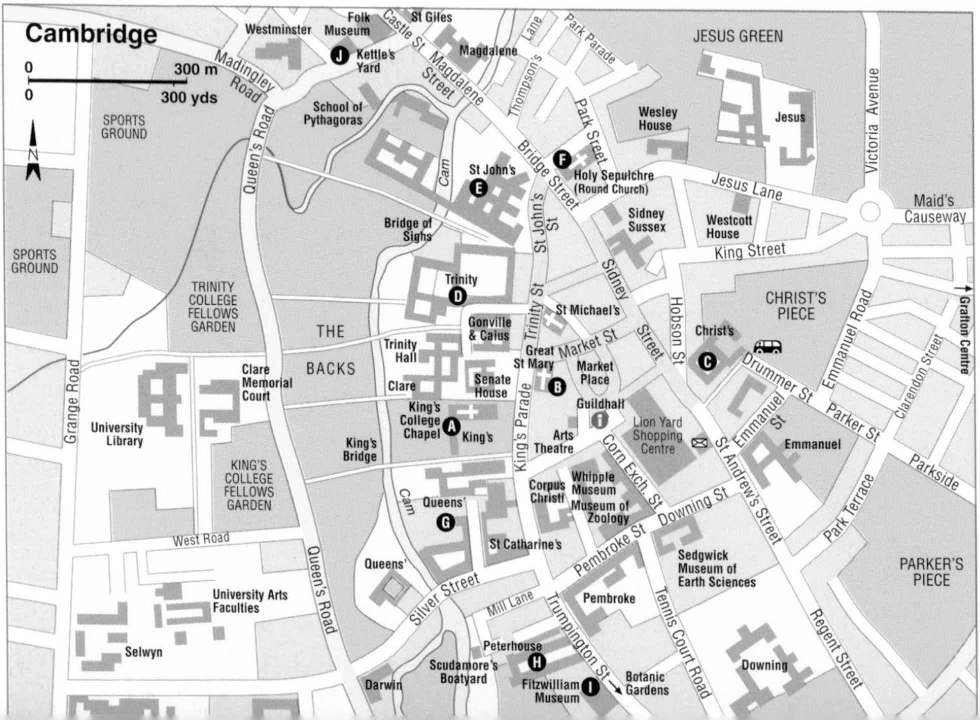

Cambridge

Recommended Restaurants and Pubs on page 203

The best way to see many colleges is to hire a punt – either self-hire or chauffered, gondolier-style – from **Scudamore's Boatyard** at the end of Mill Lane. Drift down the "Backs" (only undergraduates try to speed) from Charles Darwin's House to the Bridge of Sighs, gliding between the willows at the backs of the colleges.

The wetlands

Flat, spongy and soppy the Yarmouth area may have seemed to young Copperfield, but the **fenland** is flatter, spongier and soppier still. The village names – Landbeach, Waterbeach, Gedney Marsh and Dry Drayton – all tell the same story. Never marry a fenland woman, runs the saying, because on the wedding night you may discover she has webbed feet. For centuries no one tried to cross the marshes, let alone build on them, yet today the black fenland soil is some of the most productive land in the country.

The Romans were the first to try to drain the 2,000-sq mile (5,200-sq km) marsh that stretched from Cambridge to Lincoln, but success came only in the 17th century, when the Dutch engineer Vermuyden cut rivers through the marshes. Even he was not prepared for the dramatic land-shrinking that resulted. Today's fields are often 10 ft (3 metres) below the rivers that were cut to drain them. Only one fen remains undrained; at **Wicken Fen** ❹ (signposted off the A10, 17 miles/27 km north of Cambridge) the windpump works to keep 600 acres (240 hectares) of marshland wet, preserved by the National Trust.

Where the A10 approaches **Ely** ❺, 16 miles (25 km) north of Cambridge, the everlastingly flat skyline is broken. **Ely Cathedral** (tel: 01353 720274; opening times vary; elycathedral.org), completed in 1351, dominates the fens from its perch on what used to be called the Isle of Eels – after the staple diet of the villagers – earning it the title of "Ship of the Fens". The Isle, a knoll of dry land, was selected as a monastery site by St Etheldreda in AD 673. Some 400 years later it made an ideal refuge for Hereward the Wake when pursued by William the Conqueror. Hereward seemed unreachable on Ely (then an island), but eventually the monks tired

The Wooden Bridge joining two parts of Queen's College in Cambridge is popularly known as the Mathematical Bridge. It was first built in 1749 and rebuilt in 1866 and 1905. The reason for its name in unclear.

BELOW: Ely Cathedral.

There are 119 Saxon flint round towers in Norfolk. The Normans, however, considered the local stone undramatic. So, to build Norwich Cathedral, they shipped white stone from Normandy across the Channel and up the River Wensum.

of the siege and showed the conqueror's men the secret pathway through the marshes, giving Hereward away.

The splendour of Ely Cathedral lies in its unusual situation and in its unique lantern. In the evening, the lantern – an octagonal tower of wood and glass built high on the back of the nave in an extraordinary feat of engineering – reflects the rays of the dying sun. By night its glass gleams with the light within.

The A1101 on the left, 5 miles (8 km) north of Ely, crosses the unimaginatively named Hundred Foot Drain and passes between the rows of marching crops to **Wisbech** ❻, a market town that styles itself the capital of the fens. The two imposing Georgian streets (South Brink and North Brink) illustrate the prosperity fen drainage brought.

In the eccentric **Wisbech and Fenland Museum** on Museum Square are the complete furnishings of a Victorian post office (Tues–Sat 10am–4pm; wisbechmuseum.org free).

West of Wisbech on the A47, **Peterborough** ❼ is worth a visit for its Norman cathedral, begun in 1118. Nearby is **Flag Fen** (tel: 01733-313 414; flagfen.org), a vast archaeological centre devoted to Britain's Bronze Age.

While Wisbech has been preserved by a lack of economic development, **King's Lynn** ❽, 12 miles (20 km) northeast along the coast, has marched on. Much of the town has been rebuilt since the late 1950s but it retains many fine Georgian houses, with **King Street** marking the heart of the old town. King's Lynn is unique in having two medieval guildhalls, one the largest in Britain.

Sandringham House

Eight miles (13 km) northeast of King's Lynn, **Sandringham House** ❾ is still used as a royal country retreat. Edward VII, when Prince of Wales, built Sandringham in 1870, but it is decorated in styles ranging from Jacobean to Regency. The house is closed when a member of the royal family is in residence, but 600 acres (240 hectares) of parkland are kept open to visitors year round (house open Mar–Oct daily 11am–4.45pm, Oct until 3pm; gardens open 10.30am–5pm, Oct until 4pm; closed last week in July; tel: 01553-612908; sandringhamestate.co.uk).

BELOW: Sandringham House's gardens.

Recommended Restaurants and Pubs on page 203

Norwich

A city that retains its sense of history alongside economic success is a rare place, yet **Norwich** ⑩, the county town of Norfolk, manages to do both. It has a church for every week of the year and a pub for every day, they say, and every vista of this surprisingly hilly town confirms it. Within the city walls 32 medieval churches still stand, though some now have secular purposes. **St James' Church** is a puppet theatre; the imaginative **Elizabethan Theatre** at the Maddermarket is a combination of chapel and warehouse; and **St Peter Hungate** at the top of Elm Hill is a museum of ecclesiastical treasures.

Besides the **Cathedral** (daily 7.30am–6pm, and until 7pm mid-May–mid-Sept; cathedral.org.uk; donations welcome) and its fine **Cloisters**, worth seeing are the flinted-frame cottages and Georgian terraces in the **Cathedral Close**, and **Pull's Ferry** (last used as a river-crossing in 1939). With no source of fuel readily available to drive machines, Norwich, once the third richest town in England, was left behind by the Industrial Revolution. The city became self-sufficient and today continues to flourish. Retailing became the profession of the prosperous, and it was a succession of wealthy grocers who, century by century, added to **Strangers' Hall**. The result today is a charming museum (Wed and Sat 10.30am–4.30pm; tel: 01603-667229) with a series of interlinking rooms designed in a bewildering variety of styles. The earliest parts of the house date from 1320.

Timber-framed building in Norwich. The city's Elm Hill district has more Tudor buildings than can be found in the whole of London.

Today's wealthy grocers are no less munificent: the high street supermarket family commissioned Sir Norman Foster to design the **Sainsbury Centre for Visual Arts** (Tues–Sun 10am–5pm, Wed until 8pm; tel: 01603 593199; scva.org.uk) situated on the University of East Anglis campus. Its wide collection does not house the works of the Dutch-inspired Norwich School of Painters – these hang in the 12th-century **castle museum** (Mon–Fri 10am–4.30pm, Sat 10am–-5pm, Sun 1–5pm; museums.norfolk.gov.uk), which also hosts visiting exhibitions from the Tate.

Lottery money funded the city sky-

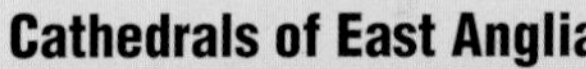

LEFT: Norwich Cathedral. **BELOW:** Ely Cathedral.

Cathedrals of East Anglia

Three enormous Norman cathedrals, all started around 1100, grace the region. Founded in 1081, Ely *(right)* is best known for its massive, octagonal lantern, built by Alan de Walsingham to cover the crossing of the nave and transepts when the Norman tower fell down in 1322. But the whole interior, with its 250-ft (76-metre) long nave is magnificent, reflecting many architectural styles, from Norman to early Renaissance.

Peterborough Cathedral, begun in 1118, is in part a good example of the late Norman style, though it was added to in nearly every later architectural period. The cathedral was severely damaged by Oliver Cromwell's troops in the 17th century. Visitors today, however, can still marvel at its painted wooden ceiling, dating from around 1220, though it has been repainted twice.

Norwich Cathedral was founded in 1096. The nave's original wooden roof was replaced in the 15th and 16th centuries by stone vaulting and embellished by carved and painted bosses illustrating Bible scenes. Norwich's spire, at 315 ft (96 metres), is second only to that of Salisbury. A very modern take on a Norman refectory, designed by Sir Michael Hopkins, was recently incorporated into the cathedral's outer flint walls.

Boats tied up at dusk on the Norfolk Broads.

line's most recent addition: the **Forum** is a striking glass-and-steel hangar housing everything Norfolk and Norwich, including the Millennium library, tourist information centre and **Origins** (daily; tel: 01603-727920), a multimedia exploration of the region's history.

In the 18th century, Norwich's textile industry was at its height. Today, the city is an excellent shopping centre. Lavish antiques shops line **Elm Hill** and in **Colman's Mustard Shop** (colmansmustard shop.com) in the Royal Arcade customers can still buy mustard for their foot baths. Elm Hill's impression of antiquity is slightly misleading, for all but the Briton's Arms was rebuilt after a fire in the 18th century. For a modern retail experience, try the city's mall, built within the castle mound.

The Norfolk Broads

Northeast of Norwich, the A1161 turns off to the village of **Woodbastwick**. As you approach it, the buzz of distant tractors fades, and is replaced by a pastoral silence. In winter, drizzle drips into the peat-dark waters of Bure marshes, and somewhere a coot grates its voice in alarm as the white triangle of the sail of a late-season yachtsman slides slowly through the brown sedge. Heeding the alarm, a cormorant splashes across the water's surface and labours into the heavy air before watchful ornithologists.

The **Norfolk Broads** ⓫ have begun. For the bird-watcher, winter is a gripping time here, but most visitors to this chain of lakes – thought to be medieval peat-diggings which have flooded over the centuries – come with the summer sun.

Hiring a boat is undoubtedly the best way of enjoying the Broads, since they are largely inaccessible by road. There are some 10,000 craft on the 200 miles (320 km) of navigable waterways, though fortunately not everyone goes

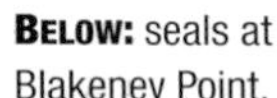

BELOW: seals at Blakeney Point.

afloat at the same time. From the water the landscape is one of church towers, windmills, reeds and sails cutting through fields, all of which would be missed from the land. Until the early part of the 20th century, sailing wherries laden with cargo used to navigate the River Yare from Norwich to the sea; one such vessel is preserved at Horning.

At **Ranworth**, the home of the floating Broadland Conservation Centre, the tower of **St Helen's Church** provides a magnificent view of the network of waterways. A little further down the River Bure stand the ruins of **St Benet's Abbey**, first built in AD 870 but now oddly misshapen thanks to the stump of a windmill (now disused) that was added to the ruins 200 years ago.

In some places the Broads are tidal, and the slightly brackish water attracts coots, heron, bittern and the nation's largest species of butterfly, the swallowtail, lives in the reeds. Plant life, however, has disappeared from the waters of all but a few Broads over the past few decades. Some blame agricultural fertilisers, others the disturbance caused by pleasure craft. The exact cause remains unknown.

The sea giveth and the sea taketh away – or so the waves seem to clamour on the shingle and hiss on the sands of East Anglia. On the north Norfolk coast **Cley-next-the-Sea** is now more than a mile (1.6 km) from the shore, but the resulting combination of salt marshes, reedbeds and lagoons attracts a remarkable number of wading birds. Nearby **Blakeney Point** attracts a host of seabirds during the summer, and it is also home to common and grey seals which bask on the sands at low tide. **Wells-next-the-Sea** ⓬ is a genuine working port, with coasters along the quay and fishing boats bringing in whelks, crabs and shrimps. Head inland via the light railway to **Little Walsingham**, a place of pilgrimage once as important as Canterbury, which has a delightful medieval high street.

The heyday for holidaying in East Anglia was undoubtedly the Victorian era, when the Great Eastern Railway Company's network opened up a dozen resorts on the sunny coastline. Two towns that have retained that atmosphere are **Sheringham** and **Cromer**, in north Norfolk, a coastline lashed by winter storms. In 1855–56 there were 500

The best places for boat hire are Wroxham and Horning (both on the River Bure near Woodbastwick, off the A1151). Broads Tours (tel: 01603-782207; www.broads.co.uk) offers all-weather trips and the Broads Authority (tel: 01603-610734; www.broads-authority.gov.uk) provides information about boat hire.

LEFT: bathing cabin, Wells-next-the-Sea. **BELOW:** traditional Punch and Judy show, Southwold.

Southwold has what must be the cheapest passenger ferry in the country (70p per person), which plies across to Walberswick, a village frequented by painters.

BELOW: Martello tower at Aldeburgh, built as a coastal defence during the Napoleonic Wars and now rented as a holiday home by the Landmark Trust.

wrecks off this shore. Even today almost every village has its own lifeboat.

Midway around the coast, **Great Yarmouth** ⓭ has kept its popularity with the tourists. Once the scene of great activity with the arrival of herring, today it is a tacky place; the golden sands of the beach are hidden behind the spires of the helter-skelters and the walls of the roller-coaster. So changed is Yarmouth that the 1969 film of *David Copperfield* had to be shot in the resort of **Southwold** ⓮, 20 miles (32 km) south. This dignified town's manicured appearance is due partly to a fire in 1659 which destroyed much of the fishing village and allowed careful reconstruction. Its tasteful image was enhanced in 2001 with the reopening of the long-neglected pier. In the town's magnificent Perpendicular Church of St Edmunds (daily June–Aug 9am–6pm, Sept–May until–4pm), Southwold Jack, a medieval figure in armour, rings in the services by striking a bell with his sword. Despite the dominance of tourism, Southwold has one of the few estuary ports still used by fishermen.

The ancient capital of **Dunwich** ⓯ at one time had eight churches; now the sea has swept most of the town away, leaving only a few cottages, the remains of a monastery and a town museum.

Aldeburgh

Across the Blythe estuary from Walberswick to **Aldeburgh** ⓰ is a rewarding, though long, walk. Benjamin Britten (1913–76) made the fishing village his home and in 1948, together with the tenor Peter Pears, started the prestigious annual music festival that runs for two weeks every June (aldeburgh.co.uk). Since then, Aldeburgh (which means "old fort") has become fashionable indeed.

Eighteen miles (29km) southwest of Aldeburgh, at Melton, is the National Trust site of **Sutton Hoo**. an atmospheric Anglo-Saxon royal burial site where ancient treasures were excavated in 1939. The burial site has been reconstructed and there are fine country walks.

Ten miles (16km) to the southwest is the Suffolk county town of **Ipswich** ⓱. It has little to recommend it apart from an atmospheric Victorian dockland, complete with lightship and sailing barges, on the River Orwell. George Orwell, the author of *Nineteen Eighty-Four,* took his pen name from the river, but the Stour, which meets the Orwell at its mouth around the North Sea passenger and cargo ports of **Harwich** and **Felixstowe**, is the more famous of the two rivers, thanks to the work of a much-loved British artist.

Constable country

The Suffolk countryside alongside the Stour is called **Constable country**. John Constable (1776–1837) painted the river, the trees and the villages with a love that has made this landscape familiar even to

Recommended Restaurants and Pubs on page 203

those who have never been here. The artist was born in the grand village of **East Bergholt** 18 (just off the A12 between Ipswich and Colchester), where the bells of the church tower, never finished, are housed in a shed in the graveyard. His father was the mill owner at **Flatford**, just down the hill. The setting had great sentiment for Constable, and he recreated it in the painting *The Hay Wain*. The water mills of nearby **Stratford St Mary** were another favourite subject. In fact, all along the River Stour is Constable's element. The National Trust arranges guided walks through "Constable scenes" from Flatford Bridge Cottage (tel: 01206-298260).

The village of **Dedham**, only a few miles up the banks of the Stour from Flatford and best approached that way, has changed little. The row of neoclassical houses that faces the church is pristine. And yet Dedham is not entirely unmodern; inside the timeless church one of the pews is decorated with medallions from the first moon landing.

Unspoilt as Dedham may seem, the villages inland are even more so. In **Kersey**, **Hadleigh** and **Lavenham**, many of the timbered houses that lean over the streets date from the early 16th century. This is wool country, and these villages were well known and wealthy for 700 years after the Norman Conquest (Kersey cloth is mentioned by Shakespeare). The rich mill owners lived in grand halls and worshipped in magnificent churches, all built with their profits. Fine examples of both of these are at **Long Melford** 19, north of Sudbury. The village's Tudor houses present a pleasing visage of turrets and moats; the two best examples are Melford Hall and Kentwell Hall.

Lavenham

In the remarkably preserved medieval village of **Lavenham** 20 many of the houses are 400 years old. The Little Hall (Easter–end summer Wed, Thur, Sat, Sun 2–5.30pm; tel: 01787 247019) and the Guildhall (Mar Wed–Sun 11am–4pm, Apr–early Nov daily 11am–5pm, mid-Nov–end Nov Sat–Sun 11am–4pm; tel: 01787 247646) are open to the public. Telegraph poles have been removed and the wires buried underground to preserve the village's Tudor appearance.

Timber-framed houses give the villages

In 1923 a water tower at Thorpeness, north of Aldeburgh, was turned into a "house in the clouds" and today has five bedrooms and three bathrooms – but there are 68 steps to climb.

BELOW: Lavenham.

Map on page 192

At Kentwell Hall, a moated Tudor manor in Long Melford, women dry wool while a man ploughs the field in a living history reenactment.

their beauty, but flint and brick dominates at **Bury St Edmunds** ㉑, the cathedral city of the area, midway between Ipswich and Cambridge on the A14. But the city is no backwater, and the narrow streets around the **Buttermarket** are jammed with people, as is the **Nutshell** on The Traverse, said to be the smallest pub in England.

On Cornhill, the **Moyse's Hall Museum** (Mon–Fri 10.30am–4.30pm, Sat–Sun 11am–4pm), built in 1180, is considered the oldest Norman house in East Anglia. It is also said to have been the house of a Jewish merchant, or even a synagogue, but with no evidence to support the claims. Inside are Bronze Age and Saxon artefacts found in the area, plus relics of the grisly Red Barn murder. At the centre of the town in Market Cross is a beautiful building by Robert Adam housing the **Bury St Edmunds Art Gallery** (Tue–Sat 10.30am–5pm, except during exhibit preparations) which stages temporary exhibitions.

The gems of Bury are the ancient **Abbey** and **Cathedral** (daily 8.30am–6pm; tel: 01284 748720). The beautiful grounds, laid out as formal gardens, are twice the size of the city centre, and the surrounding walls exclude the noise of the town. Below the Cathedral, built in the 12th century, lie the remains of the Abbey, swathed in grass.

Originally founded in the 7th century, it was an important place of pilgrimage after the body of Edmund, last king of the East Angles who was killed by the Danes, was placed there in about 900. In 1214 a group of barons swore before the altar to raise arms against King John if he refused to set his seal to the Magna Carta. He did, unwillingly, a year later, and today Bury still celebrates this event – and Edmund's burial – in its motto: Shrine of a King, Cradle of the Law. ❑

BELOW: the Abbey ruins, Bury St Edmunds.

RESTAURANTS AND PUBS

Restaurants

Prices for a three-course meal per person with a half-bottle of house wine:
£ = under £25
££ = £25–50
£££ = £50–100

Aldeburgh

The Golden Galleon Fish and Chip Shop
137 High Street
Tel: 01728-454685 **£**
If you can stand the queue you will be amply rewarded. Take your fish and chips down to the pebbly beach across the road, or sit upstairs in the restaurant.

The Lighthouse
77 High Street
Tel: 01728-453377 **£**
Fish features heavily on the menu, lovely potted Norfolk shrimps and fish soup are popular dishes. Lunch and dinner menus change daily. Sara Fox and Peter Hill also run the cookery school nearby (www.aldeburgh-cookeryschool.com) **££**

Bulmer Tye, nr Sudbury

The Bulmer Fox
Tel: 01787-312277 **£–££**
Sunday lunchtimes, and the Fox's no-booking policy together with its raging popularity mean that the car park is full before the doors have even opened. Relaxed bistro-style restaurant in Edwardian country pub.

Cambridge

Alimentum
152–154 Hills Road
Tel: 0223-413000 **££**
Ehtical values underpinned this sleek venture, from being the first UK restaurant to serve humanely produced *foie gras* right down to the biodegradeable cocktail straws. Skilfully prepared yet unfussy Modern European dishes. Closed Sun.

Midsummer House
Midsummer Common
Tel: 01223-369299 **£££**
Walled Victorian house on the banks of the Cam. Elegant modern European cuisine in stylish surroundings. Closed Sunday and Monday.

Three Horseshoes
Madingley, nr Cambridge
Tel: 01954-210221 **££**
Thatched inn in quaint village 2 miles (3 km) from Cambridge. Stunningly presented Mediterranean-style food served in the airy conservatory-cum-dining-room; lovely puddings, all well priced.

Hintlesham, nr Ipswich

Hintlesham Hall
Tel: 01473-652334 **£££**
Country-house hotel serving British food in award-winning restaurant.

Lavenham

Angel Hotel
Market Place
Tel: 01787-247388 **££**
Grilled sea bass fillet with creamed spinach and spiced pork cutlet with braised endive are just two of the mains at Lavenham's oldest inn. Dating back to 1420, the Angel still retains much of its Tudor character.

Morston, nr Blakeney

Morston Hall
Morston, Holt
Tel: 01263-741041 **£££**
A 17th-century country house hotel with an award-winning restaurant. Michelin-starred chef, Galton Black, features local produce, such as Blakeney lobster and Morston mussels, highly on the menu. Set-dinner menu changes daily.

ABOVE: fresh crabs landed at Cromer in Norfolk.

Norwich

Adlard's
79 Upper St Giles
Tel: 01603-633522 **££**
Stylish, welcoming restaurant serving modern British food with a French twist. Head chef, Jonathan Batchelor's dedication to fresh seasonal produce is apparent in all dishes.

Stanton

Leaping Hare Vineyard Restaurant
Wyken Vineyards
Tel: 01359-250287 **£–££**
Elegant café-restaurant at one of Britain's most respected vineyards. Californian-style cooking. Set on the edge of a country estate.

Swaffham

Strattons
Stratton House, 4 Ash Close
Tel: 01760-723845 **££**
Family-run hotel with a passion for local ingredients, from flour to cockles and excellent home-grown vegetables.

Pubs

In Cambridge, the **Elm Tree** on Orchard Street is cosy, with live jazz, the **Free Press** on Prospect Row is a tiny Victorian pub with imaginative, home-made food, and the **Green Dragon** on Water Street is a former coaching inn (Oliver Cromwell stayed here) with a real fire on cold days.

In Norwich, the **Coach & Horses** on Thorpe Road, an old coaching inn, has good ales and a local fire, and the **Fat Cat** on West End Street has its own brewery and more than 20 real ales.

In Aldeburgh, the **Mill Inn** on Market Cross Place is near the beach and, appropriately, serves good fish.

Recommended Restaurants and Pubs on page 217

THE SOUTHEAST

Kent and Sussex offer the hedonist a deckchair on a sunny beach, the delights of rolling countryside, the thrill of walking in high places, and the discovery of churches and rambling country houses

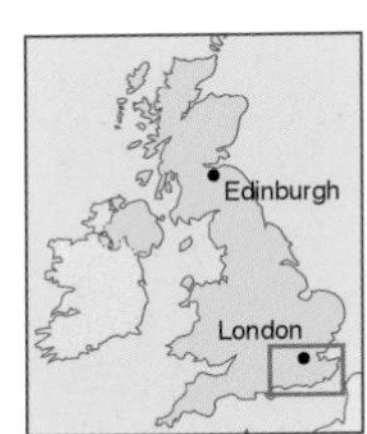

Main attractions
CHICHESTER
ARUNDEL
BRIGHTON
LEWES
GLYNDEBOURNE
PEVENSEY
RYE
SISSINGHURST CASTLE
ROYAL TUNBRIDGE WELLS
HEVER CASTLE
CHARTWELL
CHATHAM
KNOLE
CANTERBURY
MARGATE
DOVER
FOLKESTONE

The counties of **Kent** and **Sussex** in the southeast corner of England lie south of the Thames estuary, between London and the Channel. Any part of them can be seen on a day trip from the capital, particularly their historic centres such as Canterbury, Rye, Brighton and Chichester, which are best explored on foot. From London's orbital M25 motorway the M23 leads south to Brighton, principal resort of Sussex, while the M2 and M20 head for the Channel ports of Folkestone and Dover in Kent. Victoria, Charing Cross and London Bridge stations provide the rail links.

Invaders' alley

At Dover, the Kent coast is 21 miles (34 km) from France, and in 1875 the two countries were proved to be within swimming distance by Captain Matthew Webb (it took him 21 hours 45 minutes). As the nearest point to the Continent, this is the way invaders came: Romans, Angles, Saxons and Britain's last conquerors, the Normans, who scorched the date of 1066 into the history books with their triumph at the Battle of Hastings. Towers, castles and moated mansions were built to withstand later invasion attempts by France, Spain and, in the 20th century, Germany, while cathedrals rose at Chichester and Canterbury, the Church of England's spiritual home and the focus of centuries of pilgrims.

The counties have a common geology in which all the strata run east to west. Kent's North Downs mirror the Sussex South Downs and the filling in this cake is greensand, Weald clay and sandstone, repeated in reverse order. All contribute to a rich variety of landscape in a relatively small space. The chalky South Downs, with a walking trail along their summit, were hailed somewhat exaggeratedly by the eminent 18th-century natu-

PRECEDING PAGES: Arundel Castle.
LEFT: Canterbury Cathedral at night.
RIGHT: Bateman's, to the south of Burwash village in East Sussex, where the writer Rudyard Kipling lived from 1902 to 1936.

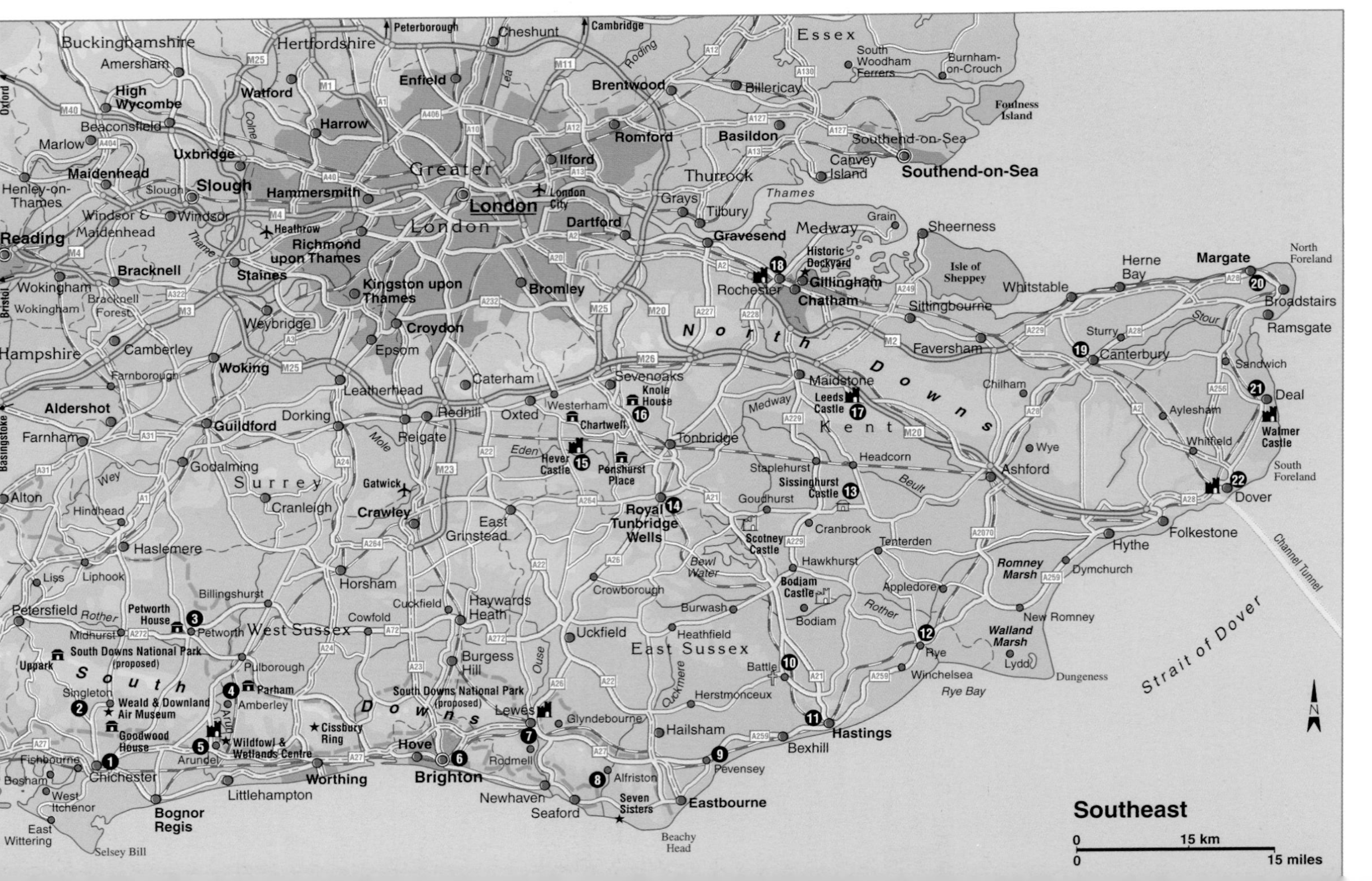

Southeast
0 15 km
0 15 miles
Strait of Dover
Channel Tunnel
North Foreland
South Foreland
Margate
Broadstairs
Ramsgate
Sandwich
Deal
Walmer Castle
Dover
Folkestone
Hythe
Dymchurch
Dungeness
New Romney
Romney Marsh
Walland Marsh
Lydd
Rye Bay
Rye
Winchelsea
Hastings
Bexhill
Pevensey
Eastbourne
Beachy Head
Seven Sisters
Alfriston
Seaford
Newhaven
Brighton
Hove
Worthing
Littlehampton
Bognor Regis
Selsey Bill
East Wittering
West Itchenor
Bosham
Fishbourne
Chichester
Goodwood House
Weald & Downland Air Museum
Singleton
Arundel
Arun
Wildfowl & Wetlands Centre
Amberley
Parham
Pulborough
Cissbury Ring
South Downs National Park (proposed)
South Downs
Lewes
Glyndebourne
Rodmell
Ouse
Burgess Hill
Haywards Heath
East Grinstead
Uckfield
Crowborough
Royal Tunbridge Wells
Heathfield
Burwash
Hailsham
Herstmonceux
Battle
Bodiam Castle
Bodiam
Hawkhurst
Cranbrook
Tenterden
Appledore
Rother
Sissinghurst Castle
Scotney Castle
Goudhurst
Staplehurst
Headcorn
Beult
Ashford
Wye
Chilham
Canterbury
Sturry
Herne Bay
Whitstable
Faversham
Sittingbourne
Isle of Sheppey
Sheerness
Grain
Medway
Historic Dockyard
Gillingham
Chatham
Rochester
Maidstone
Leeds Castle
Kent
North Downs
Tonbridge
Penshurst Place
Hever Castle
Chartwell
Knole House
Sevenoaks
Westerham
Oxted
Eden
Caterham
Redhill
Reigate
Gatwick
Crawley
Horsham
Cuckfield
Cowfold
West Sussex
Billingshurst
Petworth
Petworth House
Midhurst
Uppark
Petersfield
Liss
Liphook
Haslemere
Hindhead
Cranleigh
Surrey
Godalming
Guildford
Dorking
Mole
Leatherhead
Epsom
Croydon
Kingston upon Thames
Richmond upon Thames
Heathrow
Hammersmith
Greater London
London
London City
Bromley
Dartford
Gravesend
Tilbury
Grays
Thurrock
Thames
Basildon
Billericay
Canvey Island
Southend-on-Sea
South Woodham Ferrers
Burnham-on-Crouch
Foulness Island
Essex
Brentwood
Romford
Ilford
Cheshunt
Lea
Enfield
Harrow
Watford
Hertfordshire
Colne
Uxbridge
Slough
Windsor
Staines
Weybridge
Woking
Camberley
Farnborough
Aldershot
Farnham
Alton
Hampshire
Bracknell
Bracknell Forest
Wokingham
Reading
Windsor & Maidenhead
Maidenhead
Marlow
Henley-on-Thames
High Wycombe
Beaconsfield
Amersham
Buckinghamshire
Oxford
Bristol
Basingstoke
Peterborough
Cambridge
Roding

ralist Gilbert White as "a chain of majestic mountains". They reach the sea at the spectacular cliffs at Beachy Head, near Eastbourne; the North Downs end at the white cliffs of Dover.

In between the North and South Downs is the Weald, an excellent area for fruit growing, particularly apples, and grapes for white English wines (the chalk Downs are the same geological strata that runs through France's Champagne region). Hops grown for beer were once picked by London's East Enders in a holiday mood but barely 50 hop farms remain.

King Canute's shore

To the west lies the county town of **Chichester** ❶ where the spire of the **Cathedral** (daily; tours Mon–Sat 11.15am and 2.30pm last 45 minutes; free; chichestercathedral.org.uk) rises like a beckoning finger above this typical English rural town of notable Georgian houses. The **South Downs** provide a backdrop and the creeks and marshes of its harbour nearly reach its walls.

The 270-ft (82-metre) 14th-century cathedral spire, the only one in the country visible from the sea, was rebuilt in 1861 by George Gilbert Smith, after a storm had brought it down. Inside, the modern altar tapestry by John Piper (1903–92) is a dramatic surprise. Among many fine carvings and relief work the most remarkable is the 12th-century *Raising of Lazarus*, which can be found in the south side of the choir. There is a stained-glass window by Marc Chagall.

Pallant House Gallery (Tues–Sat 10am–5pm Thur 10am–8pm Sun 12.30–5pm; tel: 01243-774 557; pallant.org.uk; charge) is another attraction housing a unique collection of 20th-century British art in a Queen Anne townhouse and a modern building.

The 15th-century **Market Cross** is one of the finest in the country. Good local pubs with accommodation include the 15th-century Dolphin and Anchor in West Street and The Ship in North Street. To the north of the town is the **Festival Theatre**, a theatre in the round where Laurence Olivier was the first director, from 1962 to 1965.

Little of Chichester's Roman walls remain, but at **Fishbourne** (Feb–mid-Dec daily 10am–5pm; mid-Dec–Jan Sat–

Chichester Cathedral.

BELOW: Goodwood, a major racecourse close to Chichester.

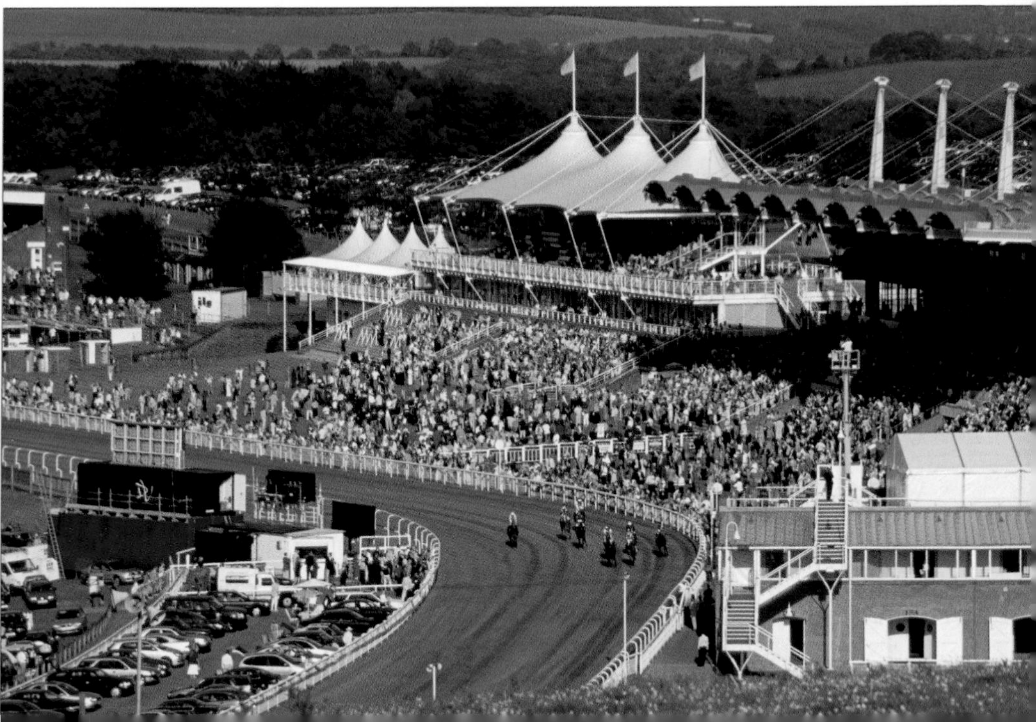

Wisley, the flagship garden of the Royal Horticultural Society, is located off the A3 east of Woking. As well as lush gardens, it has a state-of-the-art glasshouse. It is open every day and has a well-attended three-day flower show in August. Tel: 0845 2609000. www.rhs.org.uk

BELOW: *Anne Carr, Countess of Bedford* by Anthony van Dyck, part of the art collection at Petworth House.

Sun only; tel: 01243 785859), a mile to the west, Britain's largest Roman palace was uncovered in 1960. It is worth seeing for its well-preserved mosaics, including the famous *Cupid on a Dolphin*, as well as to appreciate its formidable scale and size. The estuary it stood beside has receded and Chichester's harbour now has myriad muddy inlets (harbour tours from **West Itchenor**), the most attractive being at **Bosham**.

In the South Downs behind Chichester is **Goodwood**, site of a racecourse and country house. At the summit is the hill fort of the Trundle, giving wonderful views before dropping down to **Singleton ❷** and the **Weald and Downland Open Air Museum** (Mar–Oct daily 10.30am–6pm, Nov–Feb Sat–Sun 10.30am–4pm wealddown.co.uk). For this 45-acre (18-hectare) open-air project, buildings from the 13th–19th centuries have been conserved and rebuilt.

Continuing north for 6 miles (9 km) the A286 arrives at the elderly market town of **Midhurst**, where a right turn on to the A272 leads another 6 miles to **Petworth ❸**. Here narrow streets are twisted and turned by the walls of the great 17th-century **Petworth House** (Mar–Nov Sat–Wed 11am–5pm; charge; tel: 01798-343929), seat of the Percys, Earls of Northumberland. It has a deer park (daily 8am–dusk) landscaped by Capability Brown and an exceptional art collection. J.M.W. Turner painted here in 1810 and 1830. It also has astounding wood carvings by Grinling Gibbons.

Follow the Rother downstream to join the Arun and below is **Pulborough**. This is the fishing capital of Sussex, famed for Arundel mullet and Amberley trout. **Amberley ❹**, 5 miles (8 km) to the south, has a castle (now a luxury hotel) rescued from a farm which overlooks the village of whitewashed cottages and thatch.

Just to the east lies **Parham**, a remote and carefully restored Tudor house (Apr–July, Sept Wed–Thur, Sun and bank holiday Mon 2–5pm, Aug Tues–Fri 2–5pm; gardens noon–5pm; tel: 01903-742021; parhaminsussex.co.uk); it has a delightful 4-acre (1.6-ha) walled garden with a 1920s Wendy House.

One duke's castle

The Arun finally emerges from the South Downs around **Arundel ❺**, commanded by the imposing **castle** of the Dukes of Norfolk, Earls Marshal of England, organisers of the pomp of state processions (Mar–Nov Tues–Sun noon–5pm; tel: 01903-882173; charge; arundelcastle.org). More French than English, the competing views of the castle and churches (both Anglican and Catholic under one roof at St Nicholas's) dominate the skyline. Much reconstruction through the 19th century has made the castle a sham, but it's a sham carried off with a flourish. There are splendid views of the castle from Swanborne lake in the grounds. Beyond the lake, about a mile from the castle through an avenue of trees, is the excellent **Wildfowl and Wetlands Centre** (end Oct–mid Mar daily 9.30am–4.30pm, mid Mar–end Oct until 5.30pm; charge; tel: 01903-883355; wwt.org.uk).

Earlier peoples clung to the heights around here and the Downs are littered

Recommended Restaurants and Pubs on page 217

with hill forts, flint mines, burial mounds and tracks used 2,000 years before the Romans came. The **Amberley Working Museum**, dedicated to the industrial heritage of the area, is at Houghton Bridge, Amberley (mid-Mar–Oct Wed–Sun 10am–5.30pm; amberleymuseum.co.uk), and 10 miles (16 km) east are two hills worth a climb, **Cissbury** and **Chanctonbury**, which has a crown of beeches. These are all along the **South Downs Way**, an 80-mile (130-km) footpath running from Petersfield, Hampshire to the coast at Eastbourne.

Brighton, or London-on-Sea

The history of **Brighton** ❻ is that of a poor fishing town that became the country's best-known seaside resort thanks to a local doctor, Richard Russell, who prescribed sea bathing for his patients. With the patronage of George IV (then Prince of Wales) he opened an establishment with attendants called "bathers" for men and "dippers" for women. London society followed. In 1785 the prince stayed in a villa on the Old Steine, later redesigned as the **Royal Pavilion** (daily Apr–Sept 9.30am–5.45pm, Oct–Mar 10am–5.15pm; charge; tel: 01273 290900; royalpavilion.org.uk) by John Nash, who was also responsible for London's Regent Street. Indian in style outside, Oriental within, the Pavilion, which was completed in 1822, is one of the decorative wonders of the world. It has a fascinating kitchen, and frequently has exhibitions and concerts. The adjacent **Brighton Museum and Art Gallery** (Tue 10am–7pm Wed–Sat 10am–5pm Sun 2–5pm Sun 2–5pm; tel: 01273 292882; brighton.virtualmuseum.info) is well worth a visit for its eclectic collections, ranging from archaeology to the works in its 20th-century Art and Design gallery. The **Marina** to the east of the town groups bars, restaurants, shops and cinemas around a harbour full of smart yachts and pleasure boats.

The **Palace Pier**, with its tacky amusement arcades, bars and fun fair is open until 11pm every day of the year.

Lewes ❼, the county town of East Sussex, lies to the northeast of Brighton. Its hills have been the scene of battles since Saxon times and it seems almost overburdened with history. From the Barbican entrance and the Norman

The Lanes – the square mile of narrow alleys that make up the original village of Brighton – are among the best-known haunts of antiques collectors in the south of England. The pubs, wine bars and restaurants there are worth trying.

BELOW: Brighton's Royal Pavilion, where the future George IV spent time with his lover, Mrs Maria Fitzherbert.

Oast houses are a typical feature of the Kent countryside, and a reminder of Britain's brewing industry. They were used as kilns for drying hops.

Castle to the Regency **Court Hall** and Victorian **Town Hall**, the High Street drops steeply to the river. At **Bull House**, Thomas Paine, author of *The Rights of Man*, lived from 1768 to 1774. In the same High Street, 10 men and women were burned at the stake during times of religious intolerance.

From Lewes the A27 to Eastbourne passes near **Glyndebourne**, the celebrated opera house and a key event of the summer season *(see pages 156–57)*. The area on the opposite, southern side of the highway could be described as rural Bloomsbury. At **Rodmell** Leonard and Virginia Woolf lived in **Monk's House** until Leonard's death in 1969 (Apr–Oct Wed and Sat 2–5.30pm; tel: 01323-870001).

From Berwick the River Cuckmere runs south to **Alfriston** 8. Next to the church is the thatched **Clergy House** (Apr–Oct Sat–Mon and Wed–Thur 10am–5pm Nov–Dec Sat–Mon and Wed–Thur 11am–4pm) and in the village are former smugglers' inns. Chalk cliffs, called the "Seven Sisters", lead to **Beachy Head**, at 530 ft (160 metres) the highest cliff on the coast; and to the smart resort town of **Eastbourne**, with its pier, fortress and numerous other attractions including Devonshire Park, where the famous Lawn Tennis Championships are held.

Battle

In the levels to the east, **Pevensey** 9 has the most considerable Roman monument in Sussex, but the Roman fort was incomplete and could not withstand the landing in 1066 of William, Duke of Normandy, the last man to invade Britain. The conqueror met up with Harold of England some 10 miles (16 km) inland; Senlac Field, where Harold fell, his eye pierced by an arrow, was marked by William who built upon it the high altar of the abbey church at **Battle** 10 (Apr–Oct daily 10am–6pm, Nov–March until 4pm; tel: 01424 775705) as a thanksgiving. An imposing 14th-century gatehouse leads to the grounds and ruins of the abbey.

The place where William prepared for battle is 6 miles (9 km) southeast of Battle. The hilltop Norman castle at **Hastings** 11, above a warren of caves where

BELOW: the "Seven Sisters" cliffs.

smugglers' adventures are re-enacted (Easter–Oct daily 10am–5.30pm Oct–Easter 11am–4.30pm), is now a ruin, though a siege tent inside re-tells the battle story. On the Stade, the stretch of shingle beach, tall weatherboarded sheds used by the fishermen for storing nets are architectural fantasies.

To the east is **Winchelsea**, which, like neighbouring **Rye** ⓬, has suffered from floods and the French and now lies high and dry. Edward III (1327–77) gave Rye its walls and gates. The **Landgate** and **Ypres Tower** survive, as well as much half-timbering. Today Rye is a pottery town and there is an active artists' colony whose work can be seen at the Stormont Studio in East Street (Thur–Sun; free), and the Easton Rooms in the High Street (Wed–Mon; free; tel: 01797 222433).

From Rye the land lies flat across the great expanse of **Romney Marsh**, a strange, haunted area of a special breed of sheep, of water weeds and wading birds such as the Kentish plover.

Weavers and the Weald

But before continuing in this direction, a detour back up from Rye on the B2082 to the white weatherboard town of **Tenterden**, home of a small historic railway, leads towards the **High Weald**. The region to the west of here was made rich by Flemish weavers, notably around **Cranbrook**. Daniel Defoe wrote *Robinson Crusoe* here in 1719.

Some 50 years later, during the Seven Years' War, 23-year-old Edward Gibbon, who wrote *The Decline and Fall of the Roman Empire*, was guarding French prisoners in **Sissinghurst Castle** ⓭ (Easter–Oct Fri–Tue 11am–6.30pm; tel: 01580-710701), 2 miles (3 km) to the east. The 16th-century manor house was in ruins when it was bought by Vita Sackville-West (1892–1962), poet, novelist and gardener extraordinary, and her politician husband Harold Nicolson in 1930. The beautiful gardens that they created are among the most visited in Britain. The most famous part is the White Garden, with its stunning array of white foliage and blooms in early summer.

Eight miles (13 km) west is **Goudhurst**, peaceful enough now, but in 1747 the villagers locked themselves in the church while a gang of smugglers from nearby **Hawkhurst** fought the local militia in the churchyard. From this half-timbered town there are wonderful views south over hop and fruit country and nearby are several places worth visiting. **Bodiam Castle**, to the south beyond Hawkhurst, is a classic medieval fort set in a 3-acre (1.2-hectare) moat (Feb–Oct daily 10.30am–6pm; Nov–Jan Sat–Sun 10.30am–4pm; tel: 01580-830196); while **Scotney Castle**, 5 miles (8 km) south-west, at Lamberhurst, has been described as one of the loveliest surviving landscapes in the 18th-century pictorial tradition (castle May–Sept Wed–Sun 11am–6pm; gardens Mar–Oct same hours as castle; tel: 01892-893820).

The Mermaid Inn in Rye dates from 1156 and was rebuilt in its present form in 1420.

Tunbridge Wells

Half way down the A21 between London and Hastings lies **Royal Tunbridge Wells** ⓮. Dudley, Lord North, a hypochondriac, brought fame and fortune to

BELOW: the gardens at Sissinghurst Castle, where Vita Sackville-West's library and study are open to visitors.

Many of England's finest vineyards can be found between Tenterden and Penshurst. Look out for signs offering winery and cellar tours, after which you can taste the wines.

BELOW: a pop concert at Leeds Castle. The name derives from an Old English spelling and has no connection with the city of Leeds in West Yorkshire.

the town in 1606 when he discovered the health-giving properties of a spring on the common. Court and fashion followed, and the waters, rich in iron salts, were, and still are, taken at the Pantiles. This terraced walk, with shops behind a colonnade, is named after the original tiles laid in 1638, some of which are still there.

The former home of the novelist William Thackeray in London Road (known simply as Thackeray's House) is now a restaurant and wine bar with a good reputation. There are also good second-hand bookshops in the old part of town. **Penshurst Place** (Apr–Oct daily, house noon–4pm, grounds 10.30am–6pm, Mar Sat–Sun only; tel: 01892-870307; penshurstplace.com), just to the northwest of the town, is one of Kent's finest mansions, dating from 1340 . Home of the Viscount de L'Isle, it was for two centuries the seat of the Sidney family, notably Sir Philip Sidney, the Elizabethan soldier and poet.

A few miles to the west lies **Hever Castle** ⓯ (Mar–Nov, gardens daily 10.45am–6pm, castle noon–6pm; tel: 01732-865224; hevercastle.co.uk). Henry VIII, who first met Anne Boleyn in this, her father's house, seized Hever after her execution and murdered her brother. William Waldorf Astor (1848–1919) applied his American millions to make massive and sympathetic improvements to the moated castle, 35-acre (15-hectare) lake, and gardens where flower beds are laid out just as they were in Tudor times.

Chartwell

Some 10 miles (16 km) to the north on the B2026 is **Westerham**, a town that commemorates General James Wolfe, who decisively drove the French from Canada when he stormed Quebec in 1759. South of the village is **Chartwell**, Winston Churchill's home from 1924 until his death in 1965. There is often quite a queue to see his home and studio where many of his paintings are on display (Mar–June Sept–Nov Wed–Sun 11am–5pm July, Aug Tues–Sun 11am–5pm; tel: 01732-866368).

Sevenoaks is the town 5 miles (8 km) to the east on the far side of the A21 and on its outskirts is **Knole** ⓰, one of the largest private houses in the country (Mar–Nov Wed–Sun and bank holidays noon–4pm; tel: 01732-450608). It was the Archbishop of Canterbury's residence

Canterbury Cathedral

The first church on the site was established in AD 597 by St Augustine who had been sent by Pope Gregory the Great to convert the heathen English. In 1170, Archbishop Thomas Becket, who had been quarrelling with King Henry II, was murdered in the cathedral by four of the king's knights. In 1220, his bones were transferred to a shrine in the Trinity chapel, a place of pilgrimage. In 1935, the shameful murder of Thomas Becket was recounted in verse by T.S. Eliot.

The nave – Europe's longest medieval nave – was rebuilt in 1400 and the main Bell Harry Tower was added a century later. The stunning stained glass rivals the best in France (open summer Mon–Sat 9am–5.30pm, winter 9am–5pm, Sun 12.30–2.30pm and 4.30–5.30pm; www.canterbury-cathedral.org).

Recommended Restaurants and Pubs on page 217

until confiscated by Henry VIII, and Elizabeth I gave it to Thomas Sackville who greatly extended it. It has 365 rooms, 52 stairways and seven courtyards. There are exceptionally fine portraits of the Sackville family by Gainsborough and Van Dyck, as well as some rare furniture. There is a 1,000-acre (400-hectare) deer park.

Kent's pride and joy lies to the east, 6 miles (10 km) beyond the county town of **Maidstone**. **Leeds Castle** ⓱, the castle of the queens of medieval England, is a fairytale place built on islands in a lake. It has 500 acres (200 hectares) of parkland and is a popular day out (Apr–Oct daily 10.30am–6pm, Nov–Mar until 4pm; tel: 01622-765400; charge).

Maidstone lies on the River Medway which empties into the Thames estuary between **Rochester** ⓲ and **Chatham** 10 miles (16 km) to the north. A Norman **castle** stands above the river at Rochester (Apr–Sept daily 10am–6pm, Oct–Mar until 4pm). Chatham grew around the Royal Navy dockyard established by Henry VIII. **The Historic Dockyard** (Feb–mid-Mar daily 10am 4pm mid-Mar–Oct daily 10am–6pm, Nov Sat–Sun until 4pm; tel: 01634 823807; chdt.org.uk) is now a museum, here you can discover 400 years fof maritime history. Nearby at Chatham Maritime is **Dickens World** (daily 10am–5.30pm; tel: 01634 890421; charge; dickensworld.co.uk), an indoor theme park based on the life of Charles Dickens; it gives you an authentic taste of Victorian England.

Canterbury

Canterbury ⓳ is the cradle of English Christianity. The Conqueror's Castle, the cathedral and its Thomas Becket Shrine were a magnet for pilgrims for centuries, and in St Margaret's Street the **Canterbury Tales** (Jan–Feb, Nov–Dec daily 10am–4.30pm, Mar–June Sept–Oct 10am–5pm, July–Aug 9.30am–5pm; charge) promises a "medieval adventure" with the sights, sounds and even the smells of the journey made by five of Chaucer's characters.

Despite German aerial bomb attacks in 1942, much of the town's medieval character remains, and there are a number of good pubs in its narrow streets. The town's delights include the remains of the

Chartwell, Sir Winston Churchill's old home, is run by the National Trust.

Below: Canterbury Cathedral, founded in AD 602.

Dover Castle, where you can visit the labyrinth of secret wartime tunnels built deep in Dover's White Cliffs.

original Roman wall which once enclosed it. Also worth visiting are the excavated ruins of **St Augustine's Abbey** (Mar–June Wed–Sun 10am–5pm, July, Aug daily 10am–6pm Sept–Mar Sat–Sun 11am–5pm). Further east along Longport is **St Martin's Church** where Christian worship has taken place since AD 597. In the 4th century this area was selected by rich Romans for their villas, and remains can still be seen.

The wide-ranging and newly renovated **Museum of Canterbury** is located in Stour Street (Mon–Sat 10.30am–5pm, June–Sept also Sun 1.30–5pm).

Further east lies **Margate** ⓴, which the railway opened up to London's East Enders as one of the capital's most popular seaside resorts. Bathing machines were invented here by a local Quaker and it still has a breezy holiday air. A couple of miles away is **North Foreland**, the tip of the duck's tail of Kent and Britain's most easterly spot. Immediately below is **Broadstairs**, a more up-market resort which has a sandy bay and landscaped cliffs, which Dickens described as being "left high and dry by the tide of years". When he knew it, the clifftop **Bleak House** was called Fort House. He spent his summer holidays there in the 1850s and 1860s (Mar–Nov daily 10am–6pm, Feb 11am–4pm, Jan Sat–Sun only).

BELOW: the beach at Botany Bay, Broadstairs.

Sandwich lies along the River Stour, 2 miles (3 km) from the sea. As long ago as the 9th century it was an important port, but by the 17th century the progressive silting up of the estuary left it high and dry, and it is now surrounded by a 500-acre (200-hectare) coastal bird sanctuary. In the 11th century, Sandwich became one of the original Cinque Ports, a string of safe harbours from here to Hastings fortified against invaders.

Walmer Castle (Easter–Sept daily 10am–6pm, Mar and Oct until 4pm; tel: 01304-364388) in **Deal** ㉑ is still the official residence of the Lord Warden of the Cinque Ports, a post held by the late Queen Mother for 24 years. On the shingle beach of this small resort Julius Caesar landed in 55 BC and there is a plaque commemorating the event.

Dover

Sandwich, Deal and **Dover** ㉒ are now billed as "**White Cliffs Country**", and at Dover, Britain's busiest passenger port, the chalk massif of the South Downs dramatically drops into the sea. On these cliffs the Romans built a lighthouse, the Normans a **castle** (Apr–Sept daily 10am–6pm; tel: 01314-211067 for winter hours), and from here Calais can be seen on a clear day. In the castle you can experience a medieval siege and visit tunnels used by the military in World War II. The recently-excavated **Roman Painted House** in York Street (Tue–Sat 10am–5pm, Sun 1–5pm) is also worth a visit.

It is near the neighbouring port of **Folkestone** that the Continent comes more sharply into view. The town has a large market on Sundays, but it is more famous for the nearby Channel Tunnel, which since 1994 has provided fast train and car shuttle services between England and France. It is a development that makes the coast's castles, towers and parapets look even more ancient. ❑

RESTAURANTS AND PUBS

Restaurants

Prices for a three-course meal per person with a half-bottle of house wine:

£ = under £25
££ = £25–50
£££ = £50–100

Amberley, near Arundel

Amberley Castle
On the B2139 between Storrington and Bury Hill
Tel: 01798-831992 **££**
Evocatively restored 12th-century castle. You can dine in splendour in the Queen's Room Restaurant with a splendid 16th-century mural. Classic cuisine is cooked and served with some panache.

Brighton

Gingerman
21a Norfolk Square
Tel: 01273-326688 **££**
L 12.30–1.45pm. D 7–9.30pm. Tues–Sun.
Modern European cooking with imaginative touches served in a pleasant dining space with bare wooden floors. Set menus.

Pintxo People
95 Western Road
Tel: 01273-732323
Restaurant Tues–Fri 6am–midnight Sat noon–4pm, 6pm–1am **££**
Traditional tapas cantina on the ground floor, modern tapas restaurant and cocktail bar upstairs.

Terre à Terre
71 East Street
Tel: 01273-729051
Tues–Fri noon–10.30pm (Sat 11pm, Sun 10pm). **££**
Popular restaurant offering a brilliantly innovative vegetarian menu and organic wine.

Canterbury

The Goods Shed
Station Road West
Tel: 01227-459153
L from noon, D from 6pm. **£**
A disused Victorian railway building now serves as a farmers' market and restaurant, with excellent fresh (often organic) food.

Chilgrove, near Chichester

The Fish House
High Street (B2141 Chichester to Petersfield)
Tel: 01243-519444 **££**
New restaurant, bar and hotel in a former 18th-century coaching inn. Fresh seafood dishes.

East Grinstead

Gravetye Manor
Vowels Lane (southwest of East Grinstead)
Tel: 01342-810567 **£££**
Elizabethan manor house, with wood-panelled rooms and fine gardens. Excellent traditional and modern British cooking.

Jevington

The Hungry Monk
High Street
Tel: 01323-482178 **££**
In the Cuckmere Valley, this restaurant retains its quirky rustic character. Excellent desserts and cheeseboard. Must book.

Midhurst

Loch Fyne
Rothermere, North Street
Tel: 01730-716280
Mon–Fri 9am–10pm Sat 9am–10.30pm Sun 10am–10pm. **££**
Seafood is served in a restored listed building. Terrace with views of Cowdray Park. Also non-fish and vegetarian dishes.

Rye

Landgate Bistro
5–6 Landgate
Tel: 01797-222829
D Wed–Sat from 7pm. **££**
Chef Toni Ferguson-Lees has a local following for her blend of British and Mediterranean styles. Her speciality is seafood, but that is just part of an extensive repertoire.

Tunbridge Wells

Carluccio's Café
32 Mount Pleasant Road
Tel: 01892-614968 **££**
Carluccio brings his excellent Italian cooking and flair to Tunbridge Wells. The restaurant is light and airy and there's a deli attached.

Thackeray's House
85 London Road
Tel: 01892-511921 **££–£££**
In the pretty former home of the 19th-century novelist. Good French food.

Whitstable

Whitstable Oyster Fishery Restaurant
Horsebridge
Tel: 01227-276856 **££**
Good seafood and fish served in a busy, bistro by the beach. Can get very busy at lunchtime.

Pubs

In Brighton, the **Basketmakers Arms** on Gloucester Road is decorated with old signs and has good-value food. For shoppers, the **Waggon & Horses** on Church Street has a lively atmosphere.

ABOVE: preparing a Dover sole, named after the fishing port that landed the most sole in the 19th century.

In Lewes, the **Gardener's Arms** on Cliffe High Street, has good beers.

In Chichester, the **Four Chestnuts** is noted for its beers and generous food, and has music evenings.

In Tunbridge Wells, **The Hare** on Langton Road is a pleasant pub that serves large portions of interesting food and excellent desserts.

In Canterbury, **The Phoenix** on Old Dover Road is a beamed tavern with lots of cricketing memorabilia. **Old Brewery Tavern** on High Street is a modern bistro bar.

In Dover, **Blakes** on Castle Street has a cellar bar with good ales and a pleasant upstairs restaurant with good food. The White Horse on St James Street is a tavern dating to 1365 and is about beer rather than food.

The English Garden

Britain's temperate climate nurtures an amazing diversity of gardens which blend the grand and the homely in an eclectic range of styles

The formal gardens of great houses have both followed fashion and set the style for the nation's favourite hobby. In medieval times, fruit trees, roses and herbs were grown in walled enclosures: Elvaston Country Park in Derbyshire is a good example. In the 16th century, aromatic plants were incorporated in "knots" (carpet-like patterns). Tudor Gardens (such as those at Hatfield House in Hertfordshire and Packwood House in Warwickshire) were enclosed squares of flowers in geometric patterns bordered by low hedges and gravel paths.

The Renaissance gardener also liked snipping hedges into shapes: the most inventive examples are at Hever Castle in Kent. A taste for small flower beds persisted through the 17th and 18th centuries when fountains and canals began to be introduced.

The art of the landscape

In the 1740s a rich banker, Henry Hoare, inspired by Continental art during his Grand Tour, employed William Kent (1685–1748) to turn his gardens at Stourhead in Wiltshire into a series of lakes dotted with grottoes and buildings in the classical style. This was the birth of the landscape garden, known as *le jardin anglais*, that was an entirely English invention. The style was a direct reaction to the formal gardens made in France for Louis XIV at Versailles. Nature instead of geometry was the inspiration, and the idylls of landscape painters became the idylls of gardeners too.

"Capability" Brown (*see panel, right*) rejected formal plantings in favour of natural parkland and restricted flowers to small kitchen gardens. But Humphry Repton (1752–1815) reintroduced the formal pleasure garden. The Victorians put the emphasis on plants and Gertrude Jekyll (1843–1932) promoted the idea of planting cycles to ensure that colour lasted through the year.

Left: classical statues graced many gardens in the 17th century. This one is at **Belvoir Castle**, on a Leicestershire hilltop. Until the late 18th century many statues were made of lead, but it went out of favour for a century and many garden ornaments were melted down to make bullets for wars.

Above: This Wiltshire garden at **Stourhead**, birthplace of England's landscape movement, is dotted with lakes and temples and has many rare trees and shrubs. The artful vistas were created in the 1740s, and their magnificence contrasts with the severe restraint of the Palladian house (1721–24).

ABOVE: The 4th Duke of Marlborough employed "Capability" Brown *(see right)* in 1764 to impose his back-to-nature philosophy on **Blenheim Palace**. Brown's most dramatic change was to create a large lake by damming the River Glyme.

ABOVE: Hidcote Manor, a 17th-century Cotswold house at Mickleton in Gloucestershire, has one of the most beautiful English gardens, mixing different types of plot within various species of hedges. Although covering 10 acres (4 hectares), it's like a series of cottage gardens on a grand scale, prompting Vita Sackville-West to describe it as "haphazard luxuriance".

LEFT: Thanks to the influence of the Gulf Stream, sub-tropical flora can flourish at England's south-western tip. **Tresco Abbey Gardens**, on the Isles of Scilly, were laid out on the site of a Benedictine priory and contain many rare plants.

THE GREAT GARDENERS

Lancelot Brown (1715–83), *right*, who was responsible for more than 170 gardens at some of the country's greatest houses, is generally regarded as Britain's most influential gardener. Born in Northumberland, the son of a farm labourer, he was nicknamed "Capability Brown" when he rode from one aristocratic client to the next pointing out "capabilities to improvement". His forte was presenting gardens in the natural state, and his lasting influence lay in his talent for combining simple elements to create harmonious effects. Critics called his work bland and unimaginative, and one satirist hoped he would die before Brown so that he would see Heaven before Brown had the chance to improve it.

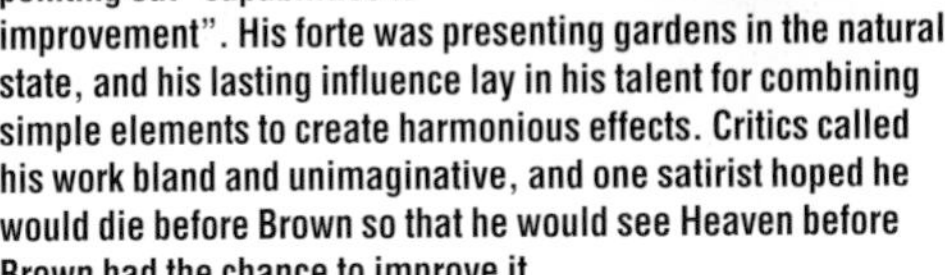

Brown liked to create elegant lakes for his parks, as at Blenheim Palace in Oxfordshire. He was also involved with the gardens at Stowe in Buckinghamshire, which the National Trust today describes as "Britain's largest work of art", and with the gardens at Kew, Britain's main botanical establishment, just outside London.

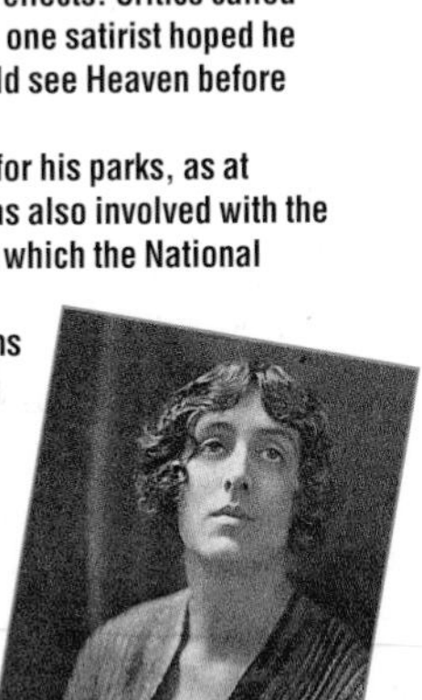

One of the 20th century's most influential gardeners was Vita Sackville-West (1892–1962), *right*, who developed her gardens at Sissinghurst Castle in Kent. She revived the 16th-century idea of dividing a garden into separate sections, combining a formal overall style with an informal choice of flowers. Although more remembered today for her relationship with the writer Virginia Woolf, she was a successful novelist and poet, and contributed an influential gardening column to *The Observer* Sunday newspaper.

BELOW: This example at Henry VIII's **Hampton Court Palace** outside London shows the Tudor liking for knots – small beds of dwarf plants or sand and gravel laid out in patterns resembling embroidery. Topiary, statues and mazes provided a counterpoint to the mathematical order.

Recommended Restaurants and Pubs on page 229

HARDY COUNTRY

Wessex, in central southern England, was immortalised by the novelist Thomas Hardy. It is especially rich in history and ancient monuments, including the magnificent stone circle at Stonehenge

Main attractions
- WINCHESTER
- SALISBURY
- STONEHENGE
- SHAFTESBURY
- LYME REGIS
- ISLE OF PORTLAND
- WEYMOUTH
- DORCHESTER
- CORFE CASTLE
- SWANAGE
- POOLE
- BOURNEMOUTH
- BEAULIEU MOTOR MUSEUM
- ISLE OF WIGHT
- SOUTHAMPTON
- PORTSMOUTH

No literary works bear the impress of place so strongly as the novels of Thomas Hardy (1840–1928) and no place has had its character and the character of its people revealed as Wessex has by Dorset's most famous son. Wessex is in fact an ancient kingdom, rather larger than the one in which the novelist's trail winds. This was the kingdom of the West Saxons, who had supremacy in England from AD 802 to 1013. It extended across the modern counties of Hampshire, Wiltshire, Dorset and Somerset and even for a short while included Devon and Cornwall.

The M3 motorway southwest of London leads to the ancient capital of Winchester in little more than an hour, and beyond it the urban sprawl of Southampton, once a transatlantic liner port. Skirting it, the A31 continues through the New Forest to the smart seaside town of Bournemouth and then to Dorchester, centre of the Hardy tours. To the north, the A303 leaves the M3 at junction 8 and heads for Salisbury Plain and Devon. Trains to London arrive at Waterloo.

There is no hurry about Wessex. The pace of life here is dictated by the cattle on its farms and the slow cycle of its growing crops. Dorset provides most of the coastline. To be lulled, go to Lyme Regis or Weymouth; to be threatened, go to Chesil Beach or Portland; to be overawed, go to the cliffs of Lulworth and Purbeck. Wessex seaside, like the country that lies behind, puts on a great show.

England's second capital

Winchester ❶ was England's first capital, as well as capital of Wessex, until all decision-making was moved to London in the 17th century. William the Conqueror had to be crowned in both places, though whether he had tea at the Old Norman Palace Tea Rooms is not so certain. Beneath the medieval and modern

LEFT: the cottage in Higher Bockhampton where Thomas Hardy was born.
RIGHT: a statue of King Alfred (reigned 871–99) surveys Winchester's high street.

Such is the allure of Stonehenge that here, on Midsummer Day, Druids celebrate their rites; in hooded white robes with mistletoe in hand, they sing and chant before dawn. Since the mid-1980s, however, all Midsummer festivities have been subject to restrictions – and sometimes banned – to prevent damage to the site.

city is a Roman town, and a Norman **Cathedral** (daily 8.30am–6pm) replaced the Saxon. Older than Canterbury and the longest in Europe, its Norman transepts and tower survive, but nave and choir were modernised by William of Wykeham in Perpendicular style towards the end of the 14th century. The organ's first notes were heard at the Crystal Palace in London's Hyde Park in 1851. The palace, cloisters, colleges and mill are all breathtaking. The Great Hall near Westgate is all that is left of Henry III's castle – but it is one of the finest in the country. Sir Walter Raleigh was condemned to death here in 1685 and it still functions as the county court.

Heading west from Winchester, the A272 drops suddenly to the broad main street of **Stockbridge** ❷, on the River Test, a delightful stop before the 15-mile (24-km) haul across the rolling countryside to Salisbury. The 12th-century coaching inn at the east end of the High Street, the White Hart (tel: 01264-810663), has plenty of atmosphere.

Salisbury ❸ ("Melchester" in the Hardy novels) has a cathedral built between 1220 and 1258, with "as many windows as days in the year, as many pillars as hours, and as many gates as moons". The spire took even longer to complete. **The Close**, a green space fringed with fine houses (mostly Georgian), distances the confusion of the modern city.

Stonehenge's secrets

About 8 miles (13 km) north of Salisbury on the A345 is Amesbury, and from there the A303 leads to that famous collection of standing stones, **Stonehenge** ❹ (daily from 9.30am, closing times vary; tel: 01980-623108; *see page 35*). On first view, it may seem disappointingly small; the American poet and essayist Ralph Waldo Emerson (1803–82) thought it "looked like a group of

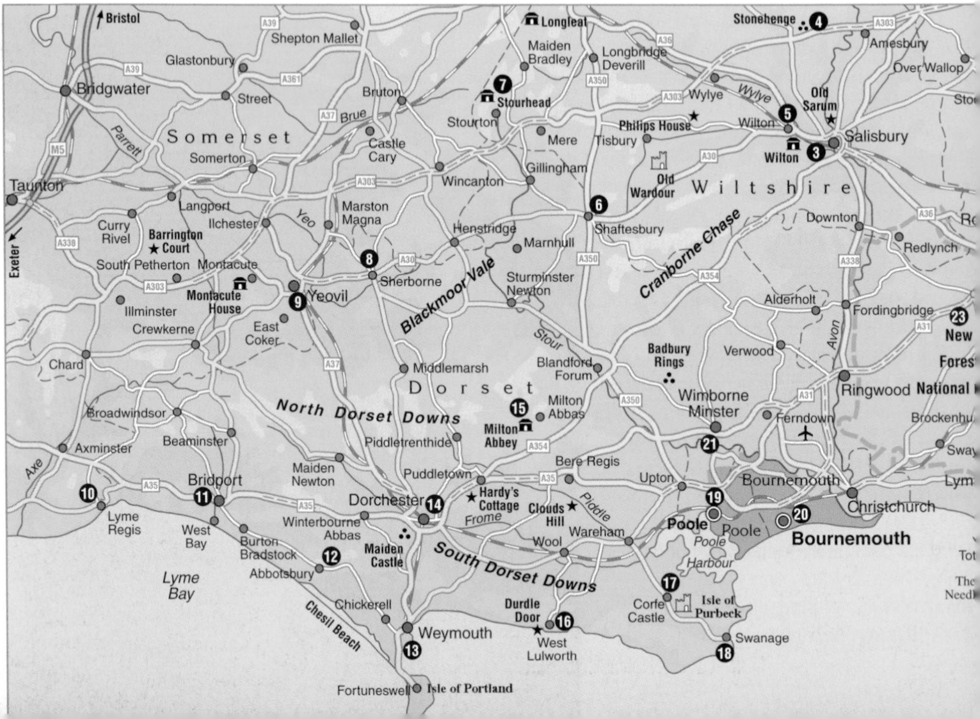

Recommended Restaurants and Pubs on page 229

brown dwarfs on the wide expanse". The largest standing trilithon is 21 ft (6 metres) high and extends more than 8 ft (2.5 metres) below ground.

Stonehenge consists of an outer ring and inner horseshoe of sarsen stone, brought from the Marlborough Downs. The blue stones are of a kind only quarried in the Prescelli Hills in Pembrokeshire. The circle's purpose is unknown, though the tumuli around the site hint at an ancient funerary significance. Some scholars suggest a link with astronomy.

Just west of Salisbury, the great house of **Wilton** ❺ (Easter–Oct daily 10.30am–5.30pm; tel: 01722-746720), the seat of the Earls of Pembroke, is splendidly framed in the entrance arch which prepares us for the sweetness and strength of Inigo Jones's rooms within. Here are the delights of a lock of Queen Elizabeth I's hair, Napoleon's despatch case, and some Rembrandts and Van Dycks. In the park, the Palladian bridge of 1737 over the River Nadder fuses function with great elegance.

Shaftesbury

Leaving Wilton, the A30 bounds the wilderness of the old hunting forest of **Cranbourne Chase** and then climbs to one of southern England's few hill towns, **Shaftesbury** ❻. Hardy renamed it "Shaston" in his 1895 novel *Jude the Obscure*. Walk the town walls above the steep drop to the horse-and-hound country of Blackmore Vale, and put the clock back centuries with a climb up the cobbled **Gold Hill** – like pilgrims to St Edward the Martyr's resting place.

In the village of Stourton, 8 miles (13 km) north of Shaftesbury near Mere, is the mansion at **Stourhead** ❼ (garden

Gold Hill, Shaftesbury.

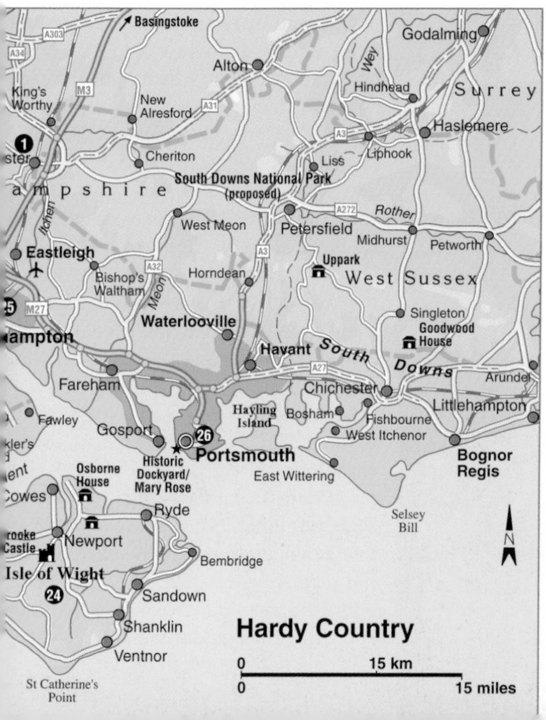

BELOW: the Temple of Apollo at Stourhead.

In the church at East Coker there's also a memorial to William Dampier (1652–1715), the ship-wrecked pirate who developed a taste for exploration and inspired Defoe's 1719 novel Robinson Crusoe.

daily 9am–7pm; house Mar–Oct Fri–Tue 11am–5pm; tel: 01747-841152), built for Henry Hoare, a banker, in 1720–24. The magnificent gardens are landscaped around the lake. There is an atmosphere of sweet melancholy about the temples to Flora and Apollo. Gothic cottages and towers are reflected in the lake's dark waters, best seen in the half light of the flint and pebble-lined grotto *(see page 218)*. Further south, 16 miles (25 km) west of Shaftesbury, is **Sherborne** ❽. Once an important centre in Wessex and the burial place of two Saxon kings, it retains a medieval flavour. You almost expect old conflicts between townsfolk and monks to flare again or to come upon Sir Walter Raleigh and his wife in their seats in the abbey chapel.

At **Yeovil** ❾, 5 miles (8 km) west of Sherborne, you stray into Somerset for a visit to **Montacute** (Easter–Oct Wed–Mon 11am–5pm; tel: 01935-823289), an Elizabethan house built for Sir Edward Phelips, a prosecuting lawyer at the trial of Guy Fawkes. In golden Ham Hill stone, the ornamental gazebos or lookouts at the corners of the forecourt are exquisite mansions in miniature.

BELOW: strolling along the seafront at Lyme Regis.

In the church at **East Coker**, 3 miles (5 km) to the south, are the ashes of T.S. Eliot (1888–1965). The poet's ancestors emigrated from here to America. "In my beginning is my end," he wrote in the poem named after the village.

Lyme Regis

There is a warm briny wind at **Lyme Regis** ❿, just east of the Devon border. This old fishing town was once as fashionable a resort as Bath, and it was popular 100 years before Bournemouth was even thought of. Regency bow windows and trellised verandas on Victorian villas line the **Parade** on the way to the tiny harbour and its curved protecting arm, the **Cobb**, where the Duke of Monmouth landed in 1685, aspiring to the crown. Its sea-lashed walls were a supporting role for Meryl Streep in the 1981 movie *The French Lieutenant's Woman*.

Austen's house, **Bay Cottage** (now a café) is near the harbour end of the parade, and she wrote much of her book here. During a visit in 1804, she stayed at Pyne House at 10 Broad Street. Charles II's illegitimate son, Monmouth, stayed at the George, in the town, and his blue ensign flew in the marketplace.

The road that hugs the sea to the east has a precarious footing above the landslips, descending to Charmouth and Jane Austen's "happiest spot for watching the flow of the tide". Hereabouts the cliffs reveal the existence of earlier visitors, like the elephant and rhinoceros, not in zoos, but in fossils. Ichthyosaurus turned up here in 1811. **Bridport** ⓫ ("Port Bredy" to Hardy) is 2 miles (3 km) from the sea, yet there is no denying its marine character. Rope and cordage, nets and tackle, this was the stuff of Bridport's prosperity.

West Bay is Bridport's improbable harbour. A narrow channel dug in the shingle bank and flanked by two high piers only feet apart offers a needle-threading operation for the small craft that lie uneasily in the little basin. In the old days coasters had to be hauled in with Bridport ropes. Visit on a Saturday and enjoy the outdoor market.

Isle of Portland

The next town east, nearby **Burton Bradstock**, is warmly summed up in thatch and smoky stone, flowers everywhere and a stream that trickles to the sea below Burton Cliff; it turned the wheel of the flax mills until the last one closed in 1930.

The dreaded Chesil Bank begins here, curving away eastwards to where it becomes the slender link that makes the **Isle of Portland** only a courtesy title. It is in fact, only a peninsula. The pebbles of the steeply shelving bank increase in size towards Portland, and at night, local fisherman docking at any point on the 16-mile (25-km) ridge can tell exactly where they are from the size of the pebbles. The bank has no mercy. To drive a boat in here spells almost certain disaster for the uninitiated. **St Catherine's Chapel**, on a green hill above the bank at **Abbotsbury** ⓬, leads a double life. A place of prayer for 500 years, it is also maintained as a mark for seamen. On the land side it overlooks the most fascinating miscellany of monastic ruin, a swannery and subtropical gardens. The 15th-century abbey barn, bigger and more splendid than many a parish church, was built as a wheat store. Further along the same road, by the salt water of Fleet, is the swan sanctuary founded in the 14th century.

Weymouth

George III did **Weymouth** ⓭ a good turn when he went there in 1789 for his convalescence after a serious illness. The grateful citizens responded by erecting the highly coloured statue that ends the half-mile esplanade.

The king bathed from his "machine" to the music of his own anthem. Fanny Burney records the occasion in the diary she kept while Second Mistress of the Robes to Queen Charlotte. George can be seen in chalk outline on a neighbouring hillside astride a horse.

There is much of the character of the 18th-century watering place about Weymouth today. Stuccoed terraces front the esplanade, the sands are golden and the sea is blue. There are museums of sea life, diving and shipwrecks. From Weymouth's jetty, ferries maintain a regular service to the Channel Isles.

Durdle Door at Lulworth Cove, 17 miles (27km) east of Weymouth. The limestone has been eroded to form a striking arch.

LEFT: King George III (reigned 1760–1820) in full regalia on Weymouth promenade.
BELOW: togetherness on Weymouth's beach.

Thomas Hardy's heartlands

To the south of Weymouth a narrow strip of land carries the road to the "island" of **Portland**. Thomas Hardy observed that the people who lived on what he called "the Gibraltar of Wessex" had manners and customs of their own. The sheer structure of Portland makes it a place apart. Everything is stone: buildings, walls, quarries – heaps of it everywhere. The lighthouse on the island's south tip overlooks the broken water of the treacherous Portland Race.

The green of the high hills inland of Weymouth comes as a welcome relief. Dorchester, 8 miles (13 km) north, is best approached from the great hill of **Maiden Castle**, *Mai Dun* ("great hill" – probably the world's largest earthwork), just before the town on the left. Excavations have shown that the hill was occupied 4,000 years ago, and a clever maze conceals the hill fort's entrance.

Dorchester ⓮, Dorset's county town, is well aware of its past, and the pace of life here, beyond the fast motorways, is noticeably slower. Thomas Hardy, Judge Jeffries and the Tolpuddle Martyrs all try to catch the visitor's eye. Hardy's statue commands his "Casterbridge" from the top of the High Street. The courtroom in the **Shire Hall** (Mon–Fri 10am–noon and 2–4pm) looks remarkably unchanged since 1834 when the Martyrs were convicted for trying to gain better working conditions. The **Dinosaur Museum** (Icen Way; 9.30am–5.30pm, Nov–Mar 10am–4.30pm; tel: 01305-269880) mixes fossils and hands-on displays.

Hardy's is perhaps the most potent influence. He was apprenticed to an architect at 39 South Street, and after he left the practice in 1885, he used his knowledge to design his own house, **Max Gate**, on the Wareham Road, where he died in 1928 (Easter–Sept Mon, Wed and Sun 2–5pm only).

There is a memorial collection devoted to Hardy in the **Dorset County Museum** on High West Street, a cast-iron building of 1880, delightfully decorated in bright primary colours. Stunning finds from **Maiden Castle** (Sept–June Mon–Sat, July–Aug daily) are here, too. Thomas Hardy was actually born in the cottage his great-grandfather built at **Higher Bockhampton**, just north of Dorchester in 1840. *Far From the Madding Crowd* and

During the Civil War of 1641–53, Abbotsbury's Benedictine abbey was used to store gunpowder, and the explosion which reduced most of its buildings to ruins provided the whole neighbourhood with material for new houses. The vicarage, farm and countless cottages in the village have the telltale white stones in their walls.

Below Right: Thomas Hardy's cottage at Higher Bockhampton.

The Genius of Thomas Hardy

Film makers today continue to be drawn to *Tess of the D'Urbervilles* and *Jude the Obscure*, finding that their strongly drawn characters and melodramatic situations translate very effectively to the screen. Yet when the novels first appeared, in the 1890s, reviewers condemned them for their pessimism and immorality. Certainly, they are much darker than Hardy's early novels such as *Under the Greenwood Tree* and *Far from the Madding Crowd*, published in the 1870s, although even these more pastoral stories convey a strong sense of the utter indifference of fate towards their protagonists – a defining characteristic of Hardy's writing.

Thomas Hardy (1840–1928) was born at Higher Bockhampton, near Dorchester, the son of a stonemason, and trained as an architect. All his major novels are set in Wessex and, despite their often bleak outlook, he draws their rustic characters with evident affection. He is also an acute observer of the natural surroundings, about which he writes poetically.

It was to poetry that he turned in his later years, with collections such as *Wessex Poems* (1898) and *Satires of Circumstance* (1914). Like his novels, his poetry has grown in critical stature with the passing of time.

Under the Greenwood Tree were written here (**Hardy's Cottage**; Easter–Oct Sun–Thur 11am–5pm; nationaltrust.org.uk).

The village of **Milton Abbas** ⓯, deep in the Dorset countryside 12 miles (20 km) to the northeast, annoyed Viscount Milton. It interfered with the view from his rebuilt mansion, **Milton Abbey** (during daylight hours), so in 1752 he moved the village as well, half a mile away, sticking to the rustic tradition of cob and thatch. The result is a uniquely harmonious parade of thatched cottages.

The 30-mile (48-km) coast from Weymouth east to Swanage, below Poole Harbour, is strictly for walking, army operations permitting, but approachable by car at **West Lulworth** ⓰, Kimmeridge and Worth Matravers.

Corfe Castle

Towards the east, the chalk hills around the **Isle of Purbeck** break at **Corfe Castle** ⓱ (daily Mar and Oct 10am–5pm, Apr–Sept 10am–6pm, Nov–Feb 10am–4pm), a too-picturesque ruin haunted by treachery, cruelty and murder. Here King Edward was murdered by his stepmother in 978, French prisoners were starved to death in the dungeons by King John, and the castle was traitorously handed over to the Roundheads in 1646 who pulled a large part of it down.

Swanage ⓲ ("Knollsea" to Thomas Hardy) "was a seaside village, lying snugly within two headlands as between a finger and a thumb". Look out for the stone globe, at Durlston Country Park, 10 ft (3 metres) in diameter, weighing 40 tons, and flanked by panels lettered with sobering information on the nature of the universe. Old Swanage, sitting on the hilltop, traps between its stone houses a mill pond.

Around Poole Harbour's creeks, mud flats and islands is **Poole** ⓳ itself, most beautiful on the quay and overlooking ships and shipyards, yachts and chandler's stores. Curving steps meet under the portico of the **Custom House** with its coat of arms representing an authority the Dorset smuggler never acknowledged. The town is famous for its pottery.

Beyond Poole are the hotels and elegant terraces of **Bournemouth** ⓴, the sedate resort built at the end of the 19th

The ruins of Corfe Castle. In the English Civil War, Parliamentary forces laid siege to the castle unsuccessfully in 1643 but captured it in 1646, using explosives to destroy its effectiveness.

BELOW: Milton Abbas, created in 1780 and thought by some to be England's first planned village.

Jet-skiing off Bournemouth.

century. To the northwest lies **Wimborne Minster** ㉑, where the church has a fine 13th-century clock. It has no hands, but rather the planets revolve with winged angels in attendance. Just east of Bournemouth is 100-year plus **Christchurch** on the mouth of the Avon. There is a turret at the **Priory** with a deliciously interlaced pattern of Norman arches that strongly recalls Pisa's leaning tower.

Hampshire haunts

Good rivers and harbours make this popular yachting country. **Lymington** ㉒ is the next safe port of call and on the River Beaulieu (pronounced *Bew-lee*) 6 miles (10 km) beyond, **Buckler's Hard** was famous for shipbuilding from the mid-18th century. Many of Nelson's warships took to the water here, launched between the two rows of shipwrights' cottages. At the end of the Napoleonic wars it all came to an abrupt end, but the **Maritime Museum** (Oct–Feb 10am–4pm, Mar–May 10am–4.30pm, June 10am–5pm, Aug–Sept 10am–5.30pm, tel: 01590-616203) captures the flavour of the past.

Beaulieu's church is unique; the monks' dining room was transformed into a pulpit. Lord Montagu runs Britain's best-known **Motor Museum** at Palace House in Beaulieu (daily 10am–5pm; tel: 01590-612345), and the local wine should be sampled.

To describe the wild, dense 100-sq mile (260-sq km) woodland of the **New Forest National Park** ㉓, which lies behind this coast, as "new" would seem to support the traditional belief that William the Conqueror had a hand in its creation. But this was always forest; William merely enforced measures to protect his deer. When driving through, remember that wild ponies have priority. Alice Lydell, Lewis Carroll's real Alice, is buried at **Lyndhurst**, the forest's capital, 8 miles (13 km) north of Lymington.

Isle of Wight

From Lymington a regular ferry crosses to the **Isle of Wight** ㉔ in 30 minutes (5.55am–9.30pm daily). The 147-sq mile (380-sq km) island is shaped like a kite, with the capital, **Newport**, just about where you might attach a string.

BELOW: riding in the New Forest.

Close by is **Carisbrooke Castle** (daily winter 10am–4pm, summer 10am–5pm; tel: 01983-522107), built by Elizabeth I as a defence against the Spanish Armada and remembered chiefly as the prison where Charles I was held before being tried and executed.

Cowes, at the mouth of the Medina River, is the venue in August for Cowes Week – the yachtsman's Ascot.

Osborne House (daily, Easter–Oct until 4.30pm, winter check times; tel: 01983-200 022) is highest Victorian, Queen Victoria's favourite residence, and left very much as it was in her lifetime. The chalk cliffs of the island shatter spectacularly in the Needles at the eastern end. Tucked behind them is **Alum Bay**, where sands come in all the colours of the rainbow, and are carried away in bottles as souvenirs. The poet John Keats took inspiration from the woods at **Shanklin**, and countless holidaymakers take to Sandown's pier. Pretty bays, thatched villages, roses and honeysuckle – England in miniature.

One way to return from Cowes is up the long arm of Southampton Water to **Southampton** ㉕. The armies that won the battles of Crécy and Agincourt embarked from here, the tiny *Mayflower* sailed for America, and many ocean liners have followed since.

Ferries also cross the Solent from the Isle of Wight to "Pompey", the important naval base of **Portsmouth** ㉖. This, too, was heavily bombed in the war, but the naval tradition could never be destroyed. The Royal Navy Museum is here, at the **Historic Dockyard** (daily Apr–Oct 10am–5.30pm, Nov–Mar 10am–5pm), but most visitors head for Admiral Lord Nelson's flagship *Victory,* on which he died at the Battle of Trafalgar in 1805, and the hulk of *Mary Rose* (daily 10am–5pm; tel: 02392-812 931), Henry VIII's "favourite warship", dredged up in 1982.

HMS Victory, Lord Nelson's flagship, on show in Portsmouth.

Soaring above the harbour, the 560-ft (170-meter) **Spinnaker Tower** (tel: 023-9285 7520; charge) has great views and displays covering the area's history. ❑

RESTAURANTS AND PUBS

Restaurants

Beaulieu

Montagu Arms Hotel
Palace Lane
Tel: 01590-612324 **£££**
Hotel and restaurant serving excellent English food. Ideal base for New Forest.

Brockenhurst

Simply Poussin
The Courtyard,
49–55 Brookley Road
Tel: 01590-623063 **£££**
First-rate French cuisine using organic local ingredients. In picturesque New Forest village, near coast.

Hordle, nr Lymington

The Mill at Gordleton
Silver Street
Tel: 01590-682219 **££**
Good-value home cooking and a good wine list make this ivy-clad mill-cum-hotel a popular venue.

Portsmouth

Lemon Sole
123 High Street, Old Portsmouth
Tel: 02392-811303 **££**
You make your selection of fresh seafood from a display and tell the staff how you would like it cooked.

Southampton

P.O.S.H.
1 Queensway
Tel: 08707-426 282 **£**
Indian restaurant decked out as an ocean liner, hence the "Port Out, Starboard Home" reference.

Stuckton

The Three Lions
Stuckton Road
Tel: 01425-652489 **££**
Michael Womersley cooks like a dream. Food admirably basic, technically consummate and deliciously flavoured.

Winchester

Hotel du Vin & Bistro
14 Southgate Street
Tel: 01962-841414 **££**
This is a wine lover's heaven, complete with an attractive menu of top-notch modern British food.

Pubs

In Brockenhurst, the unpretentious **Foresters Arms** on Brookley Road has oak beams inside and garden tables outside.

In Portsmouth, the **Hole in the Wall** on Great Southsea Street has a remarkable range of real ale and serves simple food. The **Still & West Country House** on Bath Square in Old Portsmouth has a beer garden and fine harbour views.

In Southampton, the **Duke of Wellington** on Bugle Street is a half-timbered building which became a pub in 1494.

Prices for a three-course dinner per person with a half-bottle of house wine:
£ = under £25
££ = £25–50
£££ = £50–100

THE WEST COUNTRY

Like their splendid landscape, the people of Cornwall, Devon and Somerset are a blend of rugged power and muted tranquillity – and this sets them apart from many other peoples of Britain

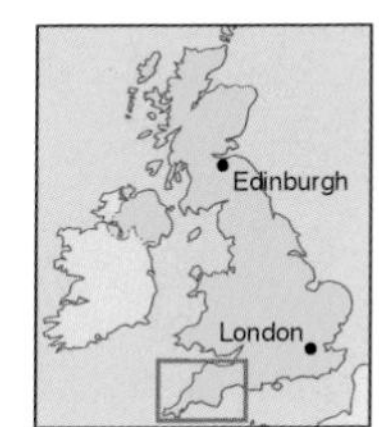

The mystique of the West Country transcends its reputation as Britain's most popular holiday region. Beneath the Bristol Channel and Wales and on the edge of the moderating Atlantic, the peninsula is made up of Somerset, Devon and Cornwall, rural counties tucked away with hidden fishing hamlets and Britain's warmest winter weather.

The West Country is also steeped in legend. This is the land of King Arthur, Camelot and the Holy Grail; the land of Jack the Giant Killer and the myth of an ancient Druid who gave weary travellers sips of water from a golden cup. History here takes on a romantic quality, with facts obscured by time and fictions embellished with tales of piracy, smuggling and shipwrecks.

An island mentality

West Country people have always considered themselves special, celebrating their Celtic origins and taking pride in their self-reliance. There's a certain island mentality here – in fact Cornwall itself is almost an island. The River Tamar flows along all but 5 miles (8 km) of the Devon border. Old traditions flourish, like the Helston Furry Dance in early May when people fill the town with flowers and dance in the streets.

Historically, the West Country has been cut off from the mainstream of British culture both by geography and choice. The peninsula was settled by hard-working Celts from Brittany who scraped a living off the essentials of the land. They dug tin and copper, grazed their sheep and cattle on windswept moors, and braved treacherous currents to take fish from the sea.

The tip of the peninsula, Land's End, is 290 miles (465 km) from London. The main artery into the region is the M5 which comes down from Birmingham, meeting the M4 from London at Bristol,

Main attractions

- BRISTOL
- ROMAN BATHS, BATH
- WELLS CATHEDRAL
- GLASTONBURY
- LONGLEAT SAFARI PARK
- EXMOOR NATIONAL PARK
- PADSTOW
- NEWQUAY
- TATE ST IVES
- LAND'S END
- ISLES OF SCILLY
- PENZANCE
- THE EDEN PROJECT
- PLYMOUTH
- DARTMOOR NATIONAL PARK
- EXETER CATHEDRAL

PRECEDING PAGES: Castle Combe.
LEFT: Somerset from Glastonbury Tor.
RIGHT: Fowey, Cornwall, is a sailing centre.

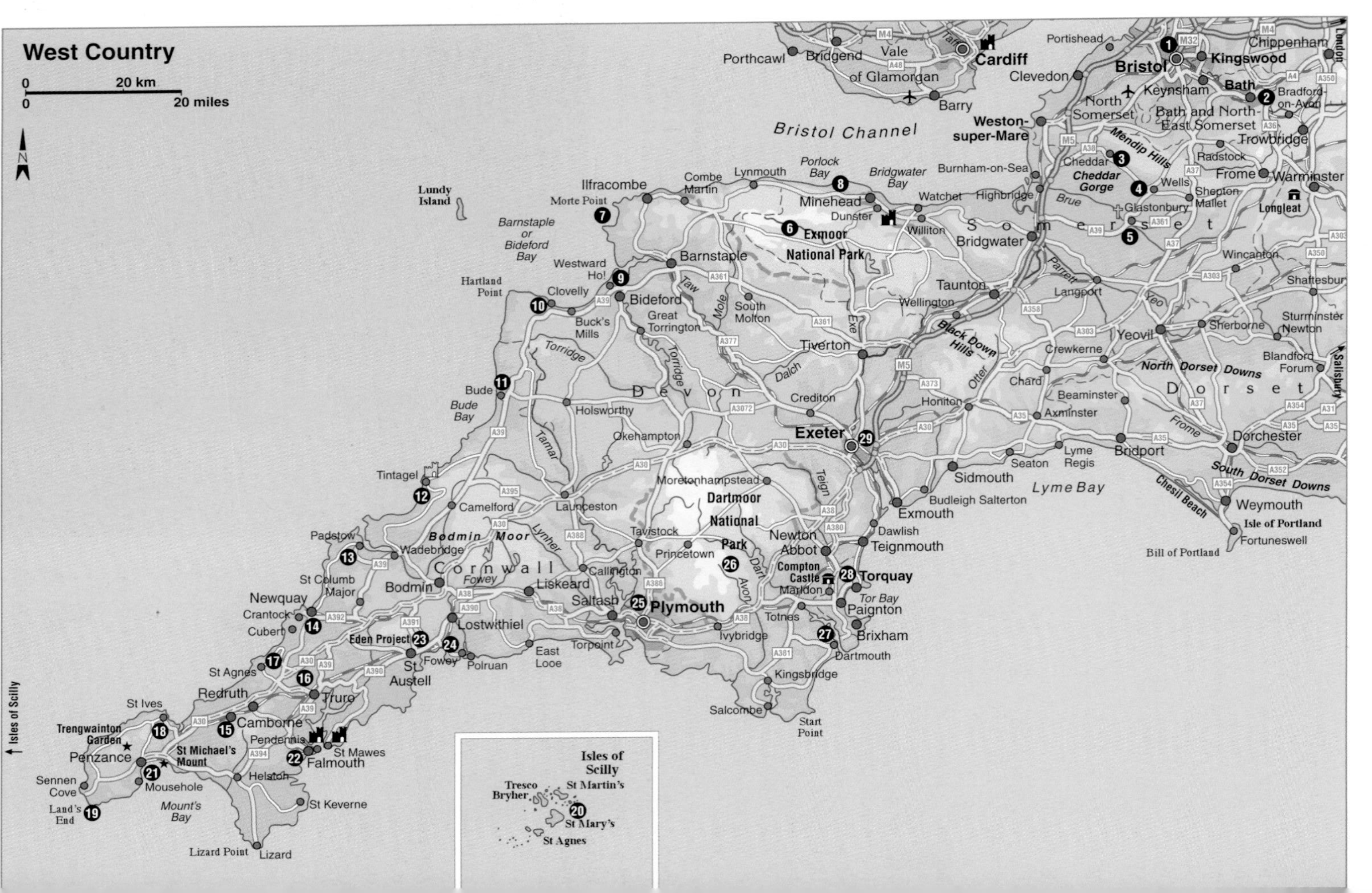

West Country
0 20 km
0 20 miles
N
Isles of Scilly
London
Salisbury
Bristol
Kingswood
Bath
Bath and North-East Somerset
Chippenham
Bradford-on-Avon
Trowbridge
Warminster
Longleat
Frome
Radstock
Keynsham
North Somerset
Portishead
Clevedon
Weston-super-Mare
Mendip Hills
Cheddar
Cheddar Gorge
Wells
Shepton Mallet
Glastonbury
Somerset
Dorset
Devon
Cornwall
Cardiff
Barry
Vale of Glamorgan
Bridgend
Porthcawl
Bristol Channel
Burnham-on-Sea
Highbridge
Bridgwater
Bridgwater Bay
Watchet
Williton
Taunton
Wellington
Black Down Hills
Minehead
Dunster
Porlock Bay
Exmoor
National Park
Lynmouth
Combe Martin
Ilfracombe
Morte Point
Barnstaple
Barnstaple or Bideford Bay
Westward Ho!
Bideford
Great Torrington
Clovelly
Buck's Mills
Hartland Point
Lundy Island
Bude
Bude Bay
Holsworthy
Okehampton
Crediton
Tiverton
South Molton
Exeter
Exmouth
Budleigh Salterton
Sidmouth
Honiton
Seaton
Lyme Regis
Lyme Bay
Axminster
Chard
Beaminster
Crewkerne
Yeovil
Sherborne
Wincanton
Shaftesbury
Sturminster Newton
Blandford Forum
North Dorset Downs
Dorchester
South Dorset Downs
Weymouth
Isle of Portland
Fortuneswell
Bill of Portland
Chesil Beach
Bridport
Langport
Dawlish
Teignmouth
Newton Abbot
Torquay
Tor Bay
Paignton
Brixham
Dartmouth
Compton Castle
Marldon
Totnes
Kingsbridge
Start Point
Salcombe
Ivybridge
Dartmoor National Park
Moretonhampstead
Princetown
Tavistock
Plymouth
Saltash
Callington
Torpoint
Launceston
Liskeard
East Looe
Lostwithiel
Polruan
Fowey
Bodmin Moor
Camelford
Tintagel
Wadebridge
Bodmin
St Austell
Eden Project
Padstow
St Columb Major
Newquay
Crantock
Cubert
Truro
St Mawes
Falmouth
Pendennis
St Keverne
St Agnes
Redruth
Camborne
Helston
Lizard
Lizard Point
St Michael's Mount
Mount's Bay
Mousehole
St Ives
Trengwainton Garden
Penzance
Sennen Cove
Land's End
Isles of Scilly
St Martin's
St Mary's
St Agnes
Tresco
Bryher

and continuing down to Exeter. On a good day the 175-mile (282-km) drive from London to Somerset will take three hours. Tourist routes are well signposted and walkers can make the most of the 500-mile (800-km) coastal footpath which extends from Minehead in Somerset to Poole in Dorset.

The region is served by train from Paddington Station in London.

Bristol

One jumping-off point into the region is the old Atlantic port of **Bristol** ❶. John Cabot set off for Newfoundland from here in 1497; later on it was a gateway to the British Empire. The excellent **British Empire and Commonwealth Museum** (10am–5pm; tel: 0117-925 4980; empiremuseum.co.uk) occupying Old Bristol Station, charts Britain's colonial expansion from 1500 until 1914.

Other attractions have flowered around the redeveloped docks, including the **Arnolfini Gallery** (Tue–Sun 10am–6pm and bank holiday Mondays; tel: 0117-917 2300; arnolfini.org.uk), a contemporary arts venue and **At-Bristol** (10am–6pm; tel: 0845-345 1235; at-bristol.org.uk), a complex of interactive science museums geared to children. Britain's most famous engineer, Isambard Kingdom Brunel (1806–59), was very active in Bristol, designing the world's first ocean-going propeller ship, **SS *Great Britain***, which can be visited in its original dock near the **Maritime Heritage Museum** (summer daily 10am–6pm, winter until 4pm; tel: 0117-926 0680).

Brunel was also responsible for the **Clifton Suspension Bridge**, which spans the Avon gorge at Clifton village (take bus Nos 8 or 9 from the cathedral).

Bath

Another jumping-off point for the West Country is **Bath** ❷, Britain's most celebrated spa town, 13 miles (21 km) southeast of Bristol. King Offa founded the **Bath Abbey** some 200 years before King Edgar was crowned King of All England there in 973. But the baths, which had been enjoyed by the Romans, were forgotten until the 18th century when bathing became fashionable.

More than 3 million people a year visit Bath on day trips.

The city owes its good looks to Bath stone and the genius of two men, the elder and younger John Wood, who in the 18th century gave its streets, squares and crescents an impressive harmony. Bath's architectural heritage has been wonderfully preserved, and the Theatre Royal and International Music Festival in May continue the strong cultural tradition. Among the architectural masterpieces are Robert Adam's **Pulteney Bridge**, which has shops on it like old London Bridge, and, in the Upper Town, the **Royal Crescent**, **The Circus**, the **Assembly Rooms** (daily 10am–5pm; free) and **Queen Square**.

But the steamy core of it all is the **Roman Baths** (Mar–June and Sept–Oct 9am–6pm, July–Aug until 9pm, Nov–Feb 9.30am–5.30pm; tel: 01225-477 785; romanbaths.co.uk), at basement level to the modern city, and its adjoining **Pump Room**.

West of the Roman Baths lies the luxurious **Thermae** spa complex (tel: 01225-331234; thermaebathspa.com), cre-

BELOW: Bath's Roman baths, with the abbey in the background.

South of Cheddar along the A371 is the Ebbor Gorge. Formed 270 million years ago, this is the most beautiful gorge of the Mendips, a lush mix of elms, oaks and ash trees, mosses, fungi and ferns. Caves here contain the remains of Stone Age pots, axes and reindeer.

ated from a cluster of historic baths at the top of Bath Street. Five minutes from here, in Gay Street, is the **Jane Austen Centre** (daily 10am–5.30pm; tel: 01225-443000 janeausten.co.uk), documenting the novelist's links with the city.

Americans can feel at home at **Claverton Manor** which houses the **American Museum** (Apr–Oct Tue–Sun 2–5pm, gardens noon–5.30pm, Aug daily, plus Christmas opening; tel: 01225-460503; americanmuseum.org), high above the Avon valley, 4 miles (6 km) south of Bath. The period-furnished rooms and displays of folk art offer an absorbing picture of American domestic life between the 17th and 19th centuries.

Ten miles (16km) notheast of Bath, in Wiltshire, is **Castle Combe**, one of several places claiming to be "the prettiest village in England." It has a good claim.

The Mendip Hills, just east of the coast and south of Bristol, mark an abrupt end to the flat, cultured landscape of the Avon Valley and the start of the wild expanses of the West Country. Across the crest of the hills runs the **West Mendip Way**, a popular hiking trail that twists from Wells, 20 miles (32 km) southwest of Bath, to the Bristol Channel and offers superb views of the countryside.

Much of the natural scenery here is simply breathtaking; **Cheddar Gorge** ❸ 12 miles (20 km) northwest of Wells, is carved by a river that now runs underground. The sheer limestone cliffs, 450 ft (135 metres) above Cheddar village below, cut through the Mendips for more than a mile. In the village itself you can visit vast underground caverns (daily 10am–5.30pm, until 5pm in winter; tel: 01934-742343; cheddarcaves.co.uk).

On the Holy Grail trail

The pride and joy of **Wells** ❹, at the southern tip of the Mendip Hills, is the **Cathedral**, a massive Gothic shrine started in about 1185 and finished four centuries later. Unlike other English cathedrals, the two main towers were built outside the church proper, thus extending the western facade into a massive gallery for 400 individual statues. More than 25 percent of the sculpture has been destroyed (most by rampaging Puritans in the 17th century) but the remaining group is an array of bishops and kings, saints and

BELOW: the ruins of Glastonbury Abbey, where the legendary King Arthur is said to have been buried.

prophets, angels and apostles. The interior is no less spectacular, especially the "hour-glass" arches at the junction of the nave and transept. These were constructed in the 14th century after the cathedral threatened to collapse under the weight of a new central tower.

Outside the cathedral, the **Vicar's Close** comprises a row of 14th-century buildings (the only complete medieval street remaining in Britain). The exteriors have changed little from their original design. But the **Bishop's Palace** (Mar–Oct Sun–Fri 10.30am–6pm, Sat until 2pm, Oct–Dec Wed–Sun 10.30am–3.30pm; tel: 01749-678691; bishopspalacewells.co.uk), south of the cathedral, is outstanding. One of the oldest inhabited houses in England, the palace is home to the Bishop of Bath and Wells. The high wall surrounding it dates from the beginning of the 13th century. Swans glide across the broad moat and, since Victorian times, have been trained to ring a bell for their food. By the Cathedral Green the **Wells Museum** (Easter–Oct Mon–Sat 11am–5pm, Sun until 4pm, Oct–Easter daily until 4pm; tel: 01749-675337; wellsmuseum.org.uk) houses plaster casts of the cathedral statues.

Glastonbury

It's a pity that the abbey at **Glastonbury** ❺, 6 miles (10 km) southwest, has not been preserved in the same way, for it was once the richest and most beautiful in England. Little remains of the great complex – a few ruined pillars and walls. But these remain an impressive monument to the power of the Roman Catholic church in England before Henry VIII's dissolution of the monasteries.

The origins of the abbey are shrouded in myths. One story claims that St Patrick founded the abbey and that St George killed the famous dragon nearby. The most popular legend centres on Joseph of Arimathea, the man who gave his tomb to Christ. Having sailed to Britain to convert the heathens in AD 60, he was leaning on his staff on Wearyall Hill, when it rooted and flowered, an omen that he should settle and found the abbey. Joseph brought with him the chalice from the Last Supper, the Holy Grail. In the 6th century King Arthur came to Glastonbury in search of the Holy Grail; tradition says he and Guinevere are buried under the abbey floor.

A short walk to the steep, conical hill called **Glastonbury Tor**, which rises up from the flat Somerset plain, is worthwhile for the view from the top, surmounted by the remains of the 15th-century St Michael's Church.

East of Glastonbury lie two of England's finest stately homes, **Longleat** (mid-Feb–Oct daily 10am–5pm; tel: 01985-844400; longleat.co.uk), the 16th-century seat of the Marquess of Bath, containing a wealth of family attractions, including a safari park; and **Stourhead**, a Palladian mansion full of Georgian treasures and famous for its landscape gardens *(see pages 218–19)*.

The boundary between Somerset and Devon falls within the confines of **Exmoor National Park** ❻, 265 sq miles (690 sq km) filled with the sights and sounds of Richard Doddridge Blackmore's novel, *Lorna Doone* (1869), the

Glastonbury Tor is the mythical home of Gwyn ap Nudd, the Lord of the Underworld and King of the Fairies.

BELOW: the abbot's kitchen re-created at Glastonbury Abbey.

Coastal path leading to the ruins of Tintagel Castle.

Exmoor ponies, direct descendants of the prehistoric horse, are the most ubiquitous animals on the moor, but there are also red deer, sheep and Devon Red cattle.

BELOW: Porlock Weir.

story of a 17th-century family of outlaws. The landscape of the park, dotted with pretty villages, transforms itself from windswept ridges covered with bracken and heather, to forested ravines carved out by white-water streams.

The undulating **Somerset and Devon Coast Path**, stretching more than 30 miles (48 km) along the shore, north of the A39, is the most fascinating of Exmoor's many hiking trails. Hugging tightly to cliffs and coves, it offers splendid views of the Bristol Channel and the far-off Atlantic. **Morte Pointe** ❼ (not safe for swimming) northwest of **Barnstaple**, and **Porlock Bay** ❽, 6 miles (10 km) west of Minehead, are good for birdwatching.

Just east of Minehead the village of **Dunster** is a pleasant stopping-place. Dunster has been a fortress site since Saxon times, but the present castle dates from the 13th century. Most of the original structure was destroyed after Charles I's execution in 1649. The graceful turrets and towers are 19th-century. The village itself is a perfect replica of feudal times, largely because one family, the Luttrells, owned it for 600 years until 1950.

King Arthur's country

Where Devon turns to Cornwall, a chain of fishing villages and hidden beauties lie beside the A39 running down to Tintagel. **Westward Ho!** ❾, by Bideford, is a popular seaside resort named after the novel by Charles Kingsley (1819–75); it has 3 miles (5 km) of sandy beach.

Clovelly ❿ is probably the most well known of these hamlets in Bideford Bay. Cars are banned from the village and donkeys carry visitors' luggage. The steep cobbled street descends 400 ft (120 metres) to the sea in a series of steps. A romantic 2-mile (3-km) walk west from the harbour leads to a magnificent range of cliffs. Nearby **Buck's Mills** is an unspoiled village of thatched cottages.

Further south and into Cornwall, the rolling waves at **Bude** ⓫ have long attracted surfers. For those who prefer calmer swimming, **Summerleaze Beach** in the town is a good spot, a sheltered, sandy expanse north of the River Neet.

The legend of King Arthur comes

Recommended Restaurants and Pubs on pages 246–7

alive at **Tintagel Castle** ⓬ (daily 10am–6pm, until 4pm in winter), a wild and romantic spot on the north Cornwall coast about 18 miles (29 km) south of Bude. Tradition claims Arthur was born or washed ashore at Tintagel, where he built a castle for Guinevere and the Knights of the Round Table. All that remains are the ruins of a 6th-century Celtic monastery and a 12th-century bastion, most of it washed away by the sea.

In the town, the 14th-century **Old Post Office**, is owned by the National Trust (Mar–Sept daily 11am–5.30pm, Oct–Nov until 4pm).

Some 20 miles (32 km) south on the A39 and then west along the A389 is **Padstow** ⓭, the only safe harbour in north Cornwall and an important port for more than 1,000 years. The town is named after St Petroc, a Celtic missionary who landed here in the 6th century to convert the heathen Cornish. The Vikings sacked Padstow in AD 981, but it later grew into a fishing centre and mineral port. The primary industry today is tourism, especially in summer. **Prideaux Place** (Easter and May–Sept Sun–Thur 12.30–5pm; tel: 01841-532411; prideauxplace.co.uk), a richly furnished Elizabethan manor in delightful grounds, overlooks the town.

Clustered around the harbour are the historic **Abbey House**, **St Petroc Church**, the **Harbour Master's Office** and **Raleigh Cottage**, where Sir Walter collected port dues as the Royal Warden of Cornwall. Every May Day the town fills up when a bizarre Hobby Horse festival creates a carnival atmosphere.

South along the coast, **Newquay** ⓮ is Cornwall's Malibu – the beach where surfers cruise the waves. It was famous in the 18th and 19th centuries as a pilchard port. Cornwall's only **zoo** (Apr–Sept daily 9.30am–6pm , Oct–Mar daily 10am–5pm; tel: 01637-873342; newquayzoo.org.uk) is in Trenance Park.

Worthwhile excursions south of Newquay include the ancient Norman church at **Crantock**. Crantock Beach is lovely, too. Still further south is **Cubert**, which features a church tower shaped curiously like a bishop's mitre. The interior of the church preserves fine Norman and 14th-century carvings and a font.

The corridor between the neighbouring towns of Redruth and **Camborne** ⓯, 18 miles (29 km) southwest and inland,

King Arthur's presence is strong at Tintagel, though it isn't backed by archaeological evidence. According to medieval histories and romances, he led the defence of Britain against the Saxon invaders in the early 6th century, but scholars can't agree on whether he really existed. The tales were given a boost in T.H. White's 1958 novel The Once and Future King *and, less reverentially, in* Monty Python and the Holy Grail.

BELOW: Clovelly, owned and preserved by an estate company.

Tate St Ives, the western outpost of the Tate group of art galleries.

was the fulcrum of Cornish tin mining for more than 200 years. Little active mining remains, but you can get some idea of what tin meant to the economy by visiting the **Cornwall Industrial Discovery Centre** (Apr–Oct Sun–Fri 11am–5pm) at Pool, just outside Camborne. Outside Camborne Library stands a statue of Richard Trevithick, the "Father of the Locomotive", who manufactured the first high-pressure steam engine in 1797.

Tin-smelting capital

Truro ⓰, 10 miles (16 km) east, is the cathedral city of Cornwall and the unofficial capital. In the 18th century it was both a centre for tin smelting and a society haunt that rivalled Bath. **Lemon Street**, laid out around 1795, features fine Georgian architecture. The **Royal Cornwall Museum** (Mon–Sat 10am–5pm; 01872-272205; royalcornwallmuseum.org.uk) has Greek, Roman and Egyptian displays, as well as local artefacts.

Out to the coast again on the A390, St Agnes Beacon, outside the village of **St Agnes** ⓱, offers a view of 32 church towers and 23 miles (40 km) of coast from 628 ft (190 metres) above. Much of the surrounding area was once mining land. Today the scars of industry give the area a melancholy beauty.

One of the last ports of call on this north coast is **St Ives** ⓲, a classic Cornish fishing village popular with artists since the end of the 19th century. Among them was the sculptor Barbara Hepworth who lived and worked here from 1949 until her death in 1975. Her home is now the **Barbara Hepworth Museum**. The works of many other local artists from St Ives' heyday – Ben Nicholson, Peter Lanyon, etc, form a small permanent exhibition, complemented by temporary exhibitions, at **Tate St Ives** (both museums Mar–Oct daily 10am–5.20pm, Nov–Feb Tue–Sun 10am–4.20pm; combined tickets available; tate.org.uk/stives), which opened in 1993 in a stunning building by Porthmeor Beach.

BELOW: the white horse at Westbury in Wlitshire, overlooking the Vale of Pewsey.

White horses

Around two dozen white horses decorate hills around England. They have been created by carving back the top layer of soil and grass to reveal the chalk underneath. Some date back to the Bronze Age (the White Horse of Uffington in Oxfordshire), though many are comparatively modern (19th century). There are also some human carvings, such as the Cerne Abbas giant, a naked man 180 ft (55 metres) long near Dorchester in Dorset. All need to be maintained to stop grass and bushes obliterating them.

What is their significance? Some may have had religious connotations, some may have represented civic pride, and others had an historical connection – the Westbury white horse, for example, may have celebrated the charger King Alfred rode when he defeated the Danes in 878.

Recommended Restaurants and Pubs on pages 246–7

Land's End – Britain's toe

Penwith is the name given to the barren and windswept knob that marks the end of Cornwall. This is a land of bleak hills and wide open spaces, surrounded by deep blue sea and sometimes thick Atlantic fog. The **Cornwall Coastal Path** traces the entire shore of Penwith, passing submerged reefs and wave-eroded cliffs, sheltered coves and weird-shaped rocks. **Land's End** ⓳, the most westerly point on mainland Britain, is an eerie but beautiful place almost constantly swept by North Atlantic storms and swirling underwater currents. The **Land's End Centre** (daily 10am–dusk; landsend-landmark.co.uk) has a discovery trail and exhibitions.

At **Sennen Cove** there's a tiny inn and a Royal Naval Coastguard Station constantly on alert for a shipwreck or yachting disaster. Tin mines at **Geevor** (Apr–Oct Sun–Fri 9am–5pm, until 4pm in winter; tel: 01736-788662; geevor.com) have tunnels that extend 250 fathoms below the sea floor. There's a mining museum with tours of the treatment plant, magnetic separators and tunnels.

The ship-eating **Isles of Scilly** (pronounced *silly*) ⓴ 28 miles (45 km) west of Land's End can be reached by ferry or helicopter from Penzance. Phoenician traders landed here before the birth of Christ in search of tin, copper and other metals. Five of the islands are inhabited and all but one, **Tresco**, is part of the Duchy of Cornwall. Highlights are the **Tresco Abbey Gardens** (daily 10am–4pm); the **Valhalla Maritime Museum**, Tresco; and the **Isles of Scilly Museum**, St Mary's. In summer there are races of six-oar gigs off St Mary's.

Back on the mainland, two picturesque villages sit on the south shore of Penwith. **Mousehole** (pronounced *mowzel*) is as tiny as the name suggests, a cluster of granite cottages and half-timbered pubs. The village is named after an old smugglers' cave called the Mouse Hole. Take a pint at the **Ship**, a friendly pub which serves good crab sandwiches, or take a walk to majestic **Merlin** and **Battery Rocks**. In nearby Newlyn, the **Newlyn Gallery** (Apr–Sept Mon–Sat 10am–5pm, Oct–Apr Wed–Sat 10am–5pm, Sun 11am–4pm; tel: 01736-363715; newlyartgallery.co.uk; donation)

Mousehole has a safe beach, popular with families.

BELOW: Land's End, once a bleak headland, has attracted theme park developers.

Pendennis Castle.

features contemporary art and the work of regional artists.

Pleasures of Penzance

Penzance ㉑ has long been the premier town of western Cornwall thanks to its commanding site on **Mount's Bay**. It has served a number of important functions over the centuries: tin shipping port for the Roman Empire and medieval Europe, passenger terminal for emigrants bound for the New World, and, most recently, a popular holiday resort. Within the town lies the **Barbican**, an 18th-century fish market transformed into a lively arts and crafts centre. The **Western Promenade** is lined with 18th- and 19th-century Regency townhouses, but the heart of Penzance lies at the junction of Chapel Street and Market Jew Street, an ancient cobblestoned quarter that retains much of the flavour of its seafaring past. There are a number of historic buildings, such as the 18th-century **Union Hotel** and **Penlee House Gallery and Museum** (Mon–Sat 10am–5pm; tel: 01736-363625; penleehouse.org.uk), which displays works by artists of the Newlyn School. The **Morrab Gardens** cultivate a variety of exotic plants. Even better is the National Trust's **Trengwainton Garden**, 2 miles (3 km) inland (Feb–Oct Sun–Thur 10.30am–5pm).

St Michael's Mount (Mar–Nov Sun–Fri 10.30am–5pm; tel: 01736-710507; stmichaelsmount.co.uk) dominates a hunk of granite in Mount's Bay. At low tide you can reach the island along a sandy causeway; at other times you go by ferry. Legend has it that a fisherman saw St Michael standing on the granite outcrop, so a Benedictine priory was founded here in 1140. It became a grandiose private house in the 17th century.

To the east, beyond the treacherous Lizard Point and the Helford River, lies **Falmouth** ㉒, steeped in the history of the seas. A famous port and fishing centre for more than 300 years, it is one of Cornwall's most interesting towns. It was a tiny hamlet until 1699 when it became the most westerly Mail Packet station in England. Ships from America, the West Indies and the Mediterranean called here to transfer their mail into stagecoaches bound for London.

Pendennis Castle (Mar–June daily 10am–5pm, July–Aug until 6pm, Sept–Mar until 4pm) guarded Falmouth for three centuries against Spanish and French raids and against Cromwell's troops during a 23-week siege in the Civil War. **Falmouth Art Gallery** (Mon–Sat 10am–5pm; tel: 01326-313863; falmouthartgallery.com; free) in the main square has some excellent exhibitions.

On the redeveloped Discovery Quay the **National Maritime Museum** (daily 10am–5pm; tel: 01326-313388 nmmc.co.uk), housed in a stunning building, is attracting hordes of visitors and has lots to interest children.

The Eden Project

Off the A390, at Bodelva, east of St Austell, is Cornwall's biggest attraction, the **Eden Project** ㉓ (Apr–Oct daily 10am–6pm, Nov–Mar until 4.30pm; tel 01726-811911; edenproject.com). Built in a disused crater, this ambitious site con

BELOW: St Michael's Mount resembles Mont St Michel in Normandy because French Benedictine monks were involved in both.

Recommended Restaurants and Pubs on pages 246–7

sists of huge covered conservatories called biomes – a humid tropical one and a warm temperate zone – plus a large outdoor landscaped area, all mimicking the planet's diverse climates. There are numerous environmentally based special exhibitions, plus educational projects. The place gets very crowded and only groups can book in advance, so be prepared for queues at busy times.

Fowey (pronounced *foy*) ㉔, on the A3082 off the A390, is a pretty little town, its ancient centre still intact, with a sheltered, deep-water working port that is also a snug harbour for pleasure craft and fishing boats. **St Catherine's Castle** (built by Henry VIII), the 18th-century Town Hall and the 14th-century **Toll Bar House** can all be visited, as can the **Daphne Du Maurier Literary Centre** (tel: 01726-833616), dedicated to the writer, who loved the town and set several of her novels in Cornwall. Take the ferry across the harbour to **Polruan**, a quaint, hilly little village.

Plymouth

Plymouth ㉕, on the Devon–Cornwall border, is a relic of the Age of Exploration, the city of Drake, Raleigh and the Pilgrim Fathers, a town where young Englishmen have long gone in search of seafaring adventure. But today's Plymouth is more than a history book, for it's still a thriving port, industrial centre, market town and cultural mecca, the largest city west of Bristol.

Francis Drake has long been Plymouth's favourite son. He sailed from the port in 1577 on his renowned global circumnavigation, and upon his return the citizens of Plymouth elected him as mayor. The Pilgrims sailed from Plymouth's West Pier in 1620 aboard the fragile *Mayflower* to the New World. (They had originally launched from Southampton, but bad weather damaged their ship and they called at Plymouth for repairs.) They took shelter in the wine cellars of the firm of James Hawker, which still carries on business today.

The Hoe still dominates Plymouth as it did in Drake's day. **Smeaton's Tower** is a red-and-white striped lighthouse that offers excellent views of the Sound. Nearby is the **Royal Citadel** (May–Sept Tues and Thur, tours at 2.30pm), a fortress built in the 17th century by Charles II to

Detail from the Royal Navy war memorial at Plymouth Hoe containing the names of 23,000 naval personnel who died in two world wars.

BELOW: the Eden Project, built in a disused china clay pit, contains the world's biggest greenhouse.

It's illegal to feed the 5,000 ponies that roam Dartmoor. They are related to Stone Age horses that have lived on this land for millions of years. The Galloway and Highland cattle and black-faced sheep are later imports.

BELOW: Haytor Rocks, Dartmoor.

stall any Republican comeback. Well landscaped into the front brow of the Hoe is the **Dome** (daily 10am–5pm), an innovative multi-media presentation of Plymouth's past and present. Down by the port is an Elizabethan quarter known as the **Barbican**, a mixture of cobblestoned streets, medieval houses and bustling piers, now containing pubs, cafés and art galleries. Many of Plymouth's historic voyages started out here and the 16th-century **Island House** is where the Pilgrims spent their last night in England. There's a fish market on the far quay, and plenty of shops, taverns and art studios to keep visitors occupied.

The huge **National Marine Aquarium** also overlooks the harbour, claiming to be the deepest in Europe and the biggest in the UK (daily Apr–Oct 10am–6pm, Nov–Mar until 5pm; tel: 01752-220084; national-aquarium.co.uk).

Impressive displays recreate the different levels of aquatic habitat, from high moorland to deepest ocean. Among species on show are sharks, turtles and even the gruesome remains of a giant Atlantic squid.

Dartmoor

Directly inland from Plymouth is **Dartmoor National Park** ㉖, an expansive 365 sq miles (915 sq km) of forest and moorland that protects the largest of the West Country's wilderness areas. Beneath all that heather and bracken is a solid core of stone, one of five granite masses that form the geological heart of the West Country. There are hundreds of miles of public footpaths and hiking trails across the moor, walked by an estimated 8 million people each year.

The visitors tend to overwhelm Dartmoor's indigenous population, the 30,000 people who live in and around the park. But the villagers still have grazing rights to the open grasslands on the moor, and they can also collect peat, stone and thatching straw for their homes. Dartmoor remains much as it has been for 1,000 years: a harsh landscape of open moors, rocky outcrops, wooded vales and muddy bogs broken only occasionally by a village or farm.

Dartmouth ㉗, directly east of Plymouth, is yet another of the West Country's famous ports. The town retains much of its seafaring heritage in the form of **Britannia Royal Naval College**, which has trained such officers as Prince Charles and the Duke of Edinburgh for the Royal Navy. Dartmouth Harbour is lined with 16th-century merchants' houses and half-timbered taverns. **Pannier Market** still sells fresh fruit and vegetables on Friday mornings, but the rest of the week it becomes a cluster of art and craft stalls.

A range of boat cruises is available from the small harbour, up the River Dart to Totnes, Kingswear and Greenway (Agatha Christie's family home) or up the coast to Torquay. One of the main operators is River Link (tel: 01803-834488; riverlink.co.uk).

Just a stone's throw up the coast lies **Torbay** ㉘, a conurbation of Torquay, Paignton and Brixham which likes to call itself the English Riviera because of its mild climate, lengthy beaches and scattered palms. **Brixham** alone maintains something of its fishing village ambience

Recommended Restaurants and Pubs on pages 246–7

with a replica of the *Golden Hinde*, Sir Francis Drake's ship that circumnavigated the globe in 1577, moored in its sheltered harbour.

Three miles (5 km) on is **Marldon**, with a lovely old church, and one mile further still is **Compton Castle** (Apr–Oct Mon, Wed and Thur 11am–5pm; tel: 01803-843235). This manor house, still the seat of the Gilbert family, was built in 1340. Sir Humphrey Gilbert (1539–83) founded Newfoundland, the first British colony in North America, and was the half-brother of Sir Walter Raleigh.

Exeter

Exeter ㉙ is a lively university and cathedral city. The immense **Cathedral** dominating the skyline was built from the 11th to 14th centuries in Norman Gothic style. The exterior displays a remarkable collection of stone statues, the largest surviving group of 14th-century sculpture in England. The lavish interior is dominated by a striking vaulted ceiling, carved to resemble the radiating branches of a palm tree. Among the church's treasures are the 14th-century Bishop's Throne and the *Exeter Book of Old English Verse*, compiled between AD 950 and 1000.

The **Royal Albert Memorial Museum and Art Gallery** on nearby Queen Street (tel: 01392-665858) is currently being refurbished, but is due to reopen in 2010. Just off Queen Street lies the **Phoenix** arts and media centre (tel: 01392-667080; exeterphoenix.org.uk), which offers a varied programme of music, theatre, film and visual arts.

Outside the cathedral, much of Exeter pales in comparison, but the old **Quayside** has been well restored, with cobbled pavements and warehouses converted into shops and cafés, a visitor centre and paths offering canalside walks. Bikes and canoes can be hired (Saddles and Paddles, tel: 01392-424241), or boat cruises (contact the visitor centre; tel: 01392-271611) down to the pretty village of **Topsham**, which has a small museum of local maritime history and wildlife (Mar–Oct Mon, Wed, Sat and Sun 2–5pm). Also interesting is **Rougemont House** (which houses an historical Discovery Centre) and the 13th-century **Underground Passages** beneath the High Street (July–Sept 10am–5pm, Oct–June Tues–Fri 2–5pm). ❑

Exeter was founded as a fortress by ther Romans in around AD 50–55. In medieval times the city prospered through farming and the wool trade, and it hallmarked its own silver until the early 19th century. Its growth as a trading centre was hampered by its position on the River Exe. As ships grew larger, the river's facilities became inadequate.

BELOW: a replica of Sir Francis Drake's ship in Brixham.

RESTAURANTS AND PUBS

Restaurants

Prices for a three-course meal per person with a half-bottle of house wine:

£ = under £25
££ = £25–50
£££ = £50–100

Barwick, near Yeovil

Little Barwick House
Tel: 01935-423902 ££
Peaceful Georgian dower house with six rooms for B&B and a great selection of seasonal dishes.

Bath

The Hole in the Wall
16 George Street
Tel: 01225-425242 £££
Long-established restaurant, revived to great acclaim. Highly imaginative haute cuisine.

Jamie's Italian
10 Milsom Place
Tel: 01225-510051 ££
Rustic Italian food overseen by celebrity chef Jamie Oliver.

The Moon and Sixpence
6A Broad Street
Tel: 01225-320088 ££
Modern British food, plus foreign imports. Old favourites with an imaginative twist. Attractive setting.

The Olive Tree
4–7 Queensbury Hotel, Russell Street
Tel: 01225-447928 £££
"Foodie" favourite. Modern British cooking with French, Italian and Spanish influences.

The Royal Crescent Hotel
16 Royal Crescent
Tel: 01225-823333 £££
Within the walled gardens of the hotel. Fine food, elegant setting.

Bristol

Bell's Diner
1–3 York Road, Montpelier
Tel: 0117-924 0357 ££
Contemporary takes on classic European dishes. A short way out of the centre, but worth the journey.

Bordeaux Quay
V-Shed, Canons Way
Tel: 0117-943 1200 ££
European cuisine, with stress on locally-sourced, organic ingredients.

Markwicks
43 Corn Street
Tel: 0117-9262658 ££
Elegant little restaurant with an excellent reputation for its trend-setting Anglo-Provençal cooking.

Chagford

22 Mill Street
Tel: 01647-432244 ££
Ex-sous chef at Gidleigh Park, Duncan Walker cooks in the Gidleigh tradition, but affordably.

Colerne

Lucknam Park
(near Bath)
Tel: 01225-742777 ££–£££
Sophisticated classic British cuisine with a serious, expensive wine list in the spacious, chandelier-lit dining room of this Georgian manor.

Dartmouth

The New Angel
2 South Embankment
Tel: 01803-839425 £££
John Burton Race's accomplished modern British and European cuisine, in a picturesque setting overlooking Dartmouth harbour and the Dart estuary. Awarded Michelin star 2005.

Drewsteignton

Hunts Tor
Tel: 01647-281228 £–££
A no-choice menu lovingly prepared with home-grown organic produce in a tiny dining room (seating eight). No children under 10.

Fowey

Q
28 Fore Street
Tel: 01726-833302 ££
In the Old Quay House hotel, right on the waterfront. Imaginative dishes, superb views. Booking advisable.

Exeter

Café Paradiso
Hotel Barcelona, Magdalen Street
Tel: 01392-281010 ££
Stylish, modern restaurant serving Mediterranean-style dishes made with seasonal ingredients, including delicious wood-fired pizzas.

The Conservatory
18 North Street
Tel: 01392-273858 ££
Excellent British and Mediterranean menu which changes daily. Relaxed, intimate setting.

Ilfracombe

11 The Quay
11 The Quay
Tel: 01271-868090 ££–£££
Damien Hirst's restaurant and art gallery, aiming to do for Ilfracombe what Rick Stein did for Padstow. The imaginative menu is strong on local seafood and West Country cheeses, as well as international dishes.

Instow

The Boathouse Restaurant
Marine Parade
Tel: 01271-861292 £
Beachfront restaurant and bar in quiet seaside town in North Devon. Good seafood and fish.

LEFT: fresh seafood is a speciality of the West Country.

ABOVE: Devon cream teas are not for serious dieters.

Kingsbridge

The Sloop Inn
Bantham, nr Kingsbridge
Tel: 01548-560489 **£**
A 16th-century Inn five minutes' walk from sandy Bantham beach and dunes. Excellent for fish and other seafood, booking advisable.

Midsomer Norton

The Moody Goose
The Old Priory Hotel, Church Square
Tel: 01761-416784 **£££**
Situated in a 12th-century priory near Bath. Exquisite modern English menu including locally-sourced poultry, meat and game.

Padstow

The Seafood Restaurant
Riverside
Tel: 01841-532700 **£££**
(Central booking number for this restaurant and the one below.)
One of the best seafood restaurants in Britain. It uses only the freshest ingredients and enthusiastic chef Rick Stein shows his passion for fish with simple dishes cooked with minimum fuss. Booking essential.

St Petroc's Bistro
4 New Street **££**
A less expensive place to try the cutting edge of Rick Stein's fish cooking, but you still need to book *(see above)*.

Plymouth

Tanners Restaurant
Prysten House, Finewell Street
Tel: 01752-252001 **££**
Fine dining in 15th-century building in the heart of Plymouth. TV chefs Chris and James Tanner offer an inspired range of dishes. Traditional local produce predominates, but prepared with artistic flair. Booking advisable.

Barbican Kitchen
Black Friars Distillery
60 Southside Street
Tel: 01752-604448 **£**
Brasserie run by the Tanner brothers *(see above)* offering a good selection dishes such as Devon red beef burgers and smoked Dartmouth haddock. Ideal for lunch.

St Ives

Alba
Wharf Road
Tel: 01736-797222 **£–££**
Minimalist décor and harbour views. Set menus (less expensive at lunch) feature lots of fish, but there's meat too and good vegetarian options.

Alfresco
Wharf Road
Tel: 01736-793737 **££**
Trendy harbourside spot. Excellent Mediterranean menu, with the emphasis on stylish fish dishes.

Taunton

Castle Hotel
Castle Green
Tel: 01823-272671 **£££**
Stylish, classic British cuisine, locally-sourced ingredients, first-class service, imposing setting.

Topsham

La Petite Maison
35 Fore Street
Tel: 01392-873660 **££**
Small, family-run restaurant in a village just outside Exeter. Excellent modern British cuisine.

Truro

Sevens
77 Lemon Street
Tel: 01872-275767 **££**
A welcome newcomer to Truro. A short, imaginative menu. Excellent Cornish lamb, as well as tempting puddings.

Pubs

In Bath, the **Old Green Tree** on Green Street is an appealing old pub but can get crowded. The **Coeur de Lion** in Northumberland Place off High Street, is even smaller but is charming. The **King William** on St Thomas Street has good beers and fresh food.

In Bristol, a Campaign for Real Ale favourite is the **Cornubia** in two 1773 Georgian houses on Temple Street.

In Plymouth, the **China House** at Sutton Harbour is a converted warehouse with good ale and good views.

In Torquay, the 16th-century **Hole in the Wall** in Park Lane, near the harbour, is atmospheric and serves real ale.

Visitors to the quaint Cornish village of Mousehole can stop at the traditional **Ship Inn**.

At the harbour front of St Ives, the **Sloop Inn**, which traces its history to 1312, is handy for the local Tate gallery.

At Polperro, the 14th-century **Crumplehorn Inn**, at the top of the village, has a nice garden and a waterwheel recalling its days as a mill.

At Fowey, the **King of Prussia** is a quayside family pub with a nautical theme. The **Ship Inn** on Trafalgar Square serves good meals upstairs.

RIGHT: Rick Stein put Padstow on the culinary map.

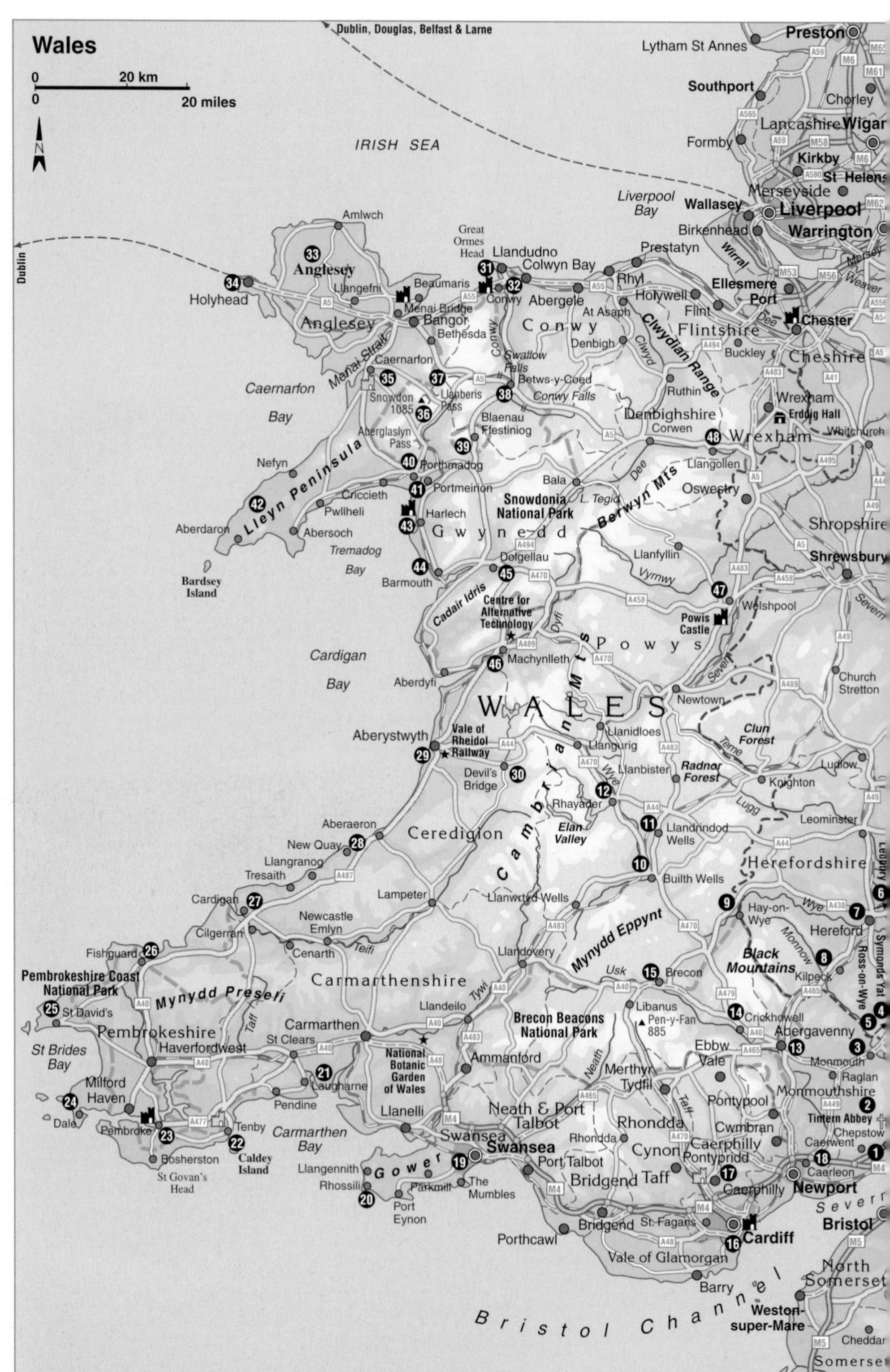

Recommended Restaurants and Pubs on page 261

THE WYE VALLEY AND SOUTH WALES

This chapter begins by following the Wye Valley into Wales from Chepstow, then crosses to Cardiff and Swansea and continues up to the beautiful Pembroke Coast

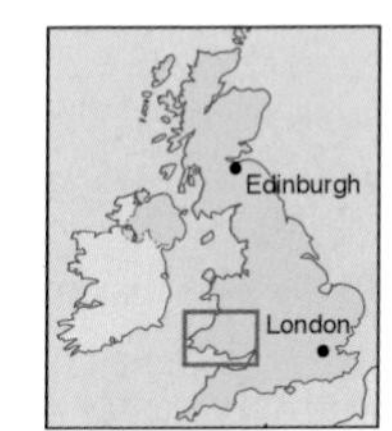

Main attractions
- TINTERN ABBEY
- MONMOUTH
- SYMONDS YAT
- ROSS-ON-WYE
- HEREFORD
- HAY-ON-WYE
- ABERGAVENNY
- BRECON BEACONS NATIONAL PARK
- CARDIFF
- CAERPHILLY CASTLE
- THE GOWER PENINSULA
- LAUGHARNE
- THE PEMBROKESHIRE COAST
- ABERYSTWYTH

Wales is little more than 135 miles (216 km) long and at one part less than 35 miles (56 km) wide. The border runs from the mouth of the Dee in Liverpool Bay in the north to the mouth of the Wye on the Severn estuary in the south. It roughly follows the lines of the dyke built to contain the Celts by Offa, the powerful Anglo-Saxon king of Mercia from 757 to 796. This 168-mile (269-km) frontier earthwork provides walkers with an introduction to Wales (a good place to start is Knighton, at about the halfway mark). Some 300 years after Offa, the Normans drove the Welsh further into the hills, establishing the Marches and the powerful Marcher Lordships along the border.

Traditionally, Wales is a melodic land of green hills and welcoming valleys, of Welshcakes, crumbling castles, poets and song. It has sweeping sandy beaches and dramatic coves. It is less populous than England, though its accessibility from southern, central and northern parts of the country make it a popular holiday haunt.

Access routes

From London and the south of England, use the M4, which skirts Bristol, crosses the Second Severn Crossing and plunges immediately into Wales, following the industrial south coast, past Newport, Cardiff and Swansea to the Gower Peninsula and the cliffs and beaches of Pembrokeshire beyond. Alternatively take the M48 which branches off the M4 just after Bristol and crosses the original Severn Bridge, taking you into Chepstow, gateway to the Wye Valley and the Vale of Usk. A toll is payable when travelling westbound on both Severn bridges. If you're coming from the Midlands, take the M5 and exit at junction 8 (about halfway between Birmingham and Bristol), where the M50 leads west towards the pretty town of Ross-on-Wye, and meets the A40 from Gloucester, crosses

PRECEDING PAGES: Welsh rugby fans at Cardiff's Millennium Stadium.
RIGHT: the Second Severn Bridge.

Beneath Symonds Yat, the village of Symonds Yat East is a popular centre for outdoors enthusiasts. Canoes and kayaks can be hired for a day or part day for excursions along the River Wye. Other centres for canoe hire are Hay-on-Wye and Glasbury, a few miles west of Hay.

BELOW RIGHT: statues in Monmouth to early aero-engine maker Henry Rolls, who lived near the town, and another local boy, Henry V.

the border at Monmouth and dives between the Black Mountains and Brecon Beacons before heading back down to the Pembrokeshire coast.

The Wye Valley

Commanding the mouth of the Wye, where it empties into the River Severn near the suspension bridge, is the small town of **Chepstow** ❶, unremarkable but for its castle. The Norman fortress, set high on a rock, remains impressively intact. Two miles (3 km) from the centre of Chepstow, heading north towards Monmouth on the A466, you pass **Chepstow Racecourse**, a popular venue for enthusiasts of steeplechasing. For most visitors, however, the true high spot of the Wye Valley is **Tintern Abbey** ❷ (Apr–Oct daily 9am–5pm, Nov–Mar Mon–Sat 9.30am–4pm, Sun 11am–4pm; admission charge), 5 miles (8 km) north of Chepstow, the most handsome and most complete of Britain's ruined monasteries. Lauded by Wordsworth and painted by Turner, this ancient abbey occupies an extraordinarily lovely spot by the river, framed by wooded slopes. It was founded by Cistercian monks in 1131, though the present remains date from the late 13th century. The area around Tintern is superb walking country, with footpaths in all directions.

Some 10 miles (16 km) further north on the A466 is **Monmouth** ❸, a market town at the confluence of the Wye and Monnow rivers. Monmouth's most famous son was Henry V, who won the battle of Agincourt. He was born in 1387 in Monmouth Castle, which was largely destroyed in the Civil War: a few walls are all that remain. Monmouth also has a **Nelson Museum** (Mar–Oct 11am–1pm and 2–5pm, Sun 2–5pm, Nov–Feb 11am–1pm and 2–4pm, Sun 2–4pm; free) dedicated to the Admiral, a celebrity in his day, who visited the city.

Seven miles (11 km) southwest of Monmouth on the A40 is **Raglan Castle** (Apr–Oct daily 9am–5pm, Nov–Mar Mon–Sat 9.30am–4pm, Sun 11am–4pm; admission charge). The late-medieval structure, which has an elegant hexagonal moated keep, was besieged during the Civil War, but the remains are impressive.

A few miles east of Monmouth is **Coleford** in the **Forest of Dean**, comprising mainly oak and beach. In the

Offa's Dyke

Offa's Dyke, an earthen bank running the length of the England–Wales border, was built at the command of King Offa (AD 757–796) as the first official boundary between England and Wales. Its exact purpose – military or administrative – is uncertain. Compared to Hadrian's Wall, built to keep the Scots at bay, it can hardly be regarded as a serious line of defence. It was not intended to be permanently manned, and neither was it a continuous structure.

The dyke ran from Prestatyn on the North Wales coast to Sedbury near Chepstow on the Severn Estuary, a distance of 142 miles (227 km). But there were many breaks along the way, especially in densely wooded river valleys. The building of the dyke must, nevertheless, have represented a monumental effort. A deep ditch was dug on the Welsh side. Above this, an earthwork barrier rose up to 20 ft (6 metres) high. The overall structure, ditch and earthwork, was in places over 70 ft (22 metres) wide.

This 1,200-year-old barrier has vanished along some of its route, but walkers can trace its course on the long-distance **Offa's Dyke Path** (www.offas-dyke.co.uk). Hay-on-Wye, Monmouth and Knighton, 17 miles/28 km west of Ludlow, are good access points.

Recommended Restaurants and Pubs on page 261

17th-century Speech House, now a hotel, Verderers, keepers of the forest, conduct their business as they always have done. This former royal hunting ground (40 sq miles/105 sq km) is crossed by trails. The **Dean Heritage Centre** (Mar–Oct daily 10am–5pm, Nov–Feb weekends only 10am–4pm; admission charge) is sited on the forest's northeast side at **Camp Mill** near **Cinderford**, where there are echoes of the old coal and iron industry. Ancient iron mines can be explored at **Clearwell Caves** (Feb–Oct daily10am–5pm, admission charge), near Coleford.

Just to the north is **Symonds Yat** ❹, a dramatic outcrop 400 ft (122 metres) over a loop in the Wye valley. The river twists along to the east of the A40 for another 8 miles (13 km) to **Ross-on-Wye** ❺, a town whose quaintness ensures it is full of visitors in summer. It centres on an arcaded 17th-century market hall where there's a market on Thursday and Saturday.

Black-and-white, half-timbered Tudor buildings are a speciality of these Welsh border towns. Above Ross are **Ledbury** ❻, which has a renowned herring-bone patterned Market House, and **Hereford** ❼, 10 miles (16 km) distant, where the Jacobean **Old House** (Tues–Sat 10am– 5pm; free) dominates the pedestrianised High Town. Hereford's **Cathedral** (Nov–Easter Mon–Sat 10am–4pm, Easter–Oct Mon–Sat 10am–5pm; admission charge) was founded by King Offa, and its greatest treasures are the *Mappa Mundi*, one of the first maps of the world, dating from around 1300, and its medieval chain library (Mon–Sat 11am–3.15pm; admission charge covers both).

Not far from Hereford, 8 miles (13 km) southwest off the A465 Abergavenny road, **Kilpeck** ❽ has a wonderfully ornate Norman church. **St Mary and St David**, built around 1140, has extraordinary carvings on its portal, including the Sheelah-na-gig, a Celtic fertility symbol.

Just off the A438, 23 miles (38 km) west of Hereford, is **Hay-on-Wye** ❾. It was transformed into a "book town" in the 1960s when the eccentric Richard Booth, seeing shops and cinemas close as they lost business to bigger towns

Hereford Cathedral, close to the Wye.

BELOW: the colourful Richard Booth, who revived the economically ailing Hay-on-Wye by buying up every vacant building and turning it into a secondhand bookshop.

Pathway leading to the Elan Valley dam.

nearby, converted them into bookstores in a bid to focus tourism. Other booksellers moved in and it soon became the biggest second-hand and antiquarian book centre in the world. Each summer (end of May), the high-profile Literary Festival (hay festival.com) is held, attracting well-known authors and celebrities from around the world. Most of the town is in Wales. William de Braose, a Marcher Lord, built a castle here to replace the one burned down by King John. Owain Glyndwr destroyed it in the 15th century, though a gateway, the keep and part of the wall remain.

The next major town on the Wye is **Builth Wells** ⓾, 20 miles (32 km) west. This is pony-trekking, walking and fishing country. The Royal Welsh Show, the principal agricultural event, is held here in July. Seven miles (10 km) to the north is **Llandrindod Wells** ⓫, a spa town which in its Victorian heyday attracted some 80,000 visitors a year who came here to "take the waters". The annual Victorian Festival in August returns the town to the leisurely days of hansom cabs, frock coats and mutton-chop whiskers.

To the west, near to the source of the Wye, lies the attractive town of **Rhayader** ⓬, where many Welsh crafts are on sale. Beyond is the **Elan Valley**, where in the late 19th century reservoirs were built to supply water to the thirsty city of Birmingham. The Elan Valley Visitor Centre, in Elan village, gives a good introduction to the lakelands and the important wildlife habitats.

The Black Mountains

On the on the south side of Hay-on-Wye is the 2,220-ft (677-metre) Hay Bluff that heralds the Black Mountains, which rise to 2,660 ft (810 metres) at Waun Fach 6 miles (10 km) beyond. To the south, the Black Mountains are cut off from the neighbouring Brecon Beacons by the Usk Valley, which the A40 follows between Abergavenny and Brecon (15 miles/24 km southwest of Hay).

Abergavenny ⓭, the area's main town, sits in a hollow surrounded by hills: the **Sugar Loaf** (1,955 ft/596 metres), **Skirrid Fach** and **Skirrid Fawr**, and the **Blorenge**, which has a lovely footpath running around its ridge

BELOW RIGHT: paragliding above Abergavenny.

Capturing the tradition of King Coal

South Wales is associated with coal like Bavaria with beer. At its peak, in 1921, some 271,000 men worked in the industry. In the 1920s there were 66 pits in the Rhondda Valley alone. All have closed.

The best place to get a feel of what it must have been like to work the coalface is the Big Pit Mining Museum (daily 9.30am–5pm; tel: 01495-790311; free; warm clothing and practical shoes recommended) in Blaenafon, near Abergavenny. The mine closed in 1980 but is now a World Heritage Site. The hour-long guided tours underground are run by former miners. Donning a miner's safety helmet, you are transported down a

300-ft (90-metre) shaft into the bowels of the earth where you can get a glimpse of what life was like for the thousands of men (and in earlier times, the women, children and pit ponies) who worked in the dank, dark tunnels. The death toll could be high.

Above ground, there's a range of colliery buildings to visit, including the engine house, blacksmith's shop, pithead baths and pitman's cabin, with a gift shop and cafeteria in what was the miners' canteen.

with far-reaching views of the surrounding countryside. The town itself is a smart shopping centre which hosts a lively annual food festival in September. Abergavenny is a splendid jumping-off point for the 80 sq miles (207 sq km) of the Black Mountains, with their opportunities for pony trekking, hang-gliding and good old-fashioned exploring.

Take the road to Capel Y Ffin running along the side of the mountains to connect with Hay-on-Wye *(see above)*, a lovely journey that takes in the romantic ruins of **Llanthony Priory**, an Augustinian monastery founded in the 12th century. Good walks lead into the hills behind the abbey, and refreshments are available in Llanthony Priory Hotel *(see page 366)* built into the abbey.

Crickhowell ⓮, 6 miles (10 km) west of Abergavenny, is another good base for exploring the Black Mountains or the Brecon Beacons. Though scarcely more than a village, it has some excellent shops and good pubs.

The Brecon Beacons

Covering 529 sq miles (1,370 sq km) and stretching 20 miles (32 km) south to Merthyr Tydfil is the **Brecon Beacons National Park**. These old red sandstone mountains are the highest in south Wales, rising to 2,906 ft (885 metres) at **Pen-y-Fan** (meaning "the top of the place"); they take their name from their use as locations for signal fires. The landscape bears the marks of long glacial history: sheer precipices hang like waves about to break over huge, semicircular valleys gouged out by the ice.

Brecon ⓯, the park's "capital", is an old market town, at the confluence of the Usk and the Honddu, internationally noted for its jazz festival held every August. William the Conqueror's half-brother built Brecon Castle; its surviving tower and battlemented section of wall are nearly all in the garden of the Castle Hotel. He also had a hand in the building of the nearby Brecon Cathedral, a largely 14th-century church, heavily restored in the 19th century. The **Brecon Beacons National Park Information Centre** (tel: 01874-624437) in the town and the **Mountain Centre**, off the A470 at **Libanus** 4 miles (6 km) south of Brecon, provide information on climbing, pony trekking and sailing on the reservoir.

TIP

If you set off walking in the benign-looking Brecon Beacons, make sure you have a map and compass and know how to use them. The weather is highly unpredictable and the rounded shapes of the mountains are very similar, making orientation difficult.

BELOW: hiking to Pen-y-Fan, the highest point in south Wales.

As a city, Cardiff (Caerdydd in Welsh) is a youngster, having nothing like the length of capital status enjoyed by either London or Edinburgh. It was designated as such only in 1955. It is also a comparatively anglicised city, where you are less likely to hear Welsh spoken than in, say, Swansea. Welsh is an advantage in Cardiff, but it is not a necessity.

A few miles southwest of Brecon is the **National Showcaves Centre** (Apr–Oct daily from 10am; admission charge) at Dan-yr-Ogof, said to be the largest showcave system in Western Europe. Apart from the underground spectacle of narrow passageways and limestone formations, the site also has a dinosaur park, an Iron-Age farm, a shire-horse centre and an indoor adventure playground, making it a popular family attraction.

Just off the A465, known as the Heads of the Valleys road, travelling along the park's southern boundary near Merthyr Tydfil, the narrow-gauge **Brecon Mountain Railway** runs a scenic 7-mile (11-km) round trip into the Beacons.

Cardiff

Between the mountains and the industrial south coast run the valleys whose names – Merthyr, Ebbw Vale, Rhondda, Neath – were once synonymous with mining, making Cardiff the world's greatest coal port. But by the beginning of the 1990s only a handful of deep mines remained. **Cardiff** ⓰ is the capital of Wales, with a population of 305,000. **Cardiff Castle** (Mar–Oct 9am–6pm, Nov–Feb 9.30am–5pm; admission charge) brings together all the strands of the city's history. The outer walls contain Roman stonework and the Norman keep, built at the end of the 11th century, still stands tall. At the height of Cardiff's prosperity, between 1867 and 1872, the Marquis of Bute (responsible for building much of the docks) added to the castle, with a clock tower and elaborate banqueting halls.

The **National Museum and Gallery Cardiff** (Tues–Sun 10am–5pm; free; tel: 029-2039 7951) boasts a wide variety of attractions, covering science, history and archaeology, and its **Art Gallery** has an Impressionist collection plus works from both English and Welsh painters.

But for those who really want to know about Wales, the **Museum of Welsh Life** (daily 10am–5pm; free), 4 miles (6 km) west of the city, is a must. Set in 100 acres (40 hectares) of parkland around the handsome Elizabethan manor house, **St Fagan's Castle**, it has brought together buildings of interest from all over the country – a toll gate, a chapel, a school room, a quarryman's cottage, a cock pit – and there are demonstrations by rural craftspeople. Of particular interest is a row of ironworkers' cottages painstakingly relocated from Rhydycar near Merthyr Tydfil. Each cottage has been restored in the style of a different era, right down to the gardens and outbuildings. They range from 1805 to 1985.

Europe's largest urban renewal scheme at **Cardiff Bay** is reuniting the city with its docks and coastline. The multi-billion pound transformation of the derelict docks into a dynamic waterfront centres on the new **Cardiff Bay Barrage**. This remarkable feat of engineering has created a vast freshwater lake and 8 miles (13 km) of coastline. The scheme can be explored in full at the pod-like **Cardiff Bay Visitor Centre** (Mon–Fri 9.30am–5pm, Sat, weekends and bank holidays 10.30am–5pm), where you can pick up information on festivals and events, water taxis and guided tours of the bay, as well as car-parking vouchers. Across from the visitor centre stands the

BELOW: the Millennium Stadium in Cardiff.

Recommended Restaurants and Pubs on page 261

Norwegian Church (daily 10am–5pm), originally built for visiting seamen, but now a cosy arts centre and café.

Close by there's **Techniquest** (Mon–Fri 9.30am–4.30pm, Sat, Sun and holidays 10.30am–5pm; admission charge), Britain's largest science exhibition centre, with over 150 hands-on exhibits, which enable you to design a tree, launch a hot-air balloon, fire a rocket, play a giant piano and much more.

The Bay is also the site for the newly opened **Wales Millennium Arts and Entertainment Centre**, a state-of-the-art theatre for musicals, opera and dance. Also being built here is the new **Assembly Building**. Visitors can witness debates from the public gallery (tickets available on the day – debating starts at 2pm Tuesday and 12.30pm Wednesday – or booked up to three weeks in advance: assemblywales.org).

Caerphilly and Carleon

Five miles (8 km) north of Cardiff, guarding the southern approaches to the Valleys is mighty **Caerphilly Castle** 17 (Mon–Sat Apr, May and Oct 9.30am–5pm, June–Sept until 6pm, Nov–Mar until 4pm; Sun 11am–4pm; admission charge). Its presence in an otherwise ordinary town is wholly unexpected. The 13th-century fortress, with its sophisticated system of water defences, concentric fortifications and leaning tower, is Britain's biggest castle after Windsor.

East of Cardiff is **Newport**, Wales's third-largest conurbation. Like Cardiff and Swansea, this rather drab industrial city on the mouth of the River Usk is the product of rapid industrial expansion in the 19th century. Of more interest to the visitor in this area is **Caerleon** 18 (Apr–Oct daily 9.30am–5pm, Nov–Mar Mon–Sat 9.30am–5pm, Sun 11am–4pm; admission charge), one of only three Roman fortress towns in Britain (Chester and York being the other two). It was built to accommodate the elite legionary troops, and you can see the impressive remains of the fortress baths, amphitheatre, barracks, and fortress walls.

The Gower Peninsula

Dylan Thomas (1914–53) described his home town, **Swansea** 19, as "an ugly,

Roman re-enactment at Caerleon.

BELOW: Cardiff's church built for Norwegian seamen and its memorial to Antarctic explorer Captain Robert Scott (1868–1912).

Three Cliffs Bay on the Gower Peninsula.

lovely town... crawling, sprawling, slummed, unplanned, jerry villa'd and smug-suburbed by the side of a long and splendid curving shore". (The poet was born in the residential Uplands district, at No. 5 Cwmdonkin Drive). Although scarred by industrialisation and World War II bombs, Swansea is nevertheless a personable city. Its main attraction is the **indoor market**, a vast glass building offering everything from ice cream to antiques and laverbread (seaweed) to carpets. To the west, a tree-lined sea wall skirts the 4-mile (6-km) bay to the Victorian pier at **The Mumbles**, a popular sailing centre and small resort, well stocked with pubs, many frequented by Dylan Thomas as a young man.

The Mumbles is the start of the **Gower Peninsula**, a small finger of land which juts out into Carmarthen Bay, designated as the first Area of Outstanding Natural Beauty in Britain. It has three National Nature Reserves and 21 Sites of Special Scientific Interest. From the Mumbles, the sheltered shoreline plunges and soars out of pine-clad limestone bays, dotted with occasional palms. **Langland Bay** is the nearest to town and popular with surfers (as is Oxwich Bay further on). At the west end of the peninsula is the gracious 3-mile (5-km) sweep of **Rhossilli beach** ⓴. The spectacular **Worms Head** promontory at one end of the beach is accessible on foot at low tide. Here there's a large seabird colony and half a dozen bed-and-breakfast establishments. The nearby **Paviland Caves** are thought to be the oldest occupied site yet excavated in Europe, dating back 100,000 years.

Llanmadoc Hill, just north of Llangennith, is topped by a hill fort – the best viewpoint at this end of the peninsula. Meanwhile, the cockle women of **Penclawdd** on the northern coast, who still traipse across the mudflats to collect the cockles and seaweed for laverbread, keep alive the region's more recent traditions.

On the mainland behind the peninsula, the River Tywi forces the road inland to **Carmarthen**, a market town with a truly Welsh atmosphere. The river charts a lazy course between Carmarthen and Llandovery to the east, flowing through tranquil green countryside. On the south side of the river is the **National Botanic Garden of Wales** (Nov–Mar daily 10am–4.30pm, Apr–Oct daily 10am–6pm; admission charge), a visionary garden dedicated to conservation and education. Its centrepiece, the Great Glasshouse designed by Lord Foster, is stunning.

To the southwest of Carmarthen is **Laugharne** ㉑. This tranquil town provided Dylan Thomas with inspiration for the wonderful creation of Llareggub (spell it backwards) in *Under Milk Wood*, his famous "play for voices". The boathouse where he spent the last few years of his life is now a museum.

BELOW: the boathouse in Laugharne where Dylan Thomas spent the last four years of his life.

The Pembrokeshire Coast

Pembrokeshire, in the extreme southwest of Wales is renowned for its rugged coastline. The **Pembrokeshire Coast National Park** stretches from Amroth in Carmarthen Bay around St David's Head and up to Cardigan in Cardigan Bay, taking in 160 miles (260 km) of spectacular coastal scenery. The only inland tracts in the park take in the **Preseli Hills**, pretty rather than dramatic, and the wooded valley of **Cwm Gaun**, which separates the Preselis from Fishguard.

Tenby ❷❷ is the major resort along this golden coast. The Harbour Beach is overlooked by the hilltop castle ruins and elegant pastel-shaded Georgian townhouses. Tenby has three more lovely beaches and its 13th-century medieval walls are almost intact. From the harbour you can take a boat to **Caldey Island**, 2½ miles (4 km) offshore, where Cistercian monks make perfume from the gorse and lavender which carpet the tiny island, to supplement their income.

The coast around **St Govan's Head**, 12 miles (20 km) west of Tenby, offers some spectacular scenery. Just behind the wave-battered cliffs lie the calm waters of **Bosherston**, man-made lakes covered in waterlilies in June. **Pembroke** ❷❸ is a few miles north at the head of an estuary in the large natural harbour of **Milford Haven**, a major oil terminal. Pembroke is more elegant than its austere industrial neighbour. A long bustling main street of Victorian and Georgian houses leads up to **Pembroke Castle** (daily: Apr–Sept 9.30am–6pm, Mar and Oct 10am–5pm, Nov–Feb 10am–4pm; admission charge), birthplace of Henry VII, founder of the Tudor dynasty. The walls of this imposing Norman fortress are 16 ft (5 metres) thick and it is bounded on three sides by a tidal inlet of the Milford Haven Waterway. There are many boating facilities in the area, particularly around the sheltered waters of **Dale** ❷❹.

St David's and Fishguard

A toll bridge leads over Milford Haven, otherwise the road around the valley via the market town of **Haverfordwest** is circuitous. The coast west of here is drawn in to sandy **St Bride's Bay** with St Ann's Head and the bird sanctuary islands of Skomer and Skokholm in the south, and Ramsey Island and St David's Head, which is Wales's western extremity, in the north.

If it weren't for its majestic cathedral, dedicated to the patron saint of Wales, **St David's** ❷❺ would be just a pretty village instead of Britain's smallest city. A cluster of shops (geared to sporty types) and restaurants surround the main square; there are a couple of hotels, a few pubs, a few chapels (backs turned resolutely to the cathedral) and that's about it. Apart

The best way of seeing the coast is to follow the Pembrokeshire Coast Path. It provides dramatic views of the sea cliffs and endless opportunities for watching gannets, fulmars, puffins, cormorants and other wildlife that thrives in the region.

BELOW: Tenby's colourful harbour.

It is believed that Ireland's patron saint, Patrick, was born close to where St David's Cathedral stands. The monastic site became a major centre of pilgrimage for kings and commoners alike. Two pilgrimages here were worth one to Rome and three were worth one to Jerusalem.

from the **Cathedral** that is. Together with the 14th-century **Bishop's Palace** (Apr–Oct daily 9am–5pm, Nov–Mar Mon–Sat 9.30am–4pm, Sun 11am–4pm), it was built into a grassy hollow, half a mile from the sea to keep it out of sight of marauders.

Only when approaching it through the south gate does the full majesty of the purple-stoned cathedral become apparent. Fears of attack on this coast were not ill-founded: the last foreign invasion was in 1797 when the French landed at **Fishguard** 26 16 miles (25 km) to the north, though they were tricked into surrendering by the townswomen. Nowadays, as well as being the main shopping centre for north Pembrokeshire, the town is a Stena Lines ferry port providing the "shortest sea route to Ireland". **Lower Fishguard**, with its charming harbour, was the setting of the 1971 film of Dylan Thomas's *Under Milk Wood*, starring Richard Burton.

Cardigan

Eighteen miles (28 km) further north on the A487 is **Cardigan** 27, a lively market town with agricultural and seafaring connections. Inland from Cardigan the road

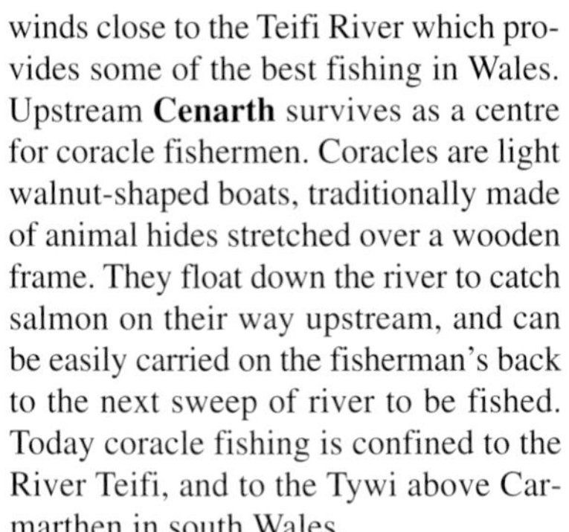

winds close to the Teifi River which provides some of the best fishing in Wales. Upstream **Cenarth** survives as a centre for coracle fishermen. Coracles are light walnut-shaped boats, traditionally made of animal hides stretched over a wooden frame. They float down the river to catch salmon on their way upstream, and can be easily carried on the fisherman's back to the next sweep of river to be fished. Today coracle fishing is confined to the River Teifi, and to the Tywi above Carmarthen in south Wales.

From Cardigan the A487 traces the coast north past attractive little inlets and coves such as **Tresaith** and **Llangrannog** before reaching the small seaside resort of **New Quay** 28, an old shipping town with a delightful quay. Just beyond, among rocky headlands, is the port of **Aberaeron**, a small well-ordered town with a stone-walled harbour and elegant sea captains' houses built during the town's 19th-century heyday.

Aberystwyth

A further 16 miles (25 km) along the coast is the university town of **Aberystwyth** 29. As well as being a commercial centre, it is a popular holiday resort (it has a large but stony beach) and a convenient base for exploring the hinterland of sheep walks and lonely lakes. It is also the headquarters of the Welsh Language Society, founded here in 1963.

Aberystwyth's Alexandra Road Station is the sea-end terminal of the steam-operated **Vale of Rheidol Railway** (tel: 01970-625819 for timetable).The countryside at **Devil's Bridge** 30, 12 miles (20 km) inland, is picturesque Wales at its most dramatic. There are in fact three bridges here, built one over the other, spanning the deep chasm of the River Mynach: the iron bridge (1901), the stone bridge (1753) and the original bridge built for the monks of **Strata Florida Abbey**, 7 miles (11 km) south. Now a ruin, this Cistercian establishment was the cultural centre of Wales in the 13th century.

East of Devil's Bridge the B4574 leads back to the lakes and high lands of the Elan Valley *(see page 254)*. ❑

BELOW: traditional coracles, used for fishing, can be carried easily, even by this 86-year-old.

RESTAURANTS AND PUBS

Restaurants

Prices for a three-course dinner per person with a half-bottle of house wine:

£ = under £25
££ = £25–50
£££ = £50–100
££££ = £100+

Aberaeron

Ty Mawr
Cilcennin
Tel: 01570 470033 **££££**
Elegant Georgian country house hotel with notable restaurant, a few miles inland from Aberaeron. Formal setting and menu featuring local produce.

Brecon

Felin Fach Griffin
On the A470 3 miles (5 km) north of Brecon
Tel: 01874 62011 **£££**
Award-winning restaurant serving well-prepared dishes using locally reared lamb, beef and pork, vegetables from its own garden, Welsh cheeses, and local seafood. Informal atmosphere, with log fires in winter and garden tables in summer.

Abergavenny

The Foxhunter
Nantyderry, nr Abergavenny
Tel: 01873-881101 **££**
In an old station-master's house, this cosy restaurant serves immaculately presented dishes made from organic produce.

The Walnut Tree
Llandewi Skirrid
(B4521 2 miles/3 km) east of Abergavenny).
Tel: 01873-852797
£££–££££
Famous restaurant newly revived under chef Shaun Hill. Good choice of fish, local meat and game, plus vegetables from the Walnut Tree Garden. Good-value set lunches.

Cardiff

Gilby's
Old Port Road,
Culverhouse Cross
Tel: 02920-670800 **££**
Converted barn with bare stone walls. Innovative menu, especially the fish.

Le Gallois
6–8 Romilly Crescent
Tel: 02920-341264 **££**
Accomplished cuisine in modern, friendly surroundings. Interesting French-Celtic fusion.

Hay-on-Wye

The Granary
Broad Street (by the Clocktower)
Tel: 01497-820790 **££**
Favourite for breakfast (from 10am), light lunches, teas and early suppers, with plenty of options for vegetarians. Low beams, old pine furniture, a fire in winter.

Hereford

Left Bank
Bridge Street
Tel: 01432-349000 **££–£££**
Good modern restaurant just around the corner from the cathedral. Book a table with river views, or in summer eat on the terrace. Set lunches.

Kington

The Stag Inn
Titley, 3 miles (5km) east of Kington (B4335), Herefordshire. Tel: 01544-230221
£££–££££
Critically acclaimed roadside inn in north Herefordshire. Emphasis is on local and home-grown produce. Great-value Sunday lunches. Essential to book.

ABOVE: Welsh rarebit is a savoury snack of melted cheese and toasted bread. The name is said to date from when the economically challenged Welsh, unable to afford rabbit, had to make do with cheese.

Llanwrtyd Wells

Carlton House
Dolycoed Road
Tel: 01591-610248 **££**
Small Edwardian hotel offering a well-priced 4-course "epicurean" menu and good-value wine list.

Swansea

L'Amuse
2 Woodville Road, Mumbles.
Tel: 01792-366006. **££**
Quirky French-style restaurant with fixed-price lunch and dinner menus and complimentary *amuse gueules*.

Solva

The Old Pharmacy
5 Main Street. Tel: 01437-720005 **££**
Good restaurants in Pembrokeshire are hard to find – this one in a coastal village is good for fish and seafood.

Tenby

D Fecci and Sons
Oxford House, Lower Frog Street. Tel: 01834-842484 **£**
Family chippie serving good fresh fare. Sit-down service available.

Pubs

The Bell in Skenfrith, near Abergavenny, is a riverside pub in a 17th-century coaching inn. It uses locally-sourced produce from the Usk valley, from lamb and cheese, to ales and ice cream.

In Cardiff, the **Cayo Arms** on Cathedral Road and **The Cottage** on St Mary Street are reliable traditional pubs.

In book town Hay-on-Wye, the central **Kilverts Inn** has an airy bar and outdoors seating.

In Swansea's pub-packed Wind Street, the **No Sign Wine Bar**, founded in 1690 and patronised by Dylan Thomas, has a Dickensian feel to it and a good range of wines and beers.

NORTH WALES

No visitor to North Wales can fail to be impressed by the dramatic mountainscape of Snowdonia or the massive, and largely preserved, fortresses of the coast

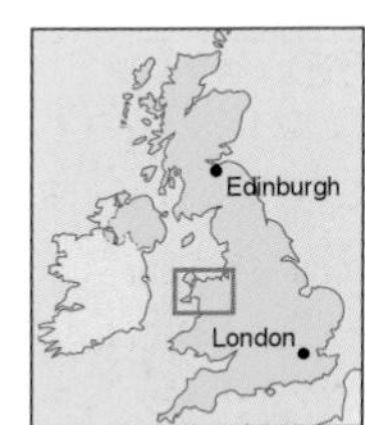

Snowdonia's great crags and gullies have long attracted hikers, rock-climbers and mountaineers. Equally deserving, though less well publicised, is the region's glorious coastline, stretching north from the Dovey peninsula round the Lleyn peninsula and Anglesey to the River Conwy. Nowhere else in Britain are high mountains and quality seaside found in such close proximity.

From Chester – largest of the towns on the English side of the border – the Dee estuary, followed by the A548, leads out to the sandy resorts of North Wales, starting with **Prestatyn** 28 miles (45 km) west. Adjoining it is **Rhyl**, which has gaudy amusements and a 3-mile (5-km) promenade, but the largest and most pleasant of these resorts is **Llandudno** ❸❶, 15 miles (24 km) further on, along the A55 North Wales Coast Expressway. Behind the town on the 679-ft (207-metre) summit of the Great Orme there are spectacular views of the North Wales coast. All these resorts are within easy reach of the Snowdonia National Park.

Conwy

Opposite Llandudno, on the far side of Thomas Telford's impressive **Conwy Suspension Bridge** (pedestrians only; Easter–Nov daily 10am–5pm), lies **Conwy** ❸❷. Enclosed by battlemented walls, Conwy is one of the best-preserved medieval fortified towns in Europe. The stunning **castle** (daily Apr–Oct 9am–5pm, Nov–Mar 9.30am–4pm; cadw.wales.gov.uk) was built under the orders of Edward I and was one of four (the others are Beaumaris, Caernarfon and Harlech) built by his Master of Works in Wales, James St George, cousin of the Count of Savoy. From these bastions Edward sallied forth to defeat the Welsh during the conquest of 1277–84. The **town walls** have survived almost unscathed; walking along the ramparts reveals bird's-eye views of the historic town and River Quay beyond, location of Britain's **smallest house**. Conwy is also home to Britain's finest Elizabethan townhouse Plas Mawr (Apr–end Oct Tues–Sun, tel:

Main attractions
- LLANDUDNO
- CONWY CASTLE
- ANGLESEY
- CAERNARFON CASTLE
- SNOWDONIA NATIONAL PARK
- FFESTINIOG NARROW-GAUGE RAILWAY
- PORTMEIRION
- HARLECH
- MACHYNLLETH
- LLANGOLLEN

LEFT: walkers on the Miners' Track, Snowdon.
BELOW: Conwy Suspension Bridge.

Conwy claims to have Britain's smallest house.

01492 580167, cadw.wales.gov.uk), notable for its elaborate plasterwork and well preserved kitchen.

St Asaph

South of Rhyl, 5 miles (8 km) along the A525, is **St Asaph** in the tranquil Vale of Clwyd – a city that's the size of a village. Its small cathedral dates back to the 1st century AD and was restored in the 19th-century by Gilbert Scott.

Further south is the market town of **Denbigh**, once home to Welsh princes and a centre of anti-English resistance. Denbigh's mighty castle (daily, Apr–Oct 10am–5pm; 10am–4pm rest of the year; cadw.wales.gov.uk) was built after the forces of Edward I crushed the town.

The A525 continues to **Ruthin**, a bustling town besieged by Owain Glyndwr in 1400. The town's former jail (daily May–Oct 10am–5pm, weekends rest of year) is now a visitor attraction and focuses on prison conditions in Victorian times. Ruthin Craft Centre (ruthincraftcentre.org.uk), on Well Street, has been redeveloped and is now the main centre for contemporary art in Wales, with craft studios, exhibition space and a cafe.

From Ruthin it is a 21-mile (35-km) journey to the town of **Wrexham**, near the English border. Two miles (3.2km) to the south is **Erddig Hall** (Sat–Wed Easter–end Oct noon–4pm, Apr–Sept noon–5pm, garden open longer; nationaltrust.org.uk), a fine 18th-century stately home with extremely well preserved servants' quarters and a walled garden with rare fruit trees.

Bangor

Bangor, a university town, is 20 miles (32 km) west and from here another Telford bridge crosses the **Menai Strait** to reach the 276-sq mile (715-sq km) island of **Anglesey** ㉝. This ancient Celtic island was the final stronghold of the Druids, who were massacred here by the Romans. The Romans settled the island and you can see the remains of a 1st-century farmstead, Din Lligwy, at Lligwy. Nearby is a Neolithic burial chamber. The Roman name for Anglesey was Mona, but the Welsh call it *Mon, mam Cymru* (Anglesey, mother of Wales) because this was the country's granary.

The Menai Suspension Bridge was built in 1826 and was the first of its kind

BELOW: Beaumaris Castle. **RIGHT:** a tribute to lifeboat crews at Moelfre Seawatch Centre on Anglesey.

Castles in North Wales

There are two distinct kinds of castle in North Wales: "native" structures and those built by Edward I following his successful campaigns against the Welsh in the late 13th century.

Those in the former category, such as Powis and Criccieth, were built by Llywellyn the Great (d.1240), who as Prince of Gwynedd devoted his life to securing the territorial integrity of Wales. His grandson, Llywellyn the Last, sought to establish his own authority as Prince of Wales, but his refusal to pay homage to Edward I resulted in the invasion that put an end to any hopes of independence. The last of the Welsh castles to fall was Castell y Bere on the western flanks of Cadair Idris, in 1283.

Edward's own castles at Conwy, Beaumaris, Caernarfon and Harlech, supported by fortified town walls, are fine examples of medieval military architecture. Their theatrical siting to guard strategic points against Welsh resistance would have intimidated any enemy. Even so, all except Caernarfon were taken, if only briefly, by the Welsh rebel Owain Glyndwr's uprising at the start of the 15th century.

Recommended Restaurants and Pubs on page 271

and the most difficult feat in the great Holyhead Road scheme which Telford engineered to link Dublin to London. Ferries still go to Ireland from **Holyhead** 34, a small island just off the west coast. On a clear day from the 722-ft (220-metre) Holyhead Mountain there is a view of Ireland to the west, and southeast to Wales's highest mountain, Snowdon. A drive across Anglesey, along its small lanes and winding roads, can be frustrating for anyone in a hurry to catch the ferry, but it is a good way to see some of the farming way of life and the small, lime-washed cottages with slurried roofs.

A warning of the island's eccentricities comes just after crossing the Strait when the A5 passes the village of **Llanfairpwllgwyngyllgogerychwyrndrobwllllantysiliogogogoch**; its name is an accurate description of the place: "St Mary's Church in the hollow of the white hazel near the rapid whirlpool of St Tysilio close to the red cave".

Beaumaris, with its fine moated castle and the nearby Penmon Priory, is towards the eastern end of the island, while **Caernarfon** 35, the largest town in the area, is at the opposite end of the Strait on the mainland. With its city walls and towers intact, Caernarfon is a fine resort, popular with yachtsmen. Its strategic position meant it was an important settlement long before the present castle was built.

The Romans arrived in AD 78 and built a fortress, Segontium; some excavated remains can be seen. Begun in 1283, the **Castle** (Apr–Oct daily 9am–5pm, Nov–Mar Mon–Sat 9.30am–4pm, Sun 11am–4pm; cadw.wales.gov.uk) was the largest of Edward I's network of fortifications. The exterior walls and three towers remain intact and are hugely impressive. Queen's Tower houses the fascinating **Regimental Museum** of the Royal Welsh Fusiliers. The Victoria Dock in Caernarfon is home to a little **Maritime Museum** (Sun–Fri, end May–mid-Sept) and **Galeri Caernarfon** (tel: 01286 685252; galericaernarfon.com), a new arts venue with a theatre, cinema and gallery.

Snowdonia

Immediately behind these coastal resorts is Eryri, the Place of Eagles. This is **Snowdonia**, Wales's most mountainous region. Fifteen summits are above 3,000 ft (1,000 metres) and **Snowdon** 36 itself,

Less energetic visitors can get to the summit of Snowdon on the Snowdon Mountain Railway, a rack railway which starts in Llanberis.

BELOW: Caernarfon Castle, where Prince Charles was invested as Prince of Wales in 1969.

Welsh fights back

Revived in schools, and with its own TV channel, Welsh is alive and well, even in the anglicised valleys of the south.

Driving into Wales on any major road supplies a painless and instant introduction to the Welsh language. The road signs are in Welsh as well as English and even the dimmest of linguists can scarcely fail to take on board sooner or later that *milltir* means miles, *lôn* lane and *toiledau* exactly what you would expect.

Welsh is now widely in evidence all over the country, *de rigueur* from railway stations to post offices, banks to supermarkets. Cities and towns carry their Welsh names as a matter of course: Cardiff/*Caerdydd*, Swansea/*Abertawe*, Newport/*Casnewydd*, Abergavenny/*Y Fenni*. A heavily subsidised Welsh television channel, S4C, backs up the language and creates a market for actors, writers and film producers working in Welsh. Its most popular soap opera, *Pobol y Cwm* (People of the Valleys) has been running for over 30 years and is watched by half of all Welsh speakers.

The language's most remarkable quality must be its powers of survival. Living in the closest possible relationship with English, one of the most all-pervading languages on earth, the miracle is that it was not swallowed without trace centuries ago. Yet, according to the 2001 census, 594,500 people (20.5 percent) speak Welsh fluently. That's a far cry from the million who spoke it in 1900, but it's holding its own better than Scots or even Irish Gaelic.

The most hopeful sign is that there has been a slight upturn in the number of Welsh speakers who are under 14. In recent years, there has been a notable surge of interest in the language, not least in anglicised South Wales where a significant number of parents want their children educated entirely through the medium of Welsh.

The Welsh equivalents of the Irish *Gaeltacht*, its language strongholds, are the north and west. Historically, in South Wales, the hold of the language was broken by the Industrial Revolution and the massive influx of immigrant workers from England and Ireland. Contemporary trends are also, it is argued, diluting the Welsh-speaking pool, as English retirees and those in search of a more peaceful way of life migrate to north and west Wales from the big cities of central and northern England.

In the north, second homes are seen as a major threat in previously homogeneous Welsh villages. Many incomers make strenuous efforts to learn Welsh, but a learned language must invariably be second best to a mother tongue.

Welsh is not easy to learn, but it holds the key to a rich literature going back through the hymns and folk ballads of the 18th century and medieval storytelling to the bards of the 6th century, and the odes and elegies of Taliesin and Aneirin. They were writing in the earliest British language – Welsh, which with Cornish belongs to the Brythonic branch of Celtic speech – and references to Catraeth (Catterick) show that their Britain went beyond present-day Wales. In a sense, therefore, Welsh belongs to the whole of Britain. ❑

ABOVE: public signs are bilingual.
LEFT: a pageant at Anglesey keeps traditions alive.

Recommended Restaurants and Pubs on page 271

some 12 miles (19 km) as the eagle flies east of Caernarfon, is the highest at 3,560 ft (1,085 metres). Sculpted by glacial activity, these mountains have been a playground for generations of climbers and walkers. Rolling green foothills rise into sheer crags, and stone sheepfolds cling impossibly to high slopes. Simply driving around Snowdonia is an exhilarating experience. Roads such as the A4086 through the sheer-sided Llanberis Pass to the east of Caernarfon, the A5 through the stunning **Ogwen Valley** between Capel Curig and Bethesda, and the A498 south of Capel Curig via the **Pass of Aberglaslyn** to Porthmadog on the coast, offer breathtaking views of the mountain scenery, which is studded with brilliant lakes. A mile (1.6 km) north of the Pass of Aberglaslyn is **Beddgelert**, a tiny, compact village nestled in the middle of beautiful scenery.

Purists insist that, like the poet William Wordsworth, visitors should climb Snowdon in order to see the dawn. The easiest and most popular path to the summit starts on its northern side at **Llanberis** ㊲ and is 5 miles (8km) long. Shorter, but more difficult, paths include the **Miners' Track** and the **Pyg Track**, both of which start at the Pen-y-Pass car park at the top of the Llanberis Pass and are 4 miles (6.4km) long. Bear in mind that the return journey doubles the length of all these walks. A new visitor centre and café has opened on the summit of Snowdon.

Betws-y-Coed

Betws-y-Coed ㊳, situated at the junction of the A5 and the A470 and at the meeting point of three valleys, Lledr, Llugwy and Conwy, is another popular centre for outdoor enthusiasts. In the Wybrnant valley 3½ miles (5 km) southwest, is a small cottage called **Ty Mawr Wybrnant** (Thur–Sun Easter–Sept noon–5pm, Oct noon–4pm), the birthplace of Bishop William Morgan (1545–1604) who first translated the Bible into Welsh. Two miles (3 km) west of Betws-y-Coed on the A5 towards Capel Curig are the famous **Swallow Falls**.

Snowdonia is full of stupendous natural scenery, but man has also left his mark on the area. Slate quarrying was once the most important industry of northwest Wales, and the huge heaps of slate spoil which overshadow places like Llanberis

TIP

Betws-y-Coed can be reached by train on the Conwy Valley Line that runs from Llandudno Junction to Blaenau Ffestiniog. Several easy walks start from the village, particularly up to Llyn Elsi by the Jubilee Path, to forest-fringed Llyn y Parc, and along the River Llugwy to the Miners Bridge. All are clearly marked.

BELOW: a mountain of slate towers over Blaenau Ffestiniog.

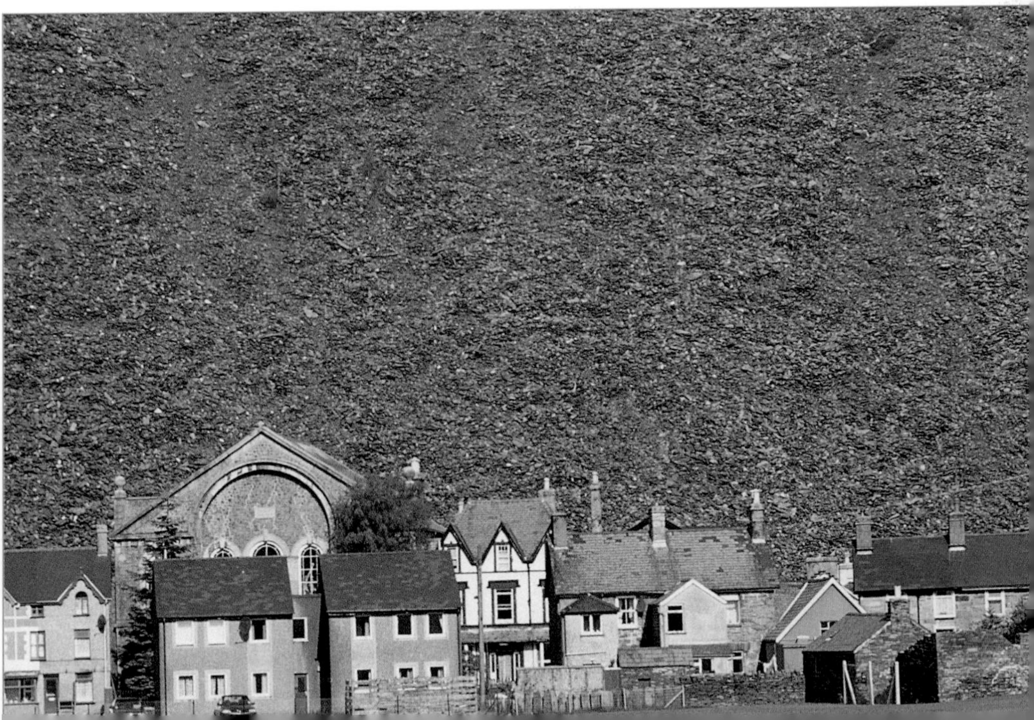

Some of the eight locomotives, such as Palmerstone *and* Prince, *powering the Ffestiniog Railway are restored from the original 1860s engines. Others have been recently constructed using old designs* – David Lloyd George *was built in 1992, for example, to look like an 1880s locomotive and is powerful enough to pull 12 carriages.*

and Bethesda, and, most famously, **Blaenau Ffestiniog** 39 on the A470 to the east, are its enduring legacy. Though the mountainsides are scarred, they do become eerily beautiful when wetted by the rain which falls so plentifully here.

The legacy of slate has also given rise to some of the region's best tourist attractions, including the **Welsh Slate Museum** at Llanberis (Easter–Oct daily 10am–5pm, Nov–Easter Sun–Fri 10am–4pm), where the sight of workmen splitting and dressing slate will make any idle onlooker feel clumsy; and, in Blaenau Ffestiniog, the **Llechwedd Slate Caverns** (daily Mar–Sept 10am–5.15pm, Oct–Feb 10am–4.15pm; llechwedd-slate-caverns.co.uk) where visitors can take a tour on Britain's deepest underground railway. For those who love activities, the **Snowdonia Rope Centre** (daily, tel: 01286 872310; ropesandladders.co.uk) is an outdoor climbing centre, next to the Welsh Slate Museum.

From Blaenau Ffestiniog, slate was transported by rail to **Porthmadog** 40. Porthmadog was the creation of William Maddocks (1773–1828), a local mill owner and parliamentarian. He constructed the mile-long embankment, called the Cob, across the river mouth which reclaimed 7,000 acres (2,800 hectares) and gave rise to the lovely town. In its industrial heyday, slate was shipped from the quaysides here all over the world.

The Ffestiniog Railway

The old **Ffestiniog Narrow Gauge Railway** (all year, tel: 01766-516024; festrail.co.uk) was rescued from oblivion in 1954 and is today very popular with visitors. The 13½-mile (22-km) journey from Porthmadog to Blaenau Ffestiniog up the beautiful Vale of Ffestiniog provides spectacular views of the mountains from the carriage windows. The rail link between Caernarfon and Porthmadog has been restored, making it possible to travel from Caernarfon to Blaenau Ffestiniog.

The architect Sir Clough William Ellis had an even more vivid imagination than Maddocks when, in 1926, he decided to build an Italianate village beside Porthmadog in the Dwyryd estuary *(see box below)*. This elaborate folly, **Portmeirion** 41 (daily 9.30am–5.30pm; tel: 01766-770000; portmeirion-village.com), incorporates a hotel. Portmeirion is also known internationally for its pottery.

BELOW AND RIGHT: Portmeirion, whose 17 cottages are let as self-catering accommodation.

The making of Portmeirion

Taking his inspiration from Portofino in Italy and buildings he had seen in Austria, Sir Clough Williams-Ellis gradually built up Portmeirion using odds and ends of houses rescued from demolition – "the home of fallen buildings," he called it. He developed "a light opera approach to architecture," aiming to produce "beauty without solemnity."

An example of this rescue process is the village's town hall. After seeing by chance that a Flintshire mansion, Emral Hall, was being torn down, Williams-Ellis bought the Hall's ballroom ceiling for £13; there were no other bidders at the auction for "so awkward and speculative a lot." At vast expense, the 17th-century ceiling was brought to Portmeirion in 100 different pieces to form the centrepiece of Hercules Hall.

The village's artistic imagination has inspired many people. Noël Coward wrote his play *Blithe Spirit* while on holiday there in 1941. It also provided the surreal backdrop for Patrick McGoohan's cult TV series *The Prisoner*, filmed there in 1967 (the 2009 remake was shot in Namibia).

Wales is sometimes depicted as an old lady throwing a ball out to sea. Her head is Anglesey, her leg Pembroke and the **Lleyn Peninsula** 42 is her arm (with Porthmadog in her armpit). Caernarfon lies on her shoulder and from **Aberdaron**, at the tip of the peninsula, **Bardsey Island**, her ball, can be reached. In the 7th century monks came to settle on the island, giving it the title "Island of 20,000 saints". Around the peninsula are tiny coastal harbours such as **Porth Dinllaen** and **Nefyn**. Travelling north of Nefyn on the B4417, the mountain range **Yr Eifl** ("The Forks") appears large on the left – 1,850 ft (564 metres) at its highest peak. On its eastern peak is the site of **Tre'r Ceiri**, an ancient Iron-Age fort.

Nearer to Porthmadog, the pleasant resort of **Criccieth** is dominated by its **castle** (daily Apr–Oct 10am–5pm, Nov–Mar Fri, Sat 9.30am–4pm, Sun 11am–4pm), which has been a ruin since it was besieged by Owain Glyndwr in the early 15th century. Just west of Criccieth is **Llanystumdwy**, childhood home of David Lloyd George, Britain's prime minister during World War I. A museum (tel: 01766 522071 for hours) is filled with memorabilia of the colourful "Welsh Wizard".

Men of Harlech

At the other side known of Tremadog Bay lies **Harlech** 43, the perfect place from which to view the Lleyn Peninsula and Snowdonia in one breathtaking gaze. The castle (tel: 01766-780552; cadw.wales.gov.uk; daily Apr–Oct 9am–5pm, Nov–Mar Mon–Sat 9.30am–4pm, Sun 11am–4pm), perched on a promontory looking out to sea, fell to Owain Glyndwr in 1404. It was recaptured by the English within five years and featured in the Wars of the Roses, when the siege (and surrender) by the Lancastrian garrison inspired the marching song *Men of Harlech* (music 1794, lyrics added in 1860, and often mistaken for Wales's national anthem).

Eleven miles (18 km) south of Harlech is the holiday resort of **Barmouth** 44, attractively built up against towering cliffs and offering superb views of **Cadair Idris** at the other side of the estuary. From here the road turns inland up the Mawddach Valley to **Dolgellau** 45,

Harlech Castle dominates the town.

BELOW: Porthmadog railway station.

Lake Bala is a major watersports centre.

an excellent base for exploring the Cadair Idris range. It's the epitome of a sturdy, close-knit Welsh community.

South of Dolgellau on the A487, 3 miles (5 km) north of Machynlleth, is the **Centre for Alternative Technology** (daily 10am–5.30pm, until dusk in winter; tel: 01654-705950; cat.org.uk). Founded in 1973, it has now found a new popularity as it demonstrates environmentally friendly approaches to energy saving and climate change.

Machynlleth

Machynlleth 46 itself is a pleasant market town at the southern edge of the Snowdonia National Park. The principal attraction here is the Owain Glyndwr Centre (daily Easter–Sept) in the Parliament House. This building incorporates the remains of an earlier structure in which Glyndwr established the country's first Parliament in 1404.

Northeast of Dolgellau, the A494 leads to **Lake Bala** (Llyn Tegid), around 18 miles (29 km) away – the largest natural expanse of water in Wales and a great centre for watersports. Just a short drive away, on the A4212, is the **National White Water Centre** (tel: 01678 521083; ukrafting.co.uk), which offers canoeing, kayaking and white water rafting.

Heading east from Dolgellau, on the A458, it's a 37-mile (60-km) drive to **Welshpool** 47, county town of Powys. There are unexpected red-brick Georgian houses here, but there are also ancient, timbered, lopsided hotels and pubs. A mile southwest is **Powis Castle** (Mar–end-Oct Mon, Thur–Sun 1pm–5pm, garden open longer, tel: 01938-55194429; nationaltrust.org.uk), built by Welsh princes around 1300. The dramatic terraced gardens were created between 1688 and 1722.

Thirty miles (48 km) to the north of Welshpool is **Llangollen** 48, home of the **International Musical Eisteddfod** and regarded as the centre of Welsh culture and music. Its two most famous residents, Lady Eleanor Butler and the Hon. Sarah Ponsonby, the eccentric "Ladies of Llangollen", lived at **Plas Newydd** cottage (daily Apr–Oct 10am–5pm). They scandalised contemporary society by setting up home together in 1780. ❑

BELOW: the Pontcysyllte Aqueduct, the highest in Britain, carries the Llangollen Canal over the valley of the River Dee.

RESTAURANTS AND PUBS

Restaurants

Prices for a three-course dinner per person with a half-bottle of house wine:

£ = under £25
££ = £25–50
£££ = £50–100

Aberdyfi

Penhelig Arms Hotel
Tel: 01654-767215. **££**
Old-fashioned country cooking in an 18th-century harbourside inn. Generous portions and excellent wine list.

Abersoch

Porth Tocyn Hotel
Tel: 01758-713303 **££**
Country house in farmland 2 miles south of town. Family-run for 40 years. Good for children.

Beaumaris

Ye Olde Bull's Head
Castle Street
Tel: 01248-810329. **££**
Anglesey restaurant above 15th-century pub near the castle.

Colwyn Bay

Café Nicoise
124 Abergele Road
Tel: 01492-531555 **££**
French-style café where the Welsh lamb is cooked to perfection and fine local fresh ingredients are used.

Dollgellau

Dylanwad Da
2 Ffos-y-Felin
Tel: 01341-422870 **£–££**
Simple restaurant offering mouth-watering food at reasonable prices. Uses local produce, such as fish and cheeses. Deserved reputation for its puddings.

Eglwysfach, nr Machynlleth

Ynyshir Hall
Tel: 01654-781209 **££**
Luxury country house hotel offers enterprising cuisine from talented chef Alan Simmonds, with fine local ingredients: Cardigan Bay seafood, wild salmon, venison, game and Welsh farmhouse cheeses.

Harlech

Castle Cottage
Y Llech
Tel: 01766-780479 **££**
Oak-beamed restaurant with rooms beneath the Castle's wing. Good value.

Llanwrst

Amser Da
Heol yr Orsaf
Tel: 01492-640215 **££**
Delicatessen and restaurant specialising in good-quality ingredients from local farms.

Llansanffraid Glan

The Old Rectory
Llanrwst Road
Tel: 01492-580611 **££**
Small hotel set in an 18th-century rectory with picturesque views across the Conwy Estuary. A married-couple team offer friendly service and a stylish set dinner.

Llanberis

Y Bistro
45 Stryd Fawr
Tel: 01286-871278 **££**
Cosy bistro dedicated to all things Welsh, especially local lamb.

Portmeirion

Portmeirion Hotel
Tel: 01766-772440 **££**
Stunning setting. Contemporary Welsh dishes with Mediterranean influence reflecting Italianate surroundings.

ABOVE: a variety of refreshments at Beddgelert.

Pwllheli

Plas Bodegroes
Nefyn Road
Tel: 01758-612363 **££**
This award-winning restaurant has a well-deserved reputation for serving good local food.

Pubs

In Llandudno, the 300-year-old **King's Head** in Old Road has an open fire in winter and a good restaurant. On Gloddaeth Street, **The Palladium** is a roomy Wetherspoons pub in a former theatre.

In Bangor, the **Harp Inn** on High Steet is an old pub, with good beers. Popular with students.

In Porthmadog, **Spooner's Bar** is situated in the terminus of the Ffestiniog Steam Railway and specialises in beers from small breweries.

In Harlech, **Y Branwen Hotel**, below the Castle, has a popular bar with cask ales and many malt whiskies.

In Llangollen, the **Corn Mill**, on Dee Lane off Castle Street, is a converted watermill with great atmosphere and decent food.

Outdoor Activities

Snowdonia's dramatic mountain peaks and deep valleys contain some of the highest and wildest land in Britain – ideal for the active visitor

By far the most popular outdoor pursuit is walking. OS maps reveal large concentrations of close-knit contour lines denoting steep ground. This is the domain of hillwalkers for whom there is an almost bewildering choice of routes. It's a good idea to pick up some of the leaflets available at information centres

Climbing **Snowdon** or **Cadair Idris** are popular goals but their often congested paths are not to everyone's taste. Each mountain range enjoys its own distinctive character. In the north the **Carneddau** offer vast grassy whaleback ridges, while the adjacent **Glyders** and **Tryfan** are strewn with frost-shattered boulders. Behind Tremadog Bay rise the **Rhinogs**, unfrequented mountains of ankle-twisting rock and deep heather.

Both the **Cadair Idris** and **Snowdon** massifs offer rugged walking, sustained gradients and wonderful views. By contrast, the featureless and often boggy **Migneint** between Bala and Ffestiniog is strictly for connoisseurs of solitude. The **Aran ridge** running north from Dinas Mawddwy to Bala Lake is regaining popularity after access problems. West and north of Blaenau Ffestiniog the **Moelwyns** are laced with the fascinating relics of slate mining.

For family groups and the less mobile there are miles of gentler footpaths and bridleways to explore. Good examples may be found in **Gwydir Forest** around Betws y Coed, in **Coed y Brenin Forest** near Dolgellau and around many of Snowdonia's more accessible **lakes**.

The dismantled **Welsh Highland Railway** at Beddgelert gives an entertaining ramble through several tunnels and there is estuary-edge walking on the **Mawddach Trail** west of Dolgellau. Sections of the **Anglesey** shoreline possess marvellous coastal paths, notably on the west and north sides of the island, and there are good stretches of path, too, around the tip of the **Lleyn Peninsula**.

Then there are the so-called **Precipice Walks**, principally around the Mawddach Estuary, the best known of which starts from from parking near Llyn Cynwch. Precipice Walks are not as hazardous as they might sound, being simply well-made footpaths which, however, traverse very steep hillsides.

Waymarked long-distance trails include the 108-mile (174-km) **Dyfi Valley Way**, the 60-mile (97-km) **North Wales Path** between Prestatyn and Bangor, and the circular 121-mile (194-km) **Anglesey Coast Path** (for information on walking trails, consult www.walking.visitwales.com).

Of various challenge walks, the most famous is the **Welsh 3000s** (www.welsh 3000s-co.uk), a gruelling 30-mile (48-km) tramp over all 15 of Snowdonia's 3,000-ft (914-metre)-plus summits within 24 hours. It is not for the faint-hearted.

Above: Off-road 4 x 4 driving events, mainly using Land-Rovers, are organised on private land near Lake Bala, the largest natural lake in Wales.

Left: A helicopter helps move heavy stones to keep pathways in the Snowdonia National Park accessible.

ABOVE: A hiker 3,060ft (933 metres) above sea level looks across the national park to Mount Snowdon.

ABOVE: The views in Snowdonia National Park are tremendous but the weather can be unpredictable and treacherous.

BELOW: The National White Water Centre, based near Bala, was founded in 1986 and is the UK's biggest rafting organisation.

THE CHOICE FOR CLIMBERS

Snowdonia's great buttresses and gullies have attracted rock climbers in ever greater numbers since before World War I when Colin Kirkus and John Menlove Edwards pioneered audacious new ascents. Later, in the 1950s, the likes of Joe Brown and Don Whillans immortalised such locations as the Llanberis Pass and Snowdon's Clogwyn Du'r Arddu.

More recently, interest has spread out from the inland crags to embrace the sea cliffs of Anglesey, the Lleyn Peninsula, Llandudno's Great Orme and the cliffs north of Tremadog.

While it is feasible for confident hillwalkers to tackle scrambling routes (requiring the use of hands as well as feet), climbing with ropes should be attempted only by experienced climbers. Courses in hillwalking, climbing, mountaineering and associated sports, including skiing and kayaking, are provided at Wales's National Mountain Centre at Plas y Brenin, Capel Curig, tel: 01690-720214; www.pyb.co.uk.

ABOVE: Climbers on Llanberis Pass. Some of the most notable breakthroughs in British climbing took place on precipices here.

RIGHT: Snowdonia has a broad appeal for birdwatchers. The variety extends from birds of prey such as kestrels and peregrine falcons to seabirds such as the red-throated diver, from buzzards and choughs to pied flycatchers and the lesser spotted woodpecker. There are eight bird reserves in the area.

Recommended Restaurants and Pubs on page 283

MERSEYSIDE AND SHROPSHIRE

Manchester and Liverpool, once industrial giants, now attract visitors with their lively cultural mix, their music and museums. There are sandy beaches to the north and Shropshire's historic towns to the south

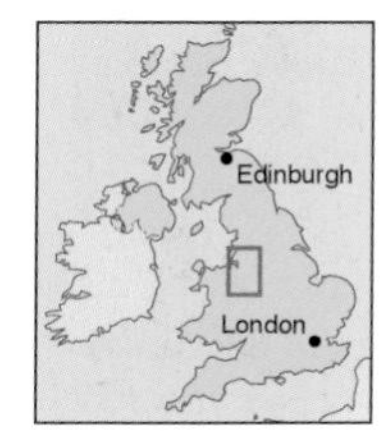

Manchester ❶ is the capital of northern England. A Victorian bastion, it was in the vanguard of the Industrial Revolution and it prospered when machinery and products from its cotton mills were transported down the 35-mile (48-km) Manchester Ship Canal to Liverpool for export. Today, it is still a relatively prosperous city, with a population of around 500,000. Many of the disused warehouses around the ship canal have been turned into smart apartment blocks.

Rolling green countryside is within easy reach of the centre. And not far away are the city's favourite holiday coasts of Lancashire and North Wales. London is 188 miles (303 km) to the south via the M6 and M1 motorways, and regular inter-city trains to London's Euston Station take about two hours 20 minutes (nationalrail.co.uk).

Music, science and art

A lively city, Manchester has three universities and a busy nightlife as well as the fine **Bridgewater Concert Hall** (bridgewater-hall.co.uk), a distinctive modern structure on the waterside that stages a wide range of performances and has a splendid auditorium that seats 2,400.

Chinatown, packed with restaurants, is well signposted by the ornate Imperial Chinese Archway, designed by a team of Beijing architects. The **Chinese Arts Centre** (Mon–Sat, 10am–5pm, Sun, 11am–4pm) features changing exhibitions by contemporary Chinese artists.

At Castleford, within walking distance of the city centre (and also accessible by both Metrolink trams and the No. 33 bus), the **Museum of Science and Industry** (daily 10am–5pm; msim.org.uk) has an impressive collection of technology from Victorian times to the Space Age, with lots to interest children. Covering a large area, it incorporates Liverpool Road, the world's first railway station.

Pre-Raphaelite art and 20th-century British works can be enjoyed in the **Manchester Art Gallery** (Tues–Sun, 10am–5pm; manchestergalleries.org), along

Main attractions
- MANCHESTER
  - WHITWORTH ART GALLERY
  - LOWRY CENTRE
- LIVERPOOL
  - TATE LIVERPOOL
  - WALKER ART GALLERY
- MORECAMBE BAY SANDS
- CHESTER CITY WALLS
- IRONBRIDGE GORGE MUSEUM

LEFT: Liverpool's Liver Building clock tower.
BELOW: *B of the Bang* sculpture, Manchester.

The Lowry Gallery displays around 350 of the artist's paintings and drawings. Because of a fondness for matchstick figures and unpopulated urban landscapes, he has been called a naive painter, although the gallery does not concur.

with an extensive collection of decorative art. On the University of Manchester campus the **Whitworth Art Gallery** (Mon–Sat, 10am–5pm, Sun 2–4pm; whitworth.manchester.ac.uk) has an outstanding collection of British watercolours and a sculpture gallery that includes major works by Hepworth, Epstein and Frink.

The **Royal Exchange Theatre** in St Ann's Square may come as a surprise to those who step through the doors of the 19th-century former Cotton Exchange to find that the theatre is enclosed in a huge glass capsule, suspended from marble pillars in the Great Hall.

The vast **Trafford Centre**, constructed after an IRA bomb devastated part of the city centre in 1996, includes a wide range of shops, high-street brands as well as designer names that run the gamut from Alexander McQueen to Vivienne Westwood, plus a 20-screen cinema (open Sun–Thur till 1am, Fri–Sat till 3am), and numerous bars and restaurants. Nearby, in Cathedral Gardens, the **Urbis Exhibition Centre** is a towering glass structure that features exhibitions on the life of the city.

In complete contrast, the city's 19th-century neo-Gothic **Town Hall** stands proudly on Albert Square. The Sculpture Hall, with a roof of Bath stone, is open to the public during working hours and tours of the building are run on Sunday and Wednesday (for bookings, contact the Tourist Information Centre in the Town Hall extension, tel: 0871-222 8223).

Manchester's **Cathedral**, set in attractive gardens, is an imposing presence whose largely 19th-century exterior conceals an interior with some interesting medieval details.

To the west of the city, on Salford Quays, the **Lowry Centre** (Sun–Fri, 11am–5pm, Sat, 10am–5pm; thelowry.com) has the world's largest collection of the work of local artist, L.S. Lowry (1887–1976). This striking multi-media arts centre also houses two theatres, bars

BELOW: Imperial War Museum North includes audiovisual displays showing the effects of war on civilians.

Map on page 276
Recommended Restaurants and Pubs on page 283

and a restaurant and won the Building of the Year Award in 2001.

The stunning, asymetrical new building opposite, designed by American architect Daniel Libeskind (his first in the UK), houses the **Imperial War Museum North** (daily, 10am–6pm, 10am–5pm winter). Tours of the building, some concentrating on the architecture, others on the museum displays, run on weekday afternoons.

Wigan

Heritage-mania at its worst can be found at **Wigan** ❷, between Manchester and Liverpool, which is trying to make up for the image George Orwell gave it in his 1937 book about working conditions in the north, *The Road to Wigan Pier*. Now the town trades on nostalgia, putting a romantic gloss on those hard times with a reconstructed shop, schoolroom, pub, cottage and even a coal mine.

Liverpool

Greater Manchester is encircled by motorways. The northbound M6 flies past it towards the Lake District and Scotland and crossing it, at junction 21A, is the M62 bound for **Liverpool** ❸. The shipping industry upon which Liverpool prospered has now all but deserted the Merseyside port, which suffered heavy unemployment through the 1970s and 1980s. But a great deal of rejuvenation has taken place and Liverpool became the European Capital of Culture in 2008.

Some tribute bands may not look too much like the Beatles, but they can still make money in Liverpool's tourist trade. The original Fab Four got started in 1960 and learned their trade through gruelling gigs at the city's Cavern Club.

Parts of the city, including much of the waterfront, were inscribed as a Unesco World Heritage Site in July 2004. The sturdy red-brick buildings of the **Albert Dock** warehousing area now house a complex of small shops, bars and restaurants as well as several museums.

Tate Liverpool (daily, 10am–5.50pm, Tues–Sun, 10am–5.50pm in winter; admission charge for special exhibitions, permanent collection free), has the largest collection of modern and contemporary art outside London and hosts some great temporary exhibitions.

The Beatles Story (daily, 9am–7pm, last admission 5pm; admission charge; tel: 0151-709 1963), is an "experience" of the city's illustrious sons which is naturally open "eight days a week" and

BELOW: Liverpool's "Three Graces" – the Royal Liver Building, the Cunard Building, and the Port of Liverpool Building.

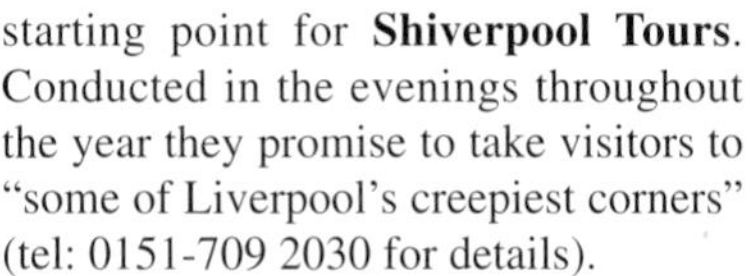

A ferry prepares to cross the Mersey from Liverpool to Birkenhead. During morning and late afternoon rush hours the direct trip takes just 10 minutes; throughout the rest of the day the service runs on the hour and takes 30 minutes (tel: 0151-330 1444).

features the Yellow Submarine and a stroll down Penny Lane. The museum, in the Britannia Pavilion, has recently doubled in size to accommodate its many visitors.

For more Beatles nostalgia you could visit the **Cavern Club** on Mathew Street for a daytime drink amid Beatles memorabilia, or to catch one of the live music performances that are staged most evenings and on weekend afternoons. This is actually the "new" Cavern Club, built on the site of the original, which closed in 1973.

Back at the dockside, the **Merseyside Maritime Museum** (daily, 10am–5pm) tells the story of this great port,including an extensive section on emigration. The building also incorporates the **International Slavery Museum**, which offers a poignant and thought-provoking view of the slave trade and its legacies. Nearby, the new **Museum of Liverpool**, replacing the Museum of Liverpool Life, is due to open at the end of 2010.

The dock's Anchor Courtyard is the starting point for **Shiverpool Tours**. Conducted in the evenings throughout the year they promise to take visitors to "some of Liverpool's creepiest corners" (tel: 0151-709 2030 for details).

From the **Pier Head** you can take the much sung-about **ferry across the Mersey** *(see margin)* to the Wirral peninsula, which protrudes between this estuary and that of the Dee to the south. If you want more time on the water, you can take a River Explorer Cruise, a 50-minute round trip with a commentary.

At the Seacombe ferry terminal on the other side of the Mersey, you could visit **Spaceport** (Tues–Sun, 10.30am–6pm, last admission at 4.30pm; admission charge) which takes you on a journey through space, complete with a space pod and planetarium.

Liverpool's architecture is on a grand scale. Down by the docks it includes the three buildings known as "The Three Graces": the imposing **Royal Liver Building**, with the mythical liver birds sitting atop the two clock towers; the Cunard Building and the Port of Liverpool Building. All three were built in the early 20th century, when the city and the port were at the height of their prosperity.

Liverpool also has two modern churches, of which the **Roman Catholic Metropolitan Cathedral**, designed by Sir Frederick W. Gibberd and consecrated in 1967, is the most striking: a circular structure topped with a spire that represents the Crown of Thorns. The crypt, begun in 1930, was the work of Sir Edwin Lutyens, and was the only part of his original design to be carried out before lack of cash halted work.

The **Anglican Cathedral**, Britain's largest, by Giles Gilbert Scott, was begun in 1904 and completed in 1978 after two world wars delayed its construction, but its neo-Gothic style gives it the appearance of a much older building.

The city is renowned for some excellent museums and galleries. The **World Museum Liverpool** in William Brown Street (daily, 10am–5pm) has something for everyone. The Bug House and the Aquarium are children's favourites,

BELOW: Liverpool's Walker Art Gallery.

Recommended Restaurants and Pubs on page 283

while the Discovery Centre displays the museum's archaeology and ethnology collections and the World Cultures section has a wealth of objects from Africa and the Americas.

The **Walker Art Gallery** (daily, 10am–5pm), also in William Brown Street, and sometimes known as "the National Gallery of the North" has an outstanding collection that ranges from the 14th century to the present, and includes works by Rembrandt and Rossetti, Monet and Hockney. There is also a new children's gallery, with lots for small kids to do.

There is a good Pre-Raphaelite collection, along with some Turners and Constables, at the **Lady Lever Art Gallery** (daily, 10am–5pm) built by William Hesketh Lever, later Lord Leverhulme (1851–1928), to house the collection he had assembled to "enrich the lives of his workforce". The gallery sits in formal gardens in the delightful model village of **Port Sunlight**, across the Mersey in Wirral. Leverhulme funded the village for employees of his soap empire. A philanthropist and an enlightened employer, Leverhulme nevertheless had a paternalistic attitude and believed that offering his workers good homes was preferable to increasing their wages. The village is a fascinating place, tranquil and seemingly detached from 21st-century life. It is a Conservation Area, and each of the 900 Grade II listed buildings is different from its neighbour. To reach Port Sunlight, take Queens Way across the Mersey if you are driving, and follow the signs, or use the Merseyrail Wirral Link to Port Sunlight or Bebington stations.

Lancashire's resorts

Some 7 miles (4km) north of Liverpool (via the A565, or 20 minutes by train from Liverpool Central station) lies Crosby, where the wide expanse of sands is peopled with 100 cast-iron naked figures, moulded from his own body by artist Antony Gormley (most famous for his Angel of the North statue, *see page 304*). Called Another Place, this haunting installation was originally a temporary one, but has now been given a permanent home here, after a certain amount of controversy.

Further north are Lancashire's traditional sandy resorts of **Southport**, **Lytham St Anne's** and **Blackpool** ❹,

Liverpool has three tourist information centres: one in the heart of the city at The 08 Place, Whitechapel; one in Anchor Courtyard at the Albert Dock; and one in the South Terminal's arrival hall at John Lennon Airport.

BELOW: Liverpool's Anglican Cathedral.

Blackpool carousel with the ferris wheel in the background.

Britain's most popular seaside resort which has not yet shed its working-class image. Up to 6 million people come here each year, their numbers swelled by trades union and political party conferences. The promenade, all 7 miles (11 km) of it, centred on a 518-ft (160-metre) Eiffel-style tower, is lit up in the autumn (end of August to end October) and these illuminations are a big event.

The famous **Blackpool Pleasure Beach** is among the resort's most popular attractions, offering a wide variety of rides that are absolutely thrilling or completely terrifying, depending on your point of view. Tickets must be booked in advance, up to 12 hours before your visit (blackpoolpleasurebeach.com). If you want to stay for more than a day, book into the adjacent 4-star Big Blue Hotel (tel: (0845) 367 3333).

Morecambe, a resort in the bay of the same name to the north, claims to have started the idea of autumn illuminations as a way of extending its summer season. Morecambe is now largely known for the walk across the sands of the bay, a trip of about 5 miles (3 km), which is fraught with the twin dangers of quicksands and unusually rapid rising tides, and involves wading through the fast-flowing River Kent. The walk must only be done with a guide and Cedric Robinson, a former fisherman who has been leading charity walks for more than 40 years, has earned the title of Queen's Sand Pilot (details, tel: 01539-532165).

The beaches all down this coast are wide and long, and sand yachting is popular at the resort of Lytham St Anne's.

BELOW: Blackpool Tower.

Chester

South of Liverpool, at the head of the Wirral peninsula and at the end of the 40-mile (64-km) M56 from Manchester, is **Chester** ❺, the most northerly and the most exciting of the timbered Tudor towns of the Welsh Marches, the hilly country bordering Wales.

Its particular architectural character can be seen by walking down Eastgate, Watergate or Bridge Street with their **Rows**, double tiers of shops and covered walkways, one on top of the other. The oldest dates from 1486, and most of them were built in the following century.

In Roman times Chester was an important stronghold called Deva and part of an **amphitheatre** can be seen just outside the city walls by St John's Street. This offers the best access to the 2-mile (3-km) round trip of the **city walls** – Chester is one of the few British cities with its medieval walls still intact.

The **Grosvenor Museum** (Mon–Sat, 10.30am–5pm, Sun, 1–4pm) records the Roman legacy with models of the fortress and tombstones from the period, and has a natural history gallery named after the Victorian writer and naturalist Charles Kingsley. Under the Normans, Chester was a near-independent state governed by a succession of earls. The tidal estuary of the Dee allowed the city to flourish as a port till the 15th century when it began to silt up, and shipping was transferred to the larger natural port of Liverpool.

The **Cathedral**, off St Werburg Street, was a Benedictine Abbey until Henry VIII's Dissolution of the Monasteries.

Recommended Restaurants and Pubs on page 283

Unusually squat, it has a short nave and a massive south transept featuring a grand, Victorian stained-glass window. At Upton, 2 miles (4 km) north of the city, is **Chester Zoo** (daily, 10am–5pm, until 4pm in winter; admission charge), the largest outside London, set in 80 acres (32 hectares) of gardens and home to more than 7,000 animals.

It is worth making a special expedition to **Little Moreton Hall** ❻ (summer Wed–Sun, 11.30–5pm, winter Sat–Sun, 11.30am–4pm, closed Jan–Feb; admission charge), due east of Chester via the A54 and A34. The ornately decorated, half-timbered, moated manor house was built in 1450–1580 and has a delightful Knot Garden. The house is now in the care of the National Trust, and there are free guided tours.

Stoke-on-Trent

Just a few miles further south lies **Stoke-on-Trent** ❼, the main town of The Potteries, the region that has supplied Britain with its finest china since the 17th century. Royal Doulton, Royal Grafton, Coalport, Minton, Spode… all the well-known porcelain and china factories are here and may be visited. A good starting point is the **Potteries Centre** by the station, where the products of two dozen local manufacturers are on display. Stoke was one of the towns featured in the Five Towns novels of Arnold Bennett (1867–1931), depicting life in the potteries during the industrial era. At Barlaston, just off the A34 to the south of Stoke, is the Wedgwood Visitor Centre (Mon–Fri, 9am–5pm, Sat–Sun, 10am–5pm), with a museum, a shop, demonstrations by potters and decorators and a factory tour (not Sat–Sun or Fri pm).

Telford

From Stoke, head south on the M6 and then west on the A518 to **Telford** ❽, a new town named after the 18th-century engineer Thomas Telford. Begun in the 1960s, the ambitious project takes in **Coalbrookdale**, where coke was first used to smelt iron, and **Ironbridge** on the River Severn, where the world's first iron bridge was built by Telford in 1773. The **Ironbridge Gorge Museum** (daily, 10am–5pm; some sites closed in winter;

Chester's Eastgate clock tower, built to commemorate Queen Victoria's Diamond Jubilee in 1897.

BELOW: Little Moreton Hall, one of Britain's finest timber-framed moated manor houses.

China kilns such as this one at Stoke-on-Trent were once common in the region, with products being transported on the canal system.

BELOW: the Iron Bridge, opened in 1781.

ironbridge.org.uk) has Abraham Darby's original coke furnace, and **Blists Hill Victorian Town** *(see box below)* recreates late 19th-century local life.

Shrewsbury ❾, home of the scientist Charles Darwin (1809–82) and World War I poet Wilfred Owen (1893–1918), is 12 miles (20 km) due west of Telford. The county town of Shropshire is beautifully situated on a meander in the River Severn, crossed by the English bridge and the Welsh bridge. It has houses dating from the 15th century, plus fine parks and gardens. The pink sandstone **castle**, near the station, was converted into a house by Telford and now incorporates the **Shropshire Regimental Museum** (daily, 10am–5pm, Tues–Sat, 10am–4pm in winter; admission charge).

Shrewsbury was also the home of the poet A.E. Housman (1859–1936) who eulogised the dreamy slopes of this agricultural land in *A Shropshire Lad*, his 1896 series of 63 nostalgic verses. All along the Welsh border, the softly rolling hills can be explored by paths, bridleways and woodland trails.

Perhaps the loveliest of the border towns is **Ludlow ❿**, where Housman's ashes lie. It has recently spearheaded an English gastronomic revival with a bounty of quality local produce. The centre is remarkably consistent architecturally, with 13th-century taverns and Tudor market buildings. It was at **Ludlow Castle**, the former seat of the presidents of the council of the Marchers, that John Milton's masque *Comus* was first performed in 1634.

Sixteen miles (25 km) west of Ludlow is **Knighton ⓫**, the centre for exploring Offa's Dyke *(see page 252)*. This 8th-century earthwork, built by King Offa to protect England from Welsh marauders, now carries a long-distance footpath. ❑

How Ironbridge Gorge drove forward the Industrial Revolution

Situated on the River Severn in the heart of Shropshire, the Ironbridge Gorge is named after the world's first ever cast-iron bridge, constructed over the river in 1779. It was designed by Thomas Farnolls Pritchard, a Shrewsbury joiner turned architect. The giant ribs for the structure were cast in open sand and raised with the aid of scaffolding. Intriguingly, the joints in the ironwork are based on traditional carpentry methods, including dovetails, wedges, mortises and tenons.

The Coalbrookdale area had been a centre of mining and ironworking since the time of Henry VIII, but by the end of the 17th century, the wood used to make charcoal to fuel the furnaces was becoming scarce. The pioneering use of a furnace to smelt iron with coke made from local coal turned the area into the busiest industrial centre anywhere in the world.

There are 10 museums around Ironbridge Gorge. The most popular is the Blists Hill Open Air Museum. Until the 1860s, Blists Hill was a thriving industrial site, but then decline set in, and by 1960 it was abandoned. Acquired by the Ironbridge Gorge Museum Trust, it was inaugurated as an open-air museum in 1973. The original furnaces, foundry, and brick and tile works are part of this working museum, but around them a "Victorian Town" has been created.

Designed to showcase 19th-century trades, most of the buildings have been dismantled from elsewhere and rebuilt. Staffed by costumed demonstrators, they include a tinsmith, a cobbler, a printer, a leather worker, a carpenter, a decorative plasterer and a candlemaker. The pub has a traditional sawdusted floor, and a bakery sells fine pies and pasties. At the end of the site, Squatters Cottages show the effects of the Industrial Revolution on the lives of working people.

RESTAURANTS AND PUBS

Restaurants

Prices for a three-course dinner per person with a half-bottle of house wine:

£ = under £25
££ = £25–50
£££ = £50–100

Blackpool

Oliver's Restaurant
Lancaster House Hotel
272 Central Drive
Tel: 01253-341 928 **££**
No, not Jamie Oliver, but a chef who knows what to do with good fresh ingredients. Morecambe Bay shrimps. Closed Mon, Sun lunch only.

Chester

Arkle Restaurant
Chester Grosvenor Hotel, Eastgate Street
Tel: 01244-324 024 **££**
This is a thoroughbred Michelin-starred restaurant in a grand hotel in central Chester. Traditional British food excellently presented and the bread board is one of the best around. Extensive but expensive wine list.

Liverpool

60 Hope Street
60 Hope Street
Tel: 0151-707 6060 **££**
Regional ingredients, tasteful preparation and smooth service in an airy venue. Typical dishes: roast crown of wood pigeon with herb risotto or sea bass with clam chowder. Closed Sun.

The Monro
92 Duke Street
Tel: 0151-707 9933 **££**
This gastropub has won plaudits for its locally sourced food, which may include Goosenargh duck breasts or leek and asparagus crêpes. Lunch only on Sun.

The London Carriage Works
Hope Street Hotel
40 Hope Street
Tel: 0151-705 2222 **££**
The restaurant of this boutique hotel offers some unusual rice and pasta dishes, plus "plates to share" – charcuterie, seafood or vegetarian based.

Yuet Ben Restaurant
1 Upper Duke Street
Tel: 0151-709 5772 **£**
A Liverpool institution since 1968, it serves well-cooked authentic Northern Chinese food at very reasonable prices.

Ludlow

La Bécasse
17 Corve Street, Ludlow
Tel: 01584-872 325 **£££**
Alan Murchison's restaurant merits its Michelin-star. Top-quality ingredients served in imaginative ways in a rustic-style dining room.

The Clive Bar and Restaurant
Bromfield
Tel: 01584-856 565 **££**
Wenlock Edge ham, Gressingham duck and local cheeses are just some of the treats in this Michelin-recommended restaurant that combines elegance with informality.

Manchester

Chaophraya Thai Restaurant
15–17 Chapel Walks
Tel: 0161-832 8342 **£–££**
A big, sometimes noisy restaurant that many believe serving very good Thai food. Reasonable prices, friendly service.

ABOVE: eating out at Liverpool's Albert Dock.

Choice
Castle Quay, Castlefor
Tel: 0161-833 3400 **££**
Puts an emphasis on local products such as black pudding and Cheshire ham, and a selection of Lakeland breads, in a pleasant canal-side setting.

Simply Heathcotes
Jacksons Row, Deansgate
Tel: 0161-835 3536 **££**
Appetising mix of modern British and European dishes, with locally sourced meat, in a contemporary setting. They are proud of their Phillippe Starck chairs. No lunch on Sat.

Pubs

Greater Manchester has a huge range of pubs. Those receiving honourable mentions from the Campaign for Real Ale include **Britons Protection** in Great Bridgewater Street, the waterside **Dukes 92** in Castle Street, and the Victorian **Marble Arch** in Rochdale Road, Ancoats.

In Liverpool, the **Philharmonic** on Hope Street is one of the most ornate Victorian pubs in the country. The **Baltic Fleet** in Wapping near the Albert Dock is a listed building with a nautical theme and the Wapping Brewery in the cellar. Other interesting Victorian pubs include **Peter Kavanagh's** in Egerton Street, the **Belvedere Arms** in Sugnall Street, and the **White Star** in Rainford Gardens.

In Chester, **The Albion** on Albion Street has a restful Victorian ambiance and World War I memorabilia. The **Bear & Billet** is located in a 1664 building in Lower Bridge Steet and has lots of original woodwork.

Recommended Restaurants and Pubs on page 291

THE PEAK DISTRICT AND EAST MIDLANDS

The Peak District's landscape may sometimes be dramatic with steep crags and heather-covered moorland, or characterised by green dales, with stone walls creating a chequerboard of fields. It is also dotted with some splendid stately homes

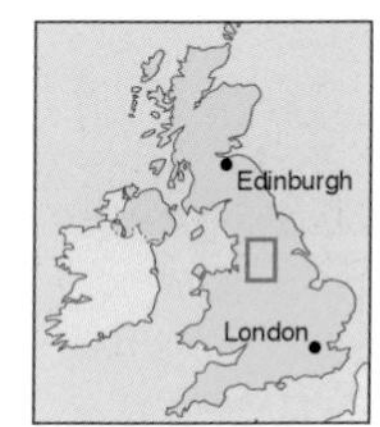

In a region littered with the relics of ancient wars, no sign remains of some comparatively recent hand-to-hand combat. Unless, that is, you count the sign that reads: "Public access to this private land has been granted by agreement with the owners."

This access was bought through direct action when, in 1932, a group of hikers, workers from the industrial cities of Manchester and Sheffield staged a mass trespass on Kinder Scout *(see page 287)*, the district's highest peak, in pursuit of their demands to be able to walk over the land for weekend recreation. They were met by owners' gamekeepers armed with clubs and guns, arrested, and five of them imprisoned. Their action received popular support and led, eventually, to the creation in 1951 of the **Peak District National Park**, the first in England.

The Peak District is like a massive English rockery garden, 30 miles long and 20 miles at its widest point (48 km by 32 km). To the west the M6 motorway heads up to Manchester; to the east the M1 runs north towards Leeds. The park begins in Derbyshire, extends northwards into Yorkshire, and offers open-air adventures to the inhabitants of half a dozen adjacent cities. Some of the summits in the area rise to 2,000 ft (610 metres), attracting hang-gliders and providing rock-climbing opportunities for novices and experts alike. Pot-holers, too, are drawn here. Sir Arthur Conan Doyle (1859–1930), creator of Sherlock Holmes, wrote: "All this country is hollow. Could you strike it with some gigantic hammer, it would boom like a drum or possibly cave in altogether."

Derby

Motorists approaching the Peak District from the south could leave the M1 motorway at junction 24 and pass through **Derby** ❶, 116 miles (187 km) northwest of London (trains to the East Midlands leave London from St Pancras). This ancient county town on the River Derwent has Britain's first real factory, a silk mill built in 1718. In the 19th

Main attractions
- PEAK DISTRICT NATIONAL PARK
- DERBY
- BUXTON
- CASTLETON CAVES
- HATHERSAGE
- CHATSWORTH HOUSE
- BAKEWELL
- SHEFFIELD
- NOTTINGHAM
- LINCOLN CATHEDRAL
- BURGHLEY HOUSE

LEFT: Chatsworth.
BELOW: hiker in the Peak District.

Fishing on the River Dove, famed for its trout.

Visiting Dovedale, Dr Samuel Johnson compared it favourably with Scotland: "He who has seen Dovedale has no need to visit the Highlands."

century railway engineering became the main employer. Rolls-Royce have had a plant here since 1908.

Highlights in the city centre include the cathedral, notable for its fine wrought-iron screen, and the **Derby Museum and Art Gallery** (Mon, 11am–5pm, Tue–Sat, 10am–5pm, Sun, 1–4pm), home to a collection of works by 18th-century local artist Joseph Wright as well as a fine collection of Derby porcelain and, strangely, two Egyptian mummies.

From Derby the A52 approaches the National Park through **Ashbourne** ❷, 12 miles (20 km) west. Its main thoroughfare, Church Street, contains a 16th-century school, 17th-century almshouse and 21st-century traffic jams. George Eliot (1819–80) described St Oswald's church as "the finest mere parish church in the kingdom". The Ashbourne Gingerbread Shop, in a half-timbered 15th-century building, is also worth a stop. Each Shrove Tuesday, Ashbourne hosts a football match in which up to 300 players a side try to score goals by touching the walls of Sturston Mill and Clifton Mill, 3 miles (5 km) apart.

Families visiting **Alton Towers** ❸, a huge theme park with some hair-raising rides (Easter–end Oct daily, 10am–5pm, till 7pm in school summer holidays; admission charge), find Ashbourne a handy place to stay, although there are two hotels within the theme park itself.

Buxton

From Ashbourne, take the A515 north into the National Park, taking the left turn down the quiet lane that twists through **Dovedale**. Sheep populate these dales, and sheepdog trials are popular summer distractions. A few miles further along the A515 – or, for the adventurous, after a delightful mystery tour through unclassified country lanes – is the attractive spa town of **Buxton** ❹, a familiar name nowadays thanks to the bottled

BELOW: rock climbing on Stanage Edge.

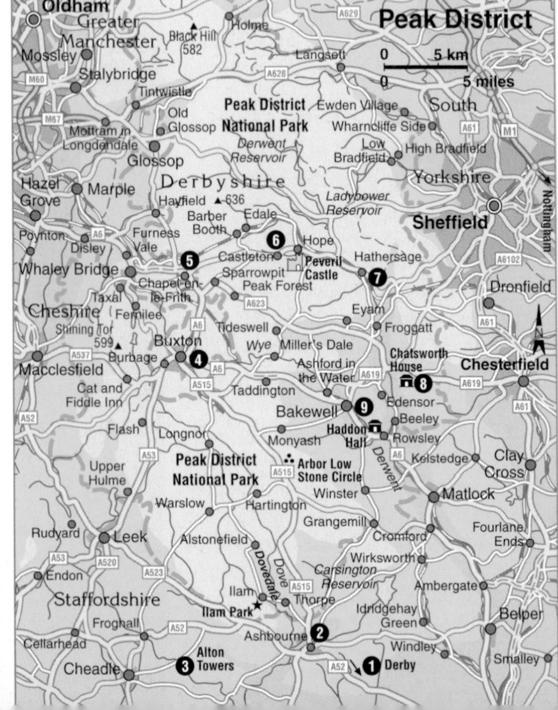

Recommended Restaurants and Pubs on page 291

product of its nine springs. Between 1570 and 1583, Mary, Queen of Scots sought treatment in Buxton for her rheumatism, a complaint doubtless aggravated by her imprisonment in a succession of draughty establishments. At the end of the 18th century, the fifth Duke of Devonshire planned and built a grand crescent here, intending the town to outshine Bath. Although this aim was never achieved, the town has its fair share of visitors who come to swim in the indoor spa-water pool at the Pavilion Gardens. The gardens themselves are a pleasant spot to spend some time, with a conservatory, a bandstand, a number of cafés and children's play areas.

Opera-lovers flock here, too, in late July, when the acclaimed **Buxton International Festival of Music and the Arts** is held at the **Opera House**, adjacent to the Pavilion Gardens. The Opera House hosts the Four-Four Time Festival in February, showcasing rock, pop, folk, blues, jazz and world music, and stages plays and musical performances all year.

Other attractions nearby include the ravine of the **Wye**, which provides a beautiful limestone route for walkers.

Chapel-en-le-Frith ❺, on the A625, is a small market town. "Frith" means "forest," but little of that is left today. Located nearby, north of the A625, is **Edale**, a tidy little village huddled at the foot of the peat-covered **Kinder Scout** peak, the challenging start of the Pennine Way hiking route, which ends in the Scottish borders.

Further along the A625, **Castleton ❻** is a centre for subterranean exploration. At the foot of **Winnats Pass**, **Speedwell Cavern** (daily, 10am–5pm; tours at regular intervals; admission charge; speedwellcavern.co.uk) is so high that rockets have gone up 450 ft (138 metres) without hitting the roof. The **Treak Cliff Cavern** has the most spectacular formations and is one of the few sources of the semi-precious Blue John stone. The mineral was much in demand in the 18th century, which meant the most substantial veins were worked out, but it is still a working mine. The blackened ceiling in the entrance to the **Peak Cavern** dates from the time when it was occupied by a community of rope-makers.

High above the village, **Peveril Castle** (summer daily, 10am–6pm, winter Thur–

The Peak District is misleadingly named. Visitors seek in vain for sharply-pointed mountain tops. In fact, the name comes from the Old English peac, *which simply meant a hill. In the 10th-century* Anglo Saxon Chronicle, *the area was known as Peaclond – the hilly land.*

BELOW: Buxton is known for its Georgian architecture, particularly the Crescent, built around 1780.

The area around Buxton is rich farming land.

Sun, 10am–4pm; charge) was the setting for Sir Walter Scott's 1823 novel *Peveril of the Peak*. The castle was built by William Peveril soon after the Norman Conquest, and it is said King Malcolm of Scotland paid homage to Henry II here in 1157.

Hathersage ❼, on the same road, is the hillside village that inspired "Morton" in Charlotte Brontë's *Jane Eyre* (1847). She also gave her heroine the surname of the local lord of the manor, Robert Eyre.

To the north of Hathersage is **Stanage Edge**, the longest and most impressive of the Peak's gritstone edges and a playground for both rock climbers and hang-gliders. The highest point is at High Neb, near the north end.

A diversion south along the B6001 leads to **Eyam** (pronounced *Eem*), a pretty village remarkable for the action of its villagers in 1665. Finding that plague germs had arrived in a box of cloth sent from London to the local tailor, they sealed off the village to confine the disease; within a year, three-quarters of the 350 inhabitants were dead. The story is told in the **Eyam Museum** (Hawkshill Road, Mar–Nov Tues–Sun 10am–4.30pm, tel: 01433-631371; charge).

Palladian palace

Near Baslow, off the A619, is **Chatsworth House** ❽ (mid-Mar–mid-Dec daily, house 11am–5.30pm, park 11am–6pm; admission charge; park open all year; free). Known as "the Palace of the Peak", this is a vast Palladian mansion built between 1687 and 1707 and set in a spacious deer park with gardens landscaped by "Capability" Brown. The seat of the Duke and Duchess of Devonshire, it houses priceless collections of books and furniture, as well as fine paintings by Rembrandt and Reynolds. Chatsworth boosts business by staging an angling fair, a brass band festival, show-jumping, horse trials and pop concerts, and has been used as a location for the 2005 film of *Pride and Prejudice* and *The Duchess* (2008), based on the life of Georgiana, Duchess of Devonshire.

Heading back south, the A6 passes through **Bakewell** ❾, a stone-built town with two medieval bridges over the Wye and famed for its "puddings" (a kind of jam and almond pastry). The town's

BELOW: Chatsworth House caters for children with milking demonstrations and daily animal handling sessions.

Recommended Restaurants and Pubs on page 291

name, however, has nothing to do with baking. An entry in the *Domesday Book* (1086) calls the town Badequella, which means Bath-well. Two of the town's iron-rich wells survive and a colourful well-dressing ceremony is held in June. Two miles (4 km) southeast, **Haddon Hall** (May–Sept daily, noon–5pm, Apr and Oct Sat–Mon; admission charge) is one of Britain's best-preserved, most atmospheric old houses, dating in parts from the 12th century.

Cutlery and crockery

Although located in Yorkshire, and that county's largest city, **Sheffield** ❿ lies just to the east of the Peak District and is ideally accessed from other major towns and areas in the region covered by this chapter – hence we have included it here *(see pages 293–307 for more on Yorkshire and the Northeast)*. Sheffield prospered at the foot of the Pennines, using the cascading water to drive grindstones manufactured from their millstone grit. However, its pre-eminent position as a steel town has been lost: Sheffield steel may still be best, but Korean cutlery costs less. The **Magna Science Adventure Centre** (daily, 10am–5pm, winter Tues–Sun; admission charge) in **Rotherham**, set within a former steel works, tells the story of the steel industry and the people whose lives depended on it, and has an adventure and water park attached (summer only) to keep children happy.

Sheffield's shopping centre is emphatically modern, neat suburbs cling to steep gradients, and the **Crucible Theatre** has a national reputation. The **Weston Park Museum** (Mon–Sat, 10am–5pm, Sun, 11am–5pm), housed in a neo-classical building, houses the former Sheffield City Museum and Mappin Art Gallery. It showcases the city's collections of archaeology, natural history, art and social history, and has won *The Guardian* newspaper's Family Friendly Museum award.

The **Millennium Galleries** (Mon–Sat, 10am–5pm) at Arundel Gate comprise four galleries in one, displaying art, craft and contemporary design, and include the **Ruskin Gallery**. Entry to all the city museums is free.

Battle re-enactments are a feature of August's Sheffield Fayre. It also includes flower shows, crafts tents and children's rides. For details, check sheffield.gov.uk

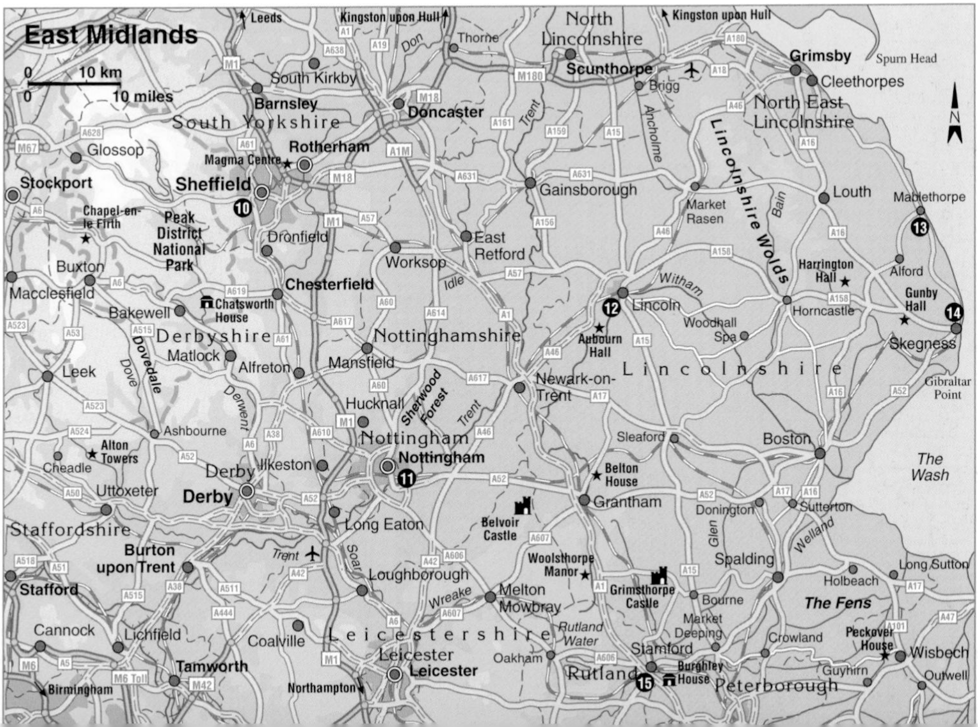

East Midlands

The mythical outlaw Robin Hood, here commemorated at Nottingham Castle, keeps the city on the tourist map.

BELOW: Lincoln Cathedral, which the writer John Ruskin (1819–1900) called "the most precious piece of architecture in the British Isles".

Out to the west on Abbeydale Road South is the **Abbeydale Industrial Hamlet** (Easter–Sept Mon–Thur, 10am–5pm, Sun, 11am–4.45pm; admission charge), a living museum of Sheffield's industrial past, where craftsmen demonstrate their traditional skills.

Nottingham

To the southeast is **Nottingham** ⓫, the cultural and nightlife hub of the East Midlands, an attractive city centred around a broad market square, with two large shopping centres, the original Paul Smith shop (he's from Nottingham), a major arts complex and myriad restaurants. Nottingham used to be known for lace making, and there is still an area called the Lace Market.

Nottingham Castle, actually a 17th-century mansion on the site of the original castle, is set in impressive grounds and houses the **Castle Museum and Art Gallery** (daily, 10am–5pm, till 4pm in winter) with collections of silver, glass, armour and paintings, and lots for children to enjoy. There are also tours of the castle caves (Mon–Sat, 11am, 2pm, 3pm; admission charge), but be warned that they are quite strenuous.

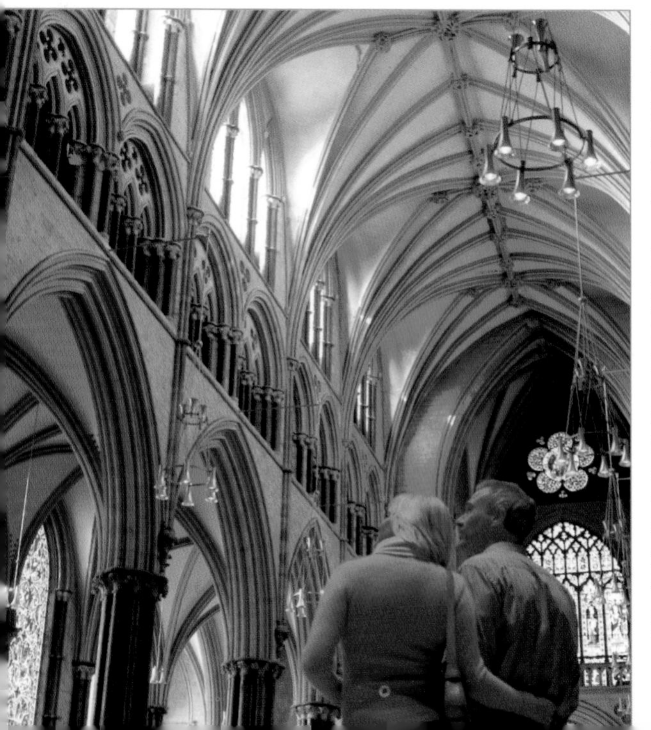

On Maid Marion Way **The Tales of Robin Hood** (daily, 10am–4.30pm; robinhood.ltd.uk) whisks you back to the Middle Ages to see, smell and browse through the outlaw's era.

Nottingham's most famous literary son is the writer D.H. Lawrence (1885–1930). There are informative tours of his **Birthplace Museum** (daily, 10am–5pm, until 4pm in winter), a modest house in the nearby village of Eastwood.

Lincolnshire

East of Nottingham, Lincolnshire has several important sights worth seeking out. **Lincoln** ⓬ is a Roman city, with some well-preserved medieval buildings which attest to the wealth derived from a flourishing wool trade. You can get a good look at the city by taking a canal trip on the *Brayford Belle* (daily, summer only; tel: (01522) 881 200). The impressive **Cathedral** is a mixture of Norman and Perpendicular styles. One of only four surviving copies of the Magna Carta of 1215 is kept in the Cathedral archives.

If you head east from Lincoln, you will reach the North Sea coast, where there are several resort towns, including **Mablethorpe** ⓭, where land yachting is popular on the long sandy beaches; and **Skegness** ⓮, a family resort for many decades, and famous as the site of the first Butlin's Holiday Camp.

If you are heading south, you can take either the A1, A15 or A16 to reach **Stamford** ⓯, 47 miles (76 km) south of Lincoln, a delightful little town on the River Welland, with stone-built houses and a 13th-century church. There you will find one of Britain's finest Elizabethan stately homes, **Burghley House** (Easter–Oct Sat–Thur, 11am–5pm; admission charge), built in 1560–87 by William Cecil, first Lord Burghley. The Gardens of Surprise incorporate mazes, fountains, and a Contemporary Sculpture Garden, and the 300-acre (120-hectare) deer park was landscaped in 1756 by "Capability" Brown *(see page 219)*. ❑

RESTAURANTS AND PUBS

Restaurants

Ashbourne

Dog and Partridge Country Inn
Swinscoe, Ashbourne
Tel: 01335-343 183 **££**
An attractive little country inn with a restaurant serving well-cooked food – trout is a speciality.

Ashford in the Water

Riverside Country House Hotel
Fennel Street, nr Bakewell
Tel: 0845-012 1760 **££**
In a beautiful position overlooking the River Wye, the conservatory restaurant of this Georgian house offers high-class English cuisine, especially game and fish.

Baslow

Fischer's at Baslow Hall
Calver Road
Tel: 01246-583 259 **£££**
Outstanding Michelin-starred restaurant serving traditional British food. Local produce might include Derbyshire spring lamb and Chatsworth venison.

Buxton

Columbine
7 Hall Bank
Tel: 01298-78752 **££**
Small friendly family-run restaurant. The fish soup is excellent and there's always an English cheeseboard.

Prices for a three-course meal per person with a half-bottle of house wine:
£ = under £25
££ = £25–50
£££ = £50–100

Dovedale, near Ashbourne

Izaak Walton Hotel
Tel: 01335-350 555 **££**
The Haddon Restaurant in this 17th-century farmhouse, set against the backdrop of the Derbyshire Peaks and overlooking Dovedale, specialises in Anglo-French dishes.

Hambleton

Hambleton Hall
Near Oakham
Tel: 01572-756 991 **£££**
Elegant dining room serving modern British cuisine in a fine country house hotel. Try the poached and roast pigeon.

Hassop

Hassop Hall Hotel
Near Bakewell
Tel: 01629-640 488 **££**
One of the finest hotel-restaurants in the Peaks, set in the Peak District National Park. Booking essential.

Hathersage

The George Hotel
Main Road
Tel: 01433-650 436 **££**
The menu includes unusual dishes such as pan-roasted loin of venison and there's a wide selection of cheeses. The George has received AA Rosettes for more than a decade.

Chequers Inn
Froggatt Edge
Tel: 01433-630 231 **££**
Locally sourced meat and produce served in a wood-floored dining room that is rustic without being fussy.

ABOVE: the Bakewell tart, more properly known as the Bakewell pudding, is widely available in the area. The jam pastry was created accidentally in 1820 when, so it's said, a cook, instead of stirring the eggs and almond paste mixture into the pastry, spread it on top of the jam. When it is topped with icing and a cherry, it is called a Bakewell cake.

Leicester

Café Bruxelles
90–92 High Street
Tel: 0116-224 3013 **£**
A trendy bar popular with most age groups. Food every day except Sunday and a range of more than 30 Belgian beers.

Nottingham

Hart's
Standard Hill, Park Row
Tel: 0115-988 1900 **££**
Innovative dishes in this popular venue include breast of duck with carrot and passion fruit purée, and there's an interesting and well-priced wine list.

Ridgeway, nr Sheffield

Old Vicarage
Tel: 0114-247 5814 **£££**
Large Victorian country house in beautiful gardens. Fixed-price menu of outstanding pedigree. Sage-roasted sadddle of Ridgeway hare is one of the specialities. The only Michelin-starred restaurant in the Sheffield area.

Sheffield

Greenhead House
84 Burncross Road, Sheffield, Chapeltown
Tel: 0114-246 9004 **££**
Offers welcoming friendly service and excellent food. Vegetables and herbs come from their own garden.

Pubs

The Peak District has many unspoilt pubs that welcome walkers: for example, **The Barrel** at Foolow, the **Millstone Inn** at Hathersage, the **Cheshire Cheese** at Hope, the **Lathkil Hotel** at Over Haddon, and **The Quiet Woman** at Earl Sterndale.

Six miles (10km) south of Buxton on the A515, near Flagg, **The Bull i' th' Thorn**, an ancient coaching inn, has Tudor panelling and stone floors.

In Bakewell, the **Castle Inn** on Bridge Street is a Georgian-fronted 17th-century pub with some atmospheric rooms.

In Nottingham, **The Olde Trip to Jerusalem**, in Brewhouse Yard below the castle, is built into the castle rock and is said to date from 1189.

In Lincoln, **The Tap & Spile** in Hungate has old posters and pictures of blues musicians. **The Victoria** in Union Road appeals to real ale fans.

Recommended Restaurants and Pubs on pages 306–7

YORKSHIRE AND THE NORTHEAST

The lands of the northeast are wild, wide-open spaces, littered with evidence of a turbulent past, but they shelter picture-book villages, bustling towns and the historic city of York

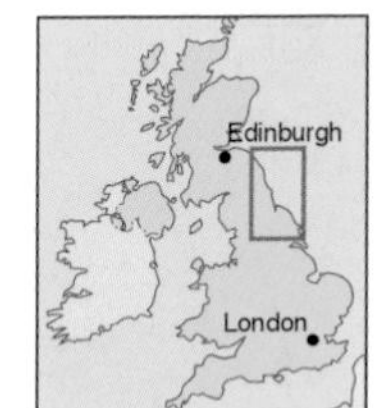

Long before Sunday-afternoon strollers trod Pennine millstone grit and mountain limestone, this corner of England was pounded by the feet of armies. The region's history is as turbulent as the sudden storms that rage on the high moors; no other part of England has more fortifications.

In AD 122, the Roman emperor Hadrian built a fortified wall for 73 miles (117 km) across the country from sea to sea to keep back "barbarian" Scots. The Wars of the Roses (1455–85) saw the Houses of Lancaster (red rose) and York (white rose) locked in a struggle to win control of the throne. The Civil War from 1641 to 1653 divided local allegiances between king and parliament.

Living traditions

Although most of the north's industries have been in upheaval, traditional life lives on. At **Huddersfield**, to the north of the Peak District and 15 miles (24 km) southwest of Leeds, the famous choral society has performed Handel's *Messiah* in the Town Hall just before Christmas every year since 1836. On the A642, half-way between Huddersfield and Wakefield, the **National Coal Mining Museum** (daily, 10am–5pm) shows the history of local coal mining during an underground tour of a former mine.

Halifax ❶, 10 miles (16 km) northwest of Huddersfield, earned its wealth from textiles. A main attraction is the award-winning **Eureka! The Children's Museum** (daily, 10am–5pm, charge), has more than 400 interactive exhibits designed for children up to the age of 11.

In nearby **Bradford** ❷, the 19th-century textile barons built solid dependability and vigour into every brick of the city's Italianate Town Hall and its Gothic Wool Exchange. One of the richest, Sir Titus Salt, enshrined his ideals in the nearby model village of **Saltaire**. In 2001 the preserved village was designated a Unesco World Heritage Site. The

Main attractions
SALTAIR MILL
NATIONAL MEDIA MUSEUM
ROYAL ARMOURIES MUSEUM
HAWORTH
YORKSHIRE DALES
HAREWOOD HOUSE
HARROGATE SPA TOWN
FOUNTAINS ABBEY
YORK MINSTER
JORVIK VIKING MUSEUM
CASTLE HOWARD
BOWES MUSEUM
DURHAM CATHEDRAL
NEWCASTLE-UPON-TYNE
HADRIAN'S WALL
BAMBURGH CASTLE
LINDISFARNE

LEFT: Castle Howard, an 18th-century gem.
RIGHT: traditional Morris dancers step out in Ripon, north Yorkshire.

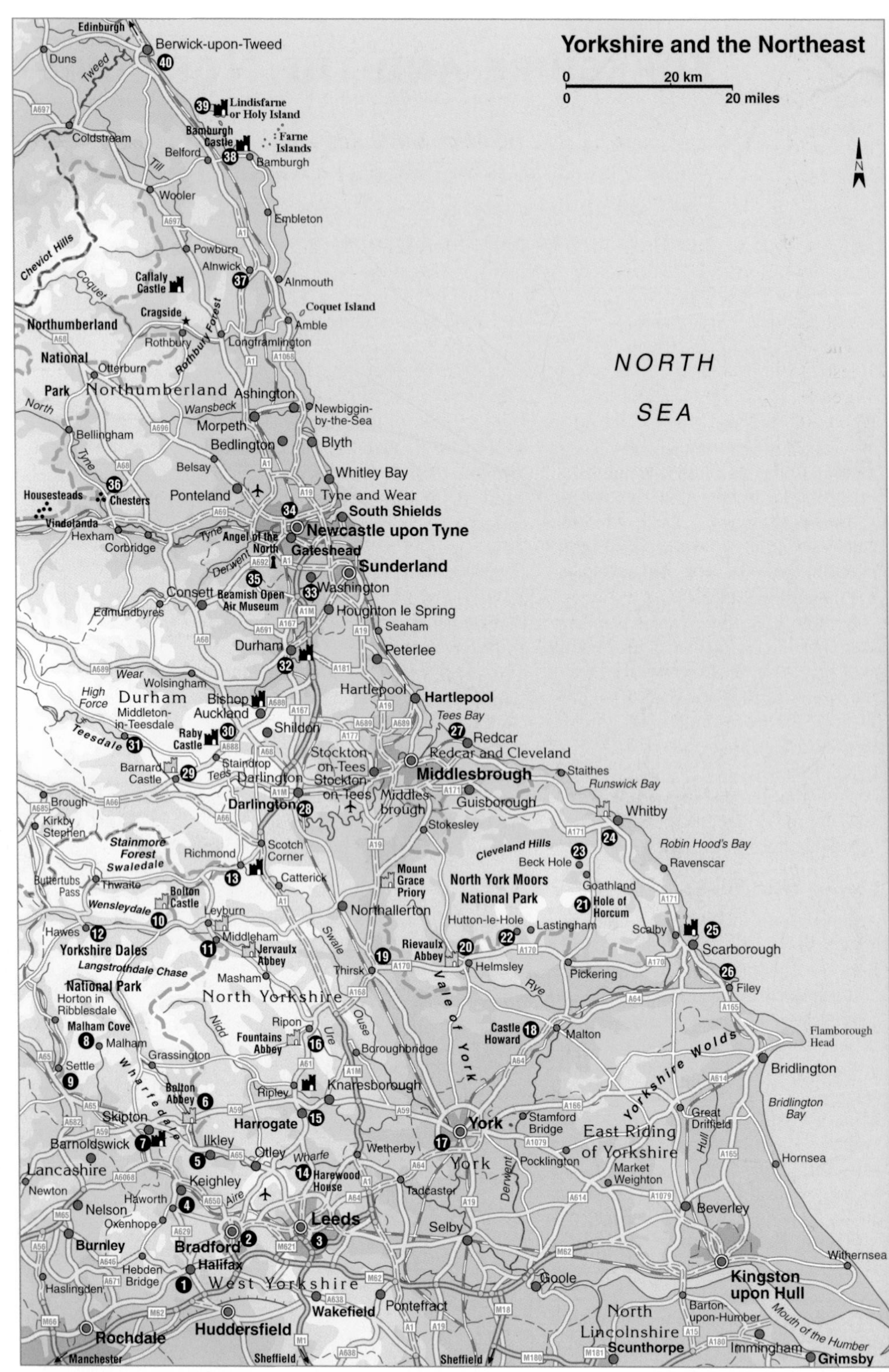
Yorkshire and the Northeast
0 20 km
0 20 miles
NORTH SEA
Edinburgh
Berwick-upon-Tweed
Duns
Tweed
Lindisfarne or Holy Island
Coldstream
Bamburgh Castle
Farne Islands
Belford
Bamburgh
Till
Wooler
Embleton
Cheviot Hills
Powburn
Alnwick
Alnmouth
Callaly Castle
Coquet
Coquet Island
Cragside
Amble
Northumberland National Park
Rothbury
Rothbury Forest
Longframlington
Otterburn
Northumberland
Ashington
North
Wansbeck
Newbiggin-by-the-Sea
Morpeth
Bellingham
Bedlington
Blyth
Tyne
Belsay
Whitley Bay
Housesteads
Chesters
Ponteland
Tyne and Wear
Vindolanda
South Shields
Hexham
Newcastle upon Tyne
Corbridge
Angel of the North
Gateshead
Derwent
Sunderland
Consett
Beamish Open Air Museum
Washington
Edmundbyres
Houghton le Spring
Seaham
Durham
Peterlee
Wear
Wolsingham
High Force
Durham
Hartlepool
Bishop Auckland
Middleton-in-Teesdale
Tees Bay
Shildon
Teesdale
Raby Castle
Redcar
Redcar and Cleveland
Stockton-on-Tees
Staindrop
Barnard Castle
Tees
Darlington
Middlesbrough
Staithes
Runswick Bay
Brough
Guisborough
Whitby
Kirkby Stephen
Stokesley
Stainmore Forest
Robin Hood's Bay
Swaledale
Richmond
Scotch Corner
Cleveland Hills
Beck Hole
Ravenscar
Buttertubs Pass
Thwaite
Catterick
Mount Grace Priory
North York Moors National Park
Goathland
Bolton Castle
Wensleydale
Leyburn
Northallerton
Hole of Horcum
Hutton-le-Hole
Lastingham
Hawes
Scalby
Middleham
Swale
Scarborough
Yorkshire Dales
Jervaulx Abbey
Rievaulx Abbey
Helmsley
Langstrothdale Chase
Thirsk
Pickering
Filey
National Park
Masham
Rye
Vale of York
Horton in Ribblesdale
North Yorkshire
Ripon
Castle Howard
Malton
Flamborough Head
Malham Cove
Malham
Nidd
Fountains Abbey
Ure
Ouse
Boroughbridge
Grassington
Settle
Wharfedale
Bridlington
Yorkshire Wolds
Knaresborough
Bolton Abbey
Ripley
Bridlington Bay
Skipton
Harrogate
Stamford Bridge
Great Driffield
York
East Riding of Yorkshire
Barnoldswick
Ilkley
Wetherby
Pocklington
Hornsea
Otley
Wharfe
Lancashire
Harewood House
Market Weighton
Newton
Keighley
Tadcaster
Haworth
Aire
Nelson
Beverley
Oxenhope
Leeds
Selby
Burnley
Bradford
Halifax
Withernsea
Hebden Bridge
Goole
Kingston upon Hull
Haslingden
West Yorkshire
Wakefield
Pontefract
North Lincolnshire
Barton-upon-Humber
Rochdale
Huddersfield
Mouth of the Humber
Scunthorpe
Immingham
Grimsby
Manchester
Sheffield
Sheffield

giant **Salt Mill** (daily 9.30am–5pm, 6pm at weekends), where all the residents worked, provides wonderful gallery space and has a one of the largest collections of art works by David Hockney, who was born in Bradford in 1937.

The wool trade attracted many immigrants to Bradford and they give the city an exotic flavour, especially during the Mela festivals in Peel Park. Asians make up 20 percent of Bradford's old city and the Muslim influence is strong.

The novelist and playwright J.B. Priestley, born here in 1894, immortalised the town as "Bruddesford" in *The Good Companions*. Festivals feature the music of Frederick Delius (1862–1934), also a native. Contemporary playwright Alan Bennett is another famous son.

The **National Media Museum** (Tues–Sun 10am–6pm; nationalmediamuseum.org.uk) is in the town centre. Its three cinemas include an IMAX screen, five storeys high by 96 ft (30 metres) wide, and BBC Bradford, which broadcasts live TV and radio from here. There are changing exhibitions in the two galleries. and the museum has the world's first negative, the earliest television footage, and what is regarded as the world's first moving pictures – Louis Le Prince's 1888 film of Leeds Bridge.

Northern attractions

Yorkshire's main city, **Leeds ❸**, is a lively university city and England's largest financial service centre outside the capital, has developed into a world centre for ready-made clothing. Its big tourist attraction is the architecturally striking **Royal Armouries Museum** at Clarence Dock (daily, 10am–5pm), displaying 3,000 years of arms, from musket balls and jousting equipment to an elephant's suit of armour and even parts of Saddam Hussein's supergun.

Presented with the matchless raw material of the Brontës, Yorkshire's tragic literary family, the engine of tourism has shifted into overdrive. Every year one million visitors tramp the steep cobbled streets of **Haworth ❹**, a hill village of grey stone houses 14 miles (22 km) west of Bradford on the B6144. A babble of nationalities queue to file through the **Brontë Parsonage** (daily Apr–Sept 10am–5.30pm, Oct–Mar 11;

Statue in Leeds of Joseph Priestley, the 18th-century theologian often credited with the discovery of oxygen.

BELOW: fencing demonstration at the Royal Armouries Museum, Leeds.

TIP

On the A65 between Ilkley and Leeds, you can dine at the world's biggest fish and chip shop, the original Harry Ramsden's. It has chandeliers, plush decor, parking for 400 cars, plus a coach park.

Below Right: Bolton Abbey was founded by the Augustinians in 1151. It ceased to be a priory in 1539 when Henry VIII dissolved the monasteries.

admission charge; bronte.org.uk), where Charlotte, Emily, Anne and their brother Branwell grew up.

Haworth station is headquarters of the **Keighley and Worth Valley Railway** (to check daily timetable call 01535 647777 or visit kwvr.co.uk), which runs steam locomotives on a 5-mile (8-km) track between **Keighley** and **Oxenhope**. Ingrow (West) station, a mile from Keighley, has a **Museum of Rail Travel**.

North of Haworth, the spa town of **Ilkley,** ❺ immortalised its rugged climate in the Yorkshire anthem *On Ilkla Moor baht 'at*, which, translated, tells you that it is not prudent to venture forth on Ilkley Moor without a hat.

The undespoiled Dales

To the north of Ilkley lies the expanse of the **Yorkshire Dales**, characterised by dry-stone walls, lively market towns, lonely farmhouses and cathedral-like caverns. The easiest excursion takes you into surrounding **Wharfedale**, an alluring mix of water, wood, crag and castle. The ruins of **Bolton Abbey** ❻ (daily, 9am–9pm, 6pm in winter; parking charge), 5 miles (8 km) northwest of Ilkley, date to the 12th century. Its stunning location by the River Wharfe has made it a major dales attraction.

West of Ilkley is the market town of **Skipton** ❼, the "gateway to the Dales", whose position on the Leeds–Liverpool Canal brought great prosperity during the Industrial Revolution. Many of the warehouses still stand, and so does the stout and well-preserved **Skipton Castle** (daily, 10am–6pm, 12– 6pm Sun; closes 4pm Oct–Feb; admission charge), which dates from the 12th century. Nearby and to the north of Malham village, is **Malham Cove** ❽, an enormous limestone crag with the largest area of limestone pavement in Britain at its top.

Further west still is the small market town of **Settle** ❾, a fine point from which to begin a circular tour of the flat-topped **Ingleborough** hill, taking in the magnificent **Ribblehead Viaduct**, built in 1869–76 to carry the Settle–Carlisle Railway across Batty Moss. To the north, **Wensleydale** is broad and wooded. The eye then catches the forbidding **Bolton Castle** ❿ (daily, 10am–5pm Mar–Oct, admission charge) perched on a hillside. Tradition has it that the mortar was

Brontë Country

Not all the relics on display at the Parsonage in Haworth may really have been owned by the Brontës: visitors gazing at a boot jump to the conclusion that the author of *Jane Eyre* must have had exceptionally small feet. But the tiny manuscripts are a reminder of the secrecy with which Charlotte *(pictured)*, Emily and Anne surrounded their work.

In the town, the church where the Brontës' father was parson scarcely exists; it was rebuilt by his successor in 1879. All the Brontës except Anne, who was buried in Scarborough, lie in the family vault near to where the Brontë pew stood in the old church. Still very visible is the congestion of old tombstones in the burial ground, recalling mid-19th-century conditions here, when average life expectancy was 28 and the town was racked with typhus and cholera.

Above Haworth, the moors retain their fabled grandeur: the wild, skyline setting at Top Withins may have inspired "Wuthering Heights" in Emily Brontë's novel. It is a popular destination for Brontë pilgrims today, reached in about an hour along a path starting at the Penistone Hill Country Park.

Recommended Restaurants and Pubs on pages 306–7

mixed with oxblood to strengthen the building. Inside, you can readily imagine yourself transported back to 1568, when Mary, Queen of Scots was imprisoned here. Nearby are the impressive **Aysgarth Falls**.

At the bottom of the dale is the town of **Middleham ⓫**, famous for its racehorse stables and its moated **castle** (daily, Mar–Oct 10am–6pm; Thur–Mon 10am–4pm in winter, admission charge), childhood home of Richard III. The 12th–14th-century remains include the massive keep, gatehouse and three chapels.

Situated at the heart of the Yorkshire Dales National Park and around 16 miles (25 km) due west on the A684, one of the main attractions of **Hawes ⓬** is the excellent **Dales Countryside Museum** (daily, 10am–5pm, admission charge) housed in the former railways station. Also worth a visit is nearby **Hardraw Force**, England's largest single drop waterfall, where water cascades an impressive 100 ft (30 metres) over the cliff. Access is via the Green Dragon pub.

Buttertubs Pass, ("buttertubs" are deep limestone shafts) is 1,730 ft (530 metres) high and links Wensleydale with **Swaledale** to the northeast. Swaledale is steep and rocky, with intricate patterns of dry-stone walls and field barns. Its market town, **Richmond ⓭**, has a cobbled square and impressive **castle** (daily, Mar–Oct 10am–6pm; Thur–Mon 10am–4pm in winter, admission charge), dramatically sited above the River Swale. It's among the oldest Norman fortresses.

A sheep farmer in the Yorkshire Dales.

Harewood House

Strike north from Leeds on the A61 and, after 9 miles (14 km), you reach the ornate **Harewood House ⓮** (Daily, 11am–4.30pm, grounds 10am–5.30pm; admission charge), a stately home and art gallery in wonderful grounds belonging to the Queen's cousin. The interiors are by Robert Adam, the furniture by Thomas Chippendale and the landscaped gardens, featuring a remarkable bird garden, were laid out by "Capability" Brown. Built in the 1760s by Edwin Lascelles, it is now the home of the Earl and Countess of Harewood.

Eight miles (13 km) further along the A61 is **Harrogate ⓯**, a handsome town

BELOW: the sweeping countryside of Swaledale, one of the more remote northern dales.

York's National Railway Museum.

and a major exhibition and conference centre. Its renown derives from its spas, and the **Royal Pump Room**, which is now part of a museum (Mon–Sat 10am–5pm; Sun 2pm–5pm, 12pm–5pm in August; 4pm Nov– Mar), which stands over the famous sulphur wells and still serves the strongest sulphur water in Europe. The museum has displays recalling Harrogate's heyday as the Queen of Inland Spas. **The Royal Hall**, Britain's last surviving Kursaal (Cure Hall), built in 1903 by the theatre designer Frank Matcham, has been renovated.

Four miles (6.5 km) east, at **Knaresborough**, is **Mother Shipton's Cave** and the Petrifying Well (daily, Apr–Oct 10am–5pm, Feb, Mar, Nov weekends only; admission charge), birthplace and home of England's most famous prophet. She supposedly foretold the Great Fire of London, the defeat of the Spanish Armada, the coming of the motor car, and her own death in 1561.

Four miles (6.5 km) north, **Ripley** is a village of cobbled squares and stone cottages conceived in the style of Alsace-Lorraine, after the French region took the fancy of Sir William Amcotts Ingilby on his travels. **Ripley Castle** (daily, guided tours 11am to 3pm. 10.30am–3.30pm; closed Mon, Wed, Fri in winter; admission charge) has been the home of the Ingleby family for 600 years and has good collections of art and armour.

Ripon ⓰, further along the A61, developed around the sombre Saxon cathedral founded by St Wilfrid in the 7th century. Three miles (5 km) to the southwest are **Fountains Abbey and Studley Royal Water Garden** (daily, 10am–5pm, 4pm in winter; entrance charge; garden open daily in daylight hours). A World Heritage Site, the Abbey was part of what was once Britain's richest Cistercian monastery, and the atmospheric remains are the largest monastic ruins in

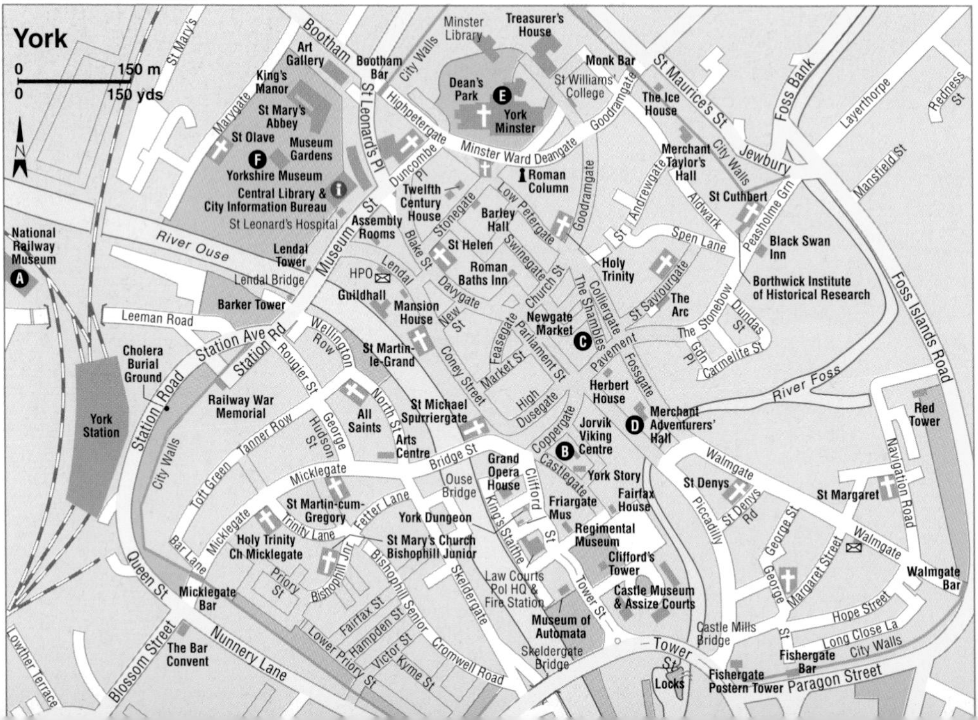

To see the production of the cheese that made Wensleydale a household name, call in at the Wensleydale Creamery Visitor Centre in Hawes.

York

0 150 m
0 150 yds

National Railway Museum (A), York Minster (E), Dean's Park, Minster Library, Treasurer's House, Monk Bar, St Williams' College, Bootham Bar, Art Gallery, King's Manor, St Mary's Abbey, St Olave, Museum Gardens (F), Yorkshire Museum, Central Library & City Information Bureau, St Leonard's Hospital, Assembly Rooms, Twelfth Century House, Roman Column, Barley Hall, St Helen, Roman Baths Inn, Lendal Tower, Lendal Bridge, Barker Tower, Guildhall, Mansion House, HPO, Holy Trinity, The Ice House, Merchant Taylor's Hall, St Cuthbert, Black Swan Inn, Borthwick Institute of Historical Research, The Arc, Newgate Market (C), The Shambles, Herbert House, Merchant Adventurers' Hall (D), Jorvik Viking Centre (B), York Story, Fairfax House, Friargate Mus, Regimental Museum, Clifford's Tower, Castle Museum & Assize Courts, Law Courts Pol HQ & Fire Station, Museum of Automata, Skeldergate Bridge, Castle Mills Bridge, Fishergate Bar, Fishergate Postern Tower, Tower St Locks, St Denys, St Margaret, Red Tower, Walmgate Bar, Cholera Burial Ground, York Station, Railway War Memorial, St Martin-le-Grand, St Michael Spurriergate, All Saints, Arts Centre, Grand Opera House, Ouse Bridge, York Dungeon, St Martin-cum-Gregory, Holy Trinity Ch Micklegate, St Mary's Church Bishophill Junior, Micklegate Bar, The Bar Convent

Bootham, St Mary's, Marygate, St Leonard's Pl, City Walls, Highpetergate, Minster Ward, Deangate, Goodramgate, St Maurice's St, Foss Bank, Jewbury, Layerthorpe, Redness St, Mansfield St, Duncombe Pl, Low Petergate, Stonegate, Blake St, Museum St, Lendal, Davygate, Swinegate, Church St, St Andrewgate, Aldwark, Spen Lane, Peasholme Grn, St Saviourgate, Colliergate, Pavement, Fossgate, The Stonebow, Dundas St, Carmelite St, Gdn Pl, River Foss, Foss Islands Road, River Ouse, Leeman Road, Station Ave, Station Rd, Station Road, Rougier St, Wellington Row, New St, Feasegate, Market St, Parliament St, Coney Street, North St, High Ousegate, Coppergate, Castlegate, Clifford St, Bridge St, King's Staithe, Skeldergate, Tower St, Walmgate, Piccadilly, St Denys Rd, George St, Margaret Street, Navigation Road, Hope Street, Long Close La, Paragon Street, Tanner Row, Hudson St, George St, Toft Green, Micklegate, Fetter Lane, Trinity Lane, Bishophill Jnr, Priory St, Bar Lane, Queen St, Fairfax St, Hampden St, Victor St, Kyme St, Bishophill Senior, Cromwell Road, Lower Priory St, Nunnery Lane, Blossom Street, Lowther Terrace

Recommended Restaurants and Pubs on pages 306–7

the country. Kitchens and dormitories survive, a tribute to old craftsmanship, giving today's visitor an unusually clear idea of medieval monastic life. The water garden has a mill and deer park.

Close to the Abbey are **Brimham Rocks**: strangely shaped sculpted sandstone dumped here during the Ice Age.

York

The Yorkshire Dales are separated from the North York Moors by the broad Vale of York, and at its centre is **York** ⓱, an eclectic city of partly Roman, mainly medieval walls and streets, an imposing Norman tower, a pub or tea shop every few yards, and the stately bulk of York Minster, the country's largest cathedral.

For an overview, take a spin on the **Yorkshire Wheel**, which rises 180 ft (55 metres) above the city. Close to the station, the wheel is part of the **National Railway Museum** Ⓐ (daily 10am–6pm; admission charge; nrm.org.uk). This is the world's largest such museum, appropriately since York was the 19th-century hub of Britain's railway system. It includes the famous *Flying Scotsman* and Queen Victoria's sumptuous carriage.

Viking life displayed at the Jorvik Viking Centre through sights, sounds and, effectively, smells.

The Romans set up a base in York in AD 71. Eight centuries later, the Vikings came, naming the settlement Jorvik. A routine archaeological dig in 1976 turned up a treasure chest of 15,000 artefacts, now the core of an inspired museum project, the **Jorvik Viking Centre** Ⓑ (daily, 10am–5pm, 4pm in winter; charge). Visitors descend into a basement below a shopping precinct and ride in electric buggies down a "time tunnel" into an authentically reconstructed 10th-century Viking village, complete with everyday sights, sounds and smells (even unpleasant ones). The buggies then pass through the actual excavation site.

Above ground you can wander through ancient alleys, such as the

BELOW: York's narrow lanes and great cathedral.

In York Minster, the Screen is decorated with the images of 15 kings of England from William I to Henry VI.

Shambles **C**, the former butchers' quarter. Now antiques and souvenirs instead of carcasses are displayed. Some alleys are so narrow that overhanging upper storeys of opposite buildings almost touch. You can walk on top of the city walls, in some parts wide enough for horses to pass – though it can take two hours to complete the circuit on foot. Medieval timber-framed buildings abound, such as **Merchant Adventurers' Hall** **D** (Apr–Sep Mon–Thur 9am–5pm, Fri–Sat 9am–3.30pm, Sun noon–4pm, Oct–Mar Mon–Sat 9am–3.30pm; charge), as do antiquarian bookshops.

It is without doubt the **Minster** **E** (daily 7am–6.30pm; admission charge, extra for Tower and Undercroft), a fusion of classical, Norman, Saxon and English influences, that dominates York. The cathedral seems to float above the city. It was constructed over a period of 250 years, as "an act of prayer by the most practical people in the world", and costs £5 a minute to maintain. Constantine the Great was declared Roman emperor in this building, providing an improbable link between Yorkshire and the founding of Constantinople. Evidence of past centuries can be seen in a fascinating display in the Undercroft, and the Tower gives a grand view of the city.

There is Roman, Anglo-Saxon and Viking history on offer in the **Yorkshire Museum** **F** (daily, 10am–5pm; gardens 7.30am–5pm, later in summer; admission charge) plus treasures such as the Middleham Jewel. You can picnic in the 10-acre (4-hectare) botanical museum gardens, where peacocks roam.

Around York

Among maritime attractions in the Museum Quarter at **Kingston-upon-Hull**, 43 miles (69 km) southeast of York, is **The Deep** (daily, 10am–6pm, admission charge) where you can find sharks and other sea creatures, both living and extinct, and on Fridays and Saturdays you can dine alongside them.

Drive 15 miles (24 km) northeast from York on the A64 into the Howardian Hills to encounter the 18th century at its most magnificent at **Castle Howard** **18** (daily, Mar–Oct 11am–4pm, grounds 10am–6.30pm; admission charge). It was

BELOW RIGHT: statue in the Temple of the Winds, Castle Howard.

York Minster's glorious glass

As the masons worked and the Minster slowly took its present form, artistry of a different kind was flourishing in small studios all over York. As a result, the whole history of English stained glass ranging from the 12th century to the present day can be seen in the Minster.

The Great East Window contains the world's largest area of medieval stained glass in a single window. It was completed in 1407 by Coventry glazier John Thornton. The window's theme is the beginning and the end of the world, using scenes from the Bible. The West Window, painted in 1338, is known as the Heart of Yorkshire because of the heart shape in the ornate tracery of the window arch. The North Transept is dominated by the stunning Five Sisters' Window, the oldest complete window in the Minster, made of green and grey "grisaille" glass set in geometric patterns.

During the two world wars all 100,000 pieces of glass were taken out and buried for safety. In the South Transept, the Rose Window narrowly escaped total destruction when lightning struck the Minster in 1984.

the creation of architect Sir John Vanbrugh (1664–1726), who you might meet along with others in period dress animating the estate *(see margin note)*.

North York Moors

Further north lie the North York Moors. Stretching from the Vale of York to the East Coast, the Moors embrace the largest expanse of heather moorland in England and Wales. They can be approached either directly from York or from the A1. Just off the A1 is the thriving market town of **Thirsk** ⑲, now famous as the "Darrowby" of the vet books by James Herriot (real name Alf Wight, 1916–95), which were translated into a 1980s TV series *All Creatures Great and Small*. Wight's former surgery is now **The World of James Herriot** (daily, Apr–Oct 10am–5pm, Nov–Mar 11am–4pm; charge) devoted to the author.

Approaching the Moors from the west or the south, most visitors will arrive in **Helmsley**, whose quaint shops give it a distinctly "Cotswolds" feel.

Nearby, tucked amid placid pastures deep in the Rye Valley, are the breathtaking ruins of **Rievaulx Abbey** ⑳ (Apr–Sept daily 10am–6pm, Oct–Mar Mon, Thur, Fri, Sat and Sun 10am–4pm; entrance charge), an extensive 12th-century Cistercian monastery.

Despite the predominant heather of the Moors, green fields are never far away. A network of dales penetrates the great dome of moorland. In some places they create dramatic natural features, such as the **Hole of Horcum** ㉑ above the Vale of Pickering; elsewhere they enfold villages and farmhouses built mainly of warm, honey-coloured sandstone. The prettiest villages include **Hutton-le-Hole** ㉒ in Farndale, with a broad green, and nearby **Lastingham**, with a splendid Norman crypt.

On the northern flanks, above Eskdale, are **Goathland** and **Beck Hole** ㉓, the latter a delightful hamlet with an arc of cottages facing a green. Across it all, for 18 miles (29km) from Pickering to Whitby, runs the steam-powered **North Yorkshire Moors Railway** (tel: 01751 472508, nymr.co.uk). For the more energetic, there is the **Lyke Wake Walk**, which traverses the Moors for 42 miles

Castle Howard was the location for the opulent 1981 TV version of Evelyn Waugh's classic 1949 novel Brideshead Revisited, *and was used again in the 2008 movie version. The Howard family helps finance it by staging concerts and allowing camping and caravanning on the extensive estate.*

BELOW: Rievaulx Abbey.

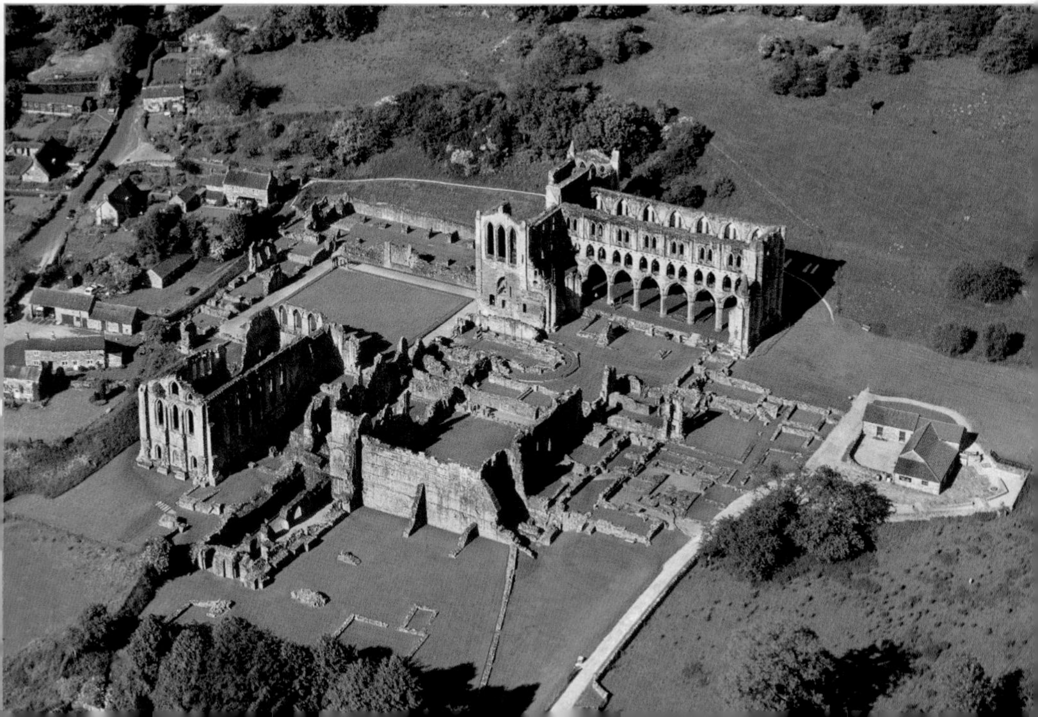

(68 km) between Osmotherley and the steep Robin Hood's Bay.

A good souvenir from Whitby is a piece of jet jewellery, which has been made in the town since Victorian days and is still produced at the Victorian Jet Works.

Coastal highlights

The Moors end at the east coast, where breaks in the precipitous cliffs provide space for pretty villages and the occasional town. **Whitby** ㉔ is a picturesque fishing port with a jumble of pantiled cottages climbing from the harbour. On **East Cliff** are the 13th-century remains of **Whitby Abbey** (Apr–Oct daily 10am–6pm, Nov–Mar 10am–4pm; charge) on which site a 7th-century monk wrote the *Song of Creation*, considered as the start of English literature.

The Pacific explorer Captain James Cook (1728–79), lived in this former whaling port. The **Captain Cook Memorial Museum** (Apr–Oct daily 9.45am–5pm, Mar Sat–Sun 11am–3pm; admission charge) in Grape Street is the focal point of a Cook heritage trail.

To the north of Whitby, steep roads lead down to **Runswick Bay**, a self-consciously pretty assortment of fishermen's cottages, and **Staithes**, where the young Cook was briefly and unhappily apprenticed to a grocer.

BELOW: Whitby and its abbey.

To the south, seekers after solitude can divert from the coastal road to find **Ravenscar**, which has fine walks, but little else except one imposing clifftop hotel. **Robin Hood's Bay**, close by, is said to have once offered sanctuary to the outlaw and was a smugglers' haunt. Today its cobbled streets and sandy beaches are popular with families.

Further south lies **Scarborough** ㉕, a posh watering hole when the **Grand Hotel** was the handsomest in Europe when it opened in 1863. The 12th-century **castle** (Apr–Sep daily 10am–6pm, Oct–Mar Mon and Thur–Sun 10am–4pm; admission charge) is worth seeing, and Anne Brontë – who, like so many invalids, came for the bracing air – is buried in the graveyard of **St Mary's Church**. The town also has an enviable theatrical reputation built around Alan Ayckbourn, the local-born playwright who premiered most of his 70-plus plays at the **Stephen Joseph Theatre** (box office 01723-370541).

Filey ㉖ offers unpretentious delights to day trippers, including amusement arcades, a splendid beach and **Filey Brigg**, the breakwater at the northern end of the bay. Off the dramatic 400-ft (130-metre) cliff at nearby **Flamborough Head**, the American squadron of John Paul Jones won a sea battle with two British men-of-war in 1779.

To Northumbria

Heading north from Whitby now and leaving Yorkshire behind, the lively sandy-beached resort of **Redcar** ㉗ is a playground for the former **Teesside** industrial centres of **Middlesbrough**, **Stockton-on-Tees** and **Darlington** ㉘. The region boomed in the 19th century, as coal and iron were discovered and the railways pioneered an undreamed-of prosperity, and it remains a centre of heavy industry. The new **Middlesbrough Institute of Modern Art** (Tues, Wed, Fri, Sat 10am–5pm, Thurs till 8pm Sun 12–4pm; tel: 01642-726720; visitmima.com) holds a large collection of Picassos, and many works by 20th and 21st-century British artists and ceramicists. George Stephen-

Recommended Restaurants and Pubs on pages 306–7

son's Locomotion No. 1 (1825) is displayed at Darlington's railway museum, **Head of Steam** (Apr–Sept Tues–Sun 10am–4pm, winter 11am–3.30pm, admission charge), near where it once ran on the world's first railway line, between Stockton and Darlington.

Sixteen miles (25 km) to the west, on the River Tees, is the the old market town of **Barnard Castle** 29. Here the château-like **Bowes Museum** (daily 10am–5pm, till 4pm Nov–Mar; charge) has a superb collection of exhibits, notably a unique 1773 clockwork silver swan.

Near **Staindrop**, on the A688 to the northeast, is the nine-towered **Raby Castle** 30 (park and gardens 11am–5.30pm, Castle 12.30–5pm May, Jun, Sept Sun–Wed, guided tours only Mon–Wed; Jul–Aug Sun–Fri; open Bank Holiday Sats; admission charge), set in a 250-acre (100-hectare) deer park.

To the northwest, off the B6277 near **Middleton-in-Teesdale** 31, the impressive **High Force** waterfall crashes down 70 ft (21 metres).

Durham 32 is a university city with a scholarly air. Until 1836, the prince-bishops of the County Palatine of Durham were granted complete sovereignty within their diocese, holding their own parliaments and minting their own coins. The mighty Romanesque **Cathedral** (Sun 7.45am–5.30pm, Mon–Sat 7.30am–6pm, until 8pm in summer; donations invited), dramatically sited above a meander in the River Wear, is one of Europe's finest. Its Chapel of the Nine Altars is the final resting place of St Cuthbert, who evangelised from Lindisfarne Abbey.

The splendid **Castle** (for guided tour tel 0191-334-3800) was the only northern stronghold not to fall to the marauding Scots, and is now occupied by the University College.

Many American visitors head for

The Bowes Museum, built by John and Joséphine Bowes, who assembled 15,000 paintings, ceramics, furniture and textiles between 1862 and 1874, when Joséphine died. John too died before the museum finally opened in 1892.

BELOW: Durham Cathedral, surrounded by the River Wear.

A section of the 73-mile (117-km) Hadrian's Wall, begun in AD122 to secure the northern boundary of Roman rule in Britain.

BELOW: the Tyne Bridge and the Sage concert hall in foreground, and in background the Gateshead Millennium Bridge and the Baltic Centre.

Washington ㉝ and the 17th-century **Old Hall** (Apr–Oct Sun–Wed 11am–5pm; admission charge). The handsome stone manor house is the ancestral home of the USA's first president.

Newcastle-upon-Tyne

Dominating the area is **Newcastle-upon-Tyne** ㉞, a sprawling former shipbuilding city, celebrated for its resilient natives ("Geordies"), whose dialect borders on impenetrability, and for its potent brew, Newcastle Brown (pronounced *broon*) Ale. Despite the setbacks caused by the decline in the coal and shipbuilding industries, Newcastle, with its famous railway bridge over the Tyne, remains an extremely vibrant place, and is the third home (after Stratford and London) of the Royal Shakespeare Company.

The striking **Millennium Bridge** links Newcastle Quayside with the new developments on **Gateshead Quays**. These include the **Baltic Centre for Contemporary Art** and the **Sage** concert hall and music education centre – the latter's shimmering shell-like form designed by Norman Foster's architectural team.

Approaching **Gateshead** by the A1 or A167, a 20-metre (66-ft) tall steel giant marks the entry into Tyneside. The *Angel of the North* stands on the site of a former coal mine and was created by Antony Gormley, partly in tribute to the coal miners who worked in darkness beneath its feet. For a realistic and lively look at what life used to be like in the northeast, visit the **Beamish Open Air Museum** ㉟ (Apr–Oct daily 10am–5pm, Nov–mid March Tues–Thur and Sat–Sun 10am–4pm; admission charge), 8 miles (13 km) southwest of Newcastle, which has a working 1913 village with buildings and artefacts collected from the region.

Hadrian's Wall

The strategic importance of the site of Newcastle was first recognised by the Romans who founded the city as a minor fort and bridge on **Hadrians's Wall** (hadrianswallcountry.org) almost 2,000 years ago. The Roman fort of **Arbeia** (Easter–Sept Mon–Sat 10am–3pm, Sun 1–5pm, Oct–Easter 10am–3.30pm, closed Sun; admission charge) has been excavated at nearby **South Shields**.

Hadrian's Wall itself, 15 ft high and 7½ ft thick (5 metres by 2½ metres), snakes westwards across the Borders for 73 miles (117 km). It has several easy points of access from the A69 but the best section is the 4 miles (7 km) between Twice Brewed and Sewingshields Crag (the site of a former castle under which, legend says, King Arthur sleeps).

You can explore Roman barracks at **Housesteads** fort and museum (daily, Apr–Sep 10am–6pm, 4pm in winter; entrance charge), the best preserved of the 16 forts along the wall, and nearby is the major site of **Vindolanda** and the **Roman Army Museum** (daily Apr–Nov 10am–6pm, earlier closing in winter).

Just above Hexham the wall crosses the River North Tyne at **Chesters** ㊱ (daily, Mar–Sept 10am– 5pm, 4pm in winter; admission charge), site of a Roman cavalry fort with a remarkably well-preserved military bath-house.

Coastal strongholds

The fortified town of **Alnwick** 37, around 34 miles (54 km) to the north of Newcastle, has one of Britain's best examples of a medieval fortress on a large scale. The **Castle** (Easter–Oct daily 11am–5pm), backdrop of Harry Potter and many other films, radiates the power the Percy family, Dukes of Northumberland, exercised over Northeast England for 600 years, and is the second largest residential castle in Britain after Windsor Castle. The magic continues in **Alnwick Garden** (daily Apr–Sept 10am–6pm, 4pm in winter; admission charge). Run as a charity by the Duchess of Northumberland, this is a great place for children, with a Poison Garden, Serpent Garden, Bamboo Labyrinth and a Tree House complex of furnished buildings linked by suspended walkways.

There are more fine fortresses along the coast, including the romantic ruins of **Dunstanburgh** and the giant keep of **Warkworth**. The most stunning is **Bamburgh Castle** 38 (Mar–Nov daily 10am–5pm; admission charge), 16 miles (25 km) north. From here, on a clear day, you can see the **Farne Islands**, 4½ miles (7 km) offshore. Boats for this former saints' sanctuary of seabirds and seals leave from Seahouses harbour (daily, every hour 10am–3pm daily).

Lindisfarne

Monks from the Scottish Isle of Iona, led by St Columbine, settled on **Lindisfarne** 39 (also called Holy Island) in the 7th century, turning it into a centre of scholarship renowned throughout Europe: the Lindisfarne Gospels, now in the British Museum, is one of the country's greatest artistic treasures.

As well as the old **Priory** ruins (daily 9.30am–5pm, earlier closing in winter; admission charge), the island, which can be reached at low tide by a 3-mile (5-km) causeway, has a small fairy-like **Castle** dating from 1550 (daily, for 5 hours, times depend on tides; admission charge). Birdwatchers also flock to the islands' breeding grounds.

On the border with Scotland is the seaport of **Berwick-upon-Tweed** 40, England's most northern town. Walk along the well-preserved Elizabethan ramparts and you can gaze down on its cobbled streets and out towards the shore-line. ❑

From the harbour at Seahouses you can take an exciting boat trip to the Farne Islands in season. The islands are famous for their breeding colonies of seabirds and their large colony of grey seals, all of which are visible from the boat.

BELOW: Alnwick Castle.

RESTAURANTS, TEARROOMS AND PUBS

Restaurants

Prices for a three-course meal per person with a half-bottle of house wine:

£ = under £25
££ = £25–50
£££ = £50–100

Bolton Abbey

Devonshire Arms Country House Hotel
Tel: 01756-718111 **£££**
The Yorkshire Restaurant in this former coaching inn owned by the Duke of Devonshire is furnished with antiques from Chatsworth. Elegant, with classic dishes given a modern touch.

Bradford

Nawaab
32 Manor Road
Tel: 01274-730371 **£**
With scores of curry houses in Bradford, you couldn't do better than start at this city centre evergreen – even Diana, Princess of Wales, sampled some of the 200 dishes.

Burnsall

Red Lion
Tel: 01756-720204 **££**
A delightful 17th-century village inn on the banks of the Wharfe, between Bolton Abbey and Grassington. The restaurant's specialities are fish and game. Also bar menu.

Chester le Street

Black Knight Restaurant
Lumley Castle Hotel
Tel: 0191-389 1111 **££**
This restaurant, 7 miles (11 km) from Durham, is in the 14th-century ancestral home if the Earl of Scarborough. Look smart and enjoy an excellent meal.

Durham

Bistro 21
Aykley Heads House, Aykley Heads
Tel: 0191-384 4354 **£**
Robust classic French country cooking in a 16th-century farmhouse on the edge of the city. Friendly and informal.

Cleckheaton

Aakash
Providence Place, Bradford Road
Tel: 01274-878866 **££**
Huge Indian restaurant, in a lavishly refurbished former church southwest of Leeds. Good food beneath chandeliers. Imran Khan has dined here. Closed Mon.

Hetton

Angel Inn
Tel: 01756-730263. **££**
Though off the beaten track, below Cracoe Fell above Wharfdale, there can be long queues for the bar brasserie meals. The restaurant offers an extensive, well-priced menu. It also has a wine cave, offering tastings.

Helmsley

Crown Hotel
Market Place
Tel: 01439-770297 **£**
Comfortable posting house. Wide choice of country-style dishes served in the bar or lounge area.

Harrogate

Drum & Monkey
Montpellier Gardens
Tel: 01423-502650 **££**
Long-standing local favourite fish restaurant on two floors, with an informal atmosphere despite a marble-top bar. Dover sole, lobster, oysters, halibut and sea bass are delivered daily.

Ilkley

Box Tree
35-37 Church Street
Tel: 01943-608484 **££**
Young Marco Pierre White cut his culinary teeth in this intimate 18th-century stone farmhouse that serves "modern French classic" dishes.

Leeds

Brasserie Forty 4
44 The Calls
Tel: 0113-234 3232 **££**
Bright, modern brasserie that's always lively, and the food provides good value for money. You might spot a well-known face here, too.

Malham

The Buck Inn
Tel: 01729-830317 **££**
Overlooking the village green. Home-cooked traditional fare in the bar, including speciality Malhan and Masham pie; à la carte in the candlelit restaurant.

Moulton

Black Bull Inn
Tel: 01325-377289 **££**
This whitewashed inn has several dining spaces with nooks and corners (Tory politician William Hague proposed to Ffion here), plus a conservatory, Fish Bar and "Hazel", a 1932 First Class Pullman dining car.

LEFT: Betty's Tea Rooms in Harrogate.

Newcastle-Upon-Tyne

Blackfriars Restaurant
Friars Street
Tel: 0191-261 2945 **££**
Reputedly the oldest purpose-built restaurant in Britain, with a medieval banqueting hall. Kevin Spacey declared it served "the best roast dinners in England".

Shangri La
38–42 Stowell Street
Tel: 0191-261 2289 **£**
One of many good, family-run Chinese restaurants on Stowell Street.

Northallerton

McCoys At The Tontine
Cleveland Tontine, Staddlebridge
Tel: 01609-882671 **£££**
Lavish, slightly faded period surroundings, in the bistro, conservatory and restaurant. A relaxed atmosphere and some very interesting food.

Seaham

Seaham Hall Hotel
Lord Byron's Walk
Tel: 01915-161 4000 **££**
Award-winning restaurant in a spa hotel 20 minutes from Newcastle. In 1815 Lord Byron was married the Byron Room.

West Witton

The Wensleydale Heifer
Tel: 01969-622322 **£**
Home cooking in a 17th-century inn in a pretty village between Leyburn and Aysgarth (A684). Voted England's Seafish Pub of the Year.

Winteringham

Winteringham Fields
Tel: 01724-733096 **££–£££**
A gem just south of the Humber Bridge: a 16th-century manor with beams, panelling and open fireplaces. This restaurant with rooms has an extensive menu, including a tasting menu and large cheese board. Swiss chef Germain Schwab takes huge pride in his mainly local ingredients, including fish fresh from Grimsby

ABOVE: the Tan Hill Inn on Swaledale, Britain's highest pub.

Whitby

The Magpie Café
14 Pier Road
Tel: 01947-602058 **££**
Legendary harbourside restaurant. Best known for superb Whitby fish and chips, but equally satisfies most other tastes. Children's menu.

York

Melton's
7 Scarcroft Road
Tel: 01904-634341 **££**
Unassuming, child-friendly restaurant with praise-worthy home cooking of Yorkshire produce served in a modern style. Good vegetarian selection.

Harville's Restaurant
47 Fossgate
Tel: 01904-654155 **££**
On three floors, this fine 1930s-style restaurant majors in chargrilled Aberdeen Angus and English Longhorn beef steaks. There is also a fish restaurant and an art deco cocktail lounge.

Tearooms

Bettys & Taylors of Harrogate
1 Parliament Street, Harrogate
Tel: 01423-814000
Founded in 1919, Bettys' family-run business is an institution with the original Tea Room in York. Now it is teamed with tea and coffee merchant Taylors of Harrogate, founded in 1886. Bettys' elegant Tea Rooms serve wonderful cakes and pastries and are also at:
Harlow Carr: RHS Gardens
Ilkley: 32 The Grove
Northallerton: High St.
York: 6–8 St Helen's Square (the original Bettys) and 28 Stonegate (Little Bettys).

Pubs

In Bradford, **Sir Titus Salt** is a Wetherspoons conversion of the old swimming baths and is handy for the National Media Museum.

Among the ornate Victorian pubs in Leeds are **The Scarborough** in Bishopsgate Street and **The Victoria** in Great George Street.

In Harrogate, **Hales Bar** in Crescent Road has good beers and retains some original gaslight fittings.

In York, **Maltings** in Tanners Moat promotes good beers, has a junk-theme decor and is handy for the Railway Museum. **The Blue Bell** in Fossgate is a small place with well-preserved Edwardian decor. **The Olde Starre** in Stonegate is popular with tourists.

In Whitby, **The Duke of York** has fine views over the harbour.

In Durham, **The Victoria** in Hallgarth Street lives up to its name with tributes to the Queen and Victorian decor. **The Dun Cow** in Old Elvet, parts of it 16th-century, dispenses the locally popular Castle Eden ale.

In Newcastle-upon-Tyne, **The Cluny** in Lime Street is a converted whisky bottling plant that also serves as an art gallery and artists' studio. For ornate architecture, try **Crown Posada** in The Side, off Dean Street. The **Centurion Bar** at the central railway station, a former first-class waiting room, has amazing tiles.

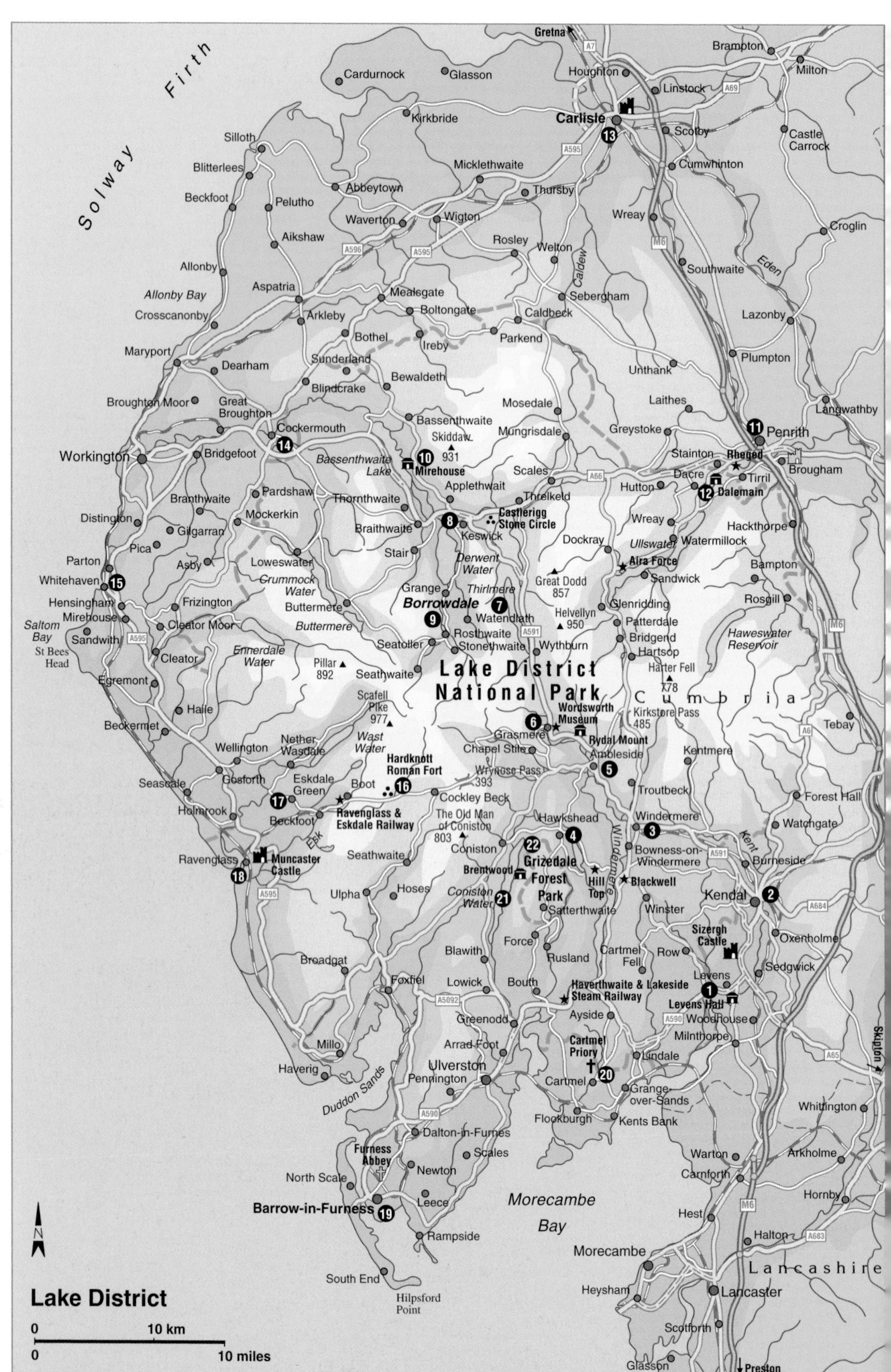
Lake District
0
10 km
0
10 miles
Solway Firth
Morecambe Bay
Lake District National Park
Cumbria
Lancashire
Carlisle
Penrith
Keswick
Kendal
Windermere
Ambleside
Cockermouth
Workington
Whitehaven
Barrow-in-Furness
Ulverston
Lancaster
Morecambe
Borrowdale
Grizedale Forest Park
Mirehouse
Dalemain
Rheged
Aira Force
Castlerigg Stone Circle
Wordsworth Museum
Rydal Mount
Hill Top
Blackwell
Brentwood
Sizergh Castle
Levens Hall
Haverthwaite & Lakeside Steam Railway
Cartmel Priory
Furness Abbey
Muncaster Castle
Ravenglass & Eskdale Railway
Hardknott Roman Fort
Skiddaw 931
Helvellyn 950
Scafell Pike 977
Pillar 892
Great Dodd 857
Harter Fell 778
The Old Man of Coniston 803
Wrynose Pass 393
Kirkstone Pass 485
Gretna
Skipton
Preston

Recommended Restaurants and Pubs on page 319

THE LAKE DISTRICT

From the time of the first guidebook to the area, Thomas West's 1778 "Guide to the Lakes", its pleasures have remained those of the eye; the landscape is what matters most

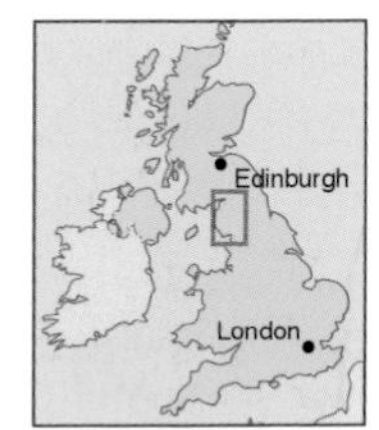

Main attractions

- AIRA FORCE
- TARN HOWS
- BEATRIX POTTER'S HILL TOP
- CASTLERIGG
- DOVE COTTAGE
- FURNESS ABBEY
- CASTLERIGG STONE CIRCLE
- DERWENT WATER
- LANGDALE

The Lake District in northwest England covers a small area, measuring scarcely more than 30 miles (48 km) from north to south and 20 miles (32 km) east to west. But as the poet William Wordsworth, who was born here at Cockermouth in 1770 and spent most of his life in the region, rightly remarked: "I do not know any tract of country in which, within so narrow a compass, may be found an equal variety in the influences of light and shadow upon the sublime or beautiful features of landscape."

The Lake District is 250 miles (400 km) from London and 75 miles (120 km) north of Manchester and it is more frequently visited by day tourists and holidaymakers than any other region of outstanding natural beauty in the British Isles. Generally it has proved remarkably able to cope with the vast numbers of visitors, but traffic congestion can be a big problem in summer.

Popular routes

The two routes which were popularised by the first tourists in the 1760s still carry the greatest share of summer traffic. One is from Penrith to Ambleside by the west shore of Ullswater (scene of Wordsworth's poem *The Daffodils*) and over the Kirkstone Pass, now the A592; the other is from Keswick to Windermere by the side of Thirlmere, Grasmere, Rydal Water and Windermere, now the A591.

Away from these it remains possible to find areas of great beauty. Here you can experience for a time the sense of being at one with nature which the first visitors and the early 19th-century Romantic poets (Wordsworth and Samuel Taylor Coleridge) valued so highly.

The central area of mountains was never much affected by industry or quarrying, and the 19th-century developments in shipbuilding, iron manufacturing, coal mining and lesser trades that once flourished by the Cumbrian coast have now almost entirely disappeared. Sheep farming was the traditional way of life of the hill folk, and it continues today throughout the area covered by the Lake District

PRECEDING PAGES: valley north of Lake Thirlmere.
BELOW: cycling is suited to the Lake District.

TIP

Plan to leave your car behind for a day. The flexible Cross Lakes Experience ticket allows you to explore the Windermere, Bowness, Hawkshead and Coniston area by boat and bus with options for walking and cycling between certain points. A bus service runs from Windermere Station to the boats at Bowness Pier 3. Tel: 015934 45161 or visit www.lakedistrict.gov.uk/map.

BELOW: sheep can create a traffic jam as they are moved between fields.

National Park, often on farms owned and leased by the National Trust.

In the early 19th century, visitors began to walk the high paths over the fells, and after about 1860 they started to climb the more difficult rock faces. Climbers still congregate in **Great Langdale**, **Borrowdale** and **Wasdale** to tackle the central heights of the **Langdales**, **Scafell Crags**, **Great Gable**, **Steeple** and **Pillar**. There are hundreds of miles of paths to tempt the walker. Paths over the high fells must be tackled with respect for the region's notoriously rapid changes of weather, and with the proper equipment, but there are innumerable easy walks by the lakesides or along the streams which anyone can enjoy.

Walking is the best way to witness the constant change of scene which is so characteristic of this small but endlessly varied district. Most of the Lake District's places of interest are museums, but they vary from permanent displays and houses to working mills and steam railways.

Approaching the Lake District from the south along the M6, a turn off at junction 36 leads to the town of **Levens** ❶. **Levens Hall**, a largely 16th-century house built around a 13th-century pele tower, with a famous topiary garden (tel: 01539-60321; levenshall.co.uk; Apr–mid-Oct Sun–Thur, house noon–4.30pm, last admission 4pm, gardens 10am–5pm; charge), is little changed since its trees were first shaped in the 17th century.

Nearby **Sizergh Castle** (tel: 015395-60951 mid-Mar–Oct Sun–Thur 1–5pm; charge) shows its origins as a medieval defensive structure even more clearly.

Fine historic buildings

Kendal ❷, a good centre for the Lakes, is a short distance north of Levens. It is, indeed, still a working town, not just a holiday centre, all the more fascinating for carrying on in the midst of fine 17th- and 18th-century buildings. Among these are old coaching inns, and a horn shop which sells items made from this material. The church is a fine, unusually broad Perpendicular building. Beside it stands **Abbot Hall** (tel: 01539-722464; abbothall.org.uk; Jan–Dec Mon–Sat 10.30am–5pm, until 4pm in Jan, Mar, Nov and Dec; charge), a mid-17th-century house which now displays a remarkable collection of furniture, china and paintings by local artists, in particular George Romney. There is also a room filled with watercolours by John Ruskin. Abbot Hall's stable block houses the **Museum of Lakeland Life** (tel: 01539-722464; lakelandmuseum.org.uk; Mon–Sat 10.30am–5pm, until 4pm in winter; charge), which has two rooms devoted to the *Swallows and Amazons* author Arthur Ransome (1884–1967).

Home of the Wordsworths

The A591 runs from Kendal to **Windermere** ❸. Below the town lies **Bowness**, with a pretty village centre, unfortunately almost always too crowded for comfort. In the town centre, **The World of Beatrix Potter** (tel: 015394-88444; hop-skip-jump.com; daily summer 10am–5.30pm, winter 10am–4.30pm; charge) creates the atmosphere of walking through Potter's books and meeting the characters. There is also a Potter-themed tearoom with tables indoors and on the garden terrace.

At Bowness, boats depart for **Belle Isle**, with the handsome late 18th-century circular house of the same name. Also at Bowness is the car ferry to Far Sawrey and **Hill Top**, Beatrix Potter's house (tel: 015394-36269; mid-Mar–Oct Sat–Thur 10.30am–4.30pm; charge), a fine example of a traditional Lakeland farmhouse. To the south of Bowness just off the A5074 is **Blackwell** (tel: 015394-46139; blackwell.org.uk; Apr–Oct and Jan daily 10.30am–5pm, Feb, Mar, Nov–Dec until 4pm; charge), the Arts and Crafts house designed by M.H. Baillie Scott for a wealthy Manchester brewery owner.

In Main Street in nearby **Hawkshead** ❹ is the **Beatrix Potter Gallery** (tel: 015394 36355; mid-Mar–Oct Sat–Thur 10.30am–4.30pm; charge) in the office of her husband, a solicitor. It has displays of many of the original drawings from her famous children's books.

William Wordsworth studied at the ancient **Grammar School** at Hawkshead, now a **museum** (hawksheadgram mar.org.uk; Apr–Sept Mon–Sat 10am–1pm and 2–5pm, Sun 1–5pm, Oct Mon–Sat 10am–1pm and 2–3.30pm, Sun 1–3.30pm; free). Downstairs, it suggests little of the excellence of its teaching in the 1780s when the Wordsworth brothers studied there. But upstairs is a superb library with books dating back to the foundation

Kendal, a town whose prosperity was based on wool, is now perhaps most famous for Kendal Mint Cake, a slabby, sweet confection which continues to be an essential part of many outdoor survival kits, whether in the Lake District or in the Himalayas.

BELOW: the lakes are replenished by generous rainfall.

Castlerigg Stone Circle, probably built around 3000BC, may have had astronomical significance.

TIP

Tarn Hows provides some of the most spellbinding views of the Lakeland fells. The best vantage point is the southern side of the lake, where the path takes to higher ground.

BELOW: the Old Mill at Ambleside.

of the school by Archbishop Sandys in Elizabeth I's reign. Wall paintings of scriptural texts are preserved in **St Michael's Church**. From beneath its east window you can take in the view of this tiny, whitewashed town with its close-packed lanes and the occasional house still sheltering the spinning gallery where the women would sit to work.

West of Hawkshead stands the medieval arched **Courthouse**, a relic of the times when the Cistercian monks from Cartmel ruled much of the southern part of the area. Further west, on the B5285, is **Tarn Hows**, considered by many to be the prettiest lake in the Lake District. Only a half-mile (800 metres) long, it was originally three smaller lakes but joined after a dam was built.

Whether you continue towards the head of Lake Windermere on this west side, or take the A591 northwest from Windermere, you will eventually reach **Ambleside** ❺, and just beyond it, Rydal Water. **Rydal Mount** (tel: 015394 33002; rydalmount.co.uk; summer daily 9.30am–5pm, winter Wed–Mon 10am–4pm; charge) was home of the Wordsworths from 1813 until William died in 1850. The house contains portraits and family mementos; the grounds are laid out in their original form and afford fine views. There is a designated picnic area and, in summer, refreshments are served in a marquee. Guided tours include Grasmere a slice of gingerbread and a glass of white wine.

Grasmere

Two miles (3 km) north lies **Grasmere** ❻. The southernmost part of the village, **Town End,** is where the poet and his sister Dorothy first settled in 1799. The white cottage is movingly simple in its furnishings, but it takes the display of manuscripts and portraits of the poet's family and friends in the nearby **Grasmere Wordsworth Museum** (tel: 015394-35748; wordsworth.org.uk; Feb–Dec daily 9.30am–5.30pm; charge) to bring home the magnitude of the poetry that was written here and the significance of Wordsworth and Coleridge in the cultural life of their day.

St Oswald's Church is a plain, rough-

Recommended Restaurants and Pubs on page 319

ly built structure with a remarkable and much-altered ancient timber roof. The Wordsworth family graves, and that of Coleridge's son Hartley, lie behind it. All about are the paths, streams and hills that Dorothy Wordworth described along with the daily life of **Dove Cottage** (included with a visit to the museum) in her 1800–02 *Journal*.

The 17-mile (28-km) journey to Keswick on the A591 passes **Thirlmere** ❼, a reservoir created out of two smaller lakes in 1890 to supply the water needs of Manchester. **Helvellyn**, the third-highest mountain in England (3,120 ft/950 metres), rises steeply to the right.

Close to Keswick you may turn off to **Castlerigg Stone Circle**, an ancient monument of 48 large stones commanding tremendous views. Early tourists associated it with the Druids. Recent scholars think the stones may have been intended as a giant calendar to show by its shadows the turn of the seasons for planting and reaping.

Pencils for poets

Keswick ❽, a Victorian town with an older centre, has been popular with visitors since the 1760s, when the poet Thomas Gray stayed there to explore its lake, **Derwent Water**. With fear and trembling, Gray ventured to the mouth of mountain-surrounded **Borrowdale** ❾, just past the southern end of the lake, which early visitors associated with the sublimity and terror of Salvator Rosa's paintings. Even today one might fear that the tottering pinnacles will detach themselves and fall upon one's head. A favourite excursion since Gray's time is the **Bowder Stone**, balanced on the side of the hill a little way up the valley. Another attraction is the waterfall at **Lodore**, near the head of Derwent Water.

Borrowdale was famed among the early tourists for the "wad" or black lead mine that enabled the manufacture of pencils in Keswick, which is now home to the **Cumberland Pencil Museum** (tel: 017687-73626; pencilmuseum.co.uk; daily 9.30am–4pm; charge).

Keswick's **Museum and Art Gallery** (tel: 017687-73263; Apr–Sept Tues–Sun 10am–4pm; free), in Fitz Park, has mementos of Coleridge, Robert Southey and Hugh Walpole, who lived nearby, and whose "Rogue Herries" novels are set in and around the area.

Coleridge settled at **Greta Hall** on the outskirts of Keswick in 1800 and persuaded his brother-in-law Robert Southey, also a writer, to join him there. **Crossthwaite Church**, which stands about half-a-mile beyond Greta Hall, has memorials to Southey and members of his family.

Northwards, the churchyard looks towards **Bassenthwaite Lake**, the eastern side of which is dominated by Skiddaw (3,050 ft/931 metres). Beneath the mountain lies **Mirehouse** ❿ (tel: 017687-72287; mirehouse.com; Apr–Nov Sun and Wed 2–4.30pm, grounds and teashop daily; charge), the 18th-century home of the Spedding family.

A 15-mile (24-km) drive eastwards from Keswick on the A66 to the old town of **Penrith** ⓫ can include a visit to **Dacre** ⓬, a few miles before the town on the right. It has a largely Norman church,

Crossthwaite Church. The poet Thomas Gray (1716–71) described the view as one which, if it could be captured "in all the softness of its living colours, would fairly sell for a thousand pounds."

BELOW: Wordsworth relics at Dove Cottage.

St Michael's Church in Lowther, 4 miles (6km) south of Penrith, displays a Viking tombstone in its porch.

even earlier carvings and views of 14th-century **Dacre Castle**. A short detour leads to **Rheged – The Village in the Hill**, just off the M6. Housed in Europe's largest grass-covered building, this innovative tourist attraction takes the visitor through 2,000 years of Cumbria's history.

Nearby is **Dalemain** (tel: 017684-86450; dalemain.com; Apr–mid-Oct Sun–Thur 11am–4pm; charge), an old house last altered in 1750 that offers fine interiors (including a Chinese drawing room with mid-18th-century wallpaper), paintings and a pleasant garden.

Dalemain lies just off the A592, which leads past **Ullswater** and over the Kirkstone Pass to Ambleside. Ullswater is the second-largest lake after Windermere. There are steamers on the lake from which one can enjoy excellent views of Helvellyn and other surrounding mountains, and **Aira Force** – on the north shore beneath Gowbarrow Fell – is one of the most impressive waterfalls in the Lake District. **Brougham Castle**, southeast of Penrith, is a Norman castle built on the foundations of a Roman fort. The ruins are impressive and the top gallery of the keep has fine views for those who climb it.

Carlisle

Carlisle ⓭, just 21 miles (34 km) north of Penrith on the M6, also deserves an excursion. The **Castle** here obtained its unusual outline when its roof was strengthened to carry early cannons. It is linked by a pedestrian subway to the **Tullie House Museum and Art Gallery** (tel: 01228-618718; tulliehouse.co.uk; daily Mon–Sat from 10am, Sun from noon, or 11am July–Aug; charge) which houses a fine collection of Roman materials and Pre-Raphaelite paintings. There is a subterranean **Millennium Gallery** (same hours) outside, with archaeological exhibits and an oral history presentation.

To the west of Keswick, on the A66, lies **Cockermouth** ⓮, an old-fashioned stone-built town stretching along a lengthy main street, very like towns across the Scottish border. **Wordsworth House** (tel: 01900-820884; wordsworthhouse.org.uk; Apr–Oct Mon–Sat 11am–4.30pm, sometimes Sat; charge) is where William and Dorothy spent their earliest years.

Adjacent to the remains of **Cockermouth Castle** (privately owned and only occasionally open to the public) is **Jennings Brewery** (tel: 0845 1297185; jen-

BELOW: a steamer arrives at Glenridding Pier, Ullswater.

Recommended Restaurants and Pubs on page 319

ningsbrewery.co.uk; guided tours Jan, Feb, Nov and Dec, Mon–Fri 2pm, Sat 11am and 2pm; charge). Established over 150 years ago, the company moved to Cockermouth in 1874. The tour includes a sample of their real ales.

The western lakes

At the **Helena Thompson Museum** in **Workington** are displays charting the maritime and social history of the town (Tues–Sun 1.30–4.30pm, Jul–Aug 10.30am–4.30pm). **Workington Hall** in Curwen Park – refuge for Mary Queen of Scots during her last night of freedom in May 1568 – is a ruin, but plaques give visitors a flavour of the hall's long history, dating from the 14th century, when it was simply a pele tower.

Whitehaven ⓯ is a stimulating town, a redstone promontory with seabirds, handy to St Bees Head. The port's role in the rum trade unfolds at **The Rum Story** (daily 10am–4.30pm), set in the Jefferson family's 18th-century premises. Delve further into the area's history at **The Beacon** (daily 10am–4.30pm) with its five floors of interactive exhibits and galleries. A footpath leads from behind the Beacon to the **Haig Colliery Mining Museum** (daily 9.30am–4.30pm; tel: 01946 599949) on the former site of the Haig Pit. The pit's mighty steam winding engine is operated on most days and guided walks may be arranged.

Roman hairpins

Southwest Lakeland is rich in interest. One of the most dramatic sites of all is best approached on the Windermere-based "Mountain Goat" mini-coach service by anyone lacking both an extremely agile car and nerves of steel. The road over the Wrynose and Hardknott passes, 10 miles (16 km) west of Ambleside, was improved by the Romans, but they probably intended their narrow road with its hairpin bends and sheer drops for pedestrians only. In summer, today's traffic conditions can make it somewhat hazardous. But the situation of **Hardknott Roman Fort** ⓰ high above **Eskdale**, with its view of the highest peaks and the distant sea, is unforgettable.

Eskdale's mines and quarries were the reason for the construction of the **Ravenglass and Eskdale Railway** (known locally as the "Ratty"), a narrow-gauge line which delights summer visitors with its beautifully maintained miniature steam engines. The line runs for about 18 miles (28 km) through lush scenery. From **Eskdale Green** ⓱ a road runs over Birker Fell to the **Duddon Valley**, an area of great natural beauty still relatively unvisited.

Ravenglass ⓲, on the coast, lies close to **Muncaster Castle** (tel: 01229-717614; muncaster.co.uk; Mar–Oct Sun–Fri noon–4.30pm, gardens 10.30am–6pm; charge), home of the Pennington family since 1325, when a new tower was built on the foundations of a Roman watchtower commanding extensive views of the fells and Eskdale. Henry VI sought refuge here and is said to have given his drinking bowl, the "Luck of Muncaster", to his host. The bowl is still in the house which, in the course of 18th- and 19th-century alterations, has grown from a medieval tower into an attractive mansion.

Just off the A6 south of Penrith is the Lakeland Bird of Prey Centre which offers daily falconry displays. Visitors who wander around may see hawks, eagles and owls.

BELOW: Ravenglass and Eskdale Railway.

TIP

Cumbria grows fine organic produce, and you can visit the apple orchards and local breweries. Tourist information centres have food-themed trail leaflets exploring the diversity of local produce. including Ale Trail, Apple Appeal, A Taste of Honey, Damson Valleys, Organic Origins, and Sausage Secrets.

Abbey lands

The southern tip of Lakeland was in medieval days the heart of the great Cistercian estate farmed by the monks of **Furness Abbey** (tel: 01229-823420; Apr–Sep daily 10am–6pm, Oct–Mar Thur–Sun 10am–4pm; charge). The impressive ruins are set in the pretty Vale of Deadly Nightshade, on the northside of the shipbuilding town, **Barrow-in-Furness** ⑲. The Abbey was the second-richest Cistercian establishment in England prior to its suppression in 1537 during Henry VIII's Dissolution of the Monasteries. Its buildings date from the 12th and 15th centuries.

To the east is **Cartmel Priory** ⑳ (daily except during services), near the resort of Grange-over-Sands on a finger of land pointing down into Morecambe Bay. It was founded in 1188 by the Baron of Cartmel and was saved from destruction by the quick-wittedness of local people who claimed that it was, in fact, their parish church. The 15th-century tower is unusual; the upper part is set diagonally across the lower stage. Inside there is good medieval carving and old glass; the lovely east window also dates from the 15th century. The village setting is very attractive.

Returning northward, the visitor approaches the foot of Windermere (from where the **Haverthwaite and Lakeside Steam Railway** runs in season) and, to the west, **Coniston Water** ㉑. Between these lies **Grizedale Forest Park** ㉒, a large tract of land the Forestry Commission has imaginatively given over to nature trails, jolly modern sculptures and a 23-seat theatre. Coniston was famous for the residence of John Ruskin (1819–1900), the great Victorian art historian and writer on social and economic themes and later by the world water speed record attempts of Donald Campbell, who died in the last attempt in 1967.

On the lake, the Victorian steam yacht ***Gondola*** operates once again, with all the elegance of a Tissot painting. Visitors can disembark at **Brantwood** (tel: 015394 41962; brantwood.org.uk; daily Apr–Oct 11am–5.30pm, Nov–Mar 11am–4.30pm; charge), on the northeast shore of Coniston Water, where many of Ruskin's paintings are preserved. The house remains much as he left it, and the grounds, with their dramatic views of lake and fell, have been improved and developed. ❑

BELOW: Coniston, where canoes and kayaks as well as larger craft can be hired.

RESTAURANTS AND PUBS

Restaurants

Prices for a three-course dinner per person with a half-bottle of house wine:

£ = under £25
££ = £25–50
£££ = £50–100

Ambleside

The Glass House Restaurant
Rydal Road
Tel: 01539-432137 **£**
A 16th-century mill; Mediterranean and modern British food.

The Drunken Duck
Barngates
Tel: 01539-36347 **££**
www.drunkenduckinn.co.uk
Award-winning gastro pub serving its own ales.

Lucy's on a Plate
Church Street
Tel: 01539-431191 **£**
Warm, relaxing café with impressive dessert menu.

Zeffirellis
Compston Road
Tel: 01539-33845 **££**
Stylish wholefood restaurant with a pleasant buzz. There is also a café, a jazz bar and a four-screen cinema. The meal-and-cinema package offers good value.

Bowness-on-Windermere

Porthole Eating House
3 Ash Street
Tel: 01539-442793 **££**
Mediterranean food in informal surroundings. Extensive wine list.

Carlisle

Garden Restaurant
Tullie House Museum and Art Gallery, Castle Street
Tel: 01228-534781 **£**
Daily specials, a salad bar, home-baked treats.

Cartmel, nr Grange-Over-Sands

L'Enclume
Cavendish Street
Tel: 01539-536362 **£££**
Modern French cuisine in a stylishly converted blacksmith's workshop.

Cavendish Arms Hotel
Cavendish Street
Tel: 01539-536240 **££**
www.drunkenduckinn.co.uk
A 16th-century coaching inn with a high reputation for its catering.

Coniston

Jumping Jenny
Brantwood
Tel: 01539-41715 **£**
Coffees, teas and lunches at Brantwood, Ruskin's old home, east of Coniston Water. Magnificent Coniston views.

Crosthwaite, nr Kendal

Punch Bowl Inn
Tel: 01539-568237 **£**
Gastro-pub featuring French-style dishes prepared with local produce, all for very reasonable prices. Traditional ales.

Eskdale

The Woolpack Inn
Holmrook
Tel: 019467-23230 **£**
This well-known hostelry in the western Lake District serves reliably good food alongside a selection of real ales.

Grasmere

The Jumble Room
Langdale Road
Tel: 015394-35188 **£**
Attractive, comfortable restaurant offering a selection of dishes from around the world.

ABOVE: Cumberland sausage, a local delicacy.

Hawkshead

Queen's Head Hotel
Main Street
Tel: 01539-36271 **£**
Traditional English cuisine served in a mellow, wood-panelled room.

Keswick

Highfield Hotel Restaurant
The Heads
Tel: 01687-72508 **££**
Imaginative modern European cuisine and wonderful Lakeland views. The menu changes daily.

Whitehaven

The Waterfront
West Strand
Tel: 01946-691130 **££**
Harbourside bar and restaurant with friendly service and a variety of daily specials.

Windermere

Lake District Visitor Centre at Brockhole
National Park, between Windermere and Ambleside
Tel: 01539-724555 **££**
The café at Brockhole serves traditional Cumbrian recipes and there is outdoor seating.

Gilpin Lodge
Crook Road
Tel: 015394-88818 **£££**
This fine Lakeland country house hotel serves fresh and unfussy dishes using local produce.

Miller Howe
Rayrigg Road
Tel: 015394-42536 **£££**
Tasty local dishes served in a delightful setting. In good weather, try for a table on the terrace overlooking Lake Windermere.

Pubs

At Ambleside, **Kirkstone Pass Inn**, Lakeland's highest pub, is hiker-friendly. All-day food.

In Kendal, **Burgundy's Wine Bar** in Lowther Street also has a good range of bottled beers.

The Travellers Rest at Grasmere is comfortable, caters for children, and can suggest walks.

In Coniston, the **Sun Hotel**, dating to the 16th century, has a warm bar in winter and a pleasant beer garden in summer. **The Black Bull** has an outdoor seating area.

At Windermere, **The Queen's Head**, Troutbeck, is cosy, with oak beams, flag floor and log fire.

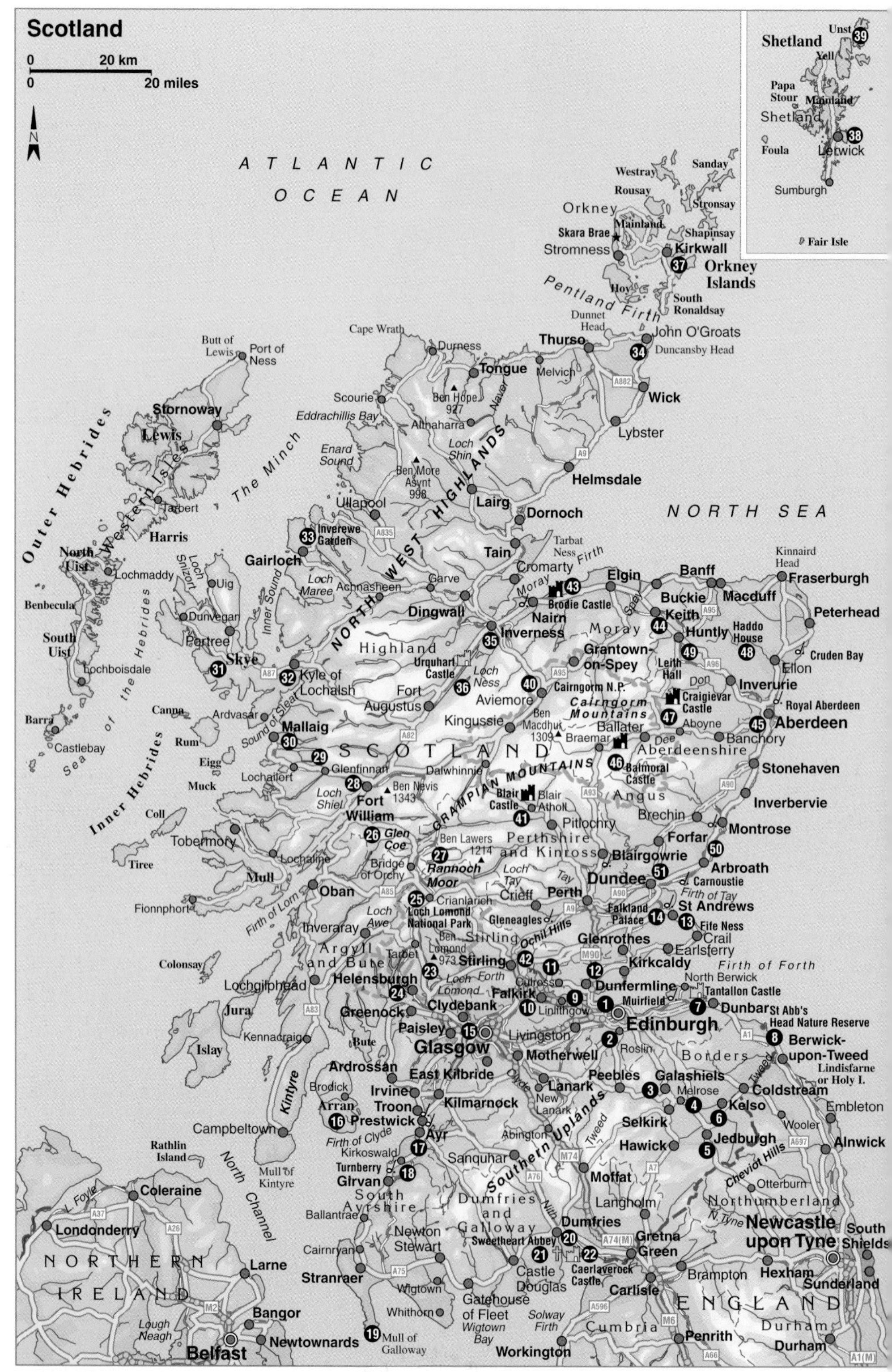
Scotland
0 20 km
0 20 miles
N
ATLANTIC OCEAN
NORTH SEA
Shetland
Unst
Yell
Papa Stour
Mainland
Shetland
Foula
Lerwick
Sumburgh
Fair Isle
Westray
Sanday
Rousay
Stronsay
Orkney
Mainland
Skara Brae
Shapinsay
Stromness
Kirkwall
Orkney Islands
Hoy
South Ronaldsay
Pentland Firth
Dunnet Head
John O'Groats
Duncansby Head
Thurso
Cape Wrath
Durness
Tongue
Melvich
Wick
Lybster
Ben Hope 927
Scourie
Eddrachillis Bay
Altnaharra
Loch Shin
Enard Sound
Ben More Assynt 998
Helmsdale
Lairg
Dornoch
Ullapool
Inverewe Garden
NORTH WEST HIGHLANDS
Tain
Tarbat Ness
Cromarty Firth
Cromarty
Gairloch
Loch Maree
Achnasheen
Garve
Dingwall
Moray Firth
Brodie Castle
Nairn
Inverness
Elgin
Banff
Buckie
Macduff
Keith
Huntly
Fraserburgh
Kinnaird Head
Peterhead
Haddo House
Cruden Bay
Ellon
Moray
Grantown-on-Spey
Leith Hall
Don
Inverurie
Craigievar Castle
Royal Aberdeen
Aberdeen
Highland
Urquhart Castle
Loch Ness
Fort Augustus
Aviemore
Cairngorm N.P.
Cairngorm Mountains
Kingussie
Ben Macdhui 1309
Braemar
Ballater
Aboyne
Banchory
Dee
Aberdeenshire
Stonehaven
SCOTLAND
GRAMPIAN MOUNTAINS
Balmoral Castle
Dalwhinnie
Blair Castle
Blair Atholl
Angus
Inverbervie
Brechin
Montrose
Pitlochry
Forfar
Perthshire and Kinross
Blairgowrie
Arbroath
Carnoustie
Dundee
Firth of Tay
Perth
St Andrews
Crieff
Falkland Palace
Fife Ness
Crail
Gleneagles
Glenrothes
Earlsferry
Kirkcaldy
Firth of Forth
North Berwick
Tantallon Castle
Ochil Hills
Stirling
Culross
Dunfermline
Falkirk
Linlithgow
Muirfield
Dunbar
St Abb's Head Nature Reserve
Edinburgh
Livingston
Roslin
Berwick-upon-Tweed
Lindisfarne or Holy I.
Motherwell
Borders
Peebles
Galashiels
Melrose
Coldstream
Lanark
New Lanark
Kelso
Embleton
Selkirk
Jedburgh
Wooler
Alnwick
Hawick
Cheviot Hills
Otterburn
Northumberland
Moffat
Langholm
N. Tyne
Newcastle upon Tyne
South Shields
Gretna Green
Dumfries
Hexham
Sunderland
Brampton
Carlisle
ENGLAND
Durham
Penrith
Cumbria
Workington
Solway Firth
Southern Uplands
Tweed
Clyde
Nith
Abington
Sanquhar
Dumfries and Galloway
Sweetheart Abbey
Castle Douglas
Caerlaverock Castle
Gatehouse of Fleet
Wigtown Bay
Wigtown
Whithorn
Mull of Galloway
Newton Stewart
Stranraer
Cairnryan
Ballantrae
South Ayrshire
Girvan
Turnberry
Kirkoswald
Firth of Clyde
Ayr
Prestwick
Troon
Irvine
Kilmarnock
East Kilbride
Ardrossan
Arran
Brodick
Bute
Glasgow
Paisley
Clydebank
Greenock
Helensburgh
Loch Lomond
Ben Lomond 973
Tarbet
Argyll and Bute
Loch Lomond National Park
Crianlarich
Loch Awe
Inveraray
Oban
Firth of Lorn
Rannoch Moor
Ben Lawers 1214
Loch Tay
Bridge of Orchy
Glen Coe
Fort William
Ben Nevis 1343
Loch Shiel
Glenfinnan
Lochailort
Mallaig
Sound of Sleat
Kyle of Lochalsh
Ardvasar
Skye
Portree
Dunvegan
Uig
Inner Sound
Loch Snizort
Lochmaddy
North Uist
Benbecula
South Uist
Lochboisdale
Barra
Castlebay
Sea of the Hebrides
Canna
Rum
Eigg
Muck
Coll
Tiree
Tobermory
Lochaline
Mull
Fionnphort
Colonsay
Jura
Islay
Lochgilphead
Kennacraig
Kintyre
Campbeltown
Mull of Kintyre
North Channel
Rathlin Island
Inner Hebrides
Outer Hebrides
Western Isles
The Minch
Butt of Lewis
Port of Ness
Stornoway
Lewis
Tarbert
Harris
Coleraine
L. Foyle
Londonderry
NORTHERN IRELAND
Larne
Lough Neagh
Bangor
Belfast
Newtownards
A882
A9
A835
A87
A82
A95
A96
A93
A90
A85
A83
M90
M74
A76
A7
A74(M)
A75
A596
M6
A66
A1
A697
A1(M)
A37
A26
M2

THE SCOTTISH LOWLANDS

Scotland is a place of endless variety: in the Lowlands there are hills and seascapes, impressive stately homes and the historic Burns country, and the vibrant cities of Edinburgh and Glasgow

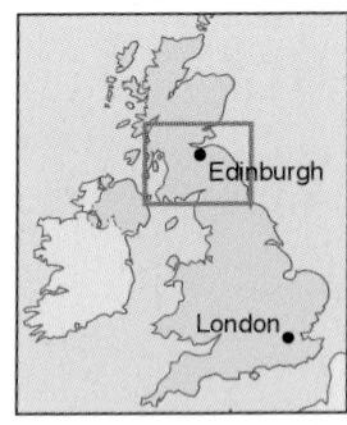

Scotland is a separate experience. The Scots themselves have a keen sense of identity, of different values, and of their own history and traditions unparalleled in Great Britain. The Scots joined England in the Union of the Crowns in 1603 – James VI of Scotland became James I of England, the first "British" monarch – and then in 1701 joined England in the Union of the Parliaments, whereby the two parliaments met jointly at Westminster. Scotland regained its own independent parliament in 1999. Throughout all they maintained their own legal and educational systems, widely regarded as superior to those in England, and continued to print their own design of bank notes – this is often the first clue to visitors that they are in a different country within Britain.

Occupying the north of Great Britain, two Roman emperors built walls across the country to keep in place the region's painted Celtic warriors, the Picts and the Scots: Hadrian's Wall *(see pages 293 and 304)* and the Antonine Wall on a line between Glasgow and Edinburgh. Scotland's 30,400 sq miles (78,740 sq km) cover one-third of Great Britain yet its population, of which more than 30 percent live in or around the three most populous cities, Edinburgh, Glasgow and Aberdeen, is less than one-tenth of the whole. Aberdeen, on the northeast coast, boomed in the 1970s with the discovery of North Sea oil.

Glasgow and Edinburgh, stimulating but quite different cities, lie only 43 miles (69 km) apart at opposite sides of the Lowlands, hidden from England by the rolling Southern Uplands and a breather before the dramatic hurdles of the Highlands. Both cities are about 380 miles (610 km) from London.

Scotland's capital

Between the Pentland Hills and the Firth (estuary) of Forth, **Edinburgh ❶** has one of the most stunning settings in the world. On the south side of its main thoroughfare of **Princes Street**, beyond sunken gardens, rises the basalt ridge on

Main attractions
EDINBURGH
ABBOTSFORD HOUSE
MELROSE ABBEY
TANTALLON CASTLE
HOPETOUN HOUSE
LINLITHGOW PALACE
DUNFERMLINE ABBEY
ST ANDREWS
GLASGOW
ROBERT BURNS COTTAGE
CULZEAN CASTLE
DUMFRIES

PRECEDING PAGES: tossing the caber. **BELOW:** Royal Mile piper, Edinburgh.

The One O'Clock Gun is fired at Edinburgh Castle.

At Edinburgh Castle don't miss the display of the Scottish crown, sceptre and sword of state – the oldest royal regalia in Europe.

which medieval Edinburgh is built. The imposing **Castle** Ⓐ (daily, Apr–Sept 9.30am–6pm, Oct–Mar till 5pm, entrance charge, edinburghcastle.gov.uk) dominates the horizon.

In the castle complex is the 12th-century **St Margaret's Chapel**, built for the wife of King Malcolm Canmore by her son, David I; the imposing **Great Hall**, which is still used for banquets and has one of the most magnificent hammer-beam ceilings in Britain; the tiny room where in 1566 Mary Queen of Scots gave birth to James VI of Scotland (James I of England); and the **National War Memorial**. Also to be seen are the crown jewels and the Stone of Destiny, or Stone of Scone, the coronation seat of Scottish kings.

The Royal Mile

Four streets – **Castlehill**, **Lawnmarket**, **High Street** and **Canongate** – make up the **Royal Mile** Ⓑ, which descends from the vast esplanade in front of the castle (where the spectacular Tattoo is held in August) and ends in the Palace of Holyroodhouse. This, the centre of Edinburgh life until the end of the 18th century, is still lively today. Along its route are some of the best examples of 16th- and 17th-century houses in Britain.

At the top is the **Scotch Whisky Heritage Centre** (daily 10am–5pm, extended hours in summer), which provides a thorough briefing of the Scottish national drink and a free dram at the end of the tour, and the nearby **Camera Obscura** (daily, entrance charge), where an extraordinary machine projects live images of the surrounding city.

Further along stands **Parliament House**, now the law courts (Mon–Fri); the **High Kirk of St Giles** Ⓒ (daily except during services) with the magnificent **Thistle Chapel**; **John Knox House**

Edinburgh

0 200 m
0 200 yds

Recommended Restaurants and Pubs on page 335

Museum (Mon–Sat 10am–5pm, Sun Jul–Sept 12–6pm), from whose windows the ruthless Protestant reformer once preached; the 16th-century **Canongate Tolbooth** (housing the **People's Story**; Mon–Sat 10am–5pm); and the Dutch-looking 17th-century **Canongate Kirk**.

The **Museum of Childhood** (High Street; tel: 0131-529 4142; vam.ac.uk; free) has displays of historical toys and daily creative activities for children.

The **Palace of Holyroodhouse** **D** (daily, Apr–Oct 9.30am–5pm, Nov–Mar until 3.30pm; royal.gov.uk; charge) is the official residence of the Queen when she visits Scotland. Tours (40 minutes) reveal French and Flemish tapestries and furniture and grant a fascinating insight into grisly times. The palace was begun in 1498 by James IV, enlarged by James V and later by Charles II and has close associations with Mary Queen of Scots. The last of the Stuarts to live here was Charles Edward Stuart (1720–88), remembered as Bonnie Prince Charlie.

The **Queen's Gallery** (daily, same times; joint ticket available), situated in front of the palace, has changing exhibits from the priceless Royal Collection.

The Royal Mile, outside the High Kirk of St Giles. The mile-long route is a mix of tourist shops, pubs and eateries, and is also the location for Scotland's main legal institutions.

Across the road is the controversial **Scottish Parliament** (open to the public daily), completed in 2004 after exceeding its £40 million building budget by more than 10 times. Nearby, under the Salisbury Crags, is **Our Dynamic Earth** (daily, 10am–5pm, Jul–Aug 6pm; admission charge) with interactive displays on the formation and evolution of the planet.

New Town classicism

The New Town, on the far side of the gardens below the castle, is a splendid example of 18th-century town planning, in marked contrast to the medieval chaos of the Old Town. This intriguing architectural juxtaposition is matched

BELOW: Edinburgh Castle is a rich architectural mix of palace, fortress, barracks, chapel and war memorial.

A statue to Greyfriars Bobby remembers the faithful Skye Terrier who kept watch for 14 years, from 1858 to 1872, over his master's grave.

nowhere else in Europe. (Both the Old and the New Town are Unesco World Heritage Sites.)

At the **Georgian House** Ⓔ (daily, Mar–Nov 10am–4.30pm; admission charge) at 7 Charlotte Square, a reconstructed elegant interior may be viewed.

To the east of Princes Street **Calton Hill**, another volcanic outcrop, offers stunning views of the city. Crowning the hill are the old **City Observatory** Ⓕ, with a Grecian-style dome; the **National Monument**, an unfinished copy of the Parthenon in Athens; and the **Nelson Monument** (Apr–Sept Mon 1–6pm, Tues–Sat, 10am–6pm, Oct–Mar Mon–Sat 10am–3pm; admission charge).

On the hill's lower slopes are the **Burns Monument** and the **Old Calton Burial Ground** where many of the great names of Scotland's 18th-century Enlightenment are interred.

North of Calton Hill is **Leith** where the decommissioned but glittering royal yacht ***Britannia*** (daily 10am–4.30pm, 3.30pm in winter; admission charge) is permanently moored at the **Ocean Terminal**, which has 75 stores, bars and restaurants as well as a 12-screen cinema.

West of the New Town lies **Dean Village**, a picturesque haunt in the deep valley of the Water of Leith. From here, a stroll along the Water of Leith Walkway leads under Thomas Telford's **Dean Bridge** and past **St Bernard's Well** within a Roman-style temple. To the north is the **Royal Botanic Garden** Ⓖ (open daily), 70 acres (28 hectares) of woodland, flora and glasshouses.

It is tempting to linger in Edinburgh to explore all its museums and art galleries, especially the **National Gallery of Scotland** Ⓗ on The Mound (daily, 10am–5pm, Thurs till 7pm; nationalgalleries.org), which has Britain's biggest collection of Old Masters outside London. Then there's the **Scottish National Portrait Gallery** Ⓘ in Queen's Street, picturing the nation's great and good, and, for local history, the **Royal Museum and Museum of Scotland** Ⓙ, both in Chambers Street; and the **Scottish National Gallery of Modern Art** and **Dean Gallery** of modern art in Belford Street (all Mon–Sat 10am–5pm, Sun noon–5pm).

In addition, there are numerous historic restaurants, colourful pubs (espe-

BELOW: the view from Calton Hill. **RIGHT:** the former royal yacht *Britannia*.

Recommended Restaurants and Pubs on page 335

cially on **Rose Street**), antique shops and sporting facilities (golf courses abound in and around the city). And visitors in August can enjoy the world's biggest arts festival. While the main Edinburgh International Festival attracts world-class companies, the Festival Fringe is where hundreds of self-financing artistes perform wherever they can – churches, toilets, elevators, streets. Concurrently, the International Book Festival, the International Jazz Festival and the International Film Festival and the Tattoo take place.

South to the Borders

Beyond the hills ringing Edinburgh to the south lie the **Borders**. This is Scotland along the frontier with England, north of the Cheviot Hills and the mouths of the rivers Esk and Tweed, the first part of Scotland to encounter the Romans, the Angles and the English on their fruitless thrusts northwards. Today, it is gentle, pastoral country with rolling green hills and bright clear streams where farming, knitwear and tweed remain the principal industries, and the passions are for trout and salmon fishing and rugby, of which the Border towns are the great Scottish stronghold.

Leaving Edinburgh by the A703 the village of **Roslin** ❷ is soon reached. The interior of the 15th-century **Rosslyn Chapel** (Mon–Sat 9.30am–6pm, Sun 12–4.45; admission charge) is covered with an abundance of fascinating stone carvings – "a Bible in Stone". It gained added renown when the novel *The Da Vinci Code* reiterated the long-held belief that within the chapel lies the Holy Grail.

Further south, 36 miles (44 km) from Edinburgh, overlooking the River Tweed outside **Galashiels** ❸, is **Abbotsford House** (daily mid-Mar–Oct 9.30am–5pm; Mar–May, Oct Sun 2–5pm; admission charge), which was the home of the popular historical novelist Sir Walter Scott (1771–1832) and which is full of Scott memorabilia. His family were Border people, and his romantic imagination was first stirred by the derring-do of his ancestors defending their land against England, the "Auld Enemy".

Historic reminders

Sitting beneath the triple mounds of the **Eildon Hills**, **Melrose** ❹, 2 miles (3 km) east of Abbotsford, was the haunt of poet and seer Thomas de Rhymer (*c*.1220–97). From the highest hill a breathtaking view of the Cheviots and the hills running westwards towards Galloway can be enjoyed. In the town stand the ruins of 12th-century **Melrose Abbey**, which despite its sacking by the English in 1544 are an architectural poem in red sandstone. Melrose is an agreeable base from which to walk the Eildon Hills, fish, or explore the Borders.

Nearby are other glorious medieval abbeys: at **Dryburgh**, 4 miles (6 km) beyond Melrose where Scott is buried; at Kelso, 10 miles (16 km) east on the A699 (Mon–Sat and Sun pm); and at **Jedburgh** ❺, 8 miles (13 km) south of Dryburgh on the A68 (All three abbeys are open daily, 9.30–5.30, 4.30 in winter; admission charge; *see page 337*).

Several impressive stately homes such as **Floors Castle** (Apr–Oct daily 10am–4.30pm; admission charge), the largest inhabited castle in Scotland and seat of the Duke of Roxburgh, just outside

Abbotsford's collection of historical relics, armour and weapons includes Rob Roy's gun, Montrose's sword and a quaich (drinking bowl) which belonged to Bonnie Prince Charlie.

BELOW: Abbotsford House and gardens.

The approach to Linlithgow Palace, where most of the Stuart kings lived.

Kelso ❻ are open to the public. Also open are the Duke of Buccleuch's house, **Bowhill**, near **Selkirk** (July only, daily; estate, visitor centre and adventure playground Apr–Aug Sat–Thur noon–5pm; admission charge), and the Adam house of **Mellerstain** on the A6089 Kelso to Gordon road (Easter and May–Sept Sun, Wed; Jul–Aug, Sun–Mon, Wed–Thur 12.30–5pm; admission charge). All have fine collections of paintings and furniture and Mellerstain has some of the best Adam ceilings in Britain.

The Firth of Forth

East Lothian, to the east of Edinburgh, has a littoral dotted with golf courses, castles and nature reserves and, beyond the Lammermuir Hills, a wide hinterland of lush farmland. Some of the best links are the four Gullane courses (including Muirfield – an Open Championship course), North Berwick, Longniddry, Luffness and Dunbar.

Charming **Dirleton Castle** stands in the centre of a delightful eponymous village on the A198 between Gullane and North Berwick while **Tantallon Castle** ❼ is an imposing ruin on a headland above the North Sea off the A198 between North Berwick and Dunbar (both sites Apr–Sept daily 9.30am–5.30pm, 4.30pm in winter; charge).

Enormous colonies of gannets and other seabirds populate the spectacular **Bass Rock** that stands 2 miles (3 km) offshore from **North Berwick**; boat excursions are available between May and September. Alternatively, state-of-the-art technology in the **Scottish Seabird Centre** shows all that is happening on Bass Rock on giant video screens (10am–6pm, shorter hours in winter; check the birdlife on live webcams at seabird.org). The same birds can be seen further south at **St Abb's Head Nature Reserve** ❽, an impressive headland jutting into the sea.

Closer to Edinburgh is **Aberlady Bay**, whose splendid dune-backed beach is a nature reserve that attracts 200 species of migrant birds. Near **Haddington**, a town of 17th- and 18th-century houses, 6 miles (10 km) inland from here, stands **Lennoxlove House** (Easter–Oct Wed, Thur and Sun 11.30am–3pm, admission charge), seat of the Dukes of Hamilton and now a smart hotel where you can sleep in a four-poster once used by Mary Queen of Scots.

BELOW: the annual Loony Dook swim on New Year's Day attracts hardy participants, many in fancy dress.

Ancient and modern

On Edinburgh's western fringe is **South Queensferry** where stands **Hopetoun House** (Apr–Oct daily 10.30am–5pm; admission charge), a glorious, massive Georgian pile belonging to the Marquess of Linlithgow. The work of several great Scottish architects, including the Adam family, it has a sumptuous interior with many "masters" that competes with the vast grounds where red and fallow deer and four-horned St Kilda's sheep graze. The observatory affords a splendid view of the Forth Bridge, a Scottish icon.

From here the M9 leads in a handful of miles to **Linlithgow** ❾, where, above a loch and park (peel), stands the roofless red sandstone shell of **Linlithgow Palace** (daily, 9.30am–5.30pm, 4.30pm in win-

Recommended Restaurants and Pubs on page 335

ter, admission charge), home of the Stewart kings, where Mary Queen of Scots was born. The adjacent **Church of St Michael** is the largest pre-Reformation church to survive in Scotland. Here, James IV saw the ghost that warned him of his defeat at Flodden Field.

A further 10 miles (16 km) leads to **Falkirk** ⑩ and the **Falkirk Wheel**, the world's first rotating boat-lift. In 2003, converging moribund canals at different levels were linked, not by customary locks, but by a 135-ft (35-metre) high rotating wheel which lifts boats in gondolas between the two canals. Visitors can enjoy the ride, too.

The Kingdom of Fife

Across the wide estuary of the Firth of Forth lies **Fife**, or "the Kingdom of Fife" as it is still known from its days of insistent independence. Coal mines and industry were ubiquitous here and although the countryside is not dramatic it has some surprises. On its western fringes, along the north bank of the Forth and upriver towards Stirling, is **Culross** ⑪, a perfectly preserved example of a small Scottish borough of the 16th and 17th centuries. It was once one of Scotland's major ports trading in coal, salt and griddle pans for making scones. Run by the National Trust for Scotland, the Palace can be visited but the Study and Town House are by guided tours only (daily June–Aug 12–5pm, Mar–May and Sept–Oct closed Tues–Wed; admission charge).

To the east is **Dunfermline** ⑫, the ancient Scottish capital, with a 12th-century **Abbey** (daily, 9.30am–5.30pm, 4.30pm, closed Fri Nov–Mar; admission charge) where Scotland's liberator Robert the Bruce was buried in 1329. The birthplace of Andrew Carnegie (1835–1918), the weaver's son who became America's greatest steel baron and one of the world's major philanthropists, is now the **Andrew Caregie Birthplace Museum** (Apr–Sept Mon–Sat 11am–5pm, Sun 2–5pm).

On the coast of the easternmost promontory of the Neuk are the pretty fishing ports of **Earlsferry**, **St Monans**, **Pittenweem**, **Anstruther** and **Crail**. A few miles northwest is Fife's most famous town, **St Andrews** ⑬, with a plethora of golf links including the Old Course where golf has been played for 600

TIP

Offshore at St Abb's is a marine nature reserve with some of the best scuba diving in Scotland. Divers must get a permit from the Ranger.

BELOW: the Falkirk Wheel, a major engineering feat that links two canals at different levels between Edinburgh and Glasgow.

Glasgow's Scottish Exhibition and Conference Centre, on the River Clyde, is popularly known as "the Armadillo."

years, and the **British Golf Museum** (Apr–Oct Mon–Sat 9.30am–5.30pm, Sun 10am–5pm; winter 10am–4pm; admission charge). Other sights in the town are one of Britain's oldest universities (founded in 1412), ecclesiastical ruins and remains of a castle with a grisly history of murders, perched on the sea's edge.

Inland is **Falkland Palace** ⓮ (Mar–Oct Mon–Sat 10am–5pm, Sun 1–5pm; admission charge), hunting lodge of the Stuarts from James IV to Mary Queen of Scots, where a "real" (or "royal") tennis court is still in use. Near **Cupar** is the elegant Edwardian mansion known as the **Hill of Tarvit** (May–Oct daily noon–5pm; closed Tues–Wed May, Sept–Oct; grounds daily 9.30am–sunset; admission charge) with a splendid selection of furniture, tapestries and paintings. Hampers are available for picnics in the grounds.

Glasgow

Glasgow ⓯ straddles the River Clyde 14 miles (23 km) from the estuary. It grew rich on shipbuilding and heavy engineering and by the end of the 19th century was Britain's second-largest city. However, the solid manufacturing base on which the city was founded was whipped from under it during the recession of the 1970s. Although unemployment rose distressingly and the population has declined to just over 600,000, an extraordinary renaissance occurred and in 1990 Glasgow was nominated City of Culture by the European Union. It has Scotland's national football stadium, at **Hampden Park**, which will be used as part of the 2012 Olympics.

Glasgow's culture is not all newly created. Its 12th-century **Cathedral** was the only Scottish medieval cathedral to escape the destruction of the Reformation. Adjacent to it is the **St Mungo Museum of Religious Life & Art**, which faces the **Provand's Lordship**, the city's oldest house (1471), now a museum (both museums open daily 10am–5pm, Fri and Sun from 11am).

In the city centre is the seminal art nouveau **School of Art** (guided tours April–Sept, 10am–5pm; gsa.ac.uk) of Charles Rennie Mackintosh. On nearby Sauchiehall Street stands the **Willow**

BELOW RIGHT: Glasgow's George Square by night.

A Tale of Two Cities

The Scottish Lowlands are divided into west and east, by character as much as by geography. Easterners regard themselves as people of taste and refinement, reflected in the ordered glory of Georgian Edinburgh. They approve of the city's sobriquet "Athens of the North". Just 43 miles (69 km) away, the westerners of industrial Glasgow consider themselves warm-hearted, less pretentious and more down-to-earth than the scions of the Scottish capital. Glasgow's ambience is closer to that of a US city than any other metropolis in Britain ("If you've got it, flaunt it!").

It's true that there is something austere in Edinburgh's beauty and this, at times, is reflected in the reserved nature of its citizens. Glaswegians, by contrast, are ebullient and demonstrative, with a black, sardonic humour nurtured by the hard times they endured when the city's industrial base, which helped power the British Empire, weakened in the 20th century.

Culturally, Edinburgh flaunts its annual arts festival, the world's biggest *(left)*. But Glaswegians point out that they don't need this annual binge – *their* culture is vibrant for 12 months of the year. There's truth in this too.

Tea-room with an immaculate Mackintosh setting. More Mackintosh can be seen in the Glasgow University area where a reconstruction of his home is an integral part of the **Hunterian Art Gallery** (Mon–Sat 9.30am–5pm), which has a superb Whistler collection. Also in this part of town is the **Kelvingrove Art Gallery & Museum** (daily, 10am–5pm, Fri and Sun from 11am), which houses an impressive collection of paintings including works from the *fin-de-siècle* Glasgow Boys, the post-war Scottish Colourists and today's Glasgow Boys.

Across the road is the excellent **Museum of Transport** (daily, 10am–5pm, Fri and Sun from 11am; free guided tours). Back in the city centre is the **Gallery of Modern Art** on Queen Street (same hours as St Mungo).

On the south bank of the River Clyde stand the futuristic buildings of the **Science Centre** (daily, 10am–5pm) together with the 423-ft (127-metre), 360-degree revolving **Glasgow Tower**, which, to minimise wind resistance, can turn along its entire height into the wind. A viewing platform is at 345 ft (105 metres) and the complex contains an IMAX cinema.

Glasgow's Museum of Transport.

Still on the south side, lustre is added to **Pollok Country Park** by the **Burrell Collection** (daily 10am–5pm, Fri and Sun from 11am), an extraordinary bequest of shipowner Sir William Burrell (1861–1958) of 8,000 ancient artefacts and Impressionist paintings. The purpose-built gallery, completed in 1983, is part of the show. Also in the park is **Pollok House** (daily 10am–5pm) with works of Goya, El Greco and William Blake.

A short taxi ride takes you to the beautiful **House for an Art Lover** (Apr–Sept Mon–Wed 10am–4pm, Thur–Sun 10am–1pm; winter Sat, Sun, 10am–1pm, weekdays vary, phone for times: 0141-353 4770; admission charge) designed by Charles Rennie Mackintosh in 1901, but not built until 1994.

Robert Burns country

Glasgow is an easy city to exit. A motorway (M8) runs through the city centre to link with the M77, which leads south to Ayrshire, the land of Robert Burns and of

LEFT: Charles Rennie Mackintosh's House for an Art Lover. **BELOW:** Kelvingrove Art Gallery.

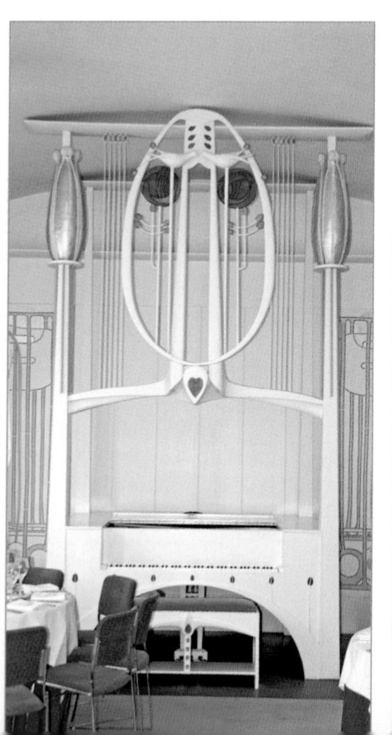

A Night with Robert Burns

Nearly a quarter of a million people around the world belong to Burns clubs – the Scottish poet's popularity has never waned

Few English people know the day on which William Shakespeare was born (23 April), but every Scot is aware that 25 January is the birthday of their country's most celebrated poet, Robert Burns. Indeed, a surprising number of people around the world suddenly recall the few drops of Scottish blood lurking in their veins.

Babbity Bowster's, a pub and hotel in a Robert Adam house in Blackfriars Street, Glasgow, has a reputation for its Burns Nights. Throughout the year its upstairs restaurant serves Scottish fare such as cullen skink (smoked haddock and potato soup), stovies (potatos cooked with onion), Loch Etive mussels and hot goat's cheese on wholemeal toast. On Burns Night it is equally traditional. Just after 7.30pm, a kilted bagpiper pipes in the first course of haggis, bashed neeps and tatties. (Haggis is made with sheep's or calf's offal, oatmeal, suet, onions and seasoning boiled in the skin of an animal's stomach, although the restaurant has a vegetarian alternative; bashed neeps are mashed turnips; tatties are potatoes.) Next comes a main course of perhaps venison in port, or beef marinaded in whisky. A chocolate pudding may round off the meal. And all this, of course, is washed down with *usquebaugh*, the water of life. In this case the whisky will be single malt (unblended and the product of one distillery). Meanwhile, guests read poems from Burns's works, starting with *Address to the Haggis*, and the evening ends after midnight as everyone crosses arms, holds hands and sings a rousing chorus of *Auld Lang Syne*.

This song was one of some 200 ballads Burns collected or re-cast for the Scots Musical Museum. "It has never been in print nor even in manuscript until I took it down from an old man singing," said Burns, though the tune may have been added later.

Burns, the "heaven-taught ploughman" was a well-educated farmer's son, born in 1759 in Alloway in Ayrshire, south of Glasgow *(see opposite page)*. The inevitable Burns Heritage Trail takes in most of the two dozen museums, mausoleum, inns and houses associated with the 37 years of his life. He was 26 when *Poems, chiefly in the Scottish Dialect* first won over Edinburgh's literary society.

Burns could write perfectly good English and the fact that some of his Scottish dialect was just as unintelligible to its audience then as it is to us now didn't matter. It was Scottish, and something to be proud of. Burns supported the French Revolution and his lines on liberty and justice have touched a chord in peoples in many nations. But most of all Burns is celebrated for his carousing, his love of drink and good company and his lack of domestic responsiblity.

No wonder women were, for so long, excluded from Burns Nights. Even today they are liable to be a minority of the 200,000 who belong to Burns clubs in about 20 countries, from the Pacific Rim to Russia, where the "Ploughman Poet", champion of the workers, is particularly revered. ❑

ABOVE: Burns's birthplace at Alloway in Ayrshire.
LEFT: the mature poet had many casual love affairs.

the seaside resorts of **Troon**, **Prestwick**, **Ayr** and **Girvan**. Before taking this route make a detour down the M70 to **New Lanark**, home to the social visionary Robert Owen (1771–1858). New Lanark was a model community based around water-powered cotton mills. At this World Heritage Site (daily 11am–5pm; charge) the visitor can see the village as it was, including working textile machinery).

North of Troon is **Adrossan** from where ferries leave for **Arran** ⓰, Glasgow's favourite holiday isle. Opulently furnished **Brodick Castle**, (Apr–Oct daily 11am–4pm; grounds daily all year 9.30am–sunset; charge), parts of which date from the 14th century and have associations with Robert the Bruce, lies at the foot of 3,000-ft (900-metre) Goatfell.

Further up the coast are **Largs** and **Wemyss Bay** from where ferries sail to the islands of **Great Cumbrae** and **Bute**.

The Ayrshire coast opposite the island of Arran has some of the best golf courses in Scotland including two Open Championship venues – Royal Troon and Turnberry. To the south of Ardrossan is **Ayr** ⓱, 35 miles (56 km) southwest of Glasgow. On the edge of the town is **Alloway** and the **Burns National Heritage Park** whose centrepiece is **Burns Cottage** (daily, Apr–Sept 9.30am– 5.30pm, Oct–Mar 10am–5pm; charge), the "auld clay biggin" where the poet was born. At **Kirkoswald** ⓲, 12 miles (20 km) south on the A77, is **Souter Johnnie's Cottage** (Mar–Sept 11.30m–5pm; charge), home of the "ancient, trusty, druthy crony" featured in Burns' poem *Tam O'Shanter* and now a museum.

On the coast, close to Kirkoswald, stands **Culzean Castle** (Apr–Oct daily 10.30am–4pm; visitor centre, shops, restaurant and grounds open in winter Thurs–Sun; admission charge), one of the greatest achievements of the 18th-century Scottish architect, Robert Adam. A suite on the top floor was given as a life tenure to General Dwight Eisenhower. In addition to paintings, weapons and porcelain, a museum commemorates the US President's achievements.

Moving south

In the southwestern-most corner of Scotland lies Dumfries and Galloway, an area full of pretty habitations along the **Solway Firth** and exquisite wild moorlands

*The coastal town of **Irvine** is the home of the **Scottish Maritime Museum** (open daily; tel: 01294-278283; admission charge). Visitors can board various lovingly restored vessels, including the steam yacht **Carola**, tour a shipyard worker's tenement flat restored to its 1920s appearance, peruse the exhibition and have a coffee in the Puffer Bar.*

BELOW: this area of Scotland has some of the country's best golf courses.

Caerlaverock Castle, originally built between 1280 and 1300 and rebuilt in the 17th century.

BELOW: the Samye Ling Buddhist Monastery and Tibetan Centre was founded in 1967 at Eskdalemuir, 26 miles (42km) northeast of Dumfries. it is possible to take a tour or stay overnight (tel: 013873-73232 ext 232).

in the interior. It culminates in the west in the **Mull of Galloway** ⓳, a hammerhead peninsula with sandy beaches, cliffs and hills. The northern inlet is **Loch Ryan**, famous for oysters, on whose east shore is **Cairnryan**, the principal departure port from Scotland to the Irish coast. **Wigtown**, on the neighbouring promontory, is Scotland's "book town" south of which is **Whithorn**, site of the first known Christian church in Britain. The area has several charming gardens – Castle Kennedy, Glenwhan, Logan – open to the public.

The A75 runs eastwards, passing close to **Kirkcudbright** (pronounced *care-***coo***-bree*), an artists' colony whose essence lies in exquisite **Broughton House** (12–5pm Mar–Jun Thur–Mon, Jul–Aug daily, Sept–Oct Thur–Mon; charge), home of artist E.A. Hornel (1864–1933).

Dumfries

And so to **Dumfries** ⓴, the largest town in southwest Scotland. Burns spent the last years of his life here, and the house where he died in 1796 is now a museum, the **Burns House** (Apr–Sept Mon–Sat 10am–5pm, Sun 2–5pm, Oct–Mar Tue–Sat 10am–1pm, 2–5pm). A statue to Burns stands on High Street and his chair is preserved in the nearby **Globe Inn**, one of his favourite taverns. The **Robert Burns Centre** on Mill Road (open as Burns House) has audio-visual displays and exhibits illustrating the life and work of the poet.

South of Dumfries, on opposite banks of the Neith where it debouches into the Solway Firth, are the red sandstone ruins of **Sweetheart Abbey** ㉑ (Apr–Sept Mon–Sat 9.30am–6.30pm, Sun 2–6pm Oct–Mar Mon–Wed, Sat, 9.30am–4.30pm, Thurs, Sun 2–4.30pm; admission charge), founded in the 14th century by Devorgilla, Lady of Galloway, in memory of her husband John Balliol, founder of Balliol College, Oxford. She carried his heart with her after his death, and it was was buried with her.

Also here are the strikingly well-preserved ruins of moated **Caerlaverock Castle** ㉒ (Apr–Sept daily 9.30–5.30, winter till 4.30pm; admission charge), a romantic setting and consequently a popular place for weddings. ❑

RESTAURANTS AND PUBS

Restaurants

Prices for a three-course meal per person with a half-bottle of house wine:

£ = under £25
££ = £25–50
£££ = £50–100

For a wide choice of restaurants in Edinburgh and Glasgow, contact the tourist offices:

Edinburgh
Tel: 0131-473 3800
www.edinburgh.org

Glasgow
Tel: 0141-204 4480
www.seeglasgow.com

Anstruther

Cellar
24 East Green
Tel: 01333-310378 **££**
Old stone walls and peat fires give this well-decorated restaurant a very cosy atmosphere. Fish is a speciality.

Cupar

The Peat Inn
Tel: 01334-840206 **££**
Food here is first-rate, based on French cuisine with local ingredients, and including a 'tasting' menu. Served stylishly in beautifully furnished rooms (there is also accommodation). Superb wine list comprising more than 400 bins.

Edinburgh

The Atrium
10 Cambridge Street
Tel: 0131-228 8882 **££**
Located in the popular Traverse Theatre, this award-winning restaurant serves good food – much of it artesan sourced – unfussily in mellow, contemporary ambience.

Oloroso
33 Castle Street
Tel: 0131-226 7614 **££**
An office block foyer and lift lead to this fashionable restaurant with two sides made entirely of glass. Innovative food is cooked to precision. Bar snacks are a good alternative. Splendid views from outdoor terrace.

The Witchery
352 Castlehill, Royal Mile
Tel: 0131-225 5613 **££**
House classics include hot smoked salmon with leeks and hollandaise and Angus beef fillet with smoked garlic broth. The upstairs restaurant is dark and deeply Gothic while downstairs is bright with lots of greenery and and a small terrace. Excellent wine list.

Glasgow

Brian Maule at Chardon D'Or
176 West Regent Street
Tel: 0141-248 3801 **££–£££**
Rich, delightful Scottish-French cuisine served in chic upmarket space.

Mother India
8 Westminster Terrace
Tel: 0141-221 1663 **£**
This is Glagow's – and possibly Scotland's – best curry house, known for its legendary home-cooked food. It is licensed but you can also bring your own bottles.

Rogano
11 Exchange Place
Tel: 0141-248 4055 **££**
This Art Deco restaurant has a slightly austere ambience. A downstairs bistro is more informal.

ABOVE: Glasgow's Willow Tea Rooms pay tribute to the design genius of Charles Rennie Mackintosh (1868–1928).

The Ubiquitous Chip
12 Ashton Lane
Tel: 0141-334 5007 **££**
Long-established, in a verdant courtyard off a cobbled street, serving fine traditional and modern Scottish cuisine. 150 malt whiskies. Light meals in brasserie.

Gullane

Greywalls
Muirfield
Tel: 1620-842144 **££–£££**
Formal dining in Lutyens-designed country house hotel. Quality Scottish produce in restaurant overlooking golf course. (Apr–Oct).

Linlithgow

Champany Inn
Tel: 01506-834532 **££–£££**
Peaceful and atmospheric with reputation as "best steakhouse in Britain". Seafood is also excellent. Many South African wines.

Troon

MacCallums' Oyster Bar
The Harbour
Tel: 01292-319339 **££**
Beautifully cooked seafood and fish in atmospheric venue in the heart of the fishmarket.

Pubs

In Edinburgh, **Abbotsford** in Rose Street is an ornate Victorian pub and restaurant. **Bow Bar**, on West Bow below the Castle, serves very well-kept beers to serious drinkers. You can sup beneath chandeliers in **Café Royal** on West Register Street. **Cloisters Bar** on Brougham Street is a former parsonage. The **Oxford Bar** on Young Street has Robert Burns memorabilia and has featured in Ian Rankin's Inspector Rebus novels.

In Glasgow, **Babbity Bowster** on Blackfriars Street is a lively mix of old and modern well liked by media types. **Blackfriars** on Bell Sreet has good beer and jazz and comedy evenings. **Bon Accord** on North Street is noted for its real ale. **The Counting House** in St Vincents Place, George Square, is a large Wetherspoons pub in a converted 1870s bank. **The Horseshoe** on Drury Street near Central Station has a bar that goes on for ever, making it easier to get served.

Castles and Abbeys

An Englishman's home may be his castle but for centuries and, in some instances even today, a Scotsman's castle has been his home

Dotted throughout the Scottish landscape are more than 2,000 castles, many in ruins but others in splendid condition. The latter, still occupied, do not fulfil the primary definition of "castle" – a fortified building – but rather meet the secondary definition: a large, magnificent house.

Either way, all are not merely part of Scottish history: they are its essence. Many carry grim and grisly tales. Thus, Hugh Macdonald was imprisoned in the bowels of Duntulum Castle and fed generous portions of salted beef, but he was denied anything – even whisky – to drink.

In 1746 Blair Castle was, on the occasion of the Jacobite uprising, the last castle in the British isles to be fired upon in anger. Today, the Duke of Atholl, the owner of Blair Castle, is the only British subject permitted to maintain a private army, the Atholl Highlanders. Prior to the siege, Bonnie Prince Charlie slept here (visitors might be excused for believing there are few castles in Scotland where either the Bonnie Prince or Mary, Queen of Scots, did not sleep at various times).

You, too, can sleep in Scottish castles. Culzean, Skibo and Inverlochy are a notable trio where accommodation is available. You will be fed no end of stories about ghostly presences: Green Ladies, wounded soldiers, the spirit of a dog… You can get married in a castle, or stage your corporate event in one. And, for those eager to become a laird, don the kilt and own a castle, several are invariably on the market. To appreciate the vastness of that market, check out www.castles.org.

Above: On the Isle of Arran, **Brodick Castle**, parts of which date from the 14th century, is the ancient seat of the Dukes of Hamilton. It is open to the public and contains various paintings and objets d'art.

Left: At Stirling Castle, an actor portrays Scottish patriot William Wallace, who resisted the English until his betrayal and execution in 1305. He was played by Mel Gibson in the film *Braveheart*.

Right: **Dunrobin**, the largest pile in the Highlands, is seat of the Dukes of Sutherland who once owned more land than anyone in Europe. Originally a fortified square keep, it was transformed into a castle and then in the 19th century into a French château with Scottish baronial overtones. The gardens are magnificent.

ABOVE: Urquhart Castle was built to guard the Great Glen. It played an important role in the Wars of Independence, being taken by Edward I and later held by Robert the Bruce. During the Jacobite troubles part of the castle was blown up to prevent it falling into "rebel" hands. Today, its walls are a strategic spot from which to sight the Loch Ness Monster.

ABOVE: Stirling Castle, once called "the key to Scotland" because of its strategic position between the Lowlands and Highlands, witnessed many bloody battles between the Scots and English – the cemetery must have been useful. Later, it became a favourite residence of Stuart monarchs. Today it houses the regimental museum of the Argyll and Sutherland Highlanders.

ABBEYS ON THE SCOTTISH BORDER

Scotland, especially the Borders, is full of abbeys that now lie ruined but were once powerful institutions with impressive buildings. During the reign of David I (1124–53), who transformed the Scottish church, more than 20 religious houses were founded. Outstanding among these is a quartet of Border abbeys – Dryburgh (Premonstratensian), Jedburgh (Augustinian), Kelso (Tironensian) and Melrose (Cistercian). All have evocative ruins, though perhaps it is Jedburgh *(above)* with tower and remarkable rose window still intact, which is Scotland's classic abbey.

It was not the Reformation (1560) that caused damage to these abbeys but rather the selfishness of pre-Reformation clergy, raids in the 14th–16th centuries by both English and Scots, the ravages of weather, and activities of 19th-century restorers. The concern of the Reformation, spearheaded by firebrand John Knox, was to preserve, not to destroy, the churches they needed.

Monasteries continued to exist as landed corporations after the Reformation. Why upset a system that suited so many interests? After all, the Pope, at the King's request, had provided priories and abbeys for five of James V's illegitimate children while they were still infants.

BELOW: Cawdor Castle, 12 miles (20km) east of Inverness, dates from the early 14th century and has links with Shakespeare's *Macbeth*. Two of its thanes (lords) were murdered. It has three gardens, a nine-hole golf course, salmon fishing, and of course the inevitable ghosts.

Recommended Restaurants on page 349

SCOTTISH HIGHLANDS

The Highlands of Scotland form one of the last great wildernesses of Europe – endless stretches of wild country, mountains, glens and moorlands probed by the long fingers of sea lochs

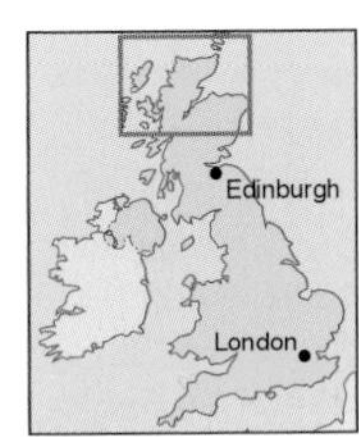

The southern edge of the Highland line runs across the country diagonally from the Mull of Kintyre, the long spit of land stretching southwards from Argyll on the western edge of the Firth of Clyde, right up to a point southwest of Aberdeen near Stonehaven. More than half of Scotland lies to the north of this line, most of it mountainous, with just a few fertile glens where crops can be grown and cattle reared. The population is sparse in the northwest – in Sutherland it is fewer than 6 people per sq mile (2.6 people per sq km), compared to the national average of 955 per sq mile (369 per sq km).

Gaelic speakers

Off the west coast lie several hundred islands, and these have the highest density of the 58,650 Gaelic speakers left in Scotland. The southernmost group comprises Gigha, Islay, Jura and Colonsay. Further north there are the large islands of Mull and Skye and the Inner Hebrides of Iona, Staffa, Tiree, Coll, Muck, Eigg, Rum and Canna; and the Outer Hebrides group of Lewis, Harris, North Uist, Benbecula, South Uist, Eriskay and Barra.

To the north of the Scottish mainland are the Orkney and Shetland groups. You can reach some of the offshore islands by air – there are services to Islay, Benbecula, Lewis, Orkney, Shetland, Fair Isle and Tiree. Ferries link the other inhabited islands to the mainland.

There is so much to see in the Highlands, such a variation in the scenery of mountain, moorland, loch and glen, that one could spend years exploring them.

The westerly A82 out of Glasgow leads almost immediately to the Highlands, turning north after Dumbarton, along the Bonnie Bonnie Banks of **Loch Lomond** ㉓, the largest freshwater lake in Britain, 23 miles (37 km) long and 5 miles (8 km) across at its widest point. Loch Lomond Shores is state-of-the-art visitor centre at the southern tip, offering information, refreshments and boat trips. Hills dominate the landscape. Across the loch is **Ben Lomond**, first of

Main attractions
- LOCH LOMOND
- BEN NEVIS
- ISLE OF SKYE
- INVERNESS
- LOCH NESS
- ORKNEY AND SHETLAND
- STIRLING CASTLE
- CULLODEN MOOR
- ABERDEEN
- BALMORAL
- DUNDEE

LEFT: Balloch Castle and Loch Lomond.
BELOW: Highland steer.

TIP

Fans of stately homes should detour west along the A83 to Loch Fyne to visit **Inveraray Castle** (tel: 01499-302203; Apr–Oct Mon–Sat & Sun pm; charge). For centuries the seat of the chiefs of Clan Campbell, the Dukes of Argyll, the present Gothic Revival building, famous for its magnificent interiors and art collection, was started in 1743.

BELOW RIGHT: climbing Ben Nevis, Britain's highest mountain.

the "Munros", Scotland's 277 mountains which rise to more than 3,000 ft (900 metres) and offer a perennial challenge to climbers from all over the country.

Scenic rail route

The A82 continues up to Fort William, a journey that can also be made by the scenic **West Highland Line** railway (firstgroup.com/scotrail). After leaving Glasgow, the railway follows the banks of the Clyde to **Helensburgh** ㉔, the small resort town where the television pioneer John Logie Baird was born in 1888. This is also where the Glasgow Modern Movement architect Charles Rennie Mackintosh built the finest extant example of his domestic style, **Hill House** (Easter–Oct daily 1.30–5.30pm, admission charge). It also has attractive formal gardens in the Mackintosh style.

The line follows the shores of Loch Long and Loch Lomond, through the narrow valley of Glen Falloch, between bronze, green and heather-purple hills, to **Crianlarich** ㉕, where the line to Oban branches off. Crianlarich to the south and Fort William to the north are both good entry points for one of the most popular "corners" of the Scottish Highlands: **Glencoe** ㉖. This deep mountain valley stretches more than 7 miles (11 km) from Loch Leven to Rannoch Moor through magnificent scenery. The often mist-shrouded peaks of the Glen are favourites among experienced rock climbers, although even the most experienced can have fatal accidents here, particularly in bad weather.

The West Highland Line train from Glasgow to Mallaig allows the best opportunity for witnessing the bleak splendour of **Rannoch Moor** ㉗, 60 sq miles (155 sq km) of peat bog, lochs and winding streams through which no road runs (one goes as far as Rannoch Station). Lying to the east of Glencoe, Rannoch is a great empty moor ringed by mountains, on which lie the two loneliest railway stations in Britain, Rannoch and Corrour, 1,370 ft (420 metres) above sea level. The moor's inhabitants are waterbirds, plovers, skylarks, eagles, herds of red deer and the succulent brown trout inhabiting peat-brown lakelets called lochans; three or four lonely households manage to exist on its surface.

At the northern edge of the moor, the

The Massacre of Glencoe

Translated literally as the Valley of Weeping, the name of Glencoe is a haunting reminder of the violent massacre that occurred here in February 1692. By order of the English King William III, more than 200 troops loyal to the English Crown commanded by Robert Campbell of Glenlyon, turned on the MacDonald clan, who had been their hosts for 12 days. Thirty-eight men, women and children were slaughtered as a punishment for the tardiness of their chief in giving allegiance to the English king.

The Massacre of Glencoe created a great deal of bad blood between the MacDonalds and Campbells and increased the clans' mistrust of central government – many Highlanders also interpreted the Jacobite Risings which took place 23 years later as revenge for Glencoe.

Reminders of the massacre are everywhere: there is a memorial to the MacDonalds near the old Invercoe Road, and the Signal Rock near the Clachaig Inn is said to be the place from which a signal was sent to the Campbells to go ahead with the massacre. The Glencoe Visitors' Centre provides further details of this notorious episode. Even today few can escape the sense of gloom as they descend the main road between the dark, brooding mountains.

Recommended Restaurants on page 349

line swings west again, past the deep cleft cut by the River Spean in Monessie Gorge, to Fort William at the head of Loch Linnhe and the foot of **Ben Nevis**, Britain's highest mountain, 4,406 ft (1,343 metres) and 24 miles (39 km) around. From here there are impressive views down the sea loch and over the mountain ranges of Ardgour and Moidart.

The Highland rail tour can be continued by changing to the train to Mallaig, a fishing port opposite the Isle of Skye. From Fort William, Ben Nevis is not much more than a stiff walk, but proper clothes and boots are essential because the weather on mountain tops in Scotland can be treacherous even in high summer. When conditions are clear, the climb really is worth the effort.

Fort William

The fortification at **Fort William** 28 was constructed in the 17th century to keep out "savage clans" and sundry other undesirables. Nothing of the fort remains today: it was demolished in the late 19th century to make way for the railway, which led to rapid expansion of the town and its environs. Nowadays, being such an important crossroads in the Scottish Highlands, "Britain's outdoor capital" is crowded with tourists. And the area yields much to the more intrepid explorer apart from Ben Nevis. A bus trip, for example, up to Loch Ness, 30 miles (48 km) to the northeast, may just result in a sighting of the famous monster *(see page 344)*.

In the town itself, near the tourist information centre, is the excellent **West Highland Museum** (Mon–Sat 10am–5pm, July–Aug also Sun 2–5pm, admission charge), which has a number of Jacobite relics including a "secret portrait" of Bonnie Prince Charlie, and contains a panelled rooms of the old fort. Younger visitors seek out the thumbscrews and torture instruments.

The train to Mallaig follows the A830

A steam train crosses the Glenfinnan viaduct, completed in 1901, which made a magic appearance in three Harry Potter films.

BELOW: Glenfinnan, with its monument to Bonnie Prince Charlie.

Mallaig harbour.

BELOW: Skye, the inspiration for the *Skye Boat Song* ("Speed, bonnie boat, like a bird on the wing…"). The words were written by Sir Harold Boulton (1859–1935) to a tune collected by Annie MacLeod (Lady Wilson) during the 1870s.

west through Bonnie Prince Charlie country, beginning with the stunning view from the viaduct at **Glenfinnan** ㉙ down Loch Shiel, and over the monument on the shore that marks the spot where the Young Pretender himself raised the Stuart standard. Here the clans gathered to begin the Jacobite Rebellion of 1745. It was in this country, too, that he hid with a price of £30,000 on his head after the defeat at Culloden.

Beyond Lochailort there is a view seawards over the bright water and rocky islets of **Loch nan Uamh**, where the Bonnie Prince landed in 1745 and from where he left 14 months later, despite all the pleadings of the haunting Jacobite songs, never to return. The pebbly beaches of Loch nan Uamh give way to the silver sands of Morar and Arisaig, shining like snow on the edge of the steel-blue sea.

Inland are the mountains looking over the dark waters of **Loch Morar**, the deepest lake in Britain at over 1,000 ft (300 metres), which is reputed to house a monster no less mysterious than the more famous one in Loch Ness.

The Isle of Skye

The busy fishing port of **Mallaig** ㉚ is one of the ferry departure points for the **Isle of Skye** (the principal crossing is over the bridge at Kyle of Lochalsh, further north). From the fjord-like sea lochs of the west, across to the sheer Cuillin Mountains in the south, and to the craggy northern tip of the Trotternish Peninsula, **Skye** ㉛ epitomises Scotland's wild Celtic appeal. The 19th-century Clearances saw whole glens emptied of their ancient settlements; since then, the population of Skye steadily decreased, but it has recovered from its lowest point and is now around 12,000. Tourism has replaced the crofters' farms as the major source of income and has produced something of a "pre-packaged" feel in some of the main centres. But a day's hike or cycle ride around the 50-mile (80-km) long island will still set you squarely in the wilderness.

The **Cuillin Mountains** are a 6-mile (10-km) arc of peaks, 15 of which exceed the 3,000 ft (900 metres) needed to make them Munros. If the summits seem forbidding, take the walk down Glen Sligachan into the heart of these mountains and through to the other side 8 miles (13 km) due south to the beach of Camasunary in Loch Scavaig. On the southern tip of Skye is **Armadale Castle Gardens and Museum of the Isles** (daily, Apr–Oct 9.30am–5.30pm, gardens year round, admission charge).

The main attraction of northwestern Skye is **Dunvegan Castle** (daily, Mar–Oct 10am–5pm, Oct–Mar 11am–4pm, admission charge), which captures the clan spirit of Scotland in its paintings and relics from Macleods. The grounds, including a walled garden, are delightful.

On the west side of the Trotternish Peninsula, **Uig** is an attractive village that encircles a bay from where ferries depart for the outer isles. This northern arm of Skye has been less altered by tourism than any part of the island. Skye's easternmost town, **Kyleakin**, is where a bridge allows the islanders to reach the mainland at **Kyle of Lochalsh** ㉜, which is also the terminus of the second part of the West Highland Line from Inverness.

The North West

The train to Inverness, the capital of the Highlands, runs along the shores of **Loch Carron**, past the pretty village of **Plockton** in a sheltered bay, with splendid views to the north of the mountains of Applecross and Wester Ross, then up Glen Carron through dramatic wild country, populated by little more than deer and eagles, wildcats and buzzards on its high tops and a few sheep and cattle among the narrow glens. As the train heads further east, so the ruggedness of the Highland landscape begins to fade. The change is first noticeable at **Garve**, where the landscape begins to melt into the civilisation of the rich farmland around the Moray Firth on the east coast. Inverness appears on the shoreline and beyond it the Monadliath mountains loom over Loch Ness.

By road, the mainland route from Kyle of Lochalsh heads north on both the A890 through **Glen Carron** and the A896 via **Shieldaig**. These roads intersect with the A832 which returns west down Glen Docherty to **Loch Maree**, one of the prettiest lochs in Scotland, and beyond to the extraordinary **Inverewe Garden** ㉝ on Loch Ewe (daily, 9.30am–8pm or sunset if earlier; shorter winter opening hours; admission charge).

Dunvegan Castle claims to be the oldest continuously inhabited castle in Scotland; it has been the seat of the chiefs of Clan Macleod for more than 700 years.

BELOW: Plockton, carefully preserved, draws artists and photographers from all over the world.

Dragon's head on the prow of a replica Viking ship in Orkney.

Begun by Osgood Mackenzie in 1860 and containing a vast array of plants from all over the world, it is hard to credit that these gardens are on a more northerly latitude than Moscow.

From Inverewe the road heads first north and then winds back to the east, giving at many points a view of the true beauty of Scotland's west coast. The road arrives at the A835, which heads north to **Ullapool**, a fishing village on Loch Broom. The further north you go past Ullapool towards Scotland's "scalp" on the north coast between Durness and **John O'Groats** 34, the longer the days are in summer, and the more the landscape takes on an eerie beauty, which is strictly for wilderness lovers.

In the opposite direction to Ullapool, the A835 is the road to Inverness.

Highland capital

Inverness 35 is the vibrant "Capital of the Highlands". For long seen as a dull backwater of Presbyterianism, has become a major shopping centre with a good choice of nightlife, especially at weekends, and is now the fastest-growing city in Britain. A number of city-centre pubs have traditional Highland live music and there are a number of top-notch restaurants. With the mouth of **Loch Ness** 36 only 5 miles (8 km) from the town, it is a good starting point for seeking out one of the world's greatest amphibian celebrities.

If the serpentine configurations don't immediately appear on the surface of the Loch as you make your way south down the A82, then make a stop at the ruins of **Urquhart Castle** (daily, Mar–Sept 9.30am–6pm, 4.30pm in winter; admission charge), which was one of the largest in Scotland until 1692 when it was blown up to prevent the Jacobites from using it. Most photos of the Loch Ness monster, known as Nessie, have been taken from this spot. The nearby **Official Loch Ness Monster Exhibition Centre** (daily, 10am–6pm, 5pm in winter; admission charge), with a scale replica of "the beastie", is one of two competing tourist centres. You can monster-watch with an on-line livecam at lochness.co.uk.

The far, far north

Inverness is also a good starting point for a journey up to the northernmost fringes

BELOW: Loch Ness and Urquhart Castle.

of Britain. The A9 follows the coast to Wick or Thurso, from where a ferry sails for **Stromness**, the **Orkney Islands**' second-largest town on Mainland, the largest of some 70 islands. Orkney, invaded by Norsemen in the 11th century, did not pass into British hands until late in the 16th century and ruins from the Norse era are all around. Everywhere in Orkney the feeling is one of being wide open to the sky, of great cliffs and rocky sea pinnacles. North of Stromness the coast offers one of the most dramatic cliff walks in Britain, from Black Craig north to the Bay of Skaill. Another excursion for wilderness lovers is the ferry to Moaness Pier on the Isle of Hoy.

Kirkwall ㊲, 10 miles (16 km) east of Stromness, is the largest town in Orkney. It is largely uninspiring except for the **Bishop's Palace**, a 12th-century ruin with a round tower added in the 16th century, and the **Earl's Palace**, one of the finest examples of Renaissance architecture in Scotland (both open daily 9.30am–5.30pm, 4.30pm in winter; admission charge). **St Magnus' Cathedral**, built in 1137, is dedicated to Magnus Erlendsson, martyred first Earl of Orkney.

Places of antiquity grace the countryside under the banner of the UNESCO World Heritage Heart of Orkney Neolithic Sites. Best known are the wonderfully preserved settlement at **Skara Brae** (daily 9.30am–6.30pm, 4.30pm in winter; admission charge; multiple entry tickets for other sites available), from c.3000 BC *(see page 34)*, and **Maes Howe** (book tours in advance, tel: 01856 761606, or at the site), a huge, chambered megalithic tomb from 2700 BC with fine, runic graffiti left by 12th-century Norse plunderers. On Papa Westray, one of the smaller Orkney islands, is the oldest extant house in Europe.

Britain's most northerly archipelago is the **Shetland Islands**, just 48 miles (78 km) north of the Orkney Islands and nearer to the Arctic circle than to London. **Lerwick** ㊳ is their only town and there is a small airport on the main island served from most Scottish airports, a frequency maintained because of Shetland's significant oil installations – it has the largest gas and oil terminal in Europe. On the last Tuesday in January, the spectacular fire ceremony of Up-Helly-Aa involves the burning of a replica Viking longship and much revelry.

The tiny island of **Mousa**, off the east coast, is the site of the world's best-preserved Iron-Age *broch* tower, a fortress that just managed to stay intact after more than 1,000 years of battering from Arctic storms. **Unst** ㊴ is the most northerly of the dozen inhabited islands, and **Muness Castle** and the ruins of **Scalloway Castle**, 6 miles (10 km) to the west of Lerwick, are also worth visiting (apply to local shops for keys). At the southern tip of the mainland, next door to Sumburgh Airport, is **Jarlshof** (daily, 9.30am–5.30pm, 4.30pm in winter; historic-scotland.gov.uk; admission charge), a remarkable "layer-cake" of an archaeological site. Bronze Age dune dwellers, *broch* builders, Vikings and medieval inhabitants all left their marks.

South from Inverness

The A9 south from Inverness leads back towards Edinburgh and Glagow through

The mixed Orcadian heritage is reflected in the shops on the Orkney Islands: here tourists are offered Nordic-style sweaters instead of the usual tartans.

BELOW: Lerwick, in the Shetland Islands.

The Wallace Monument above Stirling celebrating the 13th-century patriot whose exploits were recounted in the 1995 film Braveheart.

BELOW: show of strength at a Highland gathering.

impressive scenery in the high glens of the **Grampians**, with the massive summits of the Cairngorms towering over the ski resort of **Aviemore** ㊵. It also passes pretty **Pitlochry**, a quaint hillside town that plays patient host to an endless stream of tourist-laden vehicles. The Highland Games held here in September draw the crowds, as does the Pitlochry Festival Theatre, over the Aldour Bridge from town, which attracts first-class performers from all over the world. Eight miles (13 km) northwest of Pitlochry is 12th-century **Blair Castle** ㊶ (daily, Apr–Oct 9.30am–4.30pm). This is the seat of the Duke of Atholl, the last noble in Britain licensed to have a private army. **Perth**, generally considered the gateway to the Highlands (the first line of high hills rise over the horizon), has little of interest to the visitor.

Stirling

A fitting endpiece to the southerly hike down the A9 is a visit to **Stirling** ㊷. Equidistant from Edinburgh and Glasgow, this city still considers itself the rightful capital of Scotland. Stirling seems to have escaped the worst excesses of the Victorian Age; winding streets and medieval cobblestones are everywhere in evidence. **Stirling Castle** (daily 9.30am–6pm, 5pm in winter, admission charge) seems to have grown out of the 150-ft (77-metre) crag on which it was built. It featured prominently in the Scottish wars of succession in the 13th and 14th centuries, passing between the English and the Scots until the Scots finally won it for keeps in 1342. It was the home of the Stuart kings from 1370 to 1603 and they who shaped it into what it is today. Mary Queen of Scots and James VI of Scotland (who became James I of England) spent several years here. It also contains the regimental museum of the Argyll & Sutherland Highlanders.

A free, multi-screen presentation at the **Royal Burgh of Stirling Visitor Centre** traces the history of Stirling, bringing to life such decisive events as the Battle of Bannockburn. The centre also has an exhibition of 19th-century life in Stirling.

At the foot of the castle is the oldest part of Stirling, with a number of interesting buildings such as **Argyll's Lodging** (daily 9.30am–5.30pm, 4.30pm in winter; admission charge), the finest example of a 17th-century Scottish townhouse, and **Cowane's Hospital**, once the Guildhall and now a public venue.

Also worth visiting are two religious sites: the **Church of the Holy Rude** and the **Cambuskenneth Abbey** (both open daily, Easter–Oct; donations). The former is a 15th-century building with an unusual open timber roof and a five-sided apse in the choir. The 90-ft (28-metre) tower shows the scars of hostilities which may have occurred during the Jacobite Rebellion. Mary Queen of Scots was crowned here as a child and, following her abdication, it was the scene of the coronation of her son, James. The abbey, founded in the 11th century, is by the River Forth east of the town. In 1326 it was the site of Robert the Bruce's first Scottish Parliament.

Scotch on the rocks

A few miles east from Inverness, the B9006 runs across **Culloden Moor** where Jacobite forces under Bonnie Prince Charlie were routed in 1746. The defeat of his men by the Hanoverian army represented the end of the struggle for power by the Stuart line. On either side of the road are scattered stones marking the graves of the Highlanders. The battle is said to have centred around **Old Leanach Farmhouse** which is still standing. The Culloden Moor Visitor Centre (Feb–Dec daily) has many artefacts of the period on show.

A 16th-century tower house, **Brodie Castle** ❸ (daily Mar–Oct 10.30am–5pm, closed Fri May–Jun, Sept–Oct; garden open daily all year; admission charge), is just east of Nairn. It is packed with antiques and has a fine library.

Along the Spey from the rich farmlands of the Laigh of Moray is distillery country where most of the famous malt whiskies are made. There are distilleries on the route down the beautiful **Spey Valley** which welcome visitors to watch the process of making the *uisgebeatha*, the Gaelic "water of life". Follow the signs marked "**Whisky Trail**" (scotchwhisky.net) from **Keith** ❹ along the A95.

Royal Deeside

Aberdeen ❺, the granite city on the east coast of the Grampian region, around 54 miles (87 km) southeast of Inverness on the A96, is the oil capital of Britain,

Stirling has had to pay for its strategic position; the nearby battlefields of Stirling Bridge (1297), Bannockburn (1314) and Sauchiburn (1488) are reminders of past struggles with the English.

BELOW: Aberdeen Art Gallery.

Marischal College is the second-largest granite building in the world – the biggest is El Escorial monastery and palace complex near Madrid.

bustling with oil-related shipping in its busy harbour, set between the rivers Don and Dee. It has a widely respected university, of which the finest building is the 16th-century **King's College**, which was begun in 1500 and hailed as an outstanding example of Scottish Gothic style.

Marischal College on Broad Street, which was founded in 1593 but rebuilt in the 19th century, has the distinction of being the second-largest granite building in the world after El Escorial near Madrid. The **Art Gallery** (Tues–Sat 10am–5pm, Sun 2–5pm), on Schoolhill, is home to a wide range of English, French and Scottish paintings, with a very fine 20th-century British collection.

There is also the 14th-century **St Machar's Cathedral** (daily, 9am–5pm, 4pm in winter) and a **Maritime Museum** (Tues–Sat 10am–5pm, Sun noon–3pm) in the 16th-century Provost Ross's house in Shiprow leading down to the quays.

Balmoral

Inland from Aberdeen the A93 runs up Royal Deeside to **Balmoral** 46, where the Queen and royal family spend the most part of the summer, amid some of the most beautiful scenery in the land – a unique combination of the tumbling river, the ordered trees, the palatial houses and the wild hills beyond. The Balmoral estate, located some 50 miles (80 km) west of Aberdeen, dates from the 15th century but it did not come into the hands of the royal family until 1848, when it was bought by Prince Albert. In the **Castle**, only the **Ballroom** is open to the public, and the grounds can also be visited (Apr–July daily, 10am–5pm; admission charge; balmoralcastle.com).

Along the way to Balmoral is a cluster of superb castles. Among the most beautiful is **Drum**, the oldest property in the care of the National Trust for Scotland. **Crathes Castle** and **Castle Fraser**, to the north, off the A944, are also impressive. In addition, by the A980, is the fairy-tale **Craigievar** 47. All of these castles have a special distinction of style and furnishings, superb plaster ceilings, beautiful panelling, valuable paintings and artefacts, and are in the care of the National Trust for Scotland.

Two further NTS properties lie North of Aberdeen but still in the Grampian

BELOW: Balmoral Castle and garden.

region (of which Aberdeen is the administrative capital). **Haddo House** ❹❽ is an 18th-century palatial mansion designed by William Adam for the Earls of Aberdeen, and full of treasures. Northwest of Aberdeen, off the A96, is **Leith Hall** ❹❾, a handsome laird's house on a more modest scale. (All these NTS properties open Easter to October, with some closed days in low season; grounds open all year; nts.org.uk).

North sea ports

The A92 coast road south of Aberdeen goes through the North Sea ports of **Montrose** and **Arbroath** ❺⓿. At Arbroath are the ruins of a 12th-century **Abbey** (daily 9.30am–5.30pm, 4.30pm in winter; admission charge) where Scotland declared its independence in 1320.

Next comes **Dundee** ❺❶, the town of jam, jute and journalism looking across the estuary of the River Tay at the north coast of Fife. The three Js still play an essential part in the life of the city. D.C. Thomson produces local newspapers, Scottish weeklies and the largest collection of children's comics in Britain. Captain Scott's Antarctic ship *Discovery* is here *(see margin)*. Also in the harbour is the *Unicorn*, a 24-cannon frigate launched in 1824. Dundee is one of the largest cities in Scotland, with a Culture Quarter of art and science museums, and festivals through the year, but with acres of docklands, industry and sprawling suburbs, it is also one of the least visited.

And so across "the Silvery Tay", as the Bard of Dundee, William Topaz McGonagall, referred to it in so many of his poems, to Fife and an hour and a half's run back to Edinburgh. ❑

Discovery, the ship Captain Scott took to the Antarctic in 1910, was built in Dundee and has returned. The ship and Discovery Point exhibition are open daily 10am–6pm (5pm in winter); tel: 01382-309060; admission charge.

RESTAURANTS

Ballater

Green Inn
9 Victoria Road
Tel: 01339-755701 ££
Award-winning, serious Scottish food. Near Balmoral, with rooms.

Dunkeld

Kinnaird
Kinnaird Estate
Tel: 01796-482440 ££
Victorian hunting lodge in 7,000-acre sporting estate. First-rate ingredients, some home-grown, make up the creative modern dishes. Large wine cellar.

Fort William

Inverlochy Castle
Torlundy
Tel: 01397-702177 £££–££££
Expect full ceremony in three dining rooms. Modern British food, good value lunches.

Kingussie

The Cross
Tweed Mill Brae, Ardbroilach Road
Tel: 01540-661166 ££
Cosy atmospheric, family-run restaurant with rooms in Cairngorms. Scottish fare is cooked with pride.

Inverness

Abstract
20 Ness Bank
Tel: 01463-220 220 ££–£££
Try a tasting menu at the Chef's Table, and whisky from a wide choice in the Piano Bar.

The Mustard Seed
Fraser Street
Tel: 01463-220 220 ££
Modern, innovative restaurant with changing menu and roof terrace with views of the River Ness.

Isle of Skye

The Three Chimneys
Colbost, Dunvegan
Tel: 01470-511258 ££
Restaurant with rooms and views in remote crofters' cottage, winning awards.

Loch Lomond

Cameron House Hotel
Tel: 0845-375 2808. ££–£££
Top notch food in the Lomond Restaurant, Cameron Grill, Claret Jug and Boathouse.

Orkney

The Creel
Front Road, St Margaret's Hope
Tel: 01856-831311 ££
Friendly fish restaurant, judged "Scotland's best".

Port Appin

Pierhouse
Tel: 01631-730302 £–££
Renowned seafood restaurant in wonderfully romantic West Coast setting with views across to Mull.

Prices for a three-course dinner per person with a half-bottle of house wine:
£ = under £25
££ = £25–50
£££ = £50–100
££££ = +£100

INSIGHT GUIDES

TRAVEL TIPS

GREAT BRITAIN

TRANSPORT

GETTING THERE AND GETTING AROUND

GETTING THERE

By Air

Britain's two major international airports are Heathrow (mainly scheduled flights), which is 15 miles (24 km) to the west of London, and Gatwick (scheduled and charter flights), which is 24 miles (40 km) south of the capital. An increasing number of international flights now arrive at the regional airports of Birmingham, Manchester, Liverpool, Glasgow, Prestwick and Cardiff, and London's other airports, Stansted and Luton. The small London City Airport, a few miles from London's financial heart, is used by small aircraft to fly to European capitals.

London Airports

The Airport Travel Line, tel: (08705) 747777, gives information on coaches into Central London and between Heathrow, Gatwick and Stansted airports. Dot2Dot runs a door-to-door coach service from Heathrow and Gatwick airports to hotels in central areas of London. Booking is essential, tel: 0845 368 2368; www.dot2.com.

National Express also runs coach services connecting Heathrow, Gatwick, Stansted and Luton airports, and the first three airports with Victoria coach station in central London. For enquiries, tel: 08717 818181; www.nationalexpress.com.

Heathrow Airport, with five terminals, is sprawling – it can be a long walk to the central building.

There is a fast rail link, the Heathrow Express, between Heathrow and Paddington station. It runs every 15 minutes from 5am–midnight and takes about 20 minutes. Fares are £14.50 single and £28 return. Prices are lowest when buying online, increasing if you purchase from a machine or onboard. Paddington is on the District, Circle, Bakerloo and Hammersmith and City Line underground train lines (tel: (0845) 600 1515; www.heathrow express.com).

The cheapest way into central London is by the *Underground* (known as the Tube), which takes about 45 minutes to the West End. The Piccadilly line goes from Heathrow directly to central areas such as Kensington, Piccadilly and Covent Garden. The single fare is £4. Keep your ticket. You'll need it to exit the Underground system. For all London Transport enquiries: tel: 020-7222 1234; www.tfl.gov.uk.

Heathrow is also well-served by taxis. A ride into town in a London black cab will cost £40–£70, depending on your destination.

Gatwick Airport isn't on the Underground network, but has train and coach services into London and to other large cities. Gatwick Express trains leaves every 15 minutes from 5am until 12.35am, and take 30 minutes to London's Victoria station. For information, tel: 0845 8501530; www.gatwickexpress.com. First Capital trains to Victoria and Southern Trains to London Bridge station are much cheaper and take only a little longer, but can be very crowded at peak hours with general commuter traffic.

A black cab taxi into central London costs around £77.

Luton Airport has a regular express train service from Luton Airport Parkway (take the shuttle bus) to St Pancras Station, City Thameslink, Blackfriars and London Bridge, taking 25 minutes minimum.

Children's Fares

- **Airlines** Infants (under 2 years) either travel free or for about 10 percent of adult fare. Ages 2–12 years qualify for a child's fare, usually 80 percent of adult fare.
- **Trains** Under 5s free on your knee, aged 5–15 half-price most tickets.
- **Coaches** Under-2s free on your knee, 3–15s about half-price.

Alternatively, Green Line 757 coaches to London's Victoria Station take about an hour (tel: 0844 8017261, or easyBus coaches (up to 1 hour 40 mins during peak times).

Stansted Airport (tel: (0870) 000 0303) has the Stansted Express train service to London's Liverpool Street station. A frequent service operates 5.30am–12.30am and takes about 45 minutes (tel: (0845) 600 7245 or +44 (0) 845 600 7245 from overseas; www.stanstedexpress.com). A non-stop coach service to London Victoria is run by Terrravision, and National Express has services to Stratford (east London) and Victoria.

For those heading elsewhere in Britain other than London, there are regular National Express bus links to nearby British Rail stations.

London City Airport's major strength is its proximity to the West End (10 miles/16 km; www.london cityairport.com). There is a London City Airport DLR station (about 50 metres from the airport terminal), whose service has direct connections with the Jubilee line (at Canning Town) and Northern, Central, Circle and Waterloo and City lines (at Bank). The Transport for London website (www.tfl.gov.uk) can be used to help plan your journey.

A taxi into Central London should cost £25–£30.

English Regional Airports

Manchester Airport is 10 miles (16 km) south of the city. Frequent rail services run to Piccadilly station (20 minutes) in central Manchester, from where there are regular Intercity trains to London and other major cities. Alternatives are local buses or a taxi (approximately £15–£20). For information visit www.manchesterairport.co.uk.

Birmingham International Airport is 8 miles (13 km) southeast of Birmingham. The free Air-Rail Link shuttle connects the airport with Birmingham International station, from where trains run every 10–15 minutes to New Street station in the city centre (about 15 minutes). Intercity trains from New Street to London Euston run every half hour (about 90 minutes).

Newcastle Airport is 6 miles (9 km) northwest of Newcastle city centre on the A696 at Woolsington. The airport is a main station for the Metro underground system, which takes 23 minutes to Central Station where regular intercity trains run to London (3 hours) and Edinburgh (1 hour 30 mins).

Liverpool John Lennon Airport is 9 miles (15 km) southeast of the city centre. The Airport Airlink 500 bus runs to the city centre every 20 mins Mon–Fri and 30 mins Sat–Sun and evenings. Taxis charge about £14 for the 20-minute journey.

Kent International Airport. A 30-minute drive from Dover. Rail services from London Charing Cross and Victoria to Ramsgate from where there is an Eastonways bus to the airport (www.eastonways.co.uk). Also rail links to Ashford International from rail station Ramsgate.

Scottish Airports

Glasgow Airport (8 miles/13 km west of Glasgow) has bus services every 7 minutes at peak times to the city centre, which take about 25 minutes. These also stop at Glasgow's two rail stations, Central and Queen Street.

Prestwick Airport is 30 miles (48km) south of Glasgow on the west coast. Trains take 50 minutes to Glasgow's Central station. There are airport express buses to Glasgow and Edinburgh for people arriving outside public transport times.

Edinburgh Airport (8 miles/13 km west of Edinburgh). The Airlink bus to the city centre, which runs every 10 minutes from early morning until after midnight, takes roughly 25 minutes.

ABOVE: approaching London Heathrow.

Welsh Airports

Cardiff Airport (12 miles/19 km east) is used mainly by charter operators. There is an Airbus Xpress link to Cardiff Central Station in the city centre.

Channel Tunnel

Eurostar's regular passenger trains link France and Brussels with Britain. Services run from Paris Gare du Nord (2 hours 15 mins) and Brussels Midi (1 hour 50 minutes) to London's St Pancras International; most trains stop in Ashford, Kent.

Booking is not essential, but there are offers on tickets bought in advance. For UK bookings, tel: (08705) 186 186. From outside the UK, tel: +44 1233 617575, or visit www.eurostar.com.

By Car

"Le Shuttle" trains travel through the tunnel from Nord-Pas de Calais in France to Folkestone in Kent. At least two departures every hour during the day with a reduced service overnight (journey time 35 minutes). Booking is not essential – just turn up and take the next service. Crossings are priced on a single-leg basis and prices vary according to the level of demand; the further ahead you book, the cheaper the ticket. For UK reservations and information, tel: (08705) 35 35 35; www.eurotunnel.com.

Sea Transport

Sea services operate between 12 British ports and more than 20 Continental ones. Major ferries have full eating, sleeping and entertainment facilities. The shortest crossing is from Calais in France to Dover in Britain, which takes about 90 minutes by ferry.

Brittany Ferries sails from St. Malo, Caen and Cherbourg, France to Portsmouth, England; from Cherbourg to Poole; from Roscoff to Plymouth; and from Santander, Spain to Plymouth. Within UK tel: (08709) 076103; in France tel: 0825 82 88 28; in Spain tel: 0942 360 611; www.brittany-ferries.co.uk.

P&O Ferries run from Calais, France, to Dover; from Bilbao, Spain to Portsmouth and from Rotterdam and Zeebruge, Holland, over the North Sea to Hull on England's east coast. From France tel: 0825 120 156; Holland tel: 020 20 08 333; Spain tel: 902 020 461; UK tel: (08716) 645645; www.poferries.com.

Stena Line sail from Hook of Holland to Harwich, England. Tel: (08705) 707070 or (44) 8705 707070 from outside the UK; www.stenaline.co.uk.

Norfolkline operates between Dover and Dunkerque (approx. 1 hour 45 minutes). In the UK, tel: (0870) 870 1020; www.norfolkline.com.

If you plan to bring a vehicle over by ferry it is advisable to book, particularly during peak holiday periods. If travelling by night on a long journey it is also recommended that you book a sleeping cabin.

From the US you could arrive in style on Cunard's *Queen Mary 2* in Southampton. Operating between April and December, it takes six nights to cross the Atlantic. For information in the UK, tel: (0845) 678 0013; from the US call 1-800 223 0764; www.cunard.com.

Flight Information

- **Birmingham Airport** tel: (0870) 733 5511
- **Cardiff Airport** tel: (01446) 711111
- **Edinburgh Airport** tel: (08700) 400 007
- **Gatwick Airport** tel: (08700) 002 468
- **Glasgow Airport** tel: (08700) 400 008
- **Heathrow Airport** tel: (08700) 000 123
- **London City Airport** tel: 020-7646 0000
- **Luton Airport** tel: (01582) 405 100
- **Manchester Airport** tel: (08712) 710 711
- **Prestwick (Glasgow)** tel: (08712) 230 700
- **Stansted Airport** tel: (08700) 000 303

Speed Limits

Unless otherwise stated on signs,

- **30 mph (50 kph).**
- **60 mph (100 kph)** on normal roads away from built-up areas.
- **70 mph (112 kph)** on motorways and dual carriageways (divided highways).
- **Camping vans** or **cars towing a caravan** are restricted to 50 mph, (80 km/h) on normal roads and 60 mph (96 km/h) on dual carriageways.

Getting Around

Driving

In Britain you must drive on the left-hand side of the road and observe speed limits. It is illegal to use a mobile phone when driving. Penalties for drink driving are severe. Drivers and passengers, in both front and back seats, must wear seat belts where fitted; failure to do so can result in a fine. For further information, consult a copy of the *Highway Code* published by the DSA and widely available in bookshops. Prepare in advance by visiting www.direct.gov.uk.

If you are bringing your own car into Britain you will need a valid driving licence or International Driving Permit, plus insurance coverage and documents proving the vehicle is licensed and registered in your country and that you are resident outside the UK.

Parking

Road congestion is a problem in most town and city centres, and parking is often restricted. Never leave your car parked on a double yellow or red line, in a place marked for *permit holders only*, within a white zig-zag line close to a pedestrian crossing, or in a control zone. Also, don't park on a single yellow line when restrictions are in force, usually 8.30am–6.30pm Mon–Fri (consult signs on the kerb; if no days are shown, restrictions are in force daily). These are offences for which you can face a fine. Either use a meter or a car park (distinguished by a white P on a blue background).

Pay particular attention if leaving your car in central London. In many areas illegal parking may result in wheel clamping. This means your car is immobilised with a clamp until you pay (£70) to have it released – a process that can take several hours. Alternatively, your vehicle may be towed away to a car pound. Either way, retrieving your car will cost more than £200, plus a £40 parking fine. To ascertain whether your car has been towed, tel: 020-7747 4747.

Breakdown

The following motoring organisations operate 24-hour breakdown assistance. They have reciprocal arrangements with other national motoring clubs. All calls to these numbers are free.

AA (0800) 887766, or visit www.theaa.com
Britannia Rescue (0800) 591563, or visit www.britanniarescue.com
Green Flag (0800) 0510636, or visit www.greenflag.co.uk
RAC (0800) 828282, or visit www.rac.co.uk

Car hire/Rental

To hire a car in Britain you must be over 21 years old (over 23 for most companies) and have held a valid full driving licence for more than one year. The cost of hiring a car usually includes third-party insurance, mileage and road tax. Depending on the company, it might also incorporate insurance cover for accidental damage to the car's interior, wheels and tyres. However, it does not include insurance for other drivers without prior arrangement.

Some companies offer special weekend and holiday rates, so shop around. International companies (such as those listed below) are keen to encourage visitors to book in advance before they leave home and may offer holiday packages with discounts of up to 40 percent on advance bookings through travel agents or branches in your own country. Many hire firms provide child seats and luggage racks for a small charge.

Avis tel: (08445) 818181
Hertz tel: (08708) 448844
Budget tel: (0844) 5812231
Europcar tel: (0870) 607 5000

Driving in London

If you're staying only for a short time in the Greater London area, and are unfamiliar with the geography of the capital, don't hire a car. Central London is more than ever a nightmare to drive in, with its web of one-way streets, bad signposting, congestion charge and impatient drivers.

Parking is also a major problem in congested central London. Meters are slightly cheaper than NCP car parks, but usually allow parking for a maximum of two or four hours. If parking at a meter, do not leave your car a moment longer than your time allows or insert more money once your time has run out. For either infringement you can be fined up to £80. Some meter parking is free after 6.30pm and all day Sunday, but check the details on the meter.

You are liable to an £8 daily congestion charge if you drive in the central area between 7am and 6pm Mon–Fri. You can pay by ringing (0845) 900 1234, visiting www.tfl.gov.uk/roadusers/congestion charging, or at many small shops.

Public Transport

Domestic Flights

From the major international airports there are frequent shuttle services to Britain's many domestic airports. These give quick and easy access to many cities and offshore islands. Airlines providing domestic services include:

British Airways (the country's largest airline), reservations and general enquiries, tel: (0844) 493 0787 (from the UK); flight arrival and departure information, tel: (0844) 493 0777 (from the UK, daily 6am–8pm); from US tel: 1-800-AIRWAYS; www.britishairways.com.
bmi, British Midland International, tel: (0870) 607 0555 (within UK) or +44 1332 648181 (outside UK); www.flybmi.com
Easyjet, tel: (0871) 244 2366; www.easyjet.com
Ryanair, tel: (0871) 246 0000 (from within UK only); www.ryanair.com

Major Domestic Airports
Aberdeen tel: (08700) 400006
Bristol tel: (0871) 3344444
East Midlands tel: (0871) 9199000
Leeds-Bradford tel: (0871) 2882288
Liverpool John Lennon tel: (0871) 5218484
Newcastle upon Tyne tel: (0871) 8821121
Norwich tel: (01603) 428700
Southampton tel: (0870) 040 0009

Trains

Railways are run by 27 private regional operating companies. They are not known for punctuality, so if your arrival time is critical allow for possible delays. Avoid rush-hour travel in and out of big cities.

There are many money-saving deals, such as cheap-day returns, available. It can be difficult to find out about special offers, so if in doubt, ask again. Generally, tickets bought at least two weeks in advance are vastly cheaper than standard rates, but they sell out fast. Some saver tickets are available only if purchased abroad before arriving.

It is not usually necessary to buy tickets until the day you travel (except to get these special offers), or to make seat reservations, except over the Christmas period when InterCity trains are fully booked well in advance.

Many trains have first-class carriages with tickets up to twice the price of standard seats. It is sometimes possible to upgrade to first-class at weekends for an extra payment once you board.

On long distances overnight, it may be worth having a sleeping compartment. Available on InterCity trains, these have basic but comfortable sleeping arrangements and must be booked in advance. Information available by calling (08457) 484950; or +44 (0) 20 7278 5240 from abroad; National Rail Enquiries can then give you the phone number to book with the relevant train operator. Tickets can also be booked online at www.thetrainline.com.

The journey between London (Euston or King's Cross station) and Edinburgh or Glasgow varies between 4½ to 6 hours.

For travel in Scotland you can buy a Freedom of Scotland Travelpass giving unlimited travel throughout Scotland and the English Borders on the ScotRail network. The Travelpass also includes some coach travel and scheduled Caledonian MacBrayne ferries to the islands off the west coast. There are two options: 4 days' travel in an 8-day period, or 8 days' travel over 15 consecutive days. Call national rail enquiries or see www.firstgroup.com/scotrail.

For a really luxurious train ride, take a trip (2–7 nights) on the famous Royal Scotsman (April–October). For further information contact the Orient Express, tel: (0845) 0772222 (within UK), +44 20 7960 0500 (outside UK); www.royalscotsman.com.

Train Enquiries

- **National Rail Enquiry Service** For train times, cancellations and advance bookings by credit card, tel: (08457) 484950 or visit www.nationalrail.co.uk.
- **Rail Europe** For services from Britain, tel: (08448) 484064; www.raileurope.co.uk.

Steam Railways

Many steam rail lines have been restored by enthusiasts (www.ukhrail.uel.ac.uk). Among the most notable are:

- **Bluebell Railway**, Sheffield Park Station, Nr Uckfield, E. Sussex TN22 3QL, tel: (01825) 720800. Britain's most famous line.
- **Watercress Line**, Alresford, Hampshire S024 9JG, tel: (01962) 733810. Runs through beautiful country over steeply graded track.
- **Severn Valley Railway**, Bewdley, Worcestershire DY12 1BG, tel: (01299) 403816. Spectacular views.
- **Great Central Railway**, Loughborough, Leics LE11 1RW, tel: (01509) 230726. One of the most evocative restorations of the steam age.
- **Lakeside and Haverthwaite Railway**, Nr Ulverston, Cumbria LA12 8AL, tel: (01539) 531594. Steep ride, with connections to boats on the lake.
- **Ffestiniog Railway**, Harbour Station, Porthmadog, Gwynedd LL49 9NF, tel: (01766) 516000. Scenic ride through Snowdonia National Park.
- **North Yorkshire Moors Railway**, Pickering Station. YO18 7AJ, tel: (01751) 472508. An 18-mile (30-km) line through picturesque moorland.
- **Isle of Man Transport**, Douglas, Isle of Man, IM1 5PT, tel: (01624) 663366. Part of the UK's largest vintage network remains; 15 miles (24 km) of track.
- **Paignton and Dartmouth Steam Railway**, Queen's Park Station, Torbay Road, Paignton, Devon TQ4 6AF, tel: (01803) 555872. Beautiful coastal line, with superb views.
- **Gloucestershire–Warwickshire Railway**, Toddington, Glos GL54 5DT, tel: (01242) 621405.A 20-mile (32-km) round trip through the Cotswolds from Toddington to Cheltenham Racecourse.

Coaches and Local Buses

National Express operates a large network of long-distance bus services with comfortable coaches running on long journeys, equipped with washrooms and disabled facilities. Fares are (usually) considerably cheaper than the equivalent journey by train, although you must book your seat in advance. For enquiries and bookings, tel: (08717) 818181; www.nationalexpress.com.

National Express provides scheduled day trips to cities of interest such as Bath and Stratford-upon-Avon, as well as transport to music festivals and Wembley and Twickenham stadiums. **Green Line**, tel: (0844) 801 7261; www.greenline.co.uk), has some similar services such as to Whipsnade Animal Park.

Towns are generally well-served by buses, often owned by private companies; rural communities often have very inadequate services.

Taxis

Outside London and large cities and away from taxi ranks at stations, ports and airports you will usually have to telephone for a cab rather than expect to hail one in the street. By law cabs must be licensed and display charges on a meter. Add at least 10 percent for a tip.

London "black cab" drivers are famous for their extensive knowledge of the city's streets, but they aren't cheap, especially at night. Minicabs (unlicensed taxis, which look like private cars) are not allowed to compete with black cabs on the street and have to be hired by telephone or from a kiosk. If hiring a minicab, agree to a fee beforehand and don't expect drivers to know precise destinations. Never pick up an unsolicited minicab in the street.

If you have a complaint, make a note of the driver's licence number and contact the Public Carriage Office, tel: (0845) 300 7000.

Travelling Around London

If you are staying in London for a while it is worth investing in an *A–Z* street guide which gives detailed information of the capital's confusing complex of streets and post codes.

The Underground (Tube) is the quickest way to get across London. Althoughone of the most comprehensive systems of its kind in the world, it's also the oldest. Apart from some central stations which have been revamped recently, and the East London line redevelopment work in preparation for 2012, many remain largely unchanged since the 1930s.

The Tube service starts at 5.30am and runs until around midnight. It gets packed in the rush hours (7–9.30am and 4–7pm). Make sure that you have a valid ticket as it is illegal to travel without one and you may be fined. Smoking is prohibited. Fares are based on a zone system with a flat fare in the central zone.

A ride on the Docklands Light Railway is an excellent way to see the re-development of London's old dock area. This fully automated system has two branches connecting up with the Underground network. It operates in the same way as the Tube, with similar fares.

London buses provide a comprehensive service throughout Greater London and have their route and number clearly displayed on the front. Some buses run hourly throughout the night, with services to many parts of London departing from Trafalgar Square. Smoking is prohibited on buses.

Either pay for single journeys on London Transport (expensive, see below) or buy a one-day or three-day Travelcard *(see panel)* or Pre-pay Oyster Card. The Oyster Card is a format for organising and pre-paying for single trips. Simply touch the card on the reader in tube stations and buses. Visitor Oyster cards cost £2 and are valid for £10 or £15 worth of travel (so total cost of £12 or £17) on a pay-as-you-go basis. They can be topped up with additional credit at Tube stations, London Overground stations, Oyster Ticket Stops and London Travel Information Centres. Buy online at www.tfl.gov.uk, or tel: (0845) 330 9876. Paying cash for a single journey on the tube within zones 1 and 6 costs a daunting £4. A journey excluding zone 1 costs £3.

There is a flat fare of £1.20 for any bus journey but it is cheaper if you use Oyster Pre-Pay. Buy tickets before boarding from machines at bus stops (a few stops do not yet have machines).

A bus pass (valid in all zones) will cost £3.50 for one day or £14 for 7 days. Travelcards may be used on tube, bus, DLR and National Rail services. Prices vary according to zones covered and duration. Family Travelcards also available.

Call Transport for London on 020-7222 1234 or visit: www.tfl.gov.uk.

River Travel and Tours

London

Riverboats are an excellent way to see many major London sights whose history is intertwined with the river. During the summer these are plentiful, but there are limited winter services. Some of London Transport's travel passes allow a third off the cost of travel on scheduled Riverboat services. Boats can be boarded at: Richmond, Kew, Waterloo, Westminster, Embankment, London Bridge, the Tower of London and Greenwich piers.

Circular cruises between St Katharine's and Westminster Pier are available from: **Crown River Cruises**, Blackfriars Pier, tel: 020-7936 2033; www.crownriver.com.

Scheduled services are run by:
Thames River Services, Westminster Pier to Thames Barrier and Greenwich. March–November, tel: 020-7930 4097; www.westminsterpier.co.uk.
City Cruises Departures from Westminster, Waterloo, Tower and Greenwich Piers, tel: 020-7740 0400; www.citycruises.com.
London Duck Tours Guided tour of Westminster by road and river in amphibious vehicles used in the D-Day landings during World War II. Depart from Waterloo, tel: 020-7928 3132; www.londonducktours.co.uk.

Scotland

Ferry services between the mainland and 22 islands off the west coast of Scotland have been monopolised by Caledonian MacBrayne. Island Rover tickets allow you to visit as many islands as you wish over 8 or 15 days. Ferries to Orkney and Shetland are operated by Northlink.

You can make reservations on most services and they are strongly recommended if you wish to take a car. The ferry to the Isle of Skye from the Kyle of Lochalsh, has been replaced by a toll bridge.

P&O Irish ferries sail from Troon (Mar–Sept) and from Cairnryan to Larne in Northern Ireland. An 18-hour sailing from Rosyth (near Edinburgh) to Zeebrugge in Belgium was discontinued in 2008 but may be restarted by a new operator.

For details contact:
Caledonian MacBrayne
Tel: (01475) 650100, or visit www.calmac.co.uk
P&O Irish Ferries
Tel: (0871) 6644999
www.poirishsea.com
Northlink Orkney and Shetland Ferries
Tel: (0845) 600 0449
www.northlinkferries.co.uk

London Travel Passes

- **The Off-Peak One Day Travelcard** is a one-day pass that allows unlimited travel on the Tube, buses, Docklands Light Railway and rail services in Greater London. The card also allows a third off the cost of travel on scheduled Riverboat services. It can be used after 9.30am on a weekday or all day on a Saturday, Sunday or bank holiday, but not after 4.30am the following day, and is available from all Underground and some mainline stations.
- **Other Travelcards** are valid for 3 days, a week or a month and can be used at any time of day. To buy a pass you will need to supply a passport-sized photograph.
- For details of all available travelcards, visit www.tfl.gov.uk.

Rover Tickets

Coach
National Express, tel: (08717) 818181, offers a Brit Xplorer pass, which entitles you to unlimited travel on their coaches for specified periods.

Train
For UK residents there are several passes, including a Family, Senior Citizen's and Young Person's Railcard, valid for one year. They cost a fraction of a long-distance InterCity trip and allow you a third off the full journey fare on off-peak trains. The BritRail ticket (from European travel agents and online in US at www.britrail.com) gives you unlimited travel in Great Britain for specified periods.

British Waterways

Britain has over 2,000 miles (3,200 km) of rivers and canals, the latter a legacy of the Industrial Revolution and now extensively restored. There is a wide choice of vessels to hire. Possibilities include exploring the canals, from the Grand Union in the Midlands to the Caledonian, which stretches from coast to coast in Scotland, or taking a pleasure cruiser along major rivers such as the Thames, Avon or the Severn, or around the Norfolk Broads.

For information, contact:
Waterscape (part of British Waterways), 64 Clarendon Road, Watford, Hertfordshire WD17 1DA, tel: (01923) 201120 (Mon–Fri 9am–5.30pm); fax: (01923) 201300; www.waterscape.com.

The Inland Waterways Association is a voluntary body that fights for the restoration and maintenance of Britain's waterway network. It has saved many waterways that would otherwise have disappeared. Contact the association at: PO Box 114, Rickmansworth, Hertfordshire, WD3 1ZY, tel: (01923) 711114, www.waterways.org.uk.

ACCOMMODATION

HOTELS, INNS, BED & BREAKFASTS

Choosing a Hotel

A variety of accommodation exists in Britain, from smart luxury hotels in stately homes and castles, to bed-and-breakfast (B&B) accommodation in private family homes or country farmhouses.

By international standards, hotels in Britain are expensive, so if you are holidaying on a tight budget you should consider staying in bed-and-breakfast accommodation. Alternatively there are plenty of youth hostels, which take people of all ages *(see page 358)*. Wherever you go, always be sure to look at a room before accepting it.

Not all hotels include breakfast in their rates and they may add a service charge of 10–15 percent. However, all charges should be clearly displayed on the tariff.

It is advisable to book in advance, particularly at Christmas, Easter and throughout the summer. During the rest of the year there is generally little difficulty in finding somewhere to stay. You can book a room through a travel agent, directly with a hotel or via the Tourist Board.

Booking Services Most Tourist Information Centres *(see page 387)* will book local accommodation (free or small fee) for personal callers, whereas those involved in the Book-A-Bed-Ahead scheme will reserve you somewhere to stay in any area where there is another TIC involved in the scheme. A small fee is required, deducted from the hotel bill. Some TICs (www.enjoyengland.com) allow you to book online directly, whilst some of the larger ones can book you accommodation if you visit the centre in person and use the accommodation in the next 24 hours. All TICs supply free lists of local accommodation.

The Britain and London Visitor Centre at 1 Regent Street, London W1, www.visitbritain.com, provides general information.

Hotel awards The Enjoy England Quality Rose is the mark of England's nationwide quality assessment scheme, whose ratings (1–5 stars) assess accommodation standards in different categories eg) hotels are in a separate category to B&Bs which come under Guest Accommodation, informing you what each category has to offer.

The AA (Automobile Association) provides a simple scheme awarding between one star (good, but basic) to five stars (luxury). See www.theaa.co.uk.

Visit Scotland (the national tourism organsiation) has a single Quality Assurance Scheme for which star gradings are given by inspectors, ranging from one to five stars.

Visit Wales's assessment scheme awards 1–5 stars, reflecting facilities and quality, whilst also using accommodation categories. All these national bodies assess accommodation using the same criteria.

The Green Tourism Business Scheme has vetted more than 1,400 tourism businesses in England and Scotland since 1999, awarding bronze, silver or gold awards based on an accommodation's eco-credentials (www.green-business.co.uk).

A Michelin award is the accolade for which the most notable of hoteliers strive.

Visit Britain (tel: 020-8846 9000; fax: 020-8563 0302; www.visitbritain.com) produces a series of useful annual *Official Tourist Board* guides dealing with every type of accommodation in Britain, from farms, B&Bs and pet-friendly accommodation to camping and self-catering boating holidays. To be listed, an establishment first has to pay to be inspected and then pay to be given an enhanced listing – so the guides are not totally impartial.

VisitScotland publishes *Where To Stay* guides featuring Scottish self-catering and B&Bs. Visit Wales also publishes an annual *Where To Stay* guide covering all accommodation types in one book. Contact local Tourist Information Centres or the Visit Britain office in your own country for a list.

Stately homes Britain has many grand stately homes and castles that have been converted into country-house hotels. This growing trend in luxury accommodation has saved many historic buildings from dereliction. Most provide an extremely high standard of traditional accommodation and service, often with superb restaurants.

Hotel Listings

Many hotels offer special weekend and low-season breaks between October and April. Details can be obtained from individual hotels, chains of hotels or from Enjoy England whose website lists accomodation discounts and deals.

The suggestions in this book are for hotels in places that will serve as good bases for exploring the regions covered in the guide. Unless otherwise stated, all the rooms have private bathroom facilities.

Hotel Chains

Hotels belonging to big chains such as Holiday Inn, Marriott and Hilton tend to offer a reliable, if at times impersonal, standard of service. In addition there are a host of private hotels. The business traveller on an expense account is increasingly well catered for, in both urban and country areas, where there are many hotels offering large conference rooms and health and leisure facilities in addition to fax and secretarial services. The following groups have hotels in most parts of the country:

Premier Travel Inn tel: (0870) 242 8000 in the UK; (44) 1582 567890 outside the UK; www.premierinn.com. It's the budget leader.
Intercontinental Hotels and Resorts tel: (44) 0800 405060; www.ichotelsgroup.com.
Hilton International tel: (0870) 590 9090; www.hilton.co.uk.
Accor Hotels tel: (0870) 609 0961; www.accorhotels.com.

University Lodgings

Many universities have accommodation to let during the long summer holidays. This can be an inexpensive option (not confined to students), particularly in the capital. Some offer full board. For further information, contact the university in the town of your destination (the local tourist office will advise).

Self-catering Agencies

Blakes Country Cottages
Tel: (08700) 781 300 (UK only); +44 1282 846145 (overseas)
www.blakes-cottages.co.uk
Over 2,000 cottages in pleasant areas and villages.
Cornish Traditional Cottages
Tel: (01208) 821666
Fax: (01208) 821766
www.corncott.com
About 400 cottages in Cornwall.
English Country Cottages
Tel: (08700) 781100 (UK only); +44 1282 846137 (overseas)
Wide variety of country properties including oast houses, barns, castles and manor houses.
Farm Stay UK
Tel: (024) 7669 6909
Produces the annual Farm Stay UK guide, covering over 1200 rural retreats.
Forest Holidays
Tel: (0845) 1308223
www.forestholidays.co.uk
Rustic cabins and campsites owned by the Forestry Commission, in Yorkshire, Cornwall and Scotland.

Romantic Breaks

Many hotels have 4-poster beds and offer special packages for those seeking a romantic weekend or honeymoon. From champagne, chocolates and flowers awaiting in your room, to a candlelit dinner or a balloon flight, hotels will arrange just about anything you ask for.

Book well in advance for Valentine's Day (14 February), Britain's day for lovers.

Stepping Back in History

It is possible to stay in restored old buildings, from medieval castle to a lighthouse. Many such properties have been beautifully restored and are maintained by the Landmark Trust and the National Trust.

The Landmark Trust is a private charity, set up in 1965 to rescue historic buildings. It now has more than 180 properties to let, ranging from castles and manor houses to mills, lighthouses, forts and follies, all restored and furnished in keeping with the original character. Detailed information in a handbook available by post. The book's price is refunded against bookings. Tel: (01628) 825925; www.landmarktrust.org.uk

The National Trust and National Trust for Scotland have more than 400 cottages and smaller houses of historical interest to let, from a romantic cabin hideaway overlooking a Cornish creek to an apartment in York with clear views of the Minster. The National Trust, PO Box 536, Melksham, Wiltshire SN12 8SX, tel: (0844) 800 2070; www.nationaltrustcottages.co.uk. The National Trust for Scotland, 28 Charlotte Square, Edinburgh EH2 4ET, tel: (0844) 4932108 within UK; +44 131 2439331 outside UK; www.ntsholidays.com.

Youth Hostels

There are more than 200 youth hostels in England and Wales ranging from town houses to beach chalets. Facilities and accommodation are basic but cheap, usually comprising shared dormitories of bunk beds.

Some provide a full meals service while others have self-catering kitchens but hostels are only for those who don't mind mucking-in, communal living and a shortage of creature comforts. The maximum length of stay is 10–14 days. You must be a national or international member to stay at a hostel, although anyone of any age can join the association, overseas or in the UK.

Youth Hostel Association (YHA)
Trevelyan House, Dimple Road, Matlock, Derbyshire DE4 3YH
Tel: (01629) 592700
www.yha.org.uk
Scottish Youth Hostels Association (SYHA)
7 Glebe Crescent, Stirling FK8 2JA
Tel: +44 (0) 8701 553255
www.syha.org.uk

London Hostels

Earl's Court
38 Bolton Gardens, SW5 0AQ
Tel: 0870 7705804
186 beds.
Kensington
Holland House, Holland Walk, W8 7QU
Tel: 0870 7705866
200 beds.
St Paul's
36–8 Carter Lane, EC4V 5AB
Tel: 0870 7705764
190 beds.
Thameside
20 Salter Road, SE16 5PR
Tel: 0870 7706010
320 beds.

Inns and Pubs

Inns are a great British institution that have become increasingly popular for accommodation. They are

Reserving and Booking a Room

- When you book a hotel room, ensure that the price quoted is inclusive, and isn't going to be bumped up by a mysterious "travellers' charge" or other extras. Service is usually included in hotel bills.
- If you reserve in advance, you may be asked for a deposit. Reservations made, whether in writing or by phone, can be regarded as binding contracts, and you could lose your deposit or be charged a percentage of the cost if you fail to turn up.
- If you have reserved a room, the hotel will usually keep it for you until early evening, unless you agree otherwise. Rooms must usually be vacated by midday on the day of departure.
- Some accommodation does not allow single-night stays over the weekend.
- Most hotels offer extremely good rates if you stay for several nights, or opt for dinner, bed and breakfast. It can be worth your while to bargain. You can also save money by booking online.

cheaper and smaller than hotels and offer character and the opportunity of meeting local people.

There are many historic taverns, particularly in rural towns and villages. Many are by road sides where travelling pilgrims may have rested in the Middle Ages or stage coaches stopped. Often they retain an old-world character with open fires, low beams, ale on tap and a warm ambience. Standards and food vary from basic to sophisticated.

In urban areas pubs may have more of an institutional feel.

CAMRA (Campaign for Real Ale), 230 Hatfield Road, St Albans AL1 4LW. Tel: 01727-867201; www.camra.org.uk, publishes a guide, *Beer, Bed & Breakfast*, listing the best accommodation.

B&Bs and Guesthouses

These are generally private homes with a few rooms for rent. Standards vary, but you can usually expect friendly hospitality, a hearty breakfast of eggs and bacon with all the trimmings, and helpful advice on where to visit and eat in the area. Usually identified by a B&B sign placed outside, they are most abundant on the edge of towns, at the coast and in other prime tourist spots in rural areas.

B&Bs tend to be good value, and it is always advisable to book in advance during the peak seasons. B&B accommodation is also available in many farmhouses, which provide rural accommodation with an insight into British farm life. Contact local tourist offices for lists of recommended accommodation.

Somewhere between a hotel and a B&B in terms of size, price and facilities, guesthouses are generally small, family-run businesses. Breakfast is usually included.

Companies that specialise in B&Bs include:

Bed & Breakfast Nationwide
Tel: (01255) 831235
Fax: (01255) 831437
www.bedandbreakfastnationwide.com

London Bed & Breakfast Agency
Tel: 020-7586 2768
Fax: 020-7586 6567
www.londonbb.com

The AA publishes an annual guide to more than 4,000 inspected B&Bs, available from most good bookshops. Visit www.theaa.com.

ACCOMMODATION LISTINGS

LONDON

The price of a hotel room in London is as high as any in Europe. However, cost does not always mean quality, so try to view a room before accepting it. In Apr–Sept, it is advisable to book before you arrive as hotels fill up fast. You can book online at visitlondon.com, whilst justcalllondon.co.uk (tel: 0870 4718411) allows you to book online or call their hotel reservations centre.

The hotels listed below are located centrally and have been chosen either for their excellent positions or for providing welcoming English hospitality in characterful surroundings.

Many moderately priced hotels are small and don't have restaurants, although they may provide room service. Some hotels offer babysitting and booking services for theatres and restaurants, while smarter establishments are geared up for business travellers.

Numerous hotels, including the Ritz and the Athenaeum, offer special weekend rates depending on the season. These are well worth checking out and may include incentives such as guided tours and Champagne dinners. It's always worth checking with the hotel.

Hotel Areas

Central isn't necessarily best. Prices are high and hotels can be less characterful and sometimes more seedy than in areas a Tube ride from the West End.

SW1 Traditionally the hotel district.

Victoria There are many delightfully old-fashioned hotels in Victoria, in most price brackets, and the streets close to Victoria station are full of terraced bed-and-breakfasts.

SW5 and **SW7** Around Kensington High Street, Earl's Court and Gloucester Road is a major centre for medium-range hotels.

West End More expensive than elsewhere in London. Bloomsbury (WC1) is central yet has reasonable prices, its hotels having a dignity and providing personal touches that you won't find in the Oxford Street area.

The best areas for moderately priced B&B accommodation are **Victoria, Knightsbridge, Earl's Court, Bayswater** and **Bloomsbury**.

Top Class

Athenaeum Hotel
116 Piccadilly, W1J 7BJ
Tel: 020-7499 3464
Fax: 020-7493 1860
www.athenaeumhotel.com
Smart hotel (123 rooms) in the heart of smart London, close to shops and with views over Green Park. A very English hotel, full of character of the "gentleman's club" kind. Excellent service. **£££**

The Berkeley
Wilton Place, Knightsbridge SW1X 7RL
Tel: 020-7235 6000
Fax: 020-7235 4330
www.the-berkeley.co.uk
Many rate the Berkeley as the best in London. It's low key, with a country house, not a business atmosphere. Swimming pool. **££££**

Claridge's
Brook Street, Mayfair W1K 4HR
Tel: 020-7629 8860
Fax: 020-7499 2210
www.claridges.co.uk
Has long had a reputation for dignity and graciousness. **££££**

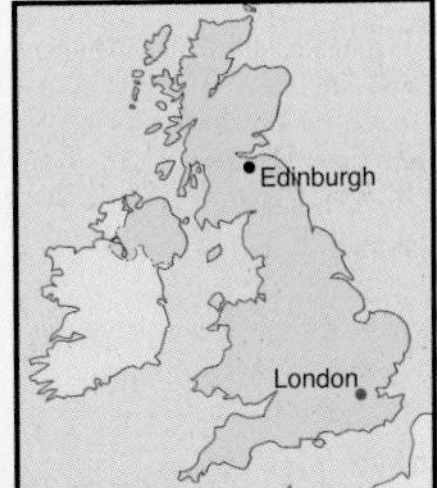

The Connaught
Carlos Place, W1K 2AL
Tel: 020-7499 7070
Fax: 020-7495 3262
www.the-connaught.co.uk
One of the best hotels in London. Superb decor, immaculate service, and a Michelin-starred restaurant. The Coburg Bar sells the rare Krug Clos d'Ambonnay 1995 champagne. **££££**

The Dorchester
Park Lane, W1K 1QA
Tel: 020-7629 8888
Fax: 020-7629 8080

PRICE CATEGORIES

Price categories are for a double room including breakfast and VAT (value added tax) at high season:

£ = under £80
££ = £80–150
£££ = £150–250
££££ = over £250

TRANSPORT
ACCOMMODATION
SHOPPING
ACTIVITIES
A – Z

www.thedorchester.com
One of the most expensive in London. Views over Hyde Park. **££££**

Durley House
115 Sloane Street, SW1X 9PJ
Tel: 020-7235 5537
Fax: 020-7259 6977
www.durleyhouse.com
Seriously luxurious suites, with all mod cons and private gardens. **££££**

The Four Seasons Hotel
Park Lane, W1A 1AZ
Tel: 020-7499 0888
Fax: 020-7493 1895
www.fourseasons.com
A temple of modern opulence. **££££**

The Lanesborough
Hyde Park Corner, SW1X 7TA
Tel: 020-7259 5599
www.lanesborough.com
Top luxury: Regency decor, high-tech facilities. Fitness centre. **££££**

Metropolitan
Old Park Lane, W1K 1LB
Tel: 020-7447 1000
Modern, minimalist and very chic. Home to the Michelin-starred Nobu restaurant. **££££**

The Sanderson
50 Berners Street, W1T 3NG
Tel: 020-7300 1400
www.sandersonlondon.com
Ultra-stylish hotel behind a plain exterior. Philippe Starck-designed interior. **££££**

The Savoy
Strand, WC2R 0EU
Tel: 020-7836 4343
www.fairmont.com/savoy
One of London's legends, with a reputation for comfort and personal service. Reopened after a dramatic £100 million renewal and convenient for theatreland and Covent Garden. **££££**

Luxury

Blakes Hotel
33 Roland Gardens, SW7 3PF
Tel: 020-7370 6701
Fax: 020-7373 0442
www.blakeshotels.com
Exotically furnished with Victorian splendour but with a cosmopolitan, laid-back style. 50 rooms. **£££–££££**

Brown's Hotel
Albemarle/Dover Street, W1S 4BP
Tel: 020-7493 6020
Fax: 020-7493 9381
www.brownshotel.com
A distinguished, very British hotel, founded by Lord Byron's valet in 1837. Smart location. 117 rooms. **££££**

Cadogan Hotel
75 Sloane Street, SW1X 9SG
Tel: 020-7235 7141
Fax: 020-7245 0994
www.cadogan.com
A 19th-century style hotel with 65 rooms. Actress Lily Langtry lived in what is now the bar. Good position in between Chelsea and Knightsbridge. **£££**

Capital Hotel
22 Basil Street, Knightsbridge, SW3 1AT
Tel: 020-7589 5171
Fax: 020-7225 0011
www.capitalhotel.co.uk
Luxurious hotel, tasteful decor. Friendly service. Michelin star restaurant. 49 rooms. **£££–££££**

Goring Hotel
Beeston Place, Grosvenor Gardens, SW1W 0JW
Tel: 020-7396 9000
Fax: 020-7834 4393
www.goringhotel.co.uk
Family-owned, delightfully traditional hotel near Buckingham Palace. Relaxed atmosphere. Homemade food. **£££–££££**

The Halkin
5 Halkin Street, Belgravia, SW1X 7DJ
Tel: 020-7333 1000
Fax: 020-7333 1100
www.halkin.como.bz
Excellent accommodation in a Georgian townhouse. Sleek design, only Michelin-starred Thai restaurant in Europe. **££££**

Landmark London
222 Marylebone Road, NW1 6JQ
Tel: 020-7631 8000
Fax: 020-7631 8080
www.landmarklondon.co.uk
Opened in 1993, eight-storey building with glass domed atrium. Good-sized rooms; all facilities. **£££**

Pelham Hotel
15 Cromwell Place, SW7 2LA
Tel: 020-7589 8288
Fax: 020-7584 8444
www.firmdale.com
Elegant Victorian town-house, with wood-panelled drawing rooms. **£££**

The Ritz
150 Piccadilly, W1J 9BR
Tel: 020-7493 8181
Fax: 020-7493 2687
www.theritzlondon.com
World-famous hotel. Not what it was, despite refurbishment. Jackets and ties required. Tea at the Ritz is one of the best. 136 rooms. **££££**

The Tower Hotel
St Katharine's Way, E1W 1LD
Tel: 0871-376 9036
www.guoman.com/the-tower
Big, modern hotel in the docklands. Breathtaking locale, with views of Tower Bridge and the river. Near the City. Brisk five-minute walk to nearest Tube station; 800+ rooms; meals. **£££**

22 Jermyn Street
22 Jermyn Street, SW1Y 6HL
Tel: 020-7734 2353
Fax: 020-7734 0750
www.22jermyn.com
Right by Piccadilly, a peaceful townhouse excellent for business trips. Concierge can secure restaurant bookings. **££££**

Moderate

Academy Town House
17–21 Gower Street, WC1E 6HG
Tel: 020-7631 4115
www.theetoncollection.com
A small, welcoming hotel. Licensed bar; evening meal available; 49 rooms, 2 with private gardens. **£££**

Elizabeth Hotel
37 Eccleston Square, Victoria, SW1V 1PB
Tel: 020-7828 6812
Fax: 020-7828 6814
www.elizabethhotel.com
Friendly hotel in elegant period square, two minutes' walk from Victoria station. There are 42 rooms, only 2 without ensuite. **££**

The Rubens at the Palace
39 Buckingham Palace Road, Victoria, SW1W 0PS
Tel: 020-7834 6600
Fax: 020-7958 7725
www.rubenshotel.com
Large traditional hotel with a smart location opposite Royal Mews. **£££**

Tophams
24-32 Ebury Street, SW1W 0LU
Tel: 020-7730 3313
Fax: 020-7730 0008
www.zolahotels.com/tophams
This luxury boutique hotel in Belgravia occupies five period houses and is very popular. Friendly and welcoming. **£££**

Inexpensive

Airways Hotel
29 St George's Drive, SW1V 4DG
Tel: 020-7834 0205
Fax: 020-7932 0007
www.airways-hotel.com
Pleasant 37-room hotel (19 with bath) close to Buckingham Place, Westminster Abbey, and Harrods. Friendly service. **££**

Clearlake Hotel
19 Prince of Wales Terrace,W8 5PQ
Tel: 020-7937 3274
Fax: 020-7376 0604
Comfortable 20 self-catering rooms and apartments in a quiet location with views of Hyde Park. Good value. **£**

County Hall Premier Inn
Belvedere Road, SE1 7PB
Tel: 0870-238 3300
www.premierinn.com
In the old County Hall by the river; listed building opposite Houses of Parliament. Advance booking essential. 314 rooms. **££**

Curzon House Hotel
58 Courtfield Gardens, SW5 0NF
Tel: 020-7581 2116
Fax: 020-7835 1319
Economical but comfortable small hotel close to Gloucester Road Underground station. Rooms vary from singles, twins and doubles to 3, 4 and 5-bed rooms to eight-bedded dormitories. **£**

Garden Court Hotel
30–31 Kensington Gardens Square, W2 4BG
Tel: 020-7229 2553
Fax: 020-7727 2749
www.gardencourthotel.co.uk
Friendly, family-run 32-room

Price Categories

Price categories are for a double room including breakfast and VAT (value added tax) at high season:

£ = under £80
££ = £80–150
£££ = £150–250
££££ = over £250

bed-and-breakfast set in a traditional English garden square. **£**

London House Hotel
81 Kensington Gardens Square W2 4DJ
Tel: 020-7243 1810
Fax: 020-7243 1723
www.londonhousehotels.com
Cheap, friendly and comfortable, in a pleasant location, close to public transport; 100 rooms in contemporary-style. **£**

Lonsdale Hotel
9–10 Bedford Place, WC1B 5JA
Tel: 020-7636 1812
Fax: 020-7580 9902
Established 40-room bed and breakfast hotel (some rooms ensuite) with real character in the heart of Bloomsbury, the capital's literary district. **££**

Hotel Strand Continental
143 Strand, WC2R 1JA
Tel: 020-7836 4880
Fax: 020-7379 6105
Despite the fancy name, a cheapest and very central hotel. There are 26 rooms, none ensuite. **£**

THE THAMES VALLEY

Aylesbury

Hartwell House
Oxford Road, nr Aylesbury HP17 8NR
Tel: (01296) 747444
Fax: (01296) 747450
www.hartwell-house.com
Country house hotel in large grounds. Antique-furnished bedrooms; excellent leisure facilities 46 rooms. No children under 6. **£££**

Henley-on-Thames

Hotel du Vin
New Street RG9 2BP
Tel: (01491) 848400
Fax: (01491) 848401
www.hotelduvin.com
Located in a converted brewery close to the river in this Oxfordshire market town, this luxury boutique hotel has 43 smart rooms and a good bistro. **£££**

Red Lion
Hart Street RG9 2AR
Tel: (01491) 572161
Fax: (01491) 410039
www.redlionhenley.co.uk
Just right for the annual regatta in early July, this comfortable, family-owned 39-room hotel close to a 1786 bridge overlooks the finishing post on the River Thames. **£££**

Taplow

Cliveden
Taplow, Berkshire, SL6 0JF
Tel: (01628) 668561
Fax: (01628) 661837
www.clivedenhouse.co.uk
Majestic, luxurious hotel. Once the home of the Prince of Wales, several dukes and the Astors, it is surrounded by 376 acres (152 hectares) of National Trust parkland. **££££**

Windsor

Oakley Court
Windsor Road, Water Oakley SL4 5UR

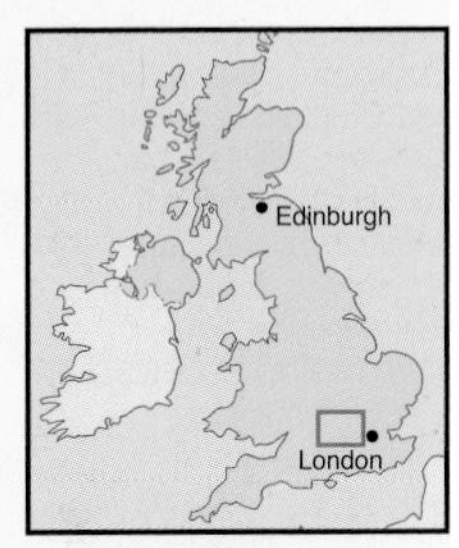

Tel: (01753) 609988
Fax: (01628) 637011
www.oakleycourt.com
Victorian house with extensive grounds running down to the Thames. 118 rooms. **£££**

OXFORD TO STRATFORD

Ampney Crucis

Crown of Crucis
Ampney Crucis, nr Cirencester GL7 5RS
Tel: (01285) 851806
Fax: (01285) 851735
www.thecrownofcrucis.co.uk
A 16th-century inn overlooking the village cricket green. Good food. **££**

Bibury

Bibury Court
Cirencester GL7 5NT
Tel: (01285) 740337
Fax: (01285) 740660
www.biburycourt.co.uk
This glorious Jacobean house fulfils everyone's idea of a Cotswold manor. Rarely does such a sense of history come with so low a price tag. **£££**

The Swan
Gloucestershire GL7 5NW
Tel: (01285) 740695
Fax: (01285) 740473
www.cotswold-inns-hotels.co.uk/swan
In a beautiful riverside setting in its own private gardens. Antique furnishings; good service; 21 rooms. **£££**

Brimingham

Jurys Inn Birmingham
245 Broad Street B1 2HQ
Tel: (0121) 6069000
Fax: (0121) 6069001
www.birminghamhotels.jurysinns.com
In the heart of the city, this 445-room hotel offers a superior standard of budget accommodation. Comfortable rooms fine for an overnight stay. **£**

Broadway, Cotswolds

The Lygon Arms
High Street
Tel: (01386) 852255
Fax: (01386) 858611
www.barcelo-hotels.co.uk
Magnificent 16th-century coaching inn; antique furnishings, log fires. **£££**

Buckland

Buckland Manor
Nr Broadway WR12 7LY
Tel: (01386) 852626
Fax: (01386) 853557
www.bucklandmanor.co.uk
13th-century manor in extensive 10 acre gardens.**££££**

Cheltenham

The Greenway
Shurdington, nr Cheltenham GL51 4UG
Tel: (01242) 862352
Fax: (01242) 862780
www.thegreenway.co.uk
Peaceful Elizabethan mansion covered in Virginia creeper. Recently refurbished rooms offer a luxurious country house feel. **£££**

Hotel On the Park
Evesham Road GL52 2AH
Tel: (01242) 518898
Fax: (01242) 511526
www.hotelonthepark.co.uk
Pretty townhouse opposite Pittville Park with tasteful, individually decorated bedrooms and luxurious bathrooms. No facilities for young children. **£££**

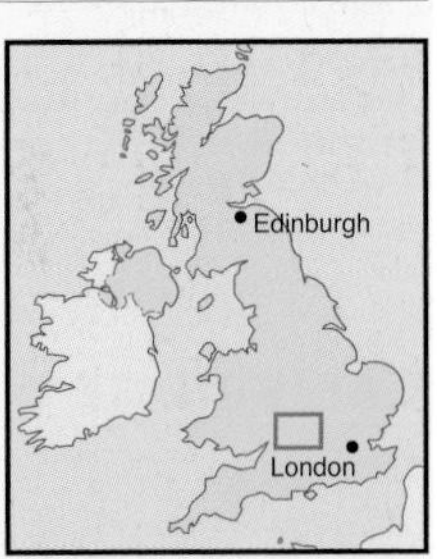

Great Milton, nr Oxford

Le Manoir aux Quat'Saisons
Church Road
Tel: (01844) 278881
Fax: (01844) 278847
www.manoir.com
Raymond Blanc's renowned restaurant and hotel. Stunning gardens, including

a Japanese tea garden. Luxurious, individually decorated rooms, some with their own terrace. **££££**

Lower Slaughter

Lower Slaughter Manor
Nr Bourton-on-the-Water, Gloucestershire GL54 2HP
Tel: (01451) 820456
Fax: (01451) 822150
www.lowerslaughter.co.uk
Luxurious 17th-century manor in own grounds, with panelled private dining room and galleried landing. Meticulous service. Stay in the manor or adjoining coach house, both magnificent with antiques, chintzy fabrics and bathrooms with twin washbasins. Superb breakfast. **££££**

Oxford

Bath Place Hotel
4–5 Bath Place OX1 3SU
Tel: (01865) 791812
Fax: (01865) 791834
www.bathplace.co.uk
Family-run 15-room hotel in the heart of Oxford occupying a group of restored 17th-century cottages. **££**

Cotswold House
363 Banbury Road OX2 7PL
Tel/fax: (01865) 310558
www.cotswoldhouse.co.uk
Recommended B&B. No smoking. **£**

Cotswold Lodge Hotel
66a Banbury Road OX2 6JP
Tel: (01865) 512121
Fax: (01865) 512490
www.cotswoldlodgehotel.co.uk
Beautiful Victorian building in a quiet conservation are a 10-minute walk from city centre; 49 rooms. **££**

Eastgate Hotel
73 High Street OX1 4BE
Tel: (01865) 248332
Fax: (01865) 791681
www.mercure.com
Traditional hotel in central location, adjacent to the site of Oxford's old East Gate, opposite the Examination Schools. Breakfast only. **£££**

The Galaxie Hotel
180 Banbury Road OX2 7BT
Tel: (01865) 515688
Fax: (01865) 556824
www.galaxie.co.uk
Friendly family-run hotel near the shopping and leisure facilities of the Summertown residential district. **££**

Old Parsonage Hotel
1 Banbury Road OX2 6NN
Tel: (01865) 310210
Fax: (01865) 311262
www.oldparsonage-hotel.co.uk
A fine hotel in a renovated old parsonage with 30 luxuriously appointed en-suite bedrooms. The restaurant is open to non-residents. **£££**

Randolph Hotel
Beaumont Street OX1 2LN
Tel: (0844) 8799132
Fax: (01865) 791678
www.randolph-hotel.com
Grand Victorian 151-room hotel in central Oxford offering traditional service with all the trimmings. **£££**

River Hotel
17 Botley Road
Tel: (01865) 243475
Fax: (01865) 724306
www.riverhotel.co.uk
Excellent riverside location, near bus and railway stations. A friendly, small and comfortable hotel within easy reach of the city centre. **£**

Stow-on-the-Wold

Grapevine Hotel
Sheep Street GL54 1AU
Tel: (01451) 830344
Fax: (01451) 832278
www.vines.co.uk
Welcoming hotel in a 17th century stone building, named after the old vine that shades the conservatory restaurant. A good base for touring the Cotswolds. 22 rooms. **££**

Stratford-upon-Avon

Shakespeare Hotel
Chapel Street CV37 6ER
Tel: (01789) 294997
Fax: (01789) 415411
www.mercure.com
This 17th-century, half-timbered building, one of Stratford's most beautiful, is the best hotel in town. Centrally located with open fires, a good restaurant and 74 rooms. **£££**

Tetbury

The Snooty Fox
Market Place GL8 8DD
Tel: (01666) 502436
Fax: (01666) 503479
www.snooty-fox.co.uk
An old Cotswold stone coaching inn on the market square of this historic town. Oak panelling, log fires, antique furniture. Fine restaurant; 12 rooms, some with four-poster beds and ensuite whirlpool bathrooms. **££**

Upper Slaughter

Lords of the Manor
Nr Bourton-on-the-Water GL54 2JD
Tel: (01451) 820243
Fax: (01451) 820696
www.lordsofthemanor.com
A 16th-century former rectory with Victorian additions set in the rolling Cotswold countryside. Many rooms have parkland and lake views. Baronial atmosphere with chintzy fabrics, Oriental rugs, antiques, paintings and family portraits. **£££–££££**

CAMBRIDGE AND EAST ANGLIA

For more hotels in Cambridge and the surrounding area, contact the tourist board on tel: (0871) 226 8006, or visit their website: www.visitcambridge.org.

Burnham Market

The Hoste Arms
The Green PE31 8HD
Tel: (01328) 738777
Fax: (01328) 730103
www.hostearms.co.uk
Characterful 17th-century inn on the green of the village near where Admiral Nelson was born and close to Sandringham's royal estate. Restaurant. **££**

Cambridge

Arundel House Hotel
53 Chesterton Road CB4 3AN
Tel: (01223) 367701
Fax: (01223) 367721
www.arundelhousehotels.co.uk
Privately owned terraced hotel overlooking the River Cam near the centre of town. Restaurant and 103 rooms. **££**

Cambridge Garden House
Granta Place, Mill Lane CB2 1RT
Tel: (01223) 259988
Fax: (01223) 316605
www.cambridgegardenhouse.com
Modern Moat House by river which provides offers on hiring punts and rowing boats. Central location. **££**

Ely

Lamb Hotel
2 Lynn Road CB7 4EJ
Tel: (01353) 663574
Fax: (01353) 662023
www.thelamb-ely.com
Former coaching house whose history can be traced to 1416. Located in the town centre and sitting in shadow of Ely's magnificent cathedral. Includes a four-poster suite. **£**

Lavenham

The Angel
Market Place, Suffolk CO10 9QZ
Tel: (01787) 247388

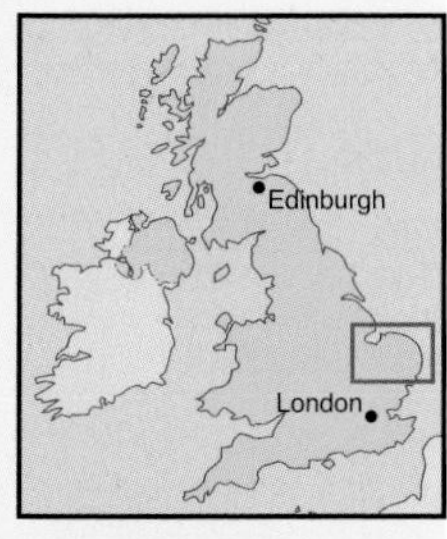

Fax: (01787) 248344
www.maypolehotels.com/angelhotel
A 15th-century inn overlooking this old wool town's market place. The recommended restaurant uses fresh local ingred-ients. Only 8 rooms. **£**

Morston, nr Holt

Morston Hall
NR25 7AA
Tel: (01263) 741041
Fax: (01263) 740419
www.morstonhall.com
Comfortable rooms in a flint manor house on the Norfolk coast. Michelin-starred chef. **£££**

Southwold

The Crown
High Street, Suffolk IP18 6DP
Tel: (01502) 722275
www.adnams.co.uk
Owned by Adnams Brewery so the beer is good. Comfortable rooms and two restaurants, one formal, one brasserie-style. **£**

The Randolph Hotel
Wangford Road, Reydon, near Southwold, Suffolk IP18 6PZ
Tel: (01502) 723603
www.therandolph.co.uk
A 15-minute walk from Southwold, this is a good base for exploring the Suffolk Heritage Coast. Ten modern, comfortable rooms. Restaurant. **££**

Wells-next-the-sea

The Crown Hotel
The Buttlands NR23 1EX
Tel: (01328) 710209
www.thecrownhotelwells.co.uk
A fine old coaching inn in a pretty port on the north Norfolk coast. Popular bar and restaurant. 10 rooms and 2 family suites. **££**

THE SOUTHEAST

Alfriston

The George Inn
High Street BN26 5SY
Tel: (01323) 870319
Fax: (01323) 871384
www.thegeorge-alfriston.com
This 14th-century pub/hotel is in the middle of a pretty village. It has oak-beamed rooms and local fish is a speciality of the restaurant. **££**

Arundel

Amberley Castle
nr Arundel BN18 9LT
Tel: (01798) 831992
Fax: (01798) 831998
www.amberleycastle.co.uk
Genuine 12th-century castle dripping with atmosphere. Opulently refurbished with antiques. Jacuzzis in every bathroom. Recommended. **££££**

Swan Hotel
27–29 High Street BN18 9AG
Tel: (01903) 882314
Fax: (01903) 883759
www.swanhotel.arundel@fullers.co.uk
A listed building at the heart of a delightful village. Comfortable and popular. Good restaurant. **££**

Brighton

The Ambassador Hotel
22–23 New Steine, Marine Parade, BN2 1PD
Tel: (01273) 676869
Fax: (01273) 689988
www.ambassadorbrighton.co.uk
Vegetarian and vegan-friendly menu. **££**

The Grand
97–99 King's Road, BN1 2FW
Tel: (01273) 224300
Fax: (01273) 224321
www.grandbrighton.co.uk
Victorian grandeur and friendly service. Overlooks the beach; indoor pool, gym and spa. **££–£££**

The New Madeira Hotel
19–23 Marine Parade, BN2 1TL
Tel: (01273) 698331
Fax: (01273) 606193
www.newmadeirahotel.com
Rooms at the front have a view of the bright lights of the pier. Weekend break special rates. **££**

Old Ship Hotel
King's Road, BN1 1NR
Tel: (01273) 329001
Fax: (01273) 820718
www.barcelo-hotels.co.uk
One of Brighton's oldest hotels. Elegant, traditional but not too grand. **££**

Hotel Pelirocco
10 Regency Square BN1 2FG
Tel: (01273) 327055
Fax: (01273) 733845
www.hotelpelirocco.co.uk
All rooms individually designed, with their own playstations, in this chic and risqué hotel in the best-preserved Regency square in town. **££**

Canterbury

Falstaff
8–10 St Dunstan's Street CT2 8AF
Tel: (01227) 462138
Fax: (01227) 463525
www.foliohotels.com/falstaff
Coaching inn, within easy reach of cathedral and shops. With 46 rooms. **££**

Chichester

The Millstream Hotel
Bosham, nr Chichester PO18 8HL
Tel: (01243) 573234
Fax: (01243) 573459
www.millstream-hotel.co.uk
Quiet country hotel near Bosham harbour. Good food. **££**

Suffolk House Hotel
3 East Row PO19 1PD
Tel: (01243) 778899
Fax: (01243) 787282
www.suffolkhousehotel.co.uk
Privately-run hotel in a fine Georgian building with restaurant and garden. **£**

Eastbourne

The Grand Hotel
King Edward's Parade BN21 4EQ
Tel: (01323) 412345
Fax: (01323) 412233
www.grandeastbourne.com
Built in 1875, with comfortable rooms, splendid service. Formal restaurant. **£££**

Midhurst

Angel Hotel
North Street GU29 9DN
Tel: (01730) 812421
Fax: (01730) 815928
www.theangelmidhurst.co.uk
A 15th-century coaching inn. Original tudor beams, antique furniture and several 4-poster beds. With 28 rooms. **££**

New Romney

Romney Bay House
Coast Road, Littlestone, TN28 8QY
Tel: (01797) 364747
Fax: (01797) 367156
www.signpost.co.uk/london_south.htm
Right by the sea with stunning views. The 10 rooms are splendidly and individually decorated. Good food and excellent cream teas. **££**

Rye

Durrant House
2 Market Street TN31 7LA
Tel: (01797) 223182

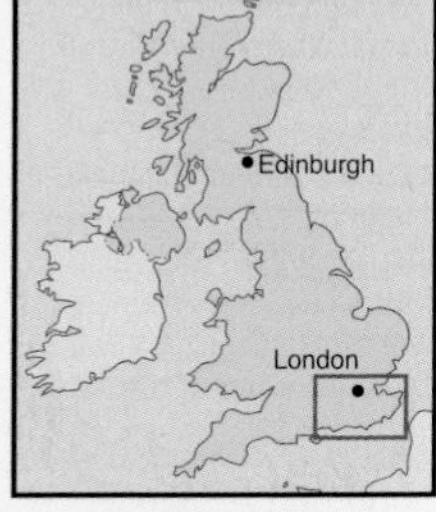

www.durranthouse.com
An attractive Georgian house. Excellent breakfasts. Only 7 rooms. No smoking. **£**

The Mermaid Inn
Mermaid Street TN31 7EY
Tel: (01797) 223065
Fax: (01797) 225069
www.mermaidinn.com
Popular 15th-century inn in this ancient coastal port. Excellent restaurant. There are 31 rooms (8 with 4-poster beds). **£–££**

Tunbridge Wells

Hotel du Vin and Bistro
Crescent Road TN1 2LY
Tel: (01892) 526455
Fax: (01892) 512044
www.hotelduvin.com
Individually decorated rooms, friendly, obliging staff, and great breakfasts are good reasons for staying here, in the centre of town. Good bistro. **££**

Price Categories

Price categories are for a double room including breakfast and VAT (value added tax) at high season:
£ = under £80
££ = £80–150
£££ = £150–250
££££ = over £250

Hardy Country

Brockenhurst

Balmer Lawn Hotel
Lyndhurst Road SO42 7ZB
Tel: (01590) 623116
Fax: (01590) 623864
www.balmerlawnhotel.com
Former hunting lodge in the heart of the New Forest with superb views. Swimming pools, tennis, squash, sauna and gym. **£££**

Careys Manor
Lyndhurst Road SO42 7RH
Tel: (01590) 623551
Fax: (01590) 622799
www.careysmanor.com
An environmentally-friendly 1888 mansion complete with Thai spa. Rooms in garden wing have balconies overlooking walled garden. Pool, gym and sauna. Choice of 3 restaurants. **££**

New Park Manor
Lyndhurst Road, SO42 7QH
Tel: (01590) 623467
Fax: (01590) 622268
www.newparkmanorhotel.co.uk
Excellent 24-room retreat, in landscaped grounds in the New Forest. Once the hunting lodge of Charles II. Excellent restaurant; croquet lawn, heated pool, spa. **££**

Evershot

Summer Lodge
Summer Lane DT2 0JR
Tel: (01935) 482000
Fax: (01935) 482040
www.summerlodgehotel.co.uk
Georgian dower house in 4 acres (1.6 hectares) of mature gardens. Tastefully furnished and noted for excellent service and hospitality. **££**

Lyme Regis

The Alexandra
Pound Street DT7 3HZ
Tel: (01297) 442010
Fax: (01297) 443229
www.hotelalexandra.co.uk
Large 18th-century house with 25 rooms set in fine grounds overlooking the bay. Comfortable and welcoming. **££**

New Milton

Chewton Glen
Christchurch Road BH25 6QS
Tel: (01425) 275341
Fax: (01425) 272310
www.chewtonglen.com

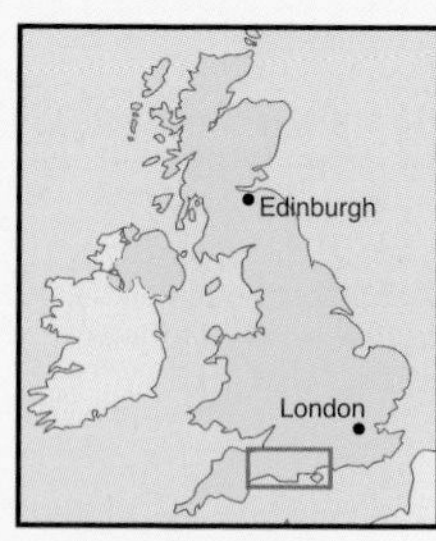

One of England's best-known country house hotels, in an elegant 18th-century mansion on the edge of the New Forest National Park. The swimming pool is modelled on the bathhouses of ancient Rome. Majority of rooms have private gardens or balconies. **££££**

The West Country

Barwick

Little Barwick House
Barwick, nr Yeovil BA22 9TD
Tel: (01935) 423902
Fax: (01935) 420908
www.litttlebarwick.co.uk
Unpretentious Georgian house with gardens. Great place to escape to. **££**

Bath

The Bath Priory
Weston Road BA1 2XT
Tel: (01225) 331922
Fax: (01225) 448276
www.thebathpriory.co.uk
Gothic-style 19th-century house in beautiful gardens. Michelin-starred restaurant. **££££**

Bath Spa Hotel
Sydney Road BA2 6JF
Tel: (0844) 8799106
Fax: (01225) 444006
www.macdonaldhotels.co.uk/bathspa
Near Sydney Gardens and set in its own extensive grounds. All comforts, including spa. Excellent restaurant. **£££**

Bloomfield House
146 Bloomfield Road BA2 2AS
Tel: (01225) 420105
Fax: (01225) 316677
www.ecobloomfield.com
Upmarket B&B in large 18th-century neoclassical house. Some 4-poster beds. No smoking. **££**

Eagle House
Church Street, Bathford BA1 7RS
Tel: (01225) 859946
Fax: (01225) 859430
www.eaglehouse.co.uk
B&B in a pretty conservation village just outside Bath. Friendly and homely but smart. **£**

Francis Hotel
Queen Square BA1 2HH
Tel: (01225) 424105
Fax: (01225) 319715
www.mercure.com
Traditional Bath stone building with comfortable interior; 95 rooms. **££**

The Hollies
Hatfield Road BA2 2BD
Tel/fax: (01225) 313366
www.theholliesbath.co.uk
Grade II listed Victorian B&B. Three attractive rooms and pretty garden. No children under 16. **£**

Holly Lodge
8 Upper Oldfield Park BA2 3JZ
Tel: (01225) 424042
Fax: (01225) 481138
www.hollylodge.co.uk
Large Victorian house on the south side of Bath. Emphasis on service and comfort. Excellent breakfasts. Frilly furnishings. **££**

The Queensberry Hotel
Russel Street BA1 2QF
Tel: (01225) 447928
Fax: (01225) 446065
www.thequeensberry.co.uk
Small boutique hotel occupying three Georgian houses knocked together. Comfortable and characterful, though some rooms are on the small side. The esteemed Olive Tree restaurant is in the basement. **££–£££**

Royal Crescent Hotel
16 Royal Crescent BA1 2LS
Tel: (01225) 823333
Fax: (01225) 339401
www.royalcrescent.co.uk
The ultimate address in Bath, with a central location. Antiques, paintings, individually decorated rooms, a noted restaurant and secluded garden at the back. With 45 rooms. **££££**

Villa Magdala Hotel
Henrietta Road BA2 6LX
Tel: (01225) 466329
Fax: (01225) 483207
www.villamagdala.co.uk
Overlooking Henrietta Park. Private car park, which is unusual in the centre of Bath. Non-smoking. **££**

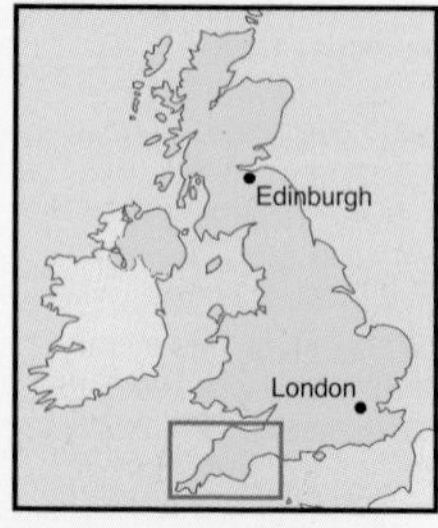

Bigbury-on-Sea

Burgh Island Hotel
South Devon TQ7 4BG
Tel: (01548) 810514
www.burghisland.com
Unusual Art Deco hotel on an island first inhabited in AD 900 by monks; access by sea tractor. Agatha Christie wrote two books here. The 25 rooms, many named for past famous

Price Categories

Price categories are for a double room including breakfast and VAT (value added tax) at high season:
£ = under £80
££ = £80–150
£££ = £150–250
££££ = over £250

guests, ooze romantic charm. Price includes dinner. **££££**

Bradford-on-Avon

Bradford Old Windmill
4 Masons Lane BA15 1QN
Tel: (01225) 866842
Fax: (01225) 866648
www.bradfordoldwindmill.co.uk
Hidden-away converted windmill. No smoking. 3 rooms **££**

Old Manor Hotel
Trowle Common, nr Bradford-on-Avon BA14 9BL
Tel: (01225) 777393
Fax: (01225) 765443
www.oldmanorhotel.com
A 16th-century manor house, newly redecorated. Restaurant. **£–££**

Castle Combe

Manor House Hotel
Castle Combe, nr Bath SN14 7HR
Tel: (01249) 782206
Fax: (01249) 782159
www.manorhouse.co.uk
Parts of this manor house are 14th-century. Best rooms have beams, exposed stone walls and quality furnishings. Golf break packages include unlimited access to the championship green although a handicap certificate is a must. **£££**

Chagford, Devon

Gidleigh Park
TQ13 8HH
Tel: (01647) 432367
Fax: (01647) 432574
www.gidleigh.com
Quintessentially English, a huge, half-timbered house in 45 acres (18 hectares) of grounds within Dartmoor National Park; babbling brook, log fires and impeccable service. Excellent restaurant, with two Michelin stars. **££££**

Mill End Hotel
Dartmoor National Park TQ13 8JN
Tel: (01647) 432282
Fax: (01647) 433106
www.millendhotel.com
Pretty old mill, complete with wheel, in peaceful setting on River Teign. Excellent for families; seasonal gourmet events by award-winning chef. **££**

Colerne, nr Bath

Lucknam Park
SN14 8AZ
Tel: (01225) 742777
Fax: (01225) 743536
www.lucknampark.co.uk
Luxurious manor with equestrian centre and spa. **££££**

Dartmouth

The Royal Castle
11 The Quay TQ6 9PS
Tel: (01803) 833033
Fax: (01803) 835445
www.royalcastle.co.uk
On Dartmouth's quayside, this 17th-century coaching inn serves good Devon cuisine. 25 rooms, some with river views). **££–£££**

Fowey

Fowey Hall
Hanson Drive PL23 1ET
Tel: (01726) 833866
www.foweyhallhotel.co.uk
Imposing turrets outside, sumptuous decor inside, but relaxed atmosphere and children are well catered for. **££**

Old Quay House
28 Fore Street PL23 1AQ
Tel: (01726) 833302
www.theoldquayhouse.com
Right on the quayside, a traditional exterior conceals sleek modern decor. The views are stupendous and the Q Restaurant is highly recommended. **££–£££**

Freshford

Homewood Park
Abbey Lane, Hinton Charterhouse BA2 7TB
Tel: (01225) 723731
Fax: (01225) 723820
www.homewoodpark.co.uk
South of Bath, this very English country house hotel has outdoor swimming pool, beautiful gardens and a cosy bar. Some rooms have Victorian free-standing baths; 19 rooms. **£££**

Marazion/ St Michael's Mount

Mount Haven Hotel
Turnpike Road, Penzance TR17 0DQ
Tel: (01736) 710249
Fax: (01736) 711658
www.mounthaven.co.uk
A pretty hotel with light, airy rooms, some with balconies and private terraces, overlooking St Michael's Mount. Near Land's End. Restaurant serves fresh fish. **££**

Monkton Combe

Combe Grove Manor Hotel
Brassknocker Hill BA2 7HS
Tel: (01225) 834644
Fax: (01255) 834961
www.barcelo-hotels.co.uk
Luxurious 18th-century house and garden lodge. Pools, gym, tennis, golf and driving range. **£££**

The Manor House
BA2 7HD
Tel: (01225) 723128
Fax: (01225) 722972
www.manorhousebath.co.uk
Attractive medieval manor offering very reasonably priced accommodation. Fig Tree Restaurant open Fri–Sat evening. **££**

Penzance

Abbey Hotel
Abbey Street TR18 4AR
Tel: (01736) 366906
Fax: (01736) 351163
http://theabbeyonline.co.uk/home.html
Delightful stuccoed building overlooking the harbour. Rooms have period features. Michelin-starred restaurant. **££**

The Queen's Hotel
The Promenade TR18 4HG
Tel: (01736) 362371
Fax: (01736) 350033
www.queens-hotel.com
Traditional English seaside hotel with wonderful views over Mounts Bay to St Michael's Mount in the distance; 70 rooms. **£–££**

The Summer House
Cornwall Terrace TR18 4HL
Tel: (01736) 363744
Fax: (01736) 360959
www.summerhouse-cornwall.com
In a blue-painted Regency building just off the seafront. Light, bright decor and a small walled garden. Open Mar–Oct; restaurant open Fri–Sun. **£–££**

St Ives

Carbis Bay Hotel
Carbis Bay TR26 2NP
Tel: (01736) 795311
Fax: (01736) 797677
www.carbisbayhotel.co.uk
Good restaurant, splendid views of one of Britain's most beautiful bays, private beach. **£–££**

Ston Easton

Ston Easton Park
Nr Bath BA3 4DF
Tel: (01761) 241631
Fax: (01761) 241377
www.stoneaston.co.uk
Most notable for its Humphrey Repton gardens, with grotto, bridges over River Norr and 18th-century ice house, this fine Palladian manor provides country house splendour in the Mendip Hills. Some rooms with Chippendale 4-posters. Restaurant's organic produce comes from the Victorian kitchen garden. **££££**

Tintagel

Michael House
Trelake Lane, Treknow, Cornwall, PL34 0EW.
Tel: (01840) 770592.
www.michael-house.co.uk
Vegetarian and vegan guest-house with sea-views, in scenic coastal resort. **£**

Truro

Royal Hotel
Lemon Street TR1 2QB
Tel: (01872) 270345
Fax: (01872) 242453
www.royalhotelcornwall.co.uk
Individually decorated rooms in an independent hotel in the heart of Truro. Executive rooms have business facilities. **£–££**

Woolacombe

Woolacombe Bay Hotel
EX34 7BN
Tel: (01271) 870388
Fax: (01271) 870 613
www.woolacombe-bay-hotel.co.uk
Built in the late 1880s and set in 6 acres (2.5 hectares) of grounds by the sea. Pools, fitness classes, squash, tennis, 9-hole pitch and putt golf course, diving, yacht charter, snooker, table tennis, gym and spa. Local surfing school. **££**

ISLES OF SCILLY

St Martin's

St Martin's on the Isle
Tel: (01720) 422090
Fax: (01720) 422298
www.stmartinshotel.co.uk
Nestling in a cove, with own quay, this hotel, looking like a cluster of granite cottages, blends with its natural surroundings. Michelin-starred chef. **£££**

St Mary's

St Mary's Hall Hotel
Church Street TR21 0JR
Tel: (01720) 422316
Fax: (01720) 422252
www.stmaryshallhotel.co.uk
On the edge of Hugh Town close to the beaches, this hotel has a long-standing reputation for good food. Price includes dinner. **££**

Tresco

Island Hotel
Tel: (01720) 422883
Fax: (01720) 423883
www.simplyscilly.co.uk
Fine hotel with great location in sub-tropical gardens near Old Grimsby. Pool and tennis court. 51 rooms. Price includes dinner. **£££**

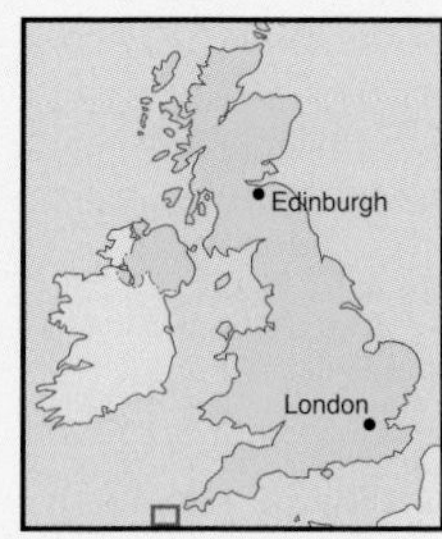

WYE VALLEY AND SOUTH WALES

Abergavenny

Llanthony Priory Hotel
Llanthony, Abergavenny, Monmouthshire, NP7 7NN
Tel: 01873 89048
www.llanthonyprioryhotel.co.uk
This small country inn is part of an Augustinian priory. The 4 rooms in the tower are furnished in 12th-century style and you have to descend a spiral staircase to reach the toilets. Fine dining room **££**

Aberystwyth

Conrah Hotel
Chancery, Ceredigion SY23 4DF
Tel: (01970) 617941
Fax: (01970) 624546
www.conrah.co.uk
Traditional country comfort at this peaceful hotel a few miles south of Aberystwyth. Good touring centre. 17 rooms. **££**

Brecon

Peterstone Court
Llanhamlach, Powys LD3 7YB
Tel: (01874) 665387
Fax: (01874) 665376
www.peterstone-court.com
Comfortable 18th-century manor with a prime location in the Brecon Beacons National Park; 12 rooms. **££**

Cardiff

St David's Hotel and Spa
Havannah Street CF10 5SD
Tel: (02920) 454045
Fax: (02920) 487056
www.principal-hayley.com
On the spectacularly transformed Cardiff Bay and within easy reach of the Wales Millennium Arts and Entertainment Centre. Airy, luxurious rooms; spectacular views; excellent restaurant. **£££**

Crickhowell

Bear Hotel
Powys NP8 1BW
Tel: (01873) 810408
Fax: (01873) 811696
www.bearhotel.co.uk
Famous inn on old stagecoach route. Atmospheric bar popular with locals and visitors. Good food and wine; comfortable rooms. **££**

Gower Peninsula

Fairyhill
Reynoldston, Swansea SA3 1BS
Tel: (01792) 390139
Fax: (01792) 391358
www.fairyhill.net
Twelve miles (20 km) west of Swansea, close to the breathtaking Gower Peninsular beaches, this 18th-century house is situated in 24 acres (9.7 hectares) of parkland. Down-to-earth and friendly, with one of the best restaurants in the area; 8 rooms. **££–£££**

Hereford

Castle House
Castle Street HR1 2NW
Tel: (01432) 356321
Fax: (01432) 365909
www.castlehse.co.uk
Former home of the Bishop of Hereford, in the centre of town, close to the cathedral, this 15-room hotel provides an excellent base. Renowned for its restaurant. **£££**

Kington

Penrhos Court
Herefordshire HR5 3LH
Tel: (01544) 230720.
Fax: (01544) 230754.
www.penrhos.com
700-year-old farm near Offa's Dyke and Black Mountains. Award-winning organic food from Daphne Lambert, chef/nutritionist and food writer. **££**

Llangammarch Wells

Lake Country House
Powys LD4 4BS
Tel: (01591) 620202
Fax: (01591) 620457
www.lakecountryhouse.co.uk
Mock-Tudor mansion set in grounds that slope down to the lake. Wonderful views from individually-designed bedrooms. Offers fishing breaks. **££**

Llyswen

Llangoed Hall
Powys LD3 0YP
Tel: (01874) 754525
Fax: (01874) 754545
www.llangoedhall.com
Luxurious 17th-century manor house on the banks of the River Wye overlooking the Black Mountains, brimming with

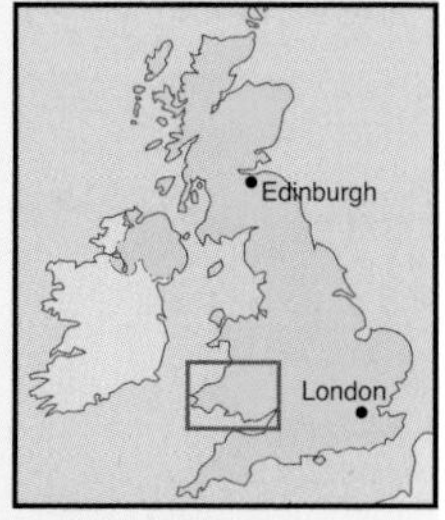

antique furniture and Elanbach fabrics (designed by Laura Ashley's widower). Parts date from 1632, but the Edwardian architect Sir Clough Williams-Ellis rebuilt it in 1919. Excellent breakfasts. **£££**

Newport

Celtic Manor
Coldra Woods, Usk Valley NP18 1HQ
Tel: (01633) 413000
Fax: (01633) 412910
www.celtic-manor.com
19th-century manor in landscaped gardens. Three golf courses (venue for 2010 Ryder Cup), indoor pool, tennis and shooting. **£££–££££**

Swansea

Norton House Hotel
Norton Road SA3 5TQ
Tel: (01792) 404891
Fax: (01792) 403210
www.nortonhousehotel.co.uk
Elegant Georgian ex-mariner's house, between Swansea Bay and the village of Mumbles. Warm welcome and sea views. **££**

ABOVE: the eccentric Portmeirion Hotel in the fantasy model village where *The Prisoner* TV series was filmed in the 1960s.

NORTH WALES

Isle of Anglesey

Ye Olde Bull's Head Inn
Castle Street, Beaumaris
Tel: (01248) 810329
Fax: (01248) 811294
www.bullsheadinn.co.uk
Historic 13-room coaching inn on the route to the Irish ferry. Comfortable oak-beamed rooms, fine restaurant and old-world charm. **££**

Betws-y-Coed

Tan-y-Foel Country House
Capel Garmon nr Betws-y-Coed
Tel: (01690) 710507
www.tyfhotel.co.uk
An award-winning stone manor hotel with stunning views and good food. Modern and informal. No children under 12. **££**

Llandrillo, nr Corwen

Tyddyn Llan
Denbighshire LL21 0ST
Tel: (01490) 440264
Fax: (01490) 440414
www.tyddynllan.co.uk
Excellent base for walking, this grey stone Georgian house in the Vale of Edeyrnion has 4 miles (6 km) of fishing on the River Dee. Elegant, antique-furnished rooms. Large gardens. Award-winning restaurant. **£–££**

Llandudno

Bodysgallen Hall
Tel: (01492) 584466
Fax: (01492) 582519
www.bodysgallen.com
Stunning sandstone manor house with superb gardens and woodland walks. Country-house feel. Spa. No children under 6. **££**

Empire Hotel
Church Walks LL30 2HE
Tel: (01492) 860555
www.empirehotel.co.uk
The third generation of the Maddock family run this elegant Victorian hotel. Quality fittings and marble bathrooms. Indoor and outdoor heated pools. **££**

St Tudno Hotel
North Parade, Promenade
Tel: (01492) 874411
Fax: (01492) 860407
www.st-tudno.co.uk
Small 18-room seaside hotel opposite the Victorian pier. Very friendly. Great for families. Excellent food. **££**

Llansanffraid Glan Conwy

The Old Rectory
Llanrwst Road
Tel: (01492) 580611
Fax: (01492) 584555
www.oldrectorycountryhouse.co.uk
Awarded 5 stars by the AA, this Georgian guest house has fine views from Conwy Castle to Snowdonia and an informal atmosphere. Six rooms with antique furnishings. Overlooks Conwy RSPB bird reserve. **££**

Eglwysfach, nr Machynlleth

Ynyshir Hall
Powys SY20 8TA
Tel: (01654) 781209
Fax: (01654) 781366
www.ynyshirhall.co.uk
Attractive 15th-century country house hotel with 9 bedrooms. It was one of Queen Victoria's hunting lodges but now has an exuberant Mediterranean feel with rooms painted in bright yellows and deep blues and the boldly coloured paintings of the owner, artist Rob Reen, on most walls. Warm service and excellent food. Nature reserve on the doorstep. **£££**

Portmeirion

Hotel Portmeirion
Tel: (01766) 770000
Fax: (01766) 770300
www.portmeirion-village.com
This eccentric 14-room hotel is central to architect Sir Clough Williams-Ellis's model fantasy village on the coast above Tremadog Bay. The interior is simple and contemporary; many rooms have direct views of the estuary. **£££**

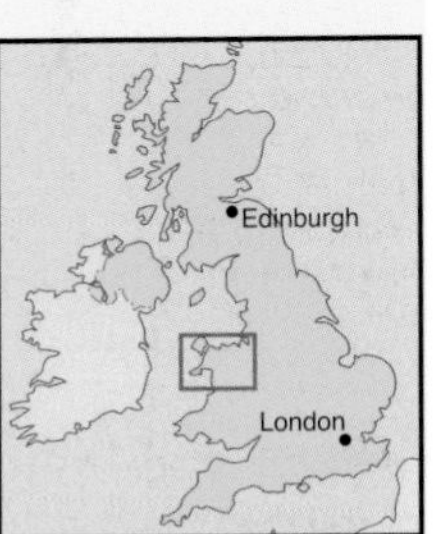

Talsarnau, nr Harlech

Maes-y-Neuadd
Gwynedd LL47 6YA
Tel: (01766) 780200
Fax: (01766) 780211
Excellent views, bar with inglenook fireplace and a friendly welcome are some of the charms of this manor house hotel, some of which dates from the 14th century. Rooms are variable, the best with the 4-poster. **££**

PRICE CATEGORIES

Price categories are for a double room including breakfast and VAT (value added tax) at high season:
£ = under £80
££ = £80–150
£££ = £150–250
££££ = over £250

MERSEYSIDE AND SHROPSHIRE

Chester

Best Western Queen Hotel
63 City Road CH1 3AH
Tel: (01244) 305000
Fax: (01244) 318483
www.bw-queenhotel.co.uk
Very handy for the station, this smart 131-room hotel has two restaurants and an Italian garden. **££**

Liverpool

Britannia Adelphi Hotel
Ranelagh Place L3 5UL
Tel: (0151) 709 7200
Fax: (0151) 708 0743
www.adelphi-hotel.co.uk
The grand classical stone facade provides a major landmark, next to Lime Street station. With 402 rooms, plus health club facilities. **££**

Crowne Plaza Liverpool
St Nicholas Place L3 1QW
Tel: (0151) 243 8000
Fax: (0151) 243 8111
www.cpliverpool.com
Good location, next to the Royal Liver Building and overlooking the Mersey. Built in 1998, it has a gym and indoor swimming pool. 159 rooms. **£££**

Hope Street Hotel
40 Hope Street L1 9DA
Tel: (0151) 709 3000
Fax: (0151) 709 2454
www.hopestreethotel.co.uk
Boutique hotel with large, light rooms, wood floors, friendly staff and excellent restaurant. Central but quiet. **££–£££**

Manchester

Malmaison Manchester
1–3 Piccadilly M1 1LS
Tel: (0161) 2781000
Fax: (0161) 2781002
www.malmaison-manchester.com
Located in a former warehouse, its red-and-black decor tries to echo the Moulin Rouge. Although it has 167 rooms, it aims for a boutique feel. Some call it pretentious. **£££**

Tulip Inn
Old Park Lane M17 8PG
Tel: (0161) 7553355
Fax: (0161) 7553344
www.tulipinnmanchester.co.uk
Opposite the 280-shop Trafford Centre, overlooking Salford Quays; 161 rooms; under-16s stay free. **£**

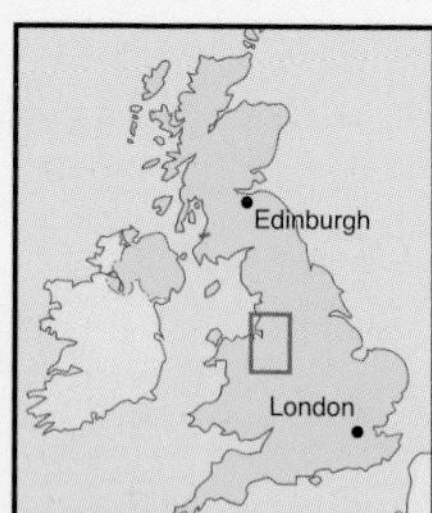

Shrewsbury

The Lion
Wyle Cop SY1 1UY
Tel: (01743) 353107
Fax: (01743) 352744
www.thelionhotelshrewsbury.co.uk
Beamed 16th-century inn in centre of this medieval town. 59 rooms. **££**

PEAK DISTRICT AND EAST MIDLANDS

Ashford in the Water

Riverside House Hotel
Bakewell DE45 1QF
Tel: (01629) 814275
Fax: (01629) 812873
www.riversidehousehotel.co.uk
Small 18th-century house on the Wye with some 4-poster beds, log fires and antiques; 15 rooms. **££**

Bakewell

Rutland Arms Hotel
The Square DE45 1BT
Tel: (01629) 812812
Fax: 01629) 812309
wwwrutlandarmsbakewell.com
Jane Austen is said to have stayed here while working on *Pride and Prejudice*. Its 54 antique clocks in public areas hint at its traditional flavour. **££**

Belton

Belton Woods Hotel
Nr Grantham NG32 2LN
Tel: (01476) 593200
Fax: (01476) 574547
www.devere-hotels.com
Lakeside hotel with two championship-standard 18-hole golf courses and one 9-hole course. 136 rooms, plus lodges in grounds. **££**

Buxton

Buckingham Hotel
1–2 Burlington Road SK17 9AS
Tel: (01298) 70481
Fax: (01298) 72186
www.buckinghamhotel.co.uk
Old and sometimes creaky building but welcoming, informal atmosphere. Bar is known for its range of real ales. 37 rooms. **££**

Old Hall Hotel
The Square SK17 6BD
Tel: (01298) 22841
Fax: (01298) 72437
www.oldhallhotelbuxton.co.uk
A landmark since the 16th century, this dignified 38-room hotel on the square overlooks Pavilion Gardens with the Opera House nearby. **£**

Dovedale

Izaak Walton Hotel
Nr Ashbourne DE6 2AY
Tel: (01335) 350555
Fax: (01335) 350539
www.izaakwaltonhotel.com
One of the Peak's most stylish and picturesque hotels, named after the 17th-century author of *The Compleat Angler* who fished in the area. In the jaws of Dovedale beneath Thorpe Cloud; 35 rooms. **££**

Hassop

Hassop Hall Hotel
Nr Bakewell DE45 1NS
Tel: (01629) 640488
Fax: (01629) 640577
www.hassophallhotel.co.uk
A classical Georgian house set in spacious parkland just 2½ miles (4 km) from Bakewell; 13 elegant rooms. **££–£££**

Hathersage

George Hotel
Main Road S32 1BB
Tel: (01433) 650436
Fax: (01433) 650099
www.george-hotel.net
Former 16th-century coaching inn; lovely courtyard and a fine restaurant. **££**

Millstone Country Inn
Sheffield Road S32 1DA
Tel: (01433) 650258
Fax: (01433) 650276
www.millstoneinn.co.uk
Above the village with fine views down the Hope Valley to Kinder Scout. **£**

Matlock

Riber Hall Hotel
DE4 5JU
Tel: (01629) 582795
Fax: (01629) 580475

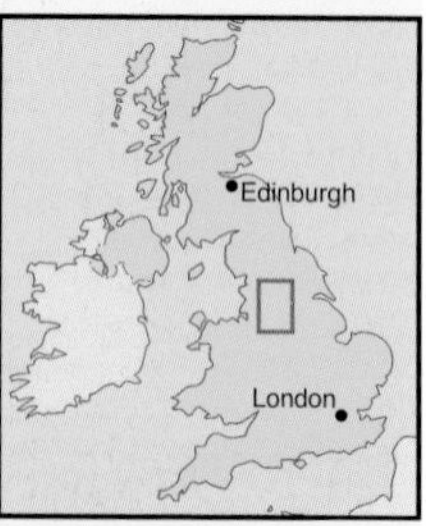

www.riber-hall.co.uk
14-room Tudor mansion high above town with wonderful views. **££**

Matlock Bath

Temple Hotel
Temple Walk DE4 3PG
Tel: (01629) 583911
Fax: (01629) 580851
www.templehotel.co.uk
On a hilltop with splendid views, this 14-room hotel, in a gorgeous Georgian building, is central and has a bar serving real ale by an open fire. **£**

Rowsley

East Lodge Country House Hotel
Matlock DE4 2EF
Tel: (01629) 734474
Fax: (01629) 733949

www.eastlodge.com
Pretty, tastefully furnished country house in 10 acres (4 hectares) of grounds, just off the A6. The restaurant has a fine reputation. **£££**

Peacock Hotel
DE4 2EB
Tel: (01629) 733518
Fax: (01629) 732671
www.thepeacockatrowsley.com
Small hotel, recently acquired by the owner of Haddon Hall. Stylish, interior-designed rooms and a restaurant headed by Daniel Smith, who has worked with well-known chef Tom Aitkins. Famous in the world of angling for the quality of fly fishing in the nearby River Wye. **££–£££**

Stapleford, nr Melton Mowbray

Stapleford Park
LE14 2EF
Tel: (01572) 787000
Fax: (01572) 787001
www.staplefordpark.com
Sumptuous 17th-century country house hotel with 55 rooms and 500 acres (200 hectares) designed by "Capability" Brown. Designers of the deluxe rooms include Nina Campbell and Mulberry and the quintessentially English style of Crabtree & Evelyn. Facilities include a spa, pool, gym, golf course, tennis courts and field sports such as shooting and falconry, plus archery and mountain biking. **££££**

YORKSHIRE AND THE NORTHEAST

Belford

The Blue Bell Hotel
Market Place NE70 7NE
Tel: (01668) 213543
www.bluebellhotel.com
Lovely hotel in 17th-century coaching inn on the east coast close to Holy Island, furnished in period style. Lovely garden; 28 rooms. **£**

Bolton Abbey

Devonshire Arms Country House Hotel
Skipton BD23 6AJ
Tel: (01756) 710441
Fax: (01756) 710564
www.thedevonshirearms.co.uk
With 40-rooms, open fires, and lounges furnished with antiques from Chatsworth, home of the Duke and Duchess of Devonshire. Visit Britain's Small Hotel of the Year 2008. **£££**

Durham

Farnley Tower Hotel
The Avenue DH1 4DX
Tel: (0191) 375 0011
Fax: (0191) 383 9694
www.farnley-tower.co.uk
Renovated Victorian house with guest-house feel situated in a quiet residential street within walking distance of the city centre. Cathedral and castle views. 13 rooms. **££**

Three Tuns Hotel
New Elvet DH1 3AQ
Tel: (0191) 3864326
www.swallow-hotels.com
Pleasant place to stay in this lovely cathedral town. Traditional atmosphere. Guests have complimentary access to leisure club in hotel lying opposite. **££**

Harrogate

The Boar's Head
Ripley Castle Estate, nr Harrogate HG3 3AY
Tel: (01423) 771888
Fax: (01423) 771509
www.boarsheadripley.co.uk
Ten minutes from Ripley. Antiques and comfy chairs. Good, plentiful, inexpensive food; 25 rooms. **££**

The Ruskin Hotel
1 Swan Road HG1 2SS
Tel: (01423) 502045
Fax: (01423) 506131
www.ruskinhotel.co.uk
Small hotel in centre. Good service and food ; beautiful gardens. **££**

Haydon Bridge

Langley Castle
Langley-on-Tyne NE47 5LU
Tel: (01434) 688888
Fax: (01434) 684019
www.langleycastle.com
A medieval fortified hotel. Individual rooms and luxury facilities. Outdoor activities plus hot air ballooning/off-road driving. **££–£££**

Helmsley

Black Swan Hotel
Market Place YO62 5BJ
Tel: (01439) 770466
www.blackswan-helmsley.co.uk
Comfortable hotel in the centre of town at the foot of the North York Moors. 45 rooms. Restaurant, tearoom and patisserie. **££**

Hexham, Priestpopple

County Hotel
NE46 1PS
Tel: (01434) 603601
www.thecountyhexham.co.uk
Excellent hospitality in a market town. Handy for exploring the Pennines, Hadrian's Wall. 8 rooms. **£**

Wensleydale

The Wheatsheaf
Carperby, nr Leyburn DL8 4DF
Tel: (01969) 663216
Fax: (01969) 663019
www.wheatsheafinwensleydale.co.uk
Where the author James Herriot and his wife spent their honeymoon. 13 rooms, some new. **£**

York

Dean Court
Duncombe Place YO1 7EF
Tel: (01904) 625082
Fax: (01904) 620305
www.deancourt-york.co.uk
Comfortable 37-room traditional hotel close to the Minster. **£££**

Elmbank
The Mount YO24 1GE
Tel: (01904) 610653
Fax: (01904) 627139
www.elmbankhotel.com
A city hotel with a country-house atmosphere. **££**

The Groves
15 St Peter's Grove YO30 6AQ
Tel: (01904) 559777
Fax: (01904) 645832
www.thegroveshotelyork.co.uk
Victorian townhouse within easy walking distance of the city centre. **£**

Ibis York Centre
77 The Mount YO24 1BN
Tel: (01904) 658301
Fax: (01904) 621224
www.ibishotel.com
Modern, functional 91-bedroom hotel within five minutes' walk of the city walls. **£**

Middlethorpe Hall
Bishopthorpe road YO23 2GB
Tel: (01904) 641241
Fax: (01904) 620176
www.middlethorpe.com
Elegant country hotel, run with style in a 17th-century house; 29 rooms. **£££**

Minster Hotel
60 Bootham
Tel: (01904) 621267
Fax: (01904) 654719
www.yorkminsterhotel.co.uk
Skilful conversion of two Victorian houses, four minutes from the Minster; rooftop garden with superb views. **££**

Park Inn
North Street YO1 6JF
Tel: (01904) 459988
Fax: (01904) 459987
www.parkinn.co.uk
On the south bank of the river, a smart seven-storey hotel with sauna, dance studio and gym. 200 modern rooms. **££**

PRICE CATEGORIES

Price categories are for a double room including breakfast and VAT (value added tax) at high season:

£ = under £80
££ = £80–150
£££ = £150–250
££££ = over £250

TRANSPORT
ACCOMMODATION
SHOPPING
ACTIVITIES
A – Z

The Lake District

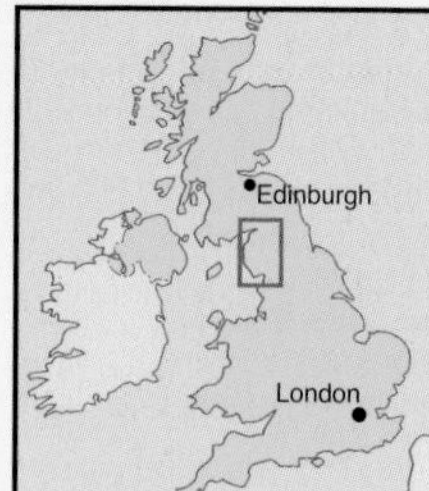

Ambleside

Rothay Manor
Rothay Bridge LA22 0EH
Tel: (01539) 433605
Fax: (01539) 433607
www.rothaymanor.co.uk
Quintessential English country house hotel with gardens. Warm and friendly. **££**

Wateredge Inn
Borrans Road, Waterhead LA22 0EP
Tel: (01539) 432332
Fax: (01539) 431878
www.wateredgeinn.co.uk
Family-run hotel with views over Lake Windermere from most rooms. Lakeshore garden. Restaurant. **£**

Cartmel, nr Grange-over-Sands

Aynsome Manor Hotel
Aynsome Lane LA11 6HH
Tel: (01539) 536653
Fax: (01539) 536016
www.aynsomemanorhotel.co.uk
16th-century main house and cottage in a picturesque lakeland village, off the tourist track. Rates include dinner. **££**

Easedale

Lancrigg Vegetarian Country House Hotel
Grasmere, Cumbria LA22 9QN
Tel: (01539) 435317
Fax: (01539) 435058
www.lancrigg.co.uk
Beautiful country house with a separate cottage. **£**

Kendal District

Heaves Hotel
Heaves LA8 8EF
Tel: (01539) 560396
Fax: (01539) 560269
www.heaveshotel.com
Well-preserved Georgian mansion with large bedrooms, a library and fine views. **£**

Keswick District

The Anchorage
14 Ambleside Road CA12 4DL
Tel: (01768) 772813
www.anchoragekeswick.co.uk
Near lake and town centre. Good views. 7 rooms. Private parking. **£**

Armathwaite Hall Country House
Bassenthwaite Lake CA12 4RE
Tel: (017687) 76551
www.armathwaite-hall.com
Gym, pool, clay shooting, jogging tracks, quad biking, archery, falconry. **££**

The Borrowdale Gates
Grange-in-Borrowdale CA12 5UQ
Tel: (01768) 777204
Fax: (01768) 777254
www.borrowdale-gates.com
Large Victorian lakeland house with sweeping views and good food. **££**

The Cottage in the Wood
Whinlatter Forest, Braithwaite CA12 5TW
Tel: (01768) 778409
www.thecottageinthewood.co.uk
Former coaching house. **£**

The Lodore Falls Hotel
Lodore Falls, Borrowdale CA12 5UX
Tel: (01768) 777285
Fax: (01768) 777343
www.lakedistricthotels.net
Luxury hotel in 40 acres (16 hectares) with excellent facilities. Some rooms overlook Derwent Water. **£–££**

The Mill Inn
Mungrisdale, Penrith CA11 0XR
Tel: (01768) 779632
Former mill cottage. Good food. **£**

The Pheasant
Bassenthwaite Lake, nr Cockermouth CA13 9YE
Tel: (01768) 776234
Fax: (01768) 776002
www.the-pheasant.co.uk
This heavily beamed former coaching inn lies in a beautifully peaceful setting. Great bar. **££**

Ullswater District

Netherdene Country House B&B
Troutbeck CA11 0SJ
Tel: 07933 826325
www.netherdene.co.uk
Small, comfortable country house set in landscaped gardens. **£**

Sharrow Bay
Sharrow Bay, Lake Ullswater CA10 2LZ
Tel: (01768) 486301
Fax: (01768) 486349
www.sharrowbay.co.uk
This Italianate luxury hotel is set in formal gardens overlooking Ullswater. The food is exquisite. **£££**

Windermere

Miller Howe Hotel
Rayrigg Road LA23 1EY
Tel: (01539) 442536
Fax: (01539) 445664
www.millerhowe.com
Prestigious luxury hotel with stunning views and fine cuisine. Rates include dinner, breakfast. **££–£££**

The Scottish Lowlands

Edinburgh

Channings
12–16 South Learmonth Gardens EH4 1EZ
Tel: (0131) 315 2226
Fax: (0131) 332 9631
www.channings.co.uk
A series of five adjoining Edwardian houses facing a cobbled, quiet street a few minutes' walk from the city centre. Shackleton's former home. There are 41 individually decorated rooms. **££–£££**

Claymore Vegetarian Guest House
68 Pilrig Street EH6 5AS
Tel: (0131) 554 2500
Red sandstone Victorian terraced villa. Rooms en suite or with private bathroom facilities. Central location. **£**

Salisbury Hotel
45 Salisbury Road
Tel/Fax: (0131) 667 1264
www.the-salisbury.co.uk
Georgian listed building with walled garden, impressive restaurant, 18 rooms and private parking. **££**

The Scotsman
20 North Bridge EH1 1YT
Tel: (0131) 556 5565
Fax: (0131) 652 3652
www.thescotsmanhotel.co.uk
Highly successful make-over of a newspaper office; rooms with all facilities; health club with pool and Cowshed spa; wonderful whisky bar. **££££**

The Sheraton Grand
Festival Square off Lothian Road
Tel: (0131) 229 9131
Fax: (0131) 228 4510
www.starwoodhotels.com
Although it has very modern facilities, this luxury 260-room hotel manages to retain some of its Scottish old-world atmosphere. Excellent health spa with large pool. **£££**

Six Mary's Place
Raeburn Place, Stockbridge EH4 1JH
Tel: (0131) 332 8965
Fax: (0131) 624 7060
www.sixmarysplace.co.uk
Highly-rated guest house, with a breakfast menu that even includes vegetarian haggis. **££**

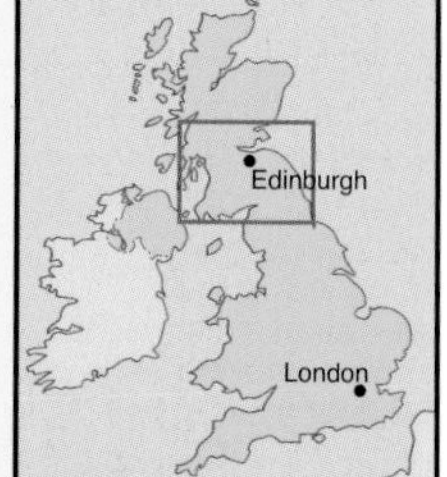

Glasgow

Malmaison
278 West George Street G2 4LL
Tel: (0141) 572 1000
Fax: (0141) 572 1002
www.malmaison-glasgow.com
Stylish hotel; decor inspired by the Paris Malmaison, in a

former church in the centre. Good atmosphere; excellent brasserie; 72 rooms. **£££**

One Devonshire Gardens
1 Devonshire Gardens G12 0UX
Tel: (0141) 339 2001
Fax: (0141) 337 1663
www.hotelduvin.com
Head and shoulders better than any other Glasgow hotel, with immaculate service. Plush rooms and oak-panelled bistro. It's worth asking for a quieter room at the rear; 49 rooms. **£££**

The Town House
4 Hughenden Terrace G12 9XR
Tel: (0141) 357 0862
Fax: (0141) 339 9605
www.thetownhouseglasgow.com
Elegantly furnished guesthouse in restored Victorian terrace in West End; 10 spacious rooms, ample parking. **£**

Dumfries

Cairndale Hotel
English Street DG1 2DF
Tel: (01387) 254111
Fax: (01387) 240288
www.cairndalehotel.co.uk
This family-owned hotel holds dinner dances and ceilidhs; fully equipped leisure club. Conference facilities for 300 people; 91 rooms. **££**

Kelso

Roxburghe Hotel
Tel: (01573) 450331
Fax: (01573) 450611
www.roxburghe.net
An 18th-century country house hotel in delightful riverside surroundings. Fishing, clay-pigeon shooting, croquet, mountain biking, championship golf course; 22 rooms. **£££**

Peebles

Cringletie House Hotel
Edinburgh Road EH45 8PL
Tel: (01721) 725750
www.cringletie.com
Set in a 28-acre (11-hectare) estate, this turreted mansion has fine food and great atmosphere; 12 rooms. **£££**

Troon

Troon Marine Hotel
8 Crosbie Road KA10 6HE
Tel: (01292) 314444
Fax: (01292) 316922
www.barcelo-hotels.co.uk
Traditional 89-room luxury hotel in the heart of Burns country, overlooking the 18th hole of Royal Troon golf course.Close to the sea with a health club and restaurant. **££**

Turnberry, nr Ayr

Westin Turnberry Resort
Tel: (01655) 331000
www.turnberry.co.uk
Luxury country club and spa with two Championship golf courses and own loch. Elegant, with gracious service; restaurants have superb views. Horse riding, tennis and off-road driving. With 219 rooms. **££££**

THE SCOTTISH HIGHLANDS

Auchterarder

Gleneagles Hotel
PH3 1NF
Tel: 0800 389 3737 (UK); (01764) 662 231 (international)
www.gleneagles.com
Famous for its golfing and sports facilities, Gleneagles is a magnificent 232-room hotel on a massive scale set in 850 acres (343 hectares) of rolling countryside. Expect to see more than a few famous faces. **££££**

Banchory

Tor-Na-Coille Hotel
Inchmarlo Road AB31 4AB
Tel: (01330) 822242
Fax: (01330) 824012
Imposing 23-room Victorian country house with a recommended restaurant. **££**

Bunchrew

Bunchrew House
Tel: (01463) 234917
Fax: (01463) 710620
www.bunchrew-inverness.co.uk
A 17th-century baronial turreted mansion. Traditional Scottish cuisine with a French influence in the restaurant which overlooks the sea. A great retreat; 16 rooms. **££**

Dunkeld

Kinnaird
Kinnaird Estate, on the B898 just off the A9
Tel: (01796) 482440
Fax: (01796) 482289
www.kinnairdestate.com
Overlooking the River Tay, with landscaped gardens, this luxurious 18th-century country house hotel retains some of the intimacy of a private home. Sofas and gas log fires in the 9 individually decorated rooms. **££££**

Fort William

Inverlochy Castle
Torlundy PH33 6SN
Tel: (01397) 702177
Fax: (01397) 702953
www.inverlochycastlehotel.com
A majestic castle in 500 acres (200 hectares) of grounds at the foot of Ben Nevis. Everything is on a grand scale, from the frescoed Great Hall and crystal chandeliers to the individually decorated bedrooms. Fine service. 17 rooms. **££££**

The Lodge on the Loch
Creag Dhu, Onich PH33 6RY
Tel: (01855) 821238
Fax: (01855) 821190
www.lodgeontheloch.com
In a stunning location perched on the edge of Loch Linnhe, this 15-room hotel provides the ideal base from which to explore the Western Highlands. Fine Scottish fare but no children under 16. **££**

Glenlivet

Minmore House
Glenlivet Crown Estate
Tel: (01807) 590378
Fax: (01807) 590472
www.minmorehousehotel.com
Small (9-room) Victorian hotel in fine grounds offering views over wonderful scenery. Bar has over 100 malt whiskies. Excellent teas. **££**

Inverness

Dunain Park
Tel: (01463) 230512
Fax: (01463) 224532
www.dunainparkhotel.co.uk
Georgian mansion with gardens and woodland, overlooking the River Ness and Caledonian Canal. Stunning views. Traditional country house feel with congenial service. More than 200 malt whiskies. Accommodation is in six suites, 5 rooms and 2 cottages. **£££**

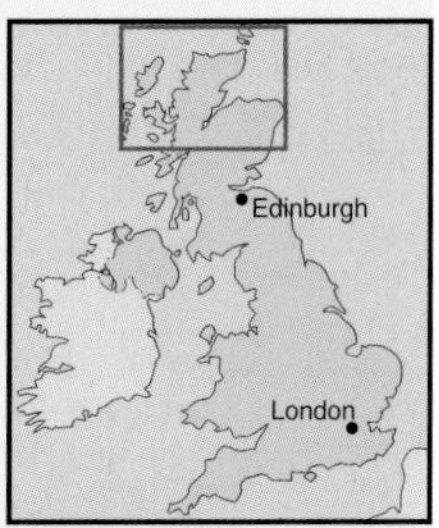

Kinbrace, Sutherland

Garvault Hotel
Tel: (01431) 831224
www.garvaulthotel.co.uk
Britain's most remote hotel. Ten miles (16 km) from the dramatic north coast of Scotland, it lies in the shadow of Ben Griann Mor, and offers trout fishing in a number of local lochs, salmon fishing on the River Helmsdale and hillwalking in a timeless location. **£**

PRICE CATEGORIES

Price categories are for a double room including breakfast and VAT (value added tax) at high season:
£ = under £80
££ = £80–150
£££ = £150–250
££££ = over £250

TRANSPORT ACCOMMODATION SHOPPING ACTIVITIES A – Z

ACTIVITIES

EVENTS, HERITAGE SITES, THE ARTS, FESTIVALS, AND SPORTS

DIARY OF EVENTS

For details of regional events, contact tourist boards *(page 387)*.

January

Burns Night (25 January) Scots celebrate birth of Robert Burns.
London International Boat Show ExCeL Exhibition Centre.

February

Chinese New Year In London and Manchester Chinatowns.
Crufts Dog Show NEC, Birmingham. Pedigree dogs compete.
Shrove Tuesday Pancake Day.
London Fashion Week.

March

Ideal Home Show Earl's Court, London.

April

April Fools' Day (1st) People play practical jokes (only until noon).
London Book Fair Earl's Court, London.
Harrogate Spring Flower Show.
Queen's Birthday (21st) Gun salute in Hyde Park and Tower of London.

May

Bath International Music Festival.
Brighton Arts Festival.
Chelsea Flower Show In grounds of Royal Hospital, London.
Hay-on-Wye Festival of Literature and the Arts. International event.
Perth Festival of the Arts.

June

Aldeburgh Festival of Arts & Music.
Beating Retreat Horse Guards Parade, London. Military bands.
Biggin Hill International Air Fair Biggin Hill, Kent.
Bournemouth Music Competitions Festival.
Dickens Festival Rochester, Kent
Glastonbury Pilgrimage Abbey Ruins, Glastonbury, Somerset.
Royal Academy of Arts Summer Exhibition, London. Large exhibition of work (till Aug). All works for sale.
Royal Highland Show Ingliston, Newbridge, Edinburgh.
Trooping the Colour Horse Guards Parade, London. The Queen's official birthday celebrations.

July

Birmingham International Jazz Festival.
Cambridge Folk Festival.
Cardiff Festival
Weekend events Jul–Aug
Cheltenham Music Festival.
Hampton Court Palace Flower Show.
Llangollen International Musical Eisteddfod Classical concerts in Llangollen, NE Wales.
Farnborough International Airshow Hampshire, biannual event.
British Motor Show Excel, London.

August

Edinburgh International Festival, Fringe Festival, Film Festival, Book Festival, Jazz and Blues Festival, Military Tattoo. It packs the city.
Notting Hill Carnival (bank holiday weekend), London. Colourful West Indian street carnival with floats, steel bands and reggae music.
Royal National Eisteddfod of Wales.

September

Abergavenny Food Festival.
London Open House Weekend. Visit buildings not normally accessible.
Salisbury Food & Drink Festival.

October

Birmingham Sidewalk Film Festival.
Cheltenham Literature Festival.
London Film Festival BFI Southbank and some West End venues.
Royal National Mod Gaelic festival, location changes annually.
Norwich Jazz Festival.
Swansea Festival of Music and Art.

November

Guy Fawkes Day (5th) Firework displays and bonfires.
London to Brighton Veteran Car Run (first Sunday).
Lord Mayor's Show London.
Military Tattoo NEC, Birmingham.
State Opening of Parliament Westminster, London.

December

Hogmanay New Year's Eve revels, four days at the end of December, best celebrated in Edinburgh.

HERITAGE SITES

Two main organisations look after Britain's old buildings, gardens and countryside. The government-funded Heritage organisations run key historic sites; the National Trust, a charity, maintains stately homes and areas of coast and countryside.

English Heritage has more than 400 properties, including Stonehenge and Dover Castle. Annual membership entitles you to free entry to all sites, plus discounts for events held at them throughout the year. A one or two-week Overseas Visitor Pass is also available. Contact: English Heritage, Customer Services Department, PO Box 569, Swindon SN2 2YP, tel: (0870) 333 1181; fax: (01793) 414926; www.english-heritage.org.uk.

Historic Scotland maintains more

than 300 properties including Glasgow Cathedral and Edinburgh Castle. Annual membership allows free access to all. Offers 3, 7 and 10 day Explorer passes to visitors. Historic Scotland, Longmore House, Salisbury Place, Edinburgh EH9 1SH, tel: (0131) 668 8831; fax: (0131) 668 8664: www.historic-scotland.gov.uk.

Cadw (Welsh Heritage) has some 100 properties, from prehistoric sites to Caernarfon Castle and Tintern Abbey. Offers 3 or 7 day Explorer Pass. Cadw, Plas Carew, Unit 5/7 Cefn Coed, Parc Nantgarw, Cardiff, CF15 7QQ, tel: (01443) 336000; fax: (01443) 336001; www.cadw.wales.gov.uk.

The National Trust was founded in 1895 as an independent charity for the conservation of places of historic interest and natural beauty. It has more than 300 properties open to the public, from large country houses and abbeys to lighthouses and industrial monuments. It also maintains more than 200 gardens and protects 612,000 acres (248,000 hectares) of countryside, including over 700 miles (1,127 km) of shoreline and woodland. The majority of its funding comes from its members.

Membership entitles you to free entry to properties and a copy of *The National Trust Handbook*. The National Trust, Membership Department, PO Box 39, Warrington WA5 7WD, tel: (0844) 800 1895; www.nationaltrust.org.uk.

The National Trust For Scotland is a separate body with more than 120 properties covering 187,000 acres (76,000 hectares). Sites in its care include castles, battlefields, islands, countryside and the birthplaces of famous Scots. The National Trust For Scotland, Wemyss House, 28 Charlotte Square, Edinburgh EH2 4ET, tel: (0844) 493 2100; fax: (0844) 493 2102; www.nts.org.uk.

All these heritage groups have reciprocal arrangements, and the NT also has reciprocal arrangements with trusts overseas, including Australia, Italy, New Zealand, Canada, the Bahamas, Malta, Jersey and Guernsey.

The **Great British Heritage Pass**, which allows unlimited access to 580 historic buildings, is a bargain for visitors interested in history. It is available exclusively for overseas visitors, can be bought online and (www.britishheritagepass.com), then sent to a home address or collected at certain visitor centres around Britain.

Top Tourist Attractions

London
The capital's top visitor attractions, according to Visit London:

- British Museum (5.4 million)
- Tate Modern (5.1 million)
- National Gallery (4.1 million)
- Natural History Museum (3.6 million)
- London Eye (3.5 million)
- Science Museum (2.7 million)
- Victoria and Albert Museum (2.4 million)
- Tower of London (2 million)
- National Maritime Museum (1.6 million)
- St Paul's Cathedral (1.6 million)

The National Trust
The 10 most visited NT properties:

- Stourhead, Wiltshire
- Fountains Abbey Estate, North Yorkshire
- Waddesdon Manor, Buckinghamshire
- Polesden Lacey, Surrey
- St Michael's Mount, Cornwall
- Penrhyn Castle, Gwynedd
- Sheffield Park Garden, East Sussex
- Belton House, Lincolnshire
- Wallington, Northumberland
- Lanhydrock, Cornwall

Historic properties
According to Visit Britain, England's most visited historic properties are:

- Tower of London
- Oldway Mansion, Devon
- Windsor Castle, Windsor
- Stonehenge, Wiltshire
- Roman Baths, Bath
- Tatton Park, Cheshire
- Old Royal Naval College, London
- Chatsworth, Derbyshire
- Hampton Court Palace, Surrey
- Portsmouth Historic Dockyard

Theme/Leisure Parks
The country's top attractions include:

- Alton Towers, Staffordshire
- Blackpool Pleasure Beach,Lancs
- Chessington World of Adventures, Surrey
- Flamingo Land, North Yorkshire
- Legoland, Windsor
- Palace Pier, Brighton
- Strathclyde Country Park, Scotland
- Thorpe Park, Surrey

Great Greenhouses

- The Eden Project, located at Bodelva, St Austell, Cornwall. Huge conservatories, or biomes, preserve plants and create climates *(see pages 242–3)*.

Private Gardens

Under the National Gardens Scheme (tel: (01483) 211535; www.ngs.org.uk) the gardens of Britain's many horticultural enthusiasts are open to the public. For a small fee visitors can explore nearly 3,500 gardens, the majority of which open in spring and summer. *The Yellow Book* (from larger bookshops) lists all gardens open each year and is published annually.

National Parks

Brecon Beacons National Park (South Wales) is made up of red sandstone mountains (including South Wales's highest peak, Pen-y-Fan: 2,907 ft/886 metres), and picturesque lowland areas of woodland, meandering rivers and rolling farmland. Attracts walkers, cyclists, sailors, canoeists, cavers and rock climbers.

The Broads Britain's largest protected wetland is situated in Norfolk and Suffolk. Rare plants and animals abound and the ideal way to explore is by water, due to the 125 miles (200km) of boating on lock-free tidal rivers.

Cairngorms National Park Taking in much of the sub-Arctic plateau of the Cairngorm Mountains, the park includes large remnants of the ancient Great Caledonian Forest. Dissected by the valley of the River Spey, home to abundant wildlife, including the rare capercaillie, largest of the grouse family.

Dartmoor Ponies roam across this expanse of Devon moorland, with granite *tors*, heath and peaty bogs. Highest point is High Willhays (2,039 ft/621 metres). Home of Dartmoor prison and setting for the 1901 Sherlock Holmes mystery *The Hound of the Baskervilles.*

Exmoor Straddling the border between Somerset and Devon, with heathery moorland and breathtaking coastline. Home to Exmoor ponies, sheep, red deer and cattle.

Lake District Stunningly beautiful countryside in Cumbria: 16 lakes are interspersed with high fells, the highest being Scafell Pike (3,210 ft/978 metres). A haven for fishing, boating, climbing and walking.

Loch Lomond and the Trossachs Centred on Loch Lomond, it includes the haunts of Scottish folk hero Rob Roy MacGregor. The Trossachs, with picturesque villages, offer breathtaking views on quieter minor routes into the Highlands.

New Forest Running from the Solent coast to the Wiltshire chalk downs and lying mainly in southwest Hampshire, this landscape combines woodland, heath, farmland and coastal saltmarsh. Originally used for hunting by William the Conqueror, the forest is home to native ponies and birds of prey.
Northumberland 405 sq miles (1,048 sq km) in the far northeast characterised by rugged moorland, wooded valleys and huge unspoilt views. The Pennine Way marches through it, from Hadrian's Wall to the Cheviot Hills on the Scottish border. Flanked on the east by spectacular coastline, Northumberland has more castles than any other British county.
North York Moors A coastline of rugged cliffs, expanses of low moorland, deep valleys and heathered uplands, this national park covers 554 sq miles (1,436 sq km), including the 110-mile (177-km) long Cleveland Way.
Peak District This well-preserved area of natural beauty at the tip of the Pennines was England's first National Park. Characterised by high, bleak moors and low, gentle limestone countryside with dramatic wooded valleys and rivers.
Pembrokeshire Coast Remote and rugged park taking up most of the coast of Pembrokeshire, southwest Wales. A coastal path stretches 186 miles (299km), from Amroth beach to Teifi near Cardigan. Popular with surfers and rock climbers.
Snowdonia A diverse area of stunning beauty covering 823 sq miles (2,130 sq km) in the northwest of Wales. Encompassing forests, lakes and torrential streams, and craggy high peaks, with Mount Snowdon the highest south of the Scottish border. Mountaineering, walking, pony trekking, canoeing, fishing, sailing.
Yorkshire Dales This wild expanse, of great natural beauty, covers 680 sq miles (1,760 sq km) in the Pennine Hills, featuring deep dales, waterfalls, caves and quarries. Made famous in fiction by vet James Herriot in books such as *All Creatures Great and Small.*

Literary Pilgrimages

Ayrshire: Robert Burns (1759–96). Scotland's literary hero. The original copy of his *Auld Lang Syne* is in the Burns National Heritage Park museum, next to the cottage where he was born in Alloway, near Ayr. During the last years of his life, he lived in a small house in a back street of Dumfries – now a museum. The Bachelors' Club in Tarbolton, a 17th-century thatched cottage where Burns and his friends formed a debating club in 1780, is now run by the National Trust for Scotland.
Dorset: Thomas Hardy (1840–1928). Hardy was born in Higher Bockhampton where he wrote *Far From the Madding Crowd* and *Under The Greenwood Tree*. He later lived in Dorchester after studying architecture, designing his own house at Max Gate on the Wareham Road. Dorset County Museum, tel: (01305) 262735; www.dorsetcountymuseum.org, in Dorchester has a Hardy memorial collection. Hardy used the 18th-century King's Arms, High Street, Dorchester, as a setting for the *Mayor of Casterbridge*, and also wrote *Tess of the d'Urbervilles* and *Jude the Obscure* there.
Hampshire: Jane Austen (1775–1817). The daughter of a Hampshire clergyman, Austen grew up in the village of Steventon. From 1809–17 she lived with her mother and sister in Chawton, Hampshire, where she wrote *Mansfield Park*, *Emma* and *Persuasion*. Now a museum (tel: (01420) 83262), it contains personal effects, letters and manuscripts. She spent time in Bath where the Jane Austen Centre, tel: (01225) 443000; www.janeausten.co.uk, can be visited; and Lyme Regis, where she wrote much of *Persuasion* from Bay Cottage on The Parade. She is buried in Winchester Cathedral.
Kent: Charles Dickens (1812–70). Most of his life was spent in Kent and London. He grew up at 11 Ordnance Terrace, Chatham, Kent. From 1837–39 he lived with his wife and son at 48 Doughty Street, London WC1, now owned by the Dickens Fellowship, housing a wide range of personal belongings, manuscripts and books (tel: 020-7405 2127). In 1856 he moved to Gad's Hill Place near Rochester (now a school), where he died. Dickens was fond of the seaside town of Broadstairs and lived there in Bleak House where he wrote part of *David Copperfield.*
The Lake District: William Wordsworth (1770–1850). In Main Street, Cockermouth, tel: (01900) 820884; www.nationaltrust.org.uk, you can visit Wordsworth's birthplace and childhood home. Dove Cottage, now a museum and art gallery, is in Town End, Grasmere, where he lived with his sister Dorothy during the most creative years of his life (tel: (01539) 435544; www.wordsworth.org.uk). Rydal Mount, his family house and garden near Ambleside, is also open to visitors, tel: (01539) 433002; www.rydalmount.co.uk.
Nottingham: D.H. Lawrence (1885–1930). The son of a miner, Lawrence grew up in Victoria Street, Eastwood, which has been restored to give an insight into his working-class childhood (Lawrence Birthplace Museum, tel: (01773) 763312. Nearby at 28 Garden Road is Breach House where the Lawrence family lived from 1887–91, the setting of the Morels' house in *Sons and Lovers*.
South Wales: Dylan Thomas (1914–53). Thomas was born in the industrial town of Swansea in Wales,

Walking Tours

There are designated, well-marked walking paths all over Britain: around the coasts, across the Pennines, over the South Downs, along Hadrian's wall, and many other places. Local tourist offices will supply information and sell detailed walkers' maps, many giving distances, estimated times and levels of difficulty.

Sightseeing Tours

- All British cities of historical interest have special double-decker buses that tour the sites. Some are open-topped and many have a commentary in several languages.
- The Original Tour is the first and biggest London sightseeing operator. Hop-on and hop-off at over 90 different stops. With commentary in wide choice of languages and a Kids' Club for 5–15 year olds. Buy tickets on bus or in advance. Operates year-round. Tel: 020-8877 1722; www.theoriginaltour.com.
- Big Bus Company operates two routes of hop-on hop-off services. Tel: 020-7233 9533; www.bigbustours.com.
- Duck Tours use World War II amphibious vehicles which drive past famous London landmarks before taking to the water. Departure from Chicheley Street, Waterloo. Tel: 020-7928 3132; www.londonducktours.co.uk.
- Golden Tours offer a wide choice of day trips for London and sites and cities all over Britain. Tel: 020-7233 7030, or within USA tel: 1-800 548 7083; www.goldentours.co.uk.

growing up in 5 Cwmdonkin Drive in the Uplands district. Follow the Dylan Thomas Uplands Trail and visit the boat house where he lived and worked in Laugharne, tel: (01994) 427420; www.dylanthomasboathouse.com. The annual Dylan Thomas Festival takes place at the end of October (www.dylanthomas.org).

Warwickshire: William Shakespeare (1564–1616). Stratford-upon-Avon is synonymous with Britain's greatest playwright. The Shakespeare Birthplace Trust, tel: (01789) 204016; www.shakespeare.org.uk, administers the following Tudor properties (inclusive admission ticket available): Shakespeare's Birthplace, Henley Street; Anne Hathaway's Cottage, Shottery; Hall's Croft, Old Town; New Place/Nash's House, Chapel Street; Mary Arden's Farm, Wilmcote, where his mother grew up (and now a museum of rural life).

Yorkshire: The Brontë Sisters: Anne (1820–49), **Charlotte** (1816–55), **Emily** (1818–48). All born in Thornton, West Yorkshire, but the family home was the Parsonage in Haworth. Now a museum run by the Brontë Society, it has been restored as it was when the family lived here (1820–61) and contains some of their furniture, manuscripts and personal belongings (tel: (01535) 642323; www.bronte.org.uk).

THE ARTS

Theatre

Britain's rich dramatic tradition is reflected in the quality of its theatre. Most towns and cities have at least one theatre that hosts productions from their own company or from touring companies that may include the Royal Shakespeare Company (RSC) and the National Theatre (NT). For comprehensive information, go to www.theatresonline.com.

It is advisable to book tickets in advance, from the box office or through commercial ticket agents in major cities.

London

Around half of London's theatres – totalling over 140, including fringe and suburban – are in the West End, centred around Shaftesbury Avenue and Covent Garden.

Tickets West End shows are popular so good tickets can be hard to obtain. If you cannot book a seat through the theatre box office, try Ticketmaster, 173 Arlington Road, NW1, tel: 0870 534 4444 (UK); +44 161 385 3211 (overseas); www.ticketmaster.co.uk.

ABOVE: the reconstructed Shakespeare's Globe in London.

Avoid ticket touts unless you're prepared to pay several times a ticket's face value for a sold-out show. The "tkts" booth at Leicester Square has unsold tickets available at bargain prices on the day of the performance. Located in the Clock Tower building and open Mon–Sat 10am–7pm, Sun 12–3pm. Payment is by cash or card and there may be long queues (www.tkts.co.uk). Some theatres, such as the National, keep back some tickets to sell at the box office from 9.30am on the day.

Fringe There is usually no problem buying a ticket on the door. Consult listings in London's weekly *Time Out* magazine, newspapers or check www.theatreguidelondon.co.uk.

Open-air plays On summer afternoons and evenings Shakespeare's plays are performed (weather permitting) at the open-air theatre in Regent's Park. Check www.openairtheatre.org for listings.

Barbican Arts Centre, Silk Street, London EC2Y 8DS, tel: 020-7638 8891. Purpose-built arts complex containing the Barbican Theatre, Concert Hall and The Pit which are well thought-out and comfortable with good acoustics, although somewhat sterile. Not easy to find your way around. Tube: Barbican.

National Theatre, South Bank, SE1, tel: 020-7452 3000; fax: 020-7452 3030. A wide range of modern and classical plays staged in three theatres in this concrete structure beside the Thames: the Olivier, the Lyttelton and the Cottesloe. Tube: Waterloo. www.nationaltheatre.org.uk

Royal Court Theatre, Sloane Square, SW1, tel: 020-7565 5000. Home to the English Stage Company, which produces plays by contemporary playwrights. Tube: Sloane Square (Circle line).

Shakespeare's Globe, 21 New Globe Walk, Bankside SE1, is a reconstruction of Shakespeare's original open-to-the-elements Elizabethan theatre. It hosts summer seasons of plays, recreating the atmosphere of the 16th-century performances. There is a choice of (recommended) bench seating or standing, actors are encouraged to interact with the audience; amplification and artificial lighting are not used. An engaging and authentic experience. The Globe Exhibition uses touch screens and includes a guided tour of the theatre (tel: 020-7902 1500; www.shakespeares-globe.org; Apr–Oct Mon–Sat 9am–12.30pm and 1–5pm, Sun 9–11.30am and 12–5pm, tours every 15–30 mins.

Stratford Upon Avon

The Royal Shakespeare Theatre, Stratford-upon-Avon. Currently being rebuilt and scheduled to open in 2010. The Royal Shakespeare Company (RSC) is meanwhile performing in the Courtyard Theatre, box office tel: 0844 800 1110. The **Swan Theatre** (an Elizabethan-style playhouse) where works by Shakespeare's contemporaries are performed is closed while the RST is being redeveloped. **The Other Place**, where modern productions are performed, will re-open as the RSC's studio theatre. The RSC season at Stratford runs from April to October. www.rsc.org.uk

Manchester

Manchester has a number of theatres, among them **The Lowry Centre**, Pier 8, Salford Quays, Manchester, tel: (0870) 787 5780, www.thelowry.com, where two theatres stage high-quality theatre and musical performances.

Newcastle-Upon-Tyne

Theatre Royal, 100 Grey Street, tel: (08448) 112121; www.theatreroyal.co.uk. Beautiful Edwardian Theatre. Drama, opera and dance. Regional home of the RSC. **Northern Stage**, Barras Bridge, tel: (0191) 230 5151; www.northernstage.co.uk. Has three stages after a £9 million refurbishment. Home of Newcastle's Northern Stage company; co-host RSC season.

Liverpool

Liverpool's **Playhouse**, Williamson Square, tel: (0151) 709 4776 and the related **Everyman**, Hope Street, tel: (0151) 709 4776 both stage excellent and sometimes innovative works. The **Empire**, Lime Street, tel: (0844) 847 2525 concentrates on light entertainment and musicals.

Scotland

Scotland's theatres include:
Royal Lyceum, Grindlay Street, Edinburgh EH3 9AX, tel: (0131) 248 4848. The Sept–May Season produces high-quality drama productions. **The Traverse**, Cambridge Street, Edinburgh EH1 2ED, tel: (0131) 228 1404. Quality contemporary productions. Commissions and supports writers and hosts numerous workshops.
Festival Theatre, 13–29 Nicholson Street, Edinburgh, tel: (0131) 529 6000. Edinburgh's showcase theatre with huge glass frontage; major opera, ballet, variety productions.
The Royal Concert Hall, 2 Sauchiehall Street, Glasgow, tel: (0141) 353 8000. Home to Royal Scottish National Orchestra. Busy venue featuring wide variety of entertainment. **The Tron Theatre**, 63 Trongate, Glasgow, tel: (0141) 552 4267. Stylish venue featuring contemporary innovative programmes of drama and dance. **Citizens' Theatre**, 119 Gorbals Street, Glasgow, tel: (0141) 429 0022. Repertory company renowned for adventurous productions.

Wales

There are a number of art centres and theatres that attract leading companies. Swansea has six theatres while Cardiff Bay's Wales Millennium Centre, tel: (08700) 402000, www.wmc.org.uk, hosts international theatre, musicals, contemporary dance, comedy, ballet and opera.

Classical Music

Many British cities have their own professional orchestras and promote seasons of concerts. These include the Royal Liverpool Philharmonic, The Hallé in Manchester, the City of Birmingham Symphony Orchestra and the spectacular ultra-modern St David's Hall in Cardiff. In London there are the London Philharmonic and, at the Barbican Arts Centre, the London Symphony Orchestra.

In the summer the Scottish National Orchestra (SNO) presents a short Promenade season in Glasgow, while in London the BBC sponsors the Proms at the Royal Albert Hall. The BBC also funds several of its own orchestras, the BBC Symphony and the BBC Scottish Symphony Orchestra.

Chamber music has considerable support in Britain and there are professional string and chamber orchestras such as the English Chamber Orchestra and The Academy of Ancient Music.

London Venues

Barbican Hall, Silk Street, London EC2Y, tel: 020-7638 8891, is home to the London Symphony Orchestra and the BBC Symphony Orchestra.
Royal Festival Hall, Belvedere Road, London SE1, tel: (0871) 663 2500, www.southbankcentre.co.uk, is the premier classical music venue. Free Friday lunchtime classical, jazz and folk performances in the foyer. Also in the South Bank complex are the Queen Elizabeth Hall (chamber concerts and solos) and the small Purcell Room.
Wigmore Hall, 36 Wigmore Street, London W1, tel: 020-7935 2141, www.wigmore-hall.org.uk, is an intimate hall renowned for its lunchtime and Sunday morning chamber recitals. There are evening peformances, too.
Royal Albert Hall, Kensington Gore, London SW7, tel: 020-7589 8212, www.royalalberthall.com, comes alive in summer for the BBC-sponsored Promenade Concerts.

Open-air concerts Summer evening concerts are performed at the Kenwood Lakeside Theatre, Kenwood House, Hampstead Lane, NW3 (tel: 0870 333 1181, www.picnicconcerts.com).

Outside London

Major venues attracting world-class performers include:
Bridgewater Hall, Manchester, tel: (0161) 907 9000.
Birmingham Symphony Hall, NEC, tel: (0121) 780 3333.
City Hall, Northumberland Road, Newcastle, tel: 0191-261 2606.
The Sage, Gateshead Quays, tel: 0191-443 4666.
Philharmonic Hall, Hope Street, Liverpool, tel: (0151) 210 2895.
The Royal Concert Hall, 2 Sauchiehall Street, Glasgow, tel: (0141) 353 8000.

Glyndebourne

For classical music lovers Glyndebourne is a highlight. Off the beaten track in Sussex, it is not the most obvious site for a major international opera festival. But ever since an ex-Eton schoolmaster inherited a mansion there and built an opera house, it has attracted top artists from around the world and become a major event. Performances are in the evening (bring your own Champagne and picnic hampers) from May until August. Tel: (01273) 815000. www.glyndebourne.com

Arts Festivals Around Britain

There are hundreds of arts festivals for music, dance, theatre and literature held throughout Britain each year.

Edinburgh The most famous of Britain's arts festivals (actually two simultaneous festivals, the official one and the "fringe"), this takes place for about 3 to 4 weeks in August and September. The city also hosts jazz, folk and film and TV festivals at other times during the year. Tel: 0845-225 5121.

Glasgow hosts the Celtic Connections in January, as well as holding its own International Jazz and International Piping festivals.

Wales The Royal National Eisteddfod of Wales dates back to 1176 and is the most important of the hundreds of *eisteddfodau* which take place in Wales annually. It is a festival devoted to music and literature in the Welsh language and is held for a week in August in a different venue each year.

The Llangollen International Eisteddfod, which takes place in the picturesque town of Llangollen in north Wales each July, was established after World War II to bring nations together in a festival of song, dance and music.

Countrywide Other notable arts festivals are held at Chichester, Brighton, Buxton, Salisbury, Harrogate and York. Music festivals are at Aldeburgh, Cheltenham, Newbury, Stratford and Bath *(for dates, see page 372).*

St David's Hall, The Hayes, Cardiff, tel: (02920) 878444.
Wales Millennium Centre, Cardiff Bay, tel: (08700) 402000.

Opera

The Royal Opera and the English National Opera perform regular seasons in London.

Royal Opera House, Bow Street, London WC2, tel: 020-7304 4000. Home to the Royal Ballet and the Royal Opera, this is a magnificent theatre with a worldwide reputation for lavish performances in original language. Dress is formal and tickets expensive unless you are prepared to stand or accept a very distant view.

London Coliseum, St Martin's Lane, London WC2N, tel: 0871 911 0200. This elegant Edwardian theatre is where the English National Opera (ENO) stages performances in English; ticket prices are lower than at the Opera House.

Welsh National Opera Its new home is the Wales Millennium Centre in Cardiff Bay, tel: (08700) 402000. Performances are also staged at theatres and concert halls throughout Wales.

Scottish Opera Scotland has its own opera company, based at the Theatre Royal, 282 Hope Street, Glasgow, tel: (0870) 060 6647. It tours Scotland and northern England, performing short seasons in Edinburgh.

Opera North Regional opera companies include Opera North, which is based in Leeds at the Grand Theatre, 46 New Briggate, LS1 6NZ, tel: (0870) 121 4901, and tours the north of England.

Buxton The Opera House, Water Street, SK17 6XN, tel: (0845) 127 2190, hosts a major opera, theatre and music festival (3 weeks in July).

Welsh Choirs

The Welsh are renowned for their fine voices. Most places in Wales have a choir. The Wales Tourist Board (www.visitwales.com, tel: (08708) 300306) has details. If you're can't get there, there's always the London Welsh Male Voice Choir (londonwelshmvc.org).

Ballet and Dance

Major venues are the Royal Opera House and the London Coliseum, home to the Royal Ballet and English National Ballet respectively.

Sadler's Wells, Rosebery Avenue, EC1R 4TN, tel: (0844) 412 4300 is a flexible state-of-the-art performance venue, with innovative programmes of contemporary and classical dance. Other performances at the Peacock Theatre, Kingsway, WC2 (same phone number for bookings).

ABOVE: for full coverage of current dance events, check www.ballet.co.uk.

Birmingham Royal Ballet, based at the Hippodrome, tel: (0121) 245 3500, tours nationwide.

Northern Ballet School Based at the Dancehouse Theatre, 10 Oxford Road, Manchester, tel: (0161) 237 9753. Tours whole UK.

Wales Leading ballet companies perform at the Wales Millennium Centre in Cardiff *(see above)*, and the Grand Theatre in Swansea, tel: (01792) 475715.

The Scottish Ballet, based in Glasgow, tel: (0141) 331 2931, tours the UK.

Jazz

There are many pubs and clubs that host live jazz, notably in London and Edinburgh. Ronnie Scott's, 47 Frith Street, W1, tel: 020-7439 0747, in London's Soho, is Britain's best-known jazz venue, showcasing top international artists.

SPORT

Tickets

Tickets for major sporting events can be purchased from agents such as Ticketmaster, tel: (0870) 534 4444; www.ticketmaster.co.uk; and Keith Prowse, tel: (0870) 840 1111; www.keithprowse.com.

Spectator Sports

Football (Soccer)

This is the country's most popular spectator and participant team sport. The professional season is August–May. England and Scotland have separate football associations (FAs), with four divisions in England (top of which is the Premier League) and four in Scotland.

Most Premier League matches can be watched only on satellite TV. The climax of the English season is the FA Cup, played at the new Wembley Stadium. Scotland's highlight is the Scottish FA Cup at Hampden Park near Glasgow.

League matches usually start Sat or Sun at 3pm, midweek 7pm. Results are aired on Saturday at 4.45pm on the main terrestrial channels (BBC and ITV). Radio 5 Live (693 or 909 AM) and talkSPORT (1053 or 1089 AM) broadcast matches and discuss the sport at length with experts and listeners.

For details of Premier League fixtures, check www.premierleague.com for club contact details; for other English fixtures, www.football-league.co.uk. For Scottish fixtures: tel: (0141) 620 4160; www.scottishfootballleague.com.

Rugby

Rugby is said to have been invented when one of the pupils of Rugby public school picked up the ball and ran in a game of football early in the 19th century. It is a national institution today, with two types (Union, played in Scotland, Wales and predominantly the South of England) and League (the north of England game).

Rugby Union, formerly for amateurs only, is now professional. The season runs from September to May, with matches played at Twickenham, Murrayfield and the Millennium Stadium. One of the highlights of the season is the Six Nations Championship, a knock-out between England, Ireland, Scotland, Wales, France and Italy.

Rugby League culminates in the Super League final at Old Trafford in September.

The Sporting Calendar

February

Rugby Six Nations Championship.

March

Football Worthington Cup Final, Cardiff Millennium Stadium.
Racing Cheltenham Gold Cup, Cheltenham, Gloucestershire.
University Boat Race Oxford and Cambridge, on the Thames between Putney and Mortlake, London.

April

Horse Racing: Grand National Race Meeting, Aintree, Liverpool.
London Marathon, Greenwich Park, London.
Rugby Union County Championship Final, Twickenham. Six Nations Cup.
Snooker World Championship, Sheffield.

May

Football FA Cup Final, Wembley Stadium.
Golf PGA Championship, Wentworth Club, Surrey.
Horse Trials Badminton, Gloucestershire.
Horse Racing 1,000 and 2,000 Guineas Stakes, Newmarket, Suffolk.
Horse Show Royal Windsor, Home Park, Windsor.
Cricket Test Matches.

June

Cycling London to Brighton bike ride.
Horse Racing Royal Ascot, Ascot, Berkshire. The Derby, Epsom, Surrey. The Oaks, Epsom, Surrey.
Tennis British Tennis Championships, Queen's Club, London. Wimbledon Lawn Tennis Championships, All England Lawn Tennis and Croquet Club: the world's most famous tennis tournament, held in southwest London suburb.
Cricket Test Matches.
Highland Games, Aberdeen.

July

Show Jumping Royal International Horse Show, Hickstead.
Motor Racing British Grand Prix, Silverstone, Northamptonshire.
Rowing Henley Royal Regatta Week, Henley-on-Thames.
Golf Open Championship, venue varies
Cricket Test Matches.
Polo Cartier International, Guards Polo Club, Surrey

August

Highland Games Cowal, Perth and Aboyne, Scotland.
Horse Racing Glorious Goodwood
Polo Cheltenham Cup
Sailing Cowes Week Regatta, Isle of Wight.
Cricket Test Matches.
Rugby League Carnegie Challenge Cup Final.

September

Braemar Royal Highland Games, Memorial Park, Scotland.
Cycling The Tour of Britain 8-day road race.
British Superbike Championship Silverstone.
Golf: World Matchplay, Wentworth, Surrey. British Masters, the Belfry, W. Midlands.

October

Great North Run, Newcastle. The world's largest half-marathon.
Golf Dunhill Links Championship, St Andrew's, Fife
Show Jumping Horse of the Year Show, NEC, Birmingham.

November

Lombard RAC Car Rally, Harrogate, North Yorkshire.
RAC London–Brighton Veteran Car Run is a 60-mile (100-km) race for 500 cars built before 1905.

December

Olympia, The London International Horse Show, Olympia, London.

For details of Rugby Union fixtures, tel: (0871) 222 2120; www.rfu.com. For Rugby League, tel: (0871) 226 1313; www.rfl.uk.com.

Cricket

Quintessentially English, cricket can be seen on village greens up and down the country throughout the summer. Usually a light-hearted performance, it is played by very amateurish amateurs, with a visit to the pub a ritual at the close of play.

England's professional teams compete in a national championship, with 4-day matches taking place all summer. But one of the most entertaining ways to be initiated into the intricacies of the game is to go along to a pacier, less serious one-day match or Twenty20 game.

On an international level, every season England plays 5-day Test Matches against one or two touring teams from Australia, India, New Zealand, Pakistan, Sri Lanka or the West Indies. These take place at half a dozen grounds in Britain including Lords and the Oval in London, Edgbaston in the Midlands and Headingly in Leeds. Test match tickets are sought-after and sell out well in advance, but there's generally less competition for seats for one-day internationals.

The governing body of the world game is Marylebone Cricket Club (MCC), based at Lord's Cricket Ground, St John's Wood, NW8, tel: 020-7616 8500; www.lords.org. Cricket can also be seen at the Oval, Kennington, SE11, tel: Surrey County Cricket Club: 08712 461100; www.surreycricket.com. For outside London, see www.play-cricket.com.

Equestrian Sports

Flat racing takes place between March and early November. The most important races are the Derby and Oaks at Epsom, the St Leger at Doncaster and the 1,000 and 2,000 Guineas at Newmarket. The Royal Ascot meeting is a major social event where racegoers dress in their finest.

Steeplechasing and hurdle racing take place from September to early June. The National Hunt Festival meeting at Cheltenham in March is the most important event; the highlight is the Gold Cup. The most famous steeplechase, watched avidly and gambled on by millions in Britain, is the Grand National held at Aintree in Liverpool.

Show jumping is the equestrian sport every young rider aspires to. Major events are the Royal International Horse Show and the British Jumping Derby at Hickstead, West Sussex, the Horse of the Year Show at the NEC, Birmingham, and the Olympia International Horse Show in London.

Polo matches take place at Windsor Great Park or Cowdray Park, Midhurst, West Sussex on summer weekends. The governing body is the Hurlingham Polo Association, tel: (01367) 242828; www.hpa-polo.co.uk).

Horse Trials are held in spring and autumn nationwide. The major 3-day events (cross-country, show jumping and dressage) are held at Badminton, Bramham, Burghley, Chatsworth and Gatcombe.

The main equestrian body in Britain is The British Horse Society, which governs the Pony Club and Riding Club. It also runs the British Equestrian Centre at Stoneleigh in Warwickshire, where it is based. For further information, contact The British Horse Society, Stoneleigh Deer Park, Kenilworth CV8 2XZ, tel: (0844) 848 1666; www.bhs.org.uk.

Athletics

Athletics are governed by the Amateur Athletics Association (AAA), with the main national sports centre for athletics at Crystal Palace, south London, tel: 020-8778 0131; www.englandathletics.org.

Highland Games are held in Scotland between May and September when they coincide with the annual gatherings of clans. Activities include such distinctive events as tossing the caber (basically an 18-ft/5.5-metre tree trunk) and throwing the hammer as well as dancing and piping competitions. The best-known games are at Braemar, near Balmoral, in September; these are sometimes attended by the Royal Family. There are also gatherings at Aboyne, Oban and Cowal. See www.visitscotland.com

Golf

The most important national golfing event is the Open Championship, which takes place every July. Other prestigious competitions include the Ryder Cup for professionals and the Walker Cup for amateurs. Both of these are played between Britain and USA every other year. Another prestigious tournament is the World Match Play Championship at Wentworth, Surrey, in September.

For information on dates and venues of tournaments contact the Professional Golfers' Association (PGA), Centenary House, The Belfry, Sutton Coldfield, West Midlands, B76 9PT, tel: (01675) 470333.

Motor Racing

The heart of motor racing worldwide, Britain has produced a number of World Champions, from Mike Hawthorn and Jim Clark to James Hunt, Nigel Mansell and Damon Hill. The British Grand Prix, the highlight of the British motor racing calendar, is traditionally held at Silverstone, however there are plans to hold it at Donington in the near future. But Britain's race tracks (most notably Brands Hatch and Donington) also host a range of race meetings, from touring cars to powerful single seaters. Rallying is also very popular.

Details of races from the Motor Sports Association, tel: (01753) 765000 or visit www.msauk.org. See also www.brdc.co.uk.

Participant Sports

For information on sports and leisure facilities in each area you can contact the local council's leisure services department. Alternatively, get in touch with Sport England, 3rd Floor, Victoria House, Bloomsbury Square, London WC1B 4SE, tel: 020-7273 1551; www.sportengland.org.

ABOVE: Wimbledon tennis championship begins in the last week of June.

The English Federation of Disability Sport promotes and develops sport for people with disabilities. For further information, contact EFDS, Manchester Metropolitan University, Alsager Campus, Hassall Road, Alsager, Stoke on Trent ST7 2HL, tel: (0161) 247 5294; www.efds.co.uk.

Angling

Fishing is Britain's top participant sport, attracting 8 million people. A useful website is www.anglingnews.net/bodies.asp, which lists many British angling clubs. For angling clubs and organisations in Scotland go to: www.fishing-uk-scotland.com.

Golf

Even the most famous clubs are open to the public. St Andrew's, however, is so much in demand that games are subject to a lottery. Courses close to London are generally heavily booked. To find a local course, visit www.uk-golfguide.com. You can book a session, often at a discount, at almost 250 clubs around the UK through www.teeofftimes.co.uk.

Horse Riding

There are plenty of public riding stables in rural areas, but most do not let riders out unaccompanied. Pony trekking is particularly popular on Dartmoor, Exmoor, in the New Forest and in Wales.

For further information and a list of approved riding stables, contact The British Horse Society, Stoneleigh Deer Park, Kenilworth CV8 2XZ, tel: (08701) 202244; www.bhs.org.uk).

Tennis

There are tennis courts in some of Britain's public parks that anyone can use free-of-charge. Contact the Lawn Tennis Association for regional offices and information on clubs and facilities: The Lawn Tennis Association, National Tennis Centre, 100 Priory Lane, Roehampton, London SW15 5JQ, tel: 020-8487 7000; www.lta.org.uk.

Watersports

Britain offers plenty of opportunities to those interested in sailing, particularly on the south coast and around Pembrokeshire, southwest Wales, but also on the lakes and lochs of the north of England and Scotland; Kielder Water, situated in northwest Northumberland, is the largest man-made reservoir in northern Europe with a shoreline of more than 27 miles (43 km). The lake offers the opportunity to take part in a variety of watersports (www.kielderwatersc.org). There are excellent facilities for canoeing, windsurfing, jet skiing and boating too on Britain's many inland waters. Cornwall is a popular surfing centre.

Superb wind surfing conditions can be found on the Scottish island of Tiree, and around John o'Groats on the north coast of Scotland.

There are National Water Sports Centres at Isle of Cumbrae, Ayrshire, Scotland, tel: (01475) 530757; www.nationalcentrecumbrae.org.uk) and Holme Pierrepont, Nottinghamshire (www.nationalwatersportsevents.co.uk).

Wimbledon Tennis Championship

The Wimbledon fortnight is one of Britain's best-loved sporting highlights, attracting nearly 400,000 spectators in person and millions of television viewers worldwide. It takes place in June/July on the immaculate grass courts at the All England Club in Wimbledon, southwest London.

Most tickets are allocated by public ballot (obtain an application form by sending a stamped SAE to the Ticket Office, AELTC, PO Box 98, Wimbledon, London SW19 5AE by the end of the previous year). For details, tel: 020-8971 2473; www.wimbledon.org. Around 1,500 tickets are kept back for some courts if you are prepared to camp out the night before, and spare seats are always to be had late-afternoon. Expect to pay more than 22p per strawberry if you want to try the strawberries and cream.

SHOPPING

BEST BUYS IN BRITAIN

WHAT TO BUY

If you are looking for something typically British to take back home, there's a remarkably wide choice.

● **Cloth and wool** Probably Britain's most famous speciality, top-quality wools and clothes worth seeking out include the wonderful hand-knitted woollens from the Scottish islands of Shetland, Arran and Fair Isle, and the Guernsey and Jersey sweaters of the Channel Islands. There is fine Harris Tweed cloth from Lewis. You can even have a kilt made in your own clan tartan. The scenic Ochil Hills north of Edinburgh have a long tradition of woollen production where visitors can take the Scottish Mill Trail.

Another important centre for the cloth and wool industry is Bradford, through which 90 percent of the wool trade passed in the 19th century. The area's many mill shops are a bargain-hunter's paradise where lengths of fabric, fine yarns and fleeces from the Yorkshire Dales can be bought. Some mills give guided tours. The Lakeland Sheep and Wool Centre in Cockermouth, Cumbria, hosts excellent daily sheep shows and sells high-quality goods. Wales, too, has many mills that produce colourful tapestry cloth in striking traditional Celtic designs.

BELOW: Britain has over 270,000 shops.

● **Shoes and lace** Nottingham is the traditional manufacturing centre for these. At the Lace Centre, Castle Road, you can watch lace being made, learn about its history and, of course, buy gifts.

● **Suits** The flagship of Britain's bespoke tailoring industry is Savile Row in London where gentlemen come from all over to have their suits crafted. Other outlets for traditional British attire are Burberry's (for raincoats and more), Aquascutum, Austin Reed and Jaeger which have branches in Oxford Street and Regent Street in London and in many department stores in other cities.

● **Fashion** Britain has a thriving fashion market, with its heart in London. Its top designers (including Caroline Charles, Jasper Conran, Katharine Hamnett, Bruce Oldfield, Stella McCartney, Paul Smith and Vivienne Westwood) are the height of haute couture and world-famous. Many top international designers can also be found in London's Knightsbridge and Mayfair, and to a lesser extent in department stores nationwide. For quality everyday clothing Marks & Spencer's stores retain their popularity. Mulberry is famous for its leather accessories, from personal organisers to weekend bags, all embossed with the classic tree logo.

● **China and porcelain** Top-price china, glass and silver items can be found in Regent Street and Mayfair in London at exclusive shops such as Waterford, Wedgwood, Thomas Goode, Asprey and Garrard. Stoke-on-Trent (in "the Potteries", Staffordshire) is the home of the great china and porcelain houses, including Wedgwood and Royal Doulton, Minton, Spode and Royal Stafford (www.thepotteries.org). All these have visitor centres where you can often pick up some real bargains. You can also visit Portmeirion in North Wales, the Caithness Glass factory at Crieff in Scotland and Dartington Crystal at Great Torrington in Devon.

● **Jewellery** The centre for British jewellery production is in Hockley, Birmingham, an industry that developed here in the 18th century along with other forms of metal working such as brass-founding and gun-smithing. Today more than 200 jewellery manufacturers and 50 silversmiths are based here.

● **Perfumes** English flower perfumes make a delightful gift. The most exclusive of these come from Floris in Jermyn Street, and Penhaligons in Covent Garden, London. The Cotswold Perfumery in the picturesque village of Bourton-on-the-Water, Gloucestershire, makes its own perfumes.

● **Antiques** If you are coming to Britain to look for antiques it is worth getting in touch with the London and Provincial Antique Dealers' Association (LAPADA), 535 King's Road, London, SW10, tel: 020-7823 3511. It runs a computer information service on the antiques situation throughout the country. A number of antiques fairs are held nationwide throughout the year and many towns such as Bath, Harrogate and Brighton have antique centres and markets.

● **Consumables** British delights that are easy to take home include Twinings or Jacksons tea, Scotch whisky and shortbread and numerous brands of chocolate. Benticks is famous for its after-dinner mints, Thornton's produces fine confectionery made from fresh ingredients while, on a more popular level, Cadbury's is a national favourite.

Britain is particularly proud of its conserves, jams, honeys, pickles and mustards (not least the famous anchovy spread, Gentleman's Relish). Local delicatessens and farm shops nationwide are often worth exploring for edible gifts. Some regional specialities to look out for include: Cornish pasties, chocolates filled with Scotch whisky, Bakewell tarts, Eccles cakes, Kendal mint cake and Kentish cobnuts in chocolate.

For Britain's food at its finest, visit Fortnum & Mason, 181 Piccadilly, London W1, an Aladdin's cave of mouthwatering goodies.

● **Crafts** Almost every town has a weekly street market where cheap clothes and domestic ware can be bought and there may also be a good presence of local crafts. There are many workshops in rural areas of Britain where potters, woodturners, leatherworkers, candlemakers and other craftspeople can be seen producing their wares. A free map can be obtained from the Crafts Council, 44a Pentonville Road, London N1, tel: 020-7806 2500. For information on Welsh crafts, contact the Wales Craft Council, tel: (01938) 555313; www.walescraftcouncil.co.uk)

● **Books** London's Charing Cross Road has long been the centre for secondhand and specialist bookshops, though there are fewer these days than there used to be. Waterstones branches nationwide are popular, and Foyles in London has five crammed floors. Outside London, university towns are the best source of books. Blackwells in Oxford and Cambridge is equally good for publications in English and most prominent foreign languages. Serious book lovers should head for Hay-on-Wye, on the border of England and Wales *(see page 253)*; it has more than 30 bookshops and also hosts a lively literary festival, with top-notch guests, in late May (www.hayfestival.com).

● **Gifts** Some of the best places to seek out tasteful presents to take home are museum gift shops (especially the ones at London's British Museum and the Victoria and Albert Museum) and the shops on National Trust properties.

Markets and Boot Sales

Many towns have regular open-air farmers' markets. Some in the south have French markets when French traders cross the Channel to sell their fresh produce.

London has several traditional markets which have become tourist attractions over the years:

● **Camden Market**, NW1. Hugely popular at the weekends, this sprawling market near Camden Lock sells clothes, jewellery, arts and crafts, food and antiques.

● **Columbia Road Flower Market**, E2. Cut flowers and houseplants are sold here at wholesale prices on Sundays, 8am–2pm. Other specialist shops on Columbia Road open to coincide with the market.

● **Petticoat Lane**, Middlesex Street, E1. London's oldest market is so-named for the undergarmets and lace once sold here by French Huguenots. Cheap clothes, fabrics and leather goods are still sold here on some of the 1,000 stalls.

● **Portobello Road**, W11. Renowned for its antiques, this is also a good place to pick up fashionable and vintage clothing, art and general bric-a-brac. It gets very crowded on Saturdays, but has a buzzing atmosphere.

● **Spitalfields**, Commercial Street, E1. This historic covered market has been gentrified with cafés and boutiques, but remains a great place to spot new talent, as many young fashion and jewellery designers sell their wares here. Music, vintage clothing, organic food and childrenswear are sold too.

A phenomenon all over Britain is the weekend **boot sale**, held in out-of-town fields or disused airfields. Participants sell all kinds of household goods – and junk – from the boot (trunk) of their car. In America, it would be known as a massive tag sale, and has the same friendly atmosphere. Some venues have hundreds of pitches.

EXPORT PROCEDURES

VAT (value added tax) is a sales tax of 17.5 percent (reduced to 15 percent during 2009) that is added to nearly all goods except food (excluding that in restaurants), books and children's clothes. It is generally included in the price marked on the item. Most large department stores and smaller gift shops operate a scheme to refund this tax to non-European visitors (Retail Export Scheme), but often require that more than a minimum amount (usually £50) is spent. For a refund you need to fill in a form from the store, have it stamped by Customs on leaving the country and post it back to the store or hand it in to a cash refund booth at the airport. If you leave the country with the goods within three months of purchase you will be refunded the tax minus an administration fee.

BELOW: Camden Passage in London's Islington mixes bric-a-brac and antiques.

A – Z

A Handy Summary of Practical Information, Arranged Alphabetically

Admission Charges

The major national museums and galleries, such as the British Museum, National Gallery, Imperial War Museum and the various Tate galleries, are free. Some municipal museums are free; others make a charge. A comprehensive website is www.24hourmuseum.org.uk.

The Great British Heritage Pass (www.britishheritagepass.com), which can be bought only outside the UK, gives entry to nearly 600 attractions; the cost of a 15-day pass would work out at less than £4 a day. This includes stately homes and gardens run by the National Trust, English Heritage and their Scottish and Welsh equivalents. Passes to cover only the properties of one of these bodies can be bought through www.visitbritaindirect.com.

If you're planning to visit a lot of attractions in the capital, it's worth looking at www.londonpass.com; prices start at £40 (adult) or £25 (child) for one day, but six-day passes are better value. Note that they don't cover some pricey attractions such as Madame Tussauds and the London Dungeon.

Business hours

Town centre shops generally open 9am–5.30pm Mon–Sat, although a few smaller shops may close for lunch in rural areas. Many small towns and villages have a half-day closing one day in the week and shopping centres in towns and cities are likely to have at least one evening of late-night shopping. Increasing numbers of shops are open on Sunday, usually 10am–4pm.

Supermarkets tend to be open 8 or 8.30am–8 to 10pm Mon–Sat and 10 or 11am–4pm on Sunday, and some branches of the larger stores are experimenting with all-night opening on certain days of the week (often Thursday or Friday night). Some local corner shops and off-licences (shops licensed to sell alcohol to be consumed off the premises) stay open until 10pm. However, there are proposals to ban off-licenses and supermarkets selling alcohol to under-21s in an effort to curb binge drinking.

Most offices operate 9am–5.30pm Mon–Fri with an hour for lunch.

British pubs' opening hours vary due to flexible closing times granted by an extended opening hours licence. Some have a 24-hour opening licence. Some may close for periods during the day, while others may just apply for the extended opening hours licence for special events such as New Year's Eve.

Children

For ideas on museums and other attractions suitable for children of various ages, see *Top Attractions for Families* on page 8.

Accommodation. Some hotels do not accept children under a certain age, so be sure to check when you book. Most restaurants accept well-behaved children, but only those that want to encourage families have children's menus and nappy-changing facilities. Only pubs with a Children's Certificate can admit children, and even these will usually restrict the hours and areas open to them. Publicans, like restaurateurs, reserve the right to refuse entry.

Public transport. Up to four children aged 11 or under can travel free on London's Underground if accompanied by a ticket-holding adult. Eleven–13-year-olds can get unlimited off-peak travel for £1 per day or "Kids for a Quid" single fares if travelling with an electronic Oyster card-holding adult, as can 14–15-year-olds providing they have a photo Oyster card (this can take up to two weeks to obtain and you need to be an EU national).

Buses are free for all children under 16, but 14–15-year-olds will need a 14–15 Oyster photocard. Buses can take up to two unfolded pushchairs (buggies) at one time (they must be parked in a special area halfway down the bus). Any further pushchairs must be folded.

Supplies. Infant formula and nappies (diapers) can be found in chemists (pharmacies) and supermarkets.

Hospitals. In a medical emergency, take your child to the Accident & Emergency department of the nearest hospital. If you require over-the-counter medications such as Calpol (liquid paracetamol) late at night in London, Bliss Pharmacy (5 Marble Arch; tel: 7723 6116) is open until midnight every day.

Climate

In a word, unpredictable. In a few words, temperate and generally mild. It is unusual for any area in the British Isles to have a dry spell for more than three weeks, even in the summer months from June to September. However, it rains most frequently in the mountainous areas of north and west Britain where temperatures are also cooler than in the south.

In summer, the average maximum temperature in the South of England is in the 70s Fahrenheit (23–25°C), although over 80°F (27°C) is not unusual. In Scotland temperatures tend to stay within the mid-60s Fahrenheit (17–19°C). During the winter (November to February), the majority of Britain, with the exception of mountainous regions in the North, tends to be cold and damp rather than snowy.

For recorded weather information, tel: (0871) 200 3985 or visit www.metoffice.org.

Clothing

Temperatures can fluctuate considerably from day to day so come prepared with suitable warm- and wet-weather clothing whatever the season. Generally, short sleeves and a jacket are fine for summer but a warm coat and woollens are recommended for winter.

On the whole the British tend to dress casually and with a few

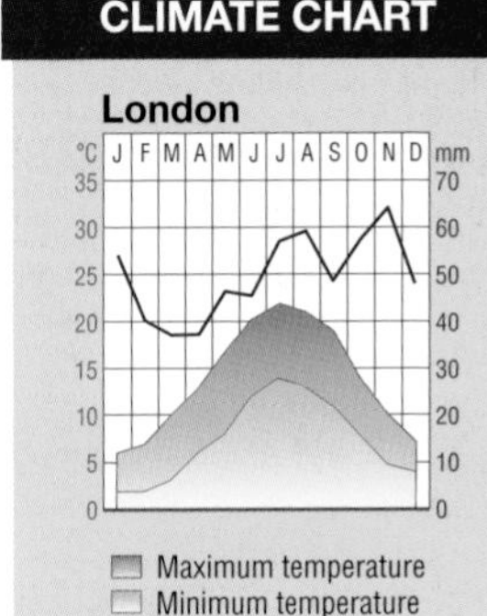

exceptions formal dress is not essential, although a jacket and tie is required by smart hotels, restaurants and clubs.

The young are particularly style-conscious and as a consequence there is a strong presence of trendy street fashion in Britain's cities. At the other end of the scale, the British reputation for conservative and traditional clothing such as waxed jackets, tweeds, woollen jumpers, cords and brogues is still evident, especially in rural areas.

Crime and Safety

Serious crime is low, but in big cities the Dickensian tradition of pick-pocketing is alive and well. Hold on tightly to purses, do not put wallets in back pockets, and do not place handbags on the ground in busy restaurants. Gangs of professional thieves target the Tube in London.

In a genuine emergency, dial 999 from any telephone (no cash required). Report routine thefts to a police station (address under Police in a telephone directory). The threat of terrorism has led to an increase in police patrols, so don't hesitate to report any suspicious packages.

Customs Regulations

If you enter the UK directly from another European Union (EU) country, you no longer need to exit Customs through a red or green channel – use the special EU blue channel, as you are not required to declare any goods you have brought in for personal use. However, if you bring in large amounts of goods such as alcohol, tobacco or perfume you may be asked to verify that they are not intended for resale.

Visitors entering the UK from non-EU countries should use the green Customs channel if they do not exceed the following allowances for goods obtained outside the EU, or purchased duty-free in the EU, or on board ship or aircraft:

- **Tobacco** 200 cigarettes *or* 100 cigarillos *or* 50 cigars *or* 250g of tobacco
- **Alcohol** 2 litres still table wine *plus* 1 litre spirits (over 22 percent by volume) *or* 2 litres fortified wine, sparkling wine or other liqueurs
- **Perfume** 60 ml of perfume *plus* 250 ml of toilet water
- **Gifts** £145 worth of gifts, souvenirs or other goods.

It is illegal to bring animals, certain drugs, firearms, obscene material and anything likely to threaten health or the environment without prior arrangement. Any amount of currency can be brought in.

For further information contact **HM Customs and Excise**, New Kings Beam House, 22 Upper Ground, London, SE1 9PJ; tel: (0845) 010 9000; www.hmce.gov.uk.

Disabled Travellers

Details of transport access for disabled people can be found on a government website, www.dft.gov.uk/transportforyou/access/

www.artsline.org.uk is a disability access website providing searchable information on over 1,000 arts venues across London.

Toilets: Britain has a system of keys to open many of the public toilets available for disabled people. To obtain a key, contact RADAR on 7250 3222. There is a charge of £3.50 (plus value-added tax – VAT) for the key and £10.25 (including post and packing) for the guidebook detailing their locations.

Electricity

230 volts. Square, three-in plugs are used, and virtually all visitors will need adaptors if planning to plug in their own equipment.

Embassies and consulates

Most countries have diplomatic representation in London *(a selection is given below)*. Others can be found through the *Yellow Pages* or by calling Directory Enquiries. Many also have consulates in Edinburgh and Cardiff.

Australia, Australia House, Strand, London WC2 4LA, tel: 020-7379 4334; www.australia.org.uk.

Canada, 1 Grosvenor Square, London W1K 4AB, tel: 020-7258 6600; www.dfait-maeci.gc.ca/canadaeuropa.

India, India House, Aldwych, London

WC2 4NA, tel: 020-7836 8484; www.hcilondon.org.
New Zealand, 80 Haymarket, London SW1Y 4TQ, tel: 020-7930 8422; www.nzembassy.com.
South Africa, South Africa House, Trafalgar Square, London WC2N 5DP, tel: 020-7451 7299; www.southafricahouse.com.
United States, 24 Grosvenor Square, London W1A 1AF, tel: 020-7499 9000; www.usembassy.org.uk.

Emergencies

Only in an absolute emergency call 999 for fire, ambulance or police. In the case of a minor accident or illness, take a taxi to the nearest casualty department of a hospital. For non-urgent calls to the police in London, dial 0300 123 1212; outside the capital, ask Directory Enquiries *(see Telecommunications entry below)* for the number of the nearest police station. They will also be able to give you the telephone number of your country's embassy or consulate if needed.

Entry Requirements

To enter the UK you need a valid passport (or any form of official identification if you are an EU citizen). Visas are not needed if you are an American, Commonwealth citizen or EU national (or come from most other European or South American countries). Health certificates are not required unless you have arrived from Asia, Africa or South America.

If you wish to stay for a protracted period or apply to work in Great Britain, contact the **Immigration and Nationality Directorate**. First look at the website: www.ind.homeoffice.gov.uk. The postal address is Croydon Public Enquiry Office (PEO), Lunar House, 40 Wellesley Road, Croydon, CR9 2BY, tel: (0870) 606 7766.

Gay and Lesbian Travellers

With Europe's largest gay and lesbian population, London has an abundance of bars, restaurants and clubs to cater for most tastes. Many of them will make space for one or more of London's free gay weekly magazines, *Boyz*, the *Pink Paper*, and *QX*. Monthly magazines on sale at newsstands include *Gay Times, Diva* and *Attitude*.

Two established websites for meeting other gay people in London are www.gaydar.co.uk and the female version, www.gaydargirls. com. Other websites reflecting Britain's gay scene include www.rainbownetwork.com and www.outuk.com.

Useful telephone contacts for advice and counselling include **London Lesbian and Gay Switchboard** (tel: 7837 7324) and **London Friend** (7.30–10pm, tel: 7837 3337). Support and advice about legal issues concerning HIV and Aids is available from the **National Aids Helpline** (tel: 0800-567 123).

Health and Medical Care

If you fall ill and are a national of the EU, you are entitled to free medical treatment. Many other countries also have reciprocal arrangements for free treatment. Most other visitors have to pay for medical and dental treatment and should ensure they have adequate health insurance.

In the case of minor accidents, your hotel will know the location of the nearest hospital with a casualty department. Self-catering accommodation should have this information, plus the number of the local GP, on a notice in the house.
Treatment: Seriously ill visitors are eligible for free emergency treatment in the Accident and Emergency departments of National Health Service hospitals. However, if they are admitted to hospital as an in-patient, even from the accident and emergency department, or referred to an out-patient clinic, they will be asked to pay unless they fall into the above exempted categories.
Walk-in clinics: There are more than 80 National Health Service walk-in centres across the country, usually open seven days a week from early morning to late evening, 365 days a year. A charge may be made to non-EU nationals.
Chemists (pharmacists): Boots is the largest chain of chemists, with many branches around the country. As well as selling over-the-counter medicines, they make up prescriptions.
Accidents: In the case of a serious accident or emergency, dial **999**.

Lost Property

If you have lost your passport, you must get in touch with your embassy as quickly as possible.

For possessions lost on trains you must contact the station where the train on which you were travelling ended its journey. The same applies if you leave something on a coach. For anything lost on public transport in London, contact the Transport For London Lost Property Office, 200 Baker Street, NW1 5RZ, tel: 020-7486 2496, fax: 020-7918 1028, from 9.30am–2pm, Mon–Fri, or fill in an enquiry form, available from any London Underground station or bus garage. Leave at least three full working days after the loss before visiting the lost property office.

Maps

Insight Guides' best-selling *FlexiMaps* are laminated for durability and easy folding and contain clear cartography as well as practical information. British titles include *London, Cornwall, the Cotswolds, Edinburgh* and the *Lake District*.

In London, map lovers should head for Stanford's (12–14 Long Acre, in the Covent Garden area), one of the world's top map and guidebook stores.

Media

Newspapers

With more than 100 daily and Sunday newspapers published nationwide, there's no lack of choice in Britain. Although free from state controland financially independent of political parties, many nationals do have pronounced political leanings. Of the quality dailies *The Times* and *The Daily Telegraph* are on the right, *The Guardian* and *The Independent* in the middle. On Sunday *The Observer* leans slightly left of centre, while the *Independent on Sunday* stands in the middle and the *Sunday Times* and *Sunday Telegraph* are on the right.

The Financial Times is renowned for the clearest, most unbiased headlines in its general news pages, plus exhaustive financial coverage.

The mass-market papers are a less formal, easy read. *The Sun, The Star* and *News of the World* (out on Sunday) are on the right and obsessed with the Royal family, soap operas and sex. *The Mirror, Sunday Mirror* and *Sunday People* are slightly left. In the mid-market sector, the *Daily Mail* and *Mail on Sunday* are slightly more upscale equivalents of the *Express* and *Sunday Express*.

Scotland's quality dailies are *The Scotsman*, based in Edinburgh and *The Herald*, based in Glasgow; *the Daily Record* is the most popular Scottish tabloid. Wales has the *Western Mail* and the *Daily Post*.

Some cities have free newspapers, paid for by advertising and often handed out at railway stations.

Listing Magazines

To find out what's on in London, the long-established weekly *Time Out* (out on Wednesdays) is supreme. But Saturday's *The Guardian* includes a

ABOVE: the big cities have newsstands – and sometimes free newspapers.

good free supplement previewing the week ahead and there are daily listings in the *Evening Standard*.

For details of events elsewhere, the quality daily newspapers have a limited listings section, but your best port of call is a Tourist Information Centre *(see page 387)*. Many local papers have a weekly section on Fridays with details of places to visit and things to do in their area. Two websites to try are: www.timeout.com and www.bbc.co.uk.

Foreign Newspapers

These can usually be found in large newsagents and railway stations nationwide. Branches of W.H. Smith, in larger towns, usually have a reasonable selection.

Television

Britain has a somewhat outdated reputation for broadcasting some of the finest television in the world. There are five national terrestial channels: BBC1, BBC2, ITV, Channel 4 (C4) and Five. Both the BBC (British Broadcasting Corporation) and ITV (Independent Television) have regional stations that broadcast local news and varying programme schedules in between links with the national networks based in London (see local newspapers for listings). The BBC is financed by compulsory annual television licence fees and therefore does not rely on advertising for funding. The independent channels, ITV, C4 and Five are funded entirely by commercials.

BBC1, ITV and Five broadcast programmes aimed at mainstream audiences, while BBC2 and C4 cater more for cultural and minority interests. However, the advent of cable and satellite channels has forced terrestrial stations to fight for audiences with a higher incidence of programmes such as soap operas and game shows. Both the BBC and ITV also have satellite channels.

There are hundreds of cable and satellite channels on offer, ranging from sport and films to cartoons and music. Pricier hotel rooms often offer a choice of cable stations, including CNN and BBC News Channel.

Radio Stations

As well as the sample of national services listed below – note that frequencies may vary in different parts of the country – there is a wide range of local radio stations which are useful for traffic reports.

BBC Radio 1 98.8FM
Britain's most popular radio station, which broadcasts mainstream pop.

BBC Radio 2 89.2FM
Easy-listening music and chat shows.

BBC Radio 3 91.3FM
24-hour classical music, plus some drama.

BBC Radio 4 93.5FM
News, current affairs, plays.

BBC Radio Five Live 909MW
Rolling news and sport.

BBC World Service 648kHz
International news.

Classic FM 100.9 FM
24-hour classical and movie music unpompously presented.

Absolute Radio 105.8FM
Middle-of-the-road rock music.

Kiss FM 100FM
24-hour dance.

Money

Most banks open between 9.30am and 4.30pm Monday–Friday, with Saturday morning banking common in shopping areas. The majority of branches have automatic teller machines (ATM) where international credit or cashpoint cards can be used, in conjunction with a personal number, to withdraw cash.

The major banks offer similar exchange rates, so it's worth shopping around only if you have large amounts of money to change. Banks charge no commission on travellers' cheques presented in sterling. If a bank is affiliated to your own bank at home, it will make no charge for cheques in other currencies either. But there is a charge for changing cash into British currency.

Some high-street travel agents, such as Thomas Cook, operate *bureaux de change* at comparable rates. There are also many privately run *bureaux de change* (some of which are open 24 hours a day) where exchange rates can be low but commissions high.

Currency: Pounds, divided into 100 pence. Scotland issues its own notes, which are not technically legal tender in England and Wales, though banks and some shops accept them. Exchange rates against the US dollar and the euro can fluctuate wildly.

Euros: A few shops, services, attractions and hotels accept euro notes, but give change in sterling. Most will charge a commission.

Credit cards: International credit cards are accepted in most shops, hotels and restaurants.

Pets

Dogs, cats and ferrets from certain countries are able to enter Britain via selected ports of entry under the pilot Pets Travel Scheme without quarantine – provided certain conditions are met. Animals other than those identified will have to be quarantined for six months at approved premises. There are no exceptions and any illegally imported animal is liable to be destroyed. Details from Department for Food and Rural Areas (www.defra.gov.uk).

Postal services

Post offices are open 9am–5.30pm Monday–Friday, and 9am–12.30pm on Saturday. London's main post office is in Trafalgar Square, behind the church of St Martin-in-the-Fields, It is open Monday–Friday until 6.30pm, till 5.30 pm on Saturday.

Stamps are sold at post offices, selected shops and newsagents, some supermarkets and from machines outside larger post offices. There is a two-tier service for mail within the UK: first class should reach its destination the next day, and second class will take a day longer. The rate to Europe for standard letters is the same as first-class post within Britain.

Mail can be forwarded to you at any post office in Britain if it is addressed c/o Poste Restante. More information at www.postoffice.co.uk.

Public holidays

Compared to most of Europe, the UK has few public holidays:
January New Year's Day (1)
March/April Good Friday, Easter Monday
May May Day (first Monday of the month), Spring Bank Holiday (last Monday)
August Summer Bank Holiday (last Monday)
December Christmas Day (25), Boxing Day (26).

On public holidays, banks and offices are closed, though most shops are open (except on Christmas Day). Roads are often a nightmare as people head for the coast or the countryside or to see relatives.

Religious Services

Although Christians, according to census returns, constitute about 71 percent of the population, half never attend church, so visitors will have no trouble finding a place in a pew. All the major varieties of Christianity are represented. Britain is a multi-faith society and other main religions, including Buddhism, Hinduism, Judaism, Islam and Sikhism, are freely practised. About 23 percent of Britons follow no particular religion.

Smoking

Smoking is banned in all enclosed public spaces, including pubs, clubs and bars (though not in outside beer gardens).

Student travel

International students can obtain various discounts at attractions, on travel services (including Eurostar) and in some shops by showing a valid ISIC card. www.isiccard.com

Telecommunications

It is usually cheaper to use public phones rather than those in hotel rooms as hotels make high profits out of this service.

British Telecom (BT) is the main telephone operating company and provides public telephone kiosks. Some public phones take coins only, some plastic phone cards and/or credit cards, and some all three. Phone cards can be bought from post offices and newsagents in varying amounts between £1 and £20.

Public telephone boxes are not as ubiquitous as they used to be. Now that so many people have mobile phones, they are not considered essential. However, you will still usually find one without going too far. Stations and shopping centres in particular are good places to look. In country areas, try a pub.

The most expensive time to use the telephone is 8am–6pm weekdays, while the cheapest is after 6pm on weekdays and all weekend. Calls are charged by distance, so a long-distance conversation on a weekday morning can eat up coins or card units in a phone box.

Numbers beginning with the prefixes 0800, 0500, 0321 or 0808 are freephone lines. Those prefixed by 0345, 0645 or 0845 are charged at local rates irrespective of distance. Those starting with 0891, 0839, 0640, 0660 and 0898 are costly.

The Directory Enquiries service, once exclusively a BT money-earner, was opened up to competition from other companies and the result was a confusing variety of expensive numbers such as 118500. A better bet is to use British Telecom's online service, www.192.com.

Cellphones: You can buy pay-as-you-go SIM cards from most mobile phone retailers and many electrical stores. If your mobile phone accepts SIM cards from companies other than the one you usually use it with, you should be able to register the SIM and use it during your trip.

Useful Numbers

- **Emergencies** 999
- **Operator** 100
- **Directory Enquiries (UK)** 118 500, 118 888 or 118 811
- **International Directory Enquiries** 118 505, 118 866 or 118 899
- **International Operator** 155
- **Telegrams** 0800 190190

Time zone

Greenwich Mean Time (GMT) is 1 hour behind Continental European Time, 5 hours ahead of Eastern Seaboard Time, and 9 hours behind Sydney, Australia. British Summer Time (GMT + one hour) runs from late March to late October.

Tipping

Most hotels and restaurants automatically add a 10–15 percent service charge to your meal bill. It's your right to deduct this amount if you're not happy with the service. Sometimes when service has been added, the final total on a credit card slip is still left blank, the implication being that a further tip is expected: you do not have to pay this. You don't tip in pubs, cinemas or theatres, but it is customary to give hairdressers, sightseeing guides, railway porters and cab drivers an extra amount of around 10 percent.

Tourist Information Offices

Visit Britain (formerly The British Tourist Authority) has offices worldwide. Visit www.visitbritain.com or write to request information.

Australia
Level 16, Gateway, 1 Macquarie Place, Sydney, NSW 2000
Tel: (02) 9377 4400
Fax: (02) 9377 4499

Canada
5915 Airport Road, Suite 120
Mississauga, Ontario, L4V 1T1
Tel: 1888 VISITUK
Fax: (905) 405 1835

New Zealand
17th Floor, NZI House, 151 Queen Street, Auckland 1
Tel: (9) 303 1446
Fax: (9) 377 6965

Singapore
01-00 GMG Building, 108 Robinson Road, Singapore 068900
Tel: (65) 6227 5400
Fax: (65) 6227 5411

South Africa
P.O.Box 41896, Lancaster Gate Hyde Park Lane, Hyde Park, 2196
Tel: (11) 325 0343
Fax: (2711) 325 0344

USA – Chicago
625 N. Michigan Avenue, Suite 1001, Chicago, IL 60611
Tel: 1 800 462 2748

USA – Los Angeles
Office not open to the public
Tel: (310) 470-2782
Fax: (310) 470-8549

USA – New York
7th Floor, 551 Fifth Avenue, New York, NY 10176-0799
Tel: 1 800 GO 2 BRIT or (212) 986-2266.

Tourist Information in London

Visit Scotland
19 Cockspur Street, London SW1Y 5BL, tel: (0845) 225 5121; fax: (01506) 832222; www.visitscotland.com.

Visit Wales Centre
Telephone line for ordering brochures, accommodation, booking and all general tourist information. Tel: (08701) 211251; fax: (08701) 211259; www.visitwales.com.

British Travel Centre
Britain and London Visitor Centre, 1 Regent Street, Piccadilly Circus, London SW1Y 4NS; www.visitbritain.com.
Lastminute.com offer a booking service for theatre tickets and accommodation throughout Britain. Tickets for rail, air and sea travel and sightseeing tours can be bought from the travel agency desk. The centre also has an internet lounge and a currency exchange bureau. The centre is open 9.30am–6.30pm Mon, 9am–6.30pm Tues–Fri and 10am–4pm weekends (during summer it is open 9am–5pm Sat).
Visit London
Britain and London Visitor Centre, 1 Regent Street, Piccadilly Circus, London SW1Y 4NS; www.visitlondon.com.
Transport for London Travel Information (Tfl) publishes various maps and guides for visitors – available from Heathrow underground station, Victoria and Euston mainline stations (main concourse). London Bridge and Hammersmith have bus information centres. For further information, tel: 020-7222 1234.

Information Centres

There are more than 800 Tourist Information Centres (TICs) throughout Britain, which provide free information and advice on local sights, activities and accommodation. Most are open office hours, which are extended to include weekends and evenings in high season or in areas where there is a high volume of visitors all year round. Some close from October to March. TICs are generally well-signposted and denoted by a distinctive *i* symbol.

For general information about the whole of the country, contact (by phone or fax only): **The English Tourist Board/British Tourist Authority**, Thames Tower, Black's Road, London W6 9EL, tel: 020-8846 9000, from US tel: 1-800-GO-2-BRIT; fax: 020-8563 0302; e-mail: travelinfo@visitbritain.org; www.visitbritain.com. This site can be used to access information from regional tourist boards by clicking on the relevant area of the map.

Alternatively, the following are information offices for different regions. You can write or telephone for information, but they are administrative offices only and cannot be visited in person.
East of England Tourist Board, Toppesfield Hall, Hadleigh, Suffolk IP7 5DN, tel: (01473) 822922; fax: (01473) 823063; www.visiteastofengland.com.
Heart of England Tourist Board, Larkhill Road, Worcester WR5 2EZ, tel: (01905) 761100; fax: (01905) 763450; www.visitheartofengland.com.
London Tourist Board and Convention Bureau, 6th Floor, Glen House, Stag Place, London SW1E 5LT, tel: 020-7234 5800; fax: 020-7932 0222; www.visitlondon.com.
Tourism Southeast, 40 Chamberlayne Road, Eastleigh, Hants SO50 5JH, tel: (02380) 625400; fax: (02380) 620010; www.gosouth.co.uk.
Southwest Tourism, Woodwater Park, Exeter EX2 5WT, tel: (01392) 360050; fax: (01392) 445112; www.visitsouthwest.co.uk.
Yorkshire Tourist Board, 312 Tadcaster Road, York YO24 1GS, tel: (01904) 707961; fax: (01904) 701414; www.yorkshirevisitor.com.
Northumbria Tourist Board, Aykley Heads, Durham DH1 5UX, tel: (0191) 375 3000; fax: (0191) 386 0899; www.visitnorthumbria.com.
Cumbria Tourist Board, Ashleigh, Holly Road, Windermere LA23 2AQ, tel: (015394) 44444; www.golakes.co.uk.
Greater Manchester Tourist Board, Churchgate House, 56 Oxford Road, Manchester M1 6EU; tel: (0161) 237 1010; www.destinationmanchester.com.
The Mersey Partnership, 12 Princes Parade, Liverpool L3 1BG, tel: (0151) 227 2727; www.merseyside.org.
Visit Scotland, 23 Ravelston Terrace, Edinburgh EH4 3EU, tel: (0131) 332 2433; fax: (0131) 343 1513; www.visitscotland.com.
Wales Tourist Board, Brunel House, 2 Fitzalan Road, Cardiff CF24 0UY, tel: (02920) 499909; fax: (02920) 485031; www.visitwales.com.

Websites

www.insightguides.com includes comprehensive hotel listings.
www.visitbritain.co.uk The official tourism site, covering just about everything. plus a booking service for flights, travel cards and rail passes.
www.visitlondon.com The capital's official tourist board site, with lots of advice, listings, links, special deals.
www.thisislondon.com Run by the *Evening Standard*; has detailed listings of events.
www.streetmap.co.uk locates the address you type in.
www.24hourmuseum.co.uk has up-to-date information of what UK museums are exhibiting.
www.bbc.co.uk is a gigantic site, particularly useful for news and weather forecasts.
www.guardian.co.uk is one of the best newspaper websites, especially good on cultural events.

Weights and measures

It's a mess, reflecting Britain's ambivalence about whether it prefers its Imperial past or its European present. So you will fill up a car with litres of fuel (which may be as well since an Imperial gallon is confusingly larger than a US gallon) but roadsigns will direct to your destination in miles. You buy beer by the pint in a pub. A supermarket will sell you a pint of milk, but most other drinks are packaged as litres. In a few controversial cases, greengrocers have been fined for selling vegetables by the pound instead of by the kilo.
The main conversions are:

Kilometres and miles
1 mile = 1.609 kilometres
1 kilometre = 0.621 miles
Litres and gallons
1 gallon = 4.546 litres
1 litre = 0.220 gallons
Kilos and pounds
1 pound = 0.453 kilos
1 kilo = 2.204 pounds

BELOW: beer is still dispensed in pints, though wine measures are metric.

FURTHER READING

Good Companions

Artist's London by David Piper, Fascinating images of London over the ages.
Cider with Rosie by Laurie Lee. Memories of an idyllic youth in Gloucestershire.
A Concise History of Scotland by Fitzroy MacLean.
The Concise Pepys by Samuel Pepys. A first-hand account of the Great Fire of London and daily life in 17th-century England.
The English: A Portrait of a People by Jeremy Paxman. Semi-serious study of English character.
Four Scottish Journeys by Andrew Eames.
A Guide through the District of the Lakes by William Wordsworth. Lyrical descriptions of the poet's beloved Lake District.
A History of Britain by Simon Schama. Readable three-volume narrative linked to a BBC series.
A History of Modern Wales by David Williams.
Hound of the Baskervilles by Sir Arthur Conan Doyle. Sherlock Holmes and mystery on the moors.
How Green was my Valley by Richard Llewellyn. Story of a Welsh mining community.
In Search Of England by Michael Wood. English identity considered through a series of intelligent yet accessible historical essays.
Jamaica Inn by Daphne du Maurier. A tale of Cornish "wreckers" who loot shipwrecks.
A Journey to the Western Isles of Scotland by Dr Samuel Johnson and **James Boswell's Journal of a Tour to the Hebrides**. Two accounts of the same trip in the 18th century by the lexicographer and his biographer.
London: A Concise History by Geoffrey Trease. Good illustrated history.
London: The Biography by Peter Ackroyd. Mammoth work on the great city, seen as a living organism.
Lorna Doone by R.D. Blackmore. The story of a tragic heroine and her lawless family on Exmoor.
The Mabinogion by Gywn Jones and Thomas Jones (translators). Eleven medieval stories from Wales.
Mary, Queen of Scots by Antonia Fraser.
Mrs Dalloway by Virginia Woolf. A day-in-the-life of an Edwardian matron in London.
Notes from a Small Island by Bill Bryson. Best-selling comic's walking tour of Britain.
Oliver Twist by Charles Dickens. The classic tale of Victorian pick-pockets in London's East End.
On the Black Hill by Bruce Chatwin.
Pride and Prejudice by Jane Austen.
The Prime of Miss Jean Brodie by Muriel Spark. The story of a strong-willed Edinburgh schoolmistress.
Secret London by Andrew Duncan. Uncovers London's hidden landscape from abandoned tube stations to the gentlemen's club.
The Literary Guide to London by Ed Glinert. A detailed, street-by-street guide to the literary lives of London.
A Shropshire Lad by A.E. Housman. Poems on the themes of Shropshire country life, and the life of a soldier.
England's Thousand Best Houses by Simon Jenkins. An invaluable guide.
Tilly Trotter by Catherine Cookson. Set in Durham, the story of a girl born into a poor family in Victorian times.
Tour Through the Whole Island of Great Britain by Daniel Defoe.
Underground London: Travels Beneath the City Streets by Stephen Smith.
Under Milkwood by Dylan Thomas.
Vanishing Cornwall by Daphne du Maurier. A perceptive view of the changing face of Cornwall.
Waverley by Sir Walter Scott. A gripping tale of Highland clans at the time of the Jacobite rising of 1745.
Westward Ho! by Charles Kingsley. Heroic tale of West Country seafarers.
Tess of the D'Urbervilles by Thomas Hardy. Rural life and tragedy in the Wessex countryside.
Wuthering Heights by Emily Brontë. Passion and repression on the brooding Yorkshire Moors.

Send Us Your Thoughts

We do our best to ensure the information in our books is as accurate and up-to-date as possible. The books are updated on a regular basis using local contacts, who painstakingly add, amend and correct as required. However, some details (such as telephone numbers and opening times) are liable to change, and we are ultimately reliant on our readers to put us in the picture.

We welcome your feedback, especially your experience of using the book "on the road". Maybe we recommended a hotel that you liked (or another that you didn't), or you came across a great bar or new attraction we missed.

We will acknowledge all contributions, and we'll offer an Insight Guide to the best letters received.

Please write to us at:
Insight Guides
PO Box 7910
London SE1 1WE
Or email us at:
insight@apaguide.co.uk

Other Insight Guides

The **Insight Guides** series includes books on *England, Scotland, Ireland, Edinburgh, London, Oxford* and *The Channel Islands*, as well as *Best Hotels: Great Britain & Ireland.*
Insight Pocket Guides series offers personal recommendations and a large-size pullout map; titles include *Scotland* and *Ireland.*
Insight Compact Guides series provides the ideal portable, fully illustrated guidebook to specific areas. A dozen titles cover every major holiday area in the UK, from *Cornwall, Edinburgh, Glasgow* and *London* to *Oxford, York* and *Bath & Surroundings*. Guides to *Scotland, Ireland* and the *Cotswolds* also feature, alongside popular national park titles such as *Devon & Exmoor, Lake District* and *Snowdonia.*
Insight Step by Step *London*, written by local experts, has 20 self-guided walks and tours, and includes a useful full-size fold-out map.
For quick reference, **Insight Smart Guide** *London*, with an A–Z format, suggests hundreds of things to see and do, ranging from architecture and theatre to shopping and pubs.

Art & Photo Credits

Apa Publications 9B, 146T, 147T, 187T, 187B, 233, 235T, 264T, 298, 299T, 299BL, 300T, 330BR, 379, 385
Natasha Babaian/Apa 131CL
David Beatty/Apa 288T, 291, 312, 313, 314T, 314B, 317T, 317B, 319
William Beckett 118BR
Brian Bell 122B
Andrew Birtwhistle/fotoLibra 264BR
Britain on View 3, 6CB, 6/7B, 9CL, 10T, 19L, 21, 66, 73, 96, 102/103, 115T, 137B, 176, 192, 193, 194, 214, 218BL, 219CL, 222, 223T, 225T, 228B, 235B, 240B, 256, 265, 272/273T, 274, 275, 276T, 277T, 277B, 281T, 282B, 283, 285, 286T, 290B, 295B, 297B, 304B, 305, 315B, 325B, 336BL, 336CR, 346B, 347
British Museum 130/131, 130BL, 131BL, 131TR, 131CR, 131BR
British Tourist Authority 7CL, 7CR, 258T, 357, 380, 387
Graham Coleman/fotoLibra 262
Christopher Cook/fotoLibra 179B
Corbis 8B, 14/15, 22, 23, 60, 61, 62, 73, 116B, 121B, 127B, 148B, 175, 209B, 210, 220, 253B, 258B, 261, 270B, 278B, 287, 288B, 299BR, 302, 307, 332B, 336/337T, 338
Country Life 1, 10B, 71, 100/101, 106, 156/157T, 157BL, 157BR, 218/219T, 227B
Alyse Dar/Apa 135T
Linton Donaldson/Apa 153
Famous Pictures & Features 69
Duncan Farquhar/fotoLibra 327, 348
Mark Ferguson/fotoLibra 337BL
Mark Follon/Imperial War Museum 276B
Glyn Genin/Apa 116T, 117B, 118BL, 121T, 122T, 123, 125B, 127T, 130BR, 132, 139T, 139B, 140T, 145T, 145B, 146B, 154T, 172T, 172BL, 173, 178B, 196, 207, 211, 212T, 216T, 227T, 375, 381
Getty Images 12/13, 16/17, 20, 57, 58, 63, 79, 80, 82, 83, 85, 86, 87, 89, 90, 92, 95, 99BL, 140B, 178T, 186, 247, 248/249, 260, 320/321, 328B, 334B
Mark Goodwin/fotoLibra 259
Paul Groom/fotoLibra 218BR
Tony Halliday/Apa 107B, 171T, 219BL, 267, 271, 273CR, 273BL, 286B, 296BR, 297T, 303T
Paul Harrison/fotoLibra 156BL
Historic Royal Palaces 118T, 136B, 155
Robert Ho/fotoStock 225BR
Hans Höfer 350
John Holmes/fotoLibra 349
David Hudson/fotoLibra 8T
Hulton Picture Company 70
Paul Hurst/fotoLibra 104/105
iStockphoto 5, 6/7T, 6CL, 6CR, 7TR, 7BR, 11C, 28B, 29T, 29R, 29B, 34BR, 34BL, 35CL, 35CR, 35B, 51B, 53, 76, 78, 98BL, 98C, 98BR, 99TR, 99BR, 137T, 152, 161, 179T, 180T, 180B, 181T, 185T, 185B, 195T, 197T, 197BL, 197BR, 198T, 200B, 201T, 202T, 203, 209T, 215T, 217, 219BR, 224, 228T, 229, 238T, 242T, 242B, 243T, 244T, 244B, 245, 246, 251, 253T, 254T, 254BL, 254BR, 255, 257T, 263, 264BL, 266T, 268BL, 268BR, 269T, 270T, 272BL, 272BR, 273CL, 273BR, 278T, 280T, 280B, 282T, 289, 290T, 293, 295T, 300BL, 304T, 311, 315T, 316T, 316B, 328T, 332T, 334T, 336BR, 337TR, 339, 340BR, 341T, 342T, 342B, 344T, 345, 346T, 353, 367, 377
Britta Jaschinksi/Apa 128, 129, 141, 143T
Caroline Jones/Apa 182, 183T, 184T, 184BL, 184BR
Kobal Collection 59, 74,91
Alex Knights 240T, 241T, 241B
Tom Le Bas/Apa 120B, 126T
Laurence Leech/fotoLibra 337BR
Siân Lezard/Apa 154
Douglas Macgilvray 4B, 323, 324, 325T, 326T, 326BL, 326BR, 329, 330T, 330BL, 331T, 331BL, 331BR, 333, 335, 372
George Mason/fotoLibra 181B
Paul Mattock/fotoLibra 266B
Iwona Medrala/fotoLibra 157TR
Roger Milam/fotoLibra 142
Robert Mort 68
Museum of London 51, 133B
National Maritime Museum 150
Richard T. Nowitz 269B
Oepkes 163T, 163B
Kim Osborn/fotoLibra 156CR
Pictorial Press 156C
Clare Peel/Apa 138T
Ramsay@Claridges 75
Alan Reed/fotoLibra 151T
Julia Rich/fotoLibra 77
Derek Roberts/fotoLibra 221
Ronnie Scott's Jazz Club 124B
Brian Shuel/Collections 134
Sir John Soane's Museum 126B
Homer Sykes 64/65
Greg Szabo/fotoLibra 306
TopFoto 81
V&A Museum 144
Peter Vallance/fotoLibra 225BL
Visit London 9TR, 67B, 112, 113, 114B, 115B, 117T, 124T, 125T, 135B, 138BL, 138BR, 143B, 147B, 149, 151B, 352, 380
Bojan Vogrin/fotoLibra 119
Von Essen hotels 162
Adrian Warren, Dae Sasitorn/Last Refuge 34/35, 98/99, 158, 195B, 215B, 243B, 279, 281B, 284, 292, 301, 303B, 308/309, 318
Bill Wassman/Apa 174, 183B, 341B, 343, 344, 348T
Ali Williams 252BR
Corrie Wingate 2/3, 4T, 18, 19R, 67T, 88, 93, 94, 97, 159, 160T, 160B, 164, 165, 166/167, 168, 169, 170, 171B, 172BR, 177B, 188/189, 190, 191, 198B, 199BL, 199BR, 200T, 201B, 202B, 204/205, 206, 212B, 213T, 230/231, 232, 236, 237T, 237B, 238B, 239
Phil Wood/Apa 84, 300BR
Philippa Wood/fotoLibra 257B, 272CR
Simon Woodcock/fotoLibra 148T
David Young/fotoLibra 157CL, 213B, 216B, 223B, 226BR
Crispin Zeeman/Apa 107T

Map Production Lovell Johns

Maps of London reproduced by permission of Geographers' A–Z Map Co. Ltd. Licence No. B4504.

Index

Numbers in italics refer to photographs

A

B

C

M

N

U

V

W

X–Z

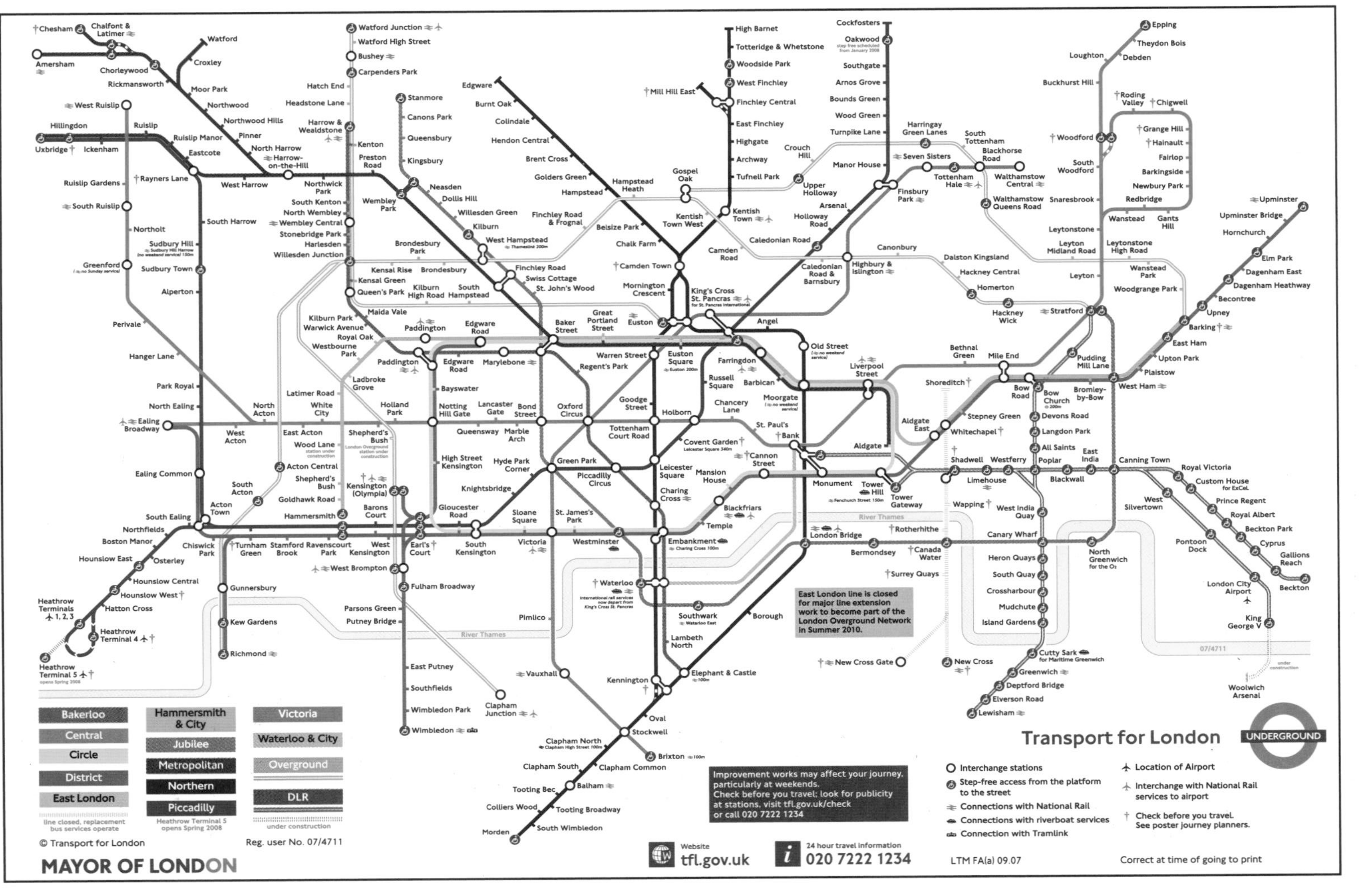

Transport for London
UNDERGROUND
Bakerloo
Central
Circle
District
East London
Hammersmith & City
Jubilee
Metropolitan
Northern
Piccadilly
Victoria
Waterloo & City
Overground
DLR
line closed, replacement bus services operate
Heathrow Terminal 5 opens Spring 2008
under construction
Interchange stations
Step-free access from the platform to the street
Connections with National Rail
Connections with riverboat services
Connection with Tramlink
Location of Airport
Interchange with National Rail services to airport
Check before you travel. See poster journey planners.
East London line is closed for major line extension work to become part of the London Overground Network in Summer 2010.
Improvement works may affect your journey, particularly at weekends. Check before you travel: look for publicity at stations, visit tfl.gov.uk/check or call 020 7222 1234
Website
tfl.gov.uk
24 hour travel information
020 7222 1234
LTM FA(a) 09.07
Correct at time of going to print
© Transport for London
Reg. user No. 07/4711
MAYOR OF LONDON
River Thames
Chesham
Chalfont & Latimer
Amersham
Chorleywood
Rickmansworth
Watford
Croxley
Moor Park
Northwood
Northwood Hills
Pinner
North Harrow
Harrow-on-the-Hill
West Harrow
Rayners Lane
Eastcote
Ruislip Manor
Ruislip
Ickenham
Hillingdon
Uxbridge
West Ruislip
Ruislip Gardens
South Ruislip
Northolt
Greenford
Perivale
Hanger Lane
Sudbury Hill
Sudbury Town
Alperton
South Harrow
Park Royal
North Ealing
Ealing Broadway
Ealing Common
West Acton
North Acton
East Acton
South Ealing
Northfields
Boston Manor
Osterley
Hounslow East
Hounslow Central
Hounslow West
Hatton Cross
Heathrow Terminals 1, 2, 3
Heathrow Terminal 4
Heathrow Terminal 5
Acton Town
South Acton
Chiswick Park
Turnham Green
Stamford Brook
Ravenscourt Park
Gunnersbury
Kew Gardens
Richmond
Watford Junction
Watford High Street
Bushey
Carpenders Park
Hatch End
Headstone Lane
Harrow & Wealdstone
Kenton
Preston Road
Northwick Park
South Kenton
North Wembley
Wembley Central
Stonebridge Park
Harlesden
Willesden Junction
Kensal Green
Queen's Park
Kensal Rise
Brondesbury Park
Brondesbury
Kilburn High Road
South Hampstead
Stanmore
Canons Park
Queensbury
Kingsbury
Wembley Park
Neasden
Dollis Hill
Willesden Green
Kilburn
West Hampstead
Finchley Road
Swiss Cottage
St. John's Wood
Edgware
Burnt Oak
Colindale
Hendon Central
Brent Cross
Golders Green
Hampstead
Hampstead Heath
Finchley Road & Frognal
Belsize Park
Chalk Farm
Camden Town
Kentish Town West
Gospel Oak
High Barnet
Totteridge & Whetstone
Woodside Park
West Finchley
Mill Hill East
Finchley Central
East Finchley
Highgate
Archway
Tufnell Park
Kentish Town
Camden Road
Caledonian Road
Caledonian Road & Barnsbury
Holloway Road
Arsenal
Upper Holloway
Crouch Hill
Cockfosters
Oakwood
Southgate
Arnos Grove
Bounds Green
Wood Green
Turnpike Lane
Manor House
Harringay Green Lanes
Seven Sisters
South Tottenham
Blackhorse Road
Walthamstow Central
Tottenham Hale
Finsbury Park
Walthamstow Queens Road
Highbury & Islington
Canonbury
Dalston Kingsland
Hackney Central
Homerton
Hackney Wick
Stratford
Epping
Theydon Bois
Loughton
Debden
Buckhurst Hill
Roding Valley
Chigwell
Woodford
Grange Hill
Hainault
Fairlop
Barkingside
Newbury Park
South Woodford
Snaresbrook
Redbridge
Wanstead
Gants Hill
Leytonstone
Leyton
Leyton Midland Road
Leytonstone High Road
Wanstead Park
Woodgrange Park
Upminster
Upminster Bridge
Hornchurch
Elm Park
Dagenham East
Dagenham Heathway
Becontree
Upney
Barking
East Ham
Upton Park
Plaistow
West Ham
Kilburn Park
Maida Vale
Warwick Avenue
Royal Oak
Westbourne Park
Paddington
Edgware Road
Marylebone
Baker Street
Great Portland Street
Euston
Mornington Crescent
King's Cross St. Pancras
Angel
Old Street
Ladbroke Grove
Latimer Road
White City
Holland Park
Shepherd's Bush
Wood Lane
Acton Central
Shepherd's Bush
Goldhawk Road
Hammersmith
Kensington (Olympia)
Barons Court
West Kensington
Earl's Court
West Brompton
Fulham Broadway
Parsons Green
Putney Bridge
East Putney
Southfields
Wimbledon Park
Wimbledon
Bayswater
Notting Hill Gate
Queensway
Lancaster Gate
Marble Arch
Bond Street
Oxford Circus
High Street Kensington
Gloucester Road
South Kensington
Knightsbridge
Hyde Park Corner
Green Park
Piccadilly Circus
Sloane Square
Victoria
St. James's Park
Westminster
Pimlico
Vauxhall
Clapham Junction
Warren Street
Regent's Park
Euston Square
Goodge Street
Tottenham Court Road
Holborn
Russell Square
Farringdon
Barbican
Chancery Lane
Moorgate
Liverpool Street
St. Paul's
Bank
Covent Garden
Leicester Square
Charing Cross
Embankment
Temple
Blackfriars
Mansion House
Cannon Street
Monument
Tower Hill
Tower Gateway
Aldgate
Aldgate East
Waterloo
Southwark
Lambeth North
London Bridge
Borough
Elephant & Castle
Kennington
Oval
Stockwell
Brixton
Clapham North
Clapham Common
Clapham South
Balham
Tooting Bec
Tooting Broadway
Colliers Wood
South Wimbledon
Morden
Shoreditch
Whitechapel
Bethnal Green
Mile End
Stepney Green
Shadwell
Wapping
Rotherhithe
Canada Water
Surrey Quays
Bermondsey
New Cross Gate
New Cross
Bow Road
Bow Church
Pudding Mill Lane
Bromley-by-Bow
Devons Road
Langdon Park
All Saints
Limehouse
Westferry
Poplar
Blackwall
East India
Canning Town
West India Quay
Canary Wharf
Heron Quays
South Quay
Crossharbour
Mudchute
Island Gardens
Cutty Sark for Maritime Greenwich
Greenwich
Deptford Bridge
Elverson Road
Lewisham
North Greenwich for the O2
Royal Victoria
Custom House for ExCeL
Prince Regent
Royal Albert
Beckton Park
Cyprus
Gallions Reach
Beckton
West Silvertown
Pontoon Dock
London City Airport
King George V
Woolwich Arsenal

London Zoo
Hampstead
Camden Lock
St Aloysius
St Pancras International Station
KING'S CROSS ST PANCRAS
King's Cross Thameslink
REGENT'S PARK
Euston Station
EUSTON
British Library
Camden Town Hall
Swinton St
King's Cross Road
Argyle St
Acton St
Outer
Albany
Hampstead Road
Euston Mosque
Eversholt St
Euston Road
Judd
REGENT'S PARK
Inner Circle
Broadwalk
Circle
Street
St Anne
Upp. Woburn Pl.
Holy Cross
Street
ST PANCRAS
British Medical Association
Euston Tower
EUSTON SQUARE
Tavistock Sq
Foundling Museum
Gray's Inn Road
Doughty St
Madame Tussauds
Holy Trinity
Euston Centre
Circle
Outer
PARK SQ GARDENS
Percival David Foundation of Chinese Art
Woburn Pl.
Brunswick Sq
CORAM FIELDS
Euston Rd
WARREN ST
University College Hospital
Gower Street
University College
Bernard St
Guilford Street
Dickens House Museum
REGENT'S PARK
Park Cr.
Fitzroy Square
Tottenham
University of London
Russell
RUSSELL SQ
Gt Ormond St Hospital for Sick Children
St Marylebone
Portland
Great Portland St
Charlotte St
Telecom Tower
RUSSELL SQ GDNS
Square
Southampton Row
Road
MARYLEBONE
Place
St Charles
American Church in London
GOODGE ST
Court
Gower St
BLOOMSBURY
Theobald's
GRAY INN
Marylebone High St
Harley Street
Broadcasting House BBC
Goodge St
Road
Bedford Square
Bloomsbury St
British Museum
HOLBORN
Langham Pl.
All Souls
Street
Mortimer
St George
Bloomsbury Way
HOLBORN
Sir John Soane's Museum
High Holborn
Wallace Collection
Wigmore Hall
Manchester Square
Wigmore
Street
TOTTENHAM COURT RD
Cartoon Museum
Lincoln Inn
New Oxford St
High Holborn
Kingsway
LINCOLN'S INN FIELDS
Cavendish Sq
Regent
OXFORD CIRCUS
Oxford
Street
Charing
St Giles High St
Great Queen St
John Lewis
Street
Street
Palladium Theatre
Photographers' Gallery
Soho Square
Phoenix Theatre
Endell St
Old Curiosity Shop
Selfridge's
Oxford
New
Hanover Square
Berwick St
Wardour St
Dean Street
Frith St
Cross
Monmouth St
Neal St
Neal's Yard
Drury La.
Royal Opera House
Bow St
Theatre Royal
Aldwych Theatre
St Clement Danes
Liberty
Carnaby St
Old Compton St
Road
COVENT GDN
St Mark
Handel House Museum
Bond
St George
SOHO
Ave
Long Acre
Covent Garden Market
Aldwych
Bush House
Roosevelt Memorial
Sotheby's
Conduit St
Savile Row
Regent Street
Golden Square
Brewer St
Shaftesbury
LEICESTER SQ
Chinatown
St Paul
London Transport Museum
Somerset House
St Martin's La.
COVENT GARDEN
Courtauld Institute
MAYFAIR
Piccadilly Circus
Trocadero Centre
Leicester Sq
London Coliseum
Strand
Lancaster Pl.
Gilbert Collection
Immaculate Conception
Berkeley Square
Old Bond St
Royal Academy of Arts
National Portrait Gallery
Adelphi Theatre
The Savoy
Faraday Museum
PICCADILLY CIRCUS
Haymarket
St Martin-in-the-Fields
VICTORIA EMBANKMENT GARDENS
Embankment
Waterloo Bridge
Grosvenor Chapel
Piccadilly
St James
National Gallery
CHARING CROSS
Fortnum & Mason
Jermyn St
Trafalgar Square
Nelson's Column
Charing Cross Station
EMBANKMENT
BFI British Film Institute
The Dorchester
St James's St
ST JAMES'S
Northumberland Ave
Queen Elizabeth Hall
South Bank Centre
Park
Curzon Street
The Ritz
Christie's
Admiralty Arch
Trafalgar Studios
Royal Festival Hall
Hayward Gallery
Lane
GREEN PARK
Mall
Duke of York Column
ICA
Shepherd Market
Pall
Chapel Royal
Marlborough House
The Admiralty
Whitehall
Old War Office
Hispaniola
Piccadilly
St James's Palace
Mall
Horse Guards Parade
Banqueting House
Tattershall Castle
Christ Church
GREEN PARK
Lancaster House
Guards Memorial
Ministry of Defence
JUBILEE GARDENS
HYDE PARK CORNER
Wellington Museum, Apsley House
Clarence House
The
Horse Guards Road
Victoria
London Eye
Wellington Mon.
ST JAMES'S PARK
Downing St Foreign Office
Cenotaph
Dali Universe
York Road
Wellington Arch
Constitution Hill
Queen Victoria Memorial
County Hall
BUCKINGHAM PALACE GARDENS
Buckingham Palace
Cabinet War Rooms & Churchill Museum
Treasury
Parliament St
WESTMINSTER
London Aquarium
Grosvenor Place
Gt George St
Big Ben
Westminster Bridge
Central Hall
Birdcage Walk
Wellington Barracks
Florence Nightingale Museum
Queen's Gallery
WESTMINSTER
Guards' Chapel & Museum
ST JAMES'S PARK
Broad Sanctuary
Houses of Parliament
Belgrave Sq
Buckingham Gate
Buckingham Gate
St Margaret St
St Thomas' Hospital
Road
Royal Mews
Westminster Abbey
T h a m e s
Upp. Belgrave St
New Scotland Yard
Westminster Chapel
Victoria Street
Jewel Tower
Palace
Belgrave Place
Hobart Pl.
Lwr Belgrave St
Grosvenor Gdns
Westminster City Hall
Church House
VICTORIA TOWER GARDENS
LAMBETH
Buckingham Palace Rd
Street
St Matthew
Great Peter St
Abingdon St
Lambeth
ARCHBISHOP'S PARK
Eaton Square
VICTORIA
Victoria
St John's Concert Hall
Millbank
Lambeth Palace
Victoria Station
Westminster R.C. Cathedral
Vauxhall Bridge Road
Rochester Row
Horseferry Road
Lambeth Bridge
Garden Museum
Eccleston St
Ebury Street
Page Street
Tate Britain